By Howard Morley Sachar

THE COURSE OF MODERN JEWISH HISTORY

ALIYAH: THE PEOPLES OF ISRAEL

FROM THE ENDS OF THE EARTH: THE PEOPLES OF ISRAEL

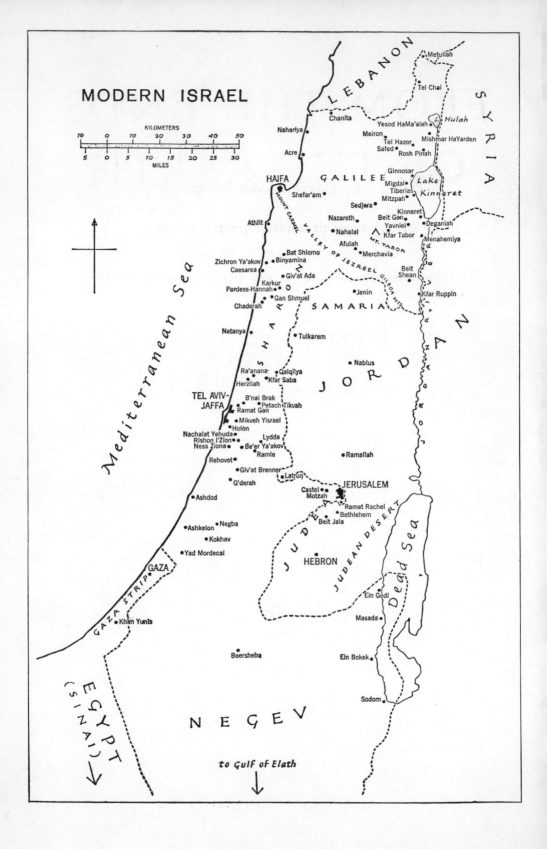

FROM THE ENDS OF THE EARTH

THE PEOPLES OF ISRAEL

‹‹‹◊›››

Howard Morley Sachar

THE WORLD PUBLISHING COMPANY

CLEVELAND AND NEW YORK

PUBLISHED BY THE WORLD PUBLISHING COMPANY
2231 WEST 110TH STREET, CLEVELAND 2, OHIO

PUBLISHED SIMULTANEOUSLY IN CANADA BY
NELSON, FOSTER & SCOTT LTD.

Library of Congress Catalog Card Number: 64-12064

FIRST EDITION

TO RACHEL AND MENAHEM

CONTENTS

MAPS

PREFACE

This volume is intended as a sequel to an earlier book, *Aliyah,* published in 1961. Its purpose, as that of its predecessor, is to describe the growth and development of the newborn Jewish Republic through "case-studies" of Israel's extraordinarily diverse population. *Aliyah* dealt primarily with the people who lived in Palestine before the emergence of the State of Israel. The present work concentrates on the immigrants who arrived after that date.

The approach of the two books is their only resemblance. For the moment of demarcation between them, May 15, 1948, is also the chasm which separates the two profoundly different nations they describe. The Jews who settled in Palestine during the late nineteenth and early twentieth centuries were, for the most part, Zionist idealists. Animated by the vision of a collective return to the soil of their ancestral homeland, they were quite prepared to endure any hardship, any danger, to fulfill their dream of revived Jewish nationhood. The immigrants who arrived in Israel after 1948 were of a radically different type. Most of the Europeans among them had lived through the Nazi inferno. By the time they arrived in Israel, few of these survivors were capable any longer of further sacrifice—for whatever cause or purpose. Others of the refugees had spent the postwar years living in semicaptivity behind the Iron Curtain. Their sense of Jewish identity had been eroded under Communist rule, and they responded slowly, even grudgingly, to the unique and uncompromising demands of Israeli citizenship.

The majority of the new immigrants was Oriental, Jews who had recently escaped from Moslem lands. These were the people least equipped of all to cope with Israel's vigorous, progressive society. For them, the shock of readjustment to a Western-oriented, twentieth-century society was hardly less than traumatic. The Orientals were religious; Israel was overwhelmingly secular. The Orientals were contemplative and passive; the tempo of life and work in Israel was strenuous and dynamic. The Orientals were backward and frequently illiterate; the challenges of Israel's industrial development and military defense required mental alertness and intellectual

9

resourcefulness. Now, therefore, transplanted to a world not of their making, the newcomers floundered badly; in the beginning they found it almost impossible to support themselves. Located in agricultural or Negev development areas, they lost heart at the first touch of adversity, and drifted back to marginal, nonproductive livelihoods in the slum sections of the larger cities—where not a few of them encamped on the doorsteps of the social welfare agencies.

For several years, the avalanche of these rudderless semimendicants threatened to extinguish the idealism of Israel's veteran European population, as well. Many of the Europeans were plainly shaken by the apparent levantinization of their Zionist utopia, and for the first time began to question their former Spartan values. In growing numbers, Israel's sabra—native-born—generation turned their backs on the kibbutz and the frontier outpost. Joining the migration to the Tel Aviv metropolitan area, they vied with the refugees in seeking out the easier life and the main chance. Few of the sabras considered themselves unpatriotic. In fact, they had always prided themselves on their devotion to their country, their determination to defend its borders, their willingness to share the burdens of housing and feeding the hundreds of thousands of destitute refugees who had returned for sanctuary to Jewish soil. But now, with Statehood, that responsibility evidently no longer required the same kind of personal commitment. A government and bureaucracy existed for the first time to care for the immigrants, to educate the youth in their civic duties, to provide farm settlements and factories with salaried instructors. In a regularized society of legal sanctions and official directives, the voluntarism, the selfless and spontaneous dedication of the pre-State era appeared somehow increasingly out of date.

In spite of occasional setbacks and failures of morale, however, the "ingathering of the exiles" has not been altogether, nor even primarily, a disheartening experience. On the contrary, there is concrete evidence that the shining hopes of the *Aliyah* epoch, the period of Zionist activism before 1948, are once again being rekindled. In other—modern, Western—societies, the lapse of idealism has traditionally been a symptom of senescence, the spiritual exhaustion of once wealthy and fecund civilizations. In Israel, conversely, suffering and protest are rather more the ordeal of birth. Remarkably, too, the nation has survived the agony of its first labor. The material circumstances of life are improving. Within the last decade Israel's agricultural production has tripled, its industrial production has quintupled. The young country's population is better fed, better housed, better dressed than at any time since the Mandatory era. The emigration of Jews from Israel, which as late as 1958 had reached the alarming total of one hundred thousand, has now been halted almost entirely. So, too, has the hemorrhage of immigrants from the outlying farm settlements and desert industrial towns.

During the 1960s, moreover, the acculturation of new citizens has proceeded rather more rapidly than could have been anticipated as recently as five years ago. The Israel government and the Jewish Agency, carefully appraising the mistakes and improvised half-measures of the early post-independence period, have devised effective new techniques for providing newcomers with job-training, for teaching them Hebrew, above all, for educating their children. Indeed, for the past few years the Israel government has deliberately adopted a policy of "positive discrimination"—that is, of offering Oriental immigrants priority in housing, jobs, and educational opportunities. In this manner it is hoped that the gap may be more effectively narrowed between the two Israels—between the dark-skinned, slum-dwelling Israel of refugees from Moslem lands, and the literate, comparatively well-employed and well-housed Israel of veteran European settlers.

That hope bears promise of fulfillment. The children of the North Africans, Iraqis, and Yemenites are beginning at last to win status for themselves in the new society. One observes the change in the growing numbers of Oriental youths who serve as officers in Israel's army, who occupy the lower managerial positions of Israel's public institutions, or who sit—a not inconsiderable minority now—in the committee rooms of Israel's parliament. One detects the change perhaps most significantly in the small but growing incidence of "mixed marriage" between Oriental and Ashkenazic (European) Jews. The Zionist experiment, a seething heterogeneity of derelicts from the four corners of the Diaspora, has confounded its critics —friends and enemies alike. Tentatively, painfully, it is beginning to work.

These successes notwithstanding, after fifteen years of sovereignty the Jewish State is still confronted with fearsome and mortal dangers to its very survival. If Israel has grown stronger since 1948, so have its enemies —incomparably stronger. At the date of writing, pro-Nasser governments have seized power in Iraq and the Yemen. It is not unlikely, too, that Syria and the Hashemite Kingdom of Jordan may yet fall within the Nasser orbit. If this happens, the Jews will find themselves surrounded by four Arab armies united by a single military command, and equipped with vast quantities of Soviet warships, tanks, bombers, and guided missiles. Neither in 1948, during the Palestine war, nor in 1956, during the Sinai Campaign, was Israel threatened by so formidable a political and military combination.

If war should come, if the Arabs should launch their long-promised "third round" in Palestine, it is unlikely that Israel will be able to rely for support upon the Western powers or the United Nations. The Jewish people has learned, from the torment of the last three decades, that its best, indeed its only, assurance of help comes from within, that the only resources upon which it can count are its own. In natural wealth, in military equipment, those resources admittedly are not impressive. And yet, whatever the paucity of its raw material, whatever the limitations of its armed forces, the little nation draws confidence from the central and compelling truth of its brief history: slowly, but inexorably, the peoples of Israel are becoming the people of Israel. It is a people determined to endure. More than any other factor, it is upon this emergent sense of peoplehood that the fate and destiny of the Jewish Republic will ultimately depend.

In the preparation of this volume I have indebted myself to a number of authorities who generously shared with me their detailed understanding of Israel's history and institutions. My thanks go to Dr. Trude Dotan, Dr. Moshe Dotan, and Dr. Chaim Tadmor of the Hebrew University for their helpful comments on Palestine archaeology and history; to Lieutenant-Colonel Netanel Lorch, formerly historian of the Army of Israel, for his suggestions on the chapter describing the War of Liberation. In the collation of immigration statistics I received invaluable resource material from Mr. Moshe Rivlin and Mr. Aharon Zisling, director of information and director of immigration, respectively, for the Jewish Agency. The chapters dealing with *Youth Aliyah* have benefited from the observations of Mr. David Oumanski, director of the placement board; of Dr. Hanoch Rinot, formerly director of education; Mr. Benjamin Jaffe, formerly secretary of the management board; of Mr. Ze'ev Weiss, formerly director of public affairs; and of Dr. Rafael Feuerstein, chief psychologist—all of *Youth Aliyah*.

Mrs. Ruth Kline, Tel Aviv district officer of the ministry of social welfare, was of great assistance in supplying me with material on Israel's welter of social cases and problems. Mr. Ezra Hadad, of the Histadrut department of Oriental affairs, provided me with vital data on the Iraqi Jewish immigration; even as Mr. Shlomo Cohen-Sidon, president of the Association of Egyptian Immigrants, offered valuable insights on his compatriots in Israel. Similarly, Mr. Ari Rath, political editor of the Jerusalem *Post,* and Mr. Jon Kimche, editor of the *Jewish Observer and Middle East Review,* kindly shared with me their specialized information on the Cairo Spy Trial and the Lavon Affair. The chapters dealing with North African Jewry owe much to discussions with Mr. Asher Hissin, president of the Association of North African Immigrants; with Mrs. Phyllis Palgi, of the ministry of social welfare; with Mr. Pesach Rudick and Mr. Efraim Millo, of the probation department of the ministry of justice; with Dr. Moshe Avidor, formerly director-general of the ministry of education; and with Dr. Aaron Siegman, professor of psychology at Bar-Ilan University.

For information relating to medicine and public health I am grateful to Dr. S. Blesh and to Dr. Joshua Cohen, director-general and assistant deputy director-general, respectively, of the ministry of health; to Dr. Israel Korn, chairman of the doctors' division of Histadrut; to Mr. Yitzhak Kancy, director of the social research institute of Kupat Holim; and, not least of all, to my brothers, Dr. Edward Sachar and Dr. David Sachar. My thanks are extended, too, to Mr. A. Shragai, director of public affairs for the Zim Steamship Company, and to Dr. Shlomo Bardin, formerly principal of the Haifa Nautical College, for material on the Israel merchant marine. Mr. Murray Greenfield, president of the Association of Americans and Canadians, supplied me with useful data on the immigration from Anglo-Saxon countries. My research on the Negev was facilitated by information and advice supplied by Mr. Shimon Yalon, deputy director-general of the ministry of development, by Mr. Michael Rothem, of the ministry of development's regional planning commission, and by Dr. Chaim Ben-Tor, director of the government geological institute.

I am particularly indebted to Major Baruch Bondet of the army information service, to Dr. Zvi Hermon, formerly chairman of the Israel prison commission, and to Mr. Aharon Turjiman, warden of Marsiyahu prison, for allowing me access to the prisoners and prison records described in this book. At their request, certain names mentioned in Chapter 5 have been changed. At the request of others without whom this book could not have been written, I have also changed names in Chapters 2, 3, 4, and 8. The events described in these and other chapters are factual.

The final draft of this volume was read, criticized, and immeasurably improved by my father, Dr. Abram L. Sachar, to whom I owe most of all for the books I have written and for any books I may write in the future.

⇨⇨⇨ I ⇦⇦⇦

The State

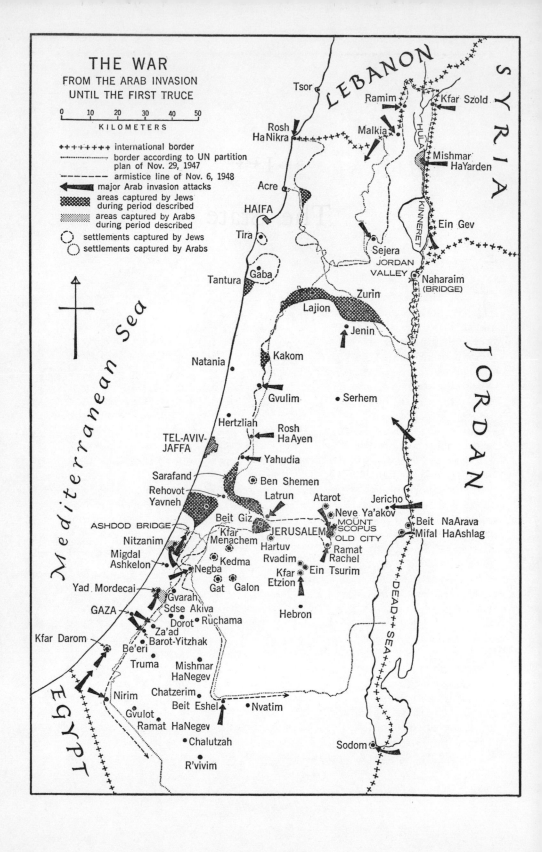

THE WAR
FROM THE ARAB INVASION
UNTIL THE FIRST TRUCE

KILOMETERS
0 10 20 30 40 50

++++++++ international border
.... border according to UN partition
plan of Nov. 29, 1947
--------- armistice line of Nov. 6, 1948
major Arab invasion attacks
areas captured by Jews
during period described
areas captured by Arabs
during period described
settlements captured by Jews
settlements captured by Arabs

LEBANON
SYRIA
JORDAN
EGYPT

Mediterranean Sea
DEAD SEA

Tsor
Ramim
Rosh HaNikra
Malkia
Kfar Szold
HULA
Mishmar HaYarden
Acre
HAIFA
Tira
KINNERET
Ein Gev
Tantura
Gaba
Sejera
JORDAN VALLEY
Naharaim (BRIDGE)
Zurin
Lajion
Jenin
Natania
Kakom
Serhem
Gvulim
Hertzliah
Rosh HaAyen
TEL-AVIV-JAFFA
Yahudia
Sarafand
Ben Shemen
Rehovot
Yavneh
Latrun
Atarot
Jericho
Neve Ya'akov
Beit Giz
MOUNT SCOPUS
Beit NaArava
ASHDOD BRIDGE
JERUSALEM OLD CITY
Mifal HaAshlag
Kfar Menachem
Nitzanim
Hartuv
Ramat Rachel
Migdal
Ashkelon
Kedma
Rvadim
Negba
Kfar Etzion
Ein Tsurim
Yad Mordecai
Gat Galon
GAZA
Gvarah
Hebron
Sdse Akiva
Dorot
Ruchama
Kfar Darom
Za'ad
Barot-Yitzhak
Be'eri
Truma
Mishmar HaNegev
Nirim
Chatzerim
Gvulot
Beit Eshel
Nvatim
Ramat HaNegev
Chalutzah
Sodom
R'vivim

CHAPTER ONE

THE ARCHAEOLOGIST

T HE LAND which extends before us is tawny. It is true that the
Jews have accomplished miracles of reforestation in the highlands of
Judea. True, also, that wheat, barley, orange and fig trees riffle gently in the
breeze drifting over the plain of Sharon. Yet even now the ochered-green
of cultivation mottles rather than engulfs the countryside. Adonis, gorse,
flax, mustard, anise, vetch, wild mignonette, and jasmine may fleck and
stipple the rolling contours of the north; but the tangled mountain range
of Galilee defiantly mocks the most strenuous exertions of farmer and
planter. The life-giving Jordan River, too, must wind its way southward
through one of the most inhospitable valleys on the earth's surface; while
further south yet lies the Wadi Aravah, the Negev desert—and wilderness.
The Jews are tough. They have wrested a living from the soil. Perhaps their
future is green. But their present is still tawny.

The reborn nation makes its home on the matrix of prehistory. For
all its harsh beauty, the land is tired, eroded, gashed and wounded by
millennia of wind and storm, by the march and countermarch of innumerable armies, and centuries of abandonment and neglect. The earth's crust
is vengeful. Its revival is slow. It warns the newcomer: civilizations fall here
as rapidly as they rise.

Is it then the shadow of Israel's past which obsesses its present? The
reader, like the author, might have learned the answer in October of 1958,
had he paid a visit to Safed, the picturesque little mountain city which
serves as "capital" of upper Galilee. There, to his dismay, he would have
discovered that no sleeping accommodations whatever were to be had in
town. Every hotel was filled to capacity, as was every *pension,* every youth
hostel, and virtually every private home. The reason for the congestion
soon became apparent. The Israel Archaeological Society was holding its
triennial congress here, and no fewer than twelve thousand archaeological
enthusiasts—more indeed than the entire population of Safed—had arrived to attend its meetings. Pre-empting every available room, the
aficionados soon overflowed into parks and fields, where they slept in tents
or simply canvas bags. Perhaps the most extraordinary feature of this

17

influx was the visitors' background—or lack of it. Hardly any of them were archaeologists by profession. Rather, their numbers included businessmen, clerks, secretaries, soldiers, kibbutz members—in fact, people of every calling and age. Yet their interest could not have been more rapt had they been graduate students attending their final seminars before examination. No physical discomfort seemed too difficult for them to bear. After all, it was not every day that one could hear Professor Yigael Yadin lecture on the excavation of Hatzor, or Professor Benjamin Mazar, or Yitzhak Ben-Zvi, President of the State, and others of equal reputation discuss the ancient communities of Galilee. The opportunity made it all worthwhile for them.

And yet the crowds that deluged the Safed congress were by no means atypical of other archaeological gatherings in Israel. In 1953, when the distinguished Christian scholar William Albright lectured in Tel Aviv on behalf of the Israel Exploration Society, at least two thousand people had to be turned away from the packed auditorium at Zionist House. Later, when Albright addressed an audience in the Negev frontier town of Beersheba, Israelis traveled to hear him from communities as far away as Nahariya and Tiberias. For that matter, whenever Professor Yigael Yadin issues a progress report at the Hebrew University on one of his numerous excavations, tickets for the lecture and parking places on the campus are at a premium.

It is doubtful, actually, if anywhere else in the world the preoccupation with historical recovery, the search for forgotten sites and relics, has so nearly approached a national pastime. For example, it is quite common on Saturday afternoons to see dozens of Israeli hiking groups, knapsacks on their backs, foraging hopefully in fields and dusty wadis for shards or clay figurines. Occasionally, too, these amateurs turn up important finds. Thus, in 1954, a shepherd in a kibbutz near Megiddo discovered a potsherd bearing cuneiform inscriptions. Investigation by the Department of Antiquities identified the inscription as the Gilgamesh Epic, the only such fragment of the Babylonian saga ever found in Palestine. Three years later Jewish farmers plowing the soil near the Gaza Strip unearthed a synagogue dating back to Byzantine times. In Shar HaGolan, a kibbutz near Lake Kinneret, children stumbled across important relics of the neolithic age. Not all private discoveries have been this newsworthy, of course; ancient Roman, Greek, and Hebrew coins and pottery are more the rule. Nevertheless, Israelis value their finds highly enough to exhibit them proudly in homemade museums. Nearly every farm settlement and school has one, as do most of the cities and towns in Israel. Many of these communities boast archaeological societies that conduct meetings at least once a month.

There are probably several reasons for this intense and at times fanatical interest in archaeological exploration. One factor is the traditional Jewish enthusiasm for intellectual activity of any kind. Israel is quite poor. Its musical, literary, and theatrical facilities, while far from insignificant, are not extensive enough to satisfy the nation's highly literate population. Archaeology, on the other hand, has proven to be a comparatively inexpensive pastime—and astonishingly productive in its cultural rewards.

Even so, a more fundamental explanation probably will be found in the Israeli's search for roots. Again and again German or Russian Jewish immigrants have asked themselves: How came I here? What am I doing in this parched, arid, impoverished little Asian land? What connection have I with this grudging soil, these undernourished valleys, this bleak and inhospitable desert wilderness? The earth gives the answer: it answers the skeptic far more satisfactorily than history lessons or Zionist propaganda. A calcified potsherd bearing Hebrew inscriptions from the era of King Ahab, a brick disinterred from Jerusalem's ancient wall, a slag-heap unearthed from King Solomon's copper mines, a column restored in a Byzantine synagogue, a parchment scroll recovered in a Dead Sea cave—each is a physical, tangible link with Israel's past. Each speaks to the immigrant: *The hands of your ancestors fashioned me. I am yours because I was theirs. This is your land because it was theirs.*

Yes, surely then it is the shadow of the past that tinctures Israel's hills and valleys with buff and lavender. History broods over its boulder-strewn face. The tinkle of camel bells in Samaria and the Negev, the plaintive yelp of jackal and hyena in the Sharon and Gilboa echo out of distant corridors of time. So, too, does the plangent thrust of shovels and picks. For the past speaks from corroded shrines and crumbled monuments. It speaks from the innumerable graves that punctuate the landscape, the resting places of ancient communities. The countryside abounds with them: conical protuberances in the earth, flattened at the top into miniature plateaus. The Arabs call them *tels*—hills, nothing more. To the archaeologist they are very special hills, however; for within them lie the remains of entire worlds passed by, the petrified memorabilia of Palestine's youth.

Now, as in decades past, experts are diligently exploring these *tels*. Hundreds of sites have already been identified and charted for future excavation. Only time and money are required for their extensive debris finally to be exposed to the clinical eye of the modern scholar. One of the largest of the *tels,* Hatzor, located in Galilee between Tiberias and Metulla, covers an ancient Canaanite city some twenty times larger than Jerusalem at the time of David. So immense is this mound, in fact, that the Israeli expedition which explored its ruins between 1955 and 1959 was able to uncover little more than one one-hundredth of its plateau. Here, as elsewhere, archaeologists have peeled back layers of habitation extending far beyond Hebrew settlement: back through the Mycenaeans, the Egyptians, the Assyrians, and the Canaanites. The earth groans with the weight of their fecundity.

One cannot escape it. Israel in the second half of the twentieth century is still a palimpsest of the civilizations that struggled, procreated, slaughtered, and ultimately died here. Their images were not fleeting. Indeed, they are engraved on the profile of the earth. From 63 B.C. to 330 A.D. there were the Romans: three centuries of Latin inscriptions, iron helmets, stone boars' heads, mahogany and rawhide ballistae, numberless gibbets and crucifixes, the imprint of a law that failed in Judea. Two centuries earlier the Hellenistic kingdoms inscribed their language, alphabet, and reliefs on Hebrew graves and monuments; and, too, for a moment, their cynicism, their worship of physical beauty, their lewdness. Strained through the Maccabean alembic, the cherished Attic gift of intellect remained, wonderfully mastered by a provincial people.

Between 1300 B.C. and 200 A.D. there were the Hebrews, too, supremely the Hebrews, who immortalized the land. They have been called austere, the God-intoxicated people of Moses, Amos, and Jeremiah, the wild-eyed soldiers of Modi'in, Jerusalem, and Masada. Yet there were backsliders among them, too, but for whose transgressions the thunder of the Prophets would not have echoed in our own day. People lived well then, and ostentatiously, when they could. Recent excavations have unearthed perfumes, paints, and spices, galbanum, stacte, labdanum, tragacanth, galena, powdered lapis lazuli, and carmine for eyes and lashes and lips; pomegranates, saffron, madder root, safflower, woad, ocher for their dyes, oils and unguents, balsam and mastic, bowls of limestone, ivory, alabaster, curling pins and hairpins and luxurious divans for the "sleek daughters of Samaria." It was still a Near Eastern land.

It was Near Eastern in its cruelty and rapacity. There were Assyrian predators, Tiglath-pileser III, Sargon, and Sennacherib, whose conquests of Hebrew border towns were grisly even by the pitiless desert standards of ancient Palestine. Friezes found at Tel Nimrud (ancient Nineveh) reveal prisoners impaled on stakes, others with eyes gouged out by spears, yet others led off into slavery by rings pierced through their upper lips. The Canaanites, their records deciphered at Ugarit in 1830, stand exposed as the lustful whoremongers of the Semitic world. The protagonists of the Ugaritic Baal epic openly reveled in incest, prostitution, and barbaric fertility rites. Their deities were classical monsters. One of them, the goddess Anath, "tied the heads of her victims as ornaments upon her back, their hands she tied upon her belt. . . . Her liver was swollen with laughter, her heart was full of joy. . . . When she was satisfied she washed her hands in streams of human blood before turning again to other things." It is evident from these revelations that more than jealousy for Yahweh motivated the furious anathemas of the Prophet Elijah. Acceptance of the Baalist deities would surely have signified the demise of the Hebrews as a civilized nation.

It was logical. These peoples were closer than neighbors; they were as intimate as only enemies can be. From Ur, Larsa, Nineveh, Phoenicia, Edom, and Moab, the civilizations of the Fertile Crescent were locked in a relentless contest for the land. In how many ways each of them resembled the others: the identical long heads, crinkled hair, black Assyriac beards and thong sandals, their nationhood an agglomeration of shepherds and goatherds, potters and moneychangers. If they burned, gutted, and deracinated, if they peered and grunted into entrails, slept with animals and their own sisters, they loved, too, and wept, pondered and wrote and sculpted, formulated imposing systems of law and literature, government and engineering. And one among the peoples was persuaded by its leaders that life was precious—and sanctified it. Search the *tels*. It is all recorded there.

It is worth noting, however, that all the major Near Eastern excavations of the nineteenth and twentieth centuries, with the single exception, in 1935, of Nelson Glueck's discovery of King Solomon's mines in the Negev desert, were carried out by non-Jews. Renan and Virolleaud at Ugarit, Rawlinson, Layard, and Smith at Nineveh, de Morgan at Susa—all were products of the romantic-historical school of the nineteenth century. It was hardly surprising that their interests carried them back to the Fertile Crescent, the very cradle of civilization. Moreover, the Palestinologists, such twentieth-century figures as Breasted, Clermont-Ganneau, Sellin, Watzinger, Albright, MacAlister, Fisher, and Starkey, were themselves deeply religious men, most of them ordained ministers and professors of biblical literature. Their investigations were undertaken with reverence for the biblical tradition—in no way compromised by the scientific techniques they brought to their profession. Indeed, the sponsoring organizations that made their excavations possible—the Palestine Exploration Fund, the Deutsche Palestine Verein, and the American School for Oriental Research—relied almost exclusively upon the patronage and financial support of Christian religious bodies.

What of the Jews, then? Did they not share in this reverence for the biblical past, this intense curiosity about people who were, after all, their own ancestors? The truth was that archaeological expeditions were a luxury few of them could indulge in. Fund-raising campaigns among Jews, even among the comparatively secure Jewry of the United States, were devoted almost exclusively to European emergency needs. The various Zionist funds and foundations were similarly preoccupied with the task of securing a Jewish agricultural foothold on Palestine. Archaeology was a science of leisure; in those days Jews had far less of it than their Christian neighbors.

And yet, of course, it was the Jews' physical presence in Palestine which ultimately accounted for the birth of their interest in archaeology. How came they there? they asked themselves. Where did their roots lie? Was their connection with this parched little land really integral enough to justify the sacrifices it demanded? The question was worth exploring. Moreover, with the establishment of the British Mandate, the Jewish community in the Holy Land was at least assured of legal status, and a minimal degree of physical protection; there was a little more breathing space now for antiquarian investigations. A group was organized, the Jewish Society for the Archaeology of Palestine, and under its auspices several Jewish scholars began their first tentative excavations.

One of the first of these archaeologists was Dr. Benjamin Meisler (now Mazar), lecturer in the newly established Hebrew University, whose investigations accounted for the discovery of the ancient Hebrew town of Beit Yerach, near the Sea of Galilee, and the magnificent Jewish necropolis of Beit She'arim, in the Carmel range. In the latter were found hundreds of Jewish ossuaries, graves of Jews whose bodies, during the first and second centuries A.D., were sent for burial to the Holy Land from all corners of the Mediterranean world. Mazar's colleague, Dr. Leo Mayer, was responsible during the Mandatory period for several truly historic finds of Moslem art and architecture, and shared with Mazar the excavation of Beit She'arim.

By far the most important of Palestine's Jewish archaeologists, however, was Professor Eliezer Sukenik of the Hebrew University. Sukenik's reputation was permanently established by his first excavation, in 1925, of Jerusalem's "third wall." The wall was alleged to have been built by King Herod Agrippa in the first century A.D. Reference to it appeared in the writings of Josephus, the celebrated Jewish historian of that era. Yet no evidence of the wall had ever been discovered. Together with Leo Mayer, Sukenik found it. With the aid of potsherds and inscriptions he succeeded in dating it. The impact of this find was felt most keenly in the Catholic world. If the ruins excavated by Sukenik were indeed those of the third wall, then the Holy Sepulcher, the most venerated site of the Christian world, could not have been the tomb of Jesus after all; Jewish law forbade burial within city limits, and the grave Christians historically worshiped was well within the confines of the third wall. To this day Catholics deny the authenticity of Sukenik's discovery. Yet nearly all professional archaeologists are inclined to accept it as valid.

Following his work on the wall, Sukenik returned to his first and keenest interest, the excavation of ancient synagogues and Jewish tombs. One of his most important finds took place at Beth Alpha, in the Palestine central plain. The mosaic floor of this ancient house of worship bore an exact date, 520 A.D., and provided fascinating examples of the Jewish folk art of 1,500 years ago. In a curious mélange, the decorations illustrated the signs of the zodiac, Noah in his ark, and Abraham's sacrifice of Isaac. The figure of the sun god, Helios, appeared in the center of the design. The hybrid village name, part Hebrew, part Greek, symbolized the diffused culture of the age, as did the inscriptions on the mosaic floor in three languages, Hebrew, Aramaic, and Greek. Others of Sukenik's excavations cast new light upon the intermingling of Jewish and pagan cultures before and after the destruction of Jewish Statehood in 70 A.D.

Long before the rise of Israel, therefore, Sukenik's innumerable finds, his articles and books, had won him recognition as the world authority on Jewish archaeology. He was, as well, a man of endearing personal qualities, and counted equally among his close friends Jewish, Christian, and Arab scholars. One of his most intimate colleagues, a French priest, Père Huguès Vincent, insisted upon paying Sukenik a courtesy visit each Rosh Hashanah, the Jewish New Year. Whenever relics and potsherds were unearthed in Palestine in those days, whether by Jews, Christian monks, or even Arab farmers, Professor Sukenik was usually the first expert whose evaluation was requested. Thus, it was hardly surprising that Sukenik should have played a principal role in the most important and dramatic archaeological event in Palestinian history—the discovery of the Dead Sea Scrolls.

The details have since been related in countless books and articles published in Israel, Europe, and the United States. Few events in the history of modern scholarship have so captured the public imagination. On November 23, 1947, Sukenik received an urgent message from a friend, an Armenian dealer in antiquities, asking the professor for an immediate appointment. These were the tension-racked days preceding the outbreak of war between Jews and Arabs, and so the two men were obliged to meet and conduct their conversation over the barricades dividing the most heavily guarded sectors of Jerusalem. Through the barbed wire, the Armenian handed over several leather scrolls for Sukenik's inspection. Instantly the professor recognized the writing on the parchment as biblical script of an unusually early period. The next day he managed to secure a pass into the Armenian's zone. Soon thereafter, at considerable personal peril, the two men traveled to Bethlehem, and to the shop of the Arab book-dealer who had first obtained the documents. There the full story was revealed. The scrolls had been discovered by several bedouin youngsters in a cave near Qumran, on the shores of the Dead Sea. The bedouin, in turn, had sold their findings to the Arab book-dealer, who promptly notified his Armenian friend.

There was reason for excitement. For one thing, these were the first ancient Hebrew scrolls ever discovered in Palestine. Until then it had been assumed that parchment materials could not survive in the damp Palestinian weather. But, evidently, the documents had been preserved by the arid climate of the Dead Sea region, and the jars in which they had been enclosed. Even more important, as far as Sukenik was concerned, was the prima facie evidence that the scrolls dated back to the biblical period. Indeed, as he read them over in the privacy of his home (he had secured permission to borrow them), it became apparent that one of the scrolls was actually an original version of the Book of Isaiah, the only such document ever discovered. It was older by a thousand years than any extant Hebrew copy of the original Sacred Writings (later a Carbon-14 test was used to date this, and the other scrolls, at about 100 B.C. to 100 A.D.). The other two parchments were hardly less important, for they contained a collection of psalms of the same period, written in biblical style, and a curious description of an imminent war between the "Sons of Light and the Sons of Darkness."

All this had fallen into Sukenik's hands at the very moment when the United Nations had decided to partition Palestine into Arab and Jewish States. Even as he pored over the three scrolls, the sound of Jews singing and shouting exultantly in the streets outside penetrated his study. It was a historic moment. For Sukenik, however, it signified the need for desperate haste to secure whatever documents yet remained, before fighting erupted between the Arab and Jewish communities. In fact, he had been informed that four other fragments were already in the hands of the Metropolitan of the monastery of St. Mark in the Old City of Jerusalem. Working with frantic speed, therefore, Sukenik managed to raise enough funds from the university to complete the purchase of the first three scrolls. And then, even as he was about to arrange payment for the second collection, the outbreak of open hostilities in Jerusalem made further contact with St. Mark's impossible; the Metropolitan withdrew the other four fragments from the antiquities market. It was a heartbreaking disappointment for the professor, perhaps the most shattering disappointment of his life. He died in 1953, convinced to the end that a priceless archaeological treasure had been irretrievably lost.

The year after his death, however, an extraordinary coincidence once again presented Israeli scholars with an opportunity to secure the missing parchments. During a lecture tour in the United States, Sukenik's son, Professor Yigael Yadin (who had Hebraized his name several years earlier), was alerted to a modest announcement which had appeared in the *Wall Street Journal*. It was a notification of the availability of "certain" scrolls— the "Dead Sea Scrolls." Yadin dared not trust his eyes. Could these possibly be the original Dead Sea documents? Subsequent investigation revealed that they were. As it turned out, the Syrian Metropolitan of St. Mark's, Mar Athanasius Samuel, had himself come to the United States to find a buyer for his treasure.

Moving quickly through intermediaries (he dared not reveal his true identity as an Israeli), Yadin succeeded in arranging the purchase of the scrolls on behalf of the Hebrew University for the (comparatively) modest sum of $250,000. Moreover, the new acquisitions turned out to be as invaluable in every respect as the original three leather parchments secured by Sukenik six years earlier. They included a second, longer version of the Book of Isaiah; a Commentary on the Book of Habakkuk; a "Manual of Discipline"—a book of rules governing the Jewish sect to which the collection belonged; and an Aramaic document, a "Genesis Apocryphon," later called the "Lamech Scroll."

What was the significance of these seven documents? The Isaiah scrolls, first of all, make it clear that the earliest surviving Masoretic—i.e., traditional —version of the Bible, dating back to 895 A.D., is surprisingly accurate. The differences that exist between this early medieval copy and the newly recovered parchment are comparatively minor, and are primarily stylistic; other fragments of the Bible, subsequently discovered at Qumran, provided further evidence of this. Second, the Habakkuk Commentary, the Commentary on the Psalms, and the Thanksgiving Hymns—all offer a vivid insight into the circumstances that brought the authors of the scrolls to the Qumran caves. These people were apparently fugitives from Jerusalem, either in hiding or in exile from the Roman administration. Evidently they bore especial animus against a certain "Wicked Priest"—perhaps a Jewish collaborator of the Romans—who had made their life impossible in the capital. There are continuous references to the sect's leader, the "Teacher of Righteousness." He was a goodly man who supervised the little group's activities in exile, and who from time to time issued ominous pronunciamentos of the impending downfall of the "Kittim" (probably the Romans) and the "Wicked Priest" who gathered wealth and spoils from the enslaved Jews.

The manner in which the downfall of the "Kittim" would take place was not left in doubt. It was described in one of the most fascinating of the scrolls, the nineteen-page document projecting a future "War of the Sons of Light against the Sons of Darkness." The "Sons of Light," of course, were the exiles at Qumran. The "Sons of Darkness" evidently included all the neighboring heathen peoples—Edomites, Moabites, Philistines, Egyptians—with special emphasis on the despised "Kittim" and their collaborators, the "Offenders against the Covenant." The scroll's version of the impending hostilities was quite specific. War would rage for no less than forty years. Angels as well as men would be mobilized for battle. The rules and tactics of warfare were clearly outlined, as well. The author spared no detail in his description of troop concentrations, attack, pursuit, and withdrawal tactics. Yigael Yadin, who has translated this scroll, suggests that these techniques were borrowed extensively from the Roman military methods of the time. Yet the elaborate system of prayers and slogans in praise of God were typically Jewish. Indeed, the visceral intensity with which the Jews continually invoked the deity confirms the information we already have of their mentality during the era of Roman rule: it was an apocalyptic age, rife with messianic rumors and expectations of salvation.

This was clearly evident in perhaps the most important of the seven parchments, the so-called "Manual of Discipline." The principles of the sect's faith required the strictest possible obedience to the laws of God, as given "through Moses and through all His servants the prophets." Rules of behavior were harsh and inflexible. Thus, the commandments of the Teacher of Righteousness and his cadre of priests were followed unquestioningly. The members of the group lived in a communal fashion. They abjured wealth, and maintained "uprightness and humility." Each novitiate in the sect was instructed that "by the spirit of uprightness and humility all his sins will be atoned, and by the submission of his soul to all ordinances of God, his flesh will be purified for the sprinkling with water for impurity . . . and he will establish his steps to walk perfectly in all the ways of God . . ." So uncompromising was this insistence upon humility, moreover, that a detailed schedule of punishments was enumerated for members who dared speak with undue levity, or in anger or blasphemy. Apparently there was a portentous reason for this cheerless asceticism. The "advent" was close at hand: the moment when, following the War of the Sons of Light against the Sons of Darkness, all evil, sin, and darkness would disappear from the world, and justice and truth would prevail.

Who, then, were the Sons of Light, the members of this curious Qumran group? The Manual of Discipline, together with relics found near the Qumran caves, suggests that they may have been Essenes, members of a devoutly religious Jewish sect which was particularly active in Palestine during the Roman period of occupation. To be sure, references to the Essenes appear in Philo of Alexandria, in Josephus, and in Pliny. With the recovery of the Dead Sea Scrolls, however, certain remarkable similarities have for the first time been noted between the Essene sect and early Christianity. The faith in the Teacher of Righteousness, the ideals of celibacy and community property, the common meal, the messianic interpretation of Scripture, the idea of the messiah begotten by God, of a triune messiah (king, priest, and prophet)—all coincide with the beliefs of the early Christian congregations. Indeed, the Qumran sect sought God in the same desert region where John the Baptist preached; and it is not impossible, therefore, that John was a member of the group. The Essenes remained intensely zealous Jews, of course. For them, the messianic age would arrive with the triumph of the Jews over the Romans, and of Judaism over the pagan creeds.

The Kingdom of God on earth, they believed, was near at hand. Neverthe-less, the way of life of at least one sectarian trend within Judaism—the Essenes—so closely paralleled that of the early Christians that biblical scholars have drawn an emphatic and surprisingly unanimous conclusion about the intertestamental period from this evidence: the sources of the New Testament were classically Jewish, rather than Greek, as had formerly been believed; Christianity's—as distinguished from Jesus'—roots in Judaism were far deeper than had ever been suspected. The new evaluation signifies a revolution in biblical criticism.

It was quite natural, as a result, that the revelations of the scrolls should have aroused the most avid scholarly interest throughout the Western world. Yet in Israel itself, the land in which Yigael Yadin and his colleagues translated and interpreted the findings of the caves, the revelations were of profound interest to far more than the community of scholars. They alto-gether fascinated the general public. The newspapers covered the story on their front pages. For weeks the discovery was a favorite topic of discussion at social gatherings. Lectures on the subject, delivered by biblical scholars, attracted record audiences. Two plays and four films dealing with the scrolls were produced. It was typical of Israel's preoccupation with its own an-tiquity. Between 1955 and 1959 Yadin's excavations at Tel Hatzor, the ancient Canaanite city of upper Galilee, was followed with almost breathless national interest. Late in 1959 Yadin's even more spectacular discovery, near the Dead Sea, of letters written by Bar Kochba, the leader of the Jewish rebellion against Rome in the second century A.D., provided school children in history classes with a choice subject for themes and pageants for weeks afterward.

Indeed, it is this historical—or, if you will, inspirational—value which accounts for archaeology's inclusion in the curriculum of Israel's State sec-ondary schools. It also accounts, in part, for the intensive course in biblical history and archaeology required of officer candidates in the Israel Army. In part, but not altogether. Knowledge of the land and its past has proved to be of the most crucial immediate value in ensuring the very survival of the Jewish State. This can be well vouched for by Eliezer Sukenik's son. Yigael Yadin's training as an archaeologist proved more than incidentally useful in other phases of his career. The government and people of Israel have taken the lesson to heart.

EARLY YEARS IN THE UNDERGROUND

It was a pleasant childhood. There was the comfortable old house in Jerusalem's Street of the Prophets, the early years in mother's own kinder-garten, games and scuffling with his younger brothers Yosef and Mattiyahu. And above all there were those wonderful outings with father. Whenever possible, Professor Sukenik took Yigael with him on his excavations. Once, when the boy was only three, he stood alone on the Mound of Saul, just north of the Old City, waiting for his father to fetch him. Silent, his finger in his mouth, the wind blowing through his hair, the child stared with fascination at the ancient walls, the fragments of uncovered potsherds. The experience was uncanny—the memory of it never left him. He heard the earth speaking.

Later, as a schoolboy, he accompanied Sukenik each Saturday morning on a round of the Old City synagogues. Together they examined walls, cornices, floors, and abutments in search of forgotten inscriptions. Occasionally they visited the monastery of St. Anne's to examine the White Fathers' superb collection of Jewish antiquities. The Catholic prelates always welcomed their Jewish guests cordially, offering them tea and cake, smiling in amusement as Sukenik pressed on in his search for undiscovered Jewish relics in the various surrounding Christian churches. He often found them, however, and once astonished his hosts by uncovering a funerary inscription of King Uzziah's tomb in the Russian convent on the Mount of Olives.

Not surprisingly, Yigael soon developed his father's intense interest in the land and its buried civilizations. Later, when he became old enough to join the Boy Scouts, he drew enthusiastically on his growing fund of archaeological information. The scout leaders insisted that their young charges know Palestine's terrain thoroughly, and were continually leading the boys on long hikes through the countryside. As the only "archaeologist" among the youngsters, Yigael quickly became a group leader, and taught his friends to avoid the main roads in favor of ancient, scarcely visible Roman and Greek pathways. It was not a mere exercise in antiquarianism. During the 1930s the scout outings were façades for Haganah (Underground defense) training exercises, and it was essential that these maneuvers not be detected by the British. If Yigael and his fellow scouts studied fieldcraft and signals, they also received intensive training as Haganah couriers. Their hiding places were often those used by the Hebrews in biblical times: the Judean wilderness, or Masada, near the Dead Sea. Years later, many of these young Palestinians would play important roles in the Haganah high command. Their knowledge of the land would not be the least of their qualifications.

Long before graduation from high school, Yigael had decided upon archaeology as a career. After a stint as an orange-picker in a co-operative farm settlement near Petach Tikvah, and later as a surveyor's assistant, he managed to accumulate enough money to enroll in the Hebrew University in 1935. Courses in Hebrew and Arabic literature supplemented his archaeology concentration. The university operated under the German system in those days; the first degree offered was the M.A., which ordinarily required four years of study. In Yigael Yadin's case, the program required ten years. Between 1935 and 1945 "security considerations" took priority.

The interruptions began in 1936, with the Grand Mufti's nationalist assault on the Jewish community and the Mandatory regime. Arab guerrilla attacks on Jewish farm settlements and British military patrols increased in frequency and intensity. Jews who ventured beyond the cities or the stockades of their kibbutzim literally took their lives in their hands. During the next two years hundreds of Jewish men, women, and children were slain in Arab ambushes. Together with several thousand other Jewish youths, therefore, Yigael was called back immediately to active duty with the Haganah.

For the next six months he was placed in charge of the defense unit at Kibbutz Kiryat Anavim, near Jerusalem. The troops under his command were fifty Jerusalem boys, who were rotated each week (to avoid detection by the British) in favor of a new group arriving from the city. Thus far the young commander had not experienced actual combat. Now, however, he and his unit were chosen by the Haganah general staff for a crucial tactical experiment. Emphasis no longer was to be placed upon static defense, as in the 1920s, but rather upon systematic ambush of Arab marauders close to their own villages. Yigael would train his boys and lead them in the operations. If the plan succeeded, the Haganah would apply it to other areas of the country.

Accordingly, Yigael and his squads fanned out from Kiryat Anavim, and lay in wait near the Arab communities of Nebi Samwil, Quetaniah, and Castel. One night, flattened on his stomach with his advance unit only a mile and a half from Nebi Samwil, Yigael heard the Arab marauders approaching. He realized that the one chance of stopping them was to allow them to come in close; his troops' armament consisted solely of pistols and grenades. When the Arabs were within thirty yards, the grenades were thrown and the pistols fired. The effect was quite devastating. Howling in terror, the guerrillas fled in all directions, leaving two dead men behind.

The impact of the raid upon Yigael and his comrades was no less decisive. They had departed for their mission as tense, nervous youths. They returned to Kiryat Anavim self-confident, eager for further battle. As far as the Haganah high command was concerned, the night attacks had proved their worth; they were swiftly launched in other areas of the country. In the north, a young Haganah lieutenant named Yigal Peicovitch (later Allon) applied the method of night attack with spectacular effectiveness, all but paralyzing the Mufti's operations throughout the entire upper Galilee.

Even the British were impressed. Under heavy assault themselves by Arab guerrillas, the Mandatory authorities reluctantly decided to accept help wherever they could find it, even from the Jews. In 1938, as a result, they incorporated several hundred Jews into the ghaffirs (the so-called supernumerary police), and armed them with British service rifles and ammunition. Yigael Yadin was appointed a ghaffir platoon leader for the Jerusalem area and its surrounding communities. By now he was well trained for the responsibility. Moreover, the troops serving under him were essentially the same Haganah members he had been commanding in that sector for the past two years. As far as they were concerned, the operation was still a Haganah one; the single advantage of ghaffir status was the opportunity it gave them to engage in self-defense legally. British weapons were welcome, too. At Yigael's disposal were two military trucks and one armored car—an unheard-of concentration of vehicles for the little Haganah band.

The youthful commander found "official" co-operation with the British a revealing experience. His ghaffirs were nominally attached to a British platoon of Highlanders stationed at Castel, overlooking the Jerusalem-Tel Aviv highway. Their task was to guard the water-pipe line which extended parallel to the road. It was dangerous territory. For months Arab infiltrators had been sabotaging the installations. The platoon commander, an English captain, had merely been waiting for Jewish reinforcements to test a pet scheme.

"I've got an idea that I've been kicking around for a while," the officer explained. "I'd like to lay a real ambush for those wogs." As Yadin listened, the captain outlined his plan. "Tomorrow is Christmas. The Arabs know that British soldiers drink on Christmas. Now suppose I take a lorry and leave it on the road with its lights on, and then put our troops in a trench nearby and have them shout and sing as if they were drunk. Naturally the Arabs will attack the lorry. That's where you chaps come in, you see. You'll be down the road a piece and can ambush the blighters on their way back —or at least those that survive us. We'll shoot a red Very light if they're coming your way. And we'll shoot a green one if they're not; in which case you and your men can go home."

Yadin agreed with alacrity. The following night he and a group of ten men lay in wait a mile down the highway from the parked lorry. They held their positions for an hour. Another hour went by. Still no light. The men grew restless. After three hours of uneventful waiting, it was apparent to Yadin that the plan had not come off. Reluctantly he ordered his men to their feet, and led them back to headquarters at Abu Ghosh. The captain and his troops were there, too. In fact, they had played their role only too well. They were dead drunk.

The idea of a decoy was essentially sound, nevertheless. With only thirty men to guard the dangerous stretch of road between Jerusalem and Ramallah, Yadin knew that it was essential to lure the Arab guerrillas into the open for ambush. Under his own direction, decoy tactics worked surprisingly well. A band of the Mufti's men would descend excitedly upon an apparently unguarded Jewish armored car, ineffectually shoot it up—and then be wiped out by a group of Jewish riflemen hiding at the side of the highway. The night was invariably a Jewish weapon; Arabs were terrified of being thrown on the defensive in darkness. In any case, the Mufti's troops were generally unfamiliar with the countryside beyond their own villages. The Haganah soldiers, on the other hand, had mastered the terrain perfectly during their endless training hikes. They were able to move rapidly from one area to another, thus convincing the enemy that their numbers were endless. By the end of 1938, guerrilla assaults in the Jerusalem area diminished markedly. Arab morale had been badly shattered there.

THE FOUNDATIONS OF AN ARMY

At the same time the members of the Haganah high command had set about re-evaluating the military lessons of the Arab-Jewish civil war. They were convinced now that well-trained officers were urgently needed; the old ragtag system of scouting and rifle practice was no longer adequate. Within two months of reaching this conclusion, therefore, the high command established a Haganah officers' training camp at Kfar Vitkin, in the central Sharon plain. Typically, it was disguised as an agricultural school. One

hundred and twenty unit leaders from all parts of the country participated
in the first training session. Yadin was chosen, of course. During his three
months at Kfar Vitkin he met the young officers who were destined for
rapid advancement in the Jewish defense effort, among them Moshe Karmel,
Moshe Dayan, Eliahu Cohen, and Yadin's own instructor, Yigal Peicovitch
(Allon). It was a demanding program. The students awoke each day at
5:00 A.M., and were given concentrated instruction in weapons and tactics.
Those who passed the course were sent back to their own communities to
organize training schools for noncommissioned officers. Yadin, appointed
chief Haganah instructor in the Jerusalem district, established five such
schools, and disguised them as *ghaffir* target ranges. Later the graduates
were assigned to key units throughout the country.

Then the Second World War began, and the Haganah high command
was suddenly faced with the task of allocating its own manpower. After
much agonizing and soul searching, the decision was ultimately taken to
assign half the Jewish Underground officers to the British army, and the rest
to home defense. Yadin was assigned to the latter category—quite against
his own wishes. His first billet was the Haganah's recently founded tactical
training college in Ein HaShofet, on the coastal plain. The instructors were
Jewish noncoms on leave from the British army. The lessons they taught
were the lessons they had learned in British officers' training camps. Yadin
rapidly won first rank among the students. Indeed, within three months he
was appointed to the school's faculty. Here again, his record was a brilliant
one. In 1941 Ya'akov Dori, the Haganah chief of staff, selected Yadin as his
aide-de-camp. From then on the young officer found himself involved in the
central planning activities of the Jewish defense effort.

It was, at first, a loosely co-ordinated effort. A standing army did not exist.
Staff organization was limited to training, planning, and intelligence. Yet
there was nothing casual or haphazard about the operation of these three
branches; they functioned with an efficiency born of grave urgency. In 1941
Rommel's Afrika Korps was dug in at the borders of Egypt. The very life
of the *Yishuv* (the Palestine Jewish community) hung in the balance. Thus,
the Haganah high command speedily devised a twofold plan. The first took
into account a possible German paratroop landing in Palestine, and envisaged full-scale warfare. The second anticipated complete German occupation of the country, and a possible Haganah retreat to the Carmel mountain
range, which would serve as a base for guerrilla activities. Neither scheme
had to be invoked, of course; within less than a year General Montgomery
succeeded in smashing the German threat at El Alamein. But although the
pressure was lifted, the experience of staff planning had proved invaluable
for the Jewish officers. They had learned the importance of dispassionate
assessment and calculation in the face of mortal peril. Ultimately this self-
discipline counted as much in forging their army as the long succession of
night skirmishes against Arab guerrillas.

Moreover, the Nazi danger had compelled Yadin and his colleagues to
prepare a long-range strategic blueprint for the defense of the *Yishuv*. The
experience was a useful one, for after the danger abated, the Haganah high

command was emboldened to drop its tactical approach to military problems, and to devise strategic goals for the postwar period. Again, the plan—"Plan D"—was twofold: the first, to secure freedom of action against the British—i.e., to ensure that the British did not interfere with the free immigration of Jews from Europe; the second, to develop a program of defense against a possible military invasion launched by neighboring Arab countries.

In the early postwar period, the British proved a far more serious threat to the Jewish National Home than the Arabs. The Haganah soon discovered that secrecy alone was not sufficient to smuggle refugees past the Royal Navy and the occupying British garrisons. Increasingly, therefore, the high command resorted to more violent measures: ordering British weapons purloined, bridges and railroads destroyed. At all times the Jewish Underground was under orders to avoid gratuitous attacks on British soldiers. Yet clashes were often unavoidable, especially during the attempts to land refugee vessels. Late in 1945, for example, Yadin—who had just been promoted to chief of operational planning—received word that a DP ship was approaching the coast. Mobilizing thousands of Haganah reserves, he ordered several concentric cordons thrown around Tel Aviv to ward off British interference. There were skirmishes. One Haganah girl was killed. But the vessel was successfully beached. Several hundred immigrants were smuggled ashore safely.

During the next two years, one refugee ship after another hurled itself against the British blockade. Within Palestine itself the Jewish Underground launched increasingly violent attacks against British armories and radar installations. Jewish bombings and sabotage, British reprisals—arrests, imprisonments, even executions—escalated rapidly into a virtual civil war. As far as the Jews were concerned, the time for half-measures was over. If the survivors of the Nazi holocaust were ever to find sanctuary, if the blockade was ever to be cracked, the British Mandate itself would have to be discredited before world opinion, and British taxpayers taught the prohibitive cost of maintaining tens of thousands of troops in the Palestine encampment. And so the violence continued. Men died on both sides. Each month the reserves of the British Exchequer were depleted by additional millions of pounds. The British Foreign Office, desperately seeking a *modus vivendi* with the Arabs, faced the mounting impatience and diplomatic pressure of the American government. Indeed, by the spring of 1947, it was plain that the Zionist leadership had calculated accurately. Exasperated beyond endurance by Jewish intransigence, British Foreign Secretary Ernest Bevin finally and reluctantly turned the Palestine issue over to the United Nations. With Bevin's capitulation, the first phase of the Haganah operations schedule had been successfully consummated.

Yadin himself, however, had left active duty at the end of 1945. A sharp, irreconcilable dispute with Yitzhak Sadeh, the Jewish Agency's military adviser, had provoked his withdrawal. To Yadin's mind, ultimate full-scale war with the Arabs was inevitable. The time had come for reorganizing the Jewish Underground on orthodox military lines—complete with divisional and battalion commands, each with a regular hierarchy of staff officers. But

Sadeh, an old night-fighter of the 1930s, insisted that the concept of a British-style army was still premature; far too many sabotage operations still lay ahead to warrant a "top-heavy" staff structure. When further discussions between the men proved fruitless, Yadin decided to return to the university.

During the war he had married. His wife, the former Carmela Ruppin, now took a job to enable Yadin to complete his long-delayed Master's dissertation on Arabic inscriptions. Immediately afterward he embarked on a doctoral project. The subject, "Problems of Biblical Warfare," had been on his mind for many years, and was unusually rich in its potentialities. Of course the thesis would have been far too ambitious for a scholar of purely orthodox academic training, or even for a soldier whose education had been exclusively military. Yadin's background as both an officer and an archaeologist was unique, however; indeed, it equipped him ideally for the undertaking.

He began by dividing his subject into four categories—weapons, fortifications, strategy, and tactics—and then set about compiling an immense card catalogue on each. With typical thoroughness, Yadin accumulated his data by poring over a vast moraine of biblical and prebiblical documents, as well as Ugaritic, Babylonian, and Assyrian sources; then by studying virtually every archaeological report published on Near Eastern excavations; and finally by consulting most of the archaeological, historical, and biblical quarterlies for possible additional clues. At every step of his research, too, he received invaluable advice and encouragement from his father. It was a fascinating project—but an immense one, as well. Although within two years Yadin had completed his examination of documentary and archaeological sources, and had card-indexed their contents, he was well aware by then that he had undertaken a topic large enough for several doctoral theses. Nevertheless, he would have continued, for he found the academic life, no less than the subject itself, profoundly congenial to his temperament. In August of 1947, however, he was suddenly called to an emergency interview with David Ben-Gurion.

Ben-Gurion was serving at the time as chairman of the Jewish Agency Executive, and in that capacity was the recognized leader of the Palestine Jewish community. With the weight of the entire *Yishuv* on his shoulders, he had little time to waste on amenities.

"The British will be withdrawing soon," Ben-Gurion stated matter-of-factly. "There's certain to be fighting with the Arabs afterward. We need you on the general staff. I'm asking you to go back in as chief of operations."

Yadin hesitated at first; he was not eager to resume the organizational wrangling with the Haganah high command. Accordingly, he asked Ben-Gurion for time to consider the offer. Within a few days after the interview, however, Ya'akov Dori, the Haifa engineer who served as Haganah chief of staff, was felled by a stroke. At that moment Yitzhak Sadeh himself asked Yadin to take over as acting chief of staff, and promised him a free hand in directing the Haganah's operations. Not without misgivings, Yadin finally accepted the responsibility. He was all of thirty years old.

At his first staff meeting, Yadin was given a full—and anxious—briefing by David Shaltiel, chief of Haganah intelligence. It appeared increasingly unlikely, Shaltiel pointed out, that hostilities would now be confined to Palestine's local Jewish and Arab communities. Reports from Haganah agents in the neighboring Arab lands made it plain that the Moslem armies would almost certainly be mobilized for invasion. A plan of general defense would have to be perfected quickly. Yadin agreed, and set to work feverishly with his staff. It was hardly too soon. On November 29, the General Assembly of the United Nations voted to partition Palestine into separate Arab and Jewish States. Within a few months, on May 15, 1948, the British would withdraw from the country. Almost immediately thereafter the armies of five Arab nations would surely cross the borders, and the Jews of Palestine —a tiny enclave of 650,000 people, their backs to the Mediterranean—would be thrown entirely upon their own resources.

THE STRUGGLE FOR POSITION

Yadin and his colleagues now concentrated their efforts on developing and refining the strategic blueprint originally worked out in 1941. The principal military scheme, the so-called "Plan D," was devised to fulfill two major objectives: protecting the internal security of the country from local Arab forces during the six-month period of British withdrawal; and defending the country against full-scale Arab invasion after May 15. The first phase of the plan, internal security, envisaged the protection of all lines of communication between the outlying Jewish settlements. It was, unfortunately, an exceptionally formidable task. Most of the roads passed through Arab territory. The Galilee and the Negev were predominantly Arab. So were the densely populated towns of Jaffa, Ramle, Lydda, and Acre. Haifa and Jerusalem were almost equally divided between Arabs and Jews.

Initially, Yadin formulated a jigsaw pattern of defense. It contemplated transforming the Jewish settlements into bristling hedgehogs, and avoiding aggressive action against the local Arab communities. If after May 15, however, the neighboring Arab countries should send their armies into Palestine, the Haganah would then be obliged to seize certain predesignated Arab cities and towns within the envisaged Jewish State.

It did not happen that way. On April 1, Yadin met with Ben-Gurion and the leading civilian and military officials of the Jewish community. The gathering took place at Ben-Gurion's home in Keren HaKayemet Street in Tel Aviv. There Yadin outlined the problems he and other members of the Haganah high command had been obliged to cope with.

"Matters have not worked out as we had hoped," Yadin explained. "You know the situation as well as I do. Jerusalem is cut off. The Etzion Bloc [a cluster of kibbutzim, near Jerusalem] is cut off. The Arabs have a stranglehold on all the main roads to Jerusalem and all the main highways in the Galilee. We're getting nowhere trying to supply our communities on a piecemeal basis. At this rate, they may well fall before May 15, and the *Yishuv* could be throttled even before full-scale Arab invasion. That leaves only one alternative. We must go on the offensive now. We must seize control of all interior communications quickly, capture all important Arab towns controlling the Jerusalem road, all the major towns in the Galilee."

It was an astonishingly bold proposal. The risks were exceptionally grave. For one thing, nation-wide mobilization was still out of the question. Although the Mandatory government already had withdrawn many of its garrisons, enough British troops were still left to interfere with a large-scale Jewish military effort. For the time being, therefore, the burden of the operation would have to be borne by Yigal Allon and his Palmach Corps, the standing shock troops of the Haganah. Unfortunately no more than six thousand of these youngsters had been mobilized, and they were already thinly dispersed throughout the country. Then, too, the problem of arms was perhaps even more critical. As long as the British remained in the country it was impossible to count on more than a trickle of weapons smuggled in on a haphazard basis. The only possible alternative would be to strip the agricultural settlements of the guns already in their possession. Yet this was a cruel sacrifice to demand of isolated and outnumbered farm communities, for they were already facing attack by well-armed Arab guerrillas.

The little group discussed the scheme for three hours, fearfully weighing the pros and cons. In the end Ben-Gurion decided the issue. He gave his approval of Yadin's proposal. Offensive operations would begin immediately. The kibbutzim would be placed under orders to hold out at all costs, not to abandon an inch of territory. It was a dangerous, indeed a heart-breaking, gamble. Ben-Gurion's willingness to take it revealed the true dimensions of his vision and courage. For as later events made clear, no decision he took—whether to declare the State of Israel, or to invade the Sinai Peninsula—ever was fraught with profounder risks. Now, however, once the die was cast, all the participants in the Tel Aviv meeting suddenly experienced a curious exhilaration. Rising, they shook hands with each other warmly. Each sensed the historic importance of the moment. Yadin and his colleagues left Ben-Gurion's home tense with excitement. The time for half-measures was over. They would move over to the attack now.

That same day at the Haganah headquarters on Tel Aviv's HaYarkon Street, Yadin made final preparations to launch the Jerusalem highway offensive. Its purpose was to seize the heights overlooking the road, once and for all clearing the route for convoys on their way to the besieged city. Colonel Shimon Avidan was appointed commander of the operation, and fifteen hundred troops were placed at his disposal. Half of them were Palmach regulars, the rest Haganah youngsters called up from the Tel Aviv area. It was a badly undermanned assault force, but there was no possibility of recruiting additional troops in time. Indeed, there would not have been sufficient weapons and ammunition for them. Typically, Yadin gave the expedition a biblical title: Operation Nachshon, after the Hebrew prince who risked the first plunge into the Red Sea during the Exodus from Egypt.

On April 6, the attack began. The first objectives were seized without undue difficulty. In less than three days the entire middle Hulda area between Tel Aviv and Jerusalem was cleared. Soon afterward all the heights near Kiryat Anavim and Motzah were captured. The one village offering the most serious resistance was Castel, the kingpin of the Arab positions overlooking the road. Here the only method of assault was a frontal attack. Both sides suffered heavy casualties as the town changed hands three times in six days. The battle was decided in favor of the Jews only after the Arab commander, Abd al-Kadar al-Husseini, a nephew of the Grand Mufti, was killed in action. Later three other key Arab villages were overrun—Colonna, Lifta, and Saris. For the time being, at least, the Jewish highway was opened. It was destined to be closed again soon afterward, when the Arabs tightened the blockade at the Bab al-Wad bottleneck from their stronghold at Latrun. But in the interval, between April 14 and April 20, three large Jewish convoys bearing stores of food and weapons succeeded in reaching Jerusalem. It was enough to restore the morale and fighting capacity of the city's Jewish population. The Har-El Brigade, one of the key Palmach units participating in the battle for the road, now was transferred to Jerusalem in time to prevent a major Arab breakthrough there.

In the north, the dramatic switch in Jewish strategy proved even more effective. Taking the initiative in the Jezreel Valley for the first time, Haganah units on April 14 cracked Fawzi al-Qawukji's siege of the Jewish settlements of Mishmar HaEmek and Ramat Yohanan. A week later, in a lightning assault, Colonel Moshe Karmel seized control of the vital port city of Haifa, smashing a badly organized Arab defense with comparatively few casualties. Soon afterward a picked company of Palmach troops, under the command of Yigal Allon, captured the Taggert fortress overlooking Rosh Pinah, then swept on to clear every Arab stronghold in the mountainous border region between Syria and Palestine. Only Safed, the "citadel of Galilee," remained in Arab hands to block the free movement of Jewish troops and supplies.

In the second week of May Allon hurled his men into a series of frontal assaults against the Syrian and Lebanese irregulars who dominated Safed's key heights. The Arabs outnumbered the attackers nearly twenty to one, and they were far better armed. In Allon, however, the Jews had their most brilliant and audacious field commander. His soldiers, too, were tough and battle-wise. These advantages proved decisive. By May 9, the Jews had routed the last of the Arab defenders from Safed. With this crucial victory, the Yishuv's interior lines of communication were reasonably secure. To be sure, Jerusalem and its life-giving artery still remained in jeopardy. But in its larger contours "Plan D" had succeeded. The Haganah had filled the vacuum left by the departing British, and had secured control of the strategic heights overlooking the main invasion routes into Palestine. When the neighboring Arab States launched their armies, the Jews, flanks secured, would be waiting for them on Palestine's actual borders.

On May 12, Ben-Gurion, now prime minister-designate of the future Jewish government, called an emergency cabinet meeting in Tel Aviv. At stake was the final decision on Jewish sovereignty. In a mere two and a half days the British Mandate was due to terminate. Administrative chaos reigned throughout the country. The prospects of a United Nations "police force" to maintain order were virtually nonexistent. Under such circumstances, Ben-Gurion asked, did the cabinet have a right to declare the establishment of a Jewish State? Here, much depended on the possibilities of a full-scale Arab invasion—and the *Yishuv*'s military capacity to repel that assault. Ben-Gurion turned to Yadin, who had been called in for consultation.

"What about it, Yigael?" he asked. "What are the chances?"

Yadin was equally blunt. "The likelihood of an Arab invasion is almost certain," he stated without hesitation. "On the other hand, the likelihood of throwing it back is anything but certain."

At this point the commander succinctly outlined the military situation for the cabinet members. The Palmach and its supporting Haganah troops had successfully consummated "Plan D." The Jews had won elbowroom for themselves, control of the interior lines of communication. Yet the situation in Jerusalem remained extremely critical. The Arabs still dominated at least half the most populous districts within the city, together with all the high ground overlooking the city, all the arteries into the city, including important stretches of the vital Tel Aviv highway. Even at that moment troops of Transjordan's British-trained Arab Legion were converging on Jerusalem along most of those roads.

The discrepancy in equipment was critical, too, Yadin pointed out. Thus far the Haganah possessed a total of 22,000 obsolescent British and captured German rifles, 11,000 automatic Sten guns (quite unreliable), 1,400 light machine guns, and 900 light and medium mortars. The Haganah's "artillery" consisted of 75 ancient PIAT antitank rifles, and 16 homemade mortars, with extremely limited quantities of ammunition. It was the factor of artillery which might well tip the balance in the fighting. The Arabs possessed large quantities of British twenty-five-pounder cannon that were already dropping shells on Jewish positions with devastating effect.

"I am now obliged to bring to this meeting heartbreaking news," Yadin added. "I have just been informed that the Etzion Bloc of settlements [near Jerusalem], after a long and heroic defense against overwhelming odds, succumbed only two hours ago to an unprecedented artillery bombardment by the Arab Legion. We simply did not have the manpower to reach those families. I regret to say that there are few survivors."

No one spoke. Golda Myerson (later Meir), the one woman in the cabinet, broke into sobs. Ben-Gurion himself remained tight-lipped. After a moment Yadin continued.

"The situation is far from favorable," he remarked soberly. "When the invasion comes the Arabs will obviously outnumber us in manpower, and in quantity and quality of weapons. However, I should like to point out that certain factors operate in our favor. The British will be leaving. This will permit full-scale mobilization for the first time. We have the morale, the planning, the tactical ability that the Arabs lack. Weapons will be coming in after May 15, and I am hopeful that this will include reasonable amounts of artillery. If we can distribute and integrate this equipment quickly enough I think we have a fifty-fifty chance."

Here Ben-Gurion added a comment of his own. "We will have manpower coming in from the Cyprus internment camps almost immediately, and from the European displaced persons' camps soon after that. These, too, are factors in our favor."

The discussion which followed was quite brief. In Yadin's presence, and with only a few dissenting votes, the cabinet members voted in favor of declaring the State. Then they filed silently from the room, their hearts heavy with the weight of their decision. On the evening of May 14, Prime Minister Ben-Gurion did indeed declare the independence of the State of Israel, reading off the proclamation solemnly before a hushed gathering in the Tel Aviv Art Museum.

THE STATE INVADED

Yadin himself was far too busy to attend the proclamation ceremony. Together with his staff in the pink stucco "red" house on HaYarkon Street, he was glued to his Haganah wireless set, waiting for news from Haifa. The first weapons were due to be unloaded at the port at any moment, and the Haganah command was fearful that the British, as a final parting gesture of friendship to the Arabs, would confiscate the supplies on the docks. After several hours of fruitless waiting, Yadin finally turned his attention to other matters. The following morning, however, the awaited information finally arrived: the first shipments had been unloaded without incident and were on their way to the quartermaster depots. Exultant, Yadin rushed directly to Ben-Gurion's home with the news. The prime minister himself opened the door.

"B.G., it's here," Yadin cried delightedly.

Ben-Gurion stared at his visitor for a moment, then turned toward the kitchen. "Paula!" he shouted to his wife. "Bring cognac."

The three of them drank a quick toast, shook hands excitedly, and then Yadin left to return to his office. As he hurried back on foot to HaYarkon Street, he heard the drone of aircraft in the distance. He recognized the sound at once as Spitfire engines. That could only mean the Egyptians. The sudden detonation of bombs from the downtown area confirmed his fears. The die was cast then. It was the certain prelude to invasion.

By the time Yadin returned to his office, his intelligence staff had begun to piece the picture together. Although the first estimates of Arab strength were exaggerated, the general outline of the invasion plan was quite accurate. It was to be a pincers movement. Transjordan's Arab Legion would concentrate on Jerusalem and its environs. Then, together with detachments of the Iraqi army, the Legion would occupy those areas of central Palestine allocated to the Palestinian Arab State. Simultaneously, in the north, the Syrians and Lebanese would move into Galilee, while other Syrian and Iraqi units would strike against the Jewish farm settlements in the Jordan

Valley. In the southwest, meanwhile, the Egyptians would move in from Sinai with a force of at least two brigades.

To block these incursions, Yadin divided his forces. The Haganah defense was based on nine territorial brigades. Three brigades were allocated to the north. Two brigades were held back in the Sharon plain to protect the Tel Aviv area. In the south, as a counterpoise to the Egyptians, a brigade was dispatched to the Rehovot-Isdud (Ashdod) area, and another to the deep south—the northern Negev region. Finally, in the Jerusalem district, one brigade was allocated for the defense of the city proper, and one to the struggle for the highway. This represented a total of twenty-five thousand fighting men, the majority recently mobilized Haganah reserves. In succeeding weeks additional thousands of recruits were pressed into service, but on May 15 Jewish military resources were still terrifyingly inadequate. At the outset, too, the vulnerability of the Jewish farm settlements weighed heavily on the high command; in response to Ben-Gurion's order of April 1, these villages had been stripped of their automatic weapons. Each kibbutz, each moshav was under strict injunction to hold out with whatever resources it could muster, and at whatever cost; not an inch of soil was to be abandoned. It was a tough warning, but it stiffened the resolve of the lightly armed farm communities. The emerging Israel army would make it up to them—once augmented in manpower and weapons. Thus it was, with both sides facing each other over borders allocated by the United Nations Partition Resolution, that the "official" Palestine war began.

On May 17 ten thousand Egyptian soldiers crossed the Sinai border into Palestine. One column, under Colonel Abd al-Aziz, moved toward Beersheba and the Hebron hills. On May 21 Aziz's advance patrols reached Bethlehem, and made preparations there for the attack on the southern outskirts of Jerusalem. Meanwhile a second, larger brigade under Colonel Mohammed Naguib moved northward along the coastal road toward Tel Aviv. Occupying Gaza, mercilessly bombarding and eventually overrunning Kibbutz Yad Mordecai, Naguib's column proceeded directly toward Isdud. Tel Aviv itself, a city of 250,000 people and the base of Haganah operations, was no more than two days' march away. By now the Jewish military situation was worse than critical; it appeared hopeless. At this point an Egyptian frigate lying only a few miles off the coast began shelling Tel Aviv with its long-range guns. Lacking a navy of their own, the Jews attacked the frigate with the only weapons available to them—several obsolete Piper Cub airplanes. The pilots flew sortie after sortie in these pathetic little craft, lobbing their homemade bombs by hand out the fuselage doors. One of the fliers was Yadin's youngest brother, Mattiyahu, who had just returned from air-lifting supplies to the isolated Negev settlements.

"You don't have to go up if you don't want to, Matti," Yadin told his brother. "Why don't you rest for a while? The other boys are fresher. They can handle the mission."

"Please stop that nonsense," Mattiyahu replied.

Joining the rest of the tiny squadron, the plane took off immediately. At the controls was David Sprinzak, son of Yosef Sprinzak, who was later to become Speaker of the Israel parliament. Yadin watched the squadron climb slowly westward, toward the Mediterranean. Then he returned to his jeep and drove back to headquarters. Several hours later, at 6:00 P.M., he reported to Ben-Gurion's home for a brief staff meeting. The prime minister seemed curiously ill at ease, and avoided Yadin's eyes as he spoke. Suddenly the young Haganah commander began to perspire. Excusing himself, he left the house. "Mundek" Pasternak, his staff assistant, was waiting for him at the door.

"What about the Egyptian destroyer?" asked Yadin.

"It was withdrawn. It was hit and frightened off," Pasternak replied. "However—we lost a plane in the operation," he added.

For a long moment Yadin hesitated. "Matti?" he asked, at last.

"Yes, Yigael. I'm sorry."

Yadin nodded. "I knew," he said quietly.

He returned to his office. For several hours he wrestled with himself and his grief. Should he fly to beleaguered Jerusalem to notify his parents? It was a visit he would not have permitted himself in other circumstances. Finally, in the evening, he decided to send a letter:

Dear Mother and Father:

I am not a man of good cheer today. Our beloved Matti has fallen in battle. This happened when a warship approached and began to bombard Tel Aviv. Several airplanes took off and among their crew was also Matti. He was always rushing into action and was the first to volunteer. He managed to hit the destroyer and thus caused it to withdraw. But his plane was hit and fell (together with him fell the son of Sprinzak). . . . I know that there is no consolation for his falling in battle. But whoever saw him in the last few weeks can have some consolation in the fact that he was happy all the time, found much interest in his work, and was loved by all because of his courage and the personal example he set. . . . Many fall every day. But it is different when the one is your brother or your son. That is our fate in this world. I know that this will be hardest of all for mother, who loved him so much. Yet in this period when everything is hanging on the edge, one must overcome these feelings, because everyone is sacrificing his life with his eyes open and without hesitation. . . . I hope that we shall be able this week to help make conditions in Jerusalem more bearable. And as you, Mother, say: "In the redemption of Israel you will find consolation." At the very end, I want to repeat what I said in the beginning. For Matti this much was clear: he and his friends knew what the pilot's fate might be. . . . Matti met death with a kiss. "May his soul know eternal life."

Your son,
Yigael

Instinctively following his military training, Yadin added the exact time—18:20—to the bottom of the page. Then he dispatched the letter to Jerusalem by courier plane.

From then on he concentrated with driving intensity on the task before him. There was no time or place now for personal sorrow. Tel Aviv had to be held at all costs.

Yadin dispatched the Givati Brigade, under Shimon Avidan, to block the Egyptian advance. Until recently Avidan's troops had been heavily involved in the fighting for the Jerusalem road, and had suffered grievous losses. The men were hollow-eyed from lack of sleep, and were seriously underequipped. Fortunately for the Jews, Mohammed Naguib, the Egyptian commander, was unaware of the actual precariousness of the Jewish position. He had already been shocked into near-immobility by the furious resistance offered by a single kibbutz, Negba; for ten days, totally isolated from the Jewish population centers in the north, the inhabitants of this collective settlement had warded off Egyptian tanks and armored cars with Molotov cocktails. Indeed, the tiny farm community continued to present a threat to Naguib's flank, and to the unimpeded movement of his troops on the Tel Aviv road. Moving with elaborate caution, as a result, the Egyptian colonel slowed his drive momentarily at Isdud, sixteen miles from the outskirts of Tel Aviv.

It was at this point that Yadin decided to mount a tactical offensive. On May 29 he ordered Avidan to circle Naguib's positions at night, and attack the Egyptian forces from the rear. The Givati Brigade consisted by now of no more than a thousand men. The Egyptians numbered four thousand. Nevertheless, the Jews found darkness and surprise effective weapons. The invaders were thrown into complete confusion by the unexpected descent upon their flank. Yadin, in turn, shrewdly exploited that confusion by calling a press conference of European correspondents, and announcing that two Egyptian brigades had been cut off from their supply lines by "overwhelming concentrations" of Israel shock troops. The "news" was immediately dispatched over the international wire services—and of course reached Cairo, as well. As Yadin had hoped, the Egyptian high command itself evidently accepted the story at face value, and radioed Naguib to pull up short and consolidate his supply lines at all costs. The bewildered colonel was more than willing to follow these instructions. His setback at the hands of the Givati Brigade proved to be the turning point of the Egyptian invasion. Although Avidan's strength was not adequate to force a major breakthrough at Ashkelon, the speed of his assault, combined with the demoralizing effect of Yadin's announcement, succeeded in halting the Egyptian drive. Tel Aviv was never again in jeopardy.

In the north, meanwhile, the Jewish defense effort was directed by Yigal Allon and Moshe Karmel, two of the most experienced and imaginative commanders in the Israel army. Their troops were well seasoned. Even before the establishment of the Jewish State, they had cleared the entire upper Galilee of Arab infiltrators. Nevertheless, at the outset of the invasion, the danger was hardly less grave here than in the other sectors of the country. Shortly after May 15 a Syrian column of two hundred heavily armored vehicles, including forty-five tanks, moved ominously toward the southern tip of Lake Kinneret. Its obvious target was the cluster of lush, prosperous Jewish settlements on both sides of the Jordan River. With comparatively little difficulty, the Syrians overran Samakh, then the Taggert fort near-by, and thereupon proceeded to attack the pioneer Zionist farm community of Deganiah, "mother of the kibbutzim."

Unfortunately, there was no possibility of blocking the column's advance without artillery; and thus far the only heavy weapons that had been unloaded at Haifa were four 65mm. howitzers, cannon that had been used by the French army as far back as the Franco-Prussian War of 1870! Yet the fate of these ancient artillery pieces was the subject of a protracted argument between Yadin and Ben-Gurion—such was the measure of the *Yishuv*'s vulnerability in those early days of the Palestine war. The prime minister was determined that the howitzers be dispatched at once to the Jerusalem Corridor. There they would prove invaluable to the Palmach troops marshaling for the battle of Latrun, the Arab stronghold blocking the passage of convoys on the road. Yadin insisted just as strenuously that the four guns would be of much less value in the mountains of Judea than in the flat country around Deganiah.

"There is a lesson for us from the past, B.G.," Yadin pointed out. "Do you remember First Kings, chapter twenty, verse twenty-three?"

In spite of the gravity of the situation Ben-Gurion could not resist a wry smile: Yadin and his biblical archaeology again. "Very well," he sighed, "I'm listening."

Yadin continued eagerly, "King Ahab faced an invasion in precisely the same spot. The Aramaeans (Syrians, for purposes of comparison) came down the same northern mountain road—the Aphek Road. Their goal was to break through into the plain and conduct the decisive battle there; for they had decided that the gods of the Israelites were the gods of the hills. Ahab knew that his best chance of destroying the Aramaean army was to intercept it just as it left the road and before it deployed in the plain. And so he crossed over the plateau with his men and caught the Aramaeans in their encampment at Aphek. He destroyed them. Well, Aphek is Deganiah, and the Syrians can be sucked into the same trap. With a little firepower we can stop them there, too."

Ben-Gurion was a better than fair biblical scholar himself. He recalled the story vividly.

"A good point, Yigael," he admitted. "Well taken. But don't forget we must defend Jerusalem, too. King Ahab never faced that problem. Jerusalem is dying and this may be our last chance to save her."

Ben-Gurion had not overstated the danger. The Arab stronghold of Latrun continued to block the highway, the jugular vein to Jerusalem; and for the prime minister Jerusalem held a mystic significance, far transcending its strategic importance. Thus, in the end, after five hours of argument, he and Yadin arrived at a compromise. Two of the artillery pieces would be dispatched to the Jerusalem Corridor. Two would be sent to Moshe Dayan's advance units at Deganiah.

The decision was reached with little time to spare. Dayan's men succeeded in assembling the antique cannon at the very moment the first Syrian tanks rumbled through the Deganiah perimeter. There were no aiming lenses on the guns. Under heavy Syrian shelling, the inexperienced Jewish artillery-men fired off a few trial shots—first to the right of the armored column, then to the left. At last, with less than twenty yards of closure left, a final shot struck home; the advance tank burst into flames. Had the Syrian commander known that these two obsolete weapons represented the entire arsenal of Jewish field guns in Deganiah—and half the Jewish cannonry in Palestine for that matter—he might well have pressed the attack. But he did not know. Indeed, it is likely that he anticipated an even heavier barrage momentarily. Shocked, and apparently unnerved by the surprising power of the Jewish defense, the commander lifted the hatch of his armored car and waved frantically to the tanks behind him. Immediately the column of vehicles swung around in its tracks, and roared back up the mountain road at full speed. It never returned. Yadin's biblical strategy was dramatically vindicated. With the exception of Kibbutz Mishmar HaYarden, which fell to a quick Syrian thrust on June 10 (it was later recaptured), the entire eastern Galilee remained firmly in Jewish hands.

Further south, in the central Jordan Valley, an Iraqi invading force of three thousand men proved equally incapable of denting the Jewish defenses. Well supported by Palmach infantrymen, the crucial border kibbutz of Gesher managed to hold firm, although suffering numerous casualties from a prolonged Arab artillery bombardment. Not every battle ended in success, however. A Jewish counterattack against the Transjordanian "wedge," protruding toward the Israel coastline further south, in the Gilboa mountains, failed with heavy loss of life. Perhaps additional numbers of troops might have blunted that wedge; but none were available. Within less than a week of the outbreak of the Palestine war, every soldier who could be spared from other fronts had been thrown into the battle for Jerusalem and the Jerusalem Corridor. And here the Jewish military position was as critical as it could possibly be.

THE BATTLE FOR JERUSALEM

Long before the outbreak of hostilities, Abdullah, King of Transjordan, had set Jerusalem as his prize objective. To the wily Hashemite monarch, conquest of this third most holy city in Islam would represent at least partial consolation for his father's loss of Mecca and Medina nearly thirty years before. He was determined to have it. Abdullah was convinced, too, that the Jewish defenders of the city were incapable for more than a few weeks of resisting a sustained attack by his Arab Legion. British-trained and British-led, this force was incomparably the most efficient army in the Arab world. It is worth noting that the Legion's British commander, Brigadier Sir John Glubb ("Glubb Pasha"), did not share Abdullah's enthusiasm for a full-scale assault on the city. As Glubb saw it, Jerusalem was a natural fortress, historically, in fact, an all-but-impregnable fortress. To the Englishman's mind it appeared far more logical to capture the surrounding plains and Judean mountains, and thus to acquire Jerusalem through an imposed peace treaty. Abdullah was adamant, however; the revered citadel must be seized at the outset, lest by some miscalculation it fall into the hands of the Egyptians. The king's decision to wage a full-scale battle for the city of Jerusalem ultimately proved to be a strategic blunder of the first magnitude. Nevertheless, for the eighty thousand Jews of Jerusalem, already badly weakened by the Arab strangle hold on their life line from the coast, the first few weeks of the Transjordanian attack very nearly proved fatal.

On May 18, Abdullah sent his first units into the walled Old City. Simultaneously he mobilized several additional companies from north of Jerusalem—a thousand soldiers in all, well equipped with modern twenty-five-pounder artillery pieces. Opposing the Arabs were approximately the same number of Jewish troops. They possessed several hundred rifles and Sten guns, quite meager quantities of ammunition, and no artillery whatever. Under the circumstances it was hardly surprising that the Legion was able rapidly to isolate Mount Scopus, with its Hebrew University and Hadassah Hospital, and to invest one Jewish quarter after another in the northern, outlying areas of Jerusalem. Thus, within the first few days of fighting, the Transjordanian forces were poised for a breakthrough at Mea-She'arim, one of the entrances to the major Jewish metropolitan area in the New City. During the next week, the fate of the Jewish population hung in the balance.

Indeed, for the haggard Jewish defenders of Jerusalem this first week of Arab invasion was the most critical period of the entire Palestine war. They were well aware of the precariousness of their position, moreover, and their frantic efforts now fully reflected this sense of desperation. Their gravest shortage was of artillery; they did not possess so much as a single cannon. Accordingly, Jewish ballistics experts and mechanics set about fashioning a number of homemade mortars from plumbing parts and grenade launchers. These "Davidkas" (after the man who conceived them) were far from accurate contraptions. Nevertheless, their projectiles, raw dynamite encased in iron, exploded with a fearsome blast that belied their actual destructive power. Brought into action for the first time during the week of May 18–24, the ungainly weapons succeeded in frightening the Arab Legionnaires and driving them back from their advance positions outside Mea-She'arim. (Today a monument to the "Davidka" may be found in one of Jerusalem's central squares.) At the end of the week Glubb decided to call off the attack in the northern part of the city. Several of his companies had lost fully half their troops.

From this point on, the Arabs switched their offensive to Jerusalem's southern suburbs. Advance units of the Egyptian army had already linked up with the Legion in Bethlehem. Thus, on May 21, under cover of a heavy Transjordanian artillery bombardment, Egyptian infantrymen stormed Ramat Rachel, a kibbutz lying astride the entrance to southern Jerusalem. For a dreadful few hours the heavily populated Jewish quarters of Talpiot, M'kor Chaim, and Katamon lay completely helpless and open to Arab occupation. Instantly, therefore, Colonel David Shaltiel, the former intelligence chief now serving as Israeli commander of the Jerusalem area, dispatched the Har-El and Etzioni Brigades with orders to reoccupy Ramat

Rachel at all costs. What followed was the most bitterly contested single battle of the Palestine war. The little kibbutz changed hands five times during the next four days. Soldiers pressing forward in bayonet attack often had to climb over bodies piled one on top of the other. But when the last attack was over, the Jews remained in control. For the moment, at least, the shadow lifted from the New City.

The Jewish quarter of the Old City was not as fortunate. For the previous six months its little enclave of seventeen hundred Orthodox Jews had been cut off from the Jewish population on the other side of the historic Wall. By May 17 the Arab Legion had penned these distraught and starving survivors into an area of no more than four hundred yards. On the afternoon of the eighteenth, the tiny community exhausted the last of its ammunition. That same night a company of Palmach troops battered its way into the Old City, and took up positions at the side of the defenders. Yet these eighty-seven youths were not enough. During the next week units of the Etzioni Brigade made several frantic attempts to break through to the Old City; but each time a murderous Arab artillery barrage drove them off. At last, on May 28, two aged rabbis approached the Legion's lines under a flag of truce, and announced the surrender of their comrades. News of the Old City's fall was received with profound shock and grief by the Jewish population of Palestine. The ancient community had been the site of the Holy Temple and the cynosure of Orthodox Jewry the world over; its capture somehow violated the deepest sensibilities even of nonreligious Jews, as if the enemy had consciously set out to defile the most cherished shrine in Jewish tradition.

Yet from the purely military point of view, the fate of the New City, with its eighty thousand Jewish inhabitants, was a matter of much graver concern to the Haganah high command. Perhaps the Arabs had thus far been unable to conquer the sprawling urban complex through direct assault: by the opening of June, nevertheless, the survival of Jewish Jerusalem was far from certain. The weeks of artillery bombardment had taken their toll in dead and wounded. So had the tightening vise of the siege itself. With the Arabs in control of the single line of supply from Tel Aviv, ammunition in the New City had all but run out. Jewish machine-gunners were under orders to fire single rounds. The water pipeline from the coast had long since been cut, and the city's taps were dry. Civilians were obliged to line up each day for rations of drinking water; there was none to spare for washing. The prospect of imminent starvation, too, faced Jerusalem. In some quarters of the city people were driven to foraging in the streets, even to eating weeds.

For Ben-Gurion, the fate of Jerusalem was of more than strategic or even humanitarian significance. Although the prime minister was no religionist, he was shrewd enough a statesman to recognize the unique political and spiritual role the Holy City had played in Jewish history. To him, Israel without Jerusalem was as unthinkable as a body without a head; indeed, he used the analogy frequently. During prolonged and anguished meetings with Yadin, therefore, Ben-Gurion insisted that military priority now be given to the opening of the Jerusalem highway—at whatever cost. Yadin accepted the responsibility, although not without misgivings. Like Glubb, he was convinced that the conquest of the rest of Palestine would ultimately, and more effectively, secure control of the great fortress-city. Nevertheless, he now concentrated his efforts on blasting open the strangled supply route.

On May 23, Yigal Allon, the Palmach commander, was called down from the north to assume tactical responsibility for the assault on Latrun, the Arab strongpoint controlling the road. There were few soldiers to spare for the operation. New recruits had to be summoned to augment the Palmach forces, and these included hundreds of recent immigrants who possessed no military experience or training whatever, who indeed had hardly learned how to handle their rifles. They were rushed up now by buses and taxis from Tel Aviv. On May 25, the attack began in a blistering *khamsin,* a desert sirocco sweeping across Palestine from the Sudan. The troops were without water. Many were white with exhaustion even as they assumed their battle stations. No time was left for reconnoitering the ground. Without adequate artillery support, the men were thrown into a direct frontal assault. As the Jewish forces scaled the rocks leading up to the well-fortified village, the Arab Legion's crack Fourth Regiment raked them with a withering mortar and artillery barrage. One hundred thirty-seven Jews died in the attack. During the next few days several additional attempts were mounted, and each time repulsed with heavy loss of life. Latrun was apparently impregnable. Indeed, the village very nearly became the graveyard of Jewish hopes for rescuing Jerusalem.

There was one other alternative, however. For several weeks Colonel David "Mickey" Marcus, the area commander, had been using a path south of Latrun and Bab el-Wad to send troops on foot through the hills to Jerusalem. Perhaps, by superhuman effort, the path could be widened sufficiently to enable vehicles to pass through. It was worth the effort. With Yadin's approval, five hundred workers were called up from both Tel Aviv and Jerusalem and immediately set about clearing boulders and blasting the rock sidings. The effort continued around the clock, often under Legion artillery fire from Latrun. It was agonizing, back-breaking, throat-parching labor. Yet there was no possibility of rest, for a United Nations truce was due to come into effect on June 11. If the "Burma Road" could not be completed before then, no further efforts would be permitted after the truce deadline. Jerusalem would starve. And so the men flailed away at the rocks until they dropped from exhaustion. Drills and explosives were carried by back, on foot. At last, by June 9, a primitive roadbed was cut through the Judean mountains. The first trucks, packed to the gunnels with cans of food and water, ventured out on the pitted makeshift highway. Several hours later they reached Jerusalem, where they were greeted ecstatically by a roaring crowd of frenzied, delirious citizens. The city was saved.

THE TEN-DAYS' CAMPAIGN

The United Nations truce, scheduled to remain in effect for one month, came as a welcome respite for both sides. The savagery of the Jewish defense had shocked and disheartened the Arab invaders. They had achieved little for their efforts—nothing more, in fact, than the Old City of Jerusalem, a fragile Syrian bridgehead in the Galilee, and an uncontested occupation of the bleak and arid Negev desert. All the Arab forces except the Egyptian suffered from a serious shortage of ammunition. What little co-ordination had ever existed between their armies was now a thing of the past. The governments of Egypt and Jordan (as the Hashemite Kingdom now called itself, controlling both sides of the river) bitterly accused each other of lethargy and cowardice, of limiting their efforts in Palestine to narrow territorial campaigns.

For the Jews, nevertheless, the situation on June 11 was hardly less precarious. The Negev still was in Arab hands; the Jewish farm communities there were shell-shocked and physically spent from innumerable artillery barrages. The Syrians threatened even yet to cut eastern Galilee in two. The Iraqi and Jordanian spearheads protruded to within ten miles of the Mediterranean. Moreover, the Jews, too, had all but exhausted their ammunition. Few Israel troops possessed serviceable military clothing, and some had been obliged to go into battle clad only in pajamas and underwear. Four thousand Palmach and Haganah men had thus far been killed, and several times that many wounded.

During the next month, as Count Folke-Bernadotte, the United Nations truce negotiator, vainly (and clumsily) attempted to work out a territorial compromise between the belligerents, the Israelis concentrated their efforts on equipping and retraining their battle-weary armies. Here the Jews were not without advantages. As early as May 20 the Czechoslovak government had turned over one of its military airfields to Haganah agents for their exclusive use; during the next three months it became the main Jewish base in Europe for the shuttle service of arms and planes. Large quantities of Czech rifles, machine guns, artillery, even dismantled Messerschmitt fighter planes, were now flown in Dakota and Commando transports to the Haganah's airstrip in Aqir, Israel. Other fighter and bomber aircraft, most of them procured illegally in the United States, were flown to Israel by Jewish veterans of the British, Canadian, American, and South African air forces. Simultaneously, freighters, loaded with surplus tanks and spare parts from such unlikely sources as Cuba and the Philippines, were now systematically disgorging their cargo at Israel ports—usually under cover of darkness, to evade the United Nations truce supervisors.

Yadin, meanwhile, worked unceasingly to reorganize his army during the four weeks at his disposal. Officers and noncoms were sent back to camp for intensive refresher courses in tactics and weapons. Twenty-five thousand new recruits were now outfitted in uniforms supplied from abroad, armed with Czech rifles, and rushed through basic training. At the same time Yadin radically altered the army's organizational structure, transforming the nine brigade commands into three front commands. The Israelis soon were better armed; their officers and more than half their men were battle-hardened. They were determined now to seize the offensive the moment the truce expired on July 8. Yadin laid his plans carefully. In the north, the Syrians were to be thrown back across the Jordan River. In the center, the Legion and its Iraqi allies would be driven from their advance salients of Lydda and Ramle, thus opening the Jerusalem Corridor at its critical juncture with the coastal plain.

And that is how it happened. A mere ten days elapsed before the United Nations forced a second truce upon the tortured land. But in that short interval the Jews moved with astonishing speed and effectiveness. Moshe Karmel, commander of the northern front, launched a slashing attack against the Syrian troops emplaced at Mishmar HaYarden. As anticipated, the Arabs dug in, committing additional troops and even fighter planes to support the defenders. Thereupon Karmel immediately dispatched his Seventh Brigade, under Chaim Laskov, into lower Galilee and Samaria. Against an inept defense thrown up by Fawzi al-Qawukji and his "Arab Liberation Army," Laskov seized Shafa Amr and Nazareth with comparatively little difficulty. Virtually all northern Palestine was now cleared to the banks of the Jordan.

Meanwhile, on the central front, Yigal Allon's brigades struck within three hours of the expiration of the truce. In a furiously contested night battle, the Legionnaires were driven out of Lydda, and then out of the international airport near-by. The next day Colonel Moshe Dayan, a one-eyed veteran of the Second World War, led a column of jeeps into the neighboring city of Ramle. Driving through the main street at full speed, machine guns blazing, the Jews sent the panic-stricken Iraqi troops fleeing for their lives. In one fell swoop the most serious Arab threat to the coastal area was shattered. Moreover, Allon's sledge-hammer campaign in the central front was not without a profound psychological effect. It convinced Jordan's King Abdullah that nothing further was to be gained by engaging the Jews in direct combat. Thus, the Legion was ordered to consolidate its conquests in Jerusalem and Arab Palestine, but to refrain from further offensive efforts against the Jews. These orders were intercepted by the Haganah. From then on, the Israel high command recognized that it was free to concentrate its forces in the south—against the Egyptians.

OPERATION TEN PLAGUES

In the final days before the imposition of the second truce, on July 18, the Jews had already succeeded in liberating a number of villages neighboring the besieged southern kibbutz of Negba. Yet most of the Negev settlements remained under blockade, and after July 18 the Egyptians tightened their line of advance positions. It was quite apparent to Yadin, therefore, that a future offensive would have to be mounted in the desert. Political as well as military considerations influenced this decision. Notwithstanding Israel's recent and substantial military victories, Count Folke-Bernadotte, the truce mediator, persisted in making cession of the Negev to the Arabs a basis for his suggested Palestine peace treaty. Increasingly certain of their strength, the Israel government contemptuously rejected Bernadotte's proposals; rather, Yadin and his staff began making preparations for an even more effective reply to the mediator. They would smash Egyptian strength in the Negev once and for all.

At first there was no unanimity on the battle plan. Moshe Karmel and Ben-Gurion himself were inclined at the outset to concentrate Israel forces against the so-called "Iron Triangle," the heavily infiltrated wedge of Arab territory projecting into central Israel at forty-five-degree angles from Jenin to Tulkarem to Nablus. Yadin persuaded them to abandon the idea, pointing out that the passage of time and Israel's military resources would permit only one offensive—and that the Egyptian danger was potentially the gravest. Allon, on the other hand, who was placed in command of the Negev front, had a favorite idea of his own.

"You know, Yigael," he said to Yadin, "the southern front is a natural staging area for an assault on Arab-held Jerusalem. I could cut straight up through Hebron to Bethlehem. The Legion is dispersed very thin there."

Yadin thought for a moment, then shook his head emphatically. "Forget it," he said. "Historically Jerusalem has never been conquered from the south."

"Never?" Allon was astonished. "With such a clear and easy approach through flat terrain a full two-thirds of the way? It hardly seems possible. Are you sure?"

"Positive," Yadin replied. "It has never been conquered that way. Not by the Sumerians, nor by the Egyptians, nor by the Hebrews, nor by the Babylonians, nor by the Greeks, nor the Romans, nor the Byzantines, nor the Arabs, nor the Turks—not by any nation that has ever captured Jerusalem. From north, east, and west, yes. But never from the south. Never."

Thereupon, to prove his point, Yadin drew upon an impressive fund of archaeological knowledge, quoting the reports of modern excavations, citing ancient parchments, wall reliefs, and offering cartographic and topographic evidence. "Not a single military cemetery, not a chariot nor an ancient storehouse or armory has even been found in that region—nothing suggests that so much as one army, one platoon, has ever gotten by those southern ramparts. They have been impregnable—right up to the time of Napoleon and even Allenby. It is barely possible, admittedly, that we could succeed where they failed. But not probable. We'll be better off concentrating our forces elsewhere."

By now Allon was convinced. The two men agreed that priority should be given instead to a full-scale offensive in the Negev. Of course there was the problem of the truce. But here the Egyptians had resolved the issue themselves. According to the terms of the July 18 cease-fire, the Jews were granted the right to send food and medical supplies to their isolated Negev settlements by unarmed convoy. From the outset, the Egyptians made their contempt for this agreement obvious. Interfering at will with the free passage of Jewish transport, they also intermittently bombed and shelled Jewish farm settlements and Jewish military positions.

"I think we'll have to call our plan Operation Ten Plagues," Yadin remarked wryly to his staff after the latest Egyptian shelling. "They won't keep any agreement until the pressure on them gets hot enough. We must make it good and hot."

He was reasonably sure now of his army's ability to apply that pressure. Although the Egyptian line, running across the northern Negev from Gaza to Hebron, was well fortified and protected by armor and artillery, it lacked defense in depth. An entire Palmach brigade had already infiltrated behind the Egyptian positions, and operated unnoticed in the vastness of the desert, maintaining contact with the Jewish settlements. Moreover, Allon now had at his disposal the single largest concentration of troops ever allocated to a front commander since the Palestine war began. These included the Givati Brigade, two battalions of the Negev Brigade, and an armored battalion, "Samson's Foxes," of Yitzhak Sadeh's brigade—thirty thousand men in all. For the first time, too, the Jews had a small air-fighter squadron at their disposal. For a veteran guerrilla fighter like Allon, the miniature army under his command was a small miracle. Once the plans for Operation Ten Plagues had been completed, he chafed impatiently to begin.

The opportunity came on October 15. With United Nations approval, the Israelis set out to provision their kibbutzim in the northern Negev by conducting an unarmed convoy across the Egyptian-controlled Faluja crossroads. Then, the moment the column drew within sight of the farm settlements, the lead vehicles were blown to bits. Yadin had expected the move—indeed, this time he had looked forward to it (although, to this day, he blandly denies that the Jews themselves dynamited the trucks). Immediately, therefore, he ordered Allon into action. The speed with which the Israelis now launched their offensive proved a shattering surprise for the Egyptians. Swooping low behind enemy lines, the fledgling Israel air force bombed and strafed the main Egyptian fighter base at Al-Arish, in the Sinai desert, as well as Gaza and other nearby depots. Simultaneously, the Yiftah Brigade (the infiltrators), operating secretly behind the fixed Arab positions, blew up the railway line near the Egyptian border, and mined the principal Egyptian supply road between Rafah and Khan Yunis. Throughout the night of October 15–16, squads of Israel commandos raided Egyptian supply dumps, battered wedges between Egyptian positions, and drove steadily up the coastal road toward Beit Hanun.

But it was all a feint. Allon's actual goal was the Faluja crossroads, the key junction controlling the highway net into the Negev desert. During the next day, while Yitzhak Sadeh hurled a battalion of tank-led infantry against the Egyptian fortification of Iraq al-Manshiyah, other detachments of Israel troops stormed into the hills overlooking the crossroads. The battle for the crossing was a particularly bloody one. Both sides suffered many dead and wounded. By the next morning, however, the strategic point was firmly in Jewish hands. The Egyptian line was badly riddled and in imminent danger of being turned. Only Huleiqat, the anchor of the enemy's fortifications, still had to be taken. Here, unfortunately, there appeared to be no alternative to a frontal assault; and Huleiqat was the most heavily defended of Egyptian bastions. The prospect would have daunted a less resolute or experienced commander than Allon. Under cover of darkness on October 20, after careful planning and a good deal of re-provisioning, the young officer launched the attack. The battle raged through the night. It was one of the most fearsome of the war. Exceptional courage was demonstrated by both Jews and Arabs. Finally, by dawn, the worst was over. Huleiqat's defenses crumbled, and the Jews occupied the fort.

The conquest of Huleiqat was the turning point of Operation Ten Plagues. The Egyptian line was now breached, and the larger number of Egyptian troops in the Negev faced the possibility of entrapment in a pocket near Faluja. At the very least, the Egyptian "finger" pointing toward Tel Aviv had been amputated once and for all. Yet there was little time to exploit this victory. Britain's Foreign Secretary Ernest Bevin was profoundly chagrined by the unexpected turn of events. His animosity toward the Jews, his friendship for the Arabs, had not waned during the half-year since the termination of the Mandate. Thus, at his instigation, the United Nations Security Council was called into session, and the British delegate, Sir Alexander Cadogan, introduced a resolution calling for a cease-fire in Palestine. The Jews had little time to waste. Without pausing to consolidate his position at Huleiqat, therefore, Allon sent his three battalions racing down the newly opened road to Beersheba, the sleepy little Arab town known as the "capital" of the Negev. The maneuver was spectacularly successful. Caught off guard, the Egyptian garrison in Beersheba surrendered after only feeble resistance. Forty-eight hours later the neighboring Lachish area was occupied by fast-moving Israel cavalry.

During the next week, as the United Nations truce settled slowly over the desert, the panic-stricken Egyptians began evacuating their detachments from the northern Negev. In the east, their positions around Hebron and Bethlehem were taken over by Jordan's Arab Legion. In the western Negev, they loaded their troops on naval vessels anchored off the coast. Even here, however, they suffered grievous losses. Two of their ships were sunk by Jewish frogmen. One of the vessels, the *Farouk*, flagship of the Egyptian navy, went down with seven hundred soldiers aboard. Finally, too, nearly three thousand of Egypt's finest troops, the crack Fourth Brigade, found themselves entirely encircled and immobilized in the northwestern Negev's Faluja "pocket." Under the command of a gallant and resourceful Sudanese, Brigadier Taha Bey (the "Black Tiger"), the soldiers of the trapped Fourth Brigade promptly dug in, tightened their lines, and mounted the single bravest defense conducted by Arab troops in the Palestine war.

Even as Israel artillery and infantry units tightened the vise on the Faluja pocket, Allon decided to establish personal communication with Taha Bey: perhaps the Egyptians could somehow be persuaded to surrender. He dispatched his aide, Major Yeruham Cohen, to arrange a meeting with the enemy officers. Under a flag of truce, Cohen, a Yemenite Jew in his early twenties, approached the Egyptian lines at Faluja. The shooting slackened, and he called out in Arabic, asking for an officer to approach him. After a pause of several minutes, three Egyptians climbed out of their trenches and walked slowly toward Cohen. One of the officers, a tall, mustachioed, hawk-nosed man, saluted the young emissary and introduced himself as Major Gamal Abd al-Nasser. Cohen extended his hand and Nasser shook it. Then the Israeli conveyed Allon's message. While Nasser continued chatting with Cohen, the other two officers returned to their lines to consult with Taha Bey. A few minutes later they returned with the announcement that their commander was willing to meet his Jewish counterpart. The appointment was set for the following day at Kibbutz Gat, two miles to the east.

The next morning Taha Bey and five officers, Nasser among them, were conducted under a white flag to the designated meeting place. Allon awaited them with his staff. After salutes and handshakes, an Israel honor guard paraded briefly before the Egyptians. Then the visitors were conducted inside the kibbutz dining hall for a meal and soft drinks. Somewhat to Allon's discomfiture, the Egyptians insisted on conducting all conversations in English—although he himself spoke fluent Arabic. Apparently they considered it a sign of breeding. Through an interpreter, therefore, Allon and Taha Bey exchanged compliments. The Egyptian general was a stocky, square-jawed Negro, gentle of manner and quick to smile. He congratulated Allon on Israel's "admirable" military victories. When Allon pointed out that the Egyptian position in the Faluja pocket was now quite hopeless, Taha Bey was quick to agree. Exploiting his advantage, the Jewish commander noted that both Egyptians and Jews had a common enemy, the British. When Taha Bey agreed again, nodding his head vigorously for emphasis, Allon observed that it would clearly be impossible for the Egyptians to fight the British as long as their army remained embroiled in Palestine. Would it not be better for the Fourth Brigade to surrender now, Allon asked, and thus avoid a needless waste of lives?

At this Taha Bey spoke gravely. "There is no doubt, honored sir," he replied, "that your position is better than ours. Your brilliant planning and the bravery of your troops have astonished us. You have broken through our most fortified lines. You have humiliated the hitherto unvanquished Egyptian army. I realize only too well that by our continued stand I will not be able to change the military situation nor save our front. But one thing I shall be able to save: the honor of the Egyptian army. And therefore I shall fight to my last bullet and my last man. Only orders from my government can stop me."

Allon, visibly disappointed, pressed the issue a little longer. But the Sudanese general remained adamant. In the end Taha Bey was conducted back to his lines, and shortly afterward the chatter of machine guns resumed. Although the Israelis had little difficulty in liquidating other isolated centers of Egyptian resistance, Taha Bey's Fourth Brigade continued to hold out fiercely. In response to United Nations pressure for another truce, both sides called a temporary halt to the fighting at the end of October. The Egyptians made it quite clear, however, that they were still unprepared to discuss a general armistice with the Jews. Indeed, throughout November, they shuttled fresh units into the Gaza Strip. Evidently their high command still anticipated breaking through to the isolated brigade at Faluja. Yadin and Allon recognized that one final, massive offensive would probably be necessary to force the Arabs to the peace table.

In the interval Allon still made fitful attempts to negotiate with the commander of the trapped Fourth Brigade. The effort was unsuccessful. Its one result was to cement the friendship between Yeruham Cohen, who continued as Israel spokesman, and Major Gamal Abd al-Nasser, who represented Taha Bey. During their conversations the two men ranged over a wide variety of political and military matters. Nasser evidenced little dislike for the Jews themselves; indeed, he seemed to regard the Palestine war as a sporting contest which had been won decisively, and honorably, by Israel. He was fascinated, too, by the kibbutzim he had seen.

"How are they organized?" he asked. "Does true socialism really exist there? How do you avoid the growth of a leisured class? That's our great problem in Egypt, you know."

Nasser's curiosity was insatiable. Everything he saw about him he insisted on comparing with his own country. He was unsparing in his criticism of the social corruption in Egypt. "We shall cure it one day," he promised Cohen, "and it will be sooner than you think."

The young Egyptian reserved his bitterest diatribes for the British, however. "They maneuvered us into this war," he noted angrily. "We didn't want it. What is Palestine to us? It was all a British trick to take our minds away from them, and their occupation of our country. Well, their time is coming, that much is certain."

Nasser questioned Cohen closely on the Jewish Underground battle against the British. How had the Jews driven them out? he asked. What techniques had been used to develop mass support among the population? Again and again he returned to the subject. At the same time he vented his wrath against Egypt's "so-called" allies. Why had Abdullah not come to the aid of the beleaguered brigade at Faluja? he wondered. The Arab Legion was encamped only seventeen miles away, in the Hebron hills. If the Jordanians had mounted even a limited offensive they could have taken the pressure off the Egyptians in the Negev. The absence of co-operation among the Arab armies was an open scandal. Some day Abdullah would pay for his "betrayal."

Nasser had other explanations, as well, for the Palestine debacle. One of his bêtes noires was the Palestine Arab population—"wretched soldiers," "shiftless, cowardly, lazy dogs." It was almost impossible to communicate with this rabble, he insisted; their dialect was unintelligible. If all those thousands of Palestine Arab refugees had not poured into Egyptian lines, the war could have been pursued more successfully. As it was, they created nothing but problems, and seriously interfered with the Egyptian war effort. He could think of no people less deserving of the blood his soldiers had spilled.

THE SEARCH FOR A ROAD

Even as Cohen and Nasser were carrying on their discussions, Yadin and Allon were making preparations for a decisive campaign to drive the enemy from its last remaining enclaves on Israel territory. The Egyptians were deployed slightly to the north of the Sinai frontier, between their own country and Israel, and formed two prongs. The northern prong, consisting of two brigades straddling Rafah and Gaza, was supported by the principal Egyptian staging base of Al-Arish. The southern prong, also of two brigades' strength, extended from Al-Auja to Bir Asluj, and aimed upward toward Beersheba. In addition to these forces, the Egyptian Fourth Brigade, locked in the Faluja pocket, tied down a Jewish unit of comparable size. Four Israel brigades remained—comparatively seasoned troops by now, and for the first time nearly as well equipped as the invaders. The Egyptians defended well-fortified positions. The Israelis enjoyed the advantage of surprise and of the choice of terrain best suited for the attack. Yadin and Allon were determined to exploit that opportunity to the maximum.

During the early weeks of December, the two young commanders made their preparations carefully, first at the Haganah "red house" in Tel Aviv, and later at Allon's Negev headquarters in Castina. The essential outlines of the plan rapidly took shape. The Egyptians would undoubtedly expect the attack to be launched against their northern line, the prong aiming at the heavily populated Jewish coastal plain. Without hesitation, therefore, Yadin and Allon discounted that alternative. Instead they would strike southward, driving toward Al-Auja, the anchor of the Egyptian position in the Negev desert. Once Al-Auja fell, the entire Egyptian army in Palestine would be outflanked. Indeed, the Israelis would then be in a position to sweep upward into the Sinai Peninsula itself, toward Al-Arish and the Mediterranean, breaking the back of the Egyptian military effort in one crushing offensive.

It was an imaginative and daring conception. But it presupposed the capture of Al-Auja; and the main road from Bir Asluj to Al-Auja, unfortunately, was well protected by formidable Egyptian artillery and tank units. Even if the enemy anticipated an attack on the northern prong (a notion Yadin encouraged by calculated leaks to newsmen), a direct assault on the southern highway could hardly be undertaken except at a heavy, even prohibitive, cost of men and equipment. Yadin and Allon grappled with the problem for the better part of a week. No matter how they viewed the campaign, however, no alternative appeared to frontal attack on the road; that would mean hundreds of casualties—perhaps several thousand, and in any case there was no guarantee of success. Yadin had not been faced with so agonizing a decision since the grim days of April, when he had ordered the Jewish farm settlements stripped of their weapons for the offensive on the Jerusalem Corridor.

Nor was the impending battle less fraught with political consequence. The British, dismayed at the unexpected turn of events in the Palestine war, were exerting pressure on the United Nations to order a final end to hostilities in the Holy Land, and to impose sanctions (presumably against Israel) in the event the orders were disobeyed. It was likely, therefore, that this offensive would be the Israelis' last chance to secure their borders. If it failed, if the Egyptians maintained their foothold in the Negev, the territorial configuration of the State of Israel would still remain in limbo, subject to continued international debate. As far as the Jews were concerned, the war had been too costly to permit that kind of attrition. Anyway, the

Negev was Israel's future, the indispensable living space for millions of immigrants—for whose anticipated arrival, after all, the State had been established.

At night, Yadin tossed on his cot, his mind anxiously wrestling with the apparently insoluble strategic problem. There was an answer, of course. It had to do with a relic. Several times he was on the verge of grasping it. But each time, as he stared fixedly at his military charts, the idea escaped him. Only the road remained, etched like a scar across the Negev terrain, and stitched by innumerable Egyptian gun and tank emplacements.

He was studying the wrong map. On December 17, the idea returned and took root. Yadin worked it out in his mind first. Then he walked quickly to his archaeological files. The old, well-thumbed folio was still there, his guide to Greco-Roman Palestine. And there was the road, just south of Al-Auja. It was in fact the barest memory of a road, a stone-knuckled pathway for the innumerable Roman legions that had trekked their way into the interior of the wilderness. For a moment, in the thrill of discovery, Yadin saw it with an archaeologist's eyes: saw the stolid janissaries' faces of the soldiers, the flash of sun on their visors and breastplates, the wind-ruffled tassels of horsehair on spears and helmet crests.

And then he saw it with a general's eyes, and the question was a different one: did the road still exist? Allon, who was hardly less excited than Yadin by the new possibility, wasted no time in finding out. Immediately he dispatched two Palmach scouts to reconnoiter the dunes above Bir Asluj. This was the no man's land northwest of the main highway, and perilously close to the Egyptian fortifications. Just before dawn the message was relayed back to command headquarters: "Kasheh, aval efshar—difficult, but possible." Those three words decided the fate of the war. The road had been found. With effort it could be made usable.

During the next ninety-six hours the effort was exerted. Under cover of darkness, engineers set to work laying boards and Bailey-bridge remnants on the most difficult stretches of the ancient pathway. The work was completed in such uncanny silence that the Egyptian outposts, less than two miles away, remained completely unsuspecting. On the night of December 21 the job was done. Twenty-four hours later the offensive began.

According to plan, Allon sent an armored column rolling ominously toward Gaza. Another brigade of infantrymen charged directly toward the main highway between Bir Asluj and Al-Auja. Actually, both these attacks were feints; and they effectively convinced the Egyptians that the Israel offensive was unfolding according to orthodox pattern. Indeed, the Arab reaction was never a matter of doubt. On the second day after fighting began, Jewish signalmen spliced into the Egyptian telephone wires, and from then on listened to a running account of the enemy's battle orders.

During the next few days, as the Egyptians braced themselves against repeated frontal assaults on their central fortifications, a powerful Israel column of half-tracks and troop carriers was already rolling swiftly along the Roman road. The troops kept strict radio silence, communicating with Allon's headquarters by means of carrier pigeons. At dawn of December

26 the Jews were within firing range of Al-Auja. The mighty fortress was silent; its garrisons had taken up positions to the north. The muzzles of the Egyptian artillery faced northward, too, covering the approaches of the main highway. Now suddenly, before the astonished defenders realized what had happened, the vanguard of the Israel army smashed into their rear, assault tanks and Bren carriers careening into the square of the town, infantrymen pouring a hail of lead into the trenches and gun emplacements. The Egyptians fought back courageously, swinging their artillery pieces around and firing at point-blank range. The Jews suffered many casualties but never lost the initiative. After a full day and night of fighting, much of it hand-to-hand, the Arabs raised the white flag. Their colonel walked out of his heavily barricaded headquarters to formalize the surrender. He was still dressed in his pajamas; the lightning attack had caught him in bed.

The fall of Al-Auja on December 27 placed the remnants of the Egyptian army in an impossible position. As their eastern axis now rapidly disintegrated, hundreds of their soldiers began surrendering, often with their battle equipment intact. Allon, determined to exploit his victory to the fullest, continued driving his battle-weary men westward into the Sinai Peninsula. In a brilliantly executed enveloping movement, the Israel columns overran Abu-Ageila, ten miles inside Egyptian territory. From here they pressed on without rest toward the Mediterranean coast—and the central Egyptian staging base of Al-Arish.

The Jews had come far in eight months of war, farther than the limited distance of mere geographical advance. In May their ill-armed little militia had faced Arab tanks less than fifteen miles from Tel Aviv. In December their battle-seasoned troops, supported by armor and fighter planes, were knifing into Egypt, to the very gates of Al-Arish, cutting the last exit routes of the entire Egyptian army. The incredible change in fortunes was as astonishing to the watching world as to the exultant Jews themselves.

The miracle of the final victory was quickly dissipated, however. On December 30, even as the conquering Israelis prepared to invest Al-Arish, Yigael Yadin suddenly received a message from Ben-Gurion. The army was ordered to evacuate the Sinai Peninsula immediately. It was an astonishing volte-face. Yadin soon enough learned what lay behind it. London had sent Ben-Gurion an ultimatum: the British government was prepared to respect its "mutual defense" pact with Egypt unless the Israelis cleared out of Egyptian territory without delay. Apparently this was Foreign Secretary Bevin's final revenge on the Jews. Of course Ben-Gurion was heartbroken by the loss of this priceless opportunity; yet he dared not risk a military encounter with a great power. Yadin shared the prime minister's grief— but at the same time he understood and accepted the decision; the Jews had won too much to gamble with their victory now. Together, Yadin and Ben-Gurion rejected Allon's anguished appeal for permission to finish the job.

At Yadin's insistence, however, the prime minister granted Allon one concession; his brigades were allowed to seize the heights above the border town of Rafah. Thus was sealed off the final escape route of the shattered Egyptian garrisons in the Gaza Strip. On January 6 the Egyptians sued for an armistice. Fighting ceased. Days passed as both sides made preparations to meet with the United Nations peace negotiator at Rhodes. At the last moment, however, the Egyptians issued an ultimatum of their own: no armistice negotiations would begin unless the Jews first evacuated the Rafah heights. To Yadin, Allon, and the Israel army staff, the demand was as preposterous as it was outrageous. Release of the encircled Egyptian troops would nullify Israel's most effective bargaining weapon, and leave Egypt with a contiguous strip of land well within Israel territory. And yet once again Ben-Gurion decided to bow before the dictates of *Realpolitik*. So far as the prime minister could determine, the only alternative to refusal was a resumption of the war, on Egyptian soil, and the inescapable threat of British intervention.

Other considerations must have weighed on Ben-Gurion's mind, as well. Israel's armies had already anchored down the greater part of the Negev. Even then a Jewish column was driving down the length of the desert on its way to Eilat, and the Red Sea. Elsewhere, under duress of battle, the Jews had accomplished more than the defense of their new republic; they had carved out an additional thousand square kilometers of territory, including western Galilee. The State was born, secured, and functioning. The other Arab nations had indicated their willingness to follow Egypt to the armistice table. Perhaps it would be wiser now to allow the Egyptians an opportunity of saving face. Even with the removal of the Israel wedge across the Gaza Strip, and the release of the trapped Egyptian brigades, it still seemed likely that the Arabs would be constrained to formalize the Rhodes truce agreements afterward with a permanent peace treaty. The gamble seemed worth taking.

Accordingly, in the second week of January, 1949, Israel withdrew its troops from the Rafah heights. The mauled and battered remnants of the Egyptian army were allowed to depart. As the Arabs assembled in formation, Yeruham Cohen, Allon's aide, watched the ceremonies from the Rafah hillside. Suddenly he spied an old friend. It was Major Nasser. Cohen shouted a greeting, and the two men ran toward each other, warmly shaking hands for the last time. To the strains of an Israel army band, the Egyptians then marched off disconsolately toward their encampment at Al-Arish.

They passed into Sinai, their trucks and gun-carriers clanking over camel thorns and brushwood. Majestic cliffs of pink and mauve granite looked down on them, aged, wind-weary slopes and gorges of amber, porphyry, and feldspar. By sunset of the next day the vanquished army was strung in a frieze across its own land. As the dust cloud opened from the east, bedouin herdsmen stared without expression at the long line of mud-skinned soldiers, flat-headed and crinkle-haired, heavy-shouldered and wide-buttocked, staring neither to right nor left as they trudged silently along the rim of the sea. No one dared ask them where they had been. No one mocked them as the scribe Aman-Appa had once been mocked:

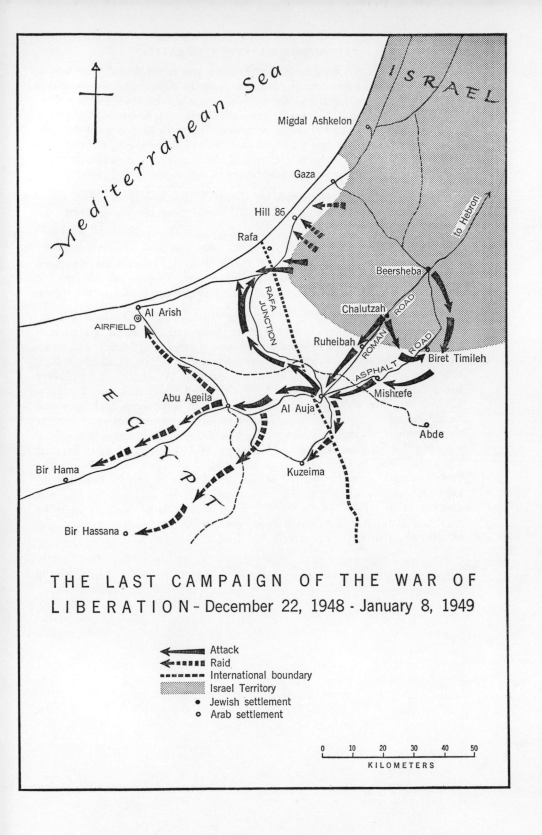

THE LAST CAMPAIGN OF THE WAR OF
LIBERATION - December 22, 1948 - January 8, 1949

Attack
Raid
International boundary
Israel Territory
• Jewish settlement
○ Arab settlement

0   10   20   30   40   50
KILOMETERS

Have you not been to Kadesh? Have you never found your way to the Lebanon where the sky is dark in broad daylight? It is overgrown with cypresses, oaks, and cedars which rise sky-high. . . . Tell me too about Sidon and Sarepta. They talk about another city that lies in the sea, the port of Tyre is its name. Water is carried to it by ship. If you go to Jaffa you will find that the fields are green. Go and look for the pretty girl who is in charge of the vineyards. She will accept you as her mate and grant you her favors. . . .

But only the king could speak for them, the pharaoh whom they served dumbly and uncomplainingly. His "triumph" was already inscribed on postage stamps, as once, thousands of years before, it had been inscribed on the mortuary of Thebes:

Canaan is despoiled and all its evil with it. Ashkelon is taken captive. Gezer is conquered. Yanoam is blotted out. The people of Israel is desolate, it has no offspring. Palestine has become a widow for Egypt.

Perhaps the proclamation did not ring entirely false. The land was indeed desolated. Its orange groves were destroyed, its fields gutted and mined. Six thousand of its young men and women were dead, and twice that many wounded. Its capital was prostrate. The nation would be a long time a-building. A new generation of Phoenicians, Amalekites, and Hittites had pulled back from its borders. But Assyria and Egypt still waxed mighty. Lachish and Megiddo lay open as reminders of what once had been and would be again: the siege guns of the invaders pushing up earth ramps, their bowmen advancing, protected by shields; and the citizens themselves, working the fire-catapults behind the city walls, the cries of their impaled kinsmen ringing in their ears. Israel was riddled with *tels*, and locked in the bowels of each were the charred and petrified relics of equally hopeful and expectant ancestors. By now the reborn nation knew its land. No one was dancing in its streets. In the exultation of victory, other nations in other ages had strutted and crowed their way across the landscape. Israel remembered them well. They were her fossils.

CHAPTER TWO

THE PARENTS

DURING the spring and summer of 1961, the people of Israel focused their attention on a courtroom in Jerusalem. In the bullet-proof dock sat the defendant, a sunken-featured, gray-skinned wisp of a man. He was Adolf Eichmann, executioner-in-chief of the "Final Solution," now diligently cloaking his record as administrator of Jewish extermination in the Byzantine complexities of German bureaucracy. At the counsel's table, Eichmann's attorney, Dr. Robert Servatius, hunched his great square head into the ridges of an ample neck and drily, tenaciously droned away at his central theses: Israel possessed no jurisdiction over the prisoner; his client had been a mere clerk, dutifully following the orders of his supervisors. It was a monotonous performance. Both Eichmann and Servatius soon lost their fascination for the public.

Gideon Hausner, the attorney general, was something else. Even the case-hardened foreign correspondents who covered the trial were shaken by his recital of the catalogue of Nazi horrors. A bald, bespectacled, round-shouldered man still in his forties, Hausner assumed something of the manner of a vengeful prophet as the sessions progressed. Long after the prisoner's twitching face had faded from memory, spectators would remember the attorney general, his accusing arm thrust like a dagger toward the defendant in the glass box. And there were the judges: Benjamin HaLevi, by his composure effectively masking the opinion of Eichmann he had expressed seven years before as a judge in this same city ("Satan," he had called him); and Yitzhak Raveh, pale-skinned, mild, and silent, perhaps the most taciturn member of the three-man panel, concentrating intently on each word, each syllable, of the testimony.

But above all it was Dr. Moshe Landau, the presiding judge, who dominated the trial from beginning to end. Like the colleagues at his side, Landau was a German Jew, formerly a practicing attorney in the nation Eichmann had inherited. Arriving in Palestine as a refugee, Landau had applied a tenacious will and an unusually brilliant mind to the challenge of a new language and a new code of laws. He mastered them both. His career as a trial lawyer was a distinguished one. After the emergence of the Jewish State, Landau was appointed judge of the district court of Haifa. Several years later, he was elevated to the supreme court. The thoroughness and acuity of his opinions were widely admired. When preparations were made for the Eichmann trial, Landau was the government's unanimous choice as chairman of the panel of judges.

Now he sat on the upper tier of the handsomely paneled proscenium, a tall, well-proportioned man in his mid-fifties, gentle blue eyes gazing thoughtfully beneath a domelike forehead fringed with red-gray hair. When questions were to be asked, he phrased them concisely and courteously. When procedure was breached, he reprimanded the offending counsel, Servatius or Hausner, with fine impartiality. The dignity of the law was embodied in the chiseled lines of his face, the deliberate caress of the documents laid out before him, the unblinking gaze with which he transfixed the actors of the drama. He was authority. Eichmann jumped like a spring, stood like a ramrod when Landau addressed him, clung as if hypnotized to the judge's every word, or to the slightest change in his features. Whatever Landau's rebuke to the prosecution, whatever his ruling on the inadmissibility of State's evidence, neither accused, accuser, nor witness doubted it: the man was justice incarnate.

Many of those who witnessed the Eichmann trial had vivid memories of another trial, a decade earlier. They had seen the application of Jewish law elsewhere. For them the jurist on the bench was still slim, his hair still red, his face all but unlined. As judges went, Landau was a young man in April of 1952. Yet he was seasoned even then by human suffering —some of it his own. He would not impose his magisterial presence on those who pleaded before him. Both sides in the case would be heard fully, fairly, completely, in their own way. No relevant fact would be obscured by mere procedure.

Counsel for the plaintiffs, standing before the bar of that same Haifa district court on April 20, 1952, had his own conviction of where justice lay. Rather less stoop-shouldered then, his skull at least partially sheltered by a thinning nest of black hair, Gideon Hausner was no less the zealous prophet in an obscure case than in the celebrated world-drama of nine years later. His performance before District Judge Landau bore all the characteristics of his later presentations as attorney general: solemnity, vigor, above all adroitness and imagination in the marshaling of witnesses. He was dealing with human lives here, too.

His clients were an immigrant family, seeking the return of a lost child, and *Youth Aliyah,* the Israel Children's Organization, acting on the parents' behalf. It was not a simple case. The reunion of one family would mean the demoralization of another. Accordingly, Hausner began slowly, whenever possible allowing his principals to speak for themselves. The mother was the first to testify. Mrs. Hemda Gruber was a short, fair-skinned, shabbily dressed woman. She was forty-two years old; but her dead-gray hair, the lattice of wrinkles at the corners of her blue eyes, the toneless weariness of her voice added another ten years to her age. She spoke in Yiddish.

Hausner: "When and where were you born, Mrs. Gruber?"

Mrs. Gruber: "In 1910, in Lodz, Poland."

Hausner: "You were married there?"

Mrs. Gruber: "Yes, in 1926. I was very young. My husband, Shlomo Rabinowitz, was a wagoner."

Hausner: "Were there children, Mrs. Gruber?"

Mrs. Gruber: "We had five children, two boys and three girls."

Hausner: "Tell us what happened after the outbreak of the war."

Mrs. Gruber did not change expression as she described the first in her series of personal tragedies. The Nazis approached Lodz, she said. There was no food. She left her three oldest children with her husband, and entrained for Warsaw with the two others. Once in the capital, she was supplied by her relatives with several boxes of canned goods. On her way back to Lodz, however, the train was stopped. The Germans had cut the rail line. The moment the passengers disembarked, Nazi troops poured out of the near-by woods, ordering all adults to return immediately to Warsaw. The children remained behind as "hostages." Hemda never saw her two youngsters again.

Months later she escaped from Warsaw with a group of other Jews, and successfully crossed into Russian-occupied territory. The Soviets transshipped the refugees to Bashkirstan, deep in the interior. Hemda subsisted there for a year as a charwoman. Later the Communist authorities permitted small groups of Jews to return westward. Eventually Hemda reached Kharkov and found employment in a glove factory. One Sabbath morning, visiting a synagogue, she encountered Shraga Gruber, a young man whom she had known in Lodz.

"I am sorry about your family, Hemda," he said. "I know what you must feel. I lost my parents and three sisters."

She went faint. "Speak," she said. "I know nothing."

He was obliged to tell her. Her husband, Shlomo Rabinowitz, had been sent to a concentration camp in Danzig. He had attempted to escape and had been hanged. The three remaining children had starved to death in Lodz.

In the ensuing months the young couple learned to comfort each other. Hemda's need for another child was obsessive and frantic. In the early summer of 1940 she and Shraga were married. And within a few weeks they were derelicts again; the German Wehrmacht launched its invasion of Russia, and battered into the Ukraine with lightning speed. The Grubers joined the migration eastward once more. Eventually they found refuge in Lubobov, a small town near the Volga, in the Saratov region of the Urals. There, on May 20, 1942, Hemda Gruber gave birth to a daughter, Tamar.

For nearly two years the child's survival was a matter of doubt. There was little food to be had. Shraga Gruber labored at slave wages in a tank factory. His wife, unable to leave her daughter to work, strapped Tamar to her back and foraged in the fields, digging up vegetables. One night her husband broke into a farm bin in a despairing effort to steal potatoes. He was caught, and sent to prison for a year and a half. Had it not been for the compassion of neighbors, mother and daughter might have perished. As it was, Tamar remained underdeveloped and spindle-boned.

For the Grubers the war ended in the late summer of 1944. The German armies had been driven from Russia and most of Poland. Soil was cleared for planting. There was a harvest. Rations improved. Movement westward was possible once again. At first the Grubers waited until there was assurance of an orderly existence in Poland before returning to Lodz. They had endured six years of vagrancy; it was enough for their lifetimes. But at the end of 1946—when the Soviet authorities began a mass repatriation of Poles and Polish Jews—Hemda, Shraga, and their child were loaded into cattle cars and shipped home.

In Lodz not a single member of their families was to be found. The Germans had left a Jewish graveyard. Nor were the Polish inhabitants eager to welcome their former neighbors back. There were outbreaks of violence. In the city of Kielce, fifty-two Jews were slain by drink-maddened gangs of unemployed laborers. It was, in fact, the Kielce pogrom which proved the final and irreparable disillusionment for those Polish Jews who had survived the war. Evidently, there was no place for Jews any longer in Christian Europe. It was time to clear out. Between 1945 and 1948 no fewer than 160,000 Polish Jews, bearing officially validated exit permits, departed for Zionist reception depots in central and southern Europe.

Yet nearly 40,000 decided to remain in Poland—if only temporarily. A few of these were Communists, or Communist sympathizers, eager to lend their talents to an avowedly anti-Fascist government. A much larger number, by far the majority, were people with technical and managerial experience whom the Warsaw regime needed badly for its development program, especially in the former German territory of Lower Silesia. They were induced now to stay on by opportunities for comfortable apartments and good salaries. The Grubers were among them. Shraga had been offered a job as a magistrate in the Silesian town of Vrotslov. Of course he and his family would not remain indefinitely; few of their Jewish neighbors had any such notions. They would stay just long enough to accumulate a few thousand zlotys, a nest egg for the new life in Palestine.

For their daughter, however, Hemda and Shraga Gruber had other, more immediate, plans. They would not keep Tamar in the Polish charnel house a day, an hour longer than it required to arrange her departure with the Jewish migration authorities. In the neighboring district, in the town of Petrolessia, a home for orphan Jewish children had been established by the Co-ordination—a committee sponsored by *Youth Aliyah,* with the financial support of the Jewish Agency and the American Joint Distribution Committee. It was one of nearly twenty such institutions from which youngsters were later sent on to Palestine. Perhaps Tamar would be accepted there.

In November of 1946 Mrs. Gruber and her daughter arrived at the children's home of Petrolessia. Mrs. Eda Rosen, the assistant to the directress, received them and filled out the registration certificate.

"The girl's father?" she asked.

"Dead," lied Mrs. Gruber. "I simply can't take care of a four-year-old child myself. She needs a new life in Palestine."

It was an old story. Mrs. Rosen nodded, completed the girl's registration, and then assigned her to a spare cot. As Tamar was led upstairs, she cried out piteously to her mother. Mrs. Gruber sobbed and rushed from the place.

She returned three weeks later. The daughter clung to her, terrified. "Why are they keeping me here, Mama?" she wailed.

"Don't fret, don't fret," murmured her mother. "They are taking you to a nice land, with other nice boys and girls. And soon Mama and Papa will join you. We are coming soon, you'll see."

When Mrs. Gruber returned home she was near hysteria. "I want her back," she insisted to her husband. "I can't leave her there. She's only four. It kills me."

"Be calm, Hemda," he said. "It's for her sake."

But the mother would not be placated. Waking or sleeping, she saw Tamar's trembling little face continually before her. In late January of 1947, Mrs. Gruber returned to Petrolessia for her second visit.

"She is gone, madam," said Mrs. Rosen, with sympathy. "That group left for Germany last week."

At the trial, as she described this final visit to Petrolessia, Mrs. Gruber's eyes clouded for the first time. "Just like that, gone," she said, turning imploringly to Judge Landau. "I did not know when I would ever see her again. If I had known then what I know now—" She shuddered, and stopped.

As it was, Mrs. Gruber still had reason for gratitude. *Youth Aliyah* had accepted her daughter without hesitation, had cared for the child at public expense, had spared no exertion or sacrifice to extricate her from Poland and provide her with a new life in Palestine. The risks and dangers surmounted by this remarkable organization far outweighed its occasional failures. Indeed, tens of thousands of children who reached the Jewish Homeland owed their security, their very lives, to the devotion and ingenuity of the *Youth Aliyah* staff. One of the members of that staff, David Oumanski, in charge of the absorption department, was called to the witness stand by Gideon Hausner and asked briefly to trace the history of the rescue effort.

The operation began in Germany, Oumanski explained, as far back as 1932, when a group of Berlin Jewish youths paid a call on the eminent Zionist leader, Mrs. Recha Freier. They were filled with foreboding; each day the Nazi Party gained in strength, and there were new assaults on Jewish homes and shops. Could Mrs. Freier suggest a solution? they wondered. Was Palestine a possibility for some of them? Mrs. Freier's response was unequivocal: Palestine was the one solution for all of them, she insisted; the time had come for them to be settled on the soil of the ancient homeland, trained to become farmers and "integral" Jews. As she outlined the idea, the youngsters were fired with enthusiasm for it. Returning to their local Zionist youth groups, they began their agricultural training at once. By February, 1934, the first group of young people—the first *Youth Aliyah* contingent—arrived in Palestine and settled in Kibbutz Ein Harod.

In succeeding years, as the destruction of European Jewry mounted, it became apparent that the departure of youngsters for Palestine would have to be organized on a large-scale emergency basis. Nor did Zionist youth groups provide the largest number of emigrants any longer. Parents— Zionist and non-Zionist alike—pleaded with *Youth Aliyah* emissaries for help in transporting their children to safety. By 1939, as a result, four thousand children had been brought to Palestine from Germany and central Europe. If the war had been delayed by a year, many times that many would probably have been saved. Instead, perhaps a million and a half Jewish children died at the hands of the Nazis.

Even after the outbreak of hostilities, however, some ten thousand youngsters managed ultimately to reach Palestine by devious routes organized with the help of *Youth Aliyah*. They tracked the earth from west to east. They came by land, sea, and air, through Iran, Turkey, Russia, and Afghanistan, through India and Iraq. They crossed the Pyrenees into Spain, continued on to Portugal and out again through Lisbon. In 1942 the first transport of children arrived in Palestine from Iraq and Yemen. A year later, in one of the most memorable episodes of human endurance, eight hundred and fifty scrawny, terrified children reached safety from eastern Europe. They had escaped in 1939, and for three and a half years had wandered through the steppes of Russia and the mountains of the Caucasus, until at last they arrived in Teheran, famished, wild-eyed little animals, more dead than alive. *Youth Aliyah* agents sent them on to Palestine.

When the war ended, the rescue operation gained momentum rapidly. Palestinian units of the British army rounded up hundreds of survivors in southern and central Europe. Haganah agents circulated through the displaced persons' camps, searching out orphans and registering them in special *Youth Aliyah* hostels. In eastern Europe the work was carried out by agents of the Co-ordination. One of the first tasks here was to reclaim some five thousand children who were repatriated from the Soviet Union. Throughout 1945 and 1946 Co-ordination representatives waited at railroad stations on the Russo-Polish border. Once the trains arrived, the workers moved rapidly through the crowd of confused, terrified orphans, interrogating them, registering them, and then transporting them to special children's homes. Often the youngsters had forgotten their true identity, and were given new names on the spot.

Within Poland proper, however, the task of registration proved far more complex. While the repatriates from Russia had escaped the Nazis by fleeing with the partisan armies, in Poland doomed Jewish parents had more frequently saved their children by turning them over to Christian families or Church officials, who then hid and guarded the youngsters at the risk of their own lives. Once the war ended, the Co-ordination began an intensive search for these missing children, tracking them down with the help of burial lists, or with clues provided by natives who sold their information for cash. Some Polish Christians were quite willing to return the boys and girls to the Jewish authorities. But others had formed deep attachments to their foster children and pleaded for the right to keep them. Not infrequently

Poles would hide a Jewish child, and deny that he or she was still alive. Priests and nuns were especially reluctant to abandon the Catholic education of their young wards. In such instances, the Co-ordination often resorted to bribery, literally buying the children back. But there were occasions, too, when agents of *Youth Aliyah* were forced to kidnap youngsters, by ruse (disguised as Polish government officials) or even by holding the Poles off at the point of a gun. Yet in spite of the most ingenious and desperate measures, the Jewish authorities were unable to retrieve more than two thousand children of the estimated five thousand remaining in Polish hands at war's end.

Those who were regained entered the Co-ordination's network of foster homes. Their stay was usually a temporary one. Occasionally they were claimed by surviving parents: anguished, distraught creatures who had hunted their children for months by trekking through the country—and often through several countries—from one foster home to another. More frequently the youngsters were sent off under staff supervision, together with tens of thousands of Jewish displaced persons already on the move to Mediterranean ports. Elaborate precautions had to be taken. Documents were forged. Names were changed. *Youth Aliyah* agents accompanying orphan children ran the risk of identification by border guards, and often had to be replaced at the last minute. Thus, in spite of the exceptional care and resourcefulness with which the entire operation was organized, some degree of confusion was inevitable. The Gruber family was one of the victims.

On the witness stand sat Moshe Ya'ari, the *Youth Aliyah* official who had first received the children upon their arrival in Palestine.

"By 1948 they were coming in at the rate of a hundred a week," he explained. "Many of them came from the British detention camps at Cyprus. Others arrived directly from Europe. My first responsibility was to identify them. Usually I had received most of the necessary information about the children well in advance."

Hausner: "Do you remember a girl named Tamar Gruber?"

Ya'ari: "Very well. In addition to the documents attached to her when she arrived, I had received previous information about her from Europe."

The facts indicated that she was born in Russia in 1944, and was delivered by her widowed mother into the care of the children's home of Petrolessia in October of 1946. In December of that year, under the care of a *Youth Aliyah* worker, she departed from Poland with a group of twenty-three other children from the same institution. For the next thirteen months Tamar Gruber remained at a children's home near Bergen-Belsen. Early in 1948 she was transferred to Marseilles, and on April 18 of that same year arrived at Haifa port aboard the S.S. *Andover*. Ya'ari registered Tamar, then arranged for her to be placed in the *Youth Aliyah* camp of Onim, in the town of Kfar Saba. On May 21 she was temporarily quartered with a family in the village of Beit Yitzhak.

Shortly afterward, on September 12, 1948, an immigrant woman of about thirty arrived at the office of the Beit Yitzhak village council. Speaking in Yiddish, the woman introduced herself as Mrs. Frume Rosenberg. She was a widow who had recently remarried; formerly her name had been Gruber. She had learned that her only daughter, Tamar, was now living with a family at Beit Yitzhak—and she had come to take the child back.

Together Mrs. Rosenberg and the secretary visited the home where the girl lived. Little Tamar was in the salon when the two women entered. The moment the child caught sight of the visitor she rushed into her arms, crying ecstatically: "Ima" [Mother]. The resemblance between the woman and the girl was marked; there seemed no doubt that they were mother and daughter. At the secretary's suggestion, therefore, Mrs. Rosenberg returned to the *Youth Aliyah* office in Tel Aviv, where, with the necessary documents, she satisfactorily proved her relationship to Tamar Gruber. Mrs. Rosenberg was living then with her husband in an abandoned Arab flat in Jaffa.

"Would you be willing to leave your daughter where she is for a while— until your circumstances improve?" asked the *Youth Aliyah* settlement officials.

"Not for a single instant," replied Mrs. Rosenberg emphatically.

Upon being questioned separately, the daughter expressed the same determination to join her mother. And so the two were united that same evening. They had lived together ever since.

"In other words," asked Gideon Hausner, when Ya'ari had finished his testimony, "there was not the slightest question that the girl, Tamar Gruber, was the daughter of Mrs. Frume Rosenberg?"

"Not the slightest then, not the slightest now," answered Ya'ari.

Nor was his story shaken in any detail by the lawyer for the defendants, who questioned him closely.

In the first week of May, Dov Or-Dan, the defense attorney, decided to follow Hausner's example. He would allow his clients, the Pollacks, to speak for themselves. Indeed, the husband, Yosef Pollack, proved to be an exceptionally effective and moving witness. He was fifty-four years old at the time of the trial, a slim, gray-haired man of medium height. As he related his story, it was apparent from his drawn, pale face and trembling hands that he was under a grave emotional strain. Yet his self-control was complete. His manner was restrained and decorous.

"Both my wife and I were born in Sokolka, Lithuania," he testified. "I myself came from a religious family, and was quite fluent in Hebrew even in Europe. Bracha, my wife, could read a bit of Hebrew, but did not speak it. And so, when we arrived in Palestine in 1925, I insisted that from then on we would speak no other language. Ours has been a Hebrew-speaking home ever since.

"We came to this country because we were Zionists and believed in what was being built here. It was always a source of pride to me that Eliahu Golomb [the founder of the Haganah] was my cousin. God was good to us from the moment of our arrival. I myself found an office job in Afula, and then two years later was offered an even better position in Haifa working for Tnuva [the Histadrut dairy combine]. When I was transferred to Kiryat Motzkin [a suburb of Haifa], my wife and I decided to build a home. We have been living there sixteen years. It is a very nice home."

It was a lovely home, airy, spacious, its third and largest room looking out on a well-tended garden. On the walls hung photographs of family patriarchs, etchings of medieval Jewish synagogues. The bookcases were well stocked with Hebrew volumes dealing variously with Jewish history and literature, Zionist lore, and translations of the Russian masters; one shelf was devoted to the Talmud and Midrashic commentaries.

The Pollacks' only child, Itamar, was born in 1930. As the years passed, he became all that parents could have wished for a son: a fine-looking boy, thorough in his studies, athletic, popular with his classmates. Enrolled in Haifa's excellent Reali High School in 1944, Itamar became especially proficient in mathematics and the sciences. Simultaneously, together with nearly all the youngsters of his age, he was a secret member of the Haganah. On evenings and weekends he participated in hikes and weapons drills.

Itamar completed his secondary studies in April, 1948, graduating from the Reali School with honors. There was little doubt about what his next step would be. The British Mandate was terminating. Fighting had already broken out between Jews and Arabs. The *Yishuv* was mobilizing. The day after he received his diploma, therefore, Itamar notified his parents that he was enlisting in the Palmach, the shock troops of the Haganah.

"You don't have to, you know," his mother reminded him, somewhat hesitantly. "They aren't calling up only sons."

"Ima, of course I have to," he chided her. "The law has nothing to do with it."

Yosef Pollack sighed. "Yes, of course he must. How would we stop him?"

Thus, at the age of seventeen and a half Itamar left for the war. His parents bade him good-by at the local bus station. Within a week the boy was already in action. As a radio operator in the Negev Brigade, he participated in the battles for Kibbutz Ruchama and Kibbutz Nirim. He survived the fighting unscathed. As the days passed, however, the situation in the south worsened. The Egyptians brought up tanks and medium artillery. Soon the fate of the vital coastal town of Ashdod hung in the balance. Outmanned and outgunned, the Palmach detachment was forced back along the heath, yard by yard. On June 3 Itamar's portable radio failed. Desperately he tampered with the receiver as bullets kicked up sand on the near-by dune.

"Come on, move," one of his comrades shouted at him.

"I don't feel well," he murmured. He tried to move, but was too late.

Avraham Bar-Don, the Kiryat Motzkin postmaster, transcribed the telegram from the defense ministry. He read it over and then wept; he had known the Pollack family for twenty years. He showed the wire to Yitzhak Shneerson, the stamp teller, and Shneerson wept. Neither could bring himself to deliver the message. Instead they kept it for two weeks. By then the entire neighborhood had the information. Only the Pollacks did not know, and no one would tell them. In the end it was a comrade of Itamar's who came to Kiryat Motzkin and informed the parents.

Two months went by and the State of Israel was secured. Yosef Pollack somehow turned up to work each day, and mechanically went through the routine of his job. Bracha Pollack cleaned her house, did the shopping, and returned each afternoon to her son's room, where she sat like a stone. In the evening friends visited the middle-aged couple, but the Pollacks gazed unseeing through the windows, and rarely spoke. Autumn came, then winter and another year. Finally, in September of 1949, the Pollacks reached a decision. They knew that if it were not fulfilled life was over for them.

In the witness box Mrs. Hava Cohen, senior social worker of *Youth Aliyah,* presented the documents relating to the Pollack affair. In September, 1949, she had written to Moshe Kol, director of *Youth Aliyah:*

> I turn to you with an unusual request . . . dealing with the Pollack family from Kiryat Motzkin who lost their only son in the War of Liberation. The parents believe that they can reconstruct their lives by adopting another child. Their financial situation is very good and makes it possible to give a child all it needs. Some of the friends of the family . . . also kindly ask you to help the parents. In Onim, near Kfar Saba, there is a girl named Tanya Gruskow, six years old, who came to Israel three years ago. So far no relatives have been found, at least we have no knowledge about them. I think she is a proper candidate.

"By the beginning of 1950," said Mrs. Cohen, "we had already sent social workers to investigate the Pollack home. There could be no question that the Pollacks and their circumstances were exemplary in all respects. Although the couple was middle aged, both husband and wife were warm, gentle, loving people. They had seen the little girl, Tanya Gruskow, at Onim. From that moment, they lived only for the opportunity to take her into their home and lavish care and affection on her. These were the factors that eventually disposed us in their favor."

On January 10, 1950, Dr. Hannoch Reinhold, Director of Education for *Youth Aliyah,* wrote to Moshe Kol:

> My general attitude toward the adoption is positive, but cautious. We should not forget that in three out of nineteen cases parents were found later, which involved a great deal of unpleasantness. In such an event the formalities do not have much value, for by then the girl has already formed close ties with the new family.
>
> Thus, we should investigate thoroughly whether this girl has parents and what their interest in her is. It seems strange that we have not heard from them so far. . . . The details about her should be published in the radio and local newspapers, asking for witnesses. We could find out through our office in Paris details of her life abroad. . . . Usually this sort of procedure has to be repeated a few times. . . .

So, indeed, it was. Under questioning by the defense attorney, Mrs. Cohen described the process. The first step was taken by the Jewish Agency's Bureau of Missing Relatives. By 1950 a full-time staff of sixty men and women worked in the Bureau's central office in Jerusalem. Sizable though it was, the number was barely adequate to deal with the hundreds of distraught immigrants who arrived each day in search of the remnants of their families. During the years immediately following the Nazi holocaust, in fact, the entire State of Israel was one vast missing persons' bureau. Questionnaires were filled out ("Inquiree's last known address and date, place of residence before World War II, occupation or trade, etc."), then cross-checked with an immense file-index containing two million biographies. This index, the largest of its kind in the world, was compiled (and continually in the process of compilation) from data supplied by Jewish municipal and communal organizations both in Israel and in other countries; and, as well, by thousands of private individuals who willingly and eagerly transmitted to the Bureau whatever personal information they possessed. Of the 300,000 Jews who passed through the office between 1945 and 1951, fully 20 per cent located their relatives through this remarkable catalogue.

If the index did not have the necessary information (as it did not, in the case of Tanya Gruskow), other expedients were resorted to. Inquiries were made abroad: through Jewish Agency offices in Europe and the United States, through the International Tracing Service at Arolsen-Waldeck, Germany, and the file indices of the International Red Cross and the International Refugee Organization. Occasionally these appeals were successful, especially in the United States, where advertisements placed by the Jewish Agency in the Yiddish-language newspapers elicited vital information. For Tanya Gruskow, however, the results were negative. It was known that she had arrived through France. Yet neither the International Refugee Organization, the Hebrew Immigrant Aid Society, the French Orphan Society, nor the Alliance Israélite Universelle was able to provide information.

There were other possibilities—within Israel itself. The girl's meager biography was sent to the Association of Polish Immigrants. The Association, in turn, sent the data to all of its 319 branch *landsmannschaften,* associations of Jews from common towns of origin. Together with the *landsmannschaften* of other countries, these amazingly effective organizations had been responsible for locating fully 30 per cent of all relatives discovered in Israel since the end of the Second World War. Tanya Gruskow, unfortunately, was not one of their successes. No one had ever heard of a Gruskow family.

The final step was advertisement through the newspapers and radio. Accordingly, on February 8, 1950, the inquiry was published in four leading dailies, one of them the Yiddish-language *Letzte Neues,* which in that period devoted nearly an entire page each day to appeals for missing relatives: "Gruskow, Tanya, six years old. Born in Russia. Came to Israel through France on board the S.S. *Alexandria,* January, 1948. We are searching for her parents. Anybody possessing additional information about this girl is kindly requested to contact *Youth Aliyah.*" Simultaneously the announcement was carried by a half-hour radio program—"Mi Makir, Mi Yodeah—Who Knows, Who Has Information"—which each afternoon broadcast descriptions of missing relatives (this program was not discontinued until 1961). Again, the results were negative. A few answers were received from various parts of the country, but these turned out to be the frantic reactions of unbalanced families who had lost their children to the Nazis, and who were convinced now that every unclaimed orphan was theirs. The girl was unknown.

Thus, on May 5, 1950, after the Pollacks had been even more thoroughly investigated and re-investigated by *Youth Aliyah* social workers, Moshe Kol instructed the director of Onim to deliver Tanya Gruskow to the Pollack family.

> We, Yosef and Bracha Pollack [read the adoption document], after serious consideration, do hereby receive into our home the girl Tanya Gruskow. We shall give this girl free board and room, and assume the financial responsibility for her education. If after two years we discover that we suit each other, and that we want this child forever, we shall make final arrangements for her adoption. We undertake not to proceed with the legal adoption unless *Youth Aliyah,* which gave us this girl, fully agree. We . . . understand that *Youth Aliyah* . . . can withhold the girl from us if they find that it is not in the interest of the girl. We understand, as well, that we may return the girl any time before the end of two years if we discover that she does not suit us. Similarly, representatives of *Youth Aliyah* are allowed to visit us any time in order to investigate this arrangement, even as we may ask such representatives to come to secure their advice if needed.

"And did the Pollacks honor their agreement to give this child good care?" asked Or-Dan, the defense attorney.

"Yes, of course," admitted Hava Cohen, on the witness stand. "They gave the girl the same devotion real parents would have given."

Perhaps even more than that. Under questioning, Mrs. Cohen described the reports of social workers who periodically visited the family. They were astonished by the change in the little girl. At Onim she had been withdrawn and silent, easily provoked to tears by the teasing of other children. After three months with the Pollacks, she had learned to smile again, to chatter happily with other youngsters at the Kiryat Motzkin elementary school. She called her foster parents "Ima" and "Abba"—Mother and Father. And with good reason. The warmth and love that once were Itamar's were now lavished upon the adopted child in equal measure. Dotingly they filled her room—Itamar's room—with dolls and games. Virtually every week the middle aged couple found an excuse to arrange a party for the youngster, inviting other children her age. When she slept they gazed adoringly at her placid face. When she played in the garden with her friends, Yosef and Bracha Pollack listened raptly to her growing Hebrew vocabulary. Friends who visited the parents found them animated once more. The Pollacks had found a reason for life.

Several thousands of miles away, in Vrotslov, Poland, another father and mother faced the growing suspicion that their own lives, painfully reconstructed from earlier tragedies, were about to be shattered once again. It was Shraga Gruber who related the events that aroused and followed that suspicion. Hausner, acting in his dual capacity as attorney for both *Youth Aliyah* and the Grubers, had the option of presenting his witnesses *non seriatim;* he had saved Gruber for this moment. As Gruber took the witness stand, spectators in the courtroom saw a slim, black-haired man of thirty-nine. His height was somewhat less than average, and his dark face seemed curiously impassive. His manner of speaking, too, was phlegmatic, almost lethargic, as if he were under sedation. But his testimony was orderly and transparently honest. Or-Dan let it stand.

The Grubers' economic circumstances in Vrotslov were not intolerable, certainly not after the hell of the war. They lived in a comfortable one-room flat, formerly occupied by Silesian Germans. Shraga kept his job as magistrate. Hemda worked in a government paper factory. The endemic anti-Semitism of their Polish neighbors was never a threat to them; the Communist police saw to that. Under ordinary conditions the family might have fulfilled its original plan: to postpone departure until it had accumulated a small nest egg, and then to leave with assurances of reasonable opportunity in Palestine. For a while Hemda Gruber seriously contemplated recalling her young daughter from the Co-ordination. To that end—and against her husband's wishes—she wrote to the Petrolessia camp in February of 1948, asking them to secure Tamar's return from the *Youth Aliyah* authorities in Darmstadt. The answer came nine days later: the girl had already arrived in Palestine.

Immediately Shraga dispatched a letter to *Youth Aliyah* headquarters in Jerusalem, requesting information of his daughter's whereabouts. Early in March he received his first reply: "Your daughter, Tamar Gruber, has recently arrived in Haifa on the S.S. *Andover.* She is presently being cared for in the children's village of Onim, near Kfar Saba." Nothing more. Subsequent inquiries elicited the same cryptic reply: "Your daughter is well," "Your daughter is being well cared for." The parents' uneasiness grew. On December 2, 1948, Hemda Gruber phrased her appeal with special urgency.

Dear Friends,

I have a great request of you. My girl, Tamar Gruber, is in Israel. She is six. She left Poland with the children's transport from Gdynia in 1946. She was in Darmstadt, Germany, until March, 1947, and left from there to Israel. Since then I know little about her, where, precisely, she is and what she does. Dear friends, please understand the heart and feelings of a mother who has nothing but this only child whose traces she has lost. We sent her to you because we were sure that we would soon be following her. Because of reasons beyond our control we were prevented from doing so. Therefore I beg you, dear friends, be so kind and look for our child and tell me in detail where she is and how she is. I thank you in advance.

Yours respectfully,
Hemda Gruber.

Something had indeed gone wrong. Under the pressure of an immigration which brought hundreds, even thousands of youngsters to Israel each month, the mysterious arrival of a Mrs. Frume Rosenberg, her reunion with the girl, Tamar Gruber, in Beit Yitzhak, had somehow gone unregistered in *Youth Aliyah* headquarters in Jerusalem. The files were brought up to date many months later. But by then the damage was done; for in the interval Shraga and Hemda Gruber continued to receive reassurances that their daughter remained in the children's village. Had the error been detected in time, *Youth Aliyah* officials presumably would have recognized that the youngster described by the Grubers was unaccountably missing— indeed, that she had to all appearances been claimed by a strange woman.

It was the Grubers themselves who first discovered that something was terribly wrong. In June, 1949, they wrote to a distant relative of Shraga's, an immigrant living in Tel Aviv, asking him to visit the local *Youth Aliyah* office and inquire into the circumstances of their daughter. The relative did as he was asked. At his request, the office checked Tamar Gruber's file— still without the information of the reunion with Mrs. Rosenberg—and then turned over to the relative the girl's immigration documents and her actual photograph. That, surely, would be reassurance enough for the parents.

"Here you have all the information you need, dear Shraga," wrote the relative. "The girl is well and happy in the village of Beit Yitzhak. I am even enclosing her original passport and the photograph that was taken of her when she arrived in Israel last year. She is a pretty little thing, and I hope that this will convince you that she has been well fed."

Shraga Gruber read the letter in Vrotslov on July 14. With trembling hands he held the photograph up to the light. His wife, too, examined the picture carefully. Then she slumped to her knees.

"Well, well, be calm," Shraga reassured her, for the thousandth time.

She gazed at him blindly. "Shraga," she cried. "This is not our daughter."

"It says Tamar Gruber," he murmured, studying the photograph again. Then he shook his head mournfully. "No, it is certainly not Tamar."

They had no more time for writing. Within the hour they had joined the line of Jews waiting outside the local passport office. Nearly three hours later the Grubers reached the inner office, where they formally applied for exit permits. The clerk answered their request with a shocker: "The fee is ninety thousand zlotys per person," he said.

"What happened?" Hemda protested, horrified. "That's more than we earn in half a year."

"Ninety thousand zlotys," repeated the clerk wearily.

A month later, the Grubers' savings and personal possessions were gone, but they had their exit permits. Nothing more could be done now but await word from the Israel Legation. Free transportation to Israel had been promised—when it was available. The crush of departing Jews was almost unmanageable, however. Two or three times a month, trains, chartered by the Jewish Agency and carrying five hundred to seven hundred passengers each, left Warsaw en route to Gdynia and the ports of southern Italy. The Grubers' turn did not come until November, 1950, more than a year after they had filed their applications. Since then, too, Shraga had lost his job as magistrate; as a would-be emigrant he was deemed "unreliable." By the time he and his wife boarded the train for Naples, they were completely penniless. Yet the moment they reached the port and caught sight of the Israel steamer, its decks packed with Jews from all corners of Europe, their confidence returned. In Israel they would not only find their daughter; they would earn back everything they had lost.

That illusion was shared by virtually every other departing Jew. Had the Grubers and the others but known it, their migration placed near-unendurable strains on the tiny country. From the moment of its independence, on May 15, 1948, the Jewish Republic had been inundated by a deluge of humanity. At the outset, 25,000 refugees arrived from the internment camps of Cyprus. These were shortly followed by 75,000 Jews from the displaced persons' camps of Germany and Austria. In succeeding months the immigrants included 33,000 Jews from Turkey; 36,000 from Bulgaria; 7,000 from Yugoslavia; 50,000 from Yemen; 40,000 from Poland. By 1950 the movement of Rumanian Jews began, bringing 88,000 additional fugitives to Israel. There were, as well, 32,000 Hungarians; 90,000 North Africans; 6,000 Persians; and nearly 100,000 Iraqis.

In all, from May 15, 1948, until the end of 1951, Israel opened its gates to nearly 650,000 newcomers. Flooding in at the rate of 18,000 a month, they doubled Palestine's Jewish population. And they were still coming. The land groaned under their weight. Almost without exception, the refugees had arrived in this arid, unendowed little country totally and desperately impoverished. They were admitted, notwithstanding, and regardless of their physical or mental condition, their degree of education, their potential value or lack of it to the State. Israel's "Law of the Return" had solemnly proclaimed that "every Jew has the right to immigrate to Israel." There were no qualifications to that law. Jews needed a homeland, and the homeland needed Jews.

Actually, the Grubers had an inkling of what awaited them the day their ship reached Haifa. At first, to be sure, Jewish Agency representatives made a valiant effort to ease the shock; they served hot coffee and sandwiches at the port while the newcomers were being registered, and handed the children bags of candy. It was only a postponement. Two hours of interrogation, classification, baggage inspection, and cursory medical examination followed. The officials thereupon arranged the newcomers in double lines and conducted them to the exit of the customs shed. Outside a fine rain was falling. Twenty ancient buses were parked in readiness. A Jewish Agency representative shouted instructions.

"You are now leaving for the reception centers," he explained in Hebrew, Yiddish, and Polish. "Check your certificate for the name of your camp. Then get into the bus carrying the same name."

Three reception centers were designated: Sha'ar HaAliyah, Beit Lid, and Givat Shaul, all located in the Haifa Bay area. The Grubers climbed aboard a Sha'ar HaAliyah bus. In a few minutes they were under way. Exhausted, they gazed silently at the passing countryside. The city of Haifa, slipping away behind them, was not unimpressive, with its crowded modern streets, its tiny houses ranked neatly on the side of the great mountain. But their eyes were on the inhabitants. It did not escape them that people here were badly dressed, their clothing drab and frequently patched. Now and then bystanders waved to them, without enthusiasm.

A half-hour later the buses rolled to a halt beside the entrance of an enormous encampment. Canvas tents extended in ordered rows as far as the eye could see. The Jewish Agency official in the lead bus had climbed out and was beckoning to the passengers.

"This is Sha'ar HaAliyah. Everyone out, please." He paused, and then repeated the announcement, his voice rising. "Please, everybody out. We have much to do yet."

As they climbed down, several of the immigrants groaned. Others began to weep. A few remained seated in the bus. The Agency official's face reddened. "It's not the Ritz-Imperial," he snapped. "We don't charge their rates either. Everybody out now."

The Grubers walked through the gate, following their guide along a path which the rain swiftly transformed into mud. Beside them the canvas flaps of the tents cracked like gunshots in the downpour. The procession ended before a low aluminum shack bearing the sign CAMP HEADQUARTERS. And inside, the camp director, a bespectacled Hungarian in his late fifties, busily checked each immigrant's registration card, then handed out accommodation and ration certificates. It did not escape Shraga Gruber that the director wore cheap khaki trousers and shirt, that his eyes were red, his hands trembling—quite obviously from exhaustion; the officials at the harbor had seemed equally harassed and work-worn. This immigration could not have been any picnic for them either.

Then Gruber and his wife moved on to a neighboring building. Here they exchanged their certificates for sheets, blankets, and straw mattresses. In the midst of the confusion one woman suddenly became hysterical. "It says I'm to sleep in Block G," she screamed. "I've been wandering in this rain for a half-hour looking for Block G. It's a jungle out there. I'm soaked. I lived two years in concentration camps that were better than this."

The other immigrants, momentarily startled, now began nodding, muttering their agreement. The Grubers were assigned to a tent at the rear of the compound. From the outside the shelter appeared spacious enough. But once inside, the Grubers discovered to their astonishment that another couple had been quartered with them. The man was young and quite dark-skinned, and both he and his wife wore Arab-style burnooses. They stared impassively at the newcomers, but said nothing. A patched U.S. Army blanket hung from the center pole as an improvised partition. Shraga and Hemda exchanged despairing glances. Then, dropping their bags, they began assembling mattresses and blankets on the steel cots; and finally they lay down exhausted, and gazed morosely at the canvas ceiling.

After several minutes Shraga sighed. "It's only for a while," he assured his wife.

"Do not speak," she replied.

At 6:00 P.M. Sha'ar HaAliyah began to tremble and roar. An army of marching legs sloshed and pounded through the paths between the barracks. Voices shouted and cursed. Pots and pans clanged. Silently the Grubers arose from their cots and donned their overcoats. They had heard the noise before—in Siberia, in the Urals, in Joint Distribution camps in Poland. It was mealtime.

They joined the file moving toward the camp dining hall. The odors of the central kitchen had already suffused the entire compound, penetrating even the rancid mildew of dripping canvas. Fully twenty minutes passed before the Grubers reached the dispensing table. Each time they approached the steaming soup tureen, people mysteriously appeared from the line behind them to edge them backward. Finally, exasperated, Shraga seized one of the offenders by the scruff of the neck. He was an aged man, dark and wrinkled as a prune. Twisting away, he cursed Shraga in Arabic.

"It's useless getting excited," whispered another immigrant, in Yiddish. "In all the months I've been here no one has been able to teach these darkies to wait in line. It's just not part of their upbringing."

Shraga looked about him. The immense dining hall was filled with a more exotic collection of humanity than he had ever seen in his life. He was familiar with the Poles and Russians, of course; they chatted easily with you in your own languages. But there were others: sallow, mustachioed Yugoslavs and Bulgarians, Greeks and Turks and Egyptians babbling away at each other in Ladino, turbaned Persians and Yemenites, bereted or burnoosed Moroccans and Tunisians, mumbling a curious Arabic patois. Hemda gazed in silent horror at their womenfolk. They wore leggings, like men. They were fat and greasy, they sweated and stank. Trembling, she clutched her husband's shoulder, waiting for him to fight his way to the serving table. The meal was dispensed from steel vats: soup, rice, eggplant, cheese stuffed with olives, and tea. The odor seemed curiously metallic—but at least it was food. The Grubers ate quickly, bolting the dinner down as if loath to taste it.

"Not bad," observed her husband. "I feel better."

They returned to the tent. The Iraqi couple smiled at them wanly, and Shraga smiled back.

"Things will be better tomorrow," he promised his wife.

The weather was better, in any case. A detachment of soldiers had arrived in camp. Their faces were young, but grave with responsibility. They were educators. The fact was that, as weeks of aimless vegetation lengthened into months, the dispirited and morose veterans of Sha'ar HaAliyah had become indifferent even to the most elementary demands of personal hygiene. They allowed dirt and sweepings to accumulate beside their cots, as well as mounds of refuse outside their tents. The soldiers, therefore, had come to direct a "military-style" cleanup. They did not hesitate to wield mop and broom themselves; but they tolerated no nonsense from slackers. Most of the immigrants followed their orders respectfully: these young conscripts had won the war, after all.

Hemda and Shraga managed to survive the first month without losing their tempers or raising their voices. Uncomplainingly, they endured the sullen and embarrassed stares of their tent partners, the hours of monotony and idle conversation in the camp compound, the infuriating pandemonium of mealtime, the trickle of rainwater through the frayed and porous canvas tent. The ordeal surely would not continue forever. Each day people were leaving the camp for other homes.

There was no way for the Grubers to know that those who departed had been waiting for a year—and longer. The little nation was almost totally unequipped to provide adequate housing for this avalanche of refugees. At the outset, to be sure, many of the newcomers had taken over abandoned Arab houses, in Haifa, Jerusalem, and Jaffa, in Safed, Ramle, and Lydda, and in smaller towns and villages. In this fashion 200,000 Jewish immigrants had pre-empted some 80,000 Arab rooms. But soon every derelict Arab village and neighborhood was full. The immigration continued. Other shelter was need, urgently.

The Jewish Agency undertook now to import thousands of prefabricated huts of Austrian, Finnish, or Swedish design. Simultaneously, a national housing corporation, Amidar, was established to build permanent immigrant housing by every known contrivance of inexpensive and accelerated construction, including homes of precast cement blocks manufactured on the spot. Most of these units were painfully functional. Space was restricted to minimum requirements; a family of four was entitled to one room plus a small alcove for washing, cooking, and storage. By the end of 1949, 25,000 such structures had been erected. A year after that, there were twice as many. But it was taking too long, much too long. In the interval, the great majority of newcomers had to be sheltered by other means.

The camp was the first and obvious solution. During the last years of the Mandate, the Jewish Agency had housed immigrants in temporary barracks at Givat Shaul, Athlit, and Bat Galim near Haifa, and at Neve Chaim near Hadera. These were supplemented in the early months of 1948 by makeshift shelters in Ra'anana and Rehovot. Although the camps accommodated up to five thousand people at a time, they were woefully inadequate for the immigration that followed the birth of Israel. Ordinarily it might have been possible to use the network of barracks recently abandoned by the British army. Following orders from London, however, the British had wantonly destroyed furniture, windows, and doors before departing; all but the shells of the buildings were left in shambles. Yet even these were temporarily repaired—and instantly packed with Jews arriving from the Cyprus internment compounds.

Thus it was that the tent cities went up. At first, they were erected as close to Haifa as possible. But within sixty days these port depots were filled to the bursting point, and the Jewish Agency was obliged to lay out immigrant camps elsewhere: by the cities of the coastal plain, in the Jerusalem Corridor, in the Galilee, even in the approaches to the northern Negev. By early 1951, 16,700 tents in 53 camps housed 97,000 men, women, and children—no less than one-tenth the population of Israel. Their circumstances were identical in each camp: food from a central kitchen, clothing from a Jewish Agency warehouse, makeshift schools provided by the Israel government. And, above all, unemployment. For with the end of the Palestine war, the demobilized veterans of the Israel army returned to their former jobs, and as a result, virtually no employment opportunities were left for the immigrants. It was a tragic fact that for the first few years after their arrival, most of the newcomers were almost total economic liabilities. Only 1 per cent of them were professionally trained. Fifty per cent of them were hopelessly unskilled. For the State, the economic burden of providing for these refugees proved all but insupportable.

As for the immigrants themselves, subsisting on the dole month after month, waking and sleeping each day in unalleviated squalor, the period between 1949 and 1951 represented more than a physical hardship; it was a psychological and spiritual trauma. More than a few of the European displaced persons had become callous and brutal after years of Nazi death-camp debasement. They passed their time now seeking out opportunities for profit on the black market, not hesitating to deal in the meager rations of their fellow inmates. Even men and women whose moral instincts had not yet been altogether blunted were gradually reduced by the immigrant camp experience to the apathy that followed despair. Divested of initiative, their instinct for self-improvement steadily and visibly atrophied.

"The Zionists are responsible," many of the tent dwellers insisted bitterly. "We had decent, comfortable barracks in the D.P. camps. There were always enough food and pocket money in Europe. The American army took good care of us there. But the Jewish Agency couldn't leave well enough alone. They had to get us here by hook or by crook—just to get their State in business. Now they can't even provide for us!"

The various political parties of Israel had their own explanations. Each day their emissaries appeared in the camps, buttonholing the immigrants, patiently making it clear to them that the true source of their misfortunes was—the other parties, of course. Each of the politicians had panaceas of his own; if the immigrants would but register with *his* party, they would be assured of work, food, housing, and loans. Nor were these appeals entirely cynical. Tent dwellers who allowed their names to be registered on one or another of the various party lists did occasionally receive special food parcels, and even small gifts of money. Not surprisingly, however, the largest number of the immigrants were repelled by this kind of party opportunism. For them, the political exploitation of their misery signified the end of a long-cherished Zionist dream. By 1952 nearly forty thousand men and women, embittered and altogether exhausted, abandoned the effort to create a new life for themselves in the Jewish State. They packed their miserable baggage and departed from the country for western Europe, South America, or Australia. Few of them ever returned.

As far back as 1950 the Israel government and the Jewish Agency had anticipated this crisis. Their planners were quite aware that the problem was psychological as much as economic. Of course poverty was debilitating. But enforced idleness was much worse; it was soul destroying. Perhaps years would pass before living conditions improved and the necessary full-time employment opportunities were generated. In the meantime the immigrants could not be permitted to wander about aimlessly and indefinitely as virtual mendicants. A temporary solution simply had to be found. At this point it occurred to the economists of the Jewish Agency that few of the original reception camps had been located near employment opportunities. Perhaps, then, this imbalance could be rectified if "mushroom" villages were erected on the outskirts of urban and other areas of industrial development, where part-time jobs were available. It was worth a try.

The first of these transit camps—or *ma'abarot,* as they were called—were located outside Tel Aviv. Physically, there was little enough to distinguish them from the original immigration depots. Shelter still was a canvas tent, a wooden hut, or at most an aluminum shack. The inhabitants still received aid from the public authorities. And yet the differences, though subtle, were important. There were occasional part-time jobs to be found near-by. In place of food and clothing, each family received a small supplementary income from the Jewish Agency—which in fact proved far less expensive to the Agency than the original camp kitchens and warehouses. In each *ma'abara,* the immigrants bought their own provisions, and did their own cooking on cheap primus stoves. For all their poverty, they enjoyed privacy at last, and were comparatively mobile. To those who had endured the shift-lessness and torpor of the immigrant camp, the *ma'abara* represented a tangible step toward self-improvement.

Encouraged by the success of the experiment, therefore, the Jewish Agency now committed its full energies to the eradication of the reception depots and the substitution of transit camps in their place. By November, 1951, no less than 127 of these *ma'abarot* had been established outside the country's urban centers. Newcomers were taken there directly. By the end of the year, six tent cities, with a population of 20,000, were either dismantled and the inhabitants transferred to *ma'abarot,* or they were themselves converted into *ma'abarot.* By early 1952, in fact, only 10,000 immigrants still remained in the reception camps, while fully 233,000 were now settled in the new transit centers.

Moreover, despite the rapid increase in the number of *ma'abarot,* an intensive effort was made to improve the standards of living within them. The number of tents was reduced by 5,000. Tin and aluminum shacks were erected instead. The government established schools, kindergartens, children's homes, synagogues, and clubs for the *ma'abarot;* while the immigrants themselves were encouraged to elect their own municipal councils and to assume a larger share in the public life of their communities. And, indeed, many of the newcomers responded eagerly to the challenge. Whatever their economic privations—and these were hardly less painful than before—they accepted the *ma'abara* in its literal meaning: as a temporary way station to employment and decent shelter. No one expected to remain there more than one or two months.

Shraga and Hemda Gruber shared this hope. It was spring when they reached their *ma'abara* near Rosh Pina, in the upper Galilee. Grass and flowers were sprouting in the fields and on the sides of the neighboring mountain range. The air was clear and pure. The couple's spirits were not dampened by their first sight of the shantytown. A new life was opening for them. They could endure a few more weeks of camp life. Within the gates of the compound three hundred corrugated-tin huts glinted brightly under the noonday sun. And inside the shack assigned to them, the Grubers found blessed privacy. The cots, the wooden table, and two chairs, the tin cups, plates, the primus stove and aluminum cooking utensils were theirs alone. Admittedly, the food was no improvement—the same rice, potatoes, bread, sugar, and tea. But at least they could eat in peace and silence. It was even possible now to endure the noisy, quarrelsome lines outside the public showers, the clinic, and the employment office. This time, after all, the arrangement was temporary.

Within ten minutes after their arrival, the Grubers lined up before the labor exchange. It was an oppressive experience, of course. The men and women around them shouted and cursed as they jostled for position. The Orientals still picked fights. Their women still wailed. The same ward heelers shuffled up and down the line, cornering their victims like birds of prey. A Herut—right-wing—politician attempted to thrust a circular into Shraga's hand. He ignored it. Finally, an hour and a half later, Gruber and his wife reached the desk inside. Here was a stroke of luck; the official was a Pole. Shraga handed over their identity cards.

"A long way from home, Pani," he murmured politely, in Polish.

The official shot him a cool glance. "Any professional training?" he asked, in Yiddish.

"I was a magistrate in Vrotslov," Gruber replied. "I understand legal procedures."

"Do you have a trade? Technical experience?"

When Gruber shook his head the official asked the same question of Hemda. Again the reply was negative. The official scribbled something on their cards, then checked a list pasted on the desk before him. "I have an opening for a charwoman," he said. "A Kupat Holim clinic in the camp. Four hours a day, eighty piasters an hour."

Hemda's eyes opened wide. "But that is next to nothing!" she exclaimed.

"It is a great deal here," the official replied, drily.

"What about me?" asked Shraga.

"You go on our unskilled list. We can give you part-time work on the kibbutzim near-by. You start at I£1.75 a day." For the first time the man looked up. He tried to put a little sympathy into his smile. "I know some others make more. But you have to understand. It's a question of seniority."

Shraga nodded, accepting his fate.

Each morning thereafter he and Hemda awoke at 5:00 A.M. After a quick breakfast of bread, tomatoes, and tea, they left the hut. They returned, exhausted, in the late afternoon. There were some days when no work at all was to be had at the kibbutzim. Occasionally Shraga earned a few extra piasters raking leaves in the *ma'abara* compound. Several times the Grubers were approached by their neighbors and invited to join in protest meetings:

hardly an afternoon went by without a noisy public demonstration before the labor exchange, or the social-welfare office. Neither Shraga nor Hemda was interested. It was only a matter of weeks until their promised flat would be ready in Safed. They were willing to wait.

Then the weeks became months, and the months became seasons. The Rosh Pina *ma'abara* was still full. So were most of the others. People were coming, not leaving. In the spring of 1952 Shraga discussed his situation once more with the camp director.

"I don't want to complain, Adon Rivlin," he said. "But it's been a year, and they still have me registered as a part-time worker. It looks like my wife and I are permanent residents. If that's the case, then we deserve a little seniority, don't you think?"

Rivlin nodded. "I want to help you, Shraga," he said. "You know what the priority is, though. First choice to families with children. It's a Histadrut rule."

"We have a child, Adon Rivlin."

"I know, I know," the official agreed quickly. "But it's not proved yet. Anyway, she's not here with you."

Gruber's voice began to shake. "I can't get her back unless I visit all the offices," he insisted. "Do you know what we've gone through since we've been here? From the first day after we came to Israel we've been traveling from one *Youth Aliyah* office to another. It's driving us crazy. Every piaster we can lay our hands on goes into the bus fare. One office after another. Haifa, Tel Aviv, Jerusalem." He began to weep. "Letters, telegrams, bus trips. My wife is almost out of her mind."

Rivlin cleared his throat. "Hold on a little longer, Shraga, " he said, putting his hand on Gruber's shoulder. "Everybody knows what you've gone through. Be patient a little longer. We are all for you. You are going to win this thing."

Gruber was crying uncontrollably now. "From the moment we arrived in Israel," he sobbed. "One office after another . . . every piaster we have . . ."

In the witness box sat Jonah Langer, director of child placement for *Youth Aliyah*'s Tel Aviv office. She was a middle-aged spinster, less than five feet tall, with an acute, birdlike face. Those who worked with the tiny social worker considered her a giant. Since the earliest days of mass immigration, no one had achieved as brilliant a record as she in tracing and reuniting Israel's broken families. The discovery of missing children was not simply Jonah Langer's official assignment; it was her personal crusade.

Late in December of 1950 the Gruber correspondence had been turned over to her. Carefully she read and reread the parents' letters. Obviously something had gone terribly wrong. Why had there been no response from the child's guardians in Onim or Beit Yitzhak? Why had the Grubers received the same routine assurances, without detailed information? Immediately, Jonah Langer sent a message to the Jerusalem office, asking for a check on Tamar Gruber's file. The answer came back three days later. The files were still in disarray. The archives had suffered a direct hit by Arab artillery during the siege of 1948, and were only now being put back in proper working order. The Gruber file would shortly be reclassified.

Jonah Langer was unwilling to wait. She left her office, and boarded a bus for Beit Yitzhak. There she interrogated Mrs. Adler, the secretary. And there she learned for the first time that the girl called Tamar Gruber had been returned to her mother. It seemed beyond belief! Could Mrs. Rosenberg actually have been the child's true mother? The secretary assured Jonah Langer that there was no possible doubt. All papers had been in order, Moreover, the youngster had recognized the woman. It was a closed case.

The little social worker worked the matter over in her mind during the return trip to Tel Aviv. The more she contemplated it, the more she was certain. Surely there must be two Tamar Grubers; and the daughter of Shraga and Hemda Gruber was missing.

Jonah Langer began painstakingly to review the data on all children who had arrived in Palestine since 1946. It was a near-hopeless task. There were no clues. What did the girl look like? When could she have come? Of course, it was always possible to write the Grubers and confess that a grievous mistake had been made, that their daughter had somehow been lost. But each time Jonah faced that possibility she rejected it: parents could not be subjected to that kind of anguish unless every other alternative was exhausted.

Then, on the morning of March 12, 1951, a shabby, middle-aged couple walked into her office. The husband addressed her in Yiddish:

"Miss Langer? Can we trouble you?"

"Please. Sit down."

"I am Shraga Gruber. This is my wife, Hemda."

"My God, the Grubers!" Jonah was on her feet, her hands outstretched. "I've had you on my mind for months now. Sit down. I'll get you some tea. Speak."

Then, between gusts of sobbing, they told her the story. Of the girl, given over to Petrolessia at the age of four, her transfer several months later to Darmstadt, then the voyage—when, they did not know—to Palestine, the correspondence between Vrotslov and the *Youth Aliyah* office in Jerusalem, the meaningless reassurances, and finally the photograph sent to them in July, 1949, the fateful, terrible photograph of a girl who was not their daughter.

"This photograph?" Jonah Langer handed them the identity card of Tamar Gruber, the youngster who had been reunited with her mother at Beit Yitzhak.

The parents examined the picture and nodded. "So you know?" said Shraga.

"I suspected for several months," said Jonah. "This girl is not your daughter, of course. There is no point in evading it now, we made a mistake." Her voice became crisp and businesslike. "Give me every bit of information about your Tamar that you can. I'll find her for you if it's the last thing I do."

The parents gazed into the social worker's determined little face, and believed her. Together, they reconstructed the details of Tamar's infancy, her appearance when last seen five years before, her illnesses. They remembered her as a shy girl, whom the early years of hunger had left thin and querulous. She had cried easily. Only the lips in her pinched, white face had been unusually full and red.

"Anything else?" asked Jonah Langer. "Think hard." A recollection was already gnawing at her.

"Nothing," said the mother after a long pause. "Her hair was dark brown —I already said that. Thin, shy. Yes, one other thing. I seem to recall that she had a birthmark on her back, near her shoulder."

Jonah Langer jotted all the information down. When she closed her notebook her mind was made up. "You can go back now. It's just a question of time and work," she promised the Grubers. "I won't rest until we find the girl."

She kept her word. Returning to the files, she analyzed carefully the description and photograph of every orphan child who had arrived in Palestine since 1946. There were nearly six thousand. Perhaps four thousand of these had come through Germany, and half that many through the children's center at Darmstadt. Jonah went over the records painstakingly. At the same time she checked the biographies of the various *Youth Aliyah* representatives who had worked at Darmstadt. There were seven. Further investigation revealed that five still remained in Israel. Jonah Langer visited each of them. And each of them vaguely remembered a Tamar Gruber—the other Tamar Gruber.

"What about a child without a name?" Jonah persisted. "A thin, frightened little girl who would have been four in 1946? She was in Darmstadt in 1947."

There were too many to remember. "Sometimes their names were changed to avoid interception by the British," one of the workers reminded her. "The girl came from Poland. Why not look for a child with a Polish name?"

Jonah nodded. The idea had long since occurred to her. By now, in fact, she was almost certain that she knew who the Gruber girl was. Once again she took the bus, this time to Jerusalem. In the *Youth Aliyah* archives she drew out the file. There was the timid, pale little face, the skull shaved nearly bare. And beneath it the name, Tanya Gruskow. The word "Gruskow" was smudged. It had obviously been crossed out and rewritten. A question mark appeared beside the name. That was all Jonah needed. She hurried down the flight of stairs to the placement office. A few minutes later she walked out with a photograph of Tanya Gruskow, taken in Israel several weeks before the child had been adopted by the Pollacks. To it she now added the pictures of four other *Youth Aliyah* girls, each approximately the same age of eight.

When, two days later, the Grubers reappeared in her office, Jonah laid the snapshots on the desk before her. "Examine these carefully," she said. "Do you think one of these children might be yours?"

The couple scrutinized the pictures. Shraga Gruber turned quite pale.

Hemda began to rock back and forth, a curious, twisted smile on her lips. "That is Tamar," whispered the father, pointing to the photograph of Tanya Gruskow. "Even after all these years I'd know her anywhere."

"Thank you," said Jonah, with evident relief. "Leave it to me now."

"Where is she?" blurted Mrs. Gruber, her voice shrill. "Take me to her."

"Try to remain calm, Mrs. Gruber, please," Jonah reassured her. "The girl is in Israel. I shall find her, I promise you. But you must leave it to me."

The Grubers were not willing to leave it to her. Six times during the next two weeks they came down from Haifa by bus or train. When they reached Jonah Langer's office they were as bedraggled, and often as famished, as hobos. They begged, pleaded, at times even threatened. And always Jonah's answer was the same: "We must be certain that this girl is your daughter. As soon as it is verified Tamar will be returned to you."

There was no leeway any longer for mistakes. Jonah Langer consulted now with Hava Cohen, the senior social worker. Mrs. Cohen did indeed remember having seen a birthmark on Tanya Gruskow's back—at the time of the adoption, when the child had been examined by the school physician in Kiryat Motzkin. The doctor had remarked then that the girl was probably older than the age listed on her immigration certificate; she still bore the symptoms of an earlier malnutrition. Even so, Mrs. Cohen was determined to investigate the matter personally once again. On March 15 she traveled to Kiryat Motzkin. She described the trip in a memorandum to Jonah Langer:

> On March 15 I went to the Pollack house and did not find anyone there. I therefore visited the school. Tanya is studying in the first grade. She is considered a rather average student, but I am told that she is now picking up interest in her studies and is quite sociable. I asked the teacher if she would escort the girl to the doctor's office. I wanted to see if Tanya had a birthmark on her back. At first both the teacher and the doctor himself resented this request. They must have suspected that Tanya's status was in doubt again. . . . Nevertheless, I finally prevailed upon the doctor to go through the motions of a physical examination. Sure enough, the moment the child removed her undershirt I saw the birthmark. It was on her right shoulder. . . .
>
> Later I returned to the Pollack home, and this time Mrs. Pollack was present. I could not bring myself to reveal the true purpose of my visit. Still, she must have sensed that something was wrong, for she was terrified. Why had I insisted that the doctor examine Tanya? she asked. I replied that it was just a routine checkup. I do not think that she believed me. Finally, being pressed, I felt obliged to point out that the doctor considered Tanya's age as closer to eight than to six—which is her registered age. As we were talking, the little girl herself returned home. She regarded my visit as perfectly natural, and paid little further attention to me.

The girl was surely Tamar Gruber, the daughter of Shraga and Hemda. Neither Hava Cohen nor Jonah Langer doubted it any longer. Nor, upon receiving a full report of these investigations, did Moshe Kol, the director of *Youth Aliyah*. The information could not be withheld from the Grubers indefinitely; they were already nearly out of their minds with frustration and grief. Yet, Mr. and Mrs. Pollack would have to be informed first. The blow would be a terrible one for them, of course. But if they were not persuaded to return the girl as quickly and painlessly as possible, the Grubers might act irresponsibly and take action—with disastrous consequences for the girl herself.

The meeting with the Pollacks took place in Jerusalem, in Hava Cohen's office. There was no way later to describe the indescribable. On the witness stand Jonah Langer confined herself to reading Hava Cohen's terse memorandum of April 15, 1951:

> The Pollack family came to my office on Friday and we had a long talk about . . . [our discovery] that Tanya Gruskow is Tamar Gruber, and that we would therefore have to take steps to return the girl to her legal parents. I am helpless to relate here the extent of their despair and pain. The discussion was protracted and heartbreaking. Near the end, however, hope seemed to revive in their hearts that perhaps our evidence is not yet sufficient. Indeed, they would insist upon additional proof, even if it were necessary to involve a lawyer. Yet, in spite of their growing resistance, their behavior was typically courteous, and even noble. They bear no grudge against us; they simply begged us not to proceed yet in any attempt to take the girl from them.

A few days later, Yosef Pollack wrote an anguished letter directly to Moshe Kol. Pleading with the director to intervene on their behalf, Pollack warned that the child could not possibly survive the shock of being taken away. Every care must be exercised to avoid undermining Tanya's security. Pollack thereupon launched into a detailed account of the youngster's happiness with her foster parents, her splendid physical and emotional development. "Everyone says that she is no longer the same child who came to our home a year ago. She is serene and self-confident with us—an adorable little angel." Only near the end of the letter did Yosef Pollack refer to himself and his wife. "We as bereaved parents turn to you to ask your help. After we lost our only son and were left lonely and miserable, we decided to adopt a girl to find a purpose in life. We have found that purpose, and that purpose is our beloved Tanya. . . . Even so, we would still be willing to give the girl up if there were one hundred per cent proof that the Grubers are her real parents. But we have sincere doubts about that." It was not a threat, simply a statement of conviction. But it was tinged with a frank appeal for mercy. "Can a thing like this be done among the people of Israel? Is there no law and justice in the land? In God's name, Mr. Kol, help us."

But *Youth Aliyah*'s first obligation was to the Grubers. The child's true identity was now being increasingly widely circulated; there was no point any longer in keeping the news from the parents. Accordingly, Shraga and Hemda Gruber were notified that Tamar had been found, that she was in the care of the Pollack family of Kiryat Motzkin. Hava Cohen assured the immigrant couple that matters would be arranged satisfactorily within a very short while, and the youngster would soon be returned. In the meantime, the Grubers would simply have to be patient. Under no circumstances were they to visit the Pollacks, or attempt any action of their own.

It was wasted breath. At first, to be sure, the Grubers were transported into a euphoria of joy and relief. But as the weeks passed, and the child remained in the hands of strangers, the aching desperation of the earlier months returned, intensified beyond endurance now that Tamar had finally been located.

> Dear Mrs. Cohen [wrote Shraga Gruber on April 28, 1951], I want to let you know that different people in the *ma'abara* suggested to me that I should take drastic action, but I did not agree to it. Dear Mrs. Cohen, why are you dragging us around for such a long time? All we want is for you to give us back our child. We are ready to undertake any action necessary, even to go through a court trial. We do not have any other witnesses because when we came back from Russia, we discovered that our entire families were lost. So you want us to lose this one, too? We do not want to give this child to anybody else, especially not in our own Jewish country, and the Agency is responsible for it. We have decided to wait three days and if we do not receive our child back by then, we shall demand a trial. I ask you to bring this to the attention of the Director of *Youth Aliyah*. . . .

> The child has not been brought to my home as promised, [He wrote again on June 20] and I call that unfinished business. I categorically demand that the girl be taken from the Pollack family. I would rather have the child put in one of your homes, but I don't want her at the Pollacks' even one more day.

The ultimatum of an impoverished immigrant couple was not to be taken seriously. Their uncontrollable terror was. Each time they trudged into Hava Cohen's office the strain of their ordeal was more evident. The frayed and patched clothes, the scuffed shoes proved nothing more than poverty. The hollow faces suggested only that food money had been spent for bus tickets. But the fixed, intent stare, the whitened lips and knuckles belonged uniquely to people on the verge of desperate, perhaps irresponsible action. So did the edged, insistent threat: "If you can't do anything about getting her back, we'll find another way. We won't wait much longer."

On July 16, Prime Minister Ben-Gurion and several members of his staff made a brief inspection tour of several *ma'abarot* in the Galilee region. The destitution of the immigrant shanty dwellers was a matter of grave personal concern to the prime minister, and he wanted them to know it. In the *ma'abara* of Rosh Pina, Ben-Gurion led his party through the maze of aluminum huts, listening solemnly to the running commentary of the camp director. Occasionally he paused amid the hundreds of silent, respectful *ma'abara* dwellers and shook the hands that were outstretched to him. Here and there he questioned the immigrants about living conditions, and then reassured them that circumstances would shortly improve. Just as Ben-Gurion reached the gate, and was about to enter his automobile, a ragged, middle-aged woman dashed out of the crowd. She thrust a piece of paper into the prime minister's hand, and then fearfully ran back into the compound.

Several days later Moshe Kol received a copy of the note from the prime minister's office.

> Dear Prime Minister of Israel, Mr. Ben-Gurion:
> This letter is written to you by a mother whose daughter has been taken from her by people who do not want to give her back. I have already written you before without having received any reply. This is my only child, who came to Israel from Germany in 1948. I went to look for her in a kibbutz where she was supposed to be but could not find her. In the kibbutz [actually Onim] I was told that she was given to other people. Now my girl is with the family named Pollack in Kiryat Motzkin, and lives in Rehov HaN'vi'im 14. They refuse to give her back. I ask you, dear Prime Minister, could you please help me to get my daughter back. Five other children of mine have been killed by the Germans. Is there a law in Israel making it possible to take children away from their parents without giving them back? I ask you, Excellency, to understand the heart of an unfortunate mother and give me back my daughter.
>
> Yours respectfully,
> Hemda Gruber.

The note was accompanied by a comment of Eliahu Gali, Ben-Gurion's secretary: "The prime minister asks you to clarify this business immediately, and to send him your results."

Of course Moshe Kol responded to the inquiry in full detail, tracing the history of the missing girl, and promising that the matter would shortly be brought to court. Kol's young associate, Benjamin Jaffe, secretary of the *Youth Aliyah* management board, had been urging this course of action for several weeks. Now, evidently, there was no other choice. Every effort had been made to persuade the Pollacks to relinquish the youngster quietly, and in her own best interest. But to no avail. As Jaffe had predicted, the public spectacle of a court trial could no longer be avoided. Thus, on September 27, 1951, Gideon Hausner, acting for *Youth Aliyah* and the Grubers, and Dov Or-Dan, representing the Pollacks, submitted their preliminary documents to the district court of Haifa.

Meanwhile, during the summer months, Jonah Langer had intensified her efforts to gather conclusive evidence of Tamar Gruber's identity. On June 1, the little social worker placed an advertisement in the newspapers requesting the addresses of all former employees of the Petrolessia camp in Poland. Soon a few responses arrived in the mail. Typically, Jonah Langer followed them up personally. At times the search proved exasperatingly circuitous. One of the former *Youth Aliyah* agents remembered Tamar Gruber, but could not identify her photograph. Another employee recognized the picture, but had no recollection of the mother, and thus could not verify Tamar's relationship to the Grubers.

Jonah Langer grimly continued her search. At her own expense, she traveled by bus and train to Jerusalem and Haifa, to smaller cities in between, and to numerous outlying farm settlements. In one of these agricultural communities, Ein HaShofet, she tracked down a former employee of Petrolessia, Mrs. Aliza Mandelbaum.

"You've come to the right place, Miss Langer," said Mrs. Mandelbaum. "I compiled a picture album of all the children who ever came to Petrolessia."

The social worker recalled later that her mouth went dry. "Can I see it?" she asked.

"Oh, it's not here," replied Mrs. Mandelbaum. "I turned my copy over to Yad v'Shem."

She was referring to the memorial musuem, half finished at the time, which was located on Mount Herzl outside Jerusalem. Yad v'Shem contained the world's largest collection of documents on the "Final Solution," the Nazi euphemism for the destruction of European Jewry.

This time Jonah left the investigation in Jerusalem to Benjamin Jaffe, Kol's associate. Jaffe visited the museum on July 21. Within a few minutes the archivist had located the album. It did not contain a photograph of Tamar Gruber.

"The archivist thinks this album isn't complete, Jonah," Jaffe explained by long-distance telephone. "He says that a man in Kibbutz Lochmei HaGhettaot has another copy which goes up through 1947. Will you try there?"

"Yes, by all means!" she shouted back. "I'll leave tonight."

Kibbutz Lochmei HaGhettaot, north of Haifa, had been founded only two years earlier by survivors of the Warsaw Ghetto revolt of 1943. One of the first buildings constructed by the kibbutz members was a small museum, displaying exhibits from the doomed ghettos and the Nazi extermination camps. As she sat in the darkened bus speeding up the coastal highway, Jonah Langer reminded herself that whatever she found in the museum would be regarded by the court as circumstantial evidence. By itself, it would not suffice. On the other hand, in conjunction with the testimony of witnesses, a photograph could be a powerful weapon. Still—there had been too many disappointments thus far. She would not allow her hopes to rise.

Arriving at Lochmei HaGhettaot at 10:00 P.M., she found the kibbutz silent; most of its members had retired for the night. Early the next morning, Jonah met the curator of the museum, and explained the purpose of her visit.

"We don't have that album on exhibit," said the curator. Then, noticing Jonah's disappointment, he added with a smile: "But that doesn't mean that the album isn't here. There are still boxes of materials we haven't even opened yet. I think I might have what you want."

Sorting through several cartons, he finally came up with another scrapbook. It was in fact the missing album. Together, the curator and Jonah scrutinized the faded snapshots on each page. It was a pathetic record. The children stared at the camera with identical listless, forlorn expressions.

Not one of them smiled. They were orphans, after all, possessing only the dimmest memories of their parents; their notion of what lay before them was even more vague. As the curator turned the sixth page, Jonah blinked several times, and raised her hand. "You can stop here, Adoni," she said.

Now, on May 14, 1952, the evidence was presented to the court. The photograph was a duplicate of the picture attached to Tanya Gruskow's identification card at the time of her arrival in Haifa: the same wistful, frightened four-year-old, her skull shaved bare.

"This was taken in Petrolessia," explained Gideon Hausner. "You will notice, Your Honor, that it is numbered precisely like the photographs of the other children in this album—with the identical slate wall for background. The ink in which her name is written is the same ink used for the other pictures. On the bottom of this snapshot you can see the words: 'Tanya Gruskow.'" Hausner turned the photograph over and handed it to Judge Landau. On the back, in the same ink, in the same handwriting, appeared the words: "Tamar Gruber, daughter of Hemda and Shraga Gruber."

Mrs. Pollack buried her head in her hands. Her huband bit his lip but did not lose his composure.

"Your Honor, if you please." Or-Dan, the Pollacks' attorney, was on his feet. He was plainly shaken. "I must point out to Your Honor that this photograph is circumstantial evidence, at best. I . . . concede that it is weighty evidence. Nor do I doubt the good faith of Miss Langer or Mr. Shamir [the curator of the museum]. But, Your Honor, many changes can be made in a snapshot, and even more in the words written on it. I should like to remind the court that the plaintiffs have not been able to produce a single witness, aside from the Grubers themselves, who can positively identify the girl Tanya Gruskow as their daughter."

But Or-Dan was wrong. For it was here that Jonah Langer's patient weeks of investigation bore fruit. She had continued her search even after the successful visit to Kibbutz Lochmei HaGhettaot. The witnesses she had discovered now took the stand, and willingly added their testimony to hers. The first of these, Saul Lachovitzky, was an old friend of the Grubers'. Indeed, he had shared their flight to Russia, and their return, in 1946, to Poland. He remembered the girl, Tamar, quite well. Recently he had accompanied Mrs. Hava Cohen to Kiryat Motzkin, and could state, with reasonable certainty, that the so-called Tanya Gruskow was in fact Tamar, the daughter of Shraga and Hemda Gruber.

Or-Dan wasted little time with Lachovitzky:

"Before your visit to Kiryat Motzkin, Mr. Lachovitzky, when was the last time you saw Tamar Gruber?"

"In 1946."

"When the child was four years old—according to the Grubers," mused Or-Dan. "And you can state with assurance that you recognize her six years after that?"

"Well, I recognize her because she resembles Shraga. She looks just like her father."

"Thank you, Mr. Lachovitzky." Or-Dan laughed. "You may step down."

Hausner and Jonah smiled, too. They had not placed much reliance on this witness. Rather, their hopes were pinned on the young woman who next took the stand.

Mrs. Devorah Katchkow was a Polish Jewess who had fled to Russia to escape the invading Wehrmacht. After the war she had returned alone to her former home. Together with several other adolescents, she was recruited by the Co-ordination to work in the children's home at Petrolessia. By the spring of that year one hundred and fifty Jewish orphans were housed in the reconverted monastery and its neighboring annex. There was never enough room. Each week scores of new youngsters arrived, usually shepherded by representatives of the Joint Distribution Committee or the Red Cross. Occasionally, too, children wandered in on their own, or with a single surviving parent. In November of 1946 Hemda Gruber arrived in Petrolessia with her little daughter.

"I remember the girl well," Mrs. Katchkow recalled. "She cried a great deal. After her mother left the last time, Tamar was inconsolable. I did what I could to cheer her up, playing with her, arranging games with the other children. After a while she stopped crying. In January the time came to send her on to Lodz, and from there to the *Youth Aliyah* camp at Darmstadt. I filled out her documents. As soon as she reached Germany her name would be Tanya Gruskow. Of course we wanted to disguise her Jewish identity. But in Tamar's case this was not the only reason. It happened that only one month before she arrived in Petrolessia, another little girl, only two years old, had been delivered to us by a mother. By a curious coincidence, that girl's name, too, was Tamar Gruber. The other Tamar Gruber left Petrolessia in December of 1946. Later—as you know—she arrived in Palestine on the *Andover*. I understand that her mother found her here shortly afterward.

"As for the older Tamar Gruber, she departed for Lodz and Darmstadt with one of our workers. However, when they reached Darmstadt, the original employee had to be replaced at the last moment. The new man evidently was not informed of Tamar's true name. He knew her only as Tanya Gruskow. Of course, in nearly all cases the original documents, bearing the original names, were sent on in advance to Palestine with the Jewish Agency emissaries. In that way the children could be properly identified when they arrived. I assume that in this instance the worker in Darmstadt erroneously sent the documents bearing the name Tanya Gruskow. That probably explains the mix-up later. That, and the partial destruction of our archives by Arab shells."

"Do you remember Tamar Gruber well enough to identify her picture?" asked Hausner.

"I think so."

A group of photographs was now handed over to Devorah Katchkow. Without hesitation she pointed to the snapshot of Tanya Gruskow. Then she identified the photograph of the other Tamar Gruber. Upon cross-examination, the witness held fast to her original testimony, even adding new details of corroboration.

Once again Or-Dan turned to the judge. "Your Honor. I have to admit how impressed I am by Mrs. Katchkow's testimony," he declared. "I have no reason to doubt her good faith. Yet I am obliged to point out that her testimony is hardly conclusive. . . . Mrs. Katchkow remembers the child in Petrolessia. But this is a question of memory, Your Honor," Or-Dan insisted. "Mrs. Katchkow's memory could be faulty. It is still possible that she identified the proper photograph entirely by chance. The Tanya Gruskow who now lives with the Pollacks might be a completely different child from the one Mrs. Katchkow remembers of six years ago. I repeat: so long as identification rests on a photograph, the evidence cannot be considered as more than circumstantial."

"Mrs. Katchkow?" This time it was Judge Landau speaking.

"Your Honor?"

He gazed thoughtfully at the soft-faced, darked-eyed woman. "Do you think that you could identify the child today?" he asked.

Mrs. Katchkow was visibly astonished. "Today, Your Honor? After so many years?"

"It would be very helpful," the judge assured her.

Mrs. Katchkow stared helplessly for a moment at Jonah Langer. The tiny social worker shrugged, her birdlike face quite pale. Then the witness consulted briefly with Hausner. Finally, looking back at Landau, she nodded silently.

Immediately the judge issued orders for the bailiff of the court to accompany the witness to Kiryat Motzkin, together with the attorneys of both sides. There, without advice from any outside party, Mrs. Katchkow would seek to identify the girl as she sat in her classroom.

Forty minutes later a taxi containing Mrs. Katchkow, Hausner, Or-Dan, and the bailiff pulled up to the front entrance of a large, yellowing stone building, the Kiryat Motzkin elementary school. The attorneys climbed out and entered the school. A few minutes later they returned, in the company of a middle-aged man.

"This is Dr. Lonherz, the school principal," said Or-Dan to Mrs. Katchkow. "He is going to take us to Tanya Pollack's class. You will look in without speaking, and then inform us if you recognize the girl."

Obviously unhappy over the visit, the principal nodded perfunctorily to Mrs. Katchkow, then led the little party to the south wing of the building. There he opened a hall door, and beckoned the others to follow. At the end of the hall he silently opened another door. "This is the class," he whispered to Mrs. Katchkow. "Look in, but don't disturb the students."

Eleven girls and nine boys sat at their desks. None of them could have been older than eight or nine. They stared at the visitors in mild curiosity for a moment, then were called back to attention by their teacher.

"Those were the Kings," the instructress was saying. "Now who can recite the Prophets?"

The hands went up, and one of the children spoke: "Amos, Isaiah, Hosea, and Ezekiel and—"

As the recitation continued, Mrs. Katchkow studied the faces of the girls. It was remarkable how each resembled the others at that age: the same clear skin, bright eyes, even the same running noses. They seemed incapable of sitting still. Some twisted and fidgeted in their seats. Others whispered to their friends, and then peeked furtively at the teacher. One scrawled pictures in her notebook. Another turned the pages of her Bible, seeking the names of the Prophets, opening and closing her rosebud mouth as she pronounced the words to herself.

Mrs. Katchkow frowned. The Tamar Gruber she remembered had been a thin, undernourished child, pale and silent, even querulous. None of these little girls fitted that description any longer. Some were smaller than others, and a few were fair-skinned, as Tamar had been. But they were all healthy-looking and quite alert; none gave the appearance of shyness. Where was that timorous little shaven-skulled youngster, with the full lips in a drawn face? Not here, surely. The task was hopeless.

As the names of the Prophets continued to peal forth, Mrs. Katchkow gazed sadly down the three rows of students. Thousands of Jewish children like these were studying the catechism in Polish schools, lost forever to their people because their parents had not returned to claim them. Perhaps, too, because she, Devorah Katchkow, and her colleagues had failed to identify them in time when the war ended. It seemed intolerable that she should fail again in a Jewish land. Inadvertently she groaned aloud. The children looked up instantly, staring at her with astonishment. Dr. Lonherz tugged angrily at her sleeve, and Mrs. Katchkow moaned again, tentatively raising her arm.

"Full lips in a drawn face," she murmured, pointing to the little rosebud mouth.

The door closed, and the adults walked back down the corridor. Dr. Lonherz shrugged:

"That was Tanya Pollack," he admitted.

Hausner's eyes filled with tears, and he pressed Mrs. Katchkow's hand.

The trial was adjourned on May 20. Judge Landau, with several other cases pending on his calendar, informed the principals that his verdict would not be ready for several weeks. The Pollacks and their foster child returned to Kiryat Motzkin. The Grubers returned to the *ma'abara* in Rosh Pina. Shraga Gruber was optimistic; the hearings had gone wonderfully well. The morning after the adjournment he paid a visit to Rivlin, the camp director. The official greeted him warmly.

"It looks good for you, Shraga," said Rivlin. "We were all praying for you and Hemda. You know that."

Gruber smiled. "I do, Adon Rivlin," he replied. "We appreciate it. Right now our one concern is to make things ready for Tamar as quickly as possible. The Pollacks have given the child every advantage. We can't match what they have done. But *something* we have to do."

Rivlin nodded. He knew what was coming.

"We must have a home for that girl," Gruber continued. "We've been on the waiting list for a flat more than a year now. Maybe others were ahead of us. But if we get Tamar back it will be our turn. It must be. We can't raise her in a tin hut, Adon Rivlin."

"Tens of thousands of children are growing up in *ma'abarot*," the official demurred mildly.

"Hundreds of thousands died in Europe," Gruber replied. "What does that prove? Does that make it right? Most of these children here never knew a better life. Tamar did. The shock of taking her away from the Pollacks will be bad enough without—all this. If we can't provide her with more than a tin hut, it's possible the judge won't even give her back to us. Anyway, Adon Rivlin, it's our turn, that's the point. You've got to get us a flat. The flats are going up by the thousands now. We only need one."

"Yes, we're working on it," Rivlin assured him, not without embarrassment. "You must remember, though, that people don't get flats unless there is some assurance of work for them near-by. We can't do everything at once."

"But things are getting better," Gruber insisted.

"Who told you?"

"I see it."

He saw tents in Rosh Pina gradually replaced by tin and aluminum huts, buildings erected in the *ma'abara* for schools, kindergartens, children's homes, clinics, synagogues, shops, and clubs for young people. Each day he saw his neighbors assigned to jobs laying approach roads, planting saplings on the mountain sides, and raising electric poles at the entrance of town. Jewish Agency instructors were training the immigrants to be farmers. Histadrut instructors were teaching men to operate lathes, and women to weave rugs. Dance and drama groups were arriving now to perform for the *ma'abara* dwellers. Of course circumstances were improving. The Grubers saw it with their own eyes.

It did not occur to them that what they saw was a palliative. The *ma'abara* was being improved, but only because there no longer existed any immediate likelihood of replacing it. More part-time work was now available—for the policy of unlimited immigration had been temporarily halted; the influx of the previous year, 176,000 people, was being systematically reduced to one seventh that number. What other alternative was there? The nation's farms were supplying less than one fourth of the population's food requirements. Industrial production was pathetically small. By the end of 1951, imports to Israel were fully five times higher than exports. Yet even the slightest reduction in essential consumer goods threatened outright famine. The diminishing reservoir of hard currency would have to be applied almost exclusively to basic food needs.

The consequences of this short-term humanitarianism were predictable. Factories slowed to a halt for lack of raw materials. The Israel pound all but collapsed in value. The official price ceiling was virtually meaningless; on the flourishing black market food costs soared daily. With inflation rampant, rationing had to be dropped. A forced indemnity was imposed upon all bank deposits. By the spring of 1952 the government of Israel was driven to seeking short-term loans from private banks. The truth was that, four years after its birth, the Jewish State teetered precariously on the edge of bankruptcy.

Rivlin attempted to explain this to Gruber. "It means grief for all of us, Shraga," he pointed out. "I know you won't believe me, but my wife and I don't live much better than any immigrant in this camp."

Gruber shook his head. "You have a roof over your head, Adoni," he murmured wearily. "You have hot food and a bedroom for your children. Never mind, I'm too tired to argue about it any more. When Tamar comes we'll discuss it again. I can tell you now we won't keep her here."

He stalked out. On the way back to the hut he passed a group of men, milling restively and angrily in front of the social-welfare office. Some of them were beating their fists on the locked door. Several pounded metal pipes against tin pots and pans.

"Gruber," cried one of the immigrants, a short, bandy-legged Rumanian. "Wait a minute."

Shraga continued walking; he was not in the mood for conversation. But the Rumanian persisted and ran after him, clutching his arm.

"Gruber," he whispered breathlessly, in Yiddish, "we're preparing a strike against the Agency. A big one this time. Five other *ma'abarot* in the area are participating."

"Leave me out of it." Shraga brushed away the man's hand. "I've had enough of your blasted strikes."

"No, no," the little Rumanian insisted. "This is different. Listen, will you? It's going to be a beauty, a nice, loud one."

Shraga laughed sourly. "Is there any other kind in these places? I'm not interested."

"A real earthquake, I tell you," the Rumanian whined. "We'll start tearing the huts down. This time we'll pound so loud they'll hear us in Safed. We need every man and woman, you hear?"

"I hear. I hear you every week. Go away."

Chagrined, his confidant dropped back, then called out once again: "And we'll strike every week until we get action. He who is not with us is against us, just remember."

"Aah, don't threaten me," Shraga growled. He entered his hut and dropped exhausted on his cot. Hemda waited for him to speak. "One thing at a time," he said finally. "Let's get the child back first."

Their chance came on June 26. Judge Landau issued his verdict that day. The reading, before the tense families and a packed courtroom (the case had received nation-wide press coverage), consumed less than an hour. There were few surprises. Succinctly and compassionately, Landau reviewed the life histories of both sets of parents.

"My decision in this case," he declared, "is based on the confidence with which the witnesses presented their evidence, primarily the parents themselves. It is true that the girl was only four years old when the mother sent her to Petrolessia—and she was identified by the parents over five years later when she was just reaching the age of nine. But I am of the opinion that a mother will not fail to identify her daughter at such an early age, even after five years. Indeed, Mrs. Gruber's recollection of the birthmark attests to this. . . .

"[Her words] . . . are also confirmed by the evidence of Mrs. Devorah Katchkow, who saw the child during the months after she left her parents' home. Mrs. Katchkow gives the impression of being dependable and just, and she surely would not twist the truth in so important a case. I hardly have to state here how especially compelling was her recent identification of the girl in the Kiryat Motzkin school. . . ."

Turning to the defense arguments, Landau observed that he was impressed only by one: Was it possible that the child would not remember her sea voyage when she was almost six? A child generally remembers such an incident in her life. If she were four years old at the time, as the defendants insisted, it was rather more likely that she forgot the trip. And yet, observed Landau, even this argument did not weigh against his conclusion. The girl even today was less developed than her age group; she suffered a great deal before she immigrated to Palestine, and it was conceivable that during all this turmoil she simply could not remember the fact of the sea crossing.

"After having observed the conduct of the witnesses on the stand, and having weighed their evidence carefully, I hereby decree that the girl Tanya Gruskow, now called Tanya Pollack, is the daughter, Tamar, of the plaintiffs Shraga and Hemda Gruber."

Landau did not stop here, however. Rather he proceeded to discuss what, to him, was a deeper issue: the legal and moral justification for removing an unwilling child from a home and people she knew and loved. "There is no common language between the girl and the Grubers," Landau pointed out, "for she has forgotten Yiddish, and her parents do not speak Hebrew. The parents live in a *ma'abara* in Rosh Pina. . . . They are among the impoverished classes. As Mr. Or-Dan has said, the transfer of the child from the Pollack home to the home of the plaintiffs would seem to her like exile from the Garden of Eden. I myself saw Tamar's conduct in the courtroom, as she burst out crying bitterly, and held the defendants with all her strength lest she be taken away and sent to the plaintiffs who seem strange and peculiar to her. . . ."

Landau hereupon pointed out that the question of child custody fell within the realm of "personal status"; and in Israel matters of personal status were decided according to religious, not civil, law. "Mr. Or-Dan claims that in accordance with the Hebrew law the operating factor must be the welfare of the child, regardless of whether the parents are alive or not. Or, as stated by our ancient sages, 'the welfare of the child lies within the discretion of the court.'. . ."

Quoting now from an impressive array of rabbinical as well as British High Court decisions, Landau concluded that "courts are obliged to be careful not to interfere between parents and their children except in cases where it cannot possibly be prevented. For example, in the case where both parents are mentally ill . . . [or] where the facts resemble the case before us, but where the child is almost at the age of maturity . . . and where it would not be useful to take the child from her surroundings and give her to her parents for a short period. But the child with whom we are now dealing is still . . . young and pliable, and therefore will adjust more easily to her new surroundings, even though there will undoubtedly be economic difficulties. It is worthwhile because these are her real parents, her own flesh and blood. . . . In any case, we shall do our best to make her transition period as easy as possible. . . .

"I therefore decide and declare that the principal plaintiff, Shraga Gruber, and the second plaintiff, Hemda Gruber, are hereby permitted to assume custody of the girl Tamar Gruber (who is also called Tanya Gruskow and Tanya Pollack), who is their legal daughter, and I order the two defendants to hand the girl over to a representative of this court, who shall be announced by me, and who shall hand her over to her parents after a period of transition."

In the second week of July, 1952, Tamar Gruber accompanied her parents from Kiryat Motzkin to Rosh Pina. Hundreds of immigrants, smiling delightedly and calling out their greetings to the child, lined the entrance to the *ma'abara* as the little party approached. Neighbors had brought flowers and small gifts of food to the Gruber hut. Inside, a small cot had been placed in the Grubers' former bedroom; the parents had moved their bed to the kitchen area.

"This is yours, Tamar," said Mrs. Gruber, pointing to the attractive quilt which covered the cot. "Our neighbors have given you this as a welcome-home present. Isn't that nice?"

Mrs. Rivlin, wife of the camp director, translated the mother's remarks into Hebrew. Tamar nodded her thanks. Then refreshments were prepared: tea, in metal cups, and cookies.

"Eat," murmured Shraga Gruber encouragingly. "It's good. Later we shall have a nice dinner. Mother has a chicken for us—a nice fresh chicken."

They sat at the table. The parents and Mrs. Rivlin nibbled at the cookies and watched the child anxiously. Tamar remained silent, her hands in her lap. Tears filled her eyes, but she did not sob. Neither did she eat.

"This is all quite new to her," said Mrs. Rivlin to the mother. "It will take a week or two for her to adjust. I wouldn't worry."

After a few more minutes of conversation Mrs. Rivlin left. The parents and the child stared at each other. Shraga Gruber attempted several words of pidgin-Hebrew. When Tamar did not answer, he lapsed into silence.

The hours passed and it was dinnertime. Mrs. Gruber turned up the oil lamp and prepared the chicken. This time Tamar made an effort to eat, picking gingerly at the wing and drumsticks laid on the tin plate before her. Occasionally she cast timorous glances at the adults' half-empty plates.

"It's all right." Mrs. Gruber smiled. "We ate before."

The child shook her head uncomprehendingly.

"Lo—raev," said the father haltingly, in broken Hebrew. "No hungry."

Tamar ate a few more bites, then sat back, exhausted. Instantly the parents jumped up and began undressing her. Then, finally, the child began to cry—quietly at first, but soon convulsively. Hemda Gruber caressed her daughter's hair, murmuring endearments. The child continued to sob. It was past midnight before she fell asleep.

The Grubers lay silently near the kitchen, behind the canvas partition once again. In the darkness they could hear the uneven rise and fall of the girl's breathing. Finally they dozed off.

Shortly before dawn a terrified scream awakened them.

"Ima, Ima," wailed the child. "Ima, Ima, Ima."

"Oh God, I'm coming," cried Hemda, jumping out of bed. She thrust the curtain aside and knelt by her daughter's bed. "Don't cry, don't cry," she begged in Yiddish. "Mother's here."

Tamar stared up at the wild-haired woman hulking above her and loosed another horrified scream. Simultaneously she flailed at Hemda's face with her small hands. Shraga rushed in with cookies.

"Ochel, ochel, Tamar," he said cajolingly. "Food, nice food."

The little girl began to choke. Shraga pounded her back, but Tamar twisted away, burrowing under the sheet. Another hour passed before the child fell silent. Then she slept again. The Grubers returned to their bed.

"We've got to get out of this place," Shraga muttered, half to himself. His strength was gone and he closed his eyes.

A few minutes later he was awakened once more. The sound of quiet sobbing again filled the hut. With a groan, he climbed out of bed and groped dazedly for the canvas partition. Tamar was sleeping, her wan face stained with tears. Confused, he turned back to his cot.

"It's all right, man," sobbed his wife. "I'll get over it."

She did not and the child did not. The days passed and nothing changed. When the youngster screamed, the parents knew that it would take more than a knowledge of Hebrew to pacify her. Everything was a question of time, Shraga muttered mechanically. Hemda no longer answered. Time would not buy a dress or fill a pot with soup. It was midsummer and the sun blazed full in the sky. Outside, dogs and the unemployed crawled for cover. Inside the aluminum shanties, walls sweated, and families gasped for air. From her stool in front of the hut, Hemda could see the child wandering the lanes of the *ma'abara* like a rag doll, kicking forlornly at orange peels and tin cans. She's safe while I can watch her, thought the mother. What happens when I go to work again?

She soon learned. On the last day of July the clinic filled with dysentery cases, and the call went out once more for charwomen. Hemda Gruber spoke to the social-welfare authorities, and it was decided that Tamar would spend each day in the children's house until her parents returned. The arrangement worked for the first week. Then, on the afternoon before the Sabbath, the mother arrived at the children's home and found several youngsters wrestling furiously in the courtyard. They were all girls, and they were grunting and tearing at each other's hair. Mrs. Gruber kneeled to pry the children apart. One of them was Tamar. Her face was matted with dirt and mucus, and her dress was shredded.

"What's happened to you?" cried Mrs. Gruber, horrified, lifting the girl to her feet. "Is this what they teach you here?"

As Tamar was led away she suddenly twisted from her mother's grasp and screeched an Arabic curse word at the other children. Mrs. Gruber seized her daughter with both hands, half carrying, half dragging her back to the hut.

That evening at dinner the mother said it first: "We've got to get out of this place."

Shraga Gruber nodded. "We are having a committee meeting tonight," he said. "The man from the housing corporation will be here. It may be good news."

"We have to get out of here right away," Hemda continued tonelessly, "or the child will be lost. Not like in Europe. Really lost, you understand?"

Shraga slowly finished his dinner of rice and eggplant. Finally, sitting back, he gazed long and thoughtfully at his daughter. Tamar's curls touched the oilskin cloth as her tongue moved catlike along the rim of her plate. Sensing Gruber's eyes on her, she looked up at him fearfully. Then, without a word, she slipped off the chair and ran to her bed. Shraga arose and left the hut.

He walked toward the noise: that would be the meeting. As he reached the Agency office he noted that the entire compound was churning with excited, gesticulating men. He walked closer. No, the men were not excited. They were infuriated, maddened. Some of them were shouting at the top of their lungs. Two Moroccans were kicking wildly at the locked office door. One Jew—a European—had seized a board and hurled it purposelessly, hysterically, against the wall of the Agency building.

"Kill them, kill them, kill them," screamed a tiny immigrant, in Yiddish. "Kill the lying, scheming Hitlers, hang them, lynch them." Completely out of control, he whirled like a dervish, then lurched into Shraga. It was the Rumanian. "You!" his fist closed on Gruber's sleeve. "Do you think you're any better than they are? Quisling, traitor, you!"

"What is it? What's the matter with you?"

" 'What's the matter with you?' " the Rumanian mocked him. "What's the matter with all of us? We've been betrayed. If people like you had joined with us it wouldn't have happened. They wouldn't have dared. The man from the housing corporation was here, that's what. He's put us back on the list. They're out of money—so, no houses, no flats, no nothing. It will take another year, at least. And even then, no promises. Now, Gruber, what do you say?"

Shraga said nothing. The news was beyond belief.

"Maybe you want to work a plot of tomatoes on a hill?" shrilled the little man. "That's what they'll give us if we're 'patient.' Right on the border where the shooting is. A nice place to raise children, eh? Otherwise you'll wait with the rest of us. Wait, wait, wait." He stamped his foot with each word. Froth had actually collected at the corners of his mouth.

"Wait," mumbled Shraga. He walked slowly back to the hut, and passed it, unseeing.

On August 9 Jonah Langer sent a memorandum to Moshe Kol: "The psychiatrist appointed by the court came by today. He informs me that he visited the *ma'abara* at Rosh Pina. The Grubers are not there. The director of the camp says that they have been missing for three days. No one knows where they have gone. I must confess that this is a most mystifying and disturbing development. According to the terms of the verdict, the parents must remain in continual touch with *Youth Aliyah*. As you know, our first report to the court on the girl's welfare is due in less than three weeks. If the Grubers fail to abide by this agreement, a very serious question may be raised about their right to keep Tamar."

The Grubers were in touch with the court. On the same day that Jonah Langer dispatched her memorandum, Shraga and Hemda Gruber were seated in Judge Landau's chambers. The Pollacks were also present. Gravely, and without comment, both couples affixed their signatures to a document. It was an addendum to the original verdict.

> It has been decided
> 1) that in spite of the decision regarding the progressive transition from the adopters [i.e., the Pollacks] to the parents, the parents agree that their girl should remain in the house of the adopters and her name should remain Tanya Pollack.
> 2) The adopters guarantee to care for the girl as they have done thus far, and to be responsible for all the expenses that are habitual in homes of their status.
> 3) The adopters guarantee to educate the girl. But they also ensure that the girl shall know the identity of her real parents, and be encouraged to love them. The adopters must take the girl for visits to the parents' home, and allow the parents to visit the girl whenever they wish.
> 4) Both sides agree that in case of misunderstanding, the arbitrator will be Rabbi Kaniel of Haifa, who has been chosen to supervise the welfare of the girl.
> 5) Both sides guarantee that the girl will never be taken from the Land of Israel without mutual agreement.
> 6) The parents abandon the rights granted them by the original verdict of the court. . . .

There was little to be said. The four parties to the agreement shook hands with Judge Landau, and thanked him for his good offices. Then the Pollacks walked out to a friend's waiting automobile. Tamar was seated in the back. They drove off together to Kiryat Motzkin. The Grubers walked to the Central Station, and there boarded a bus to the Galilee.

During the ninety-minute journey the parents sat as if frozen in their seats. Once a passenger asked Shraga for a match, repeated the request, and then noted with astonishment that the man's eyes were glazed, like a dope addict's. The wife was evidently deaf. When the bus reached the Rosh Pina *ma'abara,* the driver, who knew the Grubers well by now, called out to them twice. Finally, as if awakening from a dream, the couple picked up their small carpetbags and climbed down.

It was dusk. The huts no longer shimmered in the heat. A cool breeze floated in from the sea. It brought thunder with it. Rain? wondered Shraga. In the summer? Mealtime? wondered Hemda. This was not Sha'ar HaAliyah; there was no central kitchen or soup line here. Yet the noise, more distinct now, was the familiar, unmistakable cacophony of pots and pans, of stampeding feet and strident voices. As the Grubers entered the gate, their line of vision caught the alleyway extending into the compound. It was black with humanity. It was the strike.

The thunder rolled in from the west. From the camps of Givat Shaul, Sha'ar HaAliyah, Athlit, and Bat Galim; from the squatter cities of Neve Chaim, Ra'anana, and Kfar Azav; from the shantytowns of Beer Yaakov, Kiryat Eliahu, and Beit Etzion. From flapping canvas tents it came, from the swinging wooden shutters of welfare offices and the clanking iron tureens of soup kitchens. The clamor was the voice of the people: the anguished, the distraught, the cynical, the brutalized, the crazed, the illiterate and the cunning, the crippled and the diseased redeemed from the gas showers of Europe and the human cesspools of Asia. It was the wild, protesting cry of those who had awaited the immigrants, who had brought them to this strip of soil and who now staggered and stumbled under the agonizing, mortifying weight of them. It was the roar of the newborn Jewish Republic, back to the wall, fighting for its life.

CHAPTER THREE

THE SOCIAL CASE

O N A LATE summer day in 1958, traffic suddenly came to a stop in
Zion Circle, the heavily congested commercial center of downtown
Jerusalem. Pedestrians on the sidewalks, drivers in their automobiles stared
silently as a bizarre procession filed across the milling junction, from Ben-
Yehudah Street to Jaffa Road. Walking at the head of the group was a
lean, swarthy woman, clad in a black, ankle-length Oriental dress. She
cradled a half-naked infant in her left arm. Seven other children followed
close behind, all shabbily dressed and barefoot, and ranging in age from
about thirteen to perhaps three. The mother and four of the youngsters
clutched posters, awkwardly lettered in cursive script. "Citizens of Israel,"
read the first placard, "you see before you a penniless mother and her eight
starving children. We have wandered the length and breadth of this land
searching for help, but the government will not give us a single piaster. If
we die in the streets our blood will be on your heads." "We are without a
father to support us," announced the second poster. "We have begged the
Jewish Agency and the ministry of social welfare to give us food, but no
one has ears for us." The other signs repeated the lamentations with minor
variations.

As the family crossed the circle, the woman glared straight ahead, her
sunken features immobile, her black eyes glittering feverishly beneath a
Medusa-like tangle of gummed hair strands. None of the children uttered
a sound, not even the infant, who clung dazedly to his mother's rachitic
shoulder bone. Each of them stared morosely at the ground, apparently
oblivious to the comments of the surrounding crowd.

"Damned outrage, if you ask me," murmured one of the onlookers, a
middle-aged European. "You'd think the government would have these
people settled by now."

"Ah, the government, the government," growled his companion. "It's all
a matter of paper work to them. They're used to these 'strikes.' Last week
it was a Moroccan family—had their children camped out all night on the
ground in front of the Jewish Agency building."

The first man shook his head in disgust. "Well, what can you expect of these primitives?" he said. "If they want action they raise a howl; it's as simple as that."

And action they received. Even as the bedraggled little band took up positions at the corner of Jaffa Road, a police wagon pulled up to the curb. The sergeant, who was himself a dark-skinned Oriental, began remonstrating with the mother in Arabic. Instead of replying, the woman unexpectedly loosed a cry—an eerie wail which soared above the reviving traffic in the circle, and once again transfixed the passing crowd. Astonished, the policeman tentatively grasped the woman's arm. She made no effort to resist. Neither did her wailing cease. Somewhat unnerved, the sergeant turned to his partner for help. Together, the two men succeeded in shepherding the mother and children into the van. In a moment the vehicle had departed, moving rapidly down Jaffa Road and disappearing over the crest of Princess Mary Street.

I had watched the scene from close by, and was both moved and repelled. "What's going to happen to them?" I asked a stranger standing beside me. "They're not being carted off to jail, are they?"

The question surprised him. "To jail? Why jail? They'll be dumped at the Municipality Building. One of the city's social workers will take charge of them."

"And after that?"

He shrugged. "After that—it's the same story. If they can't get help at one office, they'll try another. You don't know these 'strikers.' They spend more time making public scandals than working. They know all the tricks."

The man's reply shocked me. Scandals? Tricks? It seemed a remarkably callous reaction to the tragedy of eight starving children.

During the next few weeks the memory of that pathetic family seldom left me. Not surprisingly, the recollection was especially painful whenever I sat down to a well-cooked evening meal. From time to time I glanced through the back columns of newspapers for a clue to the family's whereabouts. But evidently the nation had become well accustomed to these public demonstrations; the "strike" was not newsworthy. I must confess that, as the weeks passed, the vision of those ragged youngsters all but faded in my own mind, too—until early December, when it was suddenly revived. My investigation of Israel's absorption problems eventually brought me to the ministry of social welfare. It occurred to me that the plight of the Oriental mother and her children might be a useful test case.

The ministry itself, located on Jerusalem's Princess Mary Street, offered pitiless commentary on the state of siege under which all of Israel's public services operated. It was a shabby stone building at least a half-century old. The vestibule inside was quite dark, and smelled vaguely of carbolic acid. One reached the "executive" offices on the third floor by means of a creaking elevator which barely left room for the operator and two passengers. The offices, in turn, were as dimly lit as the vestibule, and nearly as damp. Clerks and secretaries warmed themselves by hissing kerosene stoves placed at strategic intervals on the chipped stone floor. Many of the employees wore sweaters under their jackets or over their dresses, and some kept scarves wrapped tightly around their necks. As I made my way to the "department of organization and supervision," my fingers involuntarily clenched and unclenched in my pockets.

Mrs. Yaffa London-Yarie, chief of the department, was a stocky East European in her middle forties. Her manner was abrupt. Without listening to my opening remarks, she glanced quickly through my letters of introduction. "What sort of material did you have in mind?" she asked.

"There was a certain case, a few months ago—a mother and eight children marching through Jerusalem with signs. I thought perhaps it might have come through your office."

Mrs. London-Yarie smiled grimly. "I remember it all right," she said. "You've certainly picked a beauty." Suddenly she turned to her secretary. "Get me the file on Habiba Boucha, will you?"

As the secretary left the office, Mrs. London-Yarie permitted herself a sigh. "You know, we get these 'strikes' all the time," she confessed. "It's an old story to us. Wherever they start out, these people usually end up here. They drop all their troubles in our laps, and if we don't solve them overnight we're 'murderers.' "

I nodded sympathetically.

"I estimate that about eight hundred thousand immigrants have arrived in this country since 1948," she continued. "At least half of them have been Orientals. And of these, half have been misfits. Cut *that* number in half and you'll find their records somewhere in our files."

"Penniless and inexperienced, of course," I ventured.

Mrs. London-Yarie scoffed. "Who isn't? Who wasn't? I can't name five Europeans who came here with enough funds to pay a month's rent. But at least they were ready to work. If they didn't have the skills this country needed, they were willing to learn. Of course, they had their share of square pegs, too. But nothing to compare with the Iraqis and the Persians."

I said: "Reading about their backgrounds, though, it seems remarkable that any of them have managed to survive in Israel at all."

Mrs. London-Yarie nodded slowly. "No, it's not their fault," she concurred. "I suppose if we thought it were, none of us would be able to stomach this work."

The secretary returned with a manila folder. Mrs. London-Yarie opened it, and fingered through its contents for several moments. Then she turned the file over to me. "Look it over—you can sit here. If you have any questions when you're through, ask them. You might start with this letter—" she pointed to a blue document bearing the insignia of the Municipality of Tel Aviv—"it's a summary of the family's situation as of last month."

The letter was dated November 4, and was addressed to the ministry of social welfare:

> The Boucha family immigrated from Iraq in 1951 with three children. Later five other children were born in Israel. The father, Saadia Boucha, was born in 1914. His wife, Habiba, was born in 1923. The eight children range from thirteen to eight months. Saadia Boucha was

unemployed, untrained in any craft useful to this country, from the moment of his arrival at Sha'ar HaAliyah [an immigrant camp near Haifa]. He was transferred to Safed, to a *ma'abara*. There he worked for a year and a half, and evidently injured himself. Since then he has suffered from an inflammation of the knee and pains in his back. He was obliged to wear an orthopedic harness, and after a while begged the Jewish Agency to transfer him to another site. Later he was moved to Moshav Chusan [a co-operative farm settlement, in the Galilee].

For five years the family raised tobacco on their own little strip of soil. In the meantime their number grew larger from year to year, and their economic plight steadily worsened. They asked help from the Jewish Agency, but never received a satisfactory answer. By then, Saadia Boucha had evidently reached the limit of his endurance. He left his family and moved to Tel Aviv. There he lived in a neglected shack on the city's outskirts, supporting himself as an agricultural field hand.

After he had deserted his family, the wife took her eight children and traveled, first to Tel Aviv, then to Jerusalem. For days she wandered the streets of these cities carrying signs which recounted her pitiful story. The institutions were apparently unwilling to help her and her large family. She and the children slept in the streets, and begged their food for nearly a month. Eventually, at the end of the summer, the Jerusalem Municipality intervened and put the wretched family up in a hotel for three days. Then they received permission to come to Machneh Yisrael [a *ma'abara* near Lydda]. . . .

We stress the fact that we have sent a letter about this case to the settlement department of the Jewish Agency. . . . The family lives without any conveniences whatever, and at the end we must again emphasize that the money [for their board in Machneh Yisrael] must be paid back, for this is a "floating" case, and it does not belong to our jurisdiction.

I must have sighed when I came to the end of the report, for Mrs. London-Yarie cocked her head in my direction, and gazed at me inquisitively for a moment. Neither of us spoke, however, and I turned back to the file. The source of Habiba Boucha's tragedy was evident enough. It was her husband. After all, a man who would have allowed his wife and eight children to become street beggars was hardly less than a murderer. I searched through the documents for a glimpse of Saadia Boucha. He was there—revealed in his own letter of May 19, 1957. He had written it several months before leaving Moshav Chusan, and had addressed it to—the prime minister! (One needs time to adjust to the Oriental mentality.)

Your Excellency [the letter read, in the florid calligraphy of a hired scribe]:

I and my family are living at Moshav Chusan, penniless and unwilling victims of the Jewish Agency's cruelty. We did not ask to be sent here. We would never have come here had our lives been in our own hands. People do not fear God here. For this is a settlement of heretics! Heretics, Your Excellency! With no compassion for human life.

When my wife became pregnant with our eighth child, I asked the *madricha* [the Jewish Agency instructress] for help. She said she could not help us, and asked: "Why do you have so many children? Now your wife is again pregnant. Let her have an abortion to lighten the burden of the family." Shocked as I was, my condition was so bad and my fear so great that I agreed to an abortion—the murder of an unborn child. My wife and I waited four months for the *madricha* to come to arrange the abortion. By then my wife was in the fifth month when it was dangerous. Finally the woman said it was our turn in the line for the abortion. But it was so dangerous by then that I did not want my wife to do it. The *madricha* became angry and said: "How do you expect to take care of all your children? Did I make them?"

Now, Mr. Prime Minister, I ask you if this is the slogan of the State: to do away with children? Or is it not the wish of the State to increase the number of children? And how does the *madricha* allow herself to say such things? This is a very painful problem. The *madricha* told my wife that she would not help her to get medical aid if she would not agree to the abortion. And then my wife went to the clinic to be treated. They threw her out.

Honored Prime Minister, I know that the son knows only his father, and the father knows only the Prime Minister, and the Prime Minister knows only God. That is why I went to you in the hope that you will intervene in my despairing condition. I have suffered so much, so many years in the hope that my children one day will at last be well off: but I awoke after I saw my situation getting only worse. That is why I write to you in this broken-hearted letter to help me immediately. There are nine of us, children from one to twelve, and no one to support us.

Prayerfully I await your immediate answer. With thanks in advance.

Saadia Boucha

When I finished reading, I put the file to one side for a moment. I was rather moved. It seemed entirely possible that Saadia Boucha, far from being indifferent to the fate of his family, was actually a decent, well-meaning man. I could sense something of the anguish that had compelled his flight from Moshav Chusan. Indeed, Boucha's departure might have been the very opposite of an act of murder. Might he not have abandoned his family to *avoid* committing the murder of his unborn children? In any case, his wife could hardly have remained at the moshav under such circumstances.

Why then had the Jewish Agency procrastinated so long before allowing

Mrs. Boucha to leave? I looked through the file again, but there was no mistake. Nearly two months. On July 7, 1958, the settlement department of the Jewish Agency had at last issued Habiba Boucha a curt official permit, authorizing her departure from Moshav Chusan. The document specifically denied such permission to her husband, however. This struck me as an especially choice example of bureaucratic vindictiveness.

"The way these things become depersonalized," I murmured to Mrs. London-Yarie.

"Have you read the whole file?" she asked.

Without waiting for my answer, she searched through the correspondence. After several moments she found the document she was looking for, and handed it to me. It was dated July 27, 1958. "This is a copy of a letter to the Jewish Agency," she explained. "It was written by Rafael Einstein, the chairman of the district council of Ma'ale HaGalil. Moshav Chusan lies within his jurisdiction. As you can see, he has his own ideas about the family."

... The Boucha family, which represents itself as being utterly destitute, has actually been engaged in a battle with the settlement department of the Jewish Agency to leave the moshav without making a final payment of its bills, as everyone else must do. And it is clear to me that if they win this battle it will be a most dangerous precedent for many families in similar conditions. I have gathered the facts of their income in 1958 (which is only halfway through) in order to obtain a picture of their "desperate condition." It is as follows:

1. Payment for tobacco, final account for produce of 1957...... 1,400
2. Advances for tobacco planting in 1958..................... 300
3. Advances for buying bulbs, seeds, manure.................. 200
4. Selling of sheep (the property of the Agency)............. 500
5. Selling of fruit harvest................................. 150
6. Selling of wheat before harvest.......................... 50

I £2,600.

I did not differentiate between the income, whose actual source was stealing from the Agency's settlement department, and I did not take into account payments that they received for work carried out according to instructions of the *madrichim*. I take the liberty of giving warning of the dangerous results of any soft-heartedness in this matter. In my opinion, the husband, Saadia Boucha, should be brought to court for illegal selling of Agency property: she for desertion of her children, and the two of them under Ordinance 16 (children in need of care and protection). They should be refused the custody of their children, and there should be publicity given to this whole matter to make an example of it, and in order that similar cases should not be produced in the near future.

I put the letter down.

"Mrs. London-Yarie," I began, "what kind of German *punktlichkeit* is this? This man Einstein—"

"You're not impressed, right?" she asked.

"But it's the same bureaucratic impersonality."

She handed me a slip of paper. It was the code number of the Boucha file. "You'll find the necessary addresses there whenever you want them," she said, "Jewish Agency settlement department, the district office of our ministry, Moshav Chusan, Machneh Yisrael, all of them." Then she smiled at me with the faintest hint of reproof. "I presume that you'll want to investigate."

Mrs. London-Yarie had not exaggerated the problem created by the influx of Oriental Jews. By 1958 they comprised the largest number of slum dwellers in Tel Aviv and Israel's other large cities. Their standard of living was far lower than that of the European Jews, for nearly all their men were either unskilled laborers or petty merchants. Indeed, poverty was often the least of their afflictions. Frequently they were diseased and illiterate. Moreover, in physical appearance, in language, in dress, diet, and social behavior, they could hardly be distinguished from Arabs. This was perhaps not surprising, since Jewish settlement in the lands of the Near and Middle East was at least as integral as, and often predated, that of the Arabs. For example, the nucleus of Iraq's Jewish population had been established as far back as the Babylonian conquest of Palestine in the sixth century B.C. So, for that matter, had the Jewish settlements in Syria and Egypt.

The proximity of Jew and Arab had not always been without its advantages. There were times when Moslem cultural traditions exerted an important stimulative influence upon the Jewish minority. The Islamic Renaissance of the Middle Ages, for example, ignited one of the most memorable sunbursts of intellectual creativity in Jewish history. Unhappily, both for Jews and Arabs, the medieval era represented the high-water mark of Moslem cultural development. After the fifteenth century a blight of spirit and mind descended upon the Arab Near East—a pall which has not lifted to this day. Inevitably, the Jews were affected by the torpor and ignorance of their Moslem neighbors. In fact, they shared it. By the nineteenth century, at a time when the Jews of Europe had begun to play a significant and growing role in the world of science and scholarship, perhaps two thirds of Oriental Jews were semiliterate and, like the Arabs around them, were imprisoned in a fantasy world of superstitions and secret terrors. They enjoyed no contact whatever with the West, nor with Western ideas.

Thus, the Zionist movement, which was consciously based upon Western nationalist premises, represented an almost totally alien concept to Oriental Jewry. Zionism's emphasis upon dynamic, secular activity, upon agricultural and industrial labor was actually quite repugnant to the mystical, contemplative Oriental. There were, to be sure, a few thousand Near and Middle Eastern Jews who returned to Palestine before the rise of Israel; but these were almost exclusively Orthodox religionists who had come to live and die within

the shadow of the ancient Temple wall. Perhaps additional thousands might
have been persuaded to come before 1948 had Zionist emissaries been sent
to the Jewish communities of the Levant and North Africa. But during
the 1920s and 1930s, the Zionist Organization preferred to concentrate its
efforts on Europe, regarding Oriental Jewry as far too backward to be
worth investment in time or money.

It required a *force majeure,* nothing less than the establishment of the
State of Israel, to propel the Jews of the Moslem hinterland toward Palestine in significant numbers for the first time. To the devoutly religious,
particularly to the Jews of Yemen, the birth of the Jewish Republic was
a messianic omen which demanded fulfillment by immediate departure for
the Holy Land. For the rest, however—for the Jews of Iraq, Syria, and
Egypt, and to a lesser extent the Jews of North Africa—the crucial and
decisive factor was neither religion nor even incipient Zionist idealism. It
was rather the sudden and violent eruption of Moslem xenophobia. The
ordeal of Saadia Boucha was typical.

His parents were Persian Jews, raised in the ghetto of Shiraz. They were
silversmiths, and like most of the other 85,000 Jews of Iran, they were dirt-
poor. It was poverty by Asian standards: squalid shacks in back alleys,
twelve people in a room, foul drinking water. Their degradation was
Oriental, as well. Few Jews dared venture beyond the ghetto; the knout
awaited them in the city's streets. When, in 1920, rumor had it that the
civilized British had moved into neighboring Iraq, the exodus began. The
Bouchas chose Basra.

The rumor was true. Life was indeed far more tolerable across the
border. Iraqi Jewry enjoyed almost complete economic and personal freedom. They plied their crafts as they pleased, and made an adequate living
as the country's most talented artisans. In the capital, Jewish millionaires
were not uncommon. Saadia Boucha was apprenticed to his father, and by
his twenty-first birthday his status as a master silversmith was established.
Only a wife was lacking. His parents arranged the match for him, of course.
At first his father toyed with the possibility of an alliance with one of the
well-born daughters of Bagdad, possibly with a family whose ancestry
traced back to Babylon.

But in the end, Saadia was betrothed to Habiba Nahmani, the daughter
of a Basra horse dealer. He was not permitted a glimpse of her until after
the wedding. Even at the betrothal ceremony Habiba was wrapped from
head to foot in a colored silk *izaar;* her face was covered by a black horse-
tail veil. It was just as well. Saadia discovered soon enough that she was
no beauty. Like most of the girls of the smaller towns, Habiba was illiterate
(although, like many Jewish girls of her class, she had been trained
to memorize entire chapters of the Book of Ezekiel). Not once did she
venture an opinion of her own. That reticence admittedly had its advantages; she was obedient and well behaved. She performed her household
chores without complaint. Where it truly mattered, moreover, she was
marvelously dependable: each year she gave birth to a fine, healthy child—
and in the third year to a boy. To his credit, too, Saadia's father provided

the grandchild with a superb *hwas welad al-bekhor,* the traditional layette in honor of the first-born male. Nor was Saadia himself overlooked. The father-in-law paid the expense of his pilgrimage to the tomb of Ezekiel the Prophet, and afterward purchased a Torah-invitation for Saadia on the night of Chanukah, the Feast of Lights.

It was a reasonably comfortable life. There was plenty of *shashlik, kebab,* oil, and rice for the table, enough *arak,* pistachio and almond nut *dragées* and watermelon for family celebrations. Although the family was still crowded together in a one-room bungalow, and the neighborhood, Zen Ma'abdin Street, was a ghetto in all but name, Saadia and his relatives and friends walked through town, traveled, pursued their livelihoods without fear of molestation. In Iraq, Jews could even aspire to a career in public life. It was well known, in fact, that five Jews actually sat in the lower house of parliament, and that Jews were heavily represented in the Iraqi civil service. Moreover, Iraq's professional and financial classes were almost exclusively Jewish. Few of the country's 110,000 Jews had cause for complaint, as a result; the evidence of their security was public and manifest.

The first warnings of change came in 1941, the year a pro-Axis clique seized control of the Iraqi government. Several months later the British overthrew the cabal; but in the interval a series of furious pogroms, erupting spontaneously, claimed the lives of hundreds of Jews. It was the Jewish community's first inkling of the depth and ferocity of Arab nationalism. In the immediate aftermath of the killings several thousand Jewish families sold their homes and businesses and migrated forthwith to Palestine. The rest remained, convinced that the xenophobia would subside once the war had ended. It seemed inconceivable to them that their identification with the nation could be called into question. They were Iraq's aristocrats, after all; many of their families had lived in the country for twenty-five hundred years. The State would not function without them. The Arabs would surely appreciate that.

It was a naïve hope. When the war ended, anti-Jewish discrimination increased. Jews were restricted in their movement throughout the country. Instances of physical violence against their homes became more common. Yet even these outrages were but a prelude to the terror of the Palestine war. On May 15, 1948, a state of emergency was announced, and two months later Zionism was branded as a crime punishable by seven years' imprisonment. For the first time the entire Iraqi Jewish community was officially stigmatized as enemy aliens and potential spies. Accordingly, Jewish public institutions were requisitioned. Wholesale dismissal of Jews from public office followed. Jews residing abroad were ordered to return at once on penalty of having their property confiscated by the State. Other thousands of Jews were dismissed from private employment. Police searches of Jewish homes were followed by public acts of extortion and blackmail. Hundreds of Jews were arrested on trumped-up charges of "spying," then tried by court-martials, and sentenced to stiff prison terms. Almost invariably their property was sequestered by the government.

For Saadia Boucha and his family, the aftermath of the Palestine war was an uninterrupted nightmare. His father's shop was boycotted by the Arabs; for that matter, few Jewish customers could afford to place orders there any longer. Eventually the old man went bankrupt. One night he ventured out to the home of an Arab friend in the hope of obtaining a loan. He was never heard from again. In later months Saadia himself managed to eke out a living by secretly taking orders from an Arab silversmith, and finishing the work at a fraction of his former prices.

For the next two years the Bouchas froze in silence whenever footsteps echoed down Zen Ma'abdin Street at night. Then, on March 3, 1950, placards went up on the walls of the Jewish quarter: Israelites wishing to emigrate to "occupied Palestine" would be permitted to do so—on condition that they renounce their Iraqi citizenship. Immediately the entire Iraqi-Jewish population was thrown into a frenzy of activity. Thousands of house-holders lined up day and night at the registration offices that had been installed in synagogues. Jews from Kurdistan poured into the larger cities from the mountains, camping on synagogue floors and in synagogue court-yards. Several weeks after registration began, the Iraqi government granted the Jewish Agency permission to use the Bagdad airport for chartered flights to Israel. The machinery of emigration was soon operating at full speed. By the end of 1950, 65,000 Jews had left the country.

Saadia Boucha's first impulse was to join them. Venturing out of the Jewish Quarter, he knocked at the door of an Arab realtor, a Moslem with whom he had enjoyed friendly business dealings for many years. He was received cordially. The two men exchanged cigarettes and polite conversa-tion. When Boucha finally reached the point of his visit, however, the sale of his home, he received a heartbreaking surprise. The panic sale of Jewish property had glutted the real-estate market. The house would not fetch more than one hundred and fifty dinars—a sum which hardly represented one twentieth of its actual value. Boucha was horror-stricken. Upon rushing to other realtors, he discovered that the answer was invariably the same: there were no longer enough buyers for Jewish property. In the end, after three weeks of soul searching, the silversmith reached a decision. He would wait. Perhaps with the passage of time the reign of terror against the Jewish community would come to an end.

During the last five months of 1950 the gravest excesses did indeed abate. Boucha began tentatively taking a few orders again under his own name. He relaxed his former precautions, and his woman became pregnant once more. The Palestine war had long since ended. Apparently the Arabs had lost interest in their Jews.

In the last week of January, 1951, Boucha returned from his shop to find his brother-in-law, Hasdai, awaiting him in the *diwan*. The man's face was gray with fear.

"They have bombed the Masouda Shemtob Synagogue, Saadia," he whispered. "The army has closed the Sayyard Bazaar. I beg you, take Habiba and the children and leave while there is still time. The troubles are truly beginning now."

Hasdai had not overstated the dangers. By mid-February mobs of Arab ruffians swarmed through the Jewish Quarter with increasing regularity, looting Jewish shops and attacking Jewish pedestrians. Far from interfering, the police clubbed and whipped those Jews who dared defend themselves. Not infrequently Jews were arrested as "smugglers," and their property confiscated outright. For Saadia there could no longer be any question of remaining. In March he returned to his Arab realtor friend and instructed him to dispose of the house for whatever he could get. The man laughed in Boucha's face.

"Don't you read the *Gazette?*" he asked. "The law of March 1 forbids Jews to sell their holdings. Everything you have now becomes State property."

Indeed, the law went further than that. Jews who emigrated were no longer permitted to take money with them. Their savings, whatever funds they still possessed, were now sequestered altogether. Boucha had waited a little too long.

On April 3, he led his wife and three children aboard the chartered Constellation at Bagdad Airport. They carried a single rucksack between them: one suit, two dresses, a blanket, and three pairs of children's shoes— nothing more. They were destitute. Boucha stared at his fellow passengers. None of them seemed better dressed than he or his family—not even old Amnon Haroun, sitting near the front of the cabin with his wife and four daughters. Haroun had once been the deputy managing director of the Basra Electric Company. Now his trousers had patches in them. Boucha turned in his seat to examine the other refugees. But at that moment the Constellation's engines roared their warning. The mighty aircraft gathered speed and then climbed slowly from the runway. The children whimpered. Habiba gazed out the window and saw the city shrinking away before her eyes. Terror-stricken, she covered her head and began mumbling compulsively from the Book of Ezekiel. Boucha struck the woman feebly with his elbow, and she fell silent, her blue lips still moving. Then he buried his face in his hands and moaned inwardly. Night had fallen. The darkness would not lift again.

Two and a half hours later the immigrants disembarked at Lydda, Israel. Slowly, fearfully, they followed the Jewish Agency representative into the customs shed. At first hot food was served and all seemed well. Yet there were men here who wore uniforms, just as in Iraq, and around their belts pistols hung. Officials asked questions, endless questions about home, education, health, occupations, and professions. For Saadia Boucha the procedure was altogether as frightening as the original registration at Basra. Then, without even a moment for rest, the immigrants were loaded into buses and driven off into the night.

Several hours later they arrived at Sha'ar HaAliyah, one of the enormous reception camps on the outskirts of Haifa. Again hot food was served. Ration books were issued to each of the newcomers. Doctors thrust needles into their arms. And once more there were the endless rounds of questions:

Did you bring any money? . . . Have you relatives here? . . . Where do they live? . . . Can they help you? . . . What can you do? . . . How much Hebrew do you know? Boucha's answers were those of nearly 100,000 other Iraqi Jews: No one awaited him; he had brought neither money nor tools with him; he had nothing. The official wrote it all down, and then told Boucha to wait.

And he and his family waited—week after week. The barracks were packed with immigrants. Not all of them were Iraqis. Moroccans and Tripolitanians predominated in the men's wards; and their Arabic dialects were all but incomprehensible to the Near Easterners. There were Kurds, too, from northeastern Iraq, swaddled in sheepskins, smelling like cattle, squatting on their haunches for hours at a time, crooning to themselves in Aramaic. Hundreds of others arrived daily, dropping their duffel bags on the floor, staring with horror at their new companions, and then falling dazedly on the iron cots.

Finally, after two months, Boucha and his family were ordered to make ready. They were being moved to Safed. Habiba's face lit up at the news. She had been raised on tales of Safed's Cabbalists and wonder-workers: the holy men there would surely find a home for her children; even as the Prophet, too, would watch over them. And indeed a home was provided. It turned out to be a one-room, tar-paper shack, covered by a tin roof— one of hundreds of such hovels clustered together along the mountain. The villagers called the shantytown a *ma'abara,* a transit camp. It would house the newcomers until proper jobs and housing could be found for them. The Jewish Agency man did not find it necessary to apologize:

"There are thirty thousand people coming in a month," he explained. "We can't build decent homes for all of them. It's the best we can do— unless you're prepared to live in tents. We've got jobs for the men on the road gangs. Some of you can hire out as field hands. We won't let anyone starve, that's a promise."

The official was right. It was a squalid existence, but it was tolerable. Boucha found odd jobs on the neighboring farms, picking olives and hoeing tomatoes. The income was not enough for food, of course, but the Agency made up the difference with free supplies of rice and lentils. Medical care was free, too. When Boucha strained his back, the clinic supplied him with an orthopedic harness. Habiba was within a few weeks of her next child, and a doctor would be available for her. For the time being, at least, the family was secure. Let the Europeans complain and make trouble if they liked, thought Boucha. They rushed and jumped and bustled, filled out forms and questionnaires and petitions, stood in line, "consulted" and "organized"—that was all *they* could do. Well, if they wanted to sweat themselves to death for fancy apartments, that was their business. As far as he was concerned, a roof, a bed, and assurance of soup for the children were worth more than the uncertainties of employment in the open market. Anyway, the pace of this land was inhuman. The Europeans seemed to do everything by the clock. They rose, washed, worked, returned, ate, rested by the clock. They probably even made love by the clock. That was their affair, of course. But by what right did they force him, Boucha, and his friends to abide by *their* schedule? Time was to be used, not measured. A man needed time to pray, to play cards with his companions, or even to sit back for a leisurely smoke on the narghile and contemplate the beauty of nature, the wisdom of the Almighty. Boucha's father-in-law (in fact, all Iraqi fathers-in-law) had understood the importance of reflective leisure, and to ensure it he had provided food and clothing for each of the grandchildren. In a Jewish State it hardly seemed reasonable that the authorities would do less.

For a year and a half the family remained in the Safed *ma'abara*. Many of the neighboring shacks were emptied in the interval. The Jewish Agency gradually found employment for the immigrants elsewhere, in the farms and factories of the country. The government erected tens of thousands of new housing units for their families. One day, in the late summer of 1952, Boucha was called to the local Jewish Agency office. A representative of the settlement department awaited him. The man was an Ashkenazi—a European—but he spoke good Arabic.

"We want to close the *ma'abara* as quickly as possible, Boucha," he said. "We can't keep you on the dole forever. There's a spot for your family at Kibbutz Cabri, in the western Galilee. I strongly advise you to take it."

Boucha's response was vigorous and emphatic: He had already heard enough about the kibbutzim. Did the Jewish Agency think that he was mad? Allow his children to be wrested away from him and raised in a collective dormitory? Eat his meals with hundreds of other men and women in a common dining hall? What kind of privacy was that for a respectable householder? Anyway, no one was going to tell him what work to do, what crops to raise. If he was going to labor he would labor for himself and his family, not for others.

The Agency official raised his hand to his brow, and slowly shook his head. These Orientals were all alike, he decided; hardly any of them showed even the faintest willingness to pioneer or sacrifice. When *he* had come to Palestine as a young man, there had not been kibbutzim enough for all the applicants. Rather than wait, the newcomers had gone into the wilderness and carved out settlements themselves. No one had guaranteed them anything. They had accomplished the task uncomplainingly by hard, grinding manual labor. Now at last there were over two hundred functioning kibbutzim, their fields cultivated, their bungalows comfortable, their market outlets guaranteed. But evidently this was not security enough for the Iraqis. No doubt *they* were accustomed to the better things of life; *their* sensibilities were more delicate than those of their predecessors.

"All right, Boucha," the man sighed. "We'll do it your way. What would you like—a moshav? We've got a house and a strip of land at Moshav Chusan, about twenty miles away. It's a good opportunity."

Again Boucha began to protest, flailing his arms wildly. He was a silversmith, a craftsman, not a peasant, not an Arab. He had no experience with the soil. How could he feed a wife and four children on his own? The Agency must help. The government must help.

"We intend to help," the official interrupted. "No one is going to throw you on the soil and leave you there to starve. We're giving you a house and land. We'll advance you seed and equipment. Our instructors will show you what to do. The village will help you market your produce. That's help, isn't it? What other country would give you that kind of help? But you'll have to help yourself, too."

And here Boucha took a different tack. His back was injured. He was incapable of doing heavy work. The doctor had instructed him to rest.

"You'll rest!" exploded the Ashkenazi. "You'll rest on your own time, not ours! We're giving you two days to make up your mind. After that we'll start charging you rent for your shanty here. And there will be no more dole, either. Two days, no more. Think it over."

Thus it was that Saadia Boucha and his family departed in the summer of 1952 for Moshav Chusan.

The moshav was one of five agricultural villages comprising the rural settlement of Ma'ale HaGalil, in the western Galilee. I visited it early in January of 1959, driving my motorbike from Naharia eastward along the Galilee mountain range. It was stunningly beautiful country. To the north, the pearl-gray hills of Lebanon drifted leisurely toward the coast. To the south, the Emek, the Valley of Jezreel, unfolded a radiant tapestry of fields between sea and mountains. This was the heartland of Israel's Arab population. Their delicately angular olive trees marched to the very edge of the road, while their flocks of sheep and goats occasionally blocked the road altogether. Frequently, too, barefoot Arab women strolled by in their brightly colored turquoise and magenta dresses, impassively bearing their head burdens of kindling or water jars.

The surroundings soon lost their charm, however, as I ascended the mountain range. Under the remorseless winter wind the fields here had turned a ferrous gray. A bus passed me, and I clung gratefully to its vacuum. When the sign announcing Ma'ale HaGalil appeared, the bus and I both turned northward, and finally rolled to a stop in front of the secretariat building. In a moment the passengers had climbed out, carrying their cardboard suitcases with them. They stood in little groups near the bus, clapping their hands for warmth, gazing dispiritedly about them. Without understanding their conversation, I nevertheless recognized their language as Rumanian. Another group of immigrants. Together, we stared at the tiny cubicle-like houses nestled on the side of the hill. All the buildings were quite new, freshly painted in white. One of them was a school. Another, not yet complete, already bore the markings of a communal clinic. If the reaction of the newcomers mirrored my own, they hardly had eyes for the beauty of the Galilee; they saw only the isolation and Spartan loneliness of the life which awaited them.

In the ten years that had passed since the birth of Israel, hundreds of thousands of Jews, nearly all of them immigrants, had confronted the same future. For them, the new Jerusalem was embodied in a cluster of modest houses and narrow vegetable patches—Ma'ale HaGalil or dozens of co-operative farm communities like it. Yet, far from representing a makeshift solution to the mass immigration, the moshav idea itself actually preceded the State. In fact, the first such co-operative village had been established as far back as 1921, in the Jezreel Valley. It was called Nahalal, and its founders bore little resemblance to the dogmatic socialists of the kibbutz. The Nahalal settlers had actually committed the "heresy" of dividing up their land, and providing each family with a small plot for individual cultivation. They cleared the soil collectively, to be sure, bought and sold jointly, even purchased and operated their heavy farm equipment together. But the holdings themselves, as well as the profits from them, remained private. So did the houses. So did family life.

Representing, thus, a cautious blend of socialism and individualism, the moshav concept attracted only a small minority of settlers before 1948. For during the 1920s and 1930s, the largest number of Jewish immigrants who settled on Palestine's soil were consumed by a fever of radical idealism; to them, the kibbutz was the classical, the all-but-sacred instrument of pioneering Zionism. By the time the State of Israel was born they had established 136 collective settlements. The number of moshavim, on the other hand, reached 91 during the same period—and seemed unlikely to go higher.

The turning point came with independence. Within a decade, immigration tripled the population of the country. The newcomers had to be settled and employed. The nation required a vast increase in its food supply, and a chain of villages in crucial defense areas. Accordingly, the initial and major emphasis of the resettlement effort was placed on agriculture. The Jewish rural population, 110,000 in 1948, rose to 325,000 by 1959. At first, too, the collective farms accounted for many of these new agriculturists; indeed, the number of kibbutzim climbed to 228 within the same period. But it was a numerical increase, not a proportional one. The truth was that few of the immigrants had ever been indoctrinated in the Zionist or socialist ideals of their predecessors. For them, the kibbutz way of life represented far too sharp a break with their former pattern of existence. This was especially true of the Orientals. The typical Moroccan or Iraqi newcomer flatly refused to settle on the soil unless he and his family could be guaranteed a home of their own, and a tangible financial return for their effort. The co-operative settlement appeared to offer the only acceptable compromise. By 1963, as a result, the number of moshavim had grown to nearly 200. Since 1948 the moshav was the key to Israel's agricultural growth.

The pattern of co-operative farming, too, was long since established. Generally, between sixty and eighty families were settled in each moshav. The Jewish Agency provided each family with its own home, and with a six- or seven-acre patch of land. The settlers farmed these strips on their own, raising the crops of their choice. On the other hand, the moshav members sold their produce and purchased all their supplies co-operatively, and invested jointly in common facilities—warehouses, grain-storage bins, refrigeration plants, dairies, machine shops, and garages; while the moshav council imposed and assessed its own taxes for the construction of schools, libraries, and recreational facilities.

The human material on these moshavim was far from outstanding. As a rule, the Oriental (and many European) immigrants were inexperienced, and were often resentful of being thrust into an alien livelihood. They floundered badly during their first few years on the soil. Not infrequently they abandoned the effort altogether, picking up stakes and returning to the slums of the larger cities. The entire moshav movement might well have become unviable had not the Jewish Agency undertaken two imaginative measures. The first was education. A specially trained agricultural instructor —the *madrich*—was assigned to work with the immigrants in each village, helping them plant their crops, teaching them the most effective methods of cultivation. The results of this supervision were soon dramatically evident. By the mid-1950s even the least experienced newcomer was turning out impressive crops of tomatoes and cucumbers. The produce was not always highly profitable. But if the farmer found temporary employment between harvests, it usually sufficed to tide him over.

The social and educational needs of the immigrants were no less important than the economic. These were now met by the adoption of an ingenious area settlement plan, based on the concept of "organic communities." Clusters of four or five villages were grouped around a common Rural Center. Here were established schools, clinics, shops, garages, occasional light industries, banks, and movie theaters. Today, these regional facilities are operating at maximum efficiency—precisely because there is now a population near-by large enough to justify their services. For the settlers, moreover, the psychological advantages of this arrangement are incalculable. Each immigrant group can live together, speaking the same language, sharing the same mores. Yet proximity to the larger unit is maintained. For example, in the regional cluster of Lachish, on the northern fringe of the Negev, the villagers of Moshav Otsem, who are Moroccans, live quite near Moshav Shahar, a settlement of Tunisians; while the neighboring community, Nir Onen, is peopled by Israeli youths, Hebrew-speaking sabras. These three moshavim—as well as Noga, also inhabited by Moroccans, and Zohar, a village of Rumanians—find their service facilities in the Rural Center. Here their children study together in school, and here the villagers meet for a theatrical performance or a movie. New friendships are made. Music and dance groups are formed. Concerts and weddings and sports events attract large and gregarious throngs of men and women. The regional "organic community" very probably represents the emergent pattern of Jewish agricultural settlement in Israel.

Such a community, in embryonic form, was Ma'ale HaGalil. Its secretary, Mr. Rafael Einstein, was the man I had come to see. He hardly represented the dour bureaucrat I had envisioned while reading his correspondence on the Boucha matter. Dressed in shabby work pants and sweater, Einstein was a tall, genial "Yecke" (German Jew) in his mid-fifties. His bubbling optimism and irrepressible good humor effectively insulated him from the freezing cold of his tiny office. "Everything is mitzuyan—excellent," he confided in his lisping Yecke accent, "especially the hardships. I love it here." He must have. He had come in the "primitive" days, back in 1935, and had worked his own plot of land ever since. "It's wonderful, why not?" he insisted. "I got in on the ground floor of the moshav movement. Now everybody is rushing to join up."

"Except the Bouchas," I said.

He grinned. "And a few others," he admitted. "We get our share of 'hard' cases." He looked at me curiously. "You read my report?"

I nodded.

"Think I'm a beast, do you?" he asked, again with that disarming smile. "Never mind, we always look heartless on paper. I want you to consider, though, the lengths to which we have gone for these people. Take the house: it was given to them practically as a gift. Their rent was nominal. Their plot of land—also a gift. Their equipment, their seed—all given to them. Schools for their children, medical care—gifts, all gifts. They didn't pay a piaster in taxes. We've got one of the best agricultural *madrichim* in the country here. He labored with Boucha endlessly. Some thanks he got."

Einstein rose suddenly, and beckoned me to follow him. We walked rapidly down the slope of the hill. "That's Chusan, you see," he said, pointing toward a necklace of twenty limestone houses in the shallow valley below. Near each house men were working their plots. Some of the farmers were pulling up weeds. Others were hoeing their rows of vegetables, the clank of metal against frozen earth echoing poignantly against the sky. Here and there women fed chickens, scoured pots from faucets attached to the walls of their homes. Every person I saw was swarthy, obviously an Oriental. The one exception was a handsome, lean giant of a man in his early forties, wearing a scarf and rubber hip boots.

Einstein introduced us. "Meet Mark Krimchansky. He's the *madrich*."

We shook hands. Krimchansky had been expecting me, and we chatted at some length. A Russian Jew, he had spent twenty years of his life in China before coming to Israel, only nine years before. He had been trained as an agronomist, and obviously delighted in the chance of teaching other immigrants.

"So, would you say it's a hard life here?" I asked.

"Sure, hard," he replied with a smile. "But does it look impossible? What about these homes?" He waved his hand at the stone houses. They were chipped and weather-beaten, but quite sturdy. The neighboring plots were well tended. Some of them nurtured peach and avocado trees of respectable size.

"No one's complaining," Krimchansky assured me. "Right, boys?" he asked suddenly, turning to two heavily mustached men bent double over the weeds in the next plot. "No one's complaining, right?"

They smiled and shook their heads. "Only you complain, Mark," one of the men replied. "We're satisfied."

"Which was the Boucha home?" I asked.

"You're leaning against it, my friend," Krimchansky replied.

"This big thing?" I was astonished. The house was empty of all furniture as I walked through it, and had obviously been badly cared for. The walls and floor were encrusted with dirt. Still, there were three rooms here. That was obviously more space than the Bouchas had ever enjoyed before, even in Basra. Outside again, I gazed at the *meshek,* the plot of land.

"Twenty-eight dunams—seven acres," Krimchansky remarked, anticipating my question. "Those are tobacco shoots," he added, pointing to the gnarled brown twigs thrusting six inches out of the ground.

The soil was rugged, but free of rocks. Krimchansky had accurately described the moshav's circumstances: hard, but not impossible. I was struck by an innovation in Boucha's *meshek;* he had apparently surrounded the land with a crude stone fence. When I commented on it, one of the farmers snorted contemptuously: "He was afraid we'd trespass. This was no ordinary man, you see. He was a 'capitalist.'"

Krimchansky nodded his agreement. "Believe me, my friend, I've had to deal with all kinds in my time," he said, "but this Boucha was the last word in impossibility. I can still remember sitting down with him over his kitchen table. He was sulking, as usual. . . ."

"Boucha," said the *madrich,* in exasperation, "I don't know how many times I have to explain it to you. You can't pack tobacco that way. It's got to be moist—moist, Boucha, you've got to wait till the rainy season. It won't last that way. You'll get low prices if you keep packing it dry. The factories only use it for wrapper then."

Boucha stared back at Krimchansky, a pained expression settling over his tight, narrow features. "The Adon asks me to wait, does he?" he murmured. "And while I wait how am I to feed my wife and children? Five children, and another one on the way?"

The *madrich* scowled. "You'll feed them the way everyone here feeds his family. With good crops raised the right way. What happened to the six hundred pounds we advanced you?"

"'What happened?'" Boucha jumped to his feet, howling as if he had been scalded. "The Adon asks what happened. It's gone into food and clothing, that's where—"

"You said it was for fertilizer and tomato plants when you applied for the loan."

Boucha thrust his sticklike arms toward the ceiling, as if supplicating the Almighty. "Am I to feed my little ones with fertilizer and tomato plants?" he croaked at last. "They are perishing before my eyes."

"Boucha, I've warned you—"

"You can't warn me any more," the Iraqi screamed, at the top of his voice. "I'm a sick man, a cripple. The doctors say I shouldn't be working at all."

Krimchansky sighed. There was nothing to be gained by arguing with this maniac. As he reached the door, he turned to Boucha once more. "I know what's in the back of your mind," he said quietly. "Don't get any ideas about leaving this place. We're not washing out your debts."

Krimchansky left him alone after that. In the spring of 1955, however, one of Boucha's neighbors, a Moroccan, whispered something in the *madrich's* ear. Krimchansky listened in astonishment, and then nodded. "I'll check it," he promised.

That afternoon he walked over to Boucha's *meshek*. The information was true. Only two men were working in the plot, and they were both Arabs. Again he seated the Iraqi at the kitchen table, and again the two men argued violently.

"You know it's against the rules," Krimchansky shouted. "You know we don't allow that."

Boucha shook his head impassively. "Has to be," he replied. "Has to be."

"Yes, 'has to be,'" the *madrich* gasped, infuriated. "Because you're too blasted lazy to do the work yourself. We don't want squires here, Boucha. If we settle a Jew on the land we want him to labor with his own hands."

A cunning, languid smile crossed Boucha's dark face. "The Adon expects me to work," he murmured softly. "But the Adon knows my back is crippled—"

"I know nothing of the sort. The doctor says you're perfectly capable of doing this work."

"—my back is crippled," Boucha continued, unfazed, "and I cannot labor like a peasant myself. These men are good workers and they ask little. Otherwise, I cannot raise my crops."

Krimchansky nodded. "Yes, they are good workers, and you are paying them with our money—the third installment we advanced you for those boxes."

Here Boucha adopted a wheedling tone. "Adoni, be reasonable," he whined, placing his hand across his chest in the classical Oriental manner. "The Agency wants us to produce crops. All right, I'm producing them. Why should it matter to you how I raise them? For me there's no longer any other way. And if I don't get my crops raised, I can't pay the Agency back, now can I?"

Krimchansky felt the blood rising to his head, and his fingers tightened on the edge of the table. Boucha anticipated the outburst, however. "Careful, Adoni," he warned. "Strong vinegar will break its jar."

No longer trusting himself to speak, the *madrich* stormed out of the house. Boucha followed him to the front yard, then stared complacently at the Ashkenazi's retreating back. As he returned he caught the eye of his Moroccan neighbor. The man stared Boucha up and down contemptuously. "Ijjamal ja yisawwi krun kessolu adhanu," he remarked, in Moghrebic. "The camel desired horns and his ears were cut off."

"Harem innakdi wula brakha biddein," Boucha shrieked back, enraged. "Better the worst thing at present than the good thing delayed. When I want your advice I'll ask for it."

That very afternoon the Iraqi instructed his two Arab helpers to set about building a stone fence around the *meshek*.

Krimchansky's last encounter with Boucha took place a year after that. This time it was Habiba who came for him. She slipped into his office like a wraith, clutching the newest child to her breast. Silently she extended her hand, palm upward.

"What-is-it-now, Habiba?" he asked slowly and carefully, in his most elementary Hebrew.

The woman did not reply. Her hand remained outstretched.

"No food?" he asked once more.

Again no response.

Wearily, the *madrich* arose, grasped the woman's elbow gently, and walked her back to her home. Two neighbors were standing by the door, one of them the Moroccan. They moved aside for Krimchansky and allowed him to look for himself. At first he saw nothing, for the room was dark. Then his nostrils flared: he recognized the sickly-sweet odor instantly. As his eyes accustomed themselves to the darkness, he discerned Boucha in the corner, seated between the two Arabs. The three men were sucking languorously on narghiles, Oriental water pipes. Bounding across the room, Krimchansky seized one of the men by the neck and tightened his powerful fingers. The Arab's hand opened slowly, and the telltale packet fell to the floor, spilling its white powder in a crescent of fine grains. Then Boucha spoke, as if in a dream.

"The life is hard here, Adoni," he whispered. "Six little ones and too many debts. You have to let me go back to the *ma'abara.*"

Krimchansky did not want me to miss the point. "That was what he was after all the time, you see. He had botched his crops. He owed money. What could be simpler than returning to the *ma'abara* and letting the government support his family? Of course, Rafael [Einstein] and I wouldn't buy that. We told him he could leave whenever he liked. After all, this is a free country. But he would have to pay his debts first. We even offered to let him pay a hundred-pound installment to the Agency, and then pay off the rest of the loan later. But of course when Einstein suggested this, Boucha flew into another one of his rages, called us butchers, child murderers, and all the rest. He threatened suicide. It was impossible to reason with him. The hashish episode was the last straw, as far as I was concerned. I was done with him."

"And with his wife and children?" I asked.

The *madrich* shrugged. "They were a social case, don't you see? Bania, our *madricha,* worked as hard with the family as I did with him. Harder, perhaps. She labored with them night and day—that woman is a saint. But there was only so much that could be done. They simply wouldn't respond."

Bania Giurtler was precisely the sort of woman Krimchansky had described. Compassion radiated from her like a halo. A short, solid Rumanian in her early forties, she had come to Israel only seven years earlier, and had immediately enrolled in a home-economics course sponsored by the Jewish Agency. After a year of training, she had volunteered to serve as *madricha* in one of the new farm settlements. Moshav Chusan was one of the toughest assignments she could have drawn. Of the fifty-one families in the community, all but six were Oriental, and many were far more primitive than the wildest gypsies Bania remembered from her own homeland.

Each morning she departed from her tiny stone flat in the valley, and made the rounds of the houses. Most of the women required the most elementary instruction in housekeeping. The *madricha* supplied it. She taught them to cook food without oil, to balance their diet with proper amounts of vegetables. Few of the newcomers possessed even the most rudimentary knowledge of hygiene. Bania trained them to wash with soap and warm water, to scour their children's scalps with disinfectant lest ringworm set in—or re-occur. If parents refused to allow their children to attend school, it was Bania who cajoled them into changing their minds. In cases of extreme family hardship it was Bania who interceded with the ministry of social welfare, pleading for more funds.

"You've got to do something about the Bouchas," she explained to Mrs. Mai, the ministry's northern district officer. "We can't hold the family responsible for the father's behavior. The wife and children have nothing. They've got to live, after all. I can hardly bring myself to walk into that house any more."

Nothing had changed in five years. Bania had paid her first visit to the family within a half-hour of their arrival at Moshav Chusan. The moment she crossed the threshhold of the stone house she stopped, appalled. The room stank unbearably. Four children squatted cross-legged on the floor, picking at themselves. The parents were flattened against the wall, glaring balefully at the intruder. The *madricha* groaned inwardly. Another "hard" case.

Indeed, it was the hardest of her experience in Chusan. The husband was a terror; reasoning with him was utterly impossible. Bania learned to wait until he had departed for work before turning up at the house.

"All right, Habiba," she would begin firmly. "Let's get the tub out and try again."

And while the mother whimpered fearfully, Bania stripped the youngsters, dropping them like frightened puppies into the foaming water and disinfectant.

"Every second day," she explained patiently to the mother. "Every second day into the tub, do you understand me, Habiba. I'm coming back the day after tomorrow, and then you shall do this before my eyes."

Sometimes Habiba complied. More often she did not. Once the *madricha* returned with a present for the youngsters, clothing provided by the ministry of social welfare. And Habiba had screamed in terror: no Western clothing for her children, it was an affront to her ancestors!

"But the neighbors are laughing at them," Bania pointed out. "Soon the girls will be going to school. They can't go in these nightgowns. They must learn to wear shoes, too."

The mother began to wail. But Bania persisted, and eventually the youngsters learned to dress themselves in the new garments. Surprisingly, the parents raised no further objection. For a while the *madricha* convinced herself that she had won the family's confidence. Her illusions were soon dispelled. In the autumn of 1955 one of the Boucha girls, Nachala, prepared to enter school. Bania noted with pleasure that the child had delicate features; with a little care she could be made presentable. On the morning of school registration, the *madricha* turned up at the Boucha house an hour early. With especial care she began to wash Nachala's scalp, and then to trim her wild mop of hair. The mother remained silent, occasionally casting frightened glances at the door. A few minutes later Saadia Boucha entered the house. He took in the sight uncomprehendingly for a moment. Then, with a howl of rage, he struck the scissors from Bania's hand.

"Whore! Daughter of perdition!" he shouted at the top of his lungs. "What doest thou to my child?"

"Boucha, control yourself—"

"Pagan! Bitch!" he roared, beside himself with fury. "Is it lust you wish to arouse among the neighbor boys? Do you wish my daughter set upon in the streets?"

"Boucha, will you listen—" Bania pleaded.

"Out, slut, before I call the police," he shrieked, aiming a spidery arm and forefinger at the door. Suddenly, in an act of inspiration, he whipped the scissors off the floor and brandished them over his daughter. "I'll kill her on the spot rather than see her shamed. Out, now, you hear?"

In despair, the *madricha* left the room. The incident left her physically ill, and she lay in her flat for two days, overcome by sudden and complete exhaustion. For weeks afterward, to her own mortification, she could not find the courage to return to the family. In the end it was the neighbors who sent for her. They urged her to hurry. Bania was still a hundred yards from the Boucha house when she heard the scream. With the Moroccan accompanying her as bodyguard, she threw open the door. The stench of burnt flesh suffused the room. The mother stood impassive against the wall, her elbows clutched in her hands. Four children lay whimpering on the floor. The middle boy, Simcha, had fallen to his knees, and gazed up in anguish at his father. Boucha still gripped the youngster's hand in his own. A knife lay on the table, its blade glowing red. With an oath, the Moroccan leaped across the room, cracking Boucha across the jaw with his fist. Then he picked up the child in his arms.

"Take him to the infirmary," Bania whispered.

The man nodded and departed with the boy.

She stood silently for a moment, looking at the father, unable to speak.

"They were stealing, Geveret," Boucha murmured weakly. "A father cannot permit his children to steal." He looked to his wife for support, but she said nothing. "They were stealing food, stealing bread."

The *madricha* found her voice at last. "Where were they stealing?" she asked.

Boucha lifted his bleeding chin scornfully. "They were stealing in this very house, stealing from their mother and father. I cannot permit that. I slave for what little we have. I, too, must eat, or I cannot work."

Bania sat down wearily. "If you needed more food you could have asked," she said.

"Have I not asked?" he replied, his voice rising to a half-wail. "Have I not asked a hundred times for money, for release from my debts? Have I not told them I am crippled and cannot work?"

Suddenly Bania, too, was screaming. "You damned barbarian. You had enough money to hire your Arab workers. Couldn't you have spared a little of that for your own children?"

"I have asked—"

"You have asked and asked, and taken and taken," she screamed. "And we have given and given, and still it's not enough for you. Now you torture your own children because they are hungry, and you think this way you'll get out of your debts. But you won't, Boucha. I'll see you in jail first."

Habiba began to sob. Bania whirled on her: "What's the matter with you now?"

Boucha answered for her. "She is with child, Geveret." His voice again had taken on a wheedling, supplicating tone. "Another child, another mouth to feed. This is our problem, you see."

Bania moved her lips, but no words came. She arose and returned to her flat.

The next day the two women met at the clinic. The *madricha* called Habiba to the corner of the waiting room.

"I have spoken to the doctor," she said quietly. "He tells me the news is true." When Habiba remained silent, Bania continued. "Do you have ears, woman? Do you listen to what I tell you? I explained what would happen if you lay with him again. The doctor showed you the pictures. Now you will have to receive injections, for you have Boucha's illness—another woman's disease."

Habiba whimpered, but still did not answer.

"Well, you can't have the child, that's all," Bania sighed. "Even if it should be born untainted, there's no assurance that you can feed it."

Habiba nodded slowly. She must not have the child, that was the solution. Would the *madricha* arrange it for her? In fact, Bania already had. The mother was registered in the clinic for the next month. On the day of the operation, Saadia Boucha came to Bania's home, and walked in without knocking.

"My woman has changed her mind," he announced. "She had not asked my permission, and I do not give it now."

With that he slammed the door and departed.

Later in the day, and in later days, Bania remonstrated with Habiba. But it was already too late. The wife fearfully parroted Boucha's words: he had not granted permission for the operation, and so there would be no operation. And eventually the baby was born, another boy. By a rare stroke of luck, the child was healthy.

In the following year, yet another child was born to the couple.

From then on Bania's contact with the Bouchas was minimal. She was only a home economist, after all, only flesh and blood. Then, in the late spring of 1958, Habiba called at the *madricha*'s home. Bania invited her in, but the woman continued standing on the doorstep, awkwardly shifting her weight from one foot to the other. At last, shamefacedly, she explained her reason for her visit. Boucha had deserted her. He had disappeared two weeks ago, without a trace, without a clue. Only God knew where he was.

Bania investigated. So did Krimchansky, Einstein, and the neighbors. Evidently Boucha had been in earnest. The endless complaints, the threats and supplications, the florid entreaties to the ministry of social welfare and to the prime minister himself—all apparently should have been taken as the warnings they were. Now at last the man was gone. He had left his debts behind him, and his wife and eight children to the mercy of the authorities.

Bania would not soon forget the two months that followed. The fate of eight helpless children preyed endlessly on her mind. Boucha himself may have been good riddance; but for the sake of the youngsters, at least, he had to be found. Habiba evidently knew nothing—except that her husband "could not bear to see his children starving." At times she mumbled vaguely that he had defected to the Arabs. Once a police report intimated that his body had been found in the Lebanon. Instantly the wife was seized by a fit of hysteria, and fell to the ground, foaming at the mouth. Then subsequent investigations revealed that the body was not Boucha's. Occasionally the *madricha* found Habiba sitting alone at night at the crossroads south of the village, crooning to the full moon, reciting disconnectedly from the Prophet Ezekiel, and waving a gall nut in the air to fend the Evil Eye away from her husband's spirit.

Somehow the wretched woman and her children would have to be cared for. At first Habiba herself made a fitful attempt to plow her *meshek*. Later the Agency found her light work as a fruit picker. It hardly sufficed to feed the family. The ministry of social welfare helped, however, by providing the mother with a small allowance of twenty pounds a month. Bania arranged for the children to be fed by the school authorities of Ma'ale HaGalil. On a short-term basis, at least, the problem of survival had apparently been solved. Again Bania had reckoned without the relentless atavism of the Oriental mind. One night early in July she was awakened by a sudden pounding on her door. Two policemen waited outside.

"Oh Lord, what now?" she muttered, still half asleep.

The sergeant touched his finger to his cap. "Are you the *madricha* at this moshav?" he asked.

"Yes, what?"

"Eight children were left with us at the Acre station early yesterday afternoon, Geveret," the man explained apologetically. "The mother promised to return for them. But she has disappeared."

Bania clutched at her throat. She could hardly breathe. Then, throwing on a robe, she followed the sergeant out to the road. All eight of the youngsters were seated in the back of the lighted police lorry. None of them so much as whimpered, not even the tiniest child. The *madricha* examined their faces carefully. They stared back at her in silent trustfulness.

"I'll take care of them," she whispered finally to the policeman. "Find the parents if it's the last thing you do. I'll be over tomorrow to file a complaint against them."

The children spent the night in Bania's bed. She herself slept on a chair. The next day she conferred with Einstein, and it was decided to farm the youngsters out among neighboring families. Temporarily the district council would pay the bill; later, hopefully, the ministry of social welfare would reimburse them.

During the next few weeks the Boucha children knew the luxury of hot, well-cooked meals. The police, in the meantime, launched a full-scale search for the parents: radio calls were issued, newspaper advertisements were circulated, inspections were carried out in the Oriental slum sections of the Galilee area.

A clue turned up less than a fortnight later. The Safed branch of Bank Le'umi reported cashing a check for Habiba—endorsed over to her by her husband.

"What do you make of it?" the *madricha* asked Einstein.

"Of course it's Boucha," he replied emphatically. "It's been Boucha all along. The whole 'desertion' was planned between them. If he couldn't get released from his debts one way or another and get back on the dole, then he would use her. I'm positive she's known where he's been from the very beginning."

Einstein was not wrong. A few days later one of the neighbors reported seeing the mother in Moshav Chusan itself, visiting at night with the oldest girl. Upon being questioned, however, the youngster, Nachala, remained secretive, insisting that she knew nothing of her parents' whereabouts. But Bania had heard enough. Packing her suitcase, she boarded the bus to Safed. If the Jewish Agency office there could not find Habiba, the *madricha* would find her on her own.

The discovery took place less than thirty minutes after Bania had arrived —and accidentally. She walked through the vestibule on her way to the resettlement office, and there was Habiba, laying siege to the receptionist with the familiar dirge of sorrows. Bania placed a firm hand on the woman's shoulder. Habiba turned, stared at the *madricha* for a moment, and then froze into terrified silence.

"Come, sit down," Bania whispered. "I won't hurt you." Unresisting, Habiba allowed herself to be led to a bench by the wall. "Now then," Bania continued, her voice gentle, "I know that what has happened is not your doing. Of course Boucha is behind it. And so I am not going to turn you over to the police." Habiba turned her head and began to weep. "Stop that!" the *madricha* ordered, quite firmly this time. "Listen to me now. I am not going to turn you over to the police if you return to the moshav immediately. I'm going to give you one minute to make up your mind."

Habiba said nothing, her lean body racked now with sobs.

"If you go to jail," the *madricha* continued, "your children will remain orphans, perhaps forever. You know that, don't you?"

Habiba nodded, wiping her eyes with the back of her hand.

"Will you come back?" Bania persisted, her voice gentle once more. "If I promise that no harm will come to you?"

Habiba nodded again, snuffling wretchedly.

The two women returned to Moshav Chusan. Neither spoke a word during the hour-long bus ride. As they walked slowly toward the Boucha home, however, the neighbor women began to gather about the pair. "Reptile," they muttered furiously at Habiba, "djinn," "child killer," "beast that you are."

"Get back to your homes," the *madricha* snapped at them. "Go on, get out. This is not your business."

The women disbanded sullenly, shouting oaths over their shoulders. Then Bania opened the door of the abandoned house. This time Habiba stopped, paralyzed with sudden terror.

"Don't be like that now," Bania warned, her temper at the breaking point. "He's not in there. No one will bother you."

But Habiba would not move. Instead she rocked back and forth on her heels, her arms crossed, wailing piteously.

During his interview with Mrs. Mai, the ministry's northern district officer, Einstein's position remained inflexible. If the family were permitted to leave the moshav a dangerous precedent would be set, he warned. It would encourage all the slackers in the district to renege on their debts to the Agency. Mrs. Mai listened patiently; but she, too, held firm. The Bouchas were quite obviously incorrigibles. If they were tied to the moshav against their will they might resort to even more drastic acts, possibly to violence. There was the safety of the children to consider. In Tel Aviv, at least, the mother would live with her brothers and sisters. The relatives had promised to care for the children, to find Habiba a job as a domestic. Nor was there any question of releasing the husband from his debts, Mrs. Mai assured Einstein. The moment Boucha was found he would be compelled to pay. And at the very least his obligations would be used to force him into a steady job.

In the end, Einstein withdrew his opposition. It was a painful disappointment—the Agency had invested heavily in the Bouchas—but he accepted it with his usual good humor. Thus, at the end of July, the ministry of social welfare recommended to the Jewish Agency that Mrs. Boucha and her children be allowed to leave the moshav. Soon afterward the permission was granted.

The day of Habiba's departure, Bania helped the mother dress the youngsters. Clothing had been supplied from the ministry's warehouse in Acre, and the *madricha* had patched the garments and washed them herself. Now she scrubbed the children's faces, and combed their hair.

"Look here, Habiba," she said at last, grasping the woman by her shoulders, "I'm giving you five pounds from my own pocket. Use it for the children. For the children, you understand me? And here are some rolls and candy, too. Don't give it to them all at once." Bania looked down again at the pathetic cluster of trusting, puppylike faces, and suddenly her lips began to tremble. "Habiba, please," she said, gazing intently into the mother's eyes. "I've put my faith in you. Don't let me down."

Habiba nodded gratefully. Her own eyes, too, were suddenly overflowing. Then, without warning, she dropped to her knees, grasped the *madricha*'s hand and kissed it.

"All right, all right," Bania muttered in sudden irritation.

A few minutes later she loaded the family onto the Eged bus. "Don't let them off until Tel Aviv," she called to the driver. He nodded. The doors closed, and the vehicle moved on. Bania waited until the bus disappeared over the brow of the hill. Then she began shivering uncontrollably.

[A letter from Mrs. Malka Me'irah, Jerusalem district, to the ministry of social welfare:]

On August 27, 1958, Mrs. Boucha appeared in our office with her eight children. . . . Since she left the moshav with her youngsters [she] has been wandering in the streets of Tel Aviv and Jerusalem, demonstrating before Agency and government authorities.

In Jerusalem, the municipality put her and her family in a hotel until the matter was discussed with the Agency. From her story we understand that her husband's sister lives in Tel Aviv. . . . [However] . . . we could not discover the address of this sister. After negotiations with the Agency, the settlement department informed the Jerusalem municipality that since the woman had been released from her debts they were willing to give her and her children a shack in the *ma'abara* of Machneh Yisrael.

Machneh Yisrael was located near Lydda, directly across the highway from Israel's international airport. I visited the *ma'abara* in February of 1959. Entering the compound's central gate, I paused for several moments before venturing further. The sight corroded one's spirit. This was misery: dilapidated huts, chipped tar-and-limestone walls and corrugated tin roofs; reeking, garbage-strewn alleyways, dividing the endless rows of shanties; the ragged Oriental children worrying a tin can between makeshift goal posts—and everywhere the clinging odor of rancid oil and unwashed bodies. I had seen and smelled it all before at Kiryat Shmoneh, Rosh HaAyen, and a half dozen other wretched immigrant encampments in other parts of the country.

"It was originally a British army camp," Mrs. Kline, the ministry's southern district director, had explained to me during our conversations in Tel Aviv. "It was one of many such camps taken over for *ma'abara* purposes during the first years of the State. Of course, as time passed and economic circumstances improved, most of the *ma'abarot* were emptied and closed up. Today [1959] only a few remain—Machneh Yisrael is unquestionably the worst of the lot. You see, it's the only *ma'abara* in the country that doesn't fall under the jurisdiction of a local council. That's the reason the municipal authorities in other towns use Machneh Yisrael as a dumping ground for their worst social cases."

I must have lifted my eyebrows, for Mrs. Kline hastened to explain.

"It's true," she insisted. "The mayors of the big cities simply refuse to accept any more social cases. The moment a chronic indigent settles anywhere in the metropolitan area his water and electricity are cut off. Sometimes local social-welfare authorities actually transport such people out of town, even to Machneh Yisrael proper. Once they're here, very few of the families ever really *want* to leave. That's the worst of it. After all, they get a roof over their heads, a room or two, and some basic furniture and utensils. They pay a nominal rental—about two pounds a month. Their water and electricity are underwritten by the ministry of health. The education of their children is covered by the ministry of education and by WIZO [the Women's International Zionist Organization]. The Histadrut will help the parents find employment. From their point of view, why should they leave?"

"But to live in all that squalor—"

Mrs. Kline smiled. "You forget that 'all that squalor' is rarely worse than the living conditions they left behind in their native lands. What kind of homes do you think they had in the *mellahs* and *hamas* of North Africa, or the ghettos of Iran and Iraq? In fact, even when cheap new housing units are ready for them, many of these people simply refuse to leave. They are terrified of facing the unknown, of moving to new neighborhoods where they may not be able to find work. Anyway, of the four thousand people in Machneh Yisrael, about thirty per cent are either incapable of real work, or else simply refuse to look for a job at all. Those are the 'hard' cases —probably the hardest cases in the entire country. They are our burden, the ministry of social welfare's. We do our best with them. So do the other agencies that work with us. And yet none of us is optimistic about the parents. It's the children we're worried about. We have to save the children at all costs."

How often had I heard that phrase. Wherever I visited—farms, settlements, towns, *ma'abarot,* clinics, schools—the reaction was always the same: despondency over the parents, but a sense of urgency bordering on desperation to "save" the children. Machneh Yisrael provided a classic example of that single-mindedness. Mrs. Ziona Dayan, the local ministry official, led me on an inspection tour of the *ma'abara's* facilities. There were the public showers, of course. One took them for granted. Persuading the camp's inhabitants to use them was another matter. None of the men and women who listlessly raked in the yards around us appeared on intimate terms with soap and water. The clinic was housed in a badly worn frame building, its packed waiting room faintly warmed by two sputtering kerosene stoves. One immigrant Polish doctor and two nurses ministered to the entire *ma'abara,* and the pressure of their duties had visibly tautened both their faces and nerves. The camp's facilities and services could hardly have been more grimly functional; and yet they were feeding the immigrants, housing them, curing them, keeping them alive. I was not allowed to forget it.

There were three schools here, and four kindergartens. Of course they were badly dilapidated and overcrowded. The odor in the classrooms was redolent of stale sweat and (I suspect) something even worse. The youngsters were the usual wild mob of Oriental moppets. It did not escape me that the teachers—most of them East European immigrants—were almost as badly dressed as their students. Not infrequently, too, they were contaminated by their pupils' ringworm and bilharziasis. Yet whatever the squalor, whatever the provocation in unruliness and even violence, the compassion of these remarkable women remained unshaken. I supposed they hardly needed a reminder that they served as parents rather more than teachers, for within moments after leaving the classroom, most of their students returned to medieval darkness.

One saw additional evidence of that devotion in the WIZO nursery for the children of working mothers. It suffused the room, palpitated, and breathed. The tots lay gurgling in their beds and playpens. Several sucked contentedly at their bottles. Others crooned to themselves on their potties. They were all Oriental, I was told. So was the young woman who cared for them, a buxom, dark-eyed sabra from Tiberias. With infinite care she fed the infants, changed them, kissed and cuddled them as if they were her own.

"Now what do you think of that child?" asked Mrs. Dayan, pointing to an especially lovely youngster of two, with glossy brown hair carefully braided and ribboned.

"A beautiful girl," I observed.

"But it is not a girl," Mrs. Dayan explained, with some amusement. "The mother wanted a girl; so she's simply raising this one as a girl." The social worker shrugged: "What can you expect? It's a Kurdish family."

"Here's a girl for you," added the nursery attendant, tenderly stroking the cheek of a pale child about five or six years old. "She's the mother's eighth daughter. The father is a seventy-five-year-old Iraqi, and quite a dangerous character. He had threatened to kill the next child if it was a girl. We still don't dare return her to her home."

Long before I left that dove's nest of babies, I recalled with a pang of remorse my early complaint to Mrs. London-Yarie—"the way these things become depersonalized . . ."

If I had not met Krimchansky, Bania Giurtler, Mrs. Mai, Mrs. Kline, or the teachers, Ziona Dayan alone would have been enough to dispel my misgivings. She was the social worker here—and in almost every respect she was the ideal choice for Machneh Yisrael. For one thing, she was emotionally unshakable. For another, she was a Sephardic Jewess; she spoke Arabic and French as fluently as Hebrew, and thus had no difficulty conversing with the Oriental inhabitants of the *ma'abara*.

Mrs. Dayan's willingness to remain at Machneh Yisrael struck me as anything but natural, however. She was still a young woman, in her early thirties. She appeared in reasonably good health; indeed, she boasted that her four children owed their strong constitutions to her. But the strain of her work had taken its toll. Her dark eyes were lackluster and edged with weariness. Her office, a damp, moldering cubicle in one of the oldest of the camp barracks, was dismal even by the wretched working standards of the ministry of welfare. There was no budget for a telephone. Here she had spent the last three years of her life coping uninterruptedly with human misery.

Her two assistants made it plain how dangerous the work could be. Machneh Yisrael's inhabitants were a tough crowd. It was their practice to hold the social workers responsible for the worst of their grievances. If the dole was not large enough, if the rooms were inadequate, if food or clothing were not plentiful enough, then pressure would have to be applied directly. The Iraqis and Moroccans were ardent believers in terror tactics. Their favorite techniques were table pounding and screaming, or at the very least sit-down strikes in the office. These methods rarely succeeded. But they did result in the nervous breakdowns and resignations of Mrs. Dayan's two predecessors.

"Why don't you keep the police here?" I asked.

Mrs. Dayan shook her head firmly. "It wouldn't work," she explained. "It would undermine whatever respect we do have around here. The furthest we can go is to have a male assistant."

Still, there were times when she had been sorely tempted to call for help. The summer months were the worst. The psychotics, the drug addicts, and alcoholics became especially restive during the hot weather. Only the August before, a Moroccan had thrown a bottle at her when she had refused to increase his relief payments; Baruch, the secretary, subdued the man before he could aim a second blow at her. On another occasion a group of middle-aged Persians surrounded her desk, threatening to beat her if she did not advance them the money to open a kiosk. Whereupon, refusing to panic, or even to lift her voice, Mrs. Dayan explained in level tones that she would not give them so much as a piaster. In fact, she added, if they did not leave her office within thirty seconds she would have them thrown out of the *ma'abara*. Taken aback by her composure, the men slunk out of the room, completely deflated. Her knees trembled for a half-hour afterward.

"Well, is it worth it?" I asked.

"It is," she replied, without a moment's hesitation. "For every 'hard' case there are two that are genuinely deserving. It means something to me to be able to dig up an old pair of shoes for a barefoot child, or to wheedle an extra ten pounds a month out of the ministry for a sick, elderly couple. Not long ago I managed to put my hands on two thousand pounds to buy a flat for a wonderful Tripolitanian woman. She had been working in a hospital for the last three years to support three ill children—one of them with polio. I tell you I made a scandal with the Jewish Agency people to get that money. When I told her the good news she kissed my hand. You should have seen her face. It made it all worth-while for me."

The entire investigation had assumed more than a professional importance to me, for that matter. Had I ever routinized my reactions to the suffering I had witnessed in this land? Very probably. And yet not long before I had criticized the ministry of social welfare for the same apparent insensitivity. The truth was that here, too, as in Moshav Chusan, the involvement was deeply and urgently personal. Judith Simhonit, Mrs. Dayan's assistant, told me about it. A slim Yemenite girl in her late twenties, she had studied every convolution in the Oriental mind during her three years at Machneh Yisrael—or thought she had. For, from the moment of their arrival, the Bouchas had taxed her resourcefulness to its final limits.

Habiba had appeared without warning on August 21, 1958. Judith looked up and the woman was standing there, her eight children ranked behind her. With the exception of the mother, who was well advanced in her pregnancy, they were all emaciated, and trembling with exhaustion. None of them spoke. With some difficulty, Judith persuaded them to sit down.

Then she served them hot tea. Two of the youngsters vomited. Immediately the social worker led the family to one of the empty huts. There she ordered the children undressed and placed on the single bed. Later she returned and interviewed the mother.

As if by rote, Habiba repeated her lament: of the years at Moshav Chusan, the husband's desertion, her own panic-stricken flight to Safed, and—later —her successful appeal to leave the moshav and settle in Tel Aviv. Yet she had not settled in the city. Instead she had wandered with her brood throughout the country, now to Haifa, now to Tel Aviv—where for two weeks she had begged alms at the Central Bus Station—and finally to Jerusalem. It was in Jerusalem that she was given authorization to come to Machneh Yisrael. Here Habiba tremulously handed Judith the certificate of permission from the ministry of social welfare.

During the ensuing weeks, the welfare office assumed complete responsibility for the family. By now the mother was in her sixth month and unable to work. Arrangements were made to supply her with eighty pounds monthly, and with script for the local food store. Judith fitted the youngsters out with second-hand clothes, then registered them in Machneh Yisrael's school and nursery, where they received their breakfasts and lunches. Once again, a local *madricha* paid daily visits, ensuring that the shack was cleaned and the children properly washed and dressed. Within a month of their arrival, the Bouchas had begun to look like human beings.

Then, shortly after Rosh Hashana, the Jewish New Year, Habiba suddenly turned morose and silent. The color drained from her withered cheeks. When Judith attempted to speak to her, the mother began trembling violently and refused to answer. On the Day of Atonement Habiba was seized with severe abdominal pains. She was rushed to Dejani hospital. That night she lost the baby. During the five days of Habiba's absence, Judith personally cared for the eight children. In spite of the social worker's endearments, however, Nachala, the oldest daughter, remained as curiously silent and secretive as her mother.

The silence continued after Habiba's return. And then, a week later, Judith received a note from Nachala: would Her Excellency kindly stop by as quickly as possible? Judith left her desk immediately and hurried to the Boucha shack. An unexpectedly foul odor greeted her. The mother lay on the bed, with the three youngest children tucked in at her side. In the corner stood a man, lean, dark, quite ragged, and stinking to the ceiling. Horn-rimmed glasses effectively masked the upper part of his face. The lower half was crumpled into a porridge of gums and yellowed tooth stumps. His spindle legs were wrapped in jodhpurs. The social worker recoiled in shock; for a moment she felt faint and gripped the iron bedpost for support. Then she whispered: "You are . . . you are? . . ."

"I am Saadia Boucha, Geveret," the man replied, tears swimming lugubriously between the diopters of his spectacles, "the ill husband of an ill wife. I have returned to the bosom of my family."

"The pieces soon fell into place," Judith explained to me. "Evidently he and his wife had been in secret contact with each other ever since his 'desertion' four months earlier. He had been using Habiba to get the family out of Moshav Chusan, and into a *ma'abara*. It took me all of five minutes to figure that out. In fact, he admitted it. Still, I had to ask him how he had dared leave a wife and eight helpless children to the mercy of others. Immediately he put on a hang-dog expression.

" 'The feeling of helplessness was too much for me,' he whined, 'the thought of my wife and children starving before my eyes.'

"I couldn't bring myself to comment on that one. Instead, I simply asked him where he had been living all this time. He said that he first had gone to Beersheba, where he had stayed with his brother. He left shortly after his brother had killed himself and his mistress in a drunken brawl. Since then, apparently, he had worked as an itinerant laborer in and around Tel Aviv, and had lived in an abandoned Arab stable.

"I wouldn't listen anymore. The man sickened me. Instead I returned to my office and talked the matter over with Ziona [Dayan]. It was a temptation to turn him over to the police, of course. Family desertion is a serious crime in Israel. But the more we discussed it, the more we were convinced that nothing would be gained by having him arrested. If he rotted in jail, Habiba and the children would be no better off than before. If he was sent back to Moshav Chusan he would only run away again. Here, at least, he was where he wanted to be. He wouldn't have to labor in the fields. It seemed likely that he would try to find a little part-time employment to supplement our dole. A few extra pounds a month would make a big difference to that family.

"And so I talked it over with him. He seemed properly penitent. 'Of course' he was sorry, he said; 'of course' he was ready to work. All he asked was for light labor; 'his back' could not tolerate the strain of anything heavier. I promised to do what I could. But I warned him that at the first sign of misbehavior I would call the police. He seemed properly impressed.

"The following week I found him a job sweeping up in the Bedek Aircraft Factory across the road. It paid seventy pounds a month. The merest pittance, of course. But then his wife also found work as a maid in Tel Aviv. Between them they were not doing at all badly. Don't forget that their children were being cared for by the schools. Free lodgings, medical care, too. They seemed satisfied. Ziona and I congratulated ourselves that we had finally gotten our case under control.

"Well, we were premature—as you must have guessed."

As Judith related it, Boucha had become progressively more sullen and unmanageable. With growing frequency, he and his wife appeared at Ziona Dayan's office, demanding larger welfare payments. The social worker turned him down. Finally Boucha switched his appeal: he wanted the government to give him a kiosk—a soda and magazine stand—to enable him to go into business for himself.

"It doesn't pay to break my back as a janitor," he whined. "I can't live on seventy pounds a month."

"Between you and Habiba you're earning one hundred and sixty pounds a month," Mrs. Dayan pointed out. "Your dole adds sixty pounds to that. We're giving you your home and educating your children free of charge. I think that's enough."

Boucha shrieked as if his life had been threatened. "Enough? Enough? I'm a sick man. My wife is sick. We can't do this heavy labor any longer." He thrust his face close to Mrs. Dayan's. "And we're not going to, understand?" At a signal from him, Habiba, too, began to caterwaul.

Mrs. Dayan refused to be provoked. "It's up to you," she shrugged. "But you're getting no kiosk from us. Now clear out. I'm tired of looking at you."

Boucha began breathing heavily. "Ka'ed tikassir hab 'alayyi?" he gasped at the social worker. "Are you cracking seeds over me [making a fool of me]?" Then, seizing his wife by the arm, he marched out of the office. "We'll be back," he shouted, and then slammed the door.

They did indeed return later in the afternoon, but only after the welfare office had closed for the day. Smashing the window with an iron plumbing fixture, Boucha crawled into the room and unlocked the door. Then he completed his business and left. The next morning Judith Simhonit and Ziona Dayan arrived at the office—and found the entire brood of Boucha children inside. They had apparently been left there the entire night. The faces of three of the smaller children seemed unusually flushed. Later, after an examination at the clinic, it developed that they had the measles. The parents had vanished.

Judith tended to the children, bedding them down and feeding them. Meanwhile, Ziona Dayan grimly requisitioned one of the *ma'abara's* trucks, and traveled straightway to the Lydda police station. The sergeant listened sympathetically to her complaint.

"I should have been in touch with you last night, Geveret," he remarked when she had finished. "The parents were here then. In fact, they drew up a complaint against you."

"Against—me?"

With an apologetic smile, the officer handed Mrs. Dayan the formal police statement. But she had lost her composure by now, and was unable to look at the document. The sergeant read it for her. The accusation was a familiar one: the welfare office was "punishing" the Bouchas; the family was deliberately given the hardest labor; the doctor had warned Boucha that he was forbidden to work altogether; the children were perishing for lack of food—etc., etc.

"Do you believe this?" she murmured at last.

"Of course not. People like these are an old story to us. Do you want me to arrest them?"

"I suppose so," she whispered. "They are incorrigibles."

The sergeant nodded. "Then why don't we wait a little longer," he counseled. Before Mrs. Dayan could protest, he hastened to explain. "Look here, we'll not finish with them this way. They may get a jail sentence, but they'll be out in a few months and you'll have to go through the same business again. If we wait a little longer we probably can catch them in something bad enough to take their children from them permanently. That's the only solution. The children have to be our main concern now, right?"

"Oh God." Mrs. Dayan suddenly began to sob. "What will happen to them?"

By the time she returned to her office she had regained control over herself. Of course the policeman was right, she realized. This sort of thing simply could not continue. The children would be better off in one of *Youth Aliyah*'s hostels.

Later in the day, Baruch, her assistant, called her to the window. She watched silently as the Bouchas shuffled past the welfare office and down the dirt patch to their barracks. Evidently they were taking no chances of losing their welfare check. She said nothing. It was merely a question of waiting for them to make their next move.

Mrs. Dayan did not have to wait long. The next morning her bus stopped fifty yards short of the entrance to Machneh Yisrael. A score of automobiles, and perhaps ten times that many onlookers blocked the way. The bus driver called back: "Better jump out here, Ziona. I think it has to do with you."

Climbing down, the social worker pushed through the crush of pedestrians. Even before reaching the center of congestion, she heard Boucha's familiar nasal howl: "Run them over, kill them, ladies and gentlemen. I beg you to proceed. It's the only merciful way."

And then she saw him, parading back and forth across the highway, haranguing the crowd. His wife followed him silently, the usual placard in hand—this one announcing simply that "The Blood of My Children Lies at the Door of the Welfare Office." Horror-stricken, Mrs. Dayan stared at the little bags of clothing strewn at intervals across the road. Were they already lifeless? She knelt down beside the first child. It was Nissim. He gazed back at her, listlessly sucking his thumb. The others, too, lay silent, but obviously unharmed. A flash of light passed over the scene, freezing it momentarily. Shielding her eyes against the photographer's bulb, Mrs. Dayan searched the crowd for Judith and Baruch.

But it was the police who arrived first. The lorry rolled to a halt, its siren dying slowly. Mrs. Dayan recognized the sergeant, and called out to him: "Don't bother with the youngsters. We'll take care of them."

The sergeant nodded, and then ordered Boucha into the van. Solemnly, with a martyred and self-righteous expression on his face, the father took his seat in the back of the lorry. Mrs. Dayan reached the mother before she could follow her husband. Seizing the hapless woman by the shoulders, the social worker shouted at the top of her voice: "You poor idiot. You had to obey him right to the end, didn't you? Now you're both going to jail. You've lost your children, Habiba. You'll never get them back. It won't be like the last time, Habiba, you understand me? The children are ours now."

"I'll take her, Geveret," the sergeant interrupted, and ushered the mother into the vehicle. Before the door swung closed, Mrs. Dayan caught a last glimpse of Habiba's tormented, preternaturally bright eyes.

"That's the situation as of this moment," Judith concluded. "The youngsters are in the care of the *ma'abara*. We're negotiating to have them transferred to the *Youth Aliyah* authorities. The Bouchas drew jail sentences, of course. They came up before an Oriental judge who understood all their tricks. He showed them no mercy." She reflected for a moment, then admitted: "We're thinking of interceding, though, to get Habiba's sentence reduced. She's given us a lot of grief, but I suppose the poor wretch really isn't to blame. Boucha has always controlled her every move. In her own way she's probably even religious—she's always mumbling something from the Bible. I can't say she deserves a jail cell."

Indeed, Habiba did not remain in the Ramle women's prison for more than two weeks. Gazing long and thoughtfully into her glittering eyes, Dr. Heller, the police surgeon, had a notion of what was wrong. He sent to the Machneh Yisrael clinic for her medical record. It suggested nothing. Neither did a blood test. The doctor's suspicion lingered. Finally, after Habiba had been X-rayed, the suspicion was confirmed.

"A nasty case, one of the worst I've seen this year," Dr. Heller stated in his report to the Malben hospital in Beer Ya'akov. "The superior lobe of the left lung has been almost entirely tuberculated. The patient is only thirty-nine years old. She has no history of previous major illnesses, except for her undoubted neurological disorders. In spite of her generally weakened condition, I do not believe that a pulmonary lobotomy is contraindicated."

Upon examining the X-ray negatives, the hospital's pathology staff agreed. Immediately, arrangements were made for Habiba to be transferred to Beer Ya'akov; the Malben hospital there, one of four managed by the Joint Distribution Committee, specialized in thoracic cases. The trip from Ramle was only six miles, and Dr. Heller drove Habiba in his own automobile. At the reception desk he personally signed the letters of transference.

"Come along, Habiba," said a brisk, middle-aged nurse. "We're going to take good care of you. Come right with me now and we'll put you in one of our pretty gowns."

Habiba hesitated, obviously terrified by the smell of iodoform, and the passing orderlies in their white jackets. She cast a last imploring glance at Heller, her black eyes rolling wildly.

"Don't be frightened," the nurse repeated, taking Habiba's hand firmly in her own. "There's nothing to be worried about here." The doctor nodded reassuringly. Together the two women moved slowly down the stone corridor.

In the ward, two young nurse's assistants began stripping the patient's clothing from her. Again Habiba balked, this time setting up a tremulous whine.

"Stop that now," one of the girls scolded. "We're not going to hurt you. Off with it—that's right."

"Elohim," murmured the other girl. "What has this woman lived on?" She gazed in astonishment at Habiba's naked body, wizened and shrunken into a foetal-like agglomeration of bone ridges and vein networks.

"Get me one of those basins," said the first assistant. "This isn't going to be easy."

And they scrubbed and scraped for twenty minutes, ignoring the woman's frantic yelps, until they had all but rubbed the skin off Habiba's body. Afterward the crusted basin was sent off for sterilization.

She lay silently at last in the iron cot, staring in confusion at the women who coughed and moaned on either side of her. From time to time a young doctor stopped at her bed, stared at a chart attached to the rail, and then moved on. In the late afternoon a Yemenite girl brought soup and vegetables on a tray. Habiba ate without appetite. Then night came and she lay without sleeping. Around her several of the strange women were crying softly in their pillows. Occasionally the white-garbed assistants padded in and out of the ward, chatting quietly with the patients. Finally she slept.

In the early morning an older doctor approached Habiba's bed. He was accompanied by two nurses and another woman, dressed in sweater and slacks.

"We're operating at eleven," the doctor explained to the social worker. "It's extremely likely that we'll also find some tuberculation in the middle lobe. We'll have to incise there, in that case."

"And afterward?" asked the woman.

"All in all, if she maintains her strength afterward, I would estimate a postoperative hospitalization of not less than five weeks."

The social worker nodded. "Her adjustment record is as bad as any I've ever seen," she said. "The one encouraging factor is the forced separation from her husband. He's locked up in Ramle with no possibility of contacting her. I think she'll behave herself as long as she's here."

This time it was the doctor's turn. "And afterward?" he asked, with a smile.

"Afterward we'll train her, of course. Weaving, sewing—it depends on which school has an opening." Here the woman leaned over the bed and stared intently at Habiba. Then she sighed, straightening up. "Whatever happens to her should be an improvement," she said.

The little group moved on.

Two hours later one of the nurses returned. Grasping the patient's arm, she rubbed it vigorously with cotton wadding. "This is to make you relax, Habiba," she said reassuringly, pressing the emaciated wrist until the vein stood out like a wire. When the hypodermic needle thrust home, Habiba peeped like a chicken. The nurse disappeared.

The clock on the wall began ticking loudly and slowly. The whimpering of the other women faded into the second level of silence. Not long afterward two dark faces peered into Habiba's.

"We are going to put you on this rolling table, Habiba," one of the men said gently, in Arabic. "It will take you into the other room. You will enjoy the ride."

She did not reply. Her lips were moving in a private litany. As the cot trundled through the corridor, she watched the copper bracings and stone fretwork in the ceiling ripple by like ocean waves. Suddenly the doors swung open before her, and the waves became a flood of light.

. . . And I sit in the house of my father on Zen Ma'abdin Street. I and my mother, and Simcha, Mordecai, Cyrus, Elijah, and Ziporah. And Father reads the words of the Prophet. He, Ezekiel, who watched over us when we came to Babylon. He who brought me here. He will not cast me adrift. Ah, he has not forsaken me among the strangers. He will not leave me to the hands of the Moscobim, the wizards, and the djinns. He feeds and clothes my children. He, Ezekiel, the Prophet who calls me back to Father's house, to the house where I was born, and to my home before I was born.

Is it time already? What do they want of me, the four who stand over me? What? He speaks with Father's voice, the Prophet. He says—

"I looked, and behold, a stormy wind came from the north, a great cloud, with fire flashing through it, and a radiance round about it, while out of the midst of it gleamed something with a luster like shining metal.

"Out of the midst of it stood forth the likeness of four living creatures, and this was their appearance: their form was like that of a man. Yet each had four faces and four wings. . . .

"Over the heads of the creatures was the likeness of a canopy, and it glittered like ice, and was stretched forth above their heads. Under the canopy one pair of their wings touched those of the next creature, while the other pair covered the body. When they moved, the sound of their wings sounded to me like the sound of mighty waters, or like the voice of the Almighty.

"Above the vault that was over their heads was the likeness of a throne, colored like sapphire; and upon the likeness of the throne was a likeness like that of a man upon it."

And I see Thee. And I wait for Thy vessel to carry me back to the River Sambation and Paradise. Now, My Master, Whose uncomplaining slave I have been, set me free at last. Thou hearest the voice of Thy gentle Habiba? O set me free.

CHAPTER FOUR

THE EFFICIENCY EXPERT

DURING the early months of my first sojourn in Israel, I did not own a private vehicle. This presented no serious difficulties as long as I remained in Jerusalem. Most of the important government and Jewish Agency offices, and nearly all my friends and acquaintances, could be found within a radius of two miles. Nor was travel between Jerusalem and other parts of the country a problem, if it was confined to normal daytime and early evening hours; buses and trains were frequent and dependable. The Sabbath was the stumbling block. On the sacred day of rest transportation between Israel's cities stopped abruptly; the religious parties had managed to win this concession from the coalition government. Even on weekdays, moreover, the interurban bus line dispatched its last Leyland Tigers at 11:30 P.M. After that, luckless travelers like myself were obliged to have recourse to the *sheroot*. I must describe the experience in some detail, for it will explain my ultimate decision to bring a car to Israel—and undergo that most fearsome of Israel institutions: ordeal by customs.

The *sheroot* is an interurban taxi. It looks like any other taxi: it has four wheels, a spare tire, room inside for seven passengers, and in its trunk and on its roof space for ten or twelve suitcases. The resemblance is deceptive, however—as deceptive as the very word *sheroot*. For *sheroot* in Hebrew means "service," and one might assume, therefore, that the interurban taxi is at the service of the traveler. This is shallow thinking. Actually it is the traveler who is at the service of the *sheroot*. For example, although the fare is apportioned among seven passengers, the *sheroot* will not budge until the full quota of passengers is reached. Admittedly, the delay is never a long one during the daylight hours, when traffic is heavy. The *sheroot* fills up reasonably quickly then. In fact, until nine or even ten at night the traveler need not wait more than ten or fifteen minutes. But after 11:00 P.M. movement between cities slows down. And of all homeward bound passengers, the most unfortunate is the poor soul traveling at that hour from bustling modern Tel Aviv to sleepy old Jerusalem. From the very moment of his arrival at Tel Aviv's central *sheroot* station, he is confronted with an imbroglio which would have tried the patience and fortitude of a Job.

137

Unhappily, I do not possess these qualities. Each Saturday night as I prepared for the return trip to Jerusalem I could feel the acid beginning its run down my stomach lining. One particular evening, as I approached the central station at 11:40, the drivers were setting up their usual nocturnal din: "Haifa! Haifa!" bellowed the dispatchers at one corner of the street. "Ramat Gan! Ramat Gan!" shouted the stationmaster at the head of another line of parked taxis. "Petach Tikvah . . . Rehovot! . . . Natanaiah! . . ." the cries echoed across the square. Finally I located my own chariot: one lonely, battered 1946 DeSoto, resting disconsolately at the darkened far corner of the station. The driver was seated on the curb, puffing glumly at a cigarette.

"Jerusalem?" I asked him hopefully.

He shrugged noncommittally. "Who knows?"

I saw his point. The cab was nearly empty. I hesitated. Already nearly midnight, and only two passengers were seated inside. The situation looked bad. One of the customers, a slim young man wearing a checkered cap, sensed my indecision.

"Get in, get in, Adoni," he urged. "We've just arrived. At this rate we'll be leaving any minute."

"Just arrived? Really?" I asked the other client, a youth still in his teens, wearing the dark blue shirt and shorts of a kibbutznik.

"Hah, are you serious?" he replied.

Such gruff honesty deserved reward. I climbed in. We waited in silence. The minutes passed. At 12:10 A.M., an aged couple walked slowly toward the *sheroot*. I could sense my fellow passengers making calculations: "Two more, that will make five of us; we're almost on our way." But as the elderly woman peered in the window, it was evident that she was making calculations of her own: "Only three passengers and after midnight? Not worth it." Shaking her head, she led her husband away.

"Charah!" muttered the kibbutznik—an unpleasant word.

Ten minutes later another couple materialized out of the darkness. Young lovers at leave-taking, they planted themselves in front of the car and tenderly, noisily began embracing. The man in the checkered cap nodded at me knowingly; one more passenger, only three to go. I soon lost track of time. People approached the *sheroot,* hesitated, then walked on. The passengers set up the usual harangue: "Get in . . . We're almost full . . . only three to go, two with you . . . Come on . . . It's too late to look for a hotel . . ." and more in this vein. All the while the young lovers continued gobbling at each other hungrily. My thoughts were on the morrow: an 8:00 A.M. appointment with a prominent member of the Knesset. I was sure to be bleary-eyed and incoherent when we met. If we met. I glanced at my watch again: 12:50 A.M. and the *sheroot* was still only half full.

At this point a prim, middle-aged little woman drew near, leading a ten-year-old child by the hand. Their faces were hardly less than angelic. Indeed, the woman resembled a kind of Israel version of Whistler's Mother, down to the shawl and brooch.

"Good evening," she said sweetly to the driver. "Jerusalem?"

"That's right, Geveret," he replied, softening visibly. "Get in and we'll have only two more to go."

Two more to go! Another ten minutes passed and not a cat stirred down the street. The Haifa and Ramat Gan taxis had long since departed. All the seated passengers remained silent. The lovers stood on the sidewalk, nuzzling each other complacently. The young man finally disentangled himself long enough to ask: "How many to go?"

"Two," we muttered, in unison.

With an exclamation of delight, he entered the *sheroot*. Then, to our utter astonishment, his girl friend climbed in with him. So they were traveling together all the time! I felt a slow gurgling in my throat.

"Take it easy," whispered checker-cap. "At least we're leaving."

But we were not. No sooner were we all in our places—checker-cap in front with the driver, the kibbutznik, the middle-aged woman and I in the back seat, the little boy and the lovers in the middle folding-seats—than an ancient and elaborate ritual began. Opening his change box, our chauffeur turned around to face us:

"That'll be four pounds apiece."

"Four?" The passengers sent up a unanimous cry of outrage. "What are you talking about? . . . It's never been more than three. . . . What kind of nonsense is this? . . . Now you pull this on us."

The driver, a burly, mustachioed Oriental, was imperturbable. He had been through this routine hundreds of times. "The daytime price is three pounds," he explained blandly. "The nighttime price is four. That's it."

"That is not it," shouted the kibbutznik, furiously. "You show me where it's written that the night price is higher than the day price."

"Kacha zeh—so it is," responded the driver, with equanimity. "I'll get back to my family at three in the morning if we leave now. I'm entitled to a higher price."

"That so?" said checker-cap. "We'll see."

He climbed out. Instantly all the other passengers followed him. Confused, and thoroughly exhausted, I sat alone for a moment. It was worth an extra pound to me to get moving. On the other hand, I did not relish playing the role of the scab. Finally, with a deep sigh of self-pity, I joined the other passengers on the sidewalk. They eyed the driver balefully. He glared back, then started his motor.

"Your last chance," he shouted. "I'm going home."

"Go to hell," snapped the young man with the girl friend.

Instantly the driver meshed his gears and drove off. "Isn't there anything we can do?" I pleaded, "I have an 8:00 A.M. appointment in Jerusalem tomorrow."

"Don't we all," replied the girl. "Just keep your pants on. He'll be back."

Sure enough, a few moments later the *sheroot* turned the corner and slowed to a crawl as it passed us. The driver looked out. The passengers held firm. He shrugged. "Shimru al HaLailah," he shouted again, "Guard the night"—and then drove off some more.

"Folks," I began, "maybe we should—"

"Relax, will you?" grunted the kibbutznik.

That was too much to ask by now, but at least I remained quiet. In five minutes the taxi made a return appearance, parking on the opposite side of the street. With an elaborate show of indifference, the driver climbed out, stared at his watch, and began to walk off. Then, as if in afterthought, he murmured—just loud enough to be heard:

"Well, I don't know. Maybe three pounds seventy-five."

"Three and a half," barked the lovers simultaneously, "and that's it."

"Three and a half?" The driver hesitated, shrugged . . . "Well, I must be crazy, but it's late . . . All right, get in."

With a low murmur of triumph, we piled into the *sheroot* once again. Good God, I would simply *have* to find another way of traveling. The motor started. I settled back. After a few moments I sat up once again. We were not moving.

"Get in, get in," cried the passengers.

All became clear in a moment. The kibbutznik was still on the sidewalk, obstinately holding out on his own.

"Three pounds is all I've got," he warned the driver, "and three is all you'll get."

The driver threw up his hands, then turned off the motor. Without another word he hunched deep into his seat, leaving the field of battle to his customers.

"What's the matter with you?" they pleaded with the kibbutznik. "You knew three pounds fifty was the going rate . . . you have to go along with us . . . Be a good fellow . . . If you wanted to make trouble you should have taken the bus . . ."

The kibbutznik remained stonily unmoved. He was a member of Ha-Shomer HaTzair, the ultra left-wing collectivist movement; with him it was a matter of principle. "Three is all I've got," he insisted flatly.

A light dawned in my mind. "Are you sure?" I asked him suddenly.

He remained silent, blinking at me uncomprehendingly.

"Because if you haven't got enough," I continued, "I'll pay the extra half-pound for you." It was an American solution.

The kibbutznik had to think for a moment on that one. Finally, principle won out. "B'Seder—O.K.," he agreed, returning to his original seat. I handed over the half-pound. The other passengers grumbled under their breath as the driver started the motor once more. It was not their idea of a solution.

We were moving. I sank back against the upholstery. Now for a little sleep. Perhaps I dozed off for a few minutes. It could not have been for long. The lapping of water awakened me. Was it raining? I looked out the window. The pane was clean. The sound continued, a kind of bubbling suction, as if a toilet plunger was at work. Soon I located the source of the disturbance. In front of me the young lovers were still feeding hungrily on each other's faces. I cleared my throat—once, twice, three times. They could not have cared less. Mouths, noses, necks, hands, and elbows were locked together in a gyrating mobile. Damn! I wanted to sleep.

"I want to sleep," the words suddenly blurted out, apparently of their own volition.

The young woman stared at me curiously for a moment. Then her face darkened. "Chutzpah—some nerve!" she muttered, and pushed her partner away. When he protested, she explained: "Hold it, he's ogling us." Then, just audibly enough for me to hear, she added: "A pity he can't find a girl of his own."

The truth hurt. Never mind, at least it was quiet now. I tried to sleep again, but the spell was broken. A woman began to talk to the driver: about the weather, driving conditions, the high cost of living, the disrespect of young people these days, the unjustness of the tax laws, the decline of public idealism. In a wheedling, oscillating singsong, the voice continued to dredge up every banality, platitude, and cliché tested by time as a sure and certain antisoporific. I opened my eyes. It was Whistler's Mother. Well, this time someone else would have to take the initiative. I looked around; was I to get no support anywhere? But the other passengers, drugged by experience more than exhaustion, huddled deeper in their seats and kept their peace. And so I kept mine. My eyes ached; I closed them again. There was no protection for the ears, unfortunately. The little madonna kept up the singsong, mingled with occasional warning to her son— "Alexanderl"—to keep his fingers out of his mouth.

After a while the fine-intensity spray of water drops began once more. This time my anger was uncontrollable. The young man appeared to be smaller than I. Perhaps then if I threatened him with physical violence he would keep that suction pump of his away from the girl friend. I raised my head, slowly, and—I hoped—ominously. But the young lovers were sitting quietly, facing front. I looked about. The window panes were flecked with moisture. Outside, the *sheroot*'s headlights reflected back from the damp road. Well, by George, it *was* rain, real rain. The other passengers had also noticed the drizzle and were sitting up, talking excitedly. "What, rain again; it just rained yesterday . . . What do you know . . . that means our steps will be tracked with mud . . . Wonder if I left my window open at home . . . and me with no umbrella . . ." etc., etc.

All right, it was raining. Big *tsimmis*. Maybe they would get the excitement out of their systems in a few moments. Not so, however. Checker-cap in the front seat had been worked to a pitch of good-fellowship by our common plight, adrift at sea in an ancient 1946 DeSoto. He began posing us riddles.

"Two children, born the same day, same hour, of the same mother and father, but not twins. What are they?" He leaned back and grinned expectantly.

I ignored him. The others remained silent. That would teach him, the nincompoop.

"Maybe they didn't have the same mother and father at the same time?" exclaimed the little boy, brightly.

"Alexanderl!" Whistler's Mother was shocked.

"No, no, at the same time," insisted checker-cap. "No tricks. It's quite a simple answer."

"How do they know it was the same mother and father?" asked the kibbutznik. "With chickens—"

"I'm telling you," snapped checker-cap, "the same mother and father. What do you want—a picture post card?"

"Yes." Young lover smirked. His girl friend giggled.

After a round of speculations, checker-cap gave us the answer. The two children belonged to a set of triplets. I groaned.

"Funny, hah?" guffawed checker-cap, looking at me.

"Noisy," I replied sourly.

Nothing daunted, he continued with other riddles, most of them mathematical. By now we had reached the Judean mountains. Another forty minutes and we would be home. Or perhaps not. The driver had slowed down to half the usual rate of climb. I looked out. Fog was drifting across the road. The headlights of approaching vehicles were barely visible until almost on top of us. This was not amusing. The driver evidently did not think so either.

"I'll watch the left lane if you'll watch the right," he proposed to us finally. "I don't want to go off the road."

And so we leaned forward in our seats, craning our necks for a glimpse of the shoulder of the highway. The stretch from Bab al-Wad to Jerusalem was perilous even in daytime, and even in the best of weather. Checker-cap's chapeau blocked my vision of the right side of the front windshield.

"Take off your cap, will you," I said.

The young man seemed offended. "What for? It's comfortable."

"We can't see out," protested the other passengers.

"I'll watch for you," he replied.

"Everyone watch," ordered the driver. "Everyone."

Checker-cap opened his mouth to protest again, then thought better of it. His youthful brow was furrowed as he worked on the problem. Finally, with a sigh, he jerked off his headpiece. The girl began giggling again, but stopped short when her boy friend poked her in the ribs. I felt like howling, too. Checker-cap deserved it, poor loudmouth. He was bald as an egg.

The rest of the journey passed like a dream. At times the *sheroot* slowed to a crawl. I knew every hairpin turn in that mountain highway by heart. Each time we reached a well-known gorge, I peered down. But even the familiar yawning chasm was no longer visible, only fog. I had not experienced a journey like that since the early months of the postwar era, when I was a train passenger on a makeshift stretch of mountain track between Pisa and La Spezia. Then the Italians around me had made the sign of the cross. Now, in the *sheroot*, my fellow riders could only groan and grunt, occasionally punctuating the silence with a few nervous wisecracks. It was comparatively quiet, a natural opportunity for sleeping. I no longer felt like it.

We finally arrived, of course—at 4:10 A.M. The taxi pulled up to

Jerusalem's central *sheroot* station, off Ben-Yehudah Street. The mother and her child disembarked. The rest of us worked our private deals to be driven to our homes. I was the first to be dropped. The driver extended his hand for the customary additional half-pound payment. As I dipped into my pocket the kibbutznik suddenly grasped my arm.

"No, you don't," he said. Then to the driver, "Don't take anything from him, you hear."

The driver seemed surprised. "What's the trouble now?" he complained. "I took him to his home, didn't I?"

"Yes, but he got us all home—including you," checker-cap reminded him. "If he hadn't paid that extra half-pound—"

"Habibi," exclaimed the driver, "I can't be responsible for all your private deals."

"Come on," I moaned, "it's late. I can't stand this any more. I *want* to pay."

"But *we* don't want you to pay," said the young lovers. "This is a matter of principle. Don't budge now."

"I'm getting up," I insisted, suiting the action to the word. Instantly the kibbutznik and the young lover pinioned my arms.

"Don't budge," warned the kibbutznik. Then, to the driver: "We're none of us leaving this *sheroot* unless he doesn't have to pay."

"Habibi," growled the driver, "don't make trouble. It's after four in the morning."

We sat there silently, all of us breathing heavily.

"I'll call a policeman," said the driver, finally.

"Good, go find one," said checker-cap. "We'll tell him how you over-charged us."

Our chauffeur thought about that one for a minute. "All right," he snarled at last. "Get out, get out. I wouldn't have your lousy money. Just don't ever get into my *sheroot* again."

Don't worry, I thought to myself, as I climbed down, I'll try to forgo the privilege. Good night, good night, good night. I stumbled into my room, tore off my clothes, and collapsed on the bed. I simply would *have* to find another means of getting around.

And in fact I tried everything: restricting my travel to the daylight hours—this worked for about a week; cadging a lift from friends and acquaintances—they began to avoid me after a few months; buying and operating a small motorbike—after about a year of this my bruised kidneys began to protest. And so, ultimately, I decided to bring a little Ford over from the United States. That is where the grief really began, you see. As far as I had been informed, no problems would arise with the customs authorities; the vehicle had been imported under a *carnet de passage,* a sort of tourist's permit to operate an automobile free of charge for one year. Nevertheless, I still had to claim the Ford at Haifa dock upon its arrival and to register it with the proper authorities before driving it off. The Automobile Association's agent in Haifa, a rotund, effervescent little man, was all confidence.

"Just leave it to me, Adoni," he promised. "We'll have that machine out of here in an hour."

I knew better. Nevertheless, I agreed. It was a fatal decision. While my agent bustled about the customs shed, conversing with friends and associates, I sat down on a bench and surveyed the incoming traffic. A real bedlam; at least sixty customs and harbor officials were attempting to shepherd ten times that many arriving passengers through the proper inspection and registration channels. It took hours. I should know, I waited that long. Occasionally I tugged at my agent's sleeve: "So, how is it going?" I asked. "Relax," was the invariable answer.

Now and then I myself approached a clerk whose manner denoted authority or importance—i.e., who carried a briefcase. "Just want to check the car through on a *carnet*," I murmured respectfully, "won't take but a minute." "Soon, soon," came the offhand answer. At 1:20 P.M. the agent finally returned, accompanied by a uniformed customs officer. Hopefully, I extended my documents for examination. How impressive they all were, signed, countersigned, stamped, and duly weighted with impressive-looking seals. It should have been enough to get a trailer truck in. "First meet Customs Officer Mizrachi," the agent exclaimed breezily, waving away my outstretched arm. "Customs Officer Mizrachi, Professor Doctor Sachar from the United States." Embarrassed by the grandiloquent title (but understanding perfectly the impression the agent intended to make on my behalf), I shook hands somewhat sheepishly.

"Now then," said the official, "I myself will examine the motor and make sure the number agrees with the *carnet*."

He did that. After inscribing the necessary information, Mizrachi looked at me carefully, examined my clothes, and especially my shoes. "Now you will have to pay," he said at last.

I was shocked. For all their reputed inefficiency, the customs officials of Israel had never been known for dishonesty. "But it's on a *carnet*," I protested. Then, resignedly—"All right, what will you settle for?"

Now it was the official's turn to be shocked. "You have to pay for the first year's license, with or without the *carnet*," he explained to me. "One hundred and fifty pounds."

So it was not a question of baksheesh, that was reassuring. One hundred and fifty pounds was still a lot of money, though. Mizrachi anticipated my reaction. "Can't pay now?" he asked, surveying my clothing again. When I hesitated, he added: "I'll give you a certificate for three months. After that you'll have to pay for the full year, though. Agreed?"

I agreed with alacrity. More forms were filled out and stamped. I signed my name four times. Apparently my business was concluded, for the agent asked me to shake hands again with Mr. Mizrachi. I did, and we parted amicably. Before we reached the door, however, I was steered into another office. We waited in line for twenty minutes. A lean, tired-eyed Sephardi finally received my papers. "Adoni," he said, "how are you getting this car to Jerusalem?"

"I thought I'd drive it."

"Do you have insurance?" he persisted.

That stumped me. "How does anyone get a car out of this port?" I countered.

"With insurance," he replied with finality.

After considerable foraging, the official came up with a list of selected insurance companies—"all with branches in Haifa," he assured me. The agent gave me a tip on a good one. I summoned a cab and sped off to the address. When I arrived, the office was closed for the afternoon recess. I went to a restaurant and ate lunch. At 4:00 P.M. I returned. At 4:40 P.M. I left, with a five-hundred-pound full-coverage policy in my hands. At 5:05 I reached the customs shed at the port. It had closed for the day. Not until 10:10 the next morning did I succeed in extricating my little auto, and setting off for Jerusalem. Sitting behind that steering wheel at last, I suddenly felt as drunk with power as a teen-ager who had just learned to drive: ah, I was my own man at last.

The wasted day (not to mention the hotel bill) was my first experience in customship. It was in the nature of an appetizer, so to speak. Three months later I returned to the port to pay off the first year's license. Had I known that a special trip from Jerusalem was necessary, I would of course have paid the entire sum at the outset. But neither the agent nor the customs official had thought it necessary to give me warning. And so seven hours were consumed in the round trip between Jerusalem and Haifa. The usual waiting in line, form filling, and the payment itself required only four hours. But there it was, another day gone.

Nine months after that, a full year after my Ford had arrived in the country, I nerved myself for the ordeal of securing an Israel registration plate for the car. By this time I had used a few personal contacts and had managed to avoid a return trip to Haifa. But—who knows?—even the Haifa customs might have been preferable to what lay in wait for me. My first stop was the local customs office on Allenby Square. Actually it was not a stop, but rather more of a camp-out. The offices, winding and twisting interminably as in a house of mirrors, were decrepit and hopelessly overcrowded. By now one took that for granted; it was a struggling country. Most of the clerks were shabbily dressed, poor fellows, and appeared vaguely undershaved. Frayed and discolored cardboard files, bulging asymmetrically like workmen's sandwiches, appeared on nearly every desk. So did glasses of lukewarm tea, the symbol of Israel clerkdom. The lighting in the building was just adequate to outline every crack in a wall, every stain on a shirt or a tooth, every wrinkle or blemish on a face. Most depressing.

Applicants were pushing and jostling their way from one room to another. They were a noisy, unhappy lot, most of them new immigrants from eastern Europe or North Africa, seeking to declare their meager baggage duty-free. A babel of languages—French, Arabic, Rumanian, Yiddish, Hebrew—flooded the waiting rooms and hallways. The applicants whined, pleaded, argued, even threatened their cases. In return, clerks shouted, expostulated, threw up their hands, mopped their brows, jumped from their seats in mock imperiousness, or resumed them with sullen exasperation. The scene reminded me somehow of a Mack Sennett movie—with sound, of course. At 8:01 A.M., hunching my head against impending disaster, I drew a deep breath and ventured into Room 14, the nerve center of the customs' chamber of horrors. The line of waiting people was already strung among tables, chairs, and filing cases. With no notion of where it began or ended, I leaned against a window sill and tried to make myself comfortable. At the end of a forty-minute wait it appeared to me that all my predecessors had been duly processed. I sidled up to the central desk. The clerk was a mild-looking Iraqi.

"I've come to pay the customs on my automobile," I explained.

"Next room," he answered pleasantly. "Mr. Melamud."

That had not taken long. In the next room I waited fifty-five minutes as the line of applicants unstrung itself. Mr. Melamud was an elderly Ashkenazi, quite short, with a round, pink face, a frozen half-smile, and long black fingernails.

"I've come to pay the customs on my automobile," I explained.

With a sigh the little man gazed at my passport, examined my *carnet de passage* and the various attached certificates. Then, from an empty orange crate at the side of his desk, he removed a file and began inserting a thick sheaf of forms and questionnaires.

"Fill these out and come back," he instructed me.

For several moments I stood there, saying nothing. Finally, adopting a tone both piteous and deferential, I asked: "Can't I fill them out here? I've been waiting two hours."

He gazed at me earnestly for a moment with his rheumy blue eyes. "You Americans are always in such a hurry," he observed, not without sympathy. "Fill these forms out and come back. I'll take you right away."

That was an improvement. And so, meticulously, painstakingly, I supplied the required information: name, father's name, place of residence in the United States, in Israel, number of passport, date of arrival in Israel, occupation, anticipated length of stay, number of my Israel visa, status in the country (new immigrant, temporary resident, permanent resident, or tourist). And then information about the automobile: its year, its make, its size, number of cylinders, cost, registration number, motor number, date of purchase, date of shipment, date of entry, number of the *carnet de passage*, date of the *carnet*'s expiration. I had nearly all the necessary data at my disposal. Only the weight of the car escaped me. I searched the *carnet* in vain for this intelligence. Somewhat apologetically I shouldered my way back to the desk, and explained my predicament to Mr. Melamud. He sighed again, then called a dark Sephardic boy from the neighboring desk.

"Shabbtai," he murmured sleepily, "when can you take this gentleman to have his car weighed?"

Shabbtai examined a schedule attached to his clipboard, and then suggested that I return the following morning at 9:00. My stomach writhed like a barrel of eels.

I arrived hopefully at 8:30 the next morning. At 9:55 A.M. Shabbtai was ready for me. We drove out along Jaffa Road, heading westward toward Romema, a suburb of Jerusalem. There I maneuvered the Ford carefully onto the platform of a small weighing station. The weighing master adjusted his dials and levers, then jotted down the information. "That'll be two pounds," he informed me, handing me my certificate. I paid. As we drove back Shabbtai examined the gas gauge on my dashboard. "You have a full gas tank," he observed. "If it had been empty the weight would have been less, and you would have paid less. Just a friendly tip."

We returned at 10:35. Stoically I waited again for my turn at Mr. Melamud's desk. When it came, twenty minutes later, the little clerk turned his cracked smile on me, then took me into his confidence. "Such noise, such crowding all morning. Look at that," he said, pointing to a full glass on his table. "My tea is cold. Haven't had a chance for more than a sip." I nodded in genuine sympathy (but not for him). He scrutinized my weight receipt, then searched his orange crate for my file, whence he deposited the slip. Then he turned the entire dossier over to me, and directed me back to my original destination, Room 14. This time the wait was a mere quarter-hour. It would have been less but for the interminable ringing of the Iraqi clerk's telephone. "Hello, no. I don't know . . . ," he replied, "you'll have to ask Chaim. Chaim's not here today . . . Hello, yes, well, I'll have to see it. Bring it in some time. Can't tell you when, I'm busy, goodbye . . . Hello, don't know, I'm busy now. Call the other office for an appointment . . . Hello, what? Don't know."

By the time my turn came I anticipated a similar brush-off—and was preparing a howl of indignation which would be heard at the other end of the hall. But to my surprise, the clerk looked through my dossier knowledgeably, nodding now and then as if its contents exactly fitted his expectations. "Yes, hmm, uh-huh, very good," he murmured from time to time. "Now we'll just figure this out: the rate is calculated at one pound fifty per kilogram." Picking up a pencil, he began multiplying a sum of figures. Double-checking, he handed the slip of paper to me. "There you have it," he explained. "Your customs comes to three thousand nine hundred pounds."

Perhaps they did not hear me at the other end of the hall, but at least the other end of the room got an earful: How? Why? What? I was not an Israeli citizen, was I? I had been informed that I need pay only 10 per cent of the usual customs, hadn't I? What did this mean?

It meant a little less than I had thought. Slowly, patiently, and (in all fairness) courteously, the clerk explained the new rules to me. Since January 1 all temporary residents were obliged to pay a full 50 per cent of the customs during the first year after the expiration of their *carnets de passage*. The remaining half of the duty might be postponed until the second year. He showed me the printed regulations. There they were, in black and white. I thought for a moment: the first installment was I£1,950; I had another year to dig up the rest. Curious mechanism, the human psyche. A few seconds ago the clerk had shocked me out of my wits with the figure of I£3,900. Now I was all but tearful with relief that he had divided the sum into two installments. I pulled out my check book, examining my last stub carefully. It was close, but I would just make it.

"What about the guarantee for the second year?" asked the clerk suddenly.

"Guarantee?"

"We must have a guarantee for the money," he insisted. "Can you get a bank to sign for you?"

At first I hesitated. Then an idea suddenly occurred to me. "I think the Association of Americans and Canadians will do it," I said. "I presume their guarantee is good with you."

"Why not?" he replied equably.

"I'll have it for you in a couple of days," I promised.

As I rose to leave, the clerk stopped me. "Your *carnet* has expired today, Adoni," he pointed out. "That means that you can't drive your car until you get your new license."

I began to tremble. If I shouted again they might call for the police. Swallowing several times, I finally observed that he and his colleagues were the ones who had kept me running around in circles for the last two days; I had been ready to settle from the first moment. The clerk shrugged: "You shouldn't have waited until the last minute," he remarked.

I opened my mouth, and then closed it again. I walked out.

For the next three days I violated the laws of Israel, for I continued driving with my expired American registration. Fortunately, no occasion arose for a policeman to stop me and examine my documents. On the morning of the fourth day my guarantee arrived from the Association of Americans and Canadians. I returned triumphantly to the customs office. Within one hour I had paid my money, collected my receipts, and walked out. All that remained now was to report to the Jerusalem branch of the bureau of motor vehicles and secure my new registration plates. That was all.

The bureau of motor vehicles was located in a long, stone, barracks-like structure a mere hundred yards from the fashionable King David Hotel. It looked innocent enough. Moreover, when I arrived in the dank, tobacco-stained waiting room at 8:00 A.M. no one was shouting—until thirty-five minutes later when the door of the registration room opened. I found myself wedged in the entrance between a brawny truck driver and a mousy-faced little Yemenite—who turned out to be one of the clerks, arriving with customary lack of punctuality. The other officials inside were barricaded behind their desks, their faces surprisingly placid as they intoned their morning prayers: "Slow down there . . . one at a time . . . pushing won't help you . . . get in line or we'll close up again . . . you there, wait outside."

Eventually the clot of applicants thinned out. I was directed to a Mr. Grynspan, a handsome, gray-haired employee at the far corner of the room. He examined my customs receipts, opened a dossier, and began filling in a detailed questionnaire. I must say that Mr. Grynspan did his level best to accommodate me. Interference came not from the other applicants, but rather from the battalion of clerks and secretaries who worked in the office. They interrupted his train of concentration every two or three minutes, thrusting certificates, documents, and often entire files in his face, asking for his signature, his advice, his instructions. The official's remarks became increasingly curt and noncommittal, his voice rose a full octave, and his face slowly turned a dull, burnished red. Without realizing it, perhaps, he vented his irritation on me, for his answers to my questions now became snappish and monosyllabic. At that moment I was vaguely aware of having met Mr. Grynspan before. Only later did it occur to me that I had seen him in innumerable government offices, banks, and waiting rooms throughout the country. His were the occupational syndromes of Israel clerkdom.

"Take this receipt to Building A and make an appointment for your automobile to be inspected," he instructed.

Make an appointment? The acid within me began to percolate once more. But I did as I was told. Arriving at Building A, I followed the pointed arrow to Office 3. It turned out to be the wrong one; the clerk inside sent me on next door with a crisp jerk of the thumb. And next door a line of perhaps fifty people was strung halfway around the building, like yard birds on a rail. By luck, one of the officials happened to leave his desk at that moment, and passed within a few feet of me. Shamelessly imitating the classical gesture of Israel waiting-room dwellers, I grasped the man by the sleeve: "Adoni," I pleaded, "how long do you think I'll have to wait to get my car inspected?"

"Grr," he said, attempting to brush me off. But I held on. "Probably not today," he muttered at last, tearing himself free.

Of course he was right. By the time I reached the desk, the morning was gone. It turned out that applicants were issued numbers here, which listed their place in the inspection line-up. Never mind, I thought, at least I would have my number for the following day. I was mistaken. The clerk behind the desk brusquely informed me that there was no possibility of further inspection before closing time at 12:30 noon, and numbers could be issued only for the current day. I would have to return to the office the following morning. Drip, drip, drip.

I returned at 7:00 A.M. the next day. Fortunately, only four people were ahead of me. A few minutes after the office opened, I was handed my number, and walked out to the inspection area behind the building. The tests, as I soon learned, were quite severe. With reason: most of the vehicles were aging, rebuilt derelicts that appeared to function on *chutzpah* more than on fuel. Lights, brakes, chassis, even motors were carefully examined. The inspectors churned the automobiles, trucks, and motorcycles around a gravel yard, meticulously listing their findings on long questionnaires. My turn did not come until 9:25, nearly two and a half hours after arrival. Well, this would not take long. After all, mine was a sturdy American Ford, only a year old. And I, alas, was a naïve American driver, not much older than that in experience with Israel officialdom. Of course the inspectors found something wrong with the car. Apparently there was too much "play" in the steering wheel. I was handed the name of an approved garage which would make the necessary repairs.

The garage was filled. I was told to return the following afternoon. I did. The "repair" was made. It cost me six pounds. I returned to the bureau of motor vehicles early the *next* morning, waiting in line, receiving my number; and one hour and five minutes after that had the Ford inspected again. It passed muster. The examiner scrutinized my motor block carefully.

"Adoni," he said at last, "I can barely make out the serial number here. In another year it will be completely obscured. I would suggest that before I register it you have it re-printed." He scribbled an address on a slip of paper. "Take your car to the ORT school [an institution for vocational training]. They will print new numbers on the block."

Numbly following instructions, I drove off to the ORT school. The new numbers were duly printed. That cost me two pounds. I returned to the bureau of motor vehicles a half-hour later. To my surprise, the examiner interrupted his inspection of another car, picked up my questionnaire, filled in the new number, and sent me off to another office. Here another clerk re-registered the necessary information, and handed me a certificate.

"To the paint shed," he instructed. "They'll paint you your new license plates."

My heart began to pound excitedly. A mere eleven applicants were lined up before me at the paint shed. Within forty minutes the new plates were painted and attached to the bumpers of my car. I was almost home.

Just one more visit—to the cashier, to pay I£150 for the new year's license fee. Actually there were three cashiers' windows, each serving a different function which I could not quite discern from my vantage point at the end of a line of twenty people. But as I drew closer it appeared as if the responsibilities of each cashier were interchangeable. Indeed the cashiers themselves were, for they were continually shifting positions as if playing a game of musical chairs. Then, as I approached even closer, I realized that this interpretation, too, was in error. Evidently a small gas ring was located at the corner of the easternmost cashier's cage. The clerks were merely taking turns heating and drinking their tea there.

These matinal transfusions were entirely "unofficial," of course. By themselves they could hardly have sustained hard-working civil servants in their moment-by-moment encounter with the pitiless citizenry. The "official" fifteen-minute coffee break occurred at 10:00 A.M. No one doubted that this recess was "official"; a sign above the cashiers' cages proclaimed it. And so did the cashiers themselves at 9:58 A.M., by slamming down the shutters of their windows. Not one window, nor two, leaving a rotating force of clerks to deal with the exasperated public—but three, all of them, simultaneously. I was rather in need of a drink myself by that time, but of course dared not leave my place in the line, not even as far as the bench near the wall. With the rest of the applicants, I stood, shifting uncomfortably from foot to foot, as the minute hand on my watch crept past the hour, and the quarter-hour, to 10:21. Then the windows popped open again. Wiping their mouths with the back of their hands, the cashiers resumed their seats in the cages.

My money was ready by the time I reached the front of the line. As the clerk accepted my certificate, and filled out the necessary forms, I counted out I£150 in cash. It was not an inconsiderable sum. But I had surely not worked as hard earning it as I had labored these last few days to give it all back to the Government of Israel. I had been ready to pay, from the very first moment of the car's arrival. Never mind, it was all behind me now. Unlike many a modern Moses, who had never been privileged to reach this Promised Land of customship, who had been gathered to his fathers prematurely on some bureaucratic Mount Pisgah, I, an undeserving Joshua from the Western wilderness, had been allowed to cross the Jordan. Before me the Canaanite's suppliant hands were extended, palms upward. As I handed the funds over to him, I remember murmuring, somewhat incoherently: "Thank you, Adoni. Thank you, thank you."

Was mine an unusually harrowing ordeal? By no means. Other car owners have even more fearsome tales to relate. The complaint columns of Israel's newspapers are full of them. For example, I think of the new immigrant who planned to buy a small, four-year-old Fiat station wagon in Europe before departing for Israel. Asking the Israel Mission in Cologne for information, he was informed that a new immigrant could bring in a car at half its usual rate of customs—i.e., at I£.75 per kilogram. The sum sounded within the immigrant's means, and so he went ahead with the purchase. Upon his arrival in Israel, however, he discovered to his horror that he would be charged the full duty of I£1.50 kilogram for the car— apparently because it had not been in his possession for at least a year. The Israel representative in Cologne had forgotten to mention this.

After a five-hour discussion with various port and customs officials, the hapless newcomer left Haifa without his car. On the advice of the customs department, however, he filed an appeal, stating that he could not possibly afford the full duty, that he had been misinformed, and that he would have come without a car had he known the full regulations. After a long wait he was at last informed that the car would be freed—but no details were given. It required further correspondence to learn, eventually, that his petition had in fact been rejected, and that the full duty would have to be paid after all—plus a fine of twenty-five pounds for not having an import license, plus port fees. Six additional weeks passed before the wretched man completed the formalities of paying the duty and freeing his car; he had been obliged to deal with no less than twenty-one different officials. At the moment of writing, his car is still standing in his yard, awaiting the time when its unfortunate owner will have sufficient funds to buy a license. He had scraped together all his savings merely to extricate the automobile from Haifa port.

And yet, in a chronic and persistent, if less expensive way, these bureaucratic annoyances faced the typical Israeli, recent immigrant and veteran alike, nearly every day of his life. It was almost as if the nation's civil servants lay awake at night conjuring up new and devilish techniques to aggravate the public. No irritation seemed too petty. I think of the (comparatively) simple process of claiming packages that arrived by mail. One day I received a notice that a box of books had come for me. I promptly set off for Jerusalem's central post office. There I entered the package department. The room was wider than it was long, and the line of waiting citizens resembled a pretzel, bending and winding back upon itself until every foot of space was filled. Uncertain where the queue began or ended, I squeezed into a vacuum that momentarily opened near the counter.

After twenty-five minutes I finally reached the package department. The clerk, a bearded Orthodox Jew, hardly five feet tall, was imperturbable in the face of the public's most indignant tirades. Did an applicant protest that latecomers were being served out of turn? The clerk lifted a hand helplessly, mumbled in his beard, and proceeded with his task. Did a citizen insist that a full ten minutes need not be consumed weighing a box and affixing the proper number of stamps? The clerk scratched one of his side-curls reflectively, blinked several times, and gargled deep from within his nest of feathers. The public shouted, swore, threatened: the package man trudged complacently back and forth, recovering parcels, registering others, refusing to be instructed, rushed, or provoked. When I appeared before him to claim my package, he accepted the claim slip from my outstretched hand, peered at it closely, then at me, and mumbled again—something about my identification papers.

"What identification papers?" I exclaimed.

He shrugged and mumbled again: I could not have my package without identifying myself properly.

"But I've brought the claim slip," I insisted. "It was mailed to me. What more do you need than that?"

He gave me the helpless lifted-hand treatment. Unfortunately my passport was in Haifa at the time, in the custody of a customs agent who was examining a carton of baggage that had recently arrived for me (that's another story). When I explained this, the package man shrugged again: no tickee, no laundry.

Fifteen days later my passport was returned to me. I rushed back to the post office, back to the package room, back to the pretzel line, and back to my friend, Mumbles. He examined my passport, trudged to the package bin, and returned ten minutes later to inform me that, in view of my failure to claim delivery within the required two weeks, my parcel had been returned to the sender. Somewhat anticlimactically, I should add here that the sender, which happened to be a university library in the United States, is still waiting for the box to arrive.

But why should I complain? Did not others, permanent residents in this country, experience similar aggravations almost daily? And, in two cases out of three, was the grief not inflicted by the ministry of posts? They did—and it was. Israel's postal clerks should not have been criticized too harshly. Certainly none of the country's other government employees were called upon to perform as wide a variety of services as they. Indeed, the Israel post office was a kind of catch basin for public debts of all kinds. National savings premiums were paid there, as were water bills, electric bills, telephone bills—even police tickets. The accommodation was positively gratuitous in its magnitude.

Actually, of all the various social services, only the telephone exchange legitimately fell within the purview of the ministry of posts. To be sure, it was not an outstandingly effective utility, nor even a passably adequate one. And not infrequently it was blameless for the more flagrant breakdowns in public communication. It was hardly responsible for the switchboards of the government ministries or the Jewish Agency. Citizens attempting to ring up offices there usually spent five to thirty minutes steadily dialing and redialing before the line was free. The reason was probably a simple one. Many a switchboard girl preferred to reduce her work load by the ingenious expedient of keeping half her lines continually "engaged"—i.e., not pulling out the plugs.

Still, in many other cases the ministry of posts bore its share of the guilt. For example, not long ago a friend of mine, after wondering about the unusual silence of her telephone, lifted the receiver and discovered that the mechanism was apparently dead. Upon calling the complaint department from a neighbor's home, she was coolly informed that her telephone had been disconnected for nonpayment of her bill. My friend checked all her bills at once and found that they had been paid punctually; the last one, February 25, had been paid at the post office and was stamped March 5. After some difficulty, she finally reached the appropriate clerk in the accounting department. The man listened sympathetically.

"Very well," he agreed. "We'll check the matter. If it turns out that your bill has been paid we'll see to it that your phone is reconnected."

"But when?"

"Soon," came the reply. "Sometime this week—maybe next."

Could one have asked for a more understanding response?

Yet matters were hardly better in any other of the country's so-called "public services." Whichever ministry of government one approached, whichever bank, clinic, insurance company, bus or rail station, the circumstances were almost invariably the same: lax, indifferent, even insolent clerks, occasionally rude, not infrequently contemptuous of the supplicants who approached their desks, never for a moment bestirring themselves to extend an unsolicited courtesy. And the public: harassed, nerve-shot, frustrated often beyond endurance, eyeing the seated public officials with disgust bordering on fury. The clerk and the citizen: dwellers on the same streets, shoppers at the same stores, parents of children in the same schools, tent mates in the same army reserve camps; but in a public office sworn antagonists.

What were the reasons? Did they lie in the presiding fact of freedom in a Jewish State, where at long last one man was as good as the next, where *chutzpah* served as proof of one's revived dignity as a Jew? Did they lie in the egalitarian nature of the social-welfare State, the fact that deference, the instinct to serve, even common politeness, were frequently associated with the alleged class consciousness of the capitalist nations? Perhaps, but only partly. The fundamental reason was probably much simpler. The Israel Civil Service had been established in the midst of the chaos wrought by the termination of the British Mandate and the outbreak of war with the Arabs. It had never recovered.

In the beginning, most of the new government's employees had to be hastily co-opted from four principal sources: Jews who had served in the Mandatory administration; officials of the Jewish Agency and of the Va'ad Leumi, the former Jewish local self-government apparatus; veterans of the Underground or men and women who had compiled outstanding records in the War of Liberation (as a rule these people were hired with scant regard for their actual job qualifications); finally, officials of the various political parties, who generally were awarded the senior posts. All the lower ranks, however—telephone operators, minor clerks, stenographers—were usually hired through the Histadrut (Labor Federation) employment exchanges. Only in the more specialized upper-middle levels did a Civil Service panel evaluate and select applicants on the basis of comparative qualifications. Yet here the procedure was often extremely complicated. Fully six months could pass before a job opening was defined and confirmed, examinations prepared, administered, and graded, and applicants finally interviewed. And so a large number of posts remained chronically unfilled. Rather than begin the entire process of examinations and interviews anew whenever employees left, ministry officials simply drew from back lists of applicants. Not surprisingly, these were often quite inferior people.

Yet it was not this haphazard selection method alone which accounted for the Civil Service's generally inferior personnel. The financial inducement was pathetically inadequate. In the Mandatory administration there had been a clear-cut hierarchy of positions and salary gradations. Salaries of top officials were usually ten times higher than those in the lowest ranks. In socialist, egalitarian Israel, on the other hand, senior Civil Service officials received only three times the salaries of those in the lowest grades (compared with a ratio of 8 to 1 in Britain, and 12 to 1 in the United States). With inflation, the rise of the cost-of-living index, and steeply graded income taxes, this ratio was later actually narrowed from 3 to 1 to 1.3 to 1. As a result, the best-qualified people either left or shunned the Civil Service altogether.

Public inefficiency could also be attributed, in large measure, to plain and simple *shlumperei* in planning. This was well documented in a series of penetrating articles by Edwin Samuel, former lecturer in public administration at the Hebrew University. Even the simplest operations were frequently wrapped in endless quantities of red tape, Samuel pointed out. Some processes, such as issuing pay checks for newly appointed officials, often went through a score of different offices, and literally took months to complete. At other times there was a great deal of overlapping. Buck passing was endemic. Some routine operations awaited individual decision by senior officials when subordinates could as easily have disposed of them—but subordinates were too often suspect because they belonged to rival political parties. Not infrequently senior officials going on leave issued strict instructions against making any decisions whatever during their absence. The ensuing chaos often required weeks and months to repair.

Perhaps the Civil Service's most serious inadequacies, however, resulted from the limitations of a new and overburdened State. Fully two thirds of the government ministries were located in ancient ramshackle buildings or

barracks that would have been considered inadequate even in the most impoverished Balkan nation. Some of the leading officials in the country sat
in offices that were narrow, ugly, badly illuminated, and frequently grimly
underfurnished. For employees on the lower levels, and certainly for the
various clerks and minor functionaries, accommodations usually resembled
third-rate shipping offices, cluttered up with old files, discarded equipment,
and teacups. Packed into these tiny rooms, three and four employees were
obliged to perform their duties while yet another clerk in their midst carried on a telephone conversation. For that matter, employees and the public
alike had perfected to a fine art the habit of walking unannounced into any
room where an interview was in progress and casually interrupting the
proceedings "just for a moment" to settle an "urgent" matter.

The hours of work proved no less debilitating than the physical accommodations. Opportunities for a hot lunch were all but nonexistent, for there
were few good, cheap restaurants to be found near government offices.
Neither did ministry buildings possess staff canteens capable of serving hot
meals. It was theoretically possible, of course, for an employee to return
home for lunch; but bus service was slow and expensive. Hence, the practice developed of a single working period, from 7:30 A.M. to 2:30 P.M., with
only a brief coffee (or tea) interval at mid-morning. Civil servants who had
breakfast at 6:30 A.M. got home for lunch eight hours and a half later, at
3:00 P.M. It was a rare employee who could generate enough energy to perform his work efficiently—or courteously—during the last hour or two of
the day.

Yet even the limited facilities that did exist for government workers were
usually acquired the hard way, by the workers themselves. During the early
months of Statehood the vacuum of responsible leadership in the Civil
Service was filled by the Histadrut, the Labor Federation. Committees of
employees began laying the ground rules for working conditions. Frankly
relieved that this responsibility was being assumed by others, the government in late 1948 went so far as to sign a contract with the Histadrut, promising that all future changes in the conditions of employment for public
servants, as well as job reclassification for present workers, would first be
negotiated with the workers' committees themselves. From the moment this
authority over jobs was abdicated, it became all but impossible for a government ministry to dismiss an inefficient or insolent employee. So-called
"disciplinary" courts existed to hear cases involving inefficient or fractious
workers; but they were usually dominated by Histadrut representatives—
who were loath to invoke serious penalties against their own. In practice
this meant simply that civil servants with a year or more of seniority were
virtually immune to dismissal. All too often the manner in which they
performed their duties reflected this smug sense of invulnerability.

Thus, the people who were inherited from the first postindependence
years stayed on. Among them, working cheek by jowl with the other competent employees, were the time servers and file fumblers, the misfits and
the uncouth. Nothing could be done about them—ever. They were chained
to their desks, butter-fingered, lead-footed, and irascible, until the age of

their mandatory retirement. But—for the future—there was a glimmer of hope. The Israel Civil Service Commission was founded in 1950. To be sure, in its early years this institution was quite shaky, for it was shuttled back and forth between the office of the State comptroller, the prime minister's office, and, finally, its present home in the ministry of the treasury. The first commissioner, Ze'ev Sharef, resigned in a huff at the failure of the Histadrut to agree to his reforms. Sharef's successor, David Rosolio, was blocked for years from inaugurating crucial improvements in the dismissal system.

Slowly, nevertheless, a workable set of procedures was evolved. The practice of indiscriminately drawing middle- and lower-rank personnel from the labor exchanges was eventually abandoned. Candidates for jobs were obliged to pass competitive examinations. Within each ministry a training division was established, offering courses in public administration, routine office management, and—not least of all—public relations. Annual prizes were offered for efficiency and courtesy. IBM machines are now operating in the larger file offices. Today the results of these efforts are increasingly visible. Routine applications are handled with fair to moderate dispatch. The younger clerks manage somehow to control their tempers. By 1963 the Israel Civil Service had nearly reached the performance level of 1947, when the British Mandatory regime controlled Palestine's affairs.

Edwin Samuel was partially responsible for the most important improvements. His university courses in public administration were widely attended by government employees. As a member of the Civil Service Commission, he persuaded his colleagues to accept some of the basic innovations worked out in the United States and in western European countries. By personal example, too, he lost no opportunity to introduce Western-style efficiency in Israel's public services.

"Sometimes people overlook the most obvious methods," he complained. "I once accompanied a department head through his employees' offices. Files were lying about in disorder, glasses of tea in open drawers, clerks were consulting outdated instructions—so many errors that the department head could hardly remember them all by the time he returned to his desk. I had to call his attention to the simple device of carrying a little black book with him, and listing errors where and when he found them. If he had worked with the Mandatory Civil Service, as I had, he would have made the little black book his rule number one."

It was a typically British approach. It had been tried before by English Jews, who, like Samuel, had participated as civil servants in various echelons of the Mandatory administration. There were never more than a few hundred of these Anglo-Jewish public officials—although the most important of them, Samuel's father, Lord Herbert Samuel, had served as the first British High Commissioner for Palestine. As late as 1963, the total Anglo-Jewish population in Israel numbered a modest six thousand. The great majority of these were comparative newcomers who had arrived during and after the establishment of the State. Nearly five hundred of them had participated in the War of Liberation. Twice that many had settled on kibbutzim. Three of the most celebrated collective farms in the land, Kfar Blum, Kfar HaNasi, and Beit HaEmek, had been founded by British Jews, and eleven others were largely Anglo-Jewish in membership.

Nevertheless, as representatives of a middle-class community, by far the largest number of British-Jewish immigrants preferred to resume their former occupations in their new homeland. Several thousand entered business and professional life; while perhaps a sixth of the entire British *aliyah* found employment in Israel's public services, as government, Jewish Agency, bank, and insurance officials. The connection was logical: in large measure the Israel Civil Service was based on the Mandatory model; as a member of the sterling bloc, moreover, Israel cleared most of its overseas financial transactions through British banks—and needed functionaries with experience in those banks. Hardly less important was the fact that the small number of British Jews who remained from Mandatory times were well-ensconced in Israel's government and economic life, and thus were in a position to hire their recently arrived countrymen. On a much smaller scale, therefore, the newcomers from England duplicated the function performed by the German-Jewish immigration wave of the 1930s: bringing order, efficiency, discipline, and thoroughness to their tasks. Where the most notable improvements appeared in the standards of clerical performance, it was not uncommon to find Britishers responsible.

These middle-class attributes were hardly less typical of other English-speaking immigrants. The South Africans, for example, demonstrated a marked propensity for business. It was not difficult in their case. They were a wealthy community, and their *émigrés* to Israel usually brought sizable deposits of capital with them. For that matter, investment in and contributions to the Jewish State had long been an honored tradition even for those who entertained no thought of emigration. The 110,000 Jews of South Africa traditionally contributed more per capita to Zionist causes than any other Jewish community in the world; until 1962, when transfer of capital from South Africa was blocked by government decree, their proportional contribution was three times larger than that of any other national Jewry. The South African rate of settlement in Israel was hardly less impressive: 3,500 newcomers since 1948—far larger proportionally than the number of immigrants from other sheltered Western countries.

There were several reasons for this unprecedented Zionist activism. The South Africans themselves insisted that it derived from the warm Jewish loyalties of a common East European ancestry. Outsiders argued, with equal validity, that South African Jews viewed Israel as a reserve homeland; no Jew could feel secure any longer under a race-baiting Boer government. Either way, Israel was the beneficiary. A fourth of the South African *aliyah* (nearly all of it post-1948) settled on the land, founding a chain of kibbutzim and moshavim, and joining other collective farms in large numbers. Many hundreds of South African Jews resumed their medical and dental practices in Israel. A rather large minority entered the foreign office and the diplomatic service, the army and air force. Two South Africans were members of the Cabinet, another a member of the Knesset. Two were mayors.

But their principal contribution was to the nation's business life. Some of the most important companies in Israel owed their growth and development to South African capital. Among them were dress factories, banks, mortgage and insurance companies, and scores of other middle-sized businesses, ranging from cold-storage plants to metalwork factories. These were invariably among the most efficient and profitable enterprises in the country.

Perhaps the South Africans' most important single contribution to Israel was the coastal city of Ashkelon. In 1953 Israel's government planners decided that the economy and defense of the country required the immediate establishment of an urban settlement on the dunes eight miles north of the Gaza Strip. Within months of this decision, South African investors, in partnership with the South African Zionist Federation and the Israel government, decided to assume responsibility for the project. Today the results of their enterprise may be seen in a lovely garden city of some fifteen thousand people. Planned on the neighborhood unit principle, Ashkelon consists of five residential areas, an industrial zone, and a shore area, all separated by green belts—superb gardens planted with colorful displays of anemones, jasmine, mignonette, violets, and rhododendrons; while in the town center there is commercial enclave, in which shops and restaurants are ranked together in a broad, handsome piazza, dominated by a graceful clock tower. Today Ashkelon is more than a defense bulwark against Arab infiltration; economically and architecturally, it is one of the showpieces of Israel.

But even for the South Africans, whose financial affluence was fully matched by Zionist enthusiasm, the State of Israel proved an investor's nightmare. Businessmen with large sums at their disposal searched in vain for information about financial opportunities. During the first two or three years after the War of Liberation, Tel Aviv rang with the cries of irate inquirers lost in a bureaucratic maze. Everywhere applicants encountered the same lack of organization and of final responsibility among conflicting and confused government bureaus. In some degree, of course, the anarchy resulted from the British departure, when basic statistical records of costs, production, markets, and other investment data had been displaced or scattered around the country. But delay and waste were compounded, as well, by an almost total governmental ignorance of investor needs. In the crucial years of 1949–1950, for example, when Israel was teetering on the edge of bankruptcy, the ministry of trade and industry—the first port of call for any likely investor—was left without any minister at all, for internal political reasons. The result was the alienation of countless Western businessmen whose capital was desperately needed.

Several more years had to pass before the Israel government finally profited from the lessons of this disastrous confusion. At the suggestion of consulting American economists, a Central Investment Center was established in Tel Aviv. Simultaneously, the Knesset passed a series of laws designed to woo the capital of even the most cautious foreign industrialists. Vital inducements were offered for non-Israelis contemplating the investment of $25,000 or more in an "approved" enterprise. These inducements included substantial government loans, land, even buildings, at the most nominal of rates—plus important tax write-offs, and the assurance that investors might withdraw no less than 10 per cent of their *gross* income in dollars annually. The new approach proved dramatically successful. By the late 1950s foreign capital began arriving in impressive quantities from South Africa, Europe, the United States, Canada, and South America. New industries sprang up, manufacturing such diverse products as chemicals, plastics, textiles, tires, motor scooters, and automobiles. Western-financed hotels and housing projects studded the countryside.

The big investor, as a result, no longer found serious cause for complaint. It was the small-business man who was overlooked in this sudden onrush of government hospitality; especially the Western immigrant, usually an American or Canadian, who arrived in Israel with a modest nest egg and grandiose notions of creating a bourgeois oasis for himself in the Labor Zionist desert. Nothing whatever was done to ease his reception. On the contrary, for him the bureaucratic rat maze was frequently even more oppressive than for the most penniless European or Oriental newcomer. For example, at the customs he was instructed to make a detailed list of all personal goods he had brought with him, or anticipated bringing to Israel within the next twelve months. Guarantees had to be secured for these items as assurance that they would not be sold to Israelis (not so for a really wealthy immigrant; he was his own guarantor). This required a trip to Tel Aviv, and to the invaluable Association of Americans and Canadians. With each shipment of personal effects the routine was repeated: a trip to Haifa, then to Tel Aviv, then back to Haifa. And in Haifa itself the familiar nightmare of customship was repeated: shuttle trips from the official who filled out the forms, to the one who inspected the goods, to the third who made the evaluations (often quite arbitrary evaluations), to the fourth who accepted and registered the guarantees. The time and money required for this procedure invariably took the bloom off the hapless newcomer's Zionist enthusiasm.

The immigrant needed a home for himself and his family. While still in the United States (or Canada, or England, or South Africa), he had been assured that housing in Israel was cheap. Indeed it was. For Moroccan or Iraqi immigrants, in fact, it was virtually free—a squalid aluminum shack empty of the most elementary human comforts. For immigrants with modest sums at their disposal, there were government- or Jewish Agency-sponsored *shikoonim,* small flats without central heating, available for a down payment of a mere two thousand pounds. But few Westerners were willing to install their families in apartments measuring no more than fifty square yards. Moreover, *shikoonim* were generally located in Oriental neighborhoods where social life by Western standards was all but impossible. As a rule, the newcomer preferred to look elsewhere.

Yet once having made this decision, the American immigrant deprived himself of all further access to officially underwritten, inexpensive housing. A friend of mine, for example, who pressed on in his search for an adequate flat, discovered to his horror that no less than twenty thousand pounds were required even for the most minimal of accommodations. He finally succeeded in extracting a housing loan of four thousand pounds from the Jewish Agency at 8 per cent interest. Of course it was not enough. He applied to a bank. The bank offered a five-thousand-pound loan at 11 per cent interest. Not enough. He applied to the Association of Americans and Canadians. The interest rates were as low at 2 per cent here, but the waiting list for loans was two years long. In the end the harassed newcomer decided to rent a flat. Here, alas, the cheapest rates were a crippling two hundred pounds a month. Nevertheless, the immigrant rented on faith, still confident somehow that he would earn enough in Israel to meet his expenses.

With the remainder of his nest egg, the Western newcomer set about opening a small business. Once again return visits were paid to the customs office in Haifa, for the settler had made provisions to import his tools of trade. These items were ostensibly duty free. But only ostensibly. From the outset, the suspicious clerks took a narrow view of what constituted a "tool of trade." If the newcomer was a hardware dealer—as my friend was—the customs official insisted that his office adding machine was a "luxury item," and assessed duty on it. Other office equipment shared the same fate. If the businessman planned to open a sweet shop, he was obliged to pay duty on his coffee-grinding machine. ("Serving coffee with sweets is for coffee shops, not sweet shops," explained the customs officials.) In one well-publicized incident, a man imported twenty hair dryers for his projected beauty salon. The clerk insisted that ten were enough, and assessed duty on the rest. Several months later the newcomer was forced to sell all his machines; the expense of paying the duty had left him flat broke.

For those Western immigrants who still remained solvent after their initial skirmishes with the customs, the next stop was to secure business premises. As a rule, these were considerably more expensive than private flats. Again, a loan was indispensable. Theoretically, the Central Investment Center was available for this purpose. But in the years that had passed since the establishment of the Center (in 1952), less than two hundred Western small-business men had succeeded in procuring funds from this institution. Apparently the ministry of commerce and industry preferred to concentrate its efforts on large-scale enterprises, those potentially capable of reaching the export market. And so the small investor turned frantically elsewhere. My friend the hardware dealer tried the banks. Understandably, the banks asked for collateral. He offered as security his "Western-style" business experience, his record of financial success in the United States. It was not enough. He turned elsewhere, this time once again to the Jewish Agency. And here, to his relieved surprise, he was at least partially successful. The Agency finally lent him ten thousand pounds—on the strength of three signed guarantees. With the remnants of his nest egg, he finally managed to open his shop.

Until that moment his troubles had not been irretrievable. They were now; my friend had committed himself. He soon discovered, for example, that the bureaucracy, which he had believed safely behind him in Haifa, had stealthily crept up on him and joined his business as a silent partner. Each receipt sent out by the employer required stamp taxes affixed at the bottom.

Each product sold required purchase taxes paid and the appropriate stamps attached in advance. Each time he paid an employee's salary he was obliged to withhold not merely the man's income tax, but also his national insurance premium, his joint savings payment, his medical and hospitalization payment, and his pension payment. This was not entirely an unfamiliar routine for American businessmen, perhaps. With the exception of the income tax, however, the Israeli employer shared all these expenses. And more: he was now obliged to pay for his employee's holidays (the Jewish calendar had nearly a month of them), as well as partial salary for the thirty-one days the employee spent on reserve duty in the defense forces.

It required, in addition, a rather formidable effort for the American to adjust to Israel's exotic business practices. For one thing, customers were opposed on principle to making payments in cash: the IOU was all but legal tender here. And even when, in a momentary fit of philanthropy, the customer did pay in "cash," he took the trouble to postdate his check. Generally speaking, suppliers were less reliable even than customers: they *never* delivered on time; the quality of their goods was *never* consistent. Little was accomplished by threatening them. They knew that their competitors were, if possible, even less reliable than they. If they seemed curiously unworried about the loss of their reputation, therefore, this was due at least in part to a vaguely comforting suspicion that neither they nor their colleagues nor their competitors had reputations to lose.

In spite of these obstacles—in red tape and business inefficiency—Americans and Canadians continued to settle in Israel. However difficult circumstances were for them, life was infinitely easier than for the majority of the immigrants—who had arrived, after all, as penniless refugees. Nevertheless, one is tempted to ask why, in any case, these Westerners should have decided to leave the comfort and security of their native lands for the lean hills of Judah. As a rule the explanation could be summed up in a single phrase: Zionist idealism. By the 1950s and 1960s the newcomers from Anglo-Saxon countries were virtually the only Zionist purists left in the Jewish world. Not all of them, of course. Several hundred were Orthodox religionists of the old school who had come to Jerusalem to live out their lives in pious semimendicancy. A few were misfits and social cases whom their families or Jewish communal agencies had sent to Israel simply to get them out of the way. Others were confused romantics or escapists who viewed the beleaguered Israel Republic as a kind of foreign legion. But there were several thousand, too, by far the majority, who were products of well-organized Zionist youth groups. Like the ardent Hebrew nationalists of the early Russian-Jewish *aliyot,* their devotion to the cause of Jewish Statehood was deeply rooted and intellectually buttressed.

Actually, American Jewish settlement in Palestine dates back even further than the Zionist immigration of the 1880s. By a strange quirk of history, its forerunner was a converted Christian, Warder Cresson, the first United States consul in Palestine. Deeply influenced (according to his own testimony) by the biblical reminders he encountered whenever he traveled in the Holy Land, Cresson embraced Judaism in 1849, had himself circumcised, and changed his name to Michael Boaz Israel. The State Department, scandalized by the consul's behavior, immediately dismissed him from his job and ordered him back to the United States. Michael Boaz Israel had different plans. Settling down permanently in Jerusalem, he established a large farm on the outskirts of the city. Within the next four years nearly two hundred Americans emigrated to join his colony, fifty-two of them Jews, the rest converts to Judaism or practicing Protestants. Yet in spite of the millenarian devotion of Boaz' coworkers, the colony gradually sank into oblivion; the opposition of the Jerusalem rabbinate, which anathematized "secular" labor, proved too formidable to withstand.

Nevertheless, in the years that followed, a trickle of American Jews continued to arrive in the Holy Land, until by 1900 over a thousand had made their home there. With few exceptions, these newcomers were European-born. Many were Orthodox pietists, others fugitives from the Russian May Laws who had been unsuccessful in the United States and who now sought employment on Baron Rothschild's plantations. But there were yet others, increasing numbers of them, who were animated by the emergent Zionist ideal, who came determined to revive the barren wilderness of their ancestral homeland. During the First World War two thousand American Jews served with the Jewish Legion, and half of these stayed in Palestine during the period of the Third *Aliyah* to become private farmers, and founders of the moshav movement. Approximately three thousand American small-business men arrived in the Fourth *Aliyah* of the mid-1920s, and nearly a thousand others up to and including the early years of World War II.

Moreover, between 1945 and 1948, in the period of the Underground rescue effort, American crews manned ten refugee vessels, and were responsible for transporting fully 40 per cent of the "illegals" to Palestine (see Chapter 11). During the War of Liberation, nearly two thousand Americans and Canadians served in the Mahal, the brigade of overseas volunteers who participated in the Jewish defense forces. Several Israel army units were made up almost entirely of English-speaking volunteers, particularly the air force, where English remained for many years afterward the principal language of command. Most of the Americans and Canadians were World War II veterans, and by now, too, nearly all of them were native-born. Eighty of these volunteers were killed in action during the Palestine war.

Inevitably, however, the major growth of the American and Canadian *aliyah* awaited the "normalcy" of Statehood. Thus, between 1948 and 1963, the total North American population in Israel swelled to fourteen thousand. Few of the newcomers actually opted for Israel citizenship. The great majority kept their former passports, registering with the ministry of the interior as "temporary" or even "permanent" residents. Yet for all practical purposes they belonged to the Israel population; they bought or rented homes in Israel, earned their livelihoods there, paid taxes and spent their money there. They founded several new kibbutzim: Sassa, Kissufim, Gesher-HaZiv, and Urim. Of the twenty-seven settlements established by English-speaking settlers, the Americans were responsible for sixteen. Several hundred other Americans and Canadians joined existing kibbutzim and moshavim.

Yet the largest number of them, perhaps 80 per cent, did not become farmers. Their Zionist idealism was beyond question, of course. It was simply that most of them preferred to contribute to their new country in ways they knew best. There were among the newcomers many hundreds of teachers, doctors, dentists, engineers, chemists, optometrists, soil agronomists, botanists, zoologists, and technicians of one sort or another. They resumed their activities in Israel. Nearly a thousand found employment in the government, the Jewish Agency, the Jewish National Fund, Bonds for Israel, the United Jewish Appeal, and other national institutions—as well as in banks, travel agencies, publishing companies, insurance offices, and the like. Two or three hundred were large-scale industrialists, or executive managers of important factories. But the rest (like our friend of several pages ago) were small-business men, or business consultants. On their own, they were determined to bring "American-style" efficiency to the economic wasteland of Israel. Despite—as we have seen—continual and persistent harassment, their accomplishments were not unimpressive. By the early 1960s the Americans had won security for themselves. Indeed, their modest, carefully operated enterprises had become models for the rest of the country.

Most of these American entrepreneurs were quite willing to share the secrets of their success. They recognized, after all, that if order, competency, and reliability could be introduced to the Israel market, opportunities for profit would be improved for everyone, native and immigrant alike. George Friedman was an effective advocate of this kind of enlightened self-interest. A native of the Bronx, educated at the City College of New York and the Harvard Business School, he had earned a comfortable living in New York as the executive manager of a hobby-tool factory. Friedman's interest in Zionism had been friendly, but perfunctory. Then, in 1956, he paid a casual tourist's visit to Israel. The experience proved a deeply moving one. Determined to return at the first opportunity, he applied for an assignment there on the U.S. Technical Cooperation Program. Finally, in 1959, the American government selected Friedman as one of a small panel of marketing experts to be sent to Israel to conduct seminars for Israel businessmen. This time he brought his wife and two children with him. When the seminars ended, he stayed on to help the Israel government establish a management school; and in 1961 he decided to open his own office in Tel Aviv as an independent marketing consultant.

Friedman had been in the country long enough by then to recognize that the field was open for him. To be sure, Israelis had made undeniable progress in technology, in the production and quality control of agricultural or manufactured goods. But their selling techniques remained hopelessly primitive. Friedman had learned this by personal experience no less than by "scientific" research. Item: His wife walked into the well-known Iwanir dress shop.

"I need a white sweater," she explained to the salesgirl.

The salesgirl looked at the sweater Mrs. Friedman was wearing: "What for?" she asked. "You've already got a sweater."

Item: Seated in a train, Friedman watched a sandwich vendor approaching, sullenly elbowing his way through the passengers crowded in the aisle.

"Sandwich?" said Friedman, fishing out some coins from his pocket.

Grumbling, the vendor plowed on through the crowd, ignoring Friedman's outstretched hand.

"Sandwich?" shouted Friedman at the man's retreating back.

"If you're that hungry," the vendor shouted over his shoulder, "you can come out onto the platform."

Item: In search of office equipment, Friedman sent off a letter to a well-known furniture company in Haifa, asking if the firm sold a certain type of filing cabinet. Weeks passed without an answer. Finally, with time running short, Friedman telephoned the company direct.

"Yes, we received your letter," admitted the salesman at the other end of the line. "But what was the point of answering? We didn't have what you wanted."

Item: On one occasion Friedman sent out letters to twenty transportation agencies, asking for bids on a special bus-service for his seminars. The answers read variously: from "Please come to our office in Tel Aviv and explain yourself more clearly," to "Your letter is not clear. Please phone us and explain exactly what you want," to no answers at all. Only two companies offered to send representatives to Friedman's office.

Something had to be done.

"You people have improved your production methods," Friedman counseled a group of businessmen, "but it won't do you a bit of good if you don't learn how to sell what you produce. You need good salesmen."

"Salesmen!" they scoffed in reply. "Who wants to be a salesman in this country? It's a dirty word, like a kind of peddler, or delivery boy. If we have the goods, people will buy."

But evidently they would not buy any longer. With statistics, Friedman proved that the seller's market was over, that it was no longer possible for a manufacturer to sell every item he produced. First-rate salesmen were needed now, as well as attractive packaging, advertising, and sales research.

"We can't afford it," was the unanimous answer. "Our expenses are too high as it is."

"You can't afford not to," Friedman insisted.

Yet in spite of his ample collection of facts, statistics, and examples, Friedman found that his Israel listeners were profoundly reluctant at first to accept this "Western" approach to the local market. Most of these businessmen were transplanted Poles or Russians; they had brought with them the lackadaisical and slovenly business methods of their native lands. In Israel, moreover, east European *shlumperei* was compounded by the provincial bargaining traditions of the Oriental bazaar—and perhaps, too, by the years of austerity that had severely restricted all possibility of business expansion. Nevertheless, by the 1960s more goods were available and consumer purchasing power was growing. So was competition, both within Israel and in the export market abroad. These were the factors, far more than his own persuasiveness, that proved decisive with Friedman's clients.

One of his first accounts was *Superior,* the largest nut and bolt manufacturer in the country, and probably the best. The owner of the firm was a deeply worried man.

"I have the finest engineers and workmen money can buy," he complained. "Our product used to be a household word among builders. Now what happens? No matter what price I offer building contractors, my competitors undercut me with a simple proposition: 'My price is *Superior's* less five per cent,' they say. And the contractors take them up on it."

Friedman had the answer before the man closed his mouth. "The very fact that they adjust their rates to yours and no one else's is a good sign," he explained. "It means that *Superior* is still a household word. But the general public has to know it. You need to advertise among the consuming public. Make them insist upon *Superior.* No contractor will dare to turn you down after that."

After some persuasion, the owner finally agreed. Friedman launched a general advertising campaign. It worked. Business picked up once again. Indeed, *Superior's* sales actually exceeded their former volume.

The Hadera Paper Mills were next. Orders for their products had been notably weak of late. The moment Friedman analyzed the situation he discovered that the company had no advertising budget whatever.

"Who needs it?" protested the managing director. "There isn't another paper company worthy of the name in Israel. If people want paper, they'll buy from us."

"Agreed," said Friedman. "And so people simply have to be persuaded to use more paper."

He tackled the problem with zest. His advertising campaign emphasized the importance of reading, of writing thoughtful holiday cards, of friendly correspondence between family and friends. Friedman sent experts to teach printers how to produce more attractive stationery. Spot radio announcements and placards on buses urged the public to buy only those products that were wrapped in paper. After four months of drum beating on this theme, the paper mills' sales began to rise.

Soon Friedman was deluged with clients. He accepted some of them. Most of them he trained voluntarily in the government-sponsored management school. In each three-month course he laid special emphasis upon the importance of courtesy in dealing with the public.

"People will judge your products by your salespeople and clerks," he insisted. "Rudeness is a luxury these days. It can turn a potential profit into a dead loss."

So would slovenly displays, insufficient advertising, careless packaging and wrapping. He made his point with countless examples drawn from his experience both in the United States and Israel. His students—businessmen, plant managers, even army officers—were fascinated. One of the most enthusiastic pupils was the owner of a medium-sized (for Israel) insurance company. A young man, still in his thirties, he accosted Friedman in the hallway after one of the lectures.

"Mr. Friedman, you're the man for me," he declared grandly. "Please call me at my office when you have a chance. I want you to handle my marketing campaign."

Friedman agreed; the account would be worth a small fortune. A week later he phoned the insurance company. The line was busy. He phoned again. Still busy. Off and on for nearly two days Friedman attempted to get an open line. Finally he succeeded.

"I want to talk to Mr. Zilberberg," he said wearily.

"Hold on," answered the operator.

He did—for ten minutes. After frantic jiggling and shouting into the mouthpiece he heard an ominous click. He had been disconnected.

On the third day he tried again. This time the line was free, and he was connected immediately with Zilberberg's secretary.

"Yes, what?" the woman snapped into the phone.

"I want to talk to Mr. Zilberberg."

"What about?" came the waspish answer.

"Geveret, I want to make an appointment with him," Friedman replied coldly.

"Sorry, he's busy all this week." Click.

Laying down the receiver, Friedman watched his hands shaking. Then he picked up the phone and dialed again. No success. And again. Finally a connection. Once more he spoke to the owner's secretary.

"Geveret, I would advise you not to hang up on me again," he warned. "Mr. Zilberberg himself asked me to call him."

"You don't say?" came the skeptical answer. "And I told you that he's busy this week. What do you want to see him about?"

"It's about a marketing campaign he wants me to handle for him."

"Write me a letter," replied the secretary.

"I don't do things that way. Suppose you make an appointment for me to see him. Right now. Open his calendar."

"Mr. Zilberberg's calendar is on his desk," said the secretary. "Anyway, I can't make any appointments without consulting him, and he's busy."

"Geveret—"

"I'll connect you with his assistant, Mr. Har-Zahav."

Before Friedman could protest, the telephone clicked again. A bedlam of voices could be heard at the other end of the line: "Get Har-Zahav . . . What, out? Where? . . . On vacation, I think . . . No, out for tea . . . Wait, maybe in Malka's office . . . Har-Zahav, Har-Zahav! HAR-ZAHAV! Answer the phone, will you . . . How do I know? Some *nudnik* [nuisance] from an advertising agency . . ."

And at last: "Har-Zahav speaking. What's the emergency?"

Icily, Friedman replied in English, enunciating his words with great care: "And this is Mr. George Friedman speaking, of the Government Management School. Mr. Zilberberg was a pupil of mine. He asked me to call him immediately about an important private matter."

"Oh, very nice," mumbled Har-Zahav. He could be heard swallowing his tea. "What about?"

"About a private matter, I said. Would you prefer that I speak in Hebrew?"

"No, I understand you all right," insisted Har-Zahav. "But I'm his chief assistant. You should tell me first."

"If I don't speak to Mr. Zilberberg within thirty seconds," replied Friedman, "I shall tell HaSneh [Zilberberg's principal competitor]. And I shall write a letter to Mr. Zilberberg explaining to him who was responsible. Do you understand me?"

A long pause at the other end. Then—"Oh well, all right. Take it easy. No need to get nasty."

Friedman eventually got his appointment. When he met Zilberberg in his office, his first suggestion was brief and pungent. "You want to sell more insurance? Then fire your telephone operators, your secretary, and your chief assistant. That's the best advice I can give you and it's free."

"Relax, Mr. Friedman," replied the owner genially. "Employees can't be fired that easily these days. Anyway, I'm sure it was just a slight misunderstanding. We get calls from so many *nudniks* telling us how to run our business, you understand."

Friedman nodded glumly: Israel employees, he knew, could not be fired easily; in fact, they could not be fired at all. For the next two hours he sat with Zilberberg, analyzing the company's record of sales, the economic circumstances of its subscribers, the number of children in the neighborhoods where sales were heaviest. By the time the interview ended a plan was already forming in Friedman's mind. He needed several days to work it out. When he returned to Zilberberg for the next meeting he had mapped his campaign in detail, with charts and graphs. It was a masterpiece, he exulted to himself; Madison Avenue could not have cooked up anything better.

"You need a new product," he explained to the owner. "You have to sell your subscribers on something HaSneh hasn't yet thought of."

"Yes?" said Zilberberg eagerly.

"A group vacation plan," said Friedman, smiling triumphantly.

"A *what*? Workers already get two weeks' paid vacation time, don't you know that?"

"A group vacation plan," Friedman persisted, "covering expenses for the whole family."

Zilberberg's face clouded over. He thought for a moment, then shook his head. "No, no. My subscribers are simple working people," he explained. "They'll never go for it."

"How do you know?" snapped Friedman. "Have you asked them?"

"No . . . but . . . vacation plans . . . it's a luxury."

"Then we'll make it a necessity. The moment people get a taste of it they'll make it part of their annual routine." Warming to his subject, Friedman explained. "You already sell unemployment, accident, health, and retirement policies. What I want you to do is to raise people's standard of expectations. Make a healthy vacation in a nice resort part of a family's normal routine."

Zilberberg remained unconvinced. "How can I sell a 'resort' idea when most people have never been to one? The only thing they know about is those little Histadrut rest houses."

Friedman sighed. "Adoni," he explained patiently, "you have to begin on a trial basis. With each new group vacation premium you'll include a bonus of one free day at a nice seaside hotel."

Zilberberg fairly shrieked, "A free—a free day in a resort hotel! That will cost me a fortune. Do you think I'm in the charity business? Do you think I'm a philanthropist?"

Friedman reasoned with him, argued, remonstrated. It was a standard merchandising technique in the United States, he explained. The expense was minimal when compared to the potential increase in business. Besides, the cost was tax-deductible. But his eloquence was wasted; Zilberberg remained adamant.

"I give up," Friedman announced at last. "You wanted my ideas. I gave them to you. Delivering a free 'sample' is the best and cheapest way I know of promoting a new policy. It can save you all the trouble and expense of a market survey, of sending out questionnaires—"

"That's it!" shouted Zilberberg.

"What's it?"

"We'll send out questionnaires to all my customers, asking them if they want a group vacation policy. That way we'll know exactly if it's worthwhile."

This time Friedman was skeptical. "It takes so much time," he pointed out. "You have to keep after people to answer. Anyway, they won't know if they want a resort vacation until they actually try it."

"No, no," Zilberberg insisted, switching his position one hundred eighty degrees. "Everyone knows what a resort is. And all they'll have to do is leave their answers in their mailboxes."

And so a "market survey" was decided upon. Friedman sat with Har-Zahav for an entire afternoon, carefully working out the details of the questionnaire. The assistant had firm ideas of his own.

"This is the way it ought to be," he declared, handing Friedman a draft copy he had prepared personally.

> Spend two weeks in a lovely hotel, ladies and gentlemen [the draft read]. It will be the healthiest, most invigorating experience of the year. The whole family will love it. It is much more enjoyable than the usual *Pension* vacation. And it is hardly more expensive. You will find payment quite painless. Just join our group policy. Better than touring the country, much more relaxing. Are you interested? Just write out your answer in longhand, and be sure to sign it. Then stick it in your mailbox. We will take care of the rest. Thanking you in advance.
>
> > [signed] Mr. Yom-Tov Zilberberg.
> > Zilberberg Insurance Company
> > (In business since 1954).

Friedman read the draft, then groaned. " 'More enjoyable than the usual *Pension* vacation,' is it? Then why should anyone buy your *Pension* convalescence insurance? 'Better than touring the country,' you say. I thought you sold travel insurance, too? And who will take the trouble to write out an answer in longhand—and sign it? Maybe you want the answer notarized, too? Come on, Har-Zahav, leave this to me, will you?"

The assistant was offended. He persisted. Friedman dismissed his ideas firmly, then with increasing impatience.

"I'll tell you what let's do," Har-Zahav said at last, in a reasonable tone. "Let's ask the office staff for their reaction. Here, Rifka," he cried, handing the draft to one of the secretaries before Friedman could reply, "what do you think of my idea? Menasha, Simcha, come over here a minute."

As Friedman sat quietly, his head in his hands, the assistant polled three secretaries, two clerks, one office boy, and one telephone operator. The reactions were far from unanimous. Har-Zahav seemed disappointed.

"So, you can see it's not a simple matter," he observed finally, as if in partial triumph. "I think this will require committee action." He thought for a moment. "Yes, that's it, definitely, committee action. I'll discuss it with Mr. Zilberg at the first opportunity."

"When?" asked Friedman quietly.

The assistant shrugged helplessly. "When? How do I know when? Mr. Zilberg is a busy man. This isn't his only problem, you know."

The meeting took place at the end of the week. Crowded into the owner's dingy office were Zilberg, Har-Zahav, Friedman, two minor stockholders, and a recording secretary. It was a committee meeting, Israel style. As each man presented his viewpoint, the others interrupted, scoffed, argued, haggled, and expostulated. Friedman's own version was brief and pithy:

> We invite you to try an exciting vacation experience: two weeks in a luxury hotel of your choice. No more cutting corners and watching budgets. We will make this remarkable opportunity yours for a small addition to your monthly retirement premium. If you are interested, just tear off the yellow tab at the perforation line and leave it in the mailbox."

It was rejected out of hand. Too short, not enthusiastic enough, no assurance of participation.

"You don't want it too complicated," Friedman insisted. "And this is a survey, isn't it? You can't make a promise until you've evaluated the returns."

In the end, after two hours and forty-five minutes of further debate— interrupted nine times by telephone calls—Har-Zahav's version was approved with only minor amendments. Zilberg had 17,000 subscribers; it was decided to print 17,000 announcements. Five days passed before all bids were in from the printers. And it was another week before the printing was completed. Friedman walked in one day to find Har-Zahav's desk piled high with the packaged brochures.

"All ready?" asked Friedman. "That's fine. When will they be circulated?"

"What circulated?" croaked the assistant. "Who will circulate? You? I?"

"Why, the agents, of course. They stand to get a commission on future sales, don't they?"

After further interrogation, Friedman discovered that the insurance agents' union had held a special meeting, and had decided that the distribution of circulars represented "extra work." They were demanding additional wages for it. In the late afternoon Zilberberg called an emergency committee meeting.

"I won't pay it," he insisted furiously, banging his fist on the table. "It will cost me another thousand pounds before they get through."

Opinion was divided. No possibility existed of forcing the agents to deliver the circulars. On the other hand, stamps or professional mailbox stuffers would cost three times as much. Arguments flew back and forth: it was a matter of principle; it was not a matter of principle. The agents' union had been getting too high and mighty lately and ought to be taught a lesson; the delivery of circulars ought not to be the occasion for teaching a lesson. A compromise ought to be offered the union—a flat payment of five hundred pounds; the company should not yield an inch for fear of setting a precedent.

All the while the telephone rang incessantly. From time to time the secretary answered, jotting down the message perfunctorily, occasionally calling Zilberberg himself to the phone. Clerks interrupted the proceedings with "urgent" papers to be signed. Now and then customers would barge in, demanding to see Har-Zahav "just for a moment." Eventually, at 7:30 P.M. the compromise offer was agreed upon. The company would propose an additional payment of seven hundred pounds. A letter was drafted and sent off to the agents' union.

As the meeting broke up Zilberberg began to glance through the day's mail, which had been lying on his desk unopened. Friedman was the last to leave. As he stood at the door he noticed the owner's face slowly turning a mottled violet.

"Anything wrong, Mr. Zilberberg?" he asked, with some concern.

"Wrong?" gasped Zilberberg. "This letter . . . from the agents' union . . . yesterday they agreed on a compromise of five hundred pounds."

During the ensuing week Friedman waited patiently for word from the company. Presumably the circulars had already been distributed and the results tallied. Knowing whom he was dealing with by now, he was not eager to rush Zilberberg and his colleagues. In their own good time they would notify him. But then another week passed, and Friedman's concern mounted. Finally, reluctantly, he picked up the phone and placed a call. The line was busy, of course. He tried again several times during the morning, but without success. In the early afternoon, just before the company's closing time, he finally reached Har-Zahav.

"Oh, ah, yes, Mr. Friedman," stammered the assistant. "Can you call back in a few days. We're swamped right now. In a few days, please." He hung up.

Friedman tried again three days later. The secretary informed him that both Har-Zahav and Zilberberg were unavailable. Something was wrong.

On a hunch, Friedman drove over to the company. As he entered Har-Zahav's office he caught a glimpse of the assistant dashing out through a rear door. Friedman began perspiring; with this band of maniacs anything could have happened. Immediately he climbed the stairs to the second floor, and Zilberberg's office. The owner's secretary stared at Friedman in astonishment and confusion.

"Mr. Zilberberg is busy . . . is out . . ." she said, her voice rising hysterically as she corrected herself.

Without a word Friedman strode to the door of the inner office and opened it. Zilberberg was sitting there, drinking tea. For a moment the glass rattled on its saucer. Then—"Ah, shalom, Mr. Friedman," cried the owner, with strained cordiality. "I was just going to call you. How is Mrs. Friedman and the children?"

By now Friedman's shirt was drenched with perspiration. He approached the owner's desk cautiously. "The circulars," he muttered. "What's happened to them?"

"The circulars?" Zilberberg seemed genuinely surprised. "Uh—oh, I thought Har-Zahav phoned you. You see, we had another meeting after you left. The committee decided not to send them out after all."

Friedman groped for a chair and sat down.

"Sure you won't have some tea?" Zilberberg asked. "No? Well, you see, this was our reasoning. If we had sent the circulars out the response might have been favorable. Right?"

Friedman said nothing.

"On the other hand," the owner continued, "the response might have been unfavorable. People might not have wanted the vacation plan after all. Then the money we would have paid our agents and all the time spent counting up the circulars would have just been wasted. Down the drain, you understand. You could hardly expect us to go to all that effort for nothing. Could you?"

Friedman nodded dazedly.

Plainly relieved Zilberberg stood up. "I hope you'll be in touch with me soon, though. We owe you a real debt of gratitude. You have . . . you have, ah, clarified our thinking. Yes, that's definitely what you've done, clarified our thinking. I'm paying your fee in full, too, Mr. Friedman. With me an agreement is an agreement. My word is my bond."

Suddenly Friedman was on his feet, too. "I don't care about the damned fee," he blurted out. "I care about all our plans and preparations. We spent weeks working on that campaign. It was efficient, it was scientific, it was modern, Zilberberg, modern, just the way you wanted this company to be. Now you're pouring all that time and money down the drain."

"My dear fellow, you're taking this entirely the wrong way." Zilberberg smiled, all affability. "I personally think your ideas are very sound. The problem is simply to adjust them to the peculiar conditions of our country, that's all. We must sit down sometime soon and decide exactly what our approach should be. We'll do it soon, too—perhaps after *miluyim*."

"*Miluyim?*"

"Yes, reserve duty. I've been called up to the army the day after tomorrow. I'll be gone for a month of training."

"Mr. Zilberberg," Friedman protested, in anguish, "do you realize—?"

"Adoni." The owner stared at his visitor severely. "Are you going to suggest that our business takes priority over the nation's defense?" As Friedman's mouth dropped open, Zilberberg continued: "Every man has to do his duty in Israel, Mr. Friedman. When the army calls, we go." His head cocked back, as if he had heard a distant trumpet. "You Americans simply have to understand that."

"Adoni," moaned Friedman, "I have nothing against defending Israel—"

"Good, good, that's the attitude. We all have to make sacrifices to see our little country through these difficult times, don't we? As long as we are free we can solve our problems. We must be strong, well trained, efficient. You don't know these Arabs. They are just waiting for the chance to wreck this country." Instinctively he gazed out the window, his shoulders squared, his chin high, ready for combat. "The Arabs can destroy us, you understand?"

━━

CHAPTER FIVE

THE REFUGEE

THE DOOR swung open, and Musa Abu Sa'ad al-Abid was brought in. The light in the tiny room was harsh, and the man shrank in sudden terror against the wall. Then, prodded by a policeman, he advanced hesitantly toward my chair. He was of average height, and quite thin. Blue cotton dungarees hung loosely on his emaciated frame. He was a Negro. Sitting down, he glanced at the guard in confusion, and I noticed the bullet scar on his left cheek.

"No one will bother you, Musa," said Major Bondet, seated beside me. "The gentleman has a few questions. Just answer them frankly. Nothing will happen."

As the remarks were translated into Arabic, the Negro stared at me for a moment, his eyes glittering, and then lowered his head. He whispered something to the guard.

"Musa is at the effendi's service," said the policeman, smiling faintly.

The interrogation began, and continued for the next hour and a half. I asked most of the questions, but occasionally Major Bondet interjected with comments or questions of his own. The prisoner's reaction did not change. No reassurances could dispel his uneasiness, not even the invitation to share coffee with us. He hugged his crippled right arm with taut fingers. At each question he gazed at the policeman in doglike submissiveness, awaiting permission to reply. When he did respond, it was in the classic Arab manner, his left hand pressed flat against his chest. The obsequiousness, the false candor of the gesture, kept the cynical smile on the guard's face.

"Now, Musa," I asked, near the end, "do you seriously expect us to believe that story? How could you have taken part in such an operation without knowing its true purpose?"

Reflectively, the fingers spread-eagled again over the heart, the wool-sack head turned from side to side. "It was not I who fired the shots," he moaned. "Yunis Umbark was the one. If you had caught him he would have told."

"The bullets matched your gun," I reminded the prisoner. "How do you explain that?"

This time both hands met on his breastbone: "Effendi, believe me," he whispered, "it was Yunis Umbark who dropped that gun. He fired the shots."

"But you knew the purpose of the mission," insisted Major Bondet.

Again the prisoner shook his head. "I knew nothing, effendi, nothing," he pleaded. "I was following Yunis Umbark's orders. Find him. He can tell you."

Here the guard, a swarthy, heavy-set Egyptian Jew, laughed out loud. "'Find him!'" he scoffed. "Maybe we ought to find Mustafa Chafatz. Dead men tell no tales." Then he repeated the remark in Arabic.

The Negro shuddered. "Yunis Umbark knows," he whispered. "Also Abu Saifan, Abu Chadar, and Saïd al-Sageh. They were all members of Egyptian Intelligence. They all worked with Colonel Chafatz. Not I. I carried their knapsacks, no more."

The guard, Bondet, and I all sighed simultaneously. Plus ça change, plus c'est la même chose.

Suddenly the prisoner repeated bitterly: "Yunis ran out and left me. But he told me not to mention his name."

"Then why did you?" asked the guard.

"Because he is a bondouk [bastard]," the reply came fiercely. "They are all bondouks."

"Are you sorry for what happened?" I asked, somewhat naïvely.

He gazed morosely at the floor for a long moment. "Yes," he said at last, "I am sorry. I am a simple man. I did not know what was going to happen. Only the best for my family, that was what I wanted. I see now that our only hope is peace with the Jews."

"Do you think Israel wants peace?" I asked again.

The prisoner nodded vigorously. "Yes, yes," he agreed. "I am sure of it. The Jews are good people. I have always liked the Jews."

Major Bondet stood up. "You know the rest of this by heart," he said to me, in English.

I did indeed. *I have always liked the Jews.* Substitute English for Jews, and Turks for English, Mamelukes for Turks, Frenchmen for Mamelukes, and Greeks for Frenchmen—and you had the formula of Arab survival for thirteen centuries of Palestine history. Before the prisoner was escorted out, I offered him my hand. He stood there uncertainly for a moment, and then accepted it, eyes averted. The guard motioned him out with a jerk of the thumb.

As the gates of Tel Mond prison closed behind us, I settled back in Major Bondet's command car for the return trip to Tel Aviv. The experience had left me quite depressed. It was possible to reach a *modus vivendi* with people of convictions; but men like Musa Abu Sa'ad al-Abid apparently had none. If betrayal of their fellow Arabs came this easily, what chance was there of an enduring agreement with the Jews? And the ease with which he had lied—"I didn't know what was going to happen."

Here, rather to my surprise, Bondet took the prisoner's part.

"That much is probably true," he explained. "Of course he recognized that he had been sent out on a death mission. But he didn't consider it murder. Arab peasants like him simply don't share the Western attitude toward the sanctity of human life. That explains the role of the blood feud in Arab society, you see. Killing is not regarded as a public crime. It's still essentially a family matter. The victim's family takes revenge on the murderer's family.

"Of course, in Musa's case, the act didn't arise from a blood feud," Bondet continued. "But he certainly didn't consider the shooting as a morally reprehensible deed. After all, let's remember that the man is a typical primitive—illiterate, superstitious, easily susceptible to outside influences. He was hired to perform a certain mission. It's very unlikely that he understood the risk he ran of being killed himself. But then he was captured. And suddenly he realized that his captors regarded the shooting as the gravest of all crimes. He was confronted with an elaborate interrogation machinery. High officers in the Israel army grilled him. It must have been a shattering experience for the wretched fellow. None of his companions had warned him that he would have to face anything like this. And so, terrified at the prospect of being killed himself, he betrayed them."

Here I asked: "Couldn't it simply be a ruse to ingratiate himself with the prison authorities?"

Bondet thought for a moment. "That probably enters into it," he admitted. "Certainly his bleating about the Jews and how much he likes us tries our patience, to put it mildly. But I think his hatred of the Arab officials is genuine enough. They got him in this mess. And don't forget his grievances toward them go back to 1948."

I had not forgotten. For the past two weeks I had been reading Musa's case history and the case histories of other captured infiltrators. Sitting in a secluded office of the central police station in Tel Aviv, I had been permitted to examine the dossiers in some detail—although under the closest supervision of armed guards. The records had sent chills up my spine. After reading through the first file I began to understand the reason for the elaborate precautions, the endless quantities of red tape I had been compelled to breach before securing access to this information. It was equally clear, too, that the border police deserved their reputation as the cleverest and best-trained unit of Israel's security forces. The frontier dividing Israel from Egypt was a death trap for Jew and Arab alike. If men like Musa Abu Sa'ad al-Abid had risked that bristling no man's land it was only because the border, with all its perils, must have seemed preferable to the living death of the refugee camps.

> I was born in the Moadi-Chanin heath [read Musa Abu Sa'ad al-Abid's file], not far from the orange grove of Mr. Ilan, the place where our tribe was living, and I never went to school. At the age of six I began to care for the sheep and eight cows belonging to my father, Chamad Abu Sa'ad. My father was one of the elders of the tribe. A few years later I wanted to earn a living for myself, and then I started working as a crate packer in orange groves not far away. Among other places, I worked in the orange grove of Mr. Ilan as well as for Musa al-Tawal, a tall Arab, whom the Jews called Bushtrand. I also worked in the orange groves of Mordecai and Yosef Lehrner.

It was all true. Bushtrand was still an itinerant field hand in Rehovot.

He remembered the prisoner. So, too, did the Lehrner brothers. Musa was a strangely quiet youth, deferential, a hard worker—more than most of the boys of his tribe. He was very black. His grandfather had been a slave of Haj Gabr Attah Chalil, the richest man in Ramle. The *haj* had freed the grandfather while the latter was still a youth, and had given him a flock of fat-tailed sheep for his own. Later Musa's father inherited enough money to buy into the protection of the Moadi-Chanin tribe. He married one of the tribe's daughters, who bore him nine children. Musa was the fourth—and blackest. The boy's earliest memory was the flat of his father's hard, calloused hand, a dark face turned away from him in disgust, and the smallest portions at the dinner table.

"Learn a trade, thou," his father had warned him more than once. "It will not help thee to watch my flock, for no part of it shall ever be thine."

And so, as a crate packer for the Jews, Musa learned a little basic carpentry. He made himself useful. During the Second World War he found employment as a hod carrier in the British army camp at Sarafand. The pay was good. In 1942 he had saved enough to buy a fellah girl from the tribe of al-Ruag. Adiyah was a good wife. She produced a baby each year, and not one of the children was darker than a Negev bedouin. When the war ended, Musa returned to his heath and again placed himself under the protection of the tribe. Moadi-Chanin's sheik was a good hiring-master; he found employment for the youths and kept only half the wages for himself. For Musa, hardly a day passed without a job awaiting him in one of the orange groves of Kubeba, Migdal, or Yibneh. Most of the owners were Arab now, and they paid much less than the Jews. But the times were troubled, and employment of any kind was welcome. There was always enough wood for the fire. The roof was well patched. There was *pitah* (flat maize-bread) and *humus* (ground chick-peas) and oil for the family table. No one went hungry.

Then the winter of 1947 brought other troubles. A man came from Jaffa, a wonderful-looking man, well-dressed, with spats on his shoes and a red tarboosh on his head. He handed each of the householders a slip of paper. Musa held the document to the light, turned it first to the right, then to the left. Finally he handed it back to the man.

"You will forgive me, effendi," he murmured in embarrassment. "I was not trained in the use of the new script. Perhaps you will read it for me."

The visitor took back the paper and began to read aloud.

O Arab, Son of the Palestine Fatherland [he recited]. The Jews who live beside you have betrayed you once again. With funds and connections from all parts of the world, the Jews have persuaded their friends and allies, the gullible and easily deceived, to divide this land into two halves. The smaller half they wish to give to us, as if by charitable pittance. The larger half they wish to keep for themselves. The million Arabs who, by the Zionist plan, will be left in the Jewish half, are marked for speedy death. Already the Jews have begun to arm. They have cast greedy eyes upon your house, and are making plans to seize it the moment the British have left. Your wife and daughter are marked for rape.

Now then, O Arab, Son of Ibrahim, Chosen of the Prophet and Noblest of Warriors, give heed to the instructions of your friends. We sit in high places, and neither are we idle. The armies of our Arab brothers are making ready for the day of reckoning. Soon they will sweep down into the land of Palestine as a bolt of lightning issues forth from the angry heavens. Blood will water the fields and pour like rivers into the sea. Take heed that this blood shall be Jewish and not your own.

The Jews will try once again to beguile you, as they have beguiled you in years gone by. They will promise you rewards if you accept the plan of partition. They will entreat your co-operation. O Arab, turn deaf ears to these adders. If you co-operate with the Jews, they will have won their victory even before the British leave. Their plans must be made unworkable. Sell them nothing. Buy nothing from them. Leave them nothing. Make room for the soldiers of liberation who are arming on your behalf. Provide them with bread and shelter. Once the land is ours your house will be yours alone. Your field will be yours. And the Jew's house will be yours, and his field and his flock will be yours.

Obey the orders that will be issued in the weeks ahead. Dark times are coming.

> [Signed] Haj Amin al-Husseini
> Jamal Bey al-Husseini
> (on behalf of the Arab Higher Committee)
> Printed in the Christian Teachers' Seminary,
> Tyre, Lebanon

Musa listened uncomprehendingly. "Well, I don't know," he muttered. "There has been no trouble here. I never bothered much about the Jews."

"You don't know," the visitor remarked disdainfully. "Of course you don't know. It is not for you to know. It is only for you to obey orders. You can either fight or you can make room for those who will fight. One or the other."

Musa stared at the ground, as was his habit when confused. He said nothing.

"Well?" said the visitor.

Musa scratched his ear. "I will think about it," he said at last.

The man departed without another word. Musa watched him pass from one hut to another. The next few weeks seemed to bear out the visitor's warning. At night shots echoed in the distance. Saïd, Adiyah's bachelor brother, arrived from Jaffa with frightful tales of bloodshed between Arabs and Jews. Late one February afternoon all the women of the village suddenly loosed a frantic wailing. Without venturing out of her hut, Adiyah, too, joined in.

"You, woman, stop that," Musa hissed, cuffing his wife on the top of her head. "What do you know?"

"I know, I know," she moaned.

He ran out. She was right. The funeral cortege swelled from house to house. The victim was Hadad Mustafa al-Chonena, the father of seven. He had joined in the ambush of a Jewish convoy moving from Haderah to Nataniah. But the convoy had been armed. Four Arabs fell, Hadah among them.

After the funeral, the *mukhtar* [headman] called the householders together. "Who among us wants war with the Jews?" he asked bluntly.

No one spoke.

"I have no objection to helping ourselves to a few Jewish orchards," the *mukhtar* continued. "I could use a new house as well as any of you. But this is the plain country. The Jews outnumber us here. I do not think any of us can do anything. Those who want war had best go into the hills. I urge the rest of you stay and tend to your work."

"Esteemed sheik," ventured one of the men, "it has been suggested that we leave the country altogether."

"Leave? Leave?" the old man croaked. "Where will you go? Have you a field in Egypt? In the Emirate? Or a flock perhaps? Speak up." But the man remained silent. For several moments the *mukhtar* stared at him contemptuously, then continued. "When the Jews come this way, we shall see about leaving," he said. "What other villages do is their affair. Right now leaving is for rich men. Not for such as we."

The *mukhtar*'s words were repeated in other parts of Arab Palestine. In spite of the Higher Committee's dire warnings of impending warfare, only thirty thousand Arabs decided to leave the country during the months immediately following the Partition Resolution. Most of these *émigrés* were businessmen and their families from Haifa, Jerusalem, and Jaffa. Liquidating their holdings, they transferred their accounts to banks in Egypt or in the Lebanon, and departed unobtrusively. No one else budged. For his part, Musa even continued working occasionally in the groves of Jewish planters. Mr. Ilan received him as cordially as before, and paid him the same wages. None of the Jewish crate packers seemed hostile. There were the usual rumors of killings, but most of these came from the hill country. The tribe itself suffered no further casualties. Once, seated in the coffee shop of Yibneh, Musa listened to a recording from Radio Cairo. It was the voice of Nuri es-Saïd, the Iraqi prime minister.

"We shall smash the Jews with our guns," es-Saïd declaimed, "and destroy and obliterate every place in which the Jews seek shelter. The Arabs should conduct their wives and children to safer areas until the fighting has died down."

Musa laughed out loud. "What fighting?" he asked his two companions. "Do you see fighting?"

The men smiled, too, but said nothing. They were Musa's neighbors; and in April, they would both be dead in the groves of Rehovot, victims of a Jewish ambush.

Indeed, for Musa and his entire tribe, April signified the beginning of the avalanche. Of course, violence had long since broken out in the fields and in highway defiles. But until then the shootings were hardly more serious than the guerrilla outbreaks of the 1930s. The frantic drum beating of Radio Cairo or Radio Damascus simply was not to be taken seriously. Until April.

On the morning of April 10, 1948, Musa's neighbors began emptying their little stone huts and loading their possessions onto carts and wagons. The entire village resounded with the whimpering of women and children, the *dih*s, *huh*s, *he*s, and *hish*s of mule drivers, and the bray and groan of the mules themselves. Trembling with frustration and rage, the *mukhtar* rushed from one man to another, berating them for their cowardice.

"Have you gone mad?" he shrieked. "Where are you going? We have nothing the Jews want. We never bothered them. They will leave us alone. Whom shall I send out to the groves now? What will happen to your homes? What about your orange trees?"

None of the men had ears any longer for the old man. Finally the *mukhtar*'s own brother pulled him aside.

"Have you heard about Deir Yassin?" he asked, referring to the Arab village southwest of the Jerusalem road. When the *mukhtar* did not answer, the brother continued: "Deir Yassin is no more. Yesterday the Jews massacred everyone there, men, women, and children. Not a dog yet lives in that town."

The *mukhtar*'s jaw dropped. "How do you know this?" he whispered, finally.

The brother nodded. "I know. I am in touch. And I tell you the Jews slaughtered everyone. Only flies are left there."

The *mukhtar* refused to meet his brother's eyes. "Women and children, too?" he muttered. "I can't believe it."

The brother smiled sourly. Each day Radio Cairo had promised a war of extermination against the Jews. Only the week before Azzam Pasha, secretary-general of the Arab League, had boasted of "a momentous massacre which will be spoken of like the Mongolian massacre and the Crusades." The fate of Jewish prisoners who fell into Arab hands was no secret. The women were raped and slain, the men disemboweled, their sex parts packed into their lifeless mouths. It was the only way to conduct a war, the only way the Arabs of Palestine could remember. Why should the Jews not retaliate in kind? To expect anything less would be the grossest naïveté.

And the truth was that few Arabs expected less. Thousands of their families on the coastal plain, convinced that the Deir Yassin raid represented the emergent pattern of Jewish assault, joined the emigration to the hills.

Yet, in spite of the turmoil of movement about him, Musa still was inclined to stay put. He had four children, and his wife was pregnant again. Moreover, there had never been trouble with the Jews of the surrounding communities. Whatever their hostility, it seemed unlikely that they would inflict harm on his family now. The Lehrner brothers actually seemed more upset about the Arab emigration than he did, for there were no longer sufficient hands to work in the groves. And so Musa stayed on, performing his chores silently. During the bus rides home from the plantation he spoke to no one. But behind him, he could feel the glare of suspicious eyes, overhear the muttered curses of Jewish passengers. Gunfire rattled through the darkness with increasing frequency. Arabs died, as well as Jews. The warnings of Radio Cairo grew more urgent. Still Musa would not move.

Then, at the end of the next week, the man with the red tarboosh awaited Musa at the entrance to his hut. This time the visitor minced no words. "Why are you staying, habibi?" he snapped.

"Why should I leave?" came the sullen response.

"You even talk like a Jew," the man snorted contemptuously. "I'll tell you why you should leave. For the same reason our people in Tiberias left last night. The Jews have taken over."

The news almost defied belief. Tiberias had been considered a major Arab stronghold. Musa remained speechless for nearly a full minute. Finally, sighing, he asked: "How will it help if I leave?"

The visitor shook his head. "It's your family I'm talking about," he explained, with a great show of patience. "Do you want them slit open, your wife defiled before your very eyes? That's why Tiberias was evacuated. We want to save your family. If you clear out now nothing will happen to them. Later—I can't promise. There will be more shooting."

Musa scratched his ear again. "I'll think it over," he promised, and then walked into the hut, closing the door. He was trembling. Adiyah looked at him wordlessly. The children were seated at the table, munching contentedly on their *pitah* bread. There were few conveniences in this stone dwelling, not even a water tap. But it was security, the only security he had ever really known. He had been cast out by his own father. There were those among his own people who scorned him for his slave origins. Now at last he was his own master. He filled his children's bellies each day. It was not a simple matter to abandon everything he had won for himself.

He decided to wait.

On April 11 the fighting came closer to home. The café in Yibneh was all but deserted. Yet the radio still played. Salach al-Towil, the proprietor, understood Hebrew, and whispered the news: Haifa had fallen to the Jews; its Arab population of more than fifty thousand people had fled to the Lebanon. As Musa listened he felt his blood turn cold in his veins. He was not a coward, but his hand began to tremble so violently that he put the cup down in its saucer for shame. The Arabs of Haifa were rich. They owned the best land in the city. They would not have fled without reason. What if the man from the Arab Higher Committee had been right?

The thought occurred to others. Along the entire coastal region scores of Arab villages were emptying almost overnight. Nearly one hundred thousand people now moved in flight from the Plain of Sharon. The terror that brooded over Haifa dropped on Yibneh faster than the news of the Jewish conquest could be communicated. Always, too, the women knew first—but it was the men who insisted on flight, for the men had seen death by violence before. If Jewish methods resembled Arab or Turkish methods, there would be mutilation. Few waited to find out. For Musa the moment of decision came on April 26. He had heard the rumble of gunfire for three days. Saïd, Adiyah's brother, brought the information. He was pale with fear.

"It's Jaffa," he said, his voice shaking. "They tore through us like a hurricane. Our people are fleeing for their lives. A terrible sight, I can't describe it—seventy thousand men, women, and children running like whipped dogs."

Now it was Musa's turn to panic. "Where are they going?" he asked. "Have they boats?"

"All by land," Saïd replied. "Father and the rest of the family are camping out near Isdud. Others are making for the Migdal heath. We want you to bring Adiyah and the children and come."

Musa looked about him, at the fruits of fifteen years of hard labor. Then, with a despairing oath, he walked rapidly to the stable. Hitching his tiny mule to the draw cart, he led the animal to the door of the house. For the next two hours he and his wife and brother-in-law loaded the family possessions into the cart. There were straw mats, jars of olive oil, wooden bread bowls, straw coverlets, a clay brazier, three copper cooking utensils, two sieves, two wooden chests, utensils for grinding, roasting, and cooking coffee. In the corners of the wagon, Musa lovingly stored his brass-bound flintlock, his goatskin water bottle and his two glass narghiles. The clay food bins were too large to carry. So was the clay fire pot. Only enough room was left for the wife and children.

As he seized the reins, Musa turned to his brother-in-law. "This house and land are mine," he cried. "I'll be back for them, don't think I won't. How long must we wait for help?"

"Two weeks."

"Two weeks and I'll be back with the first Arab army to reach Yibneh."

"Good," Saïd muttered wearily. "Let's move."

But Musa would not be stopped. "It's mine," he shouted, at the top of his voice. "I'll also have Ilan's groves and Lehrner's groves, and their houses and everything in them."

"Shut up. Let's get out of here."

As the tiny mule trudged southward, Musa continued to shout, wildly, incoherently, the spittle dropping off his lips and onto his trembling hands.

The trek southward to Migdal lasted one and a half days and could have continued beyond that, for the plain stretched in a sweeping crescent along the sea, curving toward Gaza and the Sinai Peninsula. It was a shifting ocean of scrub dunes. Until recently, in fact, the heath had been ignored altogether by the Jews, and had been only sparsely inhabited by occasional tribes of wandering bedouin. Now, however, in April of 1948, the arid no man's land was suddenly transformed into an enormous encampment for tens of thousands of terrified Palestine Arabs.

Musa Abu Sa'ad al-Abid was swept along by the torrent of refugees. They came by every road and by every conveyance, by wagon and oxcart, on donkey, camel, and horse, on foot. There were farmers among them, the kaffiyahs on their heads bound tightly with goat cords, their work-worn hands grasping at their prayer beads, their lips paralyzed by the enormity of their fear. City dwellers in Western business suits had come by auto and taxi. Dumped at the edge of the heath where the road ran off, they sat hollow-eyed and slack-jawed under their parasols, fastidiously kicking the sand and dust from their patent-leather shoes. Sheiks, *mukhtars*, muezzins, and cadis circulated among the refugees, clutching at their sashes and cords of office in frantic self-reminder of the dignity that once was theirs. Dope peddlers prowled acquisitively among the clotted throng of rustics. And, too, there were the women and children who swarmed into the heath in the wake of their masters. Whimpering softly, the mothers went through the motions of normalcy, laying out blankets and tablecloths on the sand, unpacking oil and cucumbers for the youngsters. Most of the children were too exhausted to eat, however, or even to cry. They sat huddled together, their eyes blinking froglike at the sea of humanity around them, their mouths sucking reflectively at their thumbs or their mothers' breasts.

It is a matter of a fortnight, Musa reminded himself, indeed less than that until I return.

"Only thirteen days left, O beloved," cried the imams. "The British will leave. The liberators will come."

"Less than two weeks," shrilled the muezzins, "and the armies of Egypt will pass this way, sweeping the *yahud* from his pillage. Have courage."

The fugitives were patient. They burrowed grimly into the heath, stretching their bed linen on the axles of their wagon wheels by day, burning ox-dung fires by night, rubbing and scratching the sand from their pores, and measuring, dividing the strips of dried beef, the barrels of oil, the bags of barley grits, oats, and vegetables. Musa and his friends had calculated shrewdly. There would be just enough. They waited.

And on May 17 their patience was rewarded. Exactly as Radio Cairo had predicted, the Egyptians marched into the land of Palestine. The refugees watched the approaching dust cloud in a trembling ecstasy. Winding its way up the coast from Sinai, the column of jeeps, half-tracks, and cannon caissons ground slowly across the dunes toward the Arab encampment. The committee of *mukhtars* went out to meet the convoy.

"You are our saviors, excellency," said the local headman, the mayor of Karmiyah, who spoke for the committee. "Our food is all but exhausted." He then described the plight of the refugees in graphic detail.

The commanding officer, a mild, pipe-smoking colonel named Mohammed Naguib, listened to the *mukhtar*'s appeal with obvious sympathy. "Logistics present a difficult problem, my friends," he explained regretfully. "Our resources will be taxed even to keep our troops supplied with food and ammunition. You can see that this is difficult terrain. Everything we have comes through Khan Yunis from Al-Agheila."

"How shall we eat then?" asked the *mukhtar* of Zarnuqa.

"Deal with the bedouin a little longer," came the cryptic reply. "Don't forget the rewards that await you when I have cleared the Jews from their land. It will not be long, I promise you. Just promise me, for your part, that you will stay out of our way."

The *mukhtars* promised. They kept their promise. But Naguib did not keep his—not in Palestine. The brigade's twenty-five pounders blasted away impressively at the nearby kibbutz of Yad Mordecai. After a brief siege, Egyptian soldiers even occupied the farm community. But afterward the column stopped short on the outskirts of Isdud. There was fighting. At night phosphorus star-shells lit up the darkness, and the rumble of artillery sent tremors through the dunes. Additional troops moved up the coastal road. Tens of thousands of new refugees poured out of the interior, joining the encampment on the heath. One week passed, then two. But still no word of victory.

In the interval most of the fugitives exhausted their food and water supplies. Many of them fled southward, seeking haven in Egyptian territory. But the majority still remained on the plain, unwilling to abandon their foothold on Palestine soil. There was only one possibility now of survival. With the others, Musa turned to it with dread in his heart. Hanging his head in exhaustion and humiliation, he followed the pilgrimage of supplicants who made their way to the near-by bedouin encampment. Veiled in their black robes, the wraithlike nomads awaited their visitors on the crest of the dune. Their enclosure of camel-skin tents had already been transformed into a market place. Pieces of furniture, baskets, barrels, cooking utensils, hand-wrought carpets, and narghiles, were piled high in the makeshift courtyard. The aged bedouin sheik and his "counselors" were seated cross-legged on straw mats laid out before the booty, impassively sipping their coffee. They were not constrained to hurry. The entire morning passed before Musa's turn came.

"Now then, effendi," murmured the sheik gently. "I have no wish to detain you. You look tired."

"Yes, Sidi Sheik, you know what has happened to our people."

The tribal leader nodded. He was an impressive man, heavily mustached, his torso crisscrossed with bandoleers and superbly ornamented daggers. He offered Musa a cup of coffee. As the Negro drank, he felt his bowels turn to water; it was the first hot nourishment he had known for the last three days.

"How are your children, honored sir?" asked the sheik.

"Well, well," Musa gasped faintly. "But of course they have had little to eat."

The old man clucked his tongue sadly. "What madmen would have sent you fleeing like this?" he asked. "The Jews would have robbed you, but they would not have killed you."

"I am not sure, patriarch," Musa replied. "But now we are here, in any case. And we must eat. I am prepared to do business with you."

The sheik nodded. "What would you like? Mutton, water, dates, dried greens? We have them all."

"Whatever you can spare."

The old man smiled. "What can *you* spare?" he asked.

"I have baskets," Musa ventured hopefully, "two splendid narghiles made in Damascus, copper cooking dishes . . ."

The bedouin sighed. He waved his arm at the utensils piled in the compound. "Too much of that already, I'm afraid," he said. "What else have you?"

Musa swayed slightly, then tried again: "Blankets," he whispered, "carpets, an olive-wood press—"

"Hashish?" snapped one of the sheik's companions suddenly. "We can do business with hashish. What say you to that?"

Musa felt the panic rising in his breast. "Esteemed brothers," he whispered, "I am a simple man. I have never done business in such matters. Take what I have and give me something for my children. They are faint from hunger."

"No hashish?" asked the sheik, his voice suddenly gone cold. "Then I ask again: what have you?"

"My brothers," the Negro's voice became a plaintive wail, "we are your kin. Surely you will not leave us to the vultures?"

At this the sheik's companion laughed dryly. "You are not our kin and you have never been our kin. When you had food you gave us none, neither in drought nor in famine, nor when our children perished at their mothers' breasts. If you have something to sell we shall buy. But we are not buying pity today."

Musa's hand groped at his collar button, then slid inside his shirt. Instantly the sheik's arm shot out, seizing the Negro's wrist in a grip of astonishing strength: "None of that, you hear," the old man hissed. "We shall slit your throat."

A calfskin bag dropped from Musa's nerveless fingers. The sheik's companion picked it up, loosening the drawstrings. He lifted an eyebrow.

"So, then," he muttered, counting the contents, "we have here twelve, thirteen—fifteen pounds and fourteen shillings."

Musa said nothing; his head had sagged forward on his chest. The sheik stared at the money for a long moment. Then he spoke:

"This will buy you a goat, two bags of lentils, a sack of barley, and the right to use our well—" he paused briefly—"for twelve days, and not an hour more." He turned to his companion. "Hand over these provisions to our guest."

"My brothers," Musa wept, "my brothers—"

"Others are waiting in line," the sheik interrupted.

Within the hour Musa returned with his provisions, leading the tiny goat by a rope. Adiyah saw it and said nothing. With her hollow eyes and sunken cheeks, she appeared to have aged ten years in the last month. Hers was the task of preparing and rationing the greens among the four children. The goat was permitted to munch on the sacking. After the first week, however, the animal's milk gave out and Musa had to allow it two handfuls of barley each day. By the end of the month the food was entirely gone. Musa's only alternative now was to slaughter the goat.

On the night of June 3 a sheet of flame crossed the sky. The earth shook with the roar of cannon and the rattle of machine guns. The women and children crawled under the wagons. The men lay flat on their bellies, inching toward the crests of the dunes. In the distance Musa could make out the Egyptian artillery emplacements. Soldiers crouched behind sand-bags. Occasionally trucks arrived, filled with wounded men. None of the troops moved forward. Musa licked his dry lips and noted the fact: it was now June 3 and the soldiers in the distance were clinging to their positions for dear life. Then, overhead, he heard a whistle, and yet another. The sandbags erupted suddenly in streamers of fire. Silence followed. No one moved. Only the onlookers scurried back to their camp, urinating with shock.

Beneath the wagon Adiyah was howling like a dog.

"Stop it," Musa croaked. "You hear me, I'll beat you."

The woman would not stop, and rocked back and forth, cradling her youngest child in her arms. Musa raised his hand and then lowered it. Yasmin, the girl, was hardly breathing. Her face was white as chalk. Instantly the father rushed off to the tent of the holy men. Within minutes he returned with a dervish. The aged man examined the child. Then he stared at the carcass of the goat, still impaled on the spit.

"You have been feeding her carrion," he reproached Musa. "She is poisoned." He placed his ear on the girl's chest. "And now she is dead," he added.

Musa, too, placed his head over the daughter's heart. "Yes, she is dead," he repeated dully.

Ignoring Adiyah's frenzied wail, the dervish walked over to the other three children. They sat there morosely, two boys and a girl, their brown little faces intent and wizened.

"They have all eaten from the goat," Musa whispered fearfully.

The dervish did not answer. Instead he thrust his scarecrow's hand into his velvet bag, and pulled out a cluster of dried figs. These he heated over Musa's cooking fire. Then he laid the figs on the brows of the three children. Thereupon the old man began to dance, lurching heavily from one foot to the other. As a crowd gathered, watching him awe-struck, the dervish began to circle the wagon, gaining momentum. His grizzled chin trembled, his gullet pulsated wildly, and his mouth opened and closed in a hound's bay. Flecks of spittle had collected in the pockets of his cheeks. Finally, after gyrating for a quarter-hour, the holy man stopped, exhausted, and toppled to his hands and knees.

"My elixir," he panted. "My elixir."

Musa understood immediately, and stepped forward, cupping the foam from the old man's mouth with the palm of his hand, and then smearing it on the lips of his children. Quivering on his back, the dervish crooned in a falsetto voice, snapping a pair of chicken bones between his right thumb and forefinger. Finally he arose and departed.

The darkness ebbed; the sun rose. Musa and his wife watched silently as the three remaining children lapsed into a coma. Before the eyes of the parents, the youngsters' bellies heaved and bloated. Gabr, the second boy, slowly recovered consciousness. But by sunset Fatma, the second girl, and Daud, the older of the two boys, were dead.

Musa watched the burial in silence. After the prayers were read, he returned to his wagon and curled up against a wheel. He did not move for the rest of the week. Food, when it came, was the offering of Adiyah's sister, who had arrived at the heath on the day of the burial. One afternoon a man approached the wagon. It was Saïd, the brother-in-law.

"Musa," he said, "it is time to pack and move again."

"Whither?"

"To Gaza. The news is not good from the north. Our soldiers have not taken the Jews' land. The Jews have taken ours. Yours too, and all other plots on the Moadi-Chanin heath. They have killed many of our people and have driven off the others."

"That is not what the *mukhtar*s have told us."

"The *mukhtar*s repeat what the Egyptians have told them, and the Egyptians have lied."

Musa said nothing.

"Pack, my brother," Saïd repeated gently. "There is no time to lose."

But Musa merely shook his head. "I am not moving," he said, with sudden fierceness. "The Egyptians have cannon. They will not be stopped. I shall have my house back."

Saïd remonstrated with him, but to no avail. Musa would not be moved. The brother-in-law gave up the effort. He handed Musa five British pounds, and then departed with his own family. Several thousand other refugee families also left the heath, and joined the trek southward.

Elsewhere, too, the exodus gained momentum. By June 11, the date of the first United Nations truce in Palestine, some 250,000 Arabs had fled the Jewish-occupied areas of the country. This number reached 300,000 by early July. The second truce, on July 9, put a temporary stop to the refugee movement. But October was an earthquake: the Jews launched their first Negev offensive then, and the speed and fury of their assault shocked even those Arab troops who had earlier met the Israelis in combat. After five days of fighting, much of it at close quarters, the flank of the Egyptian position was turned at Huleiqat, and the larger number of Egyptian soldiers in the Negev, trapped in a large pocket near Faluia, faced annihilation.

By the end of the month even the most credulous Palestinian Arab recognized that the Jewish State, far from succumbing helplessly to armed invasion, was in fact quite capable of waging ruthless and effective warfare on its own. Accordingly, the wave of Arab *émigrés* reached the half-million mark by November, and swelled to 700,000 in December, the month of Israel's victorious and conclusive campaign in the Negev. Of these fugitives, approximately 280,000 remained in Palestine—but in the Jordan-controlled, eastern sector of the country. An additional 70,000 crossed the river and entered the Kingdom of Jordan proper. Similarly, nearly 100,000 Palestine Arabs sought refuge in the Lebanon, another 75,000 in Syria, while smaller groups of 4,000 and 7,000 traveled on to Iraq and the Egyptian interior. There were, in addition, 190,000 refugees who had originally encamped in southern Palestine, and who now fled toward the Sinai Peninsula in the wake of the battered Egyptian army.

Musa had not been inclined to budge until the last week in December. The explosion of mortar shells was hardly unfamiliar to him by then. This time, again, the shells were Jewish, and they came perilously close to the encampment. In the distance, too, he caught his first sight of the enemy: a column of twelve jeeps, mounting twin machine guns, bounced rapidly along the winding desert road, and then veered off toward the coast. For the fugitives huddled on the Migdal plain, that first glimpse was enough. Gathering together their meager belongings, they mounted their camels and mules and galloped at full speed toward Sinai.

None of them reached their destination. The last supply depot in Palestine was Gaza, an impoverished desert community of some 45,000 souls, only twelve miles south of the heath. As Musa and his companions passed through the town, they found a roadblock awaiting them a hundred yards west of the central square. A squad of Egyptian soldiers sprawled indolently in the van of an armored troop-carrier. Two sergeants, wearing white gloves and white leggings, stood beside the crossbar, interrogating the refugees. When Musa's turn came, the Egyptians wasted few words.

"Where from?" barked one of the sergeants.

"Yibneh, effendi," Musa replied.

The Egyptian gazed offhandedly at the donkey cart and the woman and child seated there. "Where to?" he asked.

Musa shrugged. "The Jews are coming, effendi," he murmured. "We must reach the interior."

"Any relatives in Egypt?" the soldier asked.

"My brother-in-law and his family came this way last month. I expect to find them in Al-Arish."

"Al-Arish? No one gets into the interior these days. You'll find them two kilometers away, habibi, at the camp. That's where you're going."

"Camp?"

"Get moving."

Musa had little trouble finding the refugee enclave. He smelled it before he had traveled the first kilometer. And he heard it during the second kilometer. It appeared at first as a sea of cattle, surging in concentric circles around trenches and troughs. Then, as he drew closer, Musa saw that they were people, people by the thousands, by the tens of thousands, an explosion of people, more people than he imagined could ever have lived in Palestine. Yet here they were compressed into a single sweep of the eye. It made one dizzy. From the rear of the wagon Adiyah moaned in terror. Musa did not bother to silence her.

After two days of inquiry he located Saïd. The brother-in-law helped him pitch his makeshift tent, and then led him to the "secretariat." It was a tiny stone hut overlooking the refugee encampment, and bearing the modestly printed sign: AMERICAN FRIENDS SERVICE COMMITTEE.

"Be respectful now, you hear?" Saïd warned urgently. "These are Americans. If you are respectful they will give you rations. You will have enough to eat. Tell them you are a Christian. It may help."

After a two-hour wait outside the hutment, Musa's turn came. He and

Saïd entered the room. Two men and a woman sat behind the table. One of the men was an Arab, and he interpreted for the others.

"Where from?" asked the Arab.

"I am a Christian, effendi," Musa blurted.

The Arab scowled. "Where from?" he repeated.

"Yibneh, effendi," replied Musa.

"Family?"

"Only my wife and a small boy survive. My wife is with child."

"What have you brought with you?"

Musa pressed his hand flat against his chest. "I am destitute, honored sir."

One of the Americans shook his head, then stamped a card, handing it to the interpreter.

"Put in your name here," he said, "also the name of your wife and child."

Saïd filled in the information, then returned the card. The woman stamped it again, then scribbled something in a tiny notebook which she offered to Musa. He accepted it, somewhat uncertainly, with his left hand.

"This is your ration card," the woman explained. "With it, you and your family can have food each week. Without it you can have nothing. If you lose it or sell it, you go hungry."

Musa nodded deferentially, then left the room with Saïd. Together the two men made directly for the supply store. It was a large, rather dilapidated warehouse, bearing the same identification: American Friends Service Committee. Three Egyptian policemen stood at each side of the single entrance. Within, another American, thin and bespectacled, worked behind the counter with two Arab helpers. Musa presented his ration book. In return he was handed three frayed British army blankets, a small bag of sugar, another of rice, and one of beans. Wrapped in one of the blankets was a bar of soap.

Musa remained standing expectantly.

"What is it?" asked the American, in Arabic.

"This is all?"

The American flushed. "This is charity," he replied, his voice still even. "You are paying nothing for what you receive. You must not ask us such questions."

Musa grumbled under his breath before leaving. The gesture represented habit more than anger; he was far from unsatisfied. These were the first real provisions he had seen in nearly a month.

"And don't forget the medicines," whispered Saïd, once they were out of earshot of the Americans. "If you get sick they'll take care of you here. It's not a bad arrangement at all."

"How long will it last, do you think?" asked Musa.

"It's lasted the month I've been here. How many months should it be before the war is over and we go back? Two, three, let's say even four? They're good for that long."

The war ended in the winter. Each day small groups of refugees milled idly about the secretariat, waiting for news of repatriation. Thus far there was nothing. The days turned into weeks, and the weeks into months. Occasionally rumors circulated that a peace treaty was about to be signed between the Jews and Arabs. Nothing happened. Nothing moved. Torpor settled over Gaza. Musa and the others lined up each fortnight before the warehouse, collected their rations, and then returned to their tents. There they waited. In the spring Adiyah gave birth to a girl, and Musa received a new book of ration coupons from the Quaker administrators of the camp. Nothing else relieved the monotony of the family's existence.

Elsewhere, however, in the world of diplomacy, the plight of the Palestine *émigrés* commanded the immediate and urgent attention of Western statesmen. As early as July, 1948, the United Nations mediator in Palestine, Count Folke-Bernadotte, warned the General Assembly that the flight of terrified Palestine Arabs was assuming the proportions of a major tragedy. Folke-Bernadotte was an old Red Cross hand. He had seen entire peoples displaced before—Greeks and Armenians in the 1920s, Poles, White Russians, and Jews during the 1930s. He knew all too well, from personal observation, the frightful toll that exposure and hunger could take. Thus, at the mediator's suggestion, the United Nations requested that a number of international welfare organizations undertake short-term emergency relief in the areas of refugee concentration. The General Assembly appointed Sir Raphael Cilento of Australia to co-ordinate the work of these bodies.

At Cilento's behest the International Refugee Organization accepted the responsibility of caring for all refugees in Israel-occupied and Jordan-occupied areas of Palestine. The Red Cross was charged with the same task in the Lebanon, Syria, and Jordan east of the river; while the American Friends Service Committee provided for refugees in the "Gaza Strip," the thin finger of southwestern Palestine which was still occupied by Egyptian military forces. The assignments were costly ones, and obviously far beyond the resources of voluntary philanthropy. To support the work of these relief agencies, therefore, the United Nations General Assembly on November 19, 1948 voted an interim grant of $5,000,000, and asked $29,500,000 in additional contributions from member nations. Yet at best financial aid of this sort could only be a short-term palliative. A more fundamental solution had to be found—and quickly. The following month, on December 11, the General Assembly passed a resolution calling upon the Arab States and Israel to begin peace negotiations without delay. Paragraph Eleven of the resolution stated that "refugees wishing to return to their homes and live at peace with their neighbors should be permitted to do so at the earliest practicable date." The appeal was commendably humane and seemingly reasonable. The Arab response to it, however, was unequivocally negative. Their battlefield defeat had been overwhelming and shattering; yet the notion of admitting this fact to the world—or to themselves—was still anathema to them. They would not sign a permanent peace treaty with the Jews.

Neither, for their part, would the Jews give even momentary consideration to the possibility of repatriating over 700,000 fugitive Arabs. The State of Israel had very nearly been throttled at birth by thousands of Palestine Arab irregulars. If the refugees were permitted to return now as part of an indiscriminate mass influx, who could say that they would not become a Fifth Column, poised at Israel's vitals, in continual communication with their kinsmen in the surrounding countries? In any case, repatriation of the *émigrés* was unthinkable except as an integral part of a general peace treaty with the Arab states; whatever their disagreements on other matters, all of Israel's political parties were united on this issue. Despite intense and persistent diplomatic pressure exerted by the United States and Britain, therefore, the attitude of the Israel government remained implacable and unbudging: solution of the refugee problem depended first and foremost on the willingness of the Arab governments to meet the Jews at the peace table.

Confronted with this flatly uncompromising position, the United Nations was compelled to abandon its insistence upon a full-scale Arab return. Rather, the world body gradually shifted its negotiations to the possibility of modifying, rather than revoking Israel's refugee policy. And the moment the General Assembly changed its approach, Israel, too, proved to be more flexible. After some hesitation, Israel's Foreign Minister, Moshe Sharett, finally declared his country's willingness to "consider" the reunion of Arab husbands and wives, children and parents. In many instances, apparently, the separation of families was caused not merely by flight, but by a chance division of the firing lines. The reunion of these unfortunates might well eliminate at least one cause of the growing infiltration into Israel—which in turn tied down large numbers of Jewish troops. Anyway, the return of a limited number of Arab breadwinners would also ease Israel's social-welfare problem.

Accordingly, at the otherwise fruitless Lausanne Conference on Palestine, which took place between April and September of 1949, the Israeli representatives agreed to allow the return of wives and minor children of "Arab breadwinners lawfully resident in Israel, and to consider other compassionate cases for readmission. . . ." The practical effects of this concession were unimpressive. During the next year the Israel government processed tens of thousands of applications for readmission—and readmitted no more than two thousand Arabs, mainly wives and children. During 1952 and 1953 the reunion provisions were extended to include fiancées of Arabs in Israel, sons up to the age of seventeen, and a limited number of Arab students studying abroad. In addition, between 20,000 and 30,000 infiltrators were "unofficially" granted permission to remain in Israel. Yet, by 1957, the total number of readmitted Arabs amounted to a mere 35,000. The question of large-scale repatriation had long since been a dead issue.

One of the factors that killed it was the policy of the Arab governments toward their own Jewish minorities. No sooner had the Palestine war ended than the circumstances of Jews in Arab lands became altogether untenable. In Iraq, Yemen, and Syria, scores of thousands of Jews were reduced overnight to the level of pariahs: their homes and shops were confiscated, their bank accounts and virtually all their possessions were sequestered. Hundreds of Jews were arrested, tortured, and even executed on trumped-up charges of collaboration with Israel. In many Arab communities Jews took their lives in their hands whenever they ventured into the streets. Even as far west as North Africa, the venerable Jewish communities of Tunisia, Morocco, and Tripolitania were subjected to anti-Jewish assaults, and to systematic economic and legal discrimination.

Between 1948 and 1957, as a consequence of this new Islamic xenophobia, no less than 467,000 Jews were compelled to flee their homes in Moslem lands. In nearly all instances they departed as paupers, stripped by the Arab governments of everything they owned, and reduced to complete dependency upon the Jewish welfare organizations that arranged for their transportation and settlement in Israel. No heavier burden than these penniless derelicts was ever borne by the Israel government, not even the burden of the war itself. Afflicted with nearly every variety of contagious Oriental disease, large numbers of the newcomers required extensive medical treatment and hospitalization. Tens of thousands of others were illiterate, often as primitive as the Moslems among whom they had lived. Somehow they would have to be educated, trained, equipped for the task of earning their livelihoods in a modern, secular society. Indeed, during their first few years in Israel, the immigrants represented an almost total economic liability for the Jewish State.

By far Israel's most serious problem, however, was the sheer physical burden of providing living accommodations for these hundreds of thousands of refugees. They could hardly be confined indefinitely to the tent cities, the endless rows of squalid shanties that passed for "homes" during the early years of Israel's existence. Thus, even as the immigration authorities grappled with the problem, the newcomers themselves discovered one obvious, and brutally simple solution: they would move into the houses and settle on the farms left behind by the *émigré* Arabs. At first the government issued warnings against "illegal squatting." Yet once begun, the stampede could not be halted. By 1951 virtually all abandoned Arab property had been preempted by the immigrants. The "squatters" made it quite clear, moreover, that any suggestion of relinquishing their newly won shelter to Arab returnees would be resisted by force if necessary. They would not allow themselves to be expropriated twice.

As time passed, the likelihood of mass Arab repatriation became completely academic. Within three years of its independence, Israel ceased altogether to resemble the country the Arabs had left behind. New factories were erected. Hundreds of thousands of dunams of wasted soil were put to the plough and transformed into productive farmland. In all corners of the nation new collective and co-operative farm settlements sprang up. Hundreds of miles of new roads and highways were laid. Electric towers, telephone poles, and wires crisscrossed the countryside. And, above all, waves of people continued to pour into Israel's ports, cities, and agricultural communities. They were all Jews. As their older traditions yielded steadily to the tempo of Zionist progressivism, their ideas, their institutions became increasingly dynamic, increasingly "Israeli." Those Arabs who returned would surely feel ill-at-ease in this revolutionized State—as uncomfortable as the Arab minority who had stayed on since the Palestine war. For better or worse, the old way of life was gone forever.

These were the circumstances to which the Israel government continually referred as it stubbornly refused even to contemplate the repatriation of Arab refugees. There were no historical precedents for the return of exchanged populations, argued Foreign Minister Sharett. After World War I, nearly 2,000,000 persons were resettled in a population transfer between Turkey and Greece. Following World War II, 900,000 Germans were transferred to Germany from Czechoslovakia, Poland, Hungary, and Yugoslavia; while a momentous exchange of populations between Poland and Soviet Russia affected 2,520,000 Poles, Ukrainians, White Russians, and Lithuanians. In the wake of the partition of India, in 1947, an immense, two-way migration of Moslems and Hindus uprooted nearly 13,000,000 people. Exchanges of population were not reversible, Sharett pointed out. Far better to accept the exodus of Arabs and Jews as a *fait accompli,* and encourage their resettlement among their kinsmen.

In 1949 an American investigating mission reached essentially the same conclusion. Under the chairmanship of Gordon R. Clapp, then director of the Tennessee Valley Authority, the mission made a firsthand study of the resources of the Middle East, and of the possibility of reclaiming and developing the area. Later, reporting to the United States Congress in February, 1950, Clapp expressed his group's unanimous conviction that the Arab refugees ought to be integrated into the economic life of the Arab States. Once the refugee problem was disposed of, Clapp insisted, the political tensions between Arab and Jew would largely be alleviated. He made the same suggestion to the United Nations General Assembly.

The General Assembly, in turn, accepted Clapp's recommendations and acted on them the following month by terminating Cilento's *ad hoc* relief committee. In its stead a United Nations Refugee Works Administration was established with a budget of $54,000,000. Unlike its predecessor, UNRWA was not charged with the task of providing the refugees with relief, but rather with employment on relocation projects. Within eighteen months, so it was estimated, most of these fugitives would be as self-supporting as their Arab neighbors, and relief handouts could probably be ended once and for all. Apparently at no time during its committee hearings did it occur to the General Assembly that the Arab governments themselves would turn their backs on the UNRWA undertaking. After all, the refugees were their kinsmen, their blood brothers, men and women who spoke the same language, recited the same prayers, observed the same traditions, rituals, and customs. Surely the Arab nations would welcome the opportunity to succor the unfortunates in their midst.

This illusion was rapidly dispelled. From the moment UNRWA officials met with the Arab governments, they encountered a blunt, uncompromising refusal to co-operate with any plan designed for economic integration. "Paragraph Eleven of the General Assembly Resolution of December, 1948, guarantees the refugees the right to return to their homes," the Arab spokesmen argued. "We cannot participate in any scheme which may compromise that right." As it happened, the delegates of the Arab nations had themselves voted unanimously against that resolution, for it had urged them to enter into peace negotiations with Israel. Now, however, they chose to interpret Paragraph Eleven as if it stood alone, and made it a condition precedent to peace discussions. They recognized, of course, that the moment the refugees were integrated into the surrounding Arab nations, the principal diplomatic obstacle to peace with Israel would have been eliminated. During the 1950s no Arab government—with the momentary exception of Jordan—was prepared yet to accept the Jewish State as a *fait accompli*.

Repeatedly, UNRWA officials sought to reassure Israel's neighbors that the public work projects would not necessarily imply renunciation of refugee political rights in Palestine. It was wasted effort; the Arab regimes would not listen. By the end of 1950, as a result, the date which the Clapp Mission had fixed for ending relief, no more than 10,000 of the 750,000 refugees were employed—and most of these in short-term drainage projects. What actually occurred was that UNRWA took over the relief work of the Cilento committee. When the projects were finished, the refugees returned to their tents and ration lines. None of them was economically absorbed in the surrounding nations. On the contrary. The UNRWA staff soon learned, to its dismay, that it had created neither long-range improvements for the refugees nor financial relief for the United Nations. Rather, UNRWA had dispensed five times the amount necessary for plain and simple relief.

It was for the purpose of breaking this stalemate that John Blandford, the American director of UNRWA from 1951 to 1953, decided to launch a new effort to reach agreement with the States of the Arab League. His proposal envisaged the contribution of State land by the various Arab governments, in return for which UNRWA would allocate $250,000,000 over a three-year period for specific employment programs. This time no mention was made of resettlement. It was Blandford's hope, nevertheless, that with Arab refugees tilling Arab soil, responsibility for both relief and rehabilitation projects would gradually be transferred from UNRWA to the Arab states. Indeed, by underwriting this plan, the United Nations fully anticipated that the refugee problem would be liquidated by the end of 1954. And in fact the Arab governments registered no objection whatever to the expenditure of this money. It was simply that they refused to commit it to the employment or integration of the refugees. Accordingly, by the end of 1954 no more than eight thousand Palestinian Arabs had been made self-sufficient. Most of the money had been spent once again on relief, nothing more. The Arab regimes continued to evince profound disinterest in joint development projects.

Each year after 1954, therefore, the exasperated members of the General Assembly warned the Arab nations that neither the patience nor the budget of the United Nations was limitless. They argued, too, that under international precedent the Arab refugees were not refugees at all. The term "refugee" had traditionally been applied to fugitives deprived of the protection of a government, and in need of asylum and status. The Palestinian *émigrés* hardly fitted that description; they were living now in the midst of peoples whose race, language, culture, and religion they shared. Was it unreasonable, the General Assembly wondered, to ask those peoples to share the burden of their blood brothers—even as Israel had altogether accepted the responsibility for Jewish fugitives from Arab countries? Evidently the Arab States considered the request unreasonable; they continued to ignore the General Assembly's protests and recriminations. And each year, as a result, the United Nations, refusing to permit three-quarters of a million human beings to perish of hunger and exposure, grudgingly allocated new funds to UNRWA. Yet each grant was accompanied by the warning that a new, and more fundamental approach to the refugee issue would soon have to be devised. No overt reference was made to resettlement; but neither was repatriation suggested any longer as a possible solution.

By the mid-1950s it became apparent that the number of Arabs registered on the dole was steadily mounting. The birth rate alone added between 30,000 and 40,000 names to the relief rolls each year. There were, as well, countless thousands of deceased refugees whose names were never withdrawn. Their deaths were never reported. Their ration books mysteriously circulated among the survivors, reappearing in the bread lines and in the camp commissaries. By 1963 the number of refugees was no longer cited as 750,000, but rather as 900,000—even 1,000,000. By 1963, too, some $370,000,000 had been expended by the United Nations for the support of the refugee camps. The largest part of this money was supplied by the United States.

Indeed, as early as 1955, it was painfully clear to the United States government that a drastic solution to the refugee issue could not be postponed indefinitely. The presence of hundreds of thousands of embittered exiles was hopelessly complicating the task of bringing peace to the Middle East. Nor was the Eisenhower administration willing any longer to pour American and United Nations funds down an endless drain. That money could far more usefully be applied, instead, to an enforced solution of the Arab-Israel imbroglio. To that end, Secretary of State John Foster Dulles formally proposed to the Arab governments that the refugees be integrated once and for all into the countries where they were then living. Israel, too, Dulles suggested, ought to agree to the repatriation of a specific number of Palestine Arabs. If Arabs and Jews would accept this compromise, the United States in turn would be willing to underwrite the agreement financially.

Dulles' proposal may have been soundly motivated, but it was poorly timed. Egypt's Colonel Nasser was even then arming his military forces with huge quantities of Soviet weapons, and thus anticipated solving the refugee problem—indeed the entire Palestine problem—in a very different way: i.e., by obliterating the State of Israel. In the face of this ominous Egyptian arms build-up, the Jews, for their part, viewed the possibility of even token repatriation as nothing short of suicide. Both sides rejected Dulles' suggestion out of hand.

Then, in the autumn of 1956, determined to smash Egyptian military power before Nasser could fulfill his boast of conquering and destroying the Jewish State, Israel suddenly hurled thirty thousand troops across the Gaza border in a lightning invasion of the Sinai Peninsula. The campaign proved to be an almost complete strategic success. Within four days every major Egyptian staging base in Sinai had been captured, together with vast quantities of Soviet weapons and ammunition. The back of the Egyptian army was broken. For the first time in many years the Jewish State enjoyed comparative military security. The nation breathed again. This new-won confidence was reflected in a speech delivered by Israel's United Nations ambassador, Abba Eban, announcing a basic shift in his country's refugee policy. Repatriation was still out of the question, Eban declared. Nevertheless, the Israel government would be willing to discuss appropriate financial compensation for the Arab refugees—provided that the terms of payment were incorporated in a general peace treaty with the Arab States. It was a not insignificant concession. The American government, seeing a flicker of hope at last in the refugee impasse, immediately made it known that it was prepared to co-operate in any possible compensation agreement.

To the chagrin of both Israel and the United States, however, the Arab governments rejected the proposal outright. First there must be repatriation, the Arab League insisted; only afterward would peace negotiations be feasible. It was another way of saying that the Arabs were still unprepared to accept the existence of a Jewish State—the Sinai defeat notwithstanding; the refugee issue would be kept alive as the insurmountable obstacle to the peace table. Nevertheless, five years later, in 1961, the Israel government decided to make a final offer: compensation to the Arab refugees independently of peace negotiations. Two conditions were attached to the proposal. First, account would have to be taken of Jewish property confiscated in Arab countries. Secondly, the United Nations must ensure that the funds would be applied to the permanent resettlement of the refugees outside Israel. The scornful reaction of the Arab governments to this offer was by now predictable. Even so, in the following year yet another American suggestion was presented. It was the so-called Johnson Plan, which called for a "poll" among the refugees themselves to determine *their* wishes—whether they preferred repatriation or integration. Not surprisingly, both Israel and the Arab States contemptuously repudiated the proposal. And there the matter remained. The issue was apparently insoluble. The refugees were still confined to their camps. The United Nations continued to pay for their relief. And the years continued to pass.

For Musa time had lost its measurement after the first year of his arrival in Gaza. He counted the passage of the seasons by Adiyah's pregnancies. Each autumn she received her warning; and each succeeding summer she was delivered of child. All were boys save one. In the winter of 1952 Musa was given his first employment, as a construction laborer for UNRWA. Together with 1,500 other men, he was put to work building clay huts for the refugees. The dwellings possessed two rooms, with connecting outhouses. They were a marked improvement over the leaking tents of the first years.

There was a little more food, too. On the fifteenth day of each month every member of the family received a kilo of flour, a quarter-kilo of sugar, a half-kilo of rice, four bags of beans, and a half-kilo of oil. This provided 1,600 calories of food nourishment daily, the commissary officials had assured them. Perhaps it was not enough to satisfy a man's appetite, but neither was anyone fainting from hunger. Medical care improved, as well. Adiyah was assisted by a trained midwife at each of the births. Every six months an American doctor examined the children. When they became ill they received free medicines from the camp dispensary. Already the two older children were attending school in the compound.

But it was still a beggar's life. What was there to do, Musa asked himself? Where was he to go? How long was his family to be confined to the camp, denied the most elementary human comforts? Where were the opportunities to work, to travel, to live like normal people? Was each day's routine to be restricted to the same gumlike meals cooked over a foul-smelling primus stove, to the dreary round of visits to his neighbors, the same idle card games, the endless and hysterical verbalizations about reconquering Palestine and driving the Jews into the sea? Who brought us here, he asked? Who locked us in this pesthole? He thought of the Jews. But the memory of the man in the red tarboosh was no less fresh in his mind.

Elsewhere, too, the questions were being repeated. "Who brought the Palestinians to the Lebanon as refugees?" asked Beirut's Moslem weekly, *Kul-Shay*. "Who brought them over in dire straits and penniless, after they had lost their honor? The Arab States, and the Lebanon amongst them, did it." "Yes," admitted Nimer al-Hawari, the former commander of the Palestine Arab Youth Organization, "we were confused by promises and deluded by our leaders. 'Get out so that we can get in!' they told us. So we got out, but they did not get in." "The responsibility of the Arab governments is very great," declared Beirut's French-language daily, *L'Orient*. "For years they have been applying to the refugees an abstract and inhuman policy; under the pretext of cultivating in the refugees the longing for their homes in Palestine, and for the purpose of maintaining a menacing population on the frontiers of Israel, they have systematically rejected all attempts at organization and employment for the refugees."

Musa had more than once made the effort to find work. The first time he had simply climbed on the back of a gasoline truck and traveled the fourteen miles to Khan Yunis. The afternoon rest period had fallen by the time he reached the fly-specked town square. Only a handful of bedouin were to be seen, lounging at the sidewalk café, drinking coffee. They eyed Musa suspiciously as he jumped off the truck. A moment later he heard the chairs scrape, and the sound of footsteps behind him. One of the bedouin seized him fast by the arm.

"Where to, *yahud*?" growled the bedouin.

"Leave me alone." He tried to wrench his arm free.

For several moments the two men remained locked together. Then the other bedouin came huffing down the road, an Egyptian gendarme close behind. "Here he is," cried the man. "We have caught him."

Musa instantly went slack. His antagonist loosed his grip.

"What are you doing here, *yahud*?" asked the policeman, pulling his report pad from his pocket.

"*Yahud* yourself," replied Musa sullenly. "If I am a Jew you are a Jew. I came here to find work. Is that a crime?"

"Precisely so," replied the Egyptian. "It is a crime. You are not to leave the compound, do you understand?"

Musa shook his head. "But how am I to understand?" he asked. "I am a good field hand. I am not here to rob anyone. I want to work. I have a family to feed."

At this the bedouin set up a hysterical cackle. "He has a family to feed, you hear?" shrieked one.

"And do we not have families to feed?" chimed the other. "You think there's so much work in these parts that we can share it with scum like you?"

The policeman was examining Musa's ration book, painstakingly jotting down his name and serial number in a cribbed child's scrawl. "Now then, habibi," he said, clutching the Negro daintily by the throat, "your name is in my book. And from here it goes straight to the police station. Do you know what will happen to you if I catch you around here again?" He drew his finger across Musa's throat. "Get moving now."

Musa started to say something, then changed his mind. He turned his back on the men and began walking out of town. A police jeep pulled up beside him before he had reached the desert road. He was driven the rest of the way back to camp. When he returned late in the afternoon he flung himself against the side of his hut, and cursed the day he was born. His wife poked her head out the door, and he cursed her, too. Then he began to moan softly to himself.

Still, he would try again. In the autumn of 1953 one of his friends, a former neighbor from Yibneh, approached him as he stood in the ration line.

"Abu Gabr [father of Gabr]," the man addressed Musa politely, "would you like to earn an Egyptian pound?"

"Of course, and I would like to go home, too, and become the *mukhtar* of Yibneh. Leave me alone."

"I mean it," the man persisted. "I am the hiring boss for a sheik who lives near-by. He needs workers to harvest for him. A pound for a week's work. What do you say to that?"

"I say the prisoners in Acre dungeon used to get more than that."

His friend smiled. "But we *are* prisoners, Abu Gabr," he said gently. "A pound will buy seven kilos of dates." He winked. "It will buy three cartons of cigarettes."

Musa laughed mirthlessly. "That sheik has a good thing in us." Then he thought for a moment. "What if the police find out?"

"They will not find out. The farm is in Jabaliya, down the road. And we shall work only at night."

Musa agreed. The following evening he and twenty other men stole out of the camp like thieves, and walked silently toward the northern outskirts of Gaza. Two trucks awaited them, and carried them off to the fields. Nearly forty other men were already at work. Musa recognized some of them; they lived in the smaller refugee compound on the other side of Gaza. One came from his own village. That night, and on eight succeeding nights, the refugees cut, bound, and threshed the sheik's winter wheat. In the daytime they slept on straw mattresses laid out in the owner's courtyard.

It was at noon of the tenth day that the gate of the courtyard suddenly swung open. Before the startled men could climb to their feet, a squad of Egyptian gendarmes burst in among them, their truncheons whirling. Gasping in terror, Musa rolled first to the right, then to the left. But to no avail. A sweating policeman had him by the throat. The wooden club descended again and again. After the first blow, Musa flung his arms feebly about his head. But still the club descended, cracking remorselessly against his skull, shaking his back teeth, filling his nose and eyes with blood. His vision dimmed; his arms dropped. Somewhere below, the policeman's boot was probing his kidneys and his groin.

When the courtyard swam into focus again, the sheik was declaring to the police sergeant. "The nerve . . . the outrage . . . I've been made a fool of . . ." Musa could feel the welts rising on his head. His lower torso was without feeling. Around him the other men lay groaning, twitching weakly. Ignoring them, the sheik maintained his shrill protest: "No one lies to me twice. I want him jailed. What an outrage! He said nothing about using refugees, nothing. Of course, I would have had nothing to do with the scum if I had known. But how could I know? To think I nearly paid them . . ."

Within the hour the workers were bundled into police vans. One of the men was unconscious and had to be carried into the vehicle. Then the trucks drove off. At the Gaza police station the refugees were registered, and then led into a darkened foyer. A lieutenant awaited them there, an enormous fat man with a swagger stick.

"I am going to release you this time," the officer said, with a faint smile. "While I am sure you would like our accommodations, I would not want to spoil you for the camp. You might even get to like our cooking. I shall not see you again," he continued, his face hardening. "He who tries any more such tricks will not get as far as the station house next time."

Then he dismissed the prisoners. The men limped down the road back to the camp, too exhausted and humiliated to speak. Nor did they have to explain their absence when they reached the compound. The other refugees had seen the welts and bruises before, and sensed instantly what had happened. Most of them carefully avoided being seen with Musa and his companions. For several days after the incident, scores of Egyptian police circulated through the camp, fingering their truncheons menacingly, halting people at random, demanding and checking ration books.

Eventually a squadron of police was stationed permanently just outside the compound. The gendarmes did not hesitate to assert their authority—neither here, nor in eight other camps scattered through the Gaza Strip. "We fail to understand Egypt's policy," complained a Gaza dignitary in a letter to the Cairo daily, *Akhbar al-Yom*. "They degrade us by every means at their disposal. They treat us like spies and traitors . . . they tyrannize us at will and suck our blood. Many a time we have spoken up and said that these are imperialist methods—but no one hears our words." "We must frankly state," added Subhi al-Kelani in the Jordanian newspaper, *Haul al-Alam*, "that thousands of young people are fleeing the Strip in the disguise of pilgrims, in the hope of finding in Saudi Arabia a chance of a decent living and of getting away from the shame that was being heaped upon them by the Egyptian authorities in the Strip. . . ."

The possibility of flight once crossed Musa's mind, but he rejected it immediately. He would not drag a wife and children through that Sinai wilderness. He would wait a little longer.

He would wait weeks, and months. Winter came. It was a cold one. The children sat around the sputtering kerosene stove, idly sucking their thumbs and rubbing their bare feet. Adiyah served coffee once each day, and Musa closed his eyes; in his imagination he poured himself a *finjan* of steaming Turkish coffee, with jasmine leaves. Then he ran his tongue over his lips and recalled the luxuriance of tobacco smoke curling gently into his lungs. Not infrequently, too, the Egyptian police helped him recall these vanished pleasures. Somehow the gendarmes were never without cigarettes dangling from their mouths. The odor of coffee grounds never left them. The swine lacked for nothing.

"Do you know why that is, Abu Gabr?" asked his companion, Hassan al-Tafran, one day.

"Because they are well paid, that's why," grunted Musa, as he dealt out the cards.

Hassan al-Tafran laughed contemptuously. He was a city dweller, for thirty years a prosperous shopkeeper in Jaffa. He had traveled to six countries and boasted that he understood all the mysteries of human behavior.

"Yes, Abu Gabr," Hassan al-Tafran explained, "they are well paid, but not for being policemen." He winked, then rubbed his thumb and forefinger together. "They sell, Abu Gabr, and people buy."

Musa sat back on his haunches, listening attentively.

"But before they can sell," Hassan al-Tafran continued, "they too must buy. They buy anything they can get their hands on. I am in a position to know," he nodded. "I do business with them. I do business with them, and with the people who bring me the things I sell them." The man's arm rested confidentially for a moment on Musa's shoulder, and he whispered. "Lots of people in this camp are drinking fresh coffee and smoking good cigarettes because they bring me things I can sell."

"Where do they find these things?" Musa asked guardedly.

The man stared back at him for a moment, an expression of infinite pity on his face. "Where, indeed," he murmured. "Not from this camp, you can be sure. Not from Gaza." He cocked his head to the east.

Musa's eyes opened wide with astonishment. "What are you suggesting?" he asked.

"Come now," Hassan al-Tafran chided. "In this camp since 1949 and you don't know what's happening. It's been going on for years now."

It had indeed, many times each day and night, and over every one of Israel's five borders. Later, the United Nations Mixed Armistice Commission estimated that between 1949 and 1956 there had occurred no less than 11,873 counted instances of Arab infiltration and banditry. Anything that could be carried off was considered fair game: entire flocks of sheep, goats, cows, and horses, the fruit of orchards, bales and sacks of harvested crops, fodder, irrigation equipment, windowpanes, doorknobs, even shutters and entire doors. And all of it was stolen with skill and comparative impunity, for the Jewish border police were thinly dispersed. One had to know where to go, of course, and where to hide. But the Palestine refugees knew.

The night Musa departed, his companion was Ibrahim al-Salal. The two had been neighbors at Yibneh, and they remembered where the flocks grazed. Between them they carried only a bag of food, a can of water, and a pair of scissors. It was after midnight when they reached the Castel al-Almi. The stately old building had once belonged to a wealthy Arab landlord. It served no other purpose now than a border marking, for the Jews had since established a kibbutz on the neighboring land. Musa and Ibrahim crossed between the Castel and Wadi Harbiyah.

Heading north, they settled into a gentle barefoot jog across the dunes. An occasional light from a distant chicken coop flickered in the distance. Now and then a jackal yelped. But not a human being was to be seen, nor a voice to be heard. Twice the men rested. Then the sky lightened, and the two quickened their pace. It was the Migdal heath. Here Musa remembered every twist in the earth, every dip in the terrain. The lowing of cows sounded to the east. That would be Giora. The sun rose. A shepherd's pipe echoed in the morning air; Ibrahim al-Salal flung himself against the seaward side of a dune, and Musa dropped panting at his feet. A man trudged by in the distance, a dog barking behind. Then silence again.

The Arabs arose and resumed their steady trot. The sun glared directly overhead. They drank a little water. Then trees appeared.

"It's Nitzanim. We'll wait in this clump until darkness," said Musa.

"There should be cattle here," said his companion.

Musa shook his head in warning. "The farmers are too well armed. We must go further inland."

They drank a little more water, and nibbled on their greens. Musa dozed. In the distance there were voices, but no one entered the cluster of trees. The dusk settled, and darkness followed. Ibrahim laid his hand on Musa's shoulder, awakening the Negro. The men started off.

The lights were an uninterrupted necklace to the east. New farms had sprung up since 1949. New people had come. There were more orchards, too, groves of orange and fig trees. They offered protection. By dawn Musa and his companion reached Yibneh.

"Be-it Sefer Am-ami Yav-neh"—"Yavneh High School," Ibrahim al-Salal laboriously read the Hebrew lettering on the side of a distant house. "Yavneh!" He laughed harshly. "They didn't even leave us the name."

Musa's eyes were focused on a near-by banana grove. "We'll sleep there," he said. "No one should be chopping those for a while." Ibrahim nodded, and they darted quickly into the stalks. It was ideal covering. Rain fell in the afternoon, but the men remained dry. No one ventured near. Soon it was dusk again. Lights winked on in the houses. The Arabs waited. The hours passed. Lights died, one by one, then in clusters. Finally Ibrahim climbed to his feet, and Musa followed.

They slipped through the banana stalks and out to an open field. Then they circled the town to the southeast, passing to within a half-kilometer of Zarnuqa. There was a quarter-moon, and the men could see clearly. The fields were well tended, Musa admitted to himself; somehow the Jews had brought water to the place. There were new barns, too, some of them freshly painted.

"Bis," Ibrahim warned, pointing to a shed at the edge of a fig grove. A mare was lying there. "That's for us."

Quietly the men descended on the animal and coaxed it to its feet. Grasping the mare's tether, they led it slowly along the rutted dirt path toward the southern outskirts of the village. Within an hour the little group had reached the dunes, and plodded steadily southward along the heath. By morning light they had passed B'nai Darom, and skirted the eastern boundary of Ashdod Yam. At last, settling in the hollow of a dune, the men rested and ate. By now the mare had become restless, and began wheezing.

"She's hungry," said Ibrahim. "Wait here."

He set off alone over the crest of the dune. An hour passed and he did not return. Musa, fighting sleep, rubbed his eyes with sand and concentrated his gaze on the sea. When the sun no longer cast a shadow he heard footsteps. It was Ibrahim. He was leading a calf with his right hand. In his left hand he carried a sack of fodder.

Musa whistled. "In broad daylight, Abu Mohammed. You are a wizard."

"Compliments of a kibbutz," said his companion, grinning triumphantly.

Both animals were allowed to feed on the hay. To the east, automobiles and trucks hummed steadily along the coastal highway. The men sat quietly and waited. Finally, at dusk, they started off once more, the animals trotting listlessly behind. The lights of Nitzanim glowed faintly in the distance. Here Musa and Ibrahim veered off sharply toward the sea, and within the hour reached the abandoned Arab village of Be'er Shakir. The water hole was still there, untended but undefiled. The mare and the calf drank gratefully. Then the men and animals continued. By dawn they reached a clump of Santa Rosa trees, and the entrance to the Ashkelon road. This time the Arabs tethered the horse and calf to one of the trees, and then moved off a hundred yards away, to the interior of the grove.

It was a shrewd move, and it was made in the nick of time. Three minutes later a party of eight workers passed along the road, picks and shovels in hand. The two Arabs froze. These were the first Jews either of the men had seen at close range since crossing the border. Musa noted, too, to his astonishment, that the workers were quite dark. Three of them wore turbans, the kind his own father had worn. Yet the workers were Jews, there could be no question of that; they walked the land as if it was theirs. Several of the men noticed the mare and calf tethered to the Santa Rosa tree. Unsuspecting, they passed on. During the course of the day other laborers walked by. One or two of them were unmistakably Arab, for they wore *kaffiyahs*. One or two out of thirty-five or forty. Musa pondered the fact.

At nightfall Ibrahim untethered the animals, and the trek began again.

This time the men completed the last leg of the journey without incident. They reached Castel al-Almi before dawn. Two hours after that they trudged wearily into the Gaza square. Musa was faint with exhaustion and hunger. On an impulse, he suddenly entered a coffeehouse.

"Our credit should be good now, shouldn't it?" he said to Ibrahim.

As they sat down, the burly proprietor fingered his toothpick and cast an appraising glance at the mare and calf tied outside. Then he whispered into his waiter's ear, and the man departed immediately. Musa and Ibrahim had barely finished their first cup of coffee before the waiter returned, this time accompanied by Hassan al-Tafran. The former shopkeeper was all geniality.

"What have we here?" he beamed delightedly, sitting down beside the men. "Drink up, my dears. The coffee is on me." He turned to the proprietor. "Bring them some *humus* and *pitah,* too."

When Musa and his companion had finished wolfing down their food and drink, Hassan al-Tafran launched directly into business. "You must forgive me, my dears," he explained apologetically. "I am a city man, and I have never mastered the art of lengthy bargaining. I am going to pay you and then dispose of the animals immediately. These matters are best not delayed. Now then . . ."

He opened his wallet and briskly began counting out freshly printed Egyptian pound notes. The two men stared at the money in fascination. Ibrahim slowly ran his tongue over his lower lip. After several moments, Hassan al-Tafran stopped counting.

"There you have it," he said. "Twenty-one pounds. Nineteen for the mare and two for the calf."

"That is for each of us," said Musa hopefully. "Is it not?"

"It is for both of you," Hassan al-Tafran replied.

Ibrahim scowled. "But we risked our lives," he protested. "These animals are worth four times that much."

"They are worth four times that much in Alexandria," Hassan al-Tafran replied, in the same even tones. "But they cannot so much as pass into Sinai. You've seen the wretches who live here. It will be hard to find one of them who can pay even that. And don't forget, the police have to get their commission."

"And so do you," muttered Musa, his anger mounting.

The storekeeper extended his hands, palms upward. "Gentlemen, you are not obliged to do business with me," he said. "If you can find a policeman who will deal with you directly, then find him, by all means." He smiled. "But take care that you do not speak to the wrong policeman. He may arrest you for crossing the border illegally."

The two men sat silently for a while. Finally, without a word, Musa picked up the money. Turning his back on Hassan al-Tafran, he divided the notes with his partner. Then they both stalked out of the coffee shop.

Before returning to camp, Musa stopped at the general store. There he purchased a five-kilo sack of coffee, three cartons of cigarettes, and two blankets. Starting to leave, he suddenly remembered Adiyah, and bought a sweater for her. Three and a half pounds remained. He would save them.

He walked back to the compound. His wife opened the door, then retreated with wide and frightened eyes. I know, he thought to himself, you had given me up for dead. Without bothering to explain his absence, he threw himself onto the bed and slept like a stone.

During the next half-year Musa crossed the border fourteen times. Sometimes he went alone, sometimes with Ibrahim al-Salal, and occasionally with others. Now and then there were narrow escapes. Once a group of Jewish farm boys saw his shadow in a fig grove and chased him, firing several shots in his direction. But he doubled back on his tracks and outwitted them. With experience, his confidence grew. After the first few trips he learned where to expect guards, searchlights, and watchdogs. He learned how to set a mule loose from its shed as a decoy, and then to set out in the opposite direction with as many as five sheep. Nor was travel confined to the night hours now. Crevices, gulleys, fruit trees, even shadows proved to be as effective protection as the darkness itself.

Musa never came back empty-handed. Sometimes he brought sheep, sometimes a horse, or a donkey. Once he returned with an entire gasoline generator strapped to his back. At other times he filled his bag with spades, primus stoves, various kinds of wrenches, hammers, or clocks stolen from Jewish warehouses. Nothing was too large—or too small. Hassan al-Tafran purchased everything he could lay his hands on. With Egyptian pounds in his pocket, Musa managed to buy a half-dozen new ration books. The hut was well heated now. The children ate chicken with their rice. Not a night went by without coffee in the *finjan*. No risk seemed too grave when seen through a languorous blue cloud of tobacco smoke.

In February of 1954 Musa returned from his fourteenth crossing. In his sack he carried two irrigation gauges and a coil of copper wire. Following his usual routine, he made straight for the café, and the meeting with Hassan al-Tafran. This time the shopkeeper did not bother to order coffee. He glanced at the loot without enthusiasm.

"I don't know, Abu Gabr," he said skeptically. "These odds and ends are beginning to flood the market. I would have preferred animals."

Musa shrugged. "So would I, Abu Daud," he said. "But the Jews are getting smart. They keep their animals close to home these days."

"Yes, yes," Hassan al-Tafran sighed. "But I really don't believe the risk is worth the effort if this is all you can come up with. However, you've made the trip. I'll give you a pound and a half for the stuff."

Musa began to breathe heavily. "This is expensive machinery, Abu Daud. It is worth much more than that."

"To the Jews, perhaps. Not to me. Take a pound and a half now and let's not waste time haggling. I told you I was a city man. With me the first price is the last price." He began to rise.

"Not so fast, Abu Daud." Musa laid a restraining hand on the man's arm. "I risked my life for this machinery."

Hassan al-Tafran's face darkened with anger. "And I risk arrest every time I handle stolen goods," he snapped back. "Get your hand off."

But Musa tightened his grip. "Abu Daud, you have been earning a good living from me. I will not be made a fool of. Either give me ten pounds for this machinery or I will deal with someone else."

The shopkeeper sat down and stared at Musa calmly. "You will not deal with anyone else, habibi," he said in quiet, precise syllables. "I shall report your name to the police and tell them that you have been crossing the border without their knowledge. I shall teach you a very simple lesson, and then you will know what happens to people who imagine they are cleverer than I am." Suddenly his eyes bulged with alarm, and he pulled his head back. "What are you doing? Stop it . . . stop it, you crazy bushman!" His voice rose to a shriek.

"I'll stop, all right," Musa roared. "When you are food for the buzzards. *Bondouk!* Blood-sucker, you."

"Stop it . . ." gasped Hassan al-Tafran, his voice much weaker now. "I didn't mean it . . . Abu Gabr . . ."

"*Bondouk,* blood-sucker, *yahud,* you!" howled Musa at the top of his voice. "Vampire, you!"

The proprietor and two waiters wrestled him to the floor, and the heavy irrigation gauge dropped from his hand, dripping blood and bone splinters.

"*Bondouk!*" he wailed. "*Bondouk!*"

A hand struck him sharply across the face, and he caught his breath.

"Do you know what you have done, camel turd?" the proprietor whispered. "Look at him and know what you have done. You will pay now."

Several minutes later the police arrived, and Musa was dragged from the café. "*Yahud, bondouk!*" the words spewed forth of their own volition, and even the thump of truncheons could not stop them. They continued long after the cell door clanged shut. At last, with the coming of night, he lay silent on the straw pallet, quivering in rage and terror.

The next morning the door opened and two guards entered. Without a word, they pulled their truncheons from their belts and proceeded to beat Musa unconscious. Then they left. In the afternoon a bowl of rice was shoved into the cell, but Musa could not eat. When darkness came again, he began to weep silently. The next day he decided to eat, but the rice had turned maggoty. He turned his face to the wall.

On the third morning the guards entered the cell and kicked Musa to his feet. Then they led him down the corridor and into a large room. Three men sat behind a desk. They were army officers. In the color photograph on the wall behind them white teeth blazed from the smiling, vulpine face.

"Approach the court," said the officer in the middle.

The guards thrust Musa toward the desk. He stood alone, blinking at the judges in confusion.

"Musa Abu Sa'ad al-Abid?" asked the chairman. When Musa did not answer, the man held up an identity card. "This says that you are Musa Abu Sa'ad al-Abid, formerly of Moadi-Chanin heath, Yibneh, Palestine. Present residence: Gaza. Age: thirty-seven. Profession: agricultural worker. Religion: Moslem. All correct? Speak up."

The guard nudged Musa, and he cleared his throat. "Yes, Excellency," he murmured.

"You are accused of the murder of Hassan al-Tafran, also of Gaza," the officer continued. "Did you in fact kill the said Hassan al-Tafran? Answer yes or no."

Musa could only nod. The chairman was satisfied. He consulted with his colleagues for a moment. Then, gazing at the prisoner with well-rehearsed compassion, he gently intoned the judgment. "In the name of the Republic, and by authority of the Military Governor of Gaza, this court sentences you to death by pistol on Fourth Day next, February 16, 1954, Year Two of the Revolution. You will be visited by an imam the morning of your execution. Have you anything to say?"

Musa stared back at the officer uncomprehendingly. Then the guards seized his arms and led him from the room.

Adiyah was allowed to visit him the next day. But when the woman began keening, Musa lost patience and sent her away. He had other matters on his mind. He did not regret braining Hassan al-Tafran. The deed was a service to humanity, and he should have performed it long ago. Of course, there were the children to be considered. Their rations would still continue, that was a comfort. They would probably not see home again—he corrected himself, they had never seen it. But in any case return to Yibneh did not depend on him. If he went back to the camp, what could he expect? Another five years of waiting, and perhaps even five years beyond that—and perhaps to the end of his life? It was hardly worth it. He repeated the phrase and listened to it, turned it around and held it up to the light. And he knew it was a lie. He did not want to die.

On the Third Day he took a few spoons of rice, but vomited and gave up the effort. In the end he lay flat on his stomach and listened to the beating of his heart. The sound continued until late afternoon, and then stopped with the opening of the door of his cell. Musa struggled to his feet.

"You are too early," he pleaded. "He said the Fourth Day. It is only the Third Day."

"Put on your shoes," said a guard. "You are wanted."

"Without an imam?" Musa began to weep. Then he did as he was ordered and walked out between the two policemen. With shaking legs, he accompanied them to the end of the corridor, and from there to an oaken door opposite the sergeant's desk. One of the guards turned the knob and motioned Musa through. He stepped out into starlight. It was open air. People were passing by. A few of them glanced at him idly. He would have touched them, but the guard suddenly thrust him into a waiting jeep. The second policeman sat behind him in the rear seat, his hand resting on a holster. The driver pulled away from the station and drove rapidly down the main road.

A few minutes later the jeep braked to a halt in a side street, in front of a small stone house. One of the soldiers stepped forward and exchanged a few words with the guards. Then he beckoned to the prisoner. It is time, Musa said to himself. Together with the soldier he walked into the house. A lieutenant awaited them before another door. The officer glanced at Musa appraisingly for a moment. Then he turned the knob and called in softly:

"He is here." The lieutenant listened to the response, then opened the door wide and nodded.

Musa walked into an office. Files stood at one end of the room. An enormous relief map of Palestine covered the wall on the other side. Against the far wall an officer sat behind a desk. He was a slim, pale man, with intent, birdlike features.

"Sit down, prisoner," he said, motioning Musa to the chair before him. Musa did as he was ordered. "Smoke?" The officer tossed Musa a pack of German Ernte 23s. As in a dream, Musa lifted the cigarette to his lips. The officer lit it for him, then settled back, locking his delicately tapered fingers on the desk before him.

"I am Major Chafatz," he said. "I know all about you from the police chief. You have done a wicked thing. Do you know what you have done?"

"Yes, Excellency," whispered Musa.

"What was that?" the major persisted.

"I killed a man."

Chafatz lifted a graceful finger. "You killed an Arab," he smiled, "instead of a Jew. There is a difference, you know." When Musa said nothing, Chafatz lifted a folded handkerchief from a drawer in his desk and handed it to the prisoner. "Open it," he said.

Musa unfolded the handkerchief. Then he saw its contents and began to tremble. A human ear lay on the cloth.

"You are surprised, yes?" said the major, taking back the handkerchief and gently folding it again. "It is a Jew's ear. The man who brought it to me occupied your cell. Now he is once again in the bosom of his family. You shall meet him. For every ear he brings to me I give him six pounds."

A light slowly dawned in Musa's mind, but he said nothing.

Chafatz smiled. "I think we are beginning to understand each other," he said. "You see, I am giving you a choice: a bullet in the back of the head tomorrow morning, or a gun of your own—and a chance to support your family in style. What do you say to that? Answer me." His voice was suddenly quite hard.

"Excellency, what do you want me to do?" Musa whispered at last.

"Ah," the major leaned forward, all business. "First understand our purpose. It is simply stated: to return to Palestine. You would like that, wouldn't you? I certainly would. I'm not a Palestinian myself, but I was there with our army five years ago. Stayed as a prisoner of war in Nitzana Prison for a half-year. I expect to go back again someday and collect payment for that. He has promised us that trip, and I believe him."

Chafatz had inclined his head toward the photograph on the wall behind him. Musa stared again at the swarthy, hawklike features, the even row of white teeth gleaming confidently below the neatly trimmed mustache.

"I am here to execute his purpose," said the major. "We begin with violence. That means more than robbery. It means demolition. It means killing. If we can strike repeatedly, the Jews will become demoralized. Many of them will decide to leave Palestine. Those who remain will fear settling on the borders. Then the borders will be vulnerable to our armies. When the time comes to cross over in force, we shall thus encounter less resistance."

Chafatz pressed a buzzer. In a moment the lieutenant had returned. "I think our man is going to co-operate," said the major. "Take him to Yunis Umbark."

As Musa reached the door, Chafatz called after him: "Habibi, think for a moment. Six pounds for every Jew, and whatever you steal you keep." The major smiled. "You already know how to steal, I think."

The lieutenant led Musa to a back room. Ammunition boxes and guns were stacked neatly on the floor. A small, wiry man was oiling one of the weapons. "Know Yunis Umbark," said the lieutenant. "He will be your instructor." The two men nodded to each other. Then the lieutenant handed Musa a pound note. "Take this back to your family. You are free to go now. We shall send for you shortly."

When Musa returned to his hut, Adiyah stared at him for several moments, tried to speak, then fainted dead away. For nearly a week thereafter she was as a mad woman, crooning tunelessly in a wild shaking voice, occasionally seizing her children and kissing them frantically as if despairing ever of seeing them again.

The lieutenant's call was not long in coming. Two weeks later a military jeep drove into the camp compound, and a policeman searched Musa out. Together they drove back to the stone house on Zeitoun Street. Yunis Umbark was waiting in the back room. Four other men sat there. They were all refugees. Musa recognized two of them as condemned murderers. They all listened respectfully and attentively now as Yunis Umbark demonstrated the weapons to them. There were Lee-Enfield and Mauser rifles, automatic Sten and Schmeisser guns, Smith-Webley, Browning, and Beretta pistols, hand grenades, steel antivehicle mines and plastic antipersonnel mines, dynamite and gelignite tubes, detonation caps and extension electric-fuses. It was an impressive arsenal.

The lessons required four successive afternoons. On the last day Yunis Umbark outlined their first mission. "We shall cross the border tomorrow night," he informed them. "I personally shall lead you. Our task is to kill, to wreck, to destroy. We shall perform this task until I decide that it is time to return. We may be gone for several days. Under no circumstances are you to tell your families where you are going. And if you are caught, you say nothing. He who identifies me, or Major Chafatz, may be sure that his family will pay. Now then," Yunis Umbark concluded, his voice suddenly very quiet, "we are embarked on a holy cause. Each of us is a *feday*—one whose soul and life are committed to this task. We shall kill like *fedayin* and if necessary die like *fedayin*."

The men returned to their huts. Musa was quite calm. It would not be his first crossing into Jewish territory. Nor did the prospect of killing faze him any longer. In any case there was no longer an alternative.

On the night of the mission the men met once again at the stone house. Yunis Umbark passed out wrist watches and weapons. All the *fedayin* received either rifles or automatic grease guns. Musa was given the knapsack with the food: twenty *pitah* rolls, and a quantity of salt, pepper, and onions.

Yunis Umbark also carried a large knapsack on his back, as well as a Sten gun and two grenades strapped to his right shoulder. Then the party set out, Umbark in the lead, Suleiman Abd al-Rabivo, Hamid Hadad, Saïd al-Saga, and Ibrahim Attah Chalil following.

The route was a familiar one. The men crossed the border at the Wadi Harbiyah, near the sea. By 10:00 P.M. they had reached Beit Darras. In the distance a tiny light moved and a motor droned. Yunis Umbark moved closer, and then returned.

"It is a tractor," he said. "All alone. Perfect. We can start right here. Come with me, Rabivo."

The two men stole off in the darkness. Musa and the others waited. A minute passed, then another. Suddenly the night was shattered by the burst of a Sten gun. The tractor's motor continued to run. Within moments the two men raced back across the field, crouched low.

"I'll cut you all in on that one," Yunis Umbark panted. "It was too easy."

The group continued northward at a quick trot. At dawn they reached Nitzanim, and took cover in the neighboring dunes. Yunis Umbark posted a military watch, and the other men slept. At dusk Ibrahim Chalil and Umbark prepared to move out on their own.

"Stay covered," said the leader. "We'll pay a little social visit on their houses." Then the two men drifted off to the east. Again Musa and his companions waited fearfully. They were rewarded shortly by the sound of a quick, flat explosion, followed by the rattle of automatic fire. Then silence. Within minutes Yunis Umbark and Ibrahim Chalil returned. This time the leader was grinning.

"Now you know what I carried in my bag," he said. Chalil triumphantly exhibited a child's hand and a powder-stained woman's shoe.

Musa was eager to return. Every border policeman in the area was surely on the alert for them. The men were pressing their luck.

But Yunis Umbark had other ideas. The wiry little instructor was apparently nerveless; without looking back, he maintained the rapid pace northward. By 11:15 P.M. the group had passed the light-fringed coastal town of Ashdod Yam. And still the group continued. By midnight even Yibneh had long since been left behind. Soon Musa could smell the dank marsh water. That would be the Rubin stream. He began to perspire; was Yunis Umbark taking them into Tel Aviv itself? But in the marshes the leader finally called a halt. The men unloaded their gear, and dropped wearily to the ground. Musa handed out rations of *pitah* and onions.

"We shall encamp here until midnight tomorrow," Yunis Umbark informed the men. "You can forage on your own now, or steal—you can even dynamite. Only one thing—" he lifted a finger—"no killings except under my orders."

Obediently, the *fedayin* promptly dispersed in separate directions. Musa moved swiftly toward the Wadi Chanin; he had heard the cackle of geese when they had passed by earlier. Nor did his instinct fail him. The fenced enclosure contained at least two dozen plump, succulent fowl. It was a simple matter to cut the wire. Within moments he had seized three geese by their gullets and stuffed them into his bag. In the farmhouse itself no one stirred. Twenty minutes later Musa retraced his steps to the swamp. Saïd al-Saga had preceded him, and was sorting out four pairs of stolen work shoes. Together, the two men cooked and devoured one of the geese. The savor of it brought tears to Musa's eyes.

By morning light all the others had returned. Some brought chickens, some work tools. Yunis Umbark proudly exhibited a wallet filled with twelve Israel pounds. From the inner lining he removed a human ear, and held it up for admiration. Then the group prepared to move. This time the instructor changed the route. They would head inland and cover their tracks.

"Release the safety catches on your guns," he warned. "The Jews will be out after us by now."

He was right. Halfway between Shedema and Bitsaron two jeeps loaded with armed men in civilian clothes passed within hearing distance. The Arabs lay flat on their bellies in a clump of weeds. The first time they were unnoticed. Late that afternoon, however, Yunis Umbark raised a hand, stopping the procession short. On the eastern rim of Beit Ezra two border policemen were scanning the ground with mine-detection equipment. Again the group crouched low. Umbark kept them squatting on their haunches for nearly an hour. Finally the policemen returned to their automobiles and drove off.

Safety descended again with the night. Nine hours later, when darkness finally lifted, the men had covered the fifteen remaining miles to Beit Hanun, and Arab territory. The moment Musa caught sight of the first Egyptian military policeman he began to tremble violently. The trip had proved far more unnerving than his first border-crossing of two years earlier. By the time he reached Gaza's central square, he was faint. Several of the other men were stumbling in near-shock. Yunis Umbark stared at them, his lips curled slightly at the edges.

"Had enough, have you?" he said. "Go home, then, my swords of Islam. You can meet me at the major's office tomorrow at noon. We'll make our accounting then."

Musa reached his hut on will power alone.

"Woman, I am sick," he gasped to Adiyah. "Bring me the pail and do not question me."

But by mid-morning of the next day, Musa was much improved. He managed to down a warm breakfast. After the third cup of coffee, his tension finally eased. He looked forward eagerly to the noon meeting on Zeitoun Street. A real payment was due this time.

Nor was Musa disappointed. The major was in a benign mood. Sitting back comfortably in his swivel chair, Chafatz smiled approvingly at the six *fedayin*.

"Yunis Umbark has given me a good report," he said. "You obeyed his orders precisely and did not flinch in the face of danger. It is true that each of you did not individually make a killing. But together you accounted for four Jews, and one farmhouse dynamited. A good record. I promised you a reward, and a reward you shall have." He opened a brass box on his desk and removed a roll of currency. "Umbark and I have decided that eleven pounds for each of you is not excessive."

The men said nothing. Chafatz counted out the bank notes and distributed them. Then he opened the newspaper which lay folded before him. The print was Hebrew.

"Anyone read Hebrew?" asked the major. "No? Then I will tell you what it says. This is *HaAretz*, one of the Jews' leading papers. It bears this morning's date." He smiled. "I repeat: this morning's date: March 18, 1954. Our intelligence system is better than perhaps any of you realized. And the newspaper describes—admits—the following *fedayin* actions of the last few days: a tractor driver killed, a woman and a child killed, an elderly man killed, a flock of sheep worth sixty thousand Jewish pounds stolen, valuable irrigation equipment stolen, a farmhouse dynamited. Most important of all, the paper describes the ambush of a bus at Scorpion's Pass, along the road to Beersheba, with the death of eleven Jews. This happened yesterday."

There was a murmur of astonishment from the men. Major Chafatz laid the paper aside and nodded significantly. "Are you surprised? Perhaps you had imagined that you were the only infiltrators ever sent into their territory. Let me make it very clear that you are not. For the past few months we have been taking a heavy toll of Jews."

Indeed, for longer than that. Since 1949, the Israel government had admitted to 5,092 thefts committed by Arab interlopers, 203 armed robberies, 108 cases of sabotage. By early 1954 the total losses to marauders were estimated at $4,000,000. But the assault on human life was far more ominous. The ambush at Scorpion's Pass represented the 1,828th armed attack since the Palestine Armistice of 1949. Nor had Chafatz exaggerated the recent and growing intensity of terrorist activities. Since June of 1953 systematic shootings and bombings had become almost daily occurrences. During each succeeding month the number of Jewish casualties mounted, reaching 796 by March, 1954. The major left no doubt of the terrorist campaign's true purpose.

"He knows," Chafatz pointed to the photograph on the wall. "And he has promised. The Palestine war is just beginning. Before it is over, every refugee between here and the Tigris will have resumed his rightful place in his homeland. What was taken from you is the least of what will be returned to you. The houses and farms of the Jews will be yours, too. Mark his words."

Musa clenched his jaw but showed no expression. He had heard that promise five years earlier. If he had not believed it then, he would not have been here now. The major must have anticipated the thought.

"The colonel is not Farouk, gentlemen," he said. "This man is a fresh wind, and he is sweeping Egypt clean. The corrupt old days are gone forever. The effendis no longer buy and sell souls at will. Their land is being redivided. The fellahin are being given their own plots. The army has been purged of traitors. It is a sword." Here Mustafa Chafatz's voice dropped to a conspiratorial whisper. "With that sword he shall strike down the enemies of our people in every corner of the Arab world. But Palestine must come first."

Chafatz lapsed into silence, his eyes glowing as he stared intently at the photograph. Yunis Umbark motioned the men to their feet.

"We are going to strike, and strike again, my comrades," the instructor promised. "Throughout Gaza groups such as ours are being organized. The Jews shall not know a moment's rest."

In truth, the Jews were not sleeping. By the time of the Scorpion's Pass massacre, they had already begun to devise effective countermeasures against the terror raids. Hundreds of crack troops from Israel's regular army were transferred to the border police, and trained intensively in antiguerrilla tactics. In the spring of 1954, Arab marauders were trapped, captured, or killed with increasing frequency. With the unqualified approval of David Ben-Gurion, acting in his role of minister of defense, Jewish army squadrons now adopted the practice of launching savage reprisal raids against Arab infiltration lairs.

But for all the militancy of Jewish countermeasures, the *fedayin* attacks continued and steadily gained momentum. Each week new groups of convicted criminals were brought into Gaza and Bani Suheila for indoctrination and training. Most of them were refugees, but some of them came now from Egypt proper. They were given to understand that the Jewish population was thoroughly demoralized and ripe for conquest. All that was required were a few more ruthless and daring terror actions. Infiltration was not to be limited any longer to border regions. Major Chafatz made this clear, in a meeting of September, 1954.

"The Jews have concentrated their forces along the demilitarized zones," he explained. "The United Nations armistice teams are keeping watch there, too. For this reason it is important for us to penetrate into the interior now, where they least expect us."

Here Musa ventured a comment. "Excellency, many of us are familiar with the border regions, and with them alone," he said. "For me, everything east of Yibneh is new territory."

The officer regarded the questioner coolly for several moments. It was Yunis Umbark who finally spoke.

"Are you a beginner at border crossings, Abid?"

"Excuse me, Abu Rashid?"

"Do you lack experience in hiding yourself from the Jews?"

Major Chafatz resumed the thread of his explanation, ignoring Musa altogether. "We suggest that every effort be made to penetrate the interior," he said. "Of course, anyone wishing to try his luck at the near-by kibbutzim —at Nahal Oz, for example, or Nir'im—is free to do so. But he does it at his own peril. The Jews will be on careful watch. They are keeping their searchlights switched on all night." Here Chafatz arose and walked over to the enormous wall-map of Palestine. With his swagger stick he tapped the sector east of Tel Aviv. "This area embraces some of their biggest and best farm communities: Giv'at Brenner, Kfar Bilu, Be'er Ya'akov, Ekron. There are towns, too: Ness Ziona, G'derah, Rehovot, Ramle, Lydda. Ramle and Lydda, gentlemen. Do I have to tell the Palestinians among us the role Ramle and Lydda have played in the history of our people? The Jews who have moved into these towns and villages have grown prosperous and fat in peace. They read of the attacks on the border villages and they are alarmed. But in their fear they still do not dream that it can happen to them. And so they remain, conduct their affairs, and raise their children." He tapped the map again significantly. "We must put a stop to that."

The major returned to his desk. "You will operate individually," he continued. "Those who strike effectively will be appropriately rewarded. I ask only that you remember that the Jews have a way of publishing the accidents that happen to them. If a man brings me an ear which he says is an Ekron ear, and the Jews say that it is a Yad Mordecai ear—a border ear— I shall believe the Jews."

Then Yunis Umbark distributed the weapons. Each man received a new Swedish submachine gun, three magazines of cartridges, three *pitah* loaves, and two hundred Egyptian pounds. When night fell they were allowed to depart.

Musa entered Jewish territory near Erez, and turned north. This time, however, he reached no further than the eastern fringe of Kibbutz Yad Mordecai, only two miles away. The familiar bronze statue of the Jewish hero, Mordecai Anielewicz, was barely visible under a crescent moon. A dog barked in the underbrush nearby. Musa tightened his grip on the Karl-Gustav gun. There were footsteps. Suddenly a man's voice called out: "Mi zeh? Tatzor!—Who's there? Stop!" Then, in Arabic: "Andak!"

His heart pounding, Musa lifted the Karl-Gustav to his shoulder and searched wildly for his target. When a shadow moved he squeezed the trigger. The flame leaped into the surrounding thicket. There the Jew stood, only five yards away, smoke curling from his Sten gun. Musa staggered, digging his fingers into the sand. Somehow he clambered to his feet again, and then doubled back toward the border. There were no further shots. No one followed him. As he ran, the gun dropped from his right arm, and the arm itself stiffened and flopped crazily to his gait, as if it had a will of its own.

He reached Erez in a half-hour, and crossed over into demilitarized territory ten minutes after that. Finally, at Beit Hanun, Musa planted himself in the middle of the road and waited for a vehicle to come his way. It was not a long wait; the Gaza highway was congested with military traffic. Within moments a staff car braked to a halt in front of him. Musa walked erratically toward the driver.

"I have come from . . . I have come . . ." he whispered.

"I can see where you have come from, habibi," said the driver with some alarm, as blood splashed on his steering column. "Get in."

But Musa fainted.

He awoke in the army hospital at Khan Yunis. Nearby stood ten empty cots. A corporal stared at him curiously from a table at the entrance to the room.

"Have a nice rest?" asked the soldier.

"What happened?"

The corporal laughed. "You don't remember? You had three Jewish slugs in your arm, that's all. The doctor will be here soon. He'll tell you."

Musa lay back silently and waited, averting his eyes from the obscene gray cast that rested on the bed beside him. In the early afternoon the doctor arrived, a tall, heavy-set Copt in lieutenant-colonel's uniform. He lifted the stricken arm delicately, and Musa shrieked.

"Not surprising," murmured the doctor. "Elbow shattered, tendons and muscles nearly severed. I patched it all up as best I could, but you won't get much use out of it anymore. Are you right-handed?"

Musa nodded weakly.

The doctor clucked his tongue. "Rest, for the time being," he said. "We'll discharge you in a few days. When you get back to Gaza the American doctor there will tell you what to do."

But there was not much that could be done. Six weeks later, the cast was removed. The arm had become quite stiff. The American doctor recommended physiotherapy, and gave Musa a rubber ball to squeeze. Eventually the wounded man regained the use of his right hand, but the arm itself would bear little weight. He kept it covered, even in the warmest weather, for it was twisted and disfigured. And one afternoon, brooding over his injury, Musa decided to visit Major Chafatz.

The officer received him politely. "I was distressed to learn of your injury," he said, offering Musa a cigarette. "You have a creditable record here."

Musa accepted the cigarette, but said nothing.

"What are your plans?" asked Chafatz.

Musa nodded glumly; he had expected that. "What plans can I have, Excellency?" he replied. "I have been crippled. It will be years before my arm is well again—if ever. I wish to remind Your Excellency that this injury has been suffered in the service of Your Excellency."

"In the service of our people, surely," said the major amiably.

"Our people sit in these camps, Excellency. How many of them have run the risks I have run?"

"That is the fate of soldiers."

Musa's voice began to shake. "But I am not a soldier. I have not been trained as a soldier. I risked terrible, frightful dangers, alone, without an army behind me. What is to happen to me now? I have a wife and children?"

The officer sighed, and glanced out the window. "What do you want?" he asked.

The refugee placed his crippled hand against his chest. "I am a poor man, Excellency. Am I not to receive payment for the services I have rendered?"

Chafatz tapped his fingers on the surface of his desk. "But you have been well paid for your services," he observed, with growing irritation.

"Effendi, I appeal to your merciful heart. What payment can possibly compensate me?"

"Let me think about it." Chafatz rose, signaling the end of the interview.

Musa returned to the house on Zeitoun Street several times within the next few weeks. But the major was invariably too busy to see him. Finally, in exasperation, the Negro accosted Yunis Umbark as the latter sat drinking in a coffee shop.

"Peace be on you, Abu Rashid. I hesitate to disturb your privacy."

"What is it, Abid?" asked the instructor.

"May I sit down?"

"I asked you: what is it?"

Musa cleared his throat several times. "Abu Rashid, my leader, I ask your understanding, your help."

"You ask my money," said Yunis Umbark, calmly downing his coffee.

Suddenly the words spilled out before Musa could stop them. To his horror, he realized that customers and passers-by were staring at him, and that he had lost control of himself once again. "You received sixty pounds each mission, you swine, sixty pounds," he shrieked, the cords standing out on his neck. "I received eleven pounds and a crippled arm. In God's name—"

"In the name of your father," Yunis Umbark interrupted in the same even voice, his fist suddenly clenched tight on Musa's collar. "I will tell you what will happen to you if you bother me or the major again. You will be taken in a command car to the border, and there you will be sent straight into the arms of a Jewish border patrol. The Jews will show you the kind of payment you can expect. Move now, quickly. You are obstructing my sunlight."

Musa slunk back to his family. The months passed, and he found himself drifting into the camp routine once again. There were aimless strolls between hut and commissary, the endless card games played for ration cards and cigarettes. The rains came and the seasons changed. Adiyah gave birth to another daughter. More soldiers were seen each day in the Gaza coffee shops. The hypnotic smile of the president shone from every second wall and shop window. Among the refugees, the perennial rumors of invasion were repeated now with growing conviction and urgency. But for Musa nothing changed. The sun rose and set on his grievance. When his fingers closed on the rubber ball it was the throat of Major Chafatz he held in his hands. Many times Musa had seen him driving through the town square in his gray Plymouth, accompanied by the lieutenant and Yunis Umbark. One burst of the Karl-Gustav would have done the job, the Karl-Gustav he had dropped in his panic near Yad Mordecai.

Then the day his neighbor told him the news he refused to believe it. Those tales were too easily circulated, and he had heard them before. But the story persisted, and Musa finally determined to learn the answer for himself. Each day he sat silently in his old coffee shop and waited. Admittedly, the gray Plymouth was no longer to be seen. Then three more weeks passed, and still there was no sign of the major. Perhaps it is true after all, thought Musa. And in the end Army Information Headquarters at Al-Arish confirmed the rumor. Mustafa Chafatz was dead. According to the official announcement, the major had inadvertently driven his automobile over a land mine. The complete facts came out only later. Chafatz had indeed been blown to pieces, but not by a mine. He had received a package postmarked Nicosia, Cyprus. In fact, the gift was a bomb; it had been mailed—via Cyprus—by the Israel Intelligence.

God was good. At first Musa wept with happiness. Then, his eyes still swimming, he hurried off to Zeitoun Street. The stone house was evidently deserted. No matter; if Yunis Umbark was not back yet Musa would wait. His patience was limitless now.

He waited for two months. During that time neither soldiers nor police set foot in the house. Had intelligence headquarters been set up elsewhere? he wondered. But when Musa inquired at the central police station he was promptly thrown out.

"You are still on our books, murderer," shouted the sergeant. "If I catch you here again you'll go back to the death cell."

But Musa would not abandon the search that easily. Headquarters may have been relocated, but they could not have been dispensed with. There was too much activity in the Gaza Strip for that. By autumn of 1955 the street were choked with additional thousands of Egyptian troops. At night the earth trembled with the weight of Soviet-built tanks and artillery caissons. The dull explosion of heavy caliber shells echoed repeatedly from the Sinai wastes, to the southwest. It was said that there had been an arms agreement with the Russians. After September of 1955, in any case, the testing of the new Russian weapons never stopped.

Neither, for that matter, did the guerrilla forays into Israel. By the opening of the new year *fedayin* and paramilitary attacks had inflicted 1,300 Jewish casualties—465 of them the works of Gaza-based infiltrators. Between August, 1954, and March, 1955, the United Nations Mixed Armistice Commission condemned Egypt forty times, warning that the assaults were "repeated acts of planned demolition in Israel by well-trained, armed and organized groups coming from Egyptian-controlled territory." On April 13, 1955, the United Nations Security Council stressed the gravity of these attacks, and imposed upon Egypt the responsibility of stopping them. Yet, far from repudiating the terror campaign, the Egyptian president took personal responsibility for it. It was only a matter of time, he announced, "before final and terrible retribution will be visited upon the usurpers of Palestine."

By 1956 none of the Arab refugees doubted him any longer. Not when the Jews themselves admitted the loss of twenty and thirty civilians a month to the *fedayin*. No population would suffer that kind of bloodletting for long if it had an army worthy of the name. Time was running out for the Jews. The excitement in the refugee camps was thick enough to taste. Conversations were animated now. Eyes shone; energy replaced languor and indifference. Men speculated and wagered on the date of invasion. Women chatted once again about wedding feasts and long-forgotten recipes. Children amused each other with mythical descriptions of the land they had never seen.

And Musa sat at a corner of the city square and waited for his man, watching the faces of the passers-by. Emaciated, hollow-eyed natives, the

Gazans, poorest of all the refuse in the Strip, shuffled past in their tattered buffalo-hide shoes. So too, did the rumpled, mud-complexioned soldiers, itching from the dust of the desert and the chancres of Gaza's back streets. There were always the refugees, of course; one recognized them by their sallow complexions and flaccid arms and bellies. Commercial agents in business suits had poured into town. Sitting at the front tables of coffee shops, they sawed the air with ringed fingers, negotiating supply contracts with army officers. And the officers, bottomless caverns of Turkish coffee, lolled back like pashas in their seats, listening with mild curiosity to the promises of baksheesh. The best rooms in town were theirs, the latest model American automobiles.

One afternoon in April, a sleek 1956 Ford pulled up to the coffee shop. Musa jerked his head as if he had been slapped. Stepping out into the street was a familiar slim figure in a beautifully tailored olive-green uniform. It was Yunis Umbark. The two recognized each other simultaneously. But it was Musa who spoke first.

"Peace on you, Abu Rashid. All these months I have been searching for you."

"You again," sighed the officer. "Have you nothing better to do with your time?"

"I see you are a captain, Abu Rashid. God's blessing on you."

"All right. What do you want?"

"You know what I want, Abu Rashid. The major is dead. Now the authority is yours. Can you not do something for me?"

Yunis Umbark took a deep breath. "Back to that again, are we?" he said. "Let me tell you something, Abid. I go on more missions in Palestine than all the other *fedayin* put together. But if anything should happen to me, my family would get nothing. And I have a wife and four children. Now stop your sniveling and let me by."

Musa began to smile. He accompanied the officer into the coffee shop. When Yunis Umbark sat down, Musa stood beside him.

"I warn you, Abid—" the Egyptian began.

"Perhaps I can do something for you, Abu Rashid," said Musa, still smiling. "My right arm can hold a gun again. You see?" He extended his hand and squeezed the rubber ball. "Not all your men come back. But I have exchanged gunfire with a Jew, Abu Rashid, and I am here to talk about it."

The officer turned in his seat and examined Musa carefully for nearly a full minute. Then he summoned the waiter. "Bring us some coffee," he said.

The two men conversed in low tones for the next hour and a half. As they made their plans, it became quite apparent to Musa that Yunis Umbark had lost none of his courage or imagination. During the past two months he had struck again and again at the very heartland of Jewish settlement, the heavily populated Ramle-Lydda-Petach Tikvah triangle. The theory was to leap-frog the border police, who had concentrated their forces along the Gaza frontier. It had worked perfectly. During the last week alone

Yunis Umbark and his marauders had gunned down eleven Jewish civilians.

"If they expect us at night we attack in daylight," the officer explained. "If they throw barbed wire around their farms we strike at their towns. Sometimes we get buses or taxis. They can't protect everything that moves."

"What about their dogs?" Musa asked.

"On the borders, mainly. The idea is to go where the people are. Dogs lose the scent that way."

In the end the two men reached agreement. They would prowl the thickly inhabited complex of farm settlements on the plain of Shafrir. The date was set for the third night; there would be no moon then. As Musa rose to leave, Yunis Umbark tapped the table.

"You have not asked about payment, Abid?" he said.

Musa pressed his hand flat against his chest. "I trust you, Abu Rashid," he said. Then he walked out into the square.

His brows drawn together, the officer watched Musa's retreating figure intently. Long after the Negro had vanished in the crowd, Yunis Umbark continued tapping his fingers on the table.

Time passed slowly in the hut. When her husband failed to go out for his afternoon card game, Adiyah grew nervous. When he began swabbing his shoes with cooking oil, she knew. She whined. He ignored her, a dreamy smile hovering about his lips. On the third night after the others had gone to bed, he murmured: "This payment is for the children," and then lapsed into silence again. The last time he left the house he cast a fleeting glance at his wife. She looked back into his eyes and this was their good-by.

Yunis Umbark awaited him at the prearranged meeting point outside Gaza. Musa recognized the command car, its markings obliterated with black paint. He climbed in without a word. Immediately the vehicle swung back onto the road and continued toward the southwest. At Deir al-Balah it turned eastward along a sunken dirt path. Ten minutes later it stopped.

"We'll cross here," said Yunis Umbark. "It takes a little longer this way, but the Jews have the entire northeast border heavily guarded. Take this." He handed Musa a knapsack of food, an army spade, and a submachine gun. Then he strapped the identical baggage to his own back, and left the jeep.

The two men walked swiftly due east, toward the sulphur quarries. The country was seared and pitted, dank and foul-smelling. But it was safe. No infiltrator had ever been caught here. Fully six hours passed, with Sderot and Ibim left behind, before Yunis Umbark so much as released the safety catch on his Karl-Gustav. By then the derricks on the Heletz oil field were in view.

"Dig," ordered the officer. "A hole will be our only protection till mid-afternoon. The crews take their break then."

Yunis Umbark watched as Musa set to work with his spade. The Negro moved with dispatch, adroitly using his right elbow as a fulcrum, throwing his entire weight on his right leg and left arm. Within a quarter-hour the men were burrowed securely into the earth. They ate and drank sparingly, and then slept. When Musa awakened the sun blazed high in the sky. Yunis Umbark was carefully studying the horizon. Another hour passed before the officer gave the order to move again.

It was a desolate landscape. After the Heletz field nothing was to be seen except an occasional camel foal. Yunis Umbark knew the route well. Swiftly and surely he picked his way along the barren stretches of marl and sandstone protruding between the isolated Jewish farm villages. By midnight the men had reached the outskirts of G'derah. There they rested in a thicket. Musa was exhausted. They had traveled nearly forty kilometers in thirty hours. This man knows his business, Musa admitted.

He awoke with the officer's hand on his shoulder. The sky had brightened.

"It is daylight," Musa murmured anxiously.

"Are you afraid?" Yunis Umbark asked, watching him carefully. "If you were a Jewish border policeman when would you be on watch?"

Musa nodded. He arose and strapped his knapsack to his back.

"One thing," Yunis Umbark leveled a finger at his companion's chest. "You are to stay at my left at all times now, and two paces ahead. It is a system we have worked out. It offers better protection."

"As you say, Abu Rashid," Musa replied. And he thought to himself: you are smart, Yunis Umbark, but I am smarter. I shall protect your flank now because I need you. But when our mission is completed, I am going to take payment for my children.

The men moved cautiously, bending low as they skirted the thickets and clumps of trees. The area swarmed with movement, with trucks and automobiles on the highway, field hands and tractor drivers on the adjoining farm strips. Still, Yunis Umbark was right; thus far there were no police. Long experience had taught the infiltrators to stay between fifty and a hundred yards to the side of the road, where the trees served as camouflage. Despite the traffic, the men maintained a steady loping rhythm for intervals of twenty minutes or a half-hour. Whenever a farmer drew too close, they dropped to their stomachs, cradling the guns tightly in their arms. It did not happen often. By midday they had reached the southwest outskirts of Ramle. There they rested in an alfalfa field and ate.

After 2:00 P.M. torpor began to settle on the countryside. Traffic thinned on the roads. The distant chatter of children from Ramle's streets slowly ebbed. Once again Yunis Umbark cocked his head and climbed to his feet.

"Abu Rashid," cautioned Musa, "there is much movement here."

"Not for long," the officer replied. "It is *hafsaka* time, their daily break."

"The Europeans too?"

"You have been away too long, habibi," said Yunis Umbark. "Almost the only people who live here now are Orientals. They follow our timetable." Then he suddenly grasped Musa by the shoulders, glaring at him. "And listen," he hissed, "I am deciding things here. Don't question my orders."

Yes, Yunis Umbark, Musa thought to himself. It is plain that you are more frightened than I am.

But the officer was right. The sector was reasonably clear now. Only a small group of bicyclists was visible on the horizon, pumping listlessly into town. The tip of Ramle's abandoned mosque shimmered in the distant heat waves. Eight years ago the muezzin would have been chanting there, Musa recalled. Then he arose and swung out to the left of his companion.

The rest of the trek was uneventful. Ninety minutes later the men slowly ascended the Shafrir plateau. It was superb country, lush emerald-green. The ridge was stippled with well-cultivated fields and freshly painted white houses and barns. Chickens and geese gabbled from the poultry runs. An occasional cow mooed. And far below unfolded the plain of Lydda, a softly glowing mosaic of farms and factories. To the east the radio tower of Lydda's international airport presided like a stamen over the unfolding petals of white, concrete runways. Twin-engined jet airplanes casually wheeled and glided overhead. Musa stared about him in wonder.

"Keep to my left now." Yunis Umbark's voice had taken on a hard, brittle edge. "We are almost there."

Musa did as he was ordered. The officer angled quickly to his right, then to his left, alternately straightening and crouching. Finally he dropped to his stomach, breathing quickly.

"Look straight ahead," he said, his voice betraying its first excitement. "Do you see? Kfar Chabad."

Musa saw ten small white barracks, separated by narrow, neatly trimmed lawns. Adjoining the buildings were a small garden, a goose pen, and what appeared to be a playground. Children strolled through the compound. They were all boys. Musa noticed, too, that they were all quite swarthy, some nearly as dark as he.

"Jews?" he whispered.

"All Jews," replied the officer. "It's an agricultural training school. It's run by rabbis, and except for the teachers only children are here." He turned to Musa and smiled. "All children, you understand? That's why we've come so far."

Musa nodded slowly. It was an ideal target. None of the youngsters looked old enough for military training. With their skullcaps and earlocks, few of them could ever have held a gun in their hands. Nor would there be mine fields near-by—too dangerous with children about. Yes, it was unquestionably an ideal target from every point of view. You are smart, Yunis Umbark, he admitted. He waited for instructions. But the officer merely shook his head.

"Eat and rest if you like," he said. "We shall remain here till sunset."

Musa nibbled on an onion and one of the *pitah* loaves. Then he lay on his back and gazed at the sky. There was not a cloud to be seen. The air was clean, pure, and bright. It was a day worth waiting for. He closed his eyes and tasted the breeze. So it blew once on the Wadi-Chanin heath. The voices belonged to his children, scampering across the court to meet his returning mule cart. From Yibneh he had brought Fatma and Masouda two

Turkish delights, and for Gabr and Daud there were two rolls of halvah. Lovely children, his jewels. At dusk the sizzling oil crackled from Adiyah's kitchen, and the muezzin's voice echoed from Zarnuqa. He was not a religious man himself, but he had encouraged his sons to join Sidi Sheik and the men at the well. There they bowed eastward and joined in the evening devotions. The muezzin called and they answered, their voices mingled gently with the evening wind.

Yunis Umbark's hand was on his shoulder again, and he opened his eyes. The sun had set. The plaintive singsong of children's voices rose and fell from the nearest building. Yunis Umbark checked a small sheet of paper.

"This is known as the Aravit," he said. "Their evening prayers."

"I remember," said Musa.

"They are all together in that room now. This is a chance that comes once in a lifetime. We are not going to bungle it." The officer looked at his watch. "In exactly three minutes you will enter that door. When I give the signal you will fire at full automatic."

"Where will you be, Abu Rashid?"

"At the window, just across from you. You will see me. This will enable us to catch them in a cross fire. At the same time I shall be well located to pick off any instructors who come from my side. Join me when your first clip is exhausted. I will know how to get us out." He climbed to his feet. "I shall circle the building now."

The two men peered into each other's eyes intently for a moment. Neither said a word. Then Musa watched Yunis Umbark dart swiftly into the abandoned compound, and then vanish at the other end of the barracks. You will empty your clip, habibi, thought Musa, but mine will be only half-empty.

Then he stared at his watch. When the first minute and a half passed he rose. Thirty seconds later he dashed to the corner of the building and crouched there. A half-minute after that he padded softly toward the door, carefully ducking his head below the window ledges. Then he flattened himself against the wall, gripping the Karl-Gustav tightly in his left hand. At that moment the voices of the children suddenly fell silent. Musa ran his tongue over his lips. He looked again at the watch. Fifteen seconds still remained. From his vantage point the compound was quite empty. The children could not have been warned. Yet none of them spoke. The only sound was the cackle of geese. From within the room someone coughed. Nothing else. Three minutes had passed.

Musa laid a moist hand on the knob. The door sighed, releasing a sliver of light. Still not a sound from within. His chest heaving, he eased the door inward and stepped across the threshold. He saw perhaps fifty small boys praying silently, rocking their heads gently over their prayerbooks. None of them looked up. Perhaps they would have seen nothing in any case, for they were manifestly in a different world. Then Musa stared at the window across the room. His eyes widened, and he blinked twice. Instantly his heart froze within him. No one was there. My watch is wrong, screamed the unspoken thought. But the moment the possibility crossed his mind he knew it was a lie. Nothing had been left to accident. *I will know how to get us out*—the irony of Yunis Umbark's words struck Musa's poor brain like a hammer.

Suddenly a grown man, wearing a red beard and earlocks, lifted his head from the prayerbook and stared into Musa's eyes. His mouth slowly opened. Yes, and that, too, is part of the plan, sobbed Musa, as his hand flicked to the wall switch, extinguishing the light. He squeezed the trigger of his weapon. "*Yahud,* you!" he roared in anguish and hatred. In the darkness he could see their ghouls' faces clearly. The soldiers in the twelve jeeps twisting across the Migdal heath. And also brother-in-law Saïd. The man in the red tarboosh. The bedouin sheik. Hassan al-Tafran, the storekeeper. The grinning colonel with the hawk nose and the white teeth. Major Chafatz. Yunis Umbark. "*Yahud,* everyone of you!" he howled. "*Yahud!*" And the leaping, shuddering gun repeated the word—*yahud, yahud*—until the clip was exhausted.

CHAPTER SIX

THE CRIMINAL

ONE STANDS before the shopwindow and admires the display. Intricately filigreed in silver, the bracelets, earrings, and necklaces glitter in the faintest light. The pattern is indigenous to the Near East: a hived and latticed mosaic, monotonously and hypnotically geometric. It has been seen before on Arab screens and carpets. Laced and threaded now into clasps and pendants, into scarves and blouses, it captivates the shopper in hundreds of stores and curio shops throughout Israel. For if the rhythm of the design is Arabic; the workmanship is not. The craftsmen are Yemenite Jews.

Their aesthetic sense is unmistakably Arabic. In Israel one hears it as readily as one sees it. The country's most popular folk songs and folk singers are Yemenite, and they echo the plaintive and ritualized minor modes of classic Arab melody. For that matter, they look like Arabs. Even the city dwellers among them, the forlorn little maids beating rugs on Ashkenazic apartment balconies, the sad-eyed watermelon vendors and street cleaners, are all but indistinguishable from their Arab cousins in physiognomy and gait. The resemblance between Jew and Arab is particularly uncanny in the new immigrants' communities. Only the long beards and sidecurls on the men and the bandannas on the women set them apart as children of Israel.

Rosh HaAyen (or Ras al-Ain, as the Arabs formerly called it) is a case in point. Located two miles northeast of Petach Tikvah, this sprawling *ma'abara* city is inhabited almost exclusively by Yemenites. There are ten thousand of them, and they are all post-1949 newcomers to Israel. A visit there is a glimpse into another world. The dirt walking paths and market place teem with copper-skinned, curiously frail little people. Most of them are still dressed in the original costumes of their native Yemen. The men wear multicolored turbans; billowing Arab-style cassocks descend to their bare shins. The women, conversely, wear leggings and bright red puttees attached to their lower trousers; high-heeled sandals complete the bizarre effect. On festive occasions, with their tasseled capuches, gold-threaded dresses, and silver-loop earrings, Yemenite wives resemble caricatures of Arab harem women.

Their language is Arabic, of course, although well-infused with Hebrew words and phrases. Their food is typical Near Eastern fare: Indian beans and *bishas* (red peppers), onions, garlic, *pitah,* and *samne* (boiled butter). In the Arab style, many Yemenite women of Rosh HaAyen traditionally cook supper outside their homes in stone ovens. For social diversion, Rosh HaAyen's men still crouch in circles on the ground in the familiar posture of the Near East, their thighs resting on the backs of their heels for hours at a time. Like the Arabs, they enjoy smoking narghiles, long-stemmed Turkish water pipes.

The resemblance is by no means limited to superficialities. In immigrant communities like Rosh HaAyen, Arab customs are incorporated into some of the most fundamental and intimate of Yemenite Jewish folk mores. Thus, Yemenite girls until recently have been kept illiterate, required to stay at home and work in the household until a husband capable of paying *mohar* makes his appearance. Marriage at the age of thirteen or fourteen is not uncommon among the Yemenites; although now, in Israel, the legal limit has been set at eighteen. When children come, the woman frequently delivers her own babies—even in the Rosh HaAyen—refusing the aid of doctors or midwives. In true bedouin-Arab fashion, the mother squats on a piece of sacking, cutting the child's umbilical cord with a razor blade or a knife. Scorning the services of Israel's medical clinics, many Yemenites continue to resort to faith healers for their illnesses.

If it strains the Westerner's imagination today to accept these Arabized little people as "true" Jews, it was hardly less difficult in 1880, when a long, straggling procession, nearly five hundred of them, first made their appearance on the outskirts of Jerusalem. The city's "veteran" Ashkenazic and Sephardic settlers hardly knew what to make of these strangers. They called themselves Yemenites. But it seemed a kind of perversity, as if to preclude identification. For the Imamate of Yemen, a tiny, sun-scorched, and obscure kingdom tucked away in the southwestern corner of the Arabian Peninsula, was wrapped in a veil of mystery. Little was known of its inhabitants, except that presumably they were all Arabs. Now, however, the leaders of this bedraggled and exhausted band of travelers insisted that *they* were Jews, the vanguard of no less than sixty thousand Israelites still living in Yemen. It did not seem likely. They surely did not resemble any Jews ever seen before, not even the Arabic-speaking Maghrebim of North Africa, nor the ancient Morisco communities of Palestine and Syria.

Yet growing acquaintance with the newcomers soon left little doubt that their religious ritual, at least, was authentically Hebraic. Their jargon, too, was a mixture of biblical Hebrew and Arabic. And manifestly they viewed their arrival in the Holy Land as the fulfillment of a messianic decree. Moreover, with the documents, the ancient records, and the family genealogies they carried with them in their meager baggage, the Yemenites offered convincing proof that Jewish settlement in Yemen was at least as old as the Arab, extending back to the first century A.D., the period of the historic Exile from Palestine. The evidence suggested, too, that within three centuries after their initial arrival there were apparently enough Jews in southwestern Arabia to exert a powerful conversionary influence on the non-Jewish population. Indeed, by the sixth century Yemen's royal household was actually Judaized, and the monarch, Yusuf Dhu-Nuwas, secured the mass conversion to Judaism of thousands of Arabs. The clue to the contemporary Yemenites' remarkable physical resemblance to the Arabs can probably be found here: many, if not most of them, are direct lineal descendants of this original converted Jewish community.

The era of large-scale proselytization was an impressive one in the history of a refugee people—but a fleeting one as well. At the other, northern end of the Arabian Peninsula, a new faith was making important inroads of its own. By the end of the ninth century, in fact, the disciples of the Prophet had swept into their fold nearly the entire (pagan) population of the Near and Middle East. Ultimately the Jews of Yemen were transformed into a *dhimmi* (non-Moslem minority) people, subjected to poll taxes, required to behave discreetly, even obsequiously, in the presence of Moslems, and confined to an isolated quarter outside the city boundaries of Tsan'a, the capital. This was, in effect, the first ghetto in the Arab Near East. Later, similar ghetto quarters were decreed for Te'ez, Dama, and Rad'ah, towns containing smaller Jewish communities.

Even then, however, the circumstances of Jewish life in Yemen were by no means burdensome. Jews generally moved freely in the villages and markets for business purposes. Mob violence or pogroms were unknown, for Moslem legend had it that a Jew whose blood was shed cried for revenge on the Day of Resurrection. Moreover, many of the imams shared the Moslem regard for the Jew as Am al-Kitab—the People of the Book; from time to time the rulers enjoyed calling the Chief Rabbi (Haham Basha) of Tsan'a to their palace for long scholarly discussions. Although *dhimmi* peoples were forbidden to till the soil (agriculture was considered a "noble" avocation reserved for Moslems), even this restriction was not without its advantages. Specializing in craftwork, the Jews soon became Yemen's most respected artisans; pottery, goldsmithing, engraving, minting, were virtually a Jewish monopoly. Some Jews plied their trade in the towns, while others traveled about the villages and bedouin encampments to make ornaments for Arab dagger sheaths, belts, and saddles, and the jewelry the Moslems gave their women. The tradition of artisanry was so highly cherished that even rabbis, to supplement their incomes, took pride in practicing manual trades. Rare indeed was the Yemenite Jew whose standard of living was not higher than that of the Arabs, who could not afford to build a solid, blocklike house in his ghetto quarters, or who did not enjoy a reasonable degree of comfort and leisure.

At all times and under all circumstances, moreover, the overwhelming majority of Yemenite Jewry remained tenacious and uncompromising in matters of religious observance. Punctiliously they followed the minutest of religious rules and regulations, from the proper manner of cleaning before meals to rites connected with feminine hygiene and sexual relations. Their ghetto in Tsan'a might have been a labyrinth of filthy alleys, but the inhabitants themselves scrupulously attended a public bath once a week, because this was a prescribed religious ritual. The rooms of their homes might have been bare of furniture, with only carpets and mattresses on the floors; but the floors themselves were scrubbed, the walls washed white—according to the talmudic injunction. The wives who drudged uncomplainingly, cooking and washing during the week, now rested on Sabbath Eve, dressed themselves in their finest kimonos, their most lavishly ornamented silver-laced trousers, their most costly filigree jewelry. The Sabbath was holy. So was parenthood, and the authority of the father. Family life was quiet, patriarchal, and peaceful, as it was written.

Because, too, the Yemenites were devotees of Cabalah, they placed unquestioning faith in the imminence of Redemption. Indeed, the End of Days was more than a dream to them; it was an obsession which kept them in a perpetually apocalyptic state of mind. When comets appeared in the sky, when triplets were born, when the stricken mysteriously recovered from near-fatal illnesses, they saw these phenomena as portents of the Messiah's arrival. Only return to the Holy Land was required as ultimate preparation for the Day of Judgment.

Then, in 1880, the vision of Return suddenly assumed tangible contours. By sailing ship and caravan, rumors reached the Imamate of Yemen that Jews from far-off lands had arrived in the Holy Land to reclaim the ancient hope of Zion. The accounts were circulated of a wealthy Jewish prince, one Rothschild, who had purchased land for his people in the sacred sanctuary of Jerusalem; Hebrews once again were praying within the shadow of the Temple wall. Perhaps the rumors were exaggerated, even false; but even the slightest hope of redemption dared not be overlooked. In the grip of a messianic delirium, a hundred families from Tsan'a promptly sold their homes and set out for Palestine. Their voyage would have taxed the endurance of a Jonah or a Sinbad. Making their way on foot to the ports of Hudeida and Jedda, they traveled up the Red Sea in flat-bottomed sailing boats to Suez. From there they proceeded by land to Alexandria, then by steamer to Jaffa, and finally again by foot to Jerusalem. Fully a third of the women and children perished en route. But the rest reached their destination. These were the five hundred trembling and awe-struck Yemenites who, in the winter of 1880, finally entered the Holy City, and opened the window on a world passed by.

Each year they were joined by several hundred of their kinsmen. By the outbreak of World War I, in fact, no fewer than 7,400 Yemenites had arrived in Palestine. When the War ended the Imam officially prohibited further Jewish emigration. But still the exodus continued. Though all points of exit were barred to them, the Israelites somehow managed to steal or bribe their way over the border toward Aden. Between 1923 and 1946 yet an additional 17,000 of them drifted past the uncertain border, evaded camel patrols, occasionally languished in the jails of the Aden Protectorate, until their Western coreligionists bought their freedom. Even before the establishment of the State of Israel, therefore, the Yemenite population of Palestine, swollen by immigration and natural increase, had reached a total of nearly 40,000 people.

And then, with the Palestine war in 1948, Zion was the only world that mattered any longer; the rise of the State of Israel was the Apocalypse for which the Imamate's remaining Jews had waited. Even for the few to whom the Jewish Republic was not a messianic portent, it was now quite evident that life in Yemen had suddenly become intolerable. Enraged at the defeat of Arab forces on the battlefields of Palestine, bands of Moslem hooligans began pouring through the Jewish quarters of Tsan'a, Te'ez, Dama, Rad'ah —pillaging and burning. As in other Arab countries, Jews risked their lives each time they ventured into the streets. Departure now became a matter of life-and-death urgency for them.

The Imam put no obstacles in their way—not as long as the Jews left all their property and most of their possessions to the Crown. The Jewish Agency, in turn, arranged an amicable understanding with the three sheiks whose territories lay between the Imamate and the British Crown Colony of Aden. For a fixed sum, the rulers finally agreed to let the Jews pass through their domains unmolested. Across this bleak and rugged terrain, therefore, the largest numbers of Yemenite Jews made their way southward down to the coast. It was a fearsome trek, on foot, camping in the open, exposed to the ravages of malaria and tropical ulcers, to robbery and occasionally even murder by bedouin tribes. By the time the Yemenites arrived at the Joint Distribution Committee camp in Hashed, adjoining Aden, most of them were walking skeletons. Frequently weeks passed before they had recovered sufficiently for the last phase of their journey.

At last they were loaded onto awaiting planes—"The Magic Carpet." The title was the Jewish Agency's, and it was not inappropriate. Between January and November of 1949, 33,500 Yemenites were flown to Israel. During the following year and a half another 15,000 Jews were carried out. All in all, some 45,000 people—by far the bulk of Yemen's Jewish population—were borne to safety via the "Magic Carpet." The RAF airport at Khornaksar was an apiary of DC-4 passenger planes, chartered by the Agency for the flight to Israel. Coal-black Somali officials stood beside each transport and waved the Jews aboard. Huddling in the fuselage, 130 and 140 to a plane (few of the passengers weighed more than ninety pounds), the Yemenites waited in unspoken terror for the roaring birds to lift them skyward. The trip required a mere three hours. Each of those hours was measured in centuries, however. As the planes reached their cruising altitude and settled into the flight northwestward, the Middle Ages drifted back into the vanishing coastline. On the horizon the twentieth century lay in wait. And like the horizon, it was destined somehow to remain beyond the grasp of the confused and disoriented Yemenite fugitives.

Even for those whose standard of living had never been high, settlement in Israel proved to be an extraordinarily difficult, at times a traumatic, experience. The Yemenites had won physical and political security for themselves, to be sure. But in their former homeland they had been artisans. In modern, industrialized Israel the market for their craftsmanship was severely limited. Virtually the only certain livelihood now open to the newcomers was heavy manual labor: on moshavim, on road gangs, in desert drilling-stations; the wives hired themselves out as maids and laundresses. The change took its toll on these undersized, delicately boned men and women. Admittedly, their wages were the highest they had ever earned; there was food for their tables. In spite of the best medical efforts on their behalf, however, the tuberculosis rate among the Yemenites remained critically high. Few of them had the skills or education necessary for office jobs, or the better-paying opportunities that were reserved almost exclusively for the European-born.

Yet if the Yemenites were dissatisfied with their lot, they gave little outward indication of it. Quiet, apparently peaceful people, they seemed altogether immersed in the world of the spirit. In Rosh HaAyen, for example, the government met their requests by constructing five large synagogues, four religious schools, and no less than one hundred tiny prayer rooms. Each day the men scrupulously recited their prayers. Seated semicircle in the classrooms, the children droned away uncomplainingly at their Holy Writ. The Ashkenazim who watched them smiled fondly: such good, reliable people, they remarked, so gentle and law-abiding. Would that every Jew were as satisfied with his lot.

Still, the children remained a mystery. Their silence was unnerving. They regarded the bustling, secular Ashkenazic community about them with preternaturally knowing eyes. What were they thinking? How did their impressionable minds react to Western clothing, to the laconic self-assurance of Western speech, to the games and parties and handholding of European children? Did they contrast the mores and habits of the Ashkenazim with the mumbled cabalistic incantations of their parents, with the entrail reading, the amulets, charms, and talismans their elders draped about their necks, wrists, and ankles, the hands painted on walls and doorways to ward off the Evil Eye? The Ashkenazim lived in modern apartments, visited medical practitioners for their ailments, and entertained themselves at concerts and cinemas. But Yemenite parents still lived in shanties, or at best in tiny cold-water flats. They depended upon holy men and miracle workers to cure them, and sometimes even paid secret visits to the hashish dens of Jaffa and Wadi Saleb. It was written that father was king. But mother, not father, paid for the groceries. It was written that mother was queen. But mother was a maid in the Ashkenazic household. It was written that the law must be obeyed. But was the law meant for them? Ashkenazim wrote the law; Ashkenazic lawyers interpreted the law; Ashkenazic judges enforced the law. The new society was complex and unfathomable. Where did the little brown people belong?

A disproportionately large number of their youths had evidently belonged to the Stern Gang, the notorious pre-State band of anti-British terrorists. The information, which came to light in 1947, profoundly startled the inhabitants of the *Yishuv*. No one, not even Jewish Agency or university sociologists, had ever suspected before that unrest or violence churned in the breasts of these pious, silent, passive children. Close attention would have to be paid, so warned the juvenile authorities; something dangerous was happening. The warning was considered, discussed—and casually ignored.

Employers, even teachers, continued to regard their Yemenites with calm benevolence. If trouble arose, they insisted, it would come from the Moroccans or the Iraqis, not the Yemenites. Not our gentle Yemenites.

Ya'akov Merhavi's mother, a native of Palestine, was the daughter of Yemenite immigrants. Her husband was first-generation—less than two weeks off the boat from Aden when she married him. The boy was born on Yalag Street, an Arab-inhabited Haifa alleyway. Later he moved with his parents to Jeo Street. It was Jewish; its inhabitants were Moroccans, Yemenites, Bukharans. The odors, poverty, squalor were still Arab. The two-room shanty overflowed with children. By night they slept on two beds. By day they swarmed out into the alleys together with the Arab and Sephardic children, raced past the *felafel* and pepper stands, under wash lines, skittered in between bales and cartons on the wharves. Mother departed each morning to work as a maid. Father labored as a brick worker by day, a movie usher by night. Each year there was a new brother or sister, less room on the beds, a little less rice and *samne* for each on the table.

Overheard when the boy was seven: his sister telling a friend that Ya'akov was not her brother. He struck her, then ran screaming to his mother.

"Yooh, boy," the woman sighed, "time you know. You are all my children. But you alone came to me from another abba. Your abba is dead."

"Abba is dead," he peeped in terror. Who was this abba who lived with them?

The mother made a fitful effort to explain it all, then gave it up. There were too many mouths to feed in this house. Someone would have to be sent out for care elsewhere, and she knew now that it would have to be Ya'akov. He was dispatched to an orphan home.

At the orphanage he screamed, clawed, spat—and eventually escaped. Mother pleaded, but the boy would not be returned. Finally she enrolled him in a local Histadrut school for workers' children. The studies were not difficult. But for the next few years Ya'akov lived in fear. Once when he was twelve, a Yemenite classmate swore at him angrily during a scuffle in the recess period: "*Mumser*—bastard," he cried. "I curse your food and water."

For days after that Ya'akov would touch nothing but the leavings on the other students' plates. His mother asked the reason. When, at last, he answered, she gasped and ran off to market. Later she returned with a chicken, which she solemnly waved over her son's head three times.

"You can eat now," she assured him.

Still, he would not return to school. Instead he spent his daylight hours in the street, playing with the Arab urchins, filching vegetables and fruits from the grocers' stalls. One day his mother discovered that the boy was not in class, and beat him so furiously that the stepfather intervened. Finally, when Ya'akov was fourteen, the Haifa juvenile authorities sent him off to a school operated for children of broken homes.

Testimony of Ephraim Millo, probation department, ministry of social welfare:

> I knew Ya'akov Merhavi, in 1941, when the social welfare department of the Municipality of Haifa placed him in Kfar Avodah [the school]. There I worked as *madrich* and teacher. Ya'akov came to my group and class, and eventually we became friends. He was a tough, obstinate, impulsive, and aggressive youngster. . . . He was also very superstitious, like so many of the Yemenites. I remember once, in the school, when he obstinately refused his coffee. I found out that someone had cursed the coffee in Arabic. He was afraid that if he drank it he would die. . . . At first he was suspicious of me. One day he did not concentrate on his lesson, and quarreled with his classmates, then ran out to the field to try to escape. He was barefoot, and I could catch him only with difficulty. "Why did you try to escape?" I asked. Then I sensed that he was panic-stricken, and that he expected me to beat him severely. The fact that I did not shocked him. Henceforth he followed me about like a little dog. All he needed was someone to trust.

The principal of the school was not as patient as Millo. Once he seized Ya'akov by the scruff of the neck and slapped him. The boy responded by biting the principal's hand and hurling dishes at his face. Then he ran away, hitchhiking a ride home. His mother and stepfather tried to persuade him to return. They remonstrated with him. They beat him. Then for two days, they chained him to his bed without food. Still the boy remained adamant. It was finally decided that he would be sent to work.

Those were hard years for Oriental children. European craftsmen often exploited them unmercifully. Ya'akov's first employer, an Ashkenazic shoemaker, had little interest in teaching his apprentice the craft. Instead, the boy was sent out on delivery, carrying heavy sacks of leather to and from the shop. Occasionally the man beat him. Ya'akov endured it uncomplainingly until the day he stumbled under the weight of his sack, and his employer cursed him as a *"mumser ben mumser—bastard son of a bastard."* Trembling with rage, the youngster silently clenched and unclenched his fists, and then darted out of the shop. He slept in the streets for the next two nights, until he found another unpaid position, as apprentice to a carpenter. It was no improvement. Once the man broke Ya'akov's finger with a hammer. The carpenter was arrested, but Ya'akov was again in the streets.

His mother then decided to enroll him in a Histadrut youth center. And through the group he was assigned to a metalworker. Fortunately, this employer was a compassionate man. Under his guidance Ya'akov quickly learned to build drainage pipes, pails and other sheet-metal products. Soon he received his first weekly wages; proudly he turned the money over to his mother and stepfather. He had shown competence, and his competence was rewarded. He was a breadwinner. The other Yemenites in his youth group treated him with respect. Of course, the European children maintained their usual reserve, but Ya'akov assured himself that he had no need of their friendship. "Lily-skinned cowards," he called them behind their backs; he knew that he had twice their strength and courage. Indeed, when Ya'akov was fifteen he joined the Stern Gang. Fearlessly pasting anti-British placards on the walls at night, he won the admiration of his companions—Europeans and Orientals alike.

"You're a good boy, Ya'akov," his commanding officer, an Ashkenazi, once complimented him. "You don't give a damn for the entire British police force."

Indeed Ya'akov did not. He despised the blue-eyed swine.

In Ya'akov's sixteenth year, a Yemenite acquaintance stopped him in the street.

"Why have you been telling us your father is dead?" he asked. "I know that he is not dead."

Ya'akov placed his lunch pail on the ground and seized the man by the throat. "Alem umekh b'isnan—Your words in your mother's teeth," he snarled in Arabic. "Why are you lying to me?"

"Bas, bas, I am not lying," the man gasped, struggling to free himself. "Someone told me."

"Who?" the youth shrieked. He tightened his grip. "I'll strangle you unless you tell me who it was."

"Yihyeh Alkori," came the choked answer. It was a Yemenite worker who had once worked in the same neighborhood.

Releasing his grip, Ya'akov allowed the man to stagger off. Then he caught a bus to the Shemen factory, where his mother worked. He did not wait for the lunch hour before accosting her at her workbench.

"Ya, umma, you lied to me," he whispered furiously. "You said my abba was dead, and he lives."

For a moment the woman was speechless. Then, weakly, she asked: "Who told you this?"

"A friend told me. It is true, isn't it?"

She shrugged.

Ya'akov began to sob, impervious to the stares of the other workers. "Why didn't you tell me? Why did you keep it a secret?"

"I did not want you to know," she murmured. "You were too young. We were divorced before you were born. I never found out later what happened to your abba."

She would tell him nothing more. But for the boy, nothing else mattered but finding Yihyeh Alkori, the man who knew. Each day at noon he stopped work and resumed his search through the Yemenite quarter. It was a jungle of twisting streets and alleyways, all descending chaotically toward the harbor gates. Whenever Ya'akov believed that he had inspected his last doorpost, he found yet another shack, hidden in the shadow of a near-by house or stone stairway. The name was nowhere to be found. He asked friends and relatives, Arabs and Maghrebim, vendors of sunflower seeds and hashish peddlers, bearded *moris* (faith-healers) and pot-bellied saloon keepers. A shake of the head was the only answer. And one day, a month after he had embarked on his search, Hamama the whore jerked her thumb toward a dark fat man seated in a tavern. Ya'akov approached him with caution.

"Haya sidi," he said politely. "You are Mar Alkori?"

The man looked up slowly. His face bore the flush of a chronic alcoholic. "What of it?" he said.

"My mother is Esther, of Jeo Street. Nissim said you know where my father is. My real father."

The man riffled a deck of cards, still not taking his eyes from Ya'akov's face.

"Esther's son," he grunted, half to himself. Then he shook his head. "I know nothing."

Ya'akov asked him again, but the man waved him away. The youth remained in the saloon for the rest of the afternoon. When Yihyeh Alkori left for home, Ya'akov followed him.

"Mar Alkori," he begged, "tell me what you know."

"Go away," the man warned.

The next morning when Yihyeh Alkori walked out of his room, Ya'akov was waiting for him. They trudged silently toward the saloon, the boy several paces behind, neither venturing a word to the other. When the man sat, Ya'akov stood an arm's length away, tight-lipped and intent. Several times Yihyeh Alkori stared up at the youth uneasily, then quickly lowered his gaze. Finally, at sundown, he jumped from his seat and lurched at his tormenter.

"Ya heh, leave me alone," he roared, swiping wildly with his right arm.

"Tell me, tell me," Ya'akov screamed, easily evading the man's fist.

"I'll send you to the hospital, as I live," shouted Yihyeh Alkori, breathing heavily. "I don't know what you want. Maybe his name is Merhavi. I don't know."

Ya'akov ran out of the saloon. The next day he wangled two days' leave from his employer and took the bus to Jaffa. He made straight for the Yemenite quarter. They were the Yemenites he knew: the same maids and craftsmen and watermelon vendors and ditch diggers who lived in Haifa. A little more provincial, perhaps, their piety still intact. But Ya'akov talked their language.

"Do you know a man from Haifa," he asked, "one of our people who left a wife behind? He is Merhavi, my father. Perhaps he looks like me."

"What is his first name, boy?"

"His first name?" The voice lowered with shame. "I do not know his name."

The eyebrows rose. Attention focused on Ya'akov's cheeks, naked of earlocks. No, of course such a boy would not know his father.

In the end the search seemed hopeless, and Ya'akov gave it up. Instead he traveled to Tel Aviv, where his mother's father lived. The old man made his home with the other Yemenites, a short distance back of the Carmel Market. Phew, what an odor! Nothing in Haifa is this bad, thought Ya'akov to himself. He fought his way through the crowd. The vendors and house-wives haggled over fruits and vegetables; European matrons jostled bandannaed North African darkies before stalls piled high with carp and flounder, onions and radishes, cheeses and peppers, *felafel, hilbeh, humus, techina,* and sesame seeds; children competed with the flies for apple torts, halvah, honey-dips, and spun-sugar sticks; ash trays and belt buckles glinted on the shelves, rhinestone earrings and rings, plastic water bottles and handbags, cotton dresses, stockings, and lingerie flapped from clothespins and steel wires; arms shot out of the harassed swarm of shoppers, waving bits and snatches of muslin or crinoline; faces peered around necks and elbows, stared with eyes blue and brown and black, glazed with *arak* brandy, inflamed with bilharziasis, blistered and sealed over with trachoma; beggars opened their laps like refuse baskets, extended crippled hands like flies' mandibles; shouts, curses, warnings, imprecations ricocheted between the stalls in Rumanian, Arabic, Polish, Yiddish, Maghrebic, Hebrew; and well-dressed customers ducked for cover. From the Carmel Market a noise floated skyward: thousand-voiced, plaintive, choleric, horror-stricken, and resigned, the sound of East and West in collision.

Ya'akov found his grandfather at his usual vantage point, the kiosk at Nachlat Benjamin, at the neck of the market. The old man had been in the country since before the first great war, but he still insisted on wearing his purple turban and woolen cassock. Beard snow-white against his leathery skin, the grandfather rocked gently back and forth on crossed feet, sucking reflectively on his narghile. When he saw Ya'akov, his toothless mouth popped open in surprise.

"Grandson! Ma sha Allah aliha! What do you here?"

"Haya saba, I came to see you."

The old man peered closely at the youth. "Have you run away from home again?" he asked.

"Lah, saba." Ya'akov shook his head. "Umma knows I am here. I need information."

"Umm, sit down," clucked grandfather. "Eat some *kela.*" He handed his grandson a plate of dried peas.

Ya'akov squatted next to the old man and ate in silence for several minutes. Then he spoke.

"Saba, I am looking for my true abba. Tell me his name and where he is to be found."

The grandfather did not answer. He continued to suck on the narghile. Slowly, like veined and wilting petals, the heavy lids settled over his eyes.

Ya'akov persisted: "There will be no peace until I know, saba."

"Aywah, aywah," the old man murmured, as if to himself. "I felt it coming."

"Tell me."

"There is nothing to tell, grandson."

"But you know." Ya'akov lifted his voice.

"There is nothing to tell," came the stubborn reply.

"Why was I not told? All the others have a father—Nissim, Motem, Daniel, Eliahu, Malka. Why not I? Yah heh, saba, what say you?"

The grandfather sighed. "I say that if Allah had wanted you to know he would have told you. Leave it, my child." He rocked back and forth in agitation, plucking at the tassels of his prayer shawl.

Through the next hour Ya'akov pleaded and cajoled, but to no avail. The old man would tell him nothing. Finally the youth prepared to leave.

"I shall not give up until I find him," he promised.

"And when you find him what will you find?" countered the grandfather. "If he wanted you, would he not have made himself known to you? Have you not a mother? Have you not already an abba in Haifa who loves you and treats you as one of his own?"

"My mother's husband is not my abba. Everyone knows it. The neighbors look at me as if I did not belong. They call me *mumser* [the old man shuddered] and curse me behind my back. They must learn that I have an abba."

"Boy, boy," whined the grandfather, quite distraught now, "it is not worth it. Let your ears hear what your mouth is saying. You are looking for grief."

But Ya'akov had made up his mind. He departed from the kiosk in anger. The grandfather followed the boy's muscular back with rheumy eyes. "Bismillah," he thought, "so be it."

Ya'akov returned to Haifa. He told his mother nothing of where he had been. His employer, the European metalsmith, did not lack for understanding.

"Any luck, Ya'akov?" he asked in a kindly voice.

The youth shook his head morosely, and then averted his face.

During the late spring and early summer he continued to make inquiries. But if people knew, they were not talking. If Allah had wanted the boy to know, they decided, He would have told him. Esther was a good woman; her past was her own affair.

In the summer of 1946 the Histadrut youth group left for a camping trip to Kibbutz Na'an, near Rehovot. At first Ya'akov was noncommittal about joining the outing. The other youngsters meant little to him, for most of them were Ashkenazim. Still, it was a chance for a free vacation, he admitted. Finally he decided to take it. The sports competition at the kibbutz was enjoyable. Ya'akov was stronger than most of the other boys, and he excelled at wrestling and gymnastics.

The evenings were something else. When the group gathered around the campfire for song and dance fests, Ya'akov turned morose again. Those bronze faces flickering in the firelight, those eyes sparkling with gaiety and merriment—what had these people to do with him? Even the spindle-shanked Yemenites and Maghrebim from Jaffa and Petach Tikvah, they were grinning, too. As if the grass under their feet and the trees over their heads were theirs, as if the rest of the group were their comrades, or the *madrichim* were ever anything but Ashkenazim. Where did they get that kind of self-confidence? But, upon contemplation, Ya'akov knew, after all. The thought nagged and gnawed at him. And he jumped up and dashed into the woods to flee it.

One night he heard the voice of a girl crying. Running through the grove of eucalyptus trees, he found Amnon, the *madrich,* with his hands on a Yemenite girl's shoulders. He was shaking her severely. Ya'akov did not wait for explanations. With one blow, he knocked the youth leader to the ground. The *madrich* lay flat on his back for a moment, his eyes glazed. Then, wiping the blood from his nose, he climbed unsteadily to his feet.

"You'll be sorry for this," he warned Ya'akov. "I can report you."

"What sort of *madrich* picks on a girl!" came the contemptuous answer.

Amnon suddenly shook his finger at the boy. "You're a born trouble-maker," he shouted. "Ever since you joined us you've been looking for trouble. We don't need your kind."

Ya'akov spat. His *kind*. He had been expecting that.

Here the girl laid her hand on Ya'akov's arm. "He meant nothing by it," she said. "He was punishing me. It was his duty."

Ya'akov stared at her. Her tears had dried now, and her face wore a contrite expression. "I was carving on the tree," she murmured with embarrassment, pointing to the knife marks on the eucalyptus trunk. "I won't do it again."

Ya'akov lowered his eyes. He knew that injuring trees or animals was a cardinal sin at the kibbutz. The girl was lucky Amnon had not expelled her.

"All right, I'm sorry," he mumbled.

The *madrich* grunted and stalked off.

When they were alone, the girl kept her eyes on Ya'akov. "I am Mazal," she said.

"Ya'akov."

"You are very strong. I saw the beating you gave that Ashkenazi boy at the swimming hole."

Ya'akov felt a surge of pride. "He was a bully," he said.

Mazal laughed. "Such a touchy number, you are. You can't fight every bully in Eretz Yisrael." She took his hand and squeezed it. "Anyway, thank you," she said. Then she walked off.

Ya'akov watched her leave. After a moment, he examined the tree. With childish vanity, Mazal had carved her own name in the bark, and had left it deeply scarred. Gnats were settling in the dripping cortex. Suddenly Ya'akov whirled and ran.

"Mazal, come back," he shouted.

He found her at the edge of the grove. "Come back." He seized her wrist and ran with her to the tree.

"Is this your name?" he demanded, pointing to the five Hebrew letters of the second word.

"What ails you?" she asked in astonishment.

"Mazal Merhavi?"

"Herself. What of it?"

Ya'akov examined her face intently. It was a dark face, with dark eyes. But it was a Yemenite face like any other. It would not do to tell her everything. Instead he spoke of an uncle.

"Missing for years," he confided. "We looked for him in Haifa and Tel Aviv, but no one knew anything."

After she had heard the story, Mazal thought for a moment. "Well, we are from Petach Tikvah. But it can't be anyone in our immediate family,"

she decided at last. "We've always been together as long as I can remember."
Then she frowned. "Wait a moment, there is a distant relative. Yosef
Merhavi is his name. He also lives in Petach Tikvah—and I think, yes, you
resemble him. Yes, you do, Ya'akov."

She did not know the address of the man. Never mind. Ya'akov had the
name. The rest would be easy. A certainty had come over him. His heart
raced.

Three days later the youth group left the kibbutz. Ya'akov returned home.
He told his mother what had happened.

"What will you do?" she asked.

"I must go now to Petach Tikvah to find him."

Then she began to cry. "I raised you all my life and now you are going
to him."

"Perhaps he will not be there," Ya'akov said, the lump rising in his throat.

"No, no," his mother shook her head. "You are looking for him, that is
what matters. If you go now, don't come back here to live. You must
choose."

Then tears came into the boy's eyes: "Umma, I want to be by my abba for
a while so that I shall feel that I have an abba as all children do."

She held fast to his hand. "Ein imek b'isnan!" She lapsed into Arabic.
"Chew your mother's eye then. Don't forget what I have said."

He left her with an aching heart. Nevertheless he took the bus to Tel
Aviv, and from there to Petach Tikvah. The moment he reached the bus
terminal he asked the direction of the Yemenite quarter. Suddenly a voice
called to him. It was Mazal.

"Shalom, Ya'akov," she said. "I knew you would be on one of these buses."

He was embarrassed. "I've just come to talk to him about work," he lied.

"It's all right," she smiled. "I'll take you there."

It was a fifteen-minute walk to the section of town known as Machneh
Yehudah. Soon none but Orientals were to be seen. When the youngsters
reached Ein Ganim Street, Mazal pointed to a small concrete house, hardly
larger than a shanty.

"He lives there," she said. "I shall leave you now." She looked back.
"God bless you, Ya'akov."

His mouth was dry as he walked through the gate. The courtyard was
large, as in all Oriental homes. Several dark-skinned children were playing
in the grass. Before he reached the front steps the door swung open and a
fat, swarthy woman stepped out. She was in her mid-thirties and neither
looked nor dressed like a Yemenite. Her weight and the heavy gold rings
in her ears gave her away. He guessed her to be an Iraqi; and when she
spoke her accent confirmed it.

"Yes, boy, are you looking for someone?"

He began to speak, but the words would not come. He cleared his throat.
"Does Mar Yosef Merhavi live here?" he whispered.

"He does," she replied, looking at him acutely. "What do you want?"

His answer was prepared. "I am looking for work, Geveret," he said. "I
was told he could help me."

Her voice was not unkind. "He is not at home now, but he will be back in an hour."

"I will return then, Geveret," said Ya'akov. As he left the courtyard he felt her eyes following him.

He sat in a coffee shop for the next hour, and then walked back to the house. The woman was waiting for him on the front step.

"My husband has not yet returned, boy," she said. "Will you come in and sit down."

He nodded and entered. The blinds were drawn against the summer heat, but even in the semidarkness he could see that the room resembled his own family's in Haifa. The furniture was heavily ornamented, in the Oriental style. Over the *diwan* hung a hammered silver amulet containing holy parchment. The curtain separating *diwan* from sleeping room was beaded. A Yemenite menorah stood on the mantel, and beside it a framed scroll inscribed in Judeo-Arabic; Ya'akov recognized the quotation from Rav Huna, the Patriarch. On the rosewood coffee table stood a copper serving tray and *aljemina,* an Oriental coffee pot. The walls were painted blue, and occasional photographs hung there. Ya'akov searched for a picture of his mother, but there was none.

Then he stared again at the bed behind the half-drawn curtain. Someone was sitting there. The figure moved and entered the sitting room. It was an aged woman, an Iraqi, and quite obviously the mother of the woman who had let him in. Her face and hair were a grotesque mask of henna and safflower. She joined her daughter on the *diwan* and peered intently into Ya'akov's face.

"I am afraid of his eyes," she said to her daughter in Arabic. Her voice rasped like a broken wire. Then, in Hebrew, she addressed Ya'akov. "Do you speak Arabic?"

"No," he lied. Perhaps they would talk freely in his presence.

The mother stared at him without blinking. Then she nodded knowingly, setting the silver necklace ajingle on her massive bosom. "This is Esther's child," she said.

The younger woman leaned forward, an uncertain smile on her face. "Are you Esther's child?" she asked.

He shook his head. But now the old woman would not be stopped. In broken Hebrew, she persisted. "You are lying. You are exactly the same drop of water as your mother, and you came here to see your father."

Ya'akov continued shaking his head reflexively. He was very frightened.

"What is your name, boy?" asked the younger woman.

"Moshe."

"You hear that accent?" the mother grunted to the younger woman. "He probably speaks Arabic better than we do."

"His ears are listening, umma," replied the daughter, momentarily slipping into her mother's heavy Iraqi argot.

The old woman answered in kind. "I don't care. I'll hang myself if he's not Esther's child."

This time the daughter bent forward and clasped Ya'akov's face in her hands. Her voice was gentle. "Tell us if you are Esther's son," she said, "and if Yosef is your father."

Ya'akov shuddered, and then nodded. The old woman sat back triumphantly. The daughter smiled. "You are Ya'akov," she said. "Baruch HaBah—Be welcome, Ya'akov."

Then she entered the kitchen and returned with a tray of tea and cookies. "Drink, my dear," she insisted, placing the cup in his hand. "Feel yourself at home."

He pretended to drink, and then returned the cup to its tray. He suspected a curse. The younger woman had opened the door and was calling her children. Soon they entered, no less than seven boys and a girl, and none of them even of bar mitzvah age.

"These are your brothers, and this is your sister," she said to Ya'akov.

The children gazed at him in silent awe. He nodded self-consciously, and rested an awkward hand on the little girl's head. Meanwhile the mother had gone out to the courtyard. A few moments later she returned with several of the neighbor women. They crowded around Ya'akov, examining him closely, patting his cheeks in admiration. "Yooh, a fine boy," they clucked in Arabic, "such a broad back and shoulders . . . See, he has all his teeth . . . the very image of his father . . . Pretty, pretty . . ."

Ya'akov was acutely uncomfortable. "Please," he whispered to the younger woman, "when is . . . Mar Merhavi coming home."

"Not till five o'clock," she replied. Then she considered for a moment. "We need not wait. Come then. We'll go to the moshav where he works."

They went out together. At the next corner they took the bus to the northeastern edge of town. As they approached the orange groves, the woman asked Ya'akov to sit in the back of the bus.

"I want to speak to my husband privately first," she explained. "This will be the last stop. The bus will wait for ten minutes."

When the vehicle rolled to a halt she climbed out. It was already four thirty and through the window Ya'akov could see groups of field hands returning from the orchards. There were many Arabs among them, and nearly as many Yemenites. Ya'akov studied their faces, but none offered a clue. He waited silently as the bus filled with workers. A mounting terror filled his chest: perhaps the bus would leave before the woman returned; perhaps she had gone to warn his father. The youth clutched the seat rail until his knuckles turned gray, and the Arab sitting across the aisle began to stare at him curiously.

Then the woman entered the bus. She beckoned to Ya'akov, and the breath went out of him. He lurched forward into the aisle and moved toward the hydraulic door. As he descended, he saw a man standing at the woman's side. He was a small, thin, sallow man in his mid-forties. He wore neither beard nor sidecurls. The hair of his temples and mustache was flecked with gray, and the hollows under his eyes were darkly shadowed. Ya'akov peered at the man for a moment, and then looked away. His legs trembled beneath him and all was not well in his stomach. The woman pointed to her companion.

"You must know this person," she said to the youth. "He knows you."

The man spoke. His voice was thin and reedy. "Shalom, Ya'akov," he said. "I am your father." He extended his hand. Ya'akov took it, his face still turned away. His shoulders began to shake. "I am glad you have come, Ya'akov," Yosef Merhavi continued. "You are welcome here . . . Now, now, don't do that. No, boy, you mustn't do that. Don't cry now." He rested his hand on Ya'akov's quivering back.

The passing field hands stopped and gazed at the weeping youth. "It's nothing." Merhavi waved them away angrily. But still they stared. Finally Merhavi and his wife led Ya'akov back into the bus. They sat down together and shielded the boy's head.

"Are you unhappy, my son?" asked Merhavi. "Is that why you cry?"

"No, no," Ya'akov sobbed. "Just the opposite."

By the time they returned to the house the boy had regained control over himself. The old woman had prepared a festive meal in his honor. There was chicken and *shashlik, kebab, humus, techina,* sesame rolls, wine, and *arak.* Now they sat around the table, and tongues gradually loosened. The new little brothers and the sister hung on Ya'akov's neck and arms, the smallest perched on his knees. The wife piled his plate high twice over, and Merhavi kept the youth's glass filled.

"Abba, abba," Ya'akov murmured.

"That is right, my son," beamed Merhavi. "I am your abba. You are my son and I am your abba."

"Abba," the youth murmured again, and then shyly kissed the man's sunken cheek. "I have an abba."

The wife clucked, and wiped her eyes with the tablecloth. The children clapped for joy.

Later, when the dishes were put away and the children tucked in bed, father and son sat alone on the *diwan.* Merhavi smoked in silence for a while, regarding his son intently. It was Ya'akov who spoke first.

"Why did you not look for me all this time, abba?"

Merhavi sighed. "When you were a small child, I asked your mother to let me take you with me," he said. "But she refused. Since then I have not even known where your mother lives."

Ya'akov wanted to say more, but decided against it.

"As the years passed," Merhavi continued, "I built a new family. My wife is a good woman. She cares for the children. I am not a rich man, and there is much that we lack, but she puts up with it." He looked at his son, his eyes taking in Ya'akov's powerful shoulders and arms. "What do you do?" he asked. "Are you a worker?"

"I am a sheet-metal worker, abba," Ya'akov answered proudly. "I have a job in Haifa and make good money. For many years now I have paid my way at home. I earn more now than my stepfather."

"Sheet-metal," mused Merhavi. "Yes, there is good money in that."

"What the Ashkenazim don't want the English will buy," said Ya'akov.

"Even so," the father agreed. He smoked quietly for a while. "I think you should live with us now," he said at last. "Do you agree?"

Ya'akov nodded in wordless happiness.

When the wife entered the room, Merhavi said: "I should like Ya'akov to live here with us. He is a sheet-metal worker. I shall arrange a job for him here in town."

"Bismillah," said the wife.

It was arranged. Work was found without difficulty. It was less simple a matter to find room in the house. But finally that too was arranged. Each week it was Merhavi's practice to turn his salary over to his wife. Ya'akov now followed his father's example. Then, working overtime, the youth managed to save a few pounds. These he invested in a cow and two calves. When the calves were six months old he slaughtered all three animals and sold the meat in the black market. The money bought new furniture for the house. Ya'akov was a hero in the family. After the evening meal he flexed his muscles for the delighted children, and lifted even the oldest of them to the ceiling.

"He is a Samson," cackled the wife's mother, reclining comfortably on the new bed.

"A prince of his people," echoed the wife, sipping mint essence from the new *aljemina*.

Merhavi squatted on the new *diwan* and nodded agreeably over his glass narghile.

At the end of the first year in his father's home, Ya'akov wrote his mother: . . . Each time I come to see you, you fill my ears with worry, and I tell you there is no need. They treat me well. Do I look underfed? What would you have them say to me? The family is not like ours, which is always talking. Father works very hard in the orchards, and when he comes home late at night he is too tired to talk. He has little to say to his wife, either. I have told him not to work so hard. I am here to help him. I bring home good money, and they live better since I am here. The woman makes no complaints. She runs this house from top to bottom, and has her hands full with the children. No ugly word has ever passed between us. . . . Umma, I want good feeling between you and father's wife. You will not be satisfied until you meet her. I want you to come to Petach Tikvah. Take this money and buy a ticket. You do not work on Third Day: I will expect you then on the one o'clock bus.

And his mother came, stepping off at the bus terminal like a timid little bird. Ya'akov awaited her, together with Merhavi's wife. Together the three sat in a coffee shop during the afternoon. At first the women spoke politely to each other of food, clothing, children, and the household matters that women speak of. But soon they were gossiping like old friends. Each vied with the other in patting the youth's cheeks, and telling the other what a fine boy he was.

"A prince," said the wife.

"A saintly boy," said the mother.

"A David, nothing less," said the wife.

"A born leader," said the mother.

"Aywah, aywah, aywah," they both clucked and nodded.

Ya'akov snapped his fingers at the waiter and ordered more coffee for the three of them.

When the afternoon drew to a close, the women took their leave of each other, and Ya'akov accompanied his mother back to the bus terminal. Before she departed he made her promise to send his stepfather to meet his father. And in fact a month later the visit took place. This time Merhavi himself received the stepfather, and the family prepared a banquet for him at home. Friends and neighbors were invited. Wine was drunk and toasts were exchanged. The stepfather wept tears of happiness when he saw how well it was with Ya'akov. At the bus terminal he embraced the youth.

"God be with you, my son," he said. "You are in good hands."

"I am happy, ya abba," said Ya'akov.

It was the truth. He knew peace and contentment. Around him the country was going mad. Nearly every night now gunfire rattled between Jews and British, and then between Jews and Arabs. The darkness was shattered by grenades and even mortar shells. Tremors ran through homes and the people who lived in them. But Ya'akov was untouched. In the bosom of his father's family he was an island unto himself.

Then, in the first week of May, 1948, there was a knock on the door. Merhavi opened it and a bearded Yemenite youth stood there, an envelope in his hand. He asked for Ya'akov, and when Ya'akov came the visitor whispered in his ear, handed him the envelope, and departed. Ya'akov knew what it was even before reading it.

"What says the letter?" asked his father.

"It is from the Lech'i," said Ya'akov, referring to the Stern Gang.

The wife and old woman gave a simultaneous shriek and dropped their lace work. Merhavi's narrow face was grim. "And what have those bandits to do with you?" he asked.

"Abba!" Ya'akov was shocked. "They are freedom fighters, Abba, not bandits."

"I asked what have those bandits to do with you?" Merhavi repeated, his reedy voice taking on an unnatural edge.

The youth shrugged. "They have ordered me to report," he said. "I must go. There will be war soon."

The wife began to rock to and fro. "And there will be mouths to feed, too," she wailed. "What will happen to us when you are gone?"

Ya'akov stared at the woman, and then looked to his father. But Merhavi said nothing.

"Don't worry," Ya'akov murmured lamely. "It's not war yet. They just want me to report."

But his heart was filled with uneasiness. What was it that concerned them? When he packed his knapsack no one said a word. Then, as he prepared to leave, his father finally spoke.

"Be careful," he said.

"Yes, abba, I will," Ya'akov replied, breathing freely again.

The camp was located at Tel Litwinsky, a kibbutz midway between

Lydda and Tel Aviv. Three hundred men and boys had reported for duty. For the next half-week they were given medical examinations, issued uniforms, and then provided with introductory training in weapons and close-quarter combat. At the end of the fourth day the recruits were dismissed on a last furlough. Ya'akov returned to Petach Tikvah. He was eager to show off his khaki combat uniform to his family. When he walked into the house he was received excitedly by the children, who swarmed over him. The two women looked at him indifferently. When Merhavi returned from work he noted his son's uniform with some surprise, but with little enthusiasm.

"So now you are a proper Ashkenazi," the father observed. "I suppose this means you'll be leaving the shop?"

Ya'akov's face began to twitch. "I shall have to fight, abba," he said. "The English are pulling out next week."

There was no answer. Ya'akov tried again: "I have made arrangements with the authorities. The family will receive a small allowance while I am gone."

The wife showed interest at this. "How much?" she asked.

"Not much," he said. "Something. Something is better than nothing."

During the next few days he said goodbye to his friends and neighbors. Many of the boys he knew were also leaving for service. Three hours after the State of Israel was declared, and the last night of his furlough, Ya'akov sat drinking with a group of them at a coffee shop. They spoke of the military situation, the rumors they had heard of Arab invasion. Fortunately, the Mandate was ending. No one doubted by then that, without further British interference, the Jews would hurl the Arabs back across their own borders. In the excitement of the moment the friends sang and toasted each other, clasping hands in warm comradeship.

. They did not leave the coffee shop until the small hours of the morning. Three of Ya'akov's friends accompanied him to the town square. There they exchanged handshakes once more, and each went his separate way. Ya'akov walked on alone toward Machneh Yehudah. Then, suddenly, as his footsteps echoed along the silent streets, he heard the word again. It came from an alleyway and was followed by muffled laughter. There was no mistaking the word. It still hung in the rising mist, each syllable as distinct as a gunshot: *"Mum-ser."* He ran to the corner to look, but saw no one.

"Who is it?" he shouted.

But there was only silence. A coldness settled in Ya'akov's stomach, and he felt himself twitching. He broke into a trot, then into a run. By the time he reached the house he was drenched in perspiration. Without bothering to undress, he hurled himself onto his cot, his heart pounding in his ears.

The next morning he departed for the Sternist headquarters at Sheik Munis, near Tel Aviv. The unit's commander, David Friedman-Yellin, was waiting there to address his men. The time had come to join forces with the Haganah and the Irgun Zvai Le'umi, Friedman-Yellin informed his listeners. Henceforth each man was to consider himself a soldier in the army of Israel. There were more words: about courage, patriotism, duty, and self-sacrifice. They reached Ya'akov's ears and passed on. That afternoon and the next day, he went through his drills as in a fog. Several times he dropped his heavy Mauser rifle, and clumsily picked it up, barrel first; had there been ammunition to spare for target practice he could have killed either the range master or himself.

On the second night the company commander called the men together around the campfire. There he launched into an impassioned appeal for the defense of the "Fatherland." "The Fatherland is calling to us in its moment of peril," he declaimed. "Our Fatherland, the Fatherland of each of us . . ." As the voice droned on, Ya'akov decided at last that he would have to desert. Edging back into the darkness, he walked quickly to his tent. There he packed his duffelbag and ran out to the road. By dawn the next morning he had returned to Petach Tikvah.

"I am back," he shouted, as he entered the house. "I have returned."

Merhavi and his wife arose from their bed and peered at him in confusion. "What does it mean?" asked his father. "Can you do this?"

Ya'akov dropped his bag on the floor. "I am doing it," he said. "I have thought it over, and have decided that you need me more than the army does."

"What do you say," murmured the father, a tight smile slowly crossing his face.

The wife nodded. "You must be hungry, Ya'akov," she said. "I will fix you a good breakfast."

Ya'akov returned to the metal shop the same afternoon. His employer was incredulous. He questioned the youth, and received the same answer: "My parents need me more than the army."

"No doubt," the man replied. "And I can use you, too. I can use my own son, and my brother, but they are also in the army. You miserable bum!" He raised his voice. "You rotten shirker! The Arabs are at our very doorsteps and you decide to desert. Get out of here! Don't let me see your coward's face again!"

When Ya'akov related the incident to his father, Merhavi consoled him. "Don't worry, there are plenty of other jobs," he promised. "We're badly in need of workers here."

But it was not that easy. Wherever Ya'akov went he met the response. His father's Yemenite friends were the most vitriolic. *"Bondouk,* coward, traitor!" they shrieked. "Do you wish to bring disgrace down on our heads? Our brothers are dying like flies outside Jerusalem, more even the Ashkenazim. And you want to sit here in safety! Clear out, pig! Clear out!"

At the end of the week Ya'akov began suffering headaches. Each time he returned to the house the family seemed to withdraw further from him. The wife's face was stone-cold. His father had no time for conversation. Increasingly the youth found himself sitting alone in the coffee shop, the waiter his sole companion. From the distance the occasional rumble of artillery and mortars echoed into Petach Tikvah. On the street before him only children and older people were to be seen. Now and then the passers-by glanced at him and muttered sullenly to themselves.

One evening a little boy and a little girl stopped before his table and stared at him unblinkingly.

"Zeh hu," said the little girl, pointing her finger at Ya'akov, "that's the one."

The boy nodded solemnly. "He looks like Mordecai the porter," he agreed. "Mordecai was one, too."

Ya'akov jumped to his feet. "Who is calling me Mordecai the porter?" he shouted. "Get moving, you little turds." He made a move in their direction—when suddenly his arms were pinioned from behind.

"Don't fight us, Merhavi," said a man's voice. "Don't give us any trouble." Two brawny military policemen had seized him, and wrestled him away from the children.

"No one calls me a *mumser*," he roared, his shoulders pressed flat against the coffee-shop wall. "I am not a *mumser*."

"No one's calling you a *mumser*," grunted one of the policemen. "You are just a rotten deserter."

[Ya'akov Merhavi, private, in military service between May, 1948, and January, 1950. Résumé of military career, from files of Har-El Brigade, Ministry of Defense.]

Former Sternist, inducted into regular defense forces shortly after declaration of the State. Deserted briefly to family home in Petach Tikvah. Arrested by military police one week later and sent to detention camp at Kfar Syrkin. Remained in Kfar Syrkin four months. Performed routine ordinance duties without complaint, although extremely introverted and withdrawn.

During the Arab assault on Rosh HaAyen, Merhavi participated in the defense action with unusual valor, burning the cornfields where the Arab concentration was located. Played a crucial role in defending the pumping station to Jerusalem. Afterward Merhavi distinguished himself by volunteering for the most dangerous assignments. Several times risked almost certain death to rescue wounded comrades. His contempt for danger at times a problem. Once almost provoked international incident: firing at Swedish United Nations officer after First Truce had come into effect.

After Second United Nations Armistice, Merhavi's restiveness increasing source of concern to his officers. Continually imagining that his family had been insulted and his own legitimacy called into question. Would return from furloughs in unmanageable temper. Moodiness reached climax in quarrel with sergeant. Upon striking sergeant, Merhavi detached from unit, assigned to Negev Battalion. Participated in conquest of Migdal Ashkelon and Ashdod.

During celebrations following conquest Merhavi became ill, was confined to hospital for observation. Encephalographic examinations revealed no organic damage. Sedatives and other medication not helpful in relieving chronic headaches. In January, 1950, honorably discharged from army with rank of private.

The furloughs during the year and a half of service were the worst ordeals. Indeed, battle action was a relief by comparison. If he could have understood. If there had been some explanation. But the stone faces of his father and the wife, the muttered distemper of the old woman defied interrogation. No one would speak. No one would answer. Ya'akov played with the children; the wife snatched them away, making the sign of the fish over them. He repaired his father's spade; Merhavi bought a new one. The youth bought meat; the old woman paid a *mori* a fee to inspect it. But words were not spoken.

A month before his final discharge, Ya'akov took up with a Yemenite girl. She was a little slip of a thing, not much to look at, but soft and gentle. She admired Ya'akov's strength; it was uncommon among their people. He was kind to her. After three evenings together, he decided that he loved her, and on the fourth evening it was understood that they were betrothed. On the fifth evening he met her at the coffee shop and found her in tears.

"What is it, Na'ama?" he asked, cherishing her the more for her grief.

She whispered the answer in his ear. It was her father, she said; he had forbidden her to see Ya'akov again. Ya'akov smiled. He knew how to handle these old-timers. One did not have to pay *mohar* anymore these days. And then she whispered the reason.

"He says you are not your father's son, Ya'akov. Your own father has told him."

She vanished before he could argue with her, too frightened even to look back. He sat perfectly still and desperately cold. From every corner of the square the word leaped at him, from every lighted window and every passing bicycle. The pedestrians spoke it in their eyes, the children in their laughter, the coffeehouse patrons as they ordered, and the waiters as they tabulated the bills. The word swam in his coffee cup and jingled in his pocket. When he left the café the word echoed with every footstep, and thus it followed him home.

He lay on the bed, not sleeping. From behind the curtain Merhavi stirred fitfully. So the stepfather had stirred fourteen years ago when Ya'akov had learned who he was, and the child had peeked through the beads and stared at the man and refused to see a stranger by his mother's side. But not a twenty-one-year-old. A grown man did not do such things. He lay there silent, waiting for his head to explode. The night passed, but his pulse beat on.

Dawn came, the cocks crowed, the goats in the courtyard began their bleating and the wife arose to fetch milk from them. Merhavi slept, for it was the Sabbath. Then the old woman also arose and began to prepare the breakfast. Soon the kitchen hissed with frying peppers and smoking onions. The children dropped like lemmings from their beds and steered a dazed, erratic course for the outhouse. The home settled slowly into the languid, comfortable rhythm of the Sabbath. A day of peace lay ahead.

Ya'akov switched on the radio. Kol Yisrael, the State Broadcasting Service, was playing European opera. No comfort there. Radio Cairo offered cabaret music—*aya habibi, aya habibi*—even worse. He turned back to Kol Yisrael. Then the curtain suddenly parted and Merhavi's face appeared.

"Who plays that machine on the Sabbath?" he growled. "It will go off now or there will be woe in this house."

When did you become so religious? thought Ya'akov. But he switched off the radio without a word. A few minutes later Yedidah, the little sister, walked over to the radio and turned it on. The house filled with music. Instantly the curtain parted again and the father stood there glowering. Then he saw that it was Yedidah who listened; his anger subsided as quickly as it came, and he returned to his bed. Ya'akov did not wish to speak, but the word came of its own will.

"Why?" he asked softly.

"What is it?" Merhavi thrust his head menacingly through the curtain. "Did you say something, boy?"

Ya'akov took a deep breath. "Why are you doing this?" he said. "My brothers can smoke. I can't. My sister can turn on the radio. I can't. Why?" His voice rose. "What do you want from me?"

The father scowled at him for a moment. Then, without a word, he seized his spade from the wall, and in one blow smashed the little nickel-plated radio to smithereens. The house fell silent. From the other room the woman and her mother were whispering fearfully. Suddenly Ya'akov leaped to his feet. His hands closed around a vase of flowers. Merhavi stepped back, his arm before his face. As the jar exploded on the bedroom floor, screams ricocheted from the kitchen to the *diwan* and back. The younger children began to cry.

"Sh'ema, run, fetch the police quickly," cried the wife to her oldest son, her voice quavering.

Sh'ema's bare feet padded across the *diwan,* then gained speed in the courtyard. In the bedroom Ya'akov and Merhavi continued glaring at each other. Each waited for the other to speak.

"Why have you blackened my life?" whispered Ya'akov finally. "What do you want of me?"

"I want nothing of you," gasped the father.

The youth nodded, a lump rising in his throat. "I worked so hard for you," he said. "I gave your wife all my earnings so that she could wear bracelets."

"Hold your tongue, boy."

"Am I worse than the other children? Tell me?" He began to sob. Then he sat on the bed, his head in his hands. Merhavi left the room.

In a few minutes Sh'ema returned. Four policemen followed him into the house. One of them spoke briefly with the wife in Arabic, then entered the bedroom, accompanied by his companions.

"Will you come with us quietly, Ya'akov?" said the sergeant. "We have the car outside."

Ya'akov stared at the man indifferently through a cloud of cigarette smoke. "I will not come with you at all," he replied. "I am still a soldier. You will have to send for the military police."

"Don't be difficult, Ya'akov," said the sergeant.

Ya'akov climbed to his feet. "Do you want to fight with me, Shabbtai?" He raised a formidable right arm. "It will take more than four of you to bring me in."

The sergeant took the warning calmly. "We can get a military police permit," he said.

"I'm not going anywhere," the youth replied.

The men promptly left the house, Merhavi and his wife accompanying them. Ya'akov lay on his bed for another few minutes. Finally, he arose and dressed. Patting Yedidah on the head, he walked out of the house. Then he continued on alone to the police station.

When he walked into the chief's office he saw that the father and his wife had preceded him. They stopped in mid-conversation, and glared silently as Ya'akov approached the desk.

"You have done well to come," said the chief. "Do you know that I can put you in jail for disturbing the peace?"

Ya'akov shrugged. "Then put me in jail."

The chief spoke quietly now. "Boy, what do you want of this family? This man is not your father and this woman is not your mother. Why can't you leave them alone?"

The flashes of pain began the moment the words were spoken. With shaking hands Ya'akov opened his wallet and removed his military identity card. "What does it say here?" he cried. "Does it say they are my parents or does it not? I arranged for the army to pay them while I was gone. Would I have done that for strangers?"

The chief examined the document. Then he turned to Merhavi. "Why do you tell me Ya'akov is not your son when it is written here that he is?"

Merhavi's face was as tight and wrinkled as a persimmon. "I know what I know," he replied, inscrutably.

"We don't want him to live with us," chimed in the woman. "He is big enough to live alone now."

The chief agreed. "Ya'akov, take a word of advice," he said gently. "I don't know who is telling the truth, but it would be best for everyone if you left that house." When the youth said nothing, the chief continued. "If you refuse to leave I'll have to put you in jail. Don't make me do that."

Ya'akov smiled grimly and nodded. "All right, chief, I won't make you do that." He pocketed the identity card and walked out.

Returning home, Ya'akov threw his clothes into his bag. He was gone before Merhavi and the wife returned.

At first he contemplated staying at his mother's home in Haifa. But he was ashamed to admit to her what had happened. After a few days he came back to Petach Tikvah, and rented a room. Without difficulty he found employment in a sheet-metal shop. The wages were adequate for his needs, and he supplemented them occasionally by making cement blocks. Life was quiet again.

But as the months passed Ya'akov realized that nothing was the same.

His friends remained his friends, but they told him a tale no enemy would have repeated. It was Merhavi's story. The father had circulated it through Machneh Yehudah. Ya'akov was not his son, he insisted; the boy did not belong to his *hamoula* (clan).

Ya'akov listened in silence. He drank in silence. Soon he began drinking alone, avoiding his former companions. Occasionally he disappeared from work for intervals of several days, and drained a bottle of *arak* in the privacy of his room. The landlord would knock. Ya'akov would not answer. His head throbbed ceaselessly. During one eight-week period late in 1951, he could not leave his bed; the neighbors brought him food. He began borrowing to pay the rent. Finally his debts became unmanageable. Only one alternative was left. Still weak and shaken, he ventured out one evening to his father's house.

The children saw him coming and scattered from the courtyard in terror. The old woman was seated at the window and rushed to close the shutters. It was too late. Ya'akov had his foot in the door and swung it open. Merhavi was seated cross-legged on the *diwan,* sucking at his narghile. He choked when he saw his visitor.

"Shalom, abba," said Ya'akov. "Keep on smoking."

The wife entered from the kitchen. "What do you want?" she cried, her eyes dilated in fear.

Ya'akov ignored her. "I have been very ill, abba, as you can see," he said. "I did not leave my room for two months. You didn't visit me once in all that time."

Merhavi climbed to his feet. "I don't want any trouble with you," he said, his voice on edge.

"I am not looking for trouble, abba," replied Ya'akov. "I am in need of a loan of twenty-five pounds. I have been sick and cannot pay my rent."

Merhavi began to shout: "Get out of here. I won't give you anything. Get your handout from somebody else."

"I only want a loan, not a gift."

"No, and again no. Get out now."

Ya'akov walked slowly to the door. He paused for a moment. "Until now I have behaved well," he said. "Now I shall be as bad as you are."

"Get out!" screamed Merhavi.

Ya'akov walked slowly to a coffee shop, sat down and waited. At 1:00 A.M. he returned to the house. From within he could hear the sounds of sleep. He removed his shoes and climbed through the kitchen window. The father's savings box was on the pantry shelf, where it had always been. Ya'akov opened it and removed fifty pounds. My money, he thought bitterly to himself; I gave them all they have. Then he left.

The next morning he paid his landlord. He had hardly walked out to the street, however, when a police car drew up to the curb.

"Ya heh, Ya'akov," Shabbtai the sergeant greeted him. "Get in, the chief wants to see you."

Without a word, Ya'akov climbed into the back seat and was driven to the police station. Merhavi and the wife were waiting in the chief's office.

"Nu, Ya'akov," said the chief. "Now you've gotten yourself in real trouble."

"It was my money," Ya'akov replied. "I earned it for them. I only wanted to borrow some of it."

"You hear him lie?" shrilled the woman. "Bad enough that he is a drunkard and a thief."

For a moment the chief gazed at her in distaste. Then he turned his attention back to Ya'akov. "I guess it's jail, habibi," he said. "Unless you can post a bond."

Here Merhavi stepped forward, a shrewd expression on his face. "No point sending him to jail, chief," he protested. "I have no wish to press charges against the poor wretch. I just want his promise never to bother us again. Let him promise now in front of witnesses, and he can even keep the fifty pounds. It's worth it to me to be rid of him."

The chief thought for a moment. "It's all right with me," he decided. "Will you promise, boy?"

Ya'akov shrugged.

"Come now," the chief persisted. "My patience is running out."

"I promise," mumbled Ya'akov.

The chief folded his arms and assumed a stern expression. "This is the second time you've gotten off with a warning, Ya'akov," he said. "With me there is no third time." He turned to the others. "Get out now, all of you."

Ya'akov returned to the sheet-metal shop. His employer was a kind man, and gave him his job back. Ya'akov worked steadily for the next half-year. Yet he was rarely completely sober. He had since taken up with Shoshanna, another Yemenite girl, a divorcee with two children. She cared for him now, feeding him when he was without funds, paying the doctor bills when his head tormented him. Nothing he did shook her affection for him.

But once, seated with him at the same coffee shop, she asked in all naïveté, "Is it true, Ya'akov? Are you really illegitimate? It makes no difference to me—"

His hand cracked across her mouth before she finished the sentence, knocking her to the floor. As she got to her feet, he struck her again before she had time to utter a word. Then he staggered out into the street, turned around twice, clutched at his head, and collapsed.

Friends and acquaintances carried him off immediately to a physician. The doctor called in a nerve specialist, who gave Ya'akov calcium injections and confined him to the Kupat Holim hospital for a week. Once Shoshanna visited him and apologized, offering to care for him again. He threw her out.

His strength was ebbing rapidly now. He was unable to work more than two days a week. Urchins jeered him in the street. A young man whom Ya'akov had soundly thrashed in a bar months before now took his revenge, cornering Ya'akov in an alleyway and beating him senseless. He was alone, alone. One afternoon as he wandered aimlessly along Nordau Street, he unexpectedly encountered Merhavi, walking the other way.

"Shalom, abba," he mumbled.

Merhavi's face froze. "You are not my son," he spat out the words. "Do not say shalom to me." Then he walked on.

Where was there help in his loneliness? Ya'akov visited his mother in Haifa whenever he could find the money, but he would not stay with her. He would not bring the dirty word into her home. Bad enough that he heard it himself wherever he turned. He could not escape it; abba had put a curse on him. Once he visited a *mori* and begged the old man to remove the Evil Eye from him. But the faith healer said that a *mumser* was his own affliction. Enough then of this loneliness. He would take Shoshanna back. When he told her, she accepted the proposal gratefully.

They were married in the presence of the stepfather and a few of the bride's friends and relatives, and then lived together in Ya'akov's single room. The early months were not unhappy, though Ya'akov continued drinking heavily. His head felt better, and he ate three meals a day. For a while he even worked steadily as a guard in a watermelon field. But in the spring the curse revealed itself again. Ya'akov was walking with his wife. A man turned the corner before them, and it was Merhavi. Ya'akov swallowed, then approached him.

"Ya heh, abba, shalom," he said. "Won't you meet my wife?"

Merhavi cast a startled sidelong glance at Shoshanna, and then growled to Ya'akov, loud enough for her to hear. "You want it in public, do you? I told you before you are not my son. Not my son. You are not my son, understand?" Then he turned on his heel, and walked away rapidly.

Shoshanna said nothing until they had returned home. But then she questioned Ya'akov. "How much longer are you going to take this?" she asked. "Whose son does he think you are then? A man can't keep calling you . . ."

Before she could utter the word his hand was on her like a flail, blackening both her cheeks and bringing blood to her nose and mouth. He stopped only when the screams brought neighbors pounding at the door. Then he sat down on the bed beside her, exhausted.

"Leave me," he gasped between breaths. "Get a divorce quickly. I tell you this for your own good." Her hand crawled to his neck, but he brushed it off. "I've brought you nothing but suffering from the day we married," he continued. "I can't stop my drinking and I can't support you. I'm no good to anyone." He moistened a towel and wiped her face. "I'm going now," he said. "You will not see me again."

He left the room and walked directly to his father's house. Merhavi's wife saw Ya'akov coming and shouted a warning, but he thrust her aside and strode into the *diwan*. The father made for the kitchen, but Ya'akov caught him by the shoulder.

"Listen now," said the young man, his voice deadly quiet. "You have put a curse on me. You have told every householder in Machneh Yehudah that I am a *mumser*. If you go on with this it will end in blood."

"Get out, you," howled the father, struggling under Ya'akov's powerful grip.

"In blood, do you hear?" Ya'akov hissed. "I will give you thirty days to decide, as it is written. Either prove officially that I am or am not a *mumser*, or it will be the end of you."

Trembling with anger and fear, Merhavi suddenly shouted back: "I'll do no such thing until your mother is dead."

"Thirty days," Ya'akov repeated, and then left the house.

Not until he reached the watermelon field did he reflect on his father's words: "until your mother is dead." Was it possible that the wretched man still loved her, after all these years?

The weeks passed and Ya'akov did not return to his wife. Each dawn he unstrapped his revolver and bedded down in the caretaker's shack at the corner of the field. He did his cooking on a tiny primus stove. When the darkness came he sat alone in the midst of his melons, his back against a Santa Rosa tree, his eyes searching the outer world. Beneath him the Evil Eye swam silently, unblinkingly, watching his every move. Above him the Name, All-Seeing, gazed down upon him in despair. Beyond the boundaries of the field his kinsmen were sleeping, their djinns purged for the night, their children guarded by amulets and parchment from curses and the accursed. Further west yet gleamed the brilliant lights of the Ashkenazim, the fair-skinned and the bare-legged, who could not care less. And beyond them— what remained but the enemy? Where then was comfort to be found? He grappled with the thought until his brain wanted to melt. Even now the best answer was the one closest at hand. Whether good or bad, a father was a father. And a father's son was not wiped out of existence so easily.

And so when the thirtieth day arrived Ya'akov set out again for Merhavi's home. It was May 25, and darkness was settling fast. He found the father in the courtyard, tending the goats. The man had aged in a month. His meager jowl was as crumpled as tissue paper, and his eyes were riddled with venules.

"Abba," said Ya'akov quietly. Merhavi must have seen him coming, for he showed no surprise. "Abba," Ya'akov repeated. "I am here."

Merhavi straightened slowly. "You can leave as quickly as you came," he said in a dull voice.

The son approached him. "I want to talk to you, abba," he said.

Suddenly Merhavi whirled, his face contorted in hatred. "Fakleh Tok-lecha," he shrieked, "Rot take you. Leave me alone."

Still Ya'akov did not raise his voice. "Why do you not leave me and my mother alone?" he countered. "You know I want nothing from you. I do not ask for your money. I ask only proof from you that I am or am not your son."

Then the father uttered the words. Ya'akov watched his lips move, and silently repeated the vocables. They uncurled slowly: "Laich l'imcha HaZona, v'tishal otah m'azeh shuk evedim lokcha otchah—Go to your whore-mother and ask her from which slave market she took you." Without warning Ya'akov's hand dropped, and the kicking revolver came up in it. Father and son stared at each other in disbelief; then Merhavi slumped to the grass.

Ya'akov stood rooted to the spot for several moments. But when windows and doors flew open around him, he thrust the gun back in his belt and walked away. He walked without hearing or seeing. His feet knew their own way. In ten minutes they carried him to the police station.

"Take me to the chief, Shabbtai," he murmured dazedly to the sergeant.

The policeman seized Ya'akov's arm, staring closely at his eyes, and then beckoned to one of his companions. Together they escorted Ya'akov into the inner office. He laid the pistol on a desk.

"I have just shot my father," he said tonelessly. "I don't know whether he is alive or dead."

A moment later the door opened again and a lieutenant entered. The sergeant and the other policeman ran out. Ya'akov could hear the slamming doors of their patrol car. Then, with a moan, he dropped into a chair beside the desk.

"Don't grill me too hard now," he pleaded. "My head hurts."

[Cumulative progress report of July, 1953, by Dr. Zvi Rosner, director of psychiatric services for the Israel prison commission.]
Shortly after his sentencing to life imprisonment for the murder of his father, Ya'akov Merhavi was examined in Ramle prison and again in Tel Mond prison. He is a schizoid personality. He prefers to be left alone to live entirely in his own world. He has refused to take an interest in any activities, even in a mechanics course. Once lost his temper and screamed at a guard, had to be subdued physically. Reverting atavistically to primitive customs of his people, he has resembled an Arab in his behavior.

Considers himself to be different from the other prisoners. Yet he is not a psychopath in the usual sense of the term, because he can fit himself into the conditions of the prison and understand his situation quite well. He is very ambivalent, and that is perhaps the reason for the murder of his father. He is disappointed with the outside world, and is satisfied by the punishment that the court has meted out to him. But he suffers from the fact that he has not been given suitable work. He wants to be a sheet-metal worker again. Says that his stepfather apprenticed him once to a shoemaker, and later to a carpenter, but that in both of these trades he did not succeed. He received beatings, and until today suffers emotionally from these beatings and cannot work in these trades. Just the opposite case with sheet-metal work, where a proprietor once treated him well. Evidently, too, he was unusually competent in this craft. . . .

[Additional comment by Dr. Rosner, January, 1954.]
As far as we can determine, Merhavi's mother had apparently cheated on his father. According to the strict Yemenite code, she was then immediately divorced by the father. Until today no one is certain if his mother was legally married or not when the prisoner was born. Why then did the father contradict himself, saying at first he was the boy's father, later denying it? Perhaps in the early days he admitted it because the boy brought money into the family. Later, after the

prisoner went into army and was married, it may have been more convenient to disown him. Of course, if the boy was illegitimate, or the child of another man at a time his own parents were married, Yosef Merhavi might have had "religious" scruples about declaring himself the father of the boy. Even if the boy was in fact his son, father may have felt the child tinctured by the mother's shame. We have no way of knowing. . . .

On Independence Day, May 4, 1954, the president of the State announced a general amnesty, and reduced Ya'akov Merhavi's sentence to ten years. On October 11, 1954, Ya'akov Merhavi granted his wife a divorce.

[Report of Dr. Aaron Siegman, adviser to psychiatric services for Israel prison commission. June, 1955.]
First suicide attempt on part of prisoner. Attempted to burn himself by pouring gasoline on his body, approaching a primus stove. Burns appeared on his legs, but did not extend to the rest of his body. Required only minor treatment for first-degree burns. Carried to infirmary pleading to be assigned to sheet-metal work. Begs to be transferred to Shatta prison where metal shop exists. It is obvious that he takes great pride in his skills as a craftsman. One might almost say that his sense of manhood is involved.

(July, 1955) Prisoner continues resentful, weeping continually, implores to be transferred to Shatta prison. Now he requests to be used for medical experiments, for he lacks enough courage to commit suicide. I have decided to recommend his transfer to Shatta. . . .

(March, 1956) After I recommended his transfer to Shatta, it has been made clear that the prisoner has only one obsession: whether his murdered father was his real father or not. . . . He cannot get out of his mind those terrible last words of Yosef Merhavi: "Laich l'imcha HaZona, v'tishal otah m'azeh shuk evedim lokcha otchah" . . . He is searching for his father; this is the *idée fixe* which dominates him, because without the assurance of his existence he is uncertain of his place in society. . . .

[Letter to Dr. Rosner from Dr. Shmuel Mendes, deputy director of social services, Israel prison commission. July, 1956.]
After numerous discussions with the prisoner, it is clear to me that Ya'akov Merhavi's crime resulted from two factors. The first was Merhavi's dread of namelessness, of existing in limbo as an illegitimate child. To understand what illegitimacy must have meant to him we should recall that the Yemenites . . . have [for centuries] been accustomed to a close and intimate association with a *hamoula*—a clan—a complex, almost tribal interconnection of related families. Membership in a *hamoula* is almost indispensable to an Oriental Jew. It provides

him with his sense of belonging. Nothing happens in his society without reference to his kinsmen, without the assurance of their protection, support, or—if necessary—their revenge on his behalf.

Ya'akov Merhavi grew up among Yemenites transplanted to a modern society. Here in Israel, as in the Imamate, they have somehow maintained the intricate nexus of *hamoula* relationships. From the sociological point of view, those relationships have actually been quite useful in enabling the Yemenites, however slowly, to adjust to the pace and tempo of Israel's life. We must understand, therefore, what it meant to a Yemenite youngster like Merhavi to grow up in this land deprived, by his lack of a father, and later by his growing suspicion of his own illegitimacy, of all right of excess to a normal *hamoula* relationship. It must have been a traumatic experience for him. That trauma was undoubtedly exacerbated by Yemenite folklore, the ancient suspicions and curses that evidently attach to illegitimacy.

Where then would the prisoner have found a substitute for that relationship? Of course among the Ashkenazim. Yet their world was obviously closed to him. This, then, is the second factor which influenced Merhavi's behavior. He was a member of an underprivileged minority people, with very limited access (if any) to Ashkenazic society. In this sense, therefore, Dr. Siegman's statement was correct: namely, that the prisoner was uncertain of his place in society. He simply did not know where he belonged. By disclaiming him, and leaving him without connections in an alien society, his father threatened Ya'akov Merhavi's final island of security: his own identity. It is now our responsibility to try to restore that source of identity. If we cannot help the prisoner find it, he may search for it in the wrong places. . . .

Shatta prison is located twelve miles south of Tiberias, in the lush, semi-tropical fissure of land known as the Beit She'an Valley. Due west, a mere four miles away, lie the mountains of Gilboa, marking the Jordanian frontier. The border curves again, fourteen miles to the east, enclosing Shatta and the southeastern Galilee in a kind of pocket. It is green and fertile country, redolent with alfalfa and sunflowers. Even the prison itself, adjoining the Afula highway to central Israel, hardly seems out of place in the gentle patchwork of fields and meadows.

Indeed, Shatta appears at first to be a kind of agricultural storage-depot—and in fact it served that purpose during the Mandatory period. A sprawling, slate-gray polyhedron, perhaps twice the circumference of a football field, the prison rises no more than twelve feet at the highest point of its surrounding walls. From the outside, only the five watchtowers located at each corner of the stockade offer a clue to the structure's present function. From the inside one sees little more at first than a leisurely series of courtyards, and a few offices—guards' quarters—attached in a ramshackle way to the enclosure's southern base. Actually the beehive of inner walls crossing Shatta's width contains the inmates' cells; the western courtyard is divided into a registry and an armory. Yet the entire effect is anything but penal. Prisoners stroll leisurely through the inner and outer courtyards by the western wall, or perform their chores in the large open compound at the far eastern side of the prison.

Until 1958 Shatta's routine did not bely its appearance. The prisoners were required to work, primarily in the sheet-metal shop in the eastern compound. The hours were reasonable, however, and there was plenty of time for recreation and conversation in the courtyards. Guards were not lacking, nor weapons for the armory; but discipline was rarely severe, and the weapons were never ostentatiously displayed. In fact, it was not uncommon for prisoners to serve as trustees; occasionally they were even permitted to open and close the outer gates. Altogether there were only 190 prisoners in Shatta, hardly an unmanageable number.

Half of these were Arabs, primarily *fedayin* (terror raiders) who had crossed into Israel before the Sinai campaign. Most of these infiltrators had been in captivity at least two years, and to all outward appearances their behavior was quite docile. They worked together with the Jews, eating at the same tables, even sleeping in the same cell compound. Officially, discrimination did not exist at Shatta. Unofficially, however, the prisoners chose their friends from among their own: Jews with Jews, Arabs with Arabs.

Except for Ya'akov. He preferred the Arabs. In the metal shop they were his workers, and he was their boss. They took orders well for he treated them fairly. Because he was kind to them they followed him around like dogs. Poor wretches, they were not such bad fellows at all, he decided. Even the killers among them probably had had no choice.

One of the marauders, Mohammed Ksasi Kalili, told Ya'akov how it was. "I quarreled and killed a man in Egypt," he said. "Afterward I escaped to Gaza, but they finally caught me. They said that if I agreed to be a *feday,* I wouldn't have to go to prison."

At first Ya'akov did not believe him. But later Musa Abu Sa'ad al-Abid, a Negro *feday,* told him the same story, and he heard it from others, as well. Then perhaps they needed only a little kindness to become friendly. He understood that.

"Take care, Merhavi," the Jews warned him. "Don't forget, they came to Israel to kill your mother and father."

And Ya'akov laughed mirthlessly.

The Arabs admired his strength and his physical courage. Even more, they admired the act of violence which had brought him there. His Arabic was as good as theirs, and his skin as dark as theirs. Indeed, he apparently cared no more for the Jews than they did. They accepted him. He felt it. After the work routine was over, they sat for hours and talked.

"You are a good fellow, Yakub," Yusuf Abumiden told him. "Throw in your lot with us and you won't be sorry."

"Are you starting that again?"

"I am." Yusuf Abumiden leaned forward and whispered: "And when the time comes to escape you can join with us. We'll get out, all right. Then you can come live with me in Gaza. My father is a rich sheik there. You'll never have another worry in your life."

Ya'akov scowled. "I told you never to mention that," he warned. "I'm getting tired of repeating myself."

But he was flattered, and they knew it.

A tall, athletic Egyptian, Ahmed Ali Ottman, sensed Ya'akov's insecurity and exploited it. University-educated, a journalist by profession, Ottman had entered Israel openly by posing as a European correspondent. Many days and many questions passed before he was discovered and seized. Now, in Shatta, he was the acknowledged leader of the Arab prisoners. They listened respectfully to his every word. Ya'akov, too, was honored by Ottman's attention.

"The question is not whether Israel will be conquered," Ottman explained, "but only when."

"As at Sinai?" It was Ya'akov's standard retort.

Ottman leaned back and smiled knowingly. "What chance would the Jews have had without the British and French? Do you really believe that a nation of two million can defend itself against a nation of twenty-five million?"

And Ya'akov, dealing out the cards, scoffed: "No, no Abu Raziq, don't try those university lectures on me. I am a simple man. Put me on the battlefield and I'll fight. Don't stick me in a classroom and expect me to argue."

Subkhi Rajab, a young student from Gaza, placed an affectionate arm on Ya'akov's shoulder. "Fight for the colonel," he said, "and you won't be sorry."

Ottman leaned close: "Among our people you are already a big man," he explained. "You can be much bigger." He pointed then to the Jewish prisoners, kicking a soccer ball on the other side of the courtyard. "What chance have you with them? What did you ever get from them? Did they ever treat you like a man?"

Ya'akov hurled the cards to the ground, in a sudden rage. "Are we playing cards or not?" he roared. "If you don't leave me in peace with your politics I'll break all your heads in. Then I'll report you. I mean it. Leave me in peace."

The others smiled patiently and resumed the game. Their time was coming, and they did not care who knew it.

Few of the Jews knew it. The restiveness of the Arab prisoners escaped them entirely. Even the guards paid little heed to the mounting arrogance of Ottman and his companions. If an Arab snapped back at a guard or refused to work, he was beaten and the matter was forgotten. If the prisoners sat in little groups, following the movement of the sentinels on the walls with hate-filled eyes, that was simply the Arab way. What else was there for them to do but sulk and brood? They lacked the nerve to do anything else. It was well known.

But one day, July 31, 1958, the warden ordered all Jewish prisoners out of the common cell block. They were now to be transferred to newly completed quarters of their own on the southern wall of the inner courtyard.

The order did not represent favoritism, for the accommodations were no improvement. Even so, the transfer created unexpected consternation among the Arabs. Ottman began walking back and forth agitatedly in the compound, conversing in a low voice with five of his companions.

"Something's wrong," Ya'akov murmured to one of the Jewish prisoners.

"You dreaming up fantasies again?" the man scoffed.

The chief guard overheard the exchange. "Don't make trouble, Merhavi," he warned. "My eye is on you."

Ya'akov said nothing more. The afternoon passed without incident.

Then, at exactly 6:00 P.M., it began.

From his usual vantage point outside the dining hall Ya'akov heard a hinge rasp. He looked up—and saw Subkhi Rajab opening the gate to the outer courtyard. At that moment eleven Arabs suddenly emerged from their cells. They carried flaming torches. In the vanguard of the group were Ottman, Narouj Betat, and Mohammed Kalili. Without a sound, the prisoners walked quickly through the door to the outer courtyard, and converged on the registry. Ya'akov leaped to his feet. Seizing the iron bar he used for his sheet-metal work, he dashed after the men.

"A break! My God, it's a break!" he kept repeating to himself.

Just as he reached the open gate, he saw Betat's torch trace a fiery arc. The registry guard dropped to the ground, unconscious. Soundlessly, the Arabs opened the door. Inside, playing chess, sat officer Weiler, the medic, and the prisoner Philip Klapper. For a moment the Jews remained motionless, transfixed by the glare of the torches. Then, with a simultaneous cry, they jumped up and grappled with the escapees. But it was too late; they were clubbed to their knees. With a crowbar Kalili ripped the telegraph wire away from its transmitter. Betat slashed the telephone wire, then picked up Weiler's key and ran to the armory. In a moment he returned carrying two heavy snipers' rifles.

By now other guards were rushing out of their quarters. Betat and Ottman met them as they entered the registry office, knocking them senseless with the rifle butts. Ya'akov saw it all, standing only ten feet away from the registry entrance. Suddenly a policeman, Yosef Shevach, staggered out of the office. Blood was streaming from his face. He managed to unfasten his pistol, and now began firing at the escapees. For an instance Shevach's gaze crossed Ya'akov's, and their eyes locked.

"Merhavi," he gasped, "Merhavi . . . I . . . help . . . Merhavi . . ."

Ya'akov stared at him, momentarily paralyzed. From the inner yard he could hear the clang of doors and the shouts of running men. Ottman's voice sounded behind him, urging his companions to hurry.

"Merhavi," Shevach cried again, his face contorted, "they're getting into the armory."

Ya'akov shook his head. Then he wheeled and dashed in the opposite direction, toward the inner courtyard gate. His left hand stretched out and he had Ottman by the wrist. The prisoner turned, recognized him: "Come on," he shouted. "This is your chance. Let's get those cells open."

Ya'akov lifted his right arm, the iron bar swinging back. Ottman's eyes widened in disbelief. "Merhavi!" he shouted, "what are you doing? Merhavi!"

The journalist was a powerful man. He raised his own crowbar in time to ward off the blow. For several moments the two men grappled, cursing each other savagely Then Ottman wrested one arm free and brought the crowbar down. It caught Ya'akov on the shoulder, knocking him backward. At the same time two shots rang out, and another passing Arab buckled and collapsed. A sheet of flame passed before Ya'akov's eyes and Philip Klapper followed it. With all his force, the Jewish prisoner hurled the torch at Ottman's head. Flesh sizzled. But the Egyptian had the strength of a bull; clutching his scorched neck, he lumbered on toward the gate. Ya'akov was after him again. He swung twice with his iron bar, and Ottman stumbled, dropping to his knees. Yeager, a sergeant-major, rushed up and covered the prisoner with his revolver.

For a moment the escape effort apparently lost its momentum. In the outer courtyard the guards and several Jewish prisoners had double barred all Arab cells. Then, from the armory, the escapees set up an exultant shout: they had found the UZIs, lethal close-range submachine guns. Narouj Betat dashed out the door, slamming a clip into the magazine of his weapon. Ya'akov saw him; instantly he hurled his crowbar, striking the UZI on the muzzle and sending it cartwheeling from the Arab's hand. Before Ya'akov could close in the prisoner, however, Betat had rushed back into the armory. He returned seconds later with a Lee-Enfield rifle. Dropping to one knee, he pulled the trigger. A man gasped, and then cried out "I'm hit" in Hebrew. Ya'akov turned just as Yeager fell on his back. An instant later another bullet kicked up dust at the fallen man's feet; Betat was still shooting. Flattening himself against the registry wall, Ya'akov shouted at the top of his voice to the tower guard:

"Gunner, train your Bren down here!"

But the guard was apparently in shock, and did not move.

"Gunner!" Ya'akov shrieked again. "Fire, you idiot!"

Finally the guard loosed one burst of the heavy machine gun. The bullets etched themselves harmlessly into the parking shed in the eastern compound. Furious, Ya'akov turned to Weiler, who had recovered consciousness and returned from the inner courtyard.

"Tell that maniac to give me his Bren, will you," he shouted. "I'll do the shooting from down here."

Before Weiler could answer, another Jewish prisoner called to them: "Come on, quickly, quickly. Look."

The man pointed to an Arab, who was pounding open the lock to the secretariat. Ya'akov recognized Mohammed Kalili. The door suddenly sprang open and Kalili entered. His voice penetrated a momentary lull in the shooting. "I've done what I could for you," Ya'akov heard him say. "Take this. Now you're on your own."

A moment later Kalili emerged empty-handed. He ran toward the north wall, leaped on the box that had been waiting for him, and clambered over. Then Ottman emerged from the secretariat. The giant Egyptian was drenched with blood; but his hands held the Lee-Enfield with authority. Ya'akov threw himself to the ground. Without pausing to fire, however, Ottman staggered through the gate to the inner courtyard. His gun went off once, twice, three times. That many cell doors swung open. Other Arab prisoners dashed out. Then other cell doors were unlocked.

"That does it," groaned Weiler.

Ya'akov anticipated what would happen now and did not wait for it. Pushing the officer aside, he dashed into the armory and seized a grappling hook. His powerful shoulders did not fail him; moments later he was on the wall. It was a twelve-foot drop to the ground outside, but he made it without injury. And there, miraculously, at that very moment, a taxi *sheroot* was approaching on the Afula road. Ya'akov rushed to the middle of the highway and waved his arms frantically. As the vehicle slowed to a halt, the prisoner pulled open the door and climbed into the empty back seat. Before the astonished driver could say a word, Ya'akov was shouting orders: "Straight ahead to the Beit She'an police station. Full speed, you hear!"

"What is this? Who are you?" protested the driver, staring at the prison uniform in the mirror.

Ya'akov thrust his mouth against the man's ear. "I am a prisoner," he said, "and I'm serving time for murder. Right now there's a *fedayin* revolt going on in Shatta, and if I'm not in that police station in ten minutes there will be more than one dead Jew on my conscience."

The driver did not wait to hear more. Slamming his foot on the accelerator, he sped off toward Beit She'an at eighty miles an hour.

When they reached the police station Ya'akov jumped out and charged up the steps three at a time. He shouted the news of the escape before the door closed behind him. The sergeant on duty blinked in amazement for several moments. Ya'akov bellowed in the man's face: "Move, you jackass!"

The sergeant suddenly came to life. He pressed a button and bells clanged throughout the station. Instantly policemen came running from all directions. The armory door was thrown open and a lieutenant handed out UZIs to the men. Ya'akov, too, was given a gun. Within two minutes a caravan of patrol cars carrying forty policemen was racing on a back road toward Shatta.

As they approached the prison, Ya'akov, seated in the lead car, caught sight of five prisoners running through the field. The driver slowed down.

"Halt!" shouted one of the policemen. "Halt!"

Ya'akov could have struck the man. "Shoot, damn you!" he raged. "They're not going to stop after all that."

The policeman took careful aim then fired a short, sustained burst. All five Arabs dropped dead on the spot. At the same moment the car's windshield blossomed into glass threads. The driver hunched down, but kept his presence of mind; he had seen the glint of metal.

"Up there," he cried, pointing to the gun tower.

Ya'akov had seen it, too, and now he recognized the sniper. It was his friend, Yusuf Abumiden, the boy who had invited him to Gaza. Ya'akov climbed out of the car and crouched behind the fender. Taking dead aim with his UZI, he fired until Yusuf Abumiden tilted slowly forward, his brain pan dropping to the ground below. Then all the police were out of their cars and storming Shatta's main gate. They reached the first courtyard just as a dozen Arabs armed with rifles came dashing out. The prisoners hesitated for a moment. Then three dropped their guns, flinging up their hands. The rest retreated toward the registry door. Their feet were instantly knocked from under them by the police fusillade.

From the inner courtyard came the sounds of a pitched battle—the crack of rifles, the staccato of UZIs and heavier Bren guns.

"Let me have some grenades," Ya'akov said to the lieutenant. "I'll blast them out."

The officer shook his head. "You go outside and join the search," he said. "Identify the escapees for the others."

The "others" were the border police and army units who were now pouring into the area, as well as scores of kibbutz members from near-by Tel Yosef. Ya'akov accompanied them as they drove their jeeps through the fields. For the first half-hour all was quiet; the countryside seemed quite deserted. Then, as the vehicle in which Ya'akov was riding completed its arc, a man jumped up directly ahead and began running erratically to the northeast. Even in the dusk Ya'akov recognized the prisoner. It was Musa, the Negro.

"Halt!" he shouted in Arabic. "Halt, Musa!"

But the man continued running, apparently crazed with fear. Ya'akov switched his UZI to single fire. He pulled the trigger twice. On the second shot the Negro flopped to the ground like a rag doll. A moment later he was picked up, blood pouring from his cheek, and hustled into the back of the jeep. Then the car returned to the prison gate.

Ya'akov and the border police entered cautiously, their guns at the ready. By now, however, the firing had stopped. The men passed through the registry and found both the outer and inner courtyards crowded with police and soldiers. Jewish prisoners were mopping up the ground with hoses and slop buckets. The compound was a porridge of blood, clothing, and human bodies. Ya'akov saw two fingers hanging from barbed wire on the north wall. Gamal Badad was lying without a head. Next to him sprawled another Arab, his entrails under his arm. Yosef Shevach, the guard, remained where he had fallen, a bullet between his eyes. Sergeant-Major Yeager's head was a pulp, his abdomen cleanly opened from breast-bone to pelvis. Among other prostrate figures Ottman lay, still breathing, a bullet in his stomach and three others in his legs. His eyes were open and he was pumping blood like a faucet. Beside him lay the twisted remains of a Bren gun. The mighty Egyptian had gone down fighting.

During the next hour the dead were piled in the secretariat, the wounded in the kitchen. Arab prisoners still able to stand were stripped naked and thrust into the dining hall under military guard. By eleven o'clock that evening complete stock had been taken. In all, thirteen Arab prisoners and two guards had been killed, three times that many men wounded. Apparently the six prisoners who had gone over the north wall had all been killed or captured. But the majority had clambered over the south wall, using a homemade ladder they had hidden for the occasion; skirting Kibbutz Beit Alpha, they had followed a small path which snaked some four miles into the Gilboa range, and then to the Jordanian border. A few even of these fugitives had also been killed or captured. But the majority, sixty trained *fedayin,* had made good their escape.

As soon as quiet had been restored, Ya'akov realized with surprise that he was counted among the wounded. In the turmoil of the fighting he had forgotten the blow from Ottman's crowbar. Now his shoulder throbbed with intense pain. He was promptly taken off to the hospital at Kfar Ruppin and bandaged. The last sound he heard before falling into an exhausted sleep was Ottman, lying next to him, feebly cursing his fate. A few days later all surviving Arab prisoners were transported to Tel Mond prison. Most of the Jews remained in Shatta.

The Israel prison commission had other plans in store for Ya'akov, however. When he testified before the commission on the events of the Shatta uprising, Dr. Zvi Hermon, the chairman, greeted him personally and rose to shake his hand. After the hearing all the commissioners congratulated Ya'akov warmly.

"We are glad to note that you acted like a faithful citizen of your country," said commissioner Etzioni. "I hope this will be taken into account."

"L'hitraot," said the other two delegates, "till we meet again."

And Dr. Hermon winked, saying: "Perhaps outside."

Ya'akov was thereupon transferred to Marsiyahu Prison in Ramle. It was a "minimum security" institution for trustworthy prisoners. There were no walls and few guards; living and working conditions were generally easier. The day after his arrival at Marsiyahu, his mother and stepfather were brought to see him. Both had aged badly in the last few years.

"Yooh, Ya'akov," Esther blinked in confusion, "what are they doing to you? What have you done now?"

He smiled. "Don't they read you the newspapers, umma?" he said. "There was a prisoners' revolt at Shatta. I caught some of them."

"Blessed be the Name," she exclaimed in astonishment. "Our people or the others?"

"The others, umma," he said proudly.

"Blessed be the Name," she repeated. "You caught the Ashkenazim."

Ya'akov leaned back and laughed until the tears came to his eyes. The stepfather wiped his eyes, too.

"Masha Allah aliha, Ya'akov," said the old man. "This is the first time I have seen you laugh since you were a little boy."

Ya'akov's face was still wreathed in smiles when it appeared on the front page of Israel's newspapers on September 23, 1958, the eve of Yom Kippur, the Day of Atonement. His flowing Oriental mustache had been neatly trimmed, his hair cut. His suitcase was in his hand. He was going home. The president of the State had granted him a pardon, subject to monthly parole reports and two psychiatric examinations each year.

"What will you do, Merhavi?" the reporters asked him.

"I shall be a sheet-metal worker," was the reply. "I hope to provide for my mother and her family."

"Will you live with her?"

"No, no. I shall live where I shall live. I prefer not to say."

And then he left the prison. A police van drove him in the direction of Tel Aviv, then turned back sharply on a side road before the reporters' taxi could follow. His whereabouts since then have been known only to the parole officer, his family, and his closest friends.

But ideas are not lacking. It has been said that he is sitting behind one of the curio stalls in Tel Aviv's Carmel Market, displaying his wares. If that is so there will not be many customers, for the Europeans prefer to buy factory goods these days. Is his labor without value then, he wonders? Surely not. Patience, ancestral skill, and hand labor have gone into his metal work; someone must come along who can appreciate it. He will wait with silent and stoic dignity.

Others suspect that he can be found in the Lachish area, bordering the northern Negev. He will be hitched to a mule there, trying his hand on the little strip of land that was denied his forebears. The kibbutz is not a place for him; better to bear the loneliness of the moshav in silence, keeping his pride and privacy. But if not there, then perhaps he is seated at the loom of the near-by textile factory, working a machine that does in one hour what his mother did in two weeks. The cloth will endure as long, of course; but no one will know that the work was his. His foreman will tell him when to begin and when to stop. He will not complain.

Nor will he protest if he must wait in line outside the labor exchange in Jaffa. The government has filled its bulletin board with announcements. Accountants are needed at Maskit, the chain of women's fashion stores. There are openings for electronic engineers at Amcor, the radio factory at Tel Litwinsky. Lathe operators are required at the furniture factory in Ramat Gan. The Ashkenazim surround the desk; for each position they have a trained man. No matter, there are other openings for the Yemenites: as garbage collectors, brick workers, pipe layers, road pavers.

He lives somewhere. The Wadi Saleb section of Haifa is not unlikely, a paradigm of limestone walls and galvanized-iron roofs, corkscrew clay stairways, wash lines, and barefoot children, mingled aromas of *hilbeh* and *kemah,* onions, garlic, and safflower oil. There is room enough to breathe, and little more. But they will not ask for more, these people, these maids and porters, waitresses and orange pickers and pepper salesmen, these religious, law-abiding, peaceful people, these beloved of Israel. It is their tradition, passed from mother to daughter and father to son, visible in the homes and classrooms and synagogues where neither a hand nor a voice is raised in protest.

There they sit, the gentle youngsters, cross-legged in a semicircle around the *mori,* who chants in a singsong of Rav Huna and Rav Hisda, of the Taj and the Rambam and of Moshe Rabenu. At the feet of abba the children learn Gematria, construing the words as numbers and exchanging them with words of equal value; and Notarikon, the symbolism of the alphabet's letters. In the kitchen mother teaches daughter the mysteries of the chicken's entrails, the traps and lairs construed by the Evil Eye, and the charms, amulets, and incantations, the sign of the fish, that offer protection for the soul.

On the street the Ashkenazim drive by in their automobiles. It is the eve of the Sabbath, and the Europeans are off to their parties and dances. Their women sing and laugh and wave their bare arms at the children who have rushed from the alleyways to watch them. There is pride and self-assurance in the Ashkenazic laughter. Then, suddenly, abba calls, and his voice is stern: "Ye sons of perdition, have ye no shame?"

The very words umma had used on him in the bedroom that afternoon, exhausted after her day's work in the Ashkenazi's household.

But the students return: in Machneh Yehudah, Wadi Saleb, in Jaffa, Nachlat Benjamin, Rosh HaAyen, and every other squatter town in the land. They resume their cross-legged positions, rock dutifully back and forth, and chant their lessons. And here, among this inscrutable band of little children, black eyes gleaming from their copper skins, Ya'akov Merhavi will be found. One of them, and more, is surely he.

CHAPTER SEVEN

THE SOLDIER

TWO MILES behind us, as the coast curved, downtown Tel Aviv cast a net of dancing neon into the sea. Before us Jaffa's Andromeda Rock guarded its share of the waters, rinsed and pale under a full moon. "Ayn ma l'hashvot," Israelis say, "There is nothing to compare." Nothing to compare between the lurid exuberance of the metropolis and the plaintive charm of venerable Jaffa. The sages had their own explanation: "All the silver and gold and precious stones that are wrecked with the ships in all the seas flow to Jaffa," they pointed out, ". . . [and this treasure] will be yielded up in the fullness of time with the advent of the Messiah, who will apportion it to each righteous man according to his merits. . . ."

It can be apportioned now by those with an eye for sleeping beauty. There are ancient roads and lanes twisting erratically through clusters of stone villas and sunken gardens. Massive archways and corridors link courtyards by pavement and roof top. Windows peep out of superb filigree and latticework. The Hassen Bek and Mahmudiye mosques loom silently over town squares that once echoed to the muezzin's wail. For Jaffa was Arab. Not in ancient times, to be sure, when the town was the major port of the Davidic and Hasmonean dynasties, nor even later when Roman and Byzantine galleys unloaded their cargoes at the city's quays. But afterward, when Mamelukes and Ottomans governed the ravaged land, and Arab merchants and artisans rushed in by land to supply garrisons pouring in by sea. Long before the twentieth century, the city had become a rancid bedlam. Camels and donkeys left their droppings in the rutted roadways. Peddlers and hucksters stridently reviled the ancestors of their competitors. Prostitutes of both sexes minced and leered in back alleys. Thugs lay in wait for wayfarers and their savings.

Yet beneath the corruption the beauty remained: the slim and tremulous minarets, the steaming Turkish bathing pools, the drying fish nets hanging in gentle parabolas between the interlocking stone corridors, the rock buttresses flying majestically into the sea. Above all the sea, treacherous and deep-throated beneath its horizons, mottled green by day, lambent as glycerine by night. Ancient Joppa—the Arabs could not destroy its muted grandeur. Neither could the Jews who were their successors.

The Zionists began arriving during the late nineteenth and early twentieth centuries. Yet as late as 1948 they numbered no more than five thousand in the midst of ten times that many Arabs; for Tel Aviv, once a tiny Jewish suburb of the famed seaport, had been the principal magnet for Jewish settlement since 1914. It was the Palestine war and the rise of Israel which precisely reversed the ratio of populations in Jaffa. The battle for the town was a savage one, uninhibited by the rules of the Geneva Convention. The Jews won. The Arabs fled, leaving only a tiny residue of their people behind. Today Jaffa is Jewish. At first, to be sure, the difference is not apparent. Most of the town's inhabitants are still dark. Many of the men wear cassocks and turbans. The women's ears are pierced for Arab-style loop earrings. Yet they are Jews, the majority of them North African, Iraqi, or Yemenite immigrants who have arrived since the establishment of the State. Marginally employed, impoverished, the newcomers make their homes in the abandoned slum dwellings of their Arab predecessors.

Their frustrations occasionally bring them afoul of the law. We drove closer toward the sound of music. Before us Ariadne's flickered white in the glare of Jaffa's lighthouse. It was a cheap Greek casino, mingling the strains of bazukoys (guitars) and tambourines with the conversation and laughter of patrons. Fifty yards down the road a sinister old Turkish prison blocked further traffic. The police sergeant eased the auto to the curb. Before climbing out, Lev, the detective, snapped on the radio transmitter and reported his whereabouts to the central police station. Then probation officer Rudick and I joined him as he walked briskly toward a tiny kiosk on the far side of Ariadne's. For several minutes Lev chatted animatedly with the proprietor, a swarthy Iraqi.

"The kiosk owner is a former convict," Rudick explained. "He's one of our most reliable informers now. Nothing happens in this neighborhood that he doesn't know about."

But nothing had happened. "No activity tonight," said the detective, rejoining us. We returned to the police van. "Straight on to Omar Khayyam's," Lev ordered the sergeant.

The auto pulled out and we cruised the few short blocks to HaShetach HaGadol, the "Great Sector." It was one of Israel's more celebrated vistas. The hill mushroomed high over the harbor, then descended in gentle gradients toward the waves. Light from strategically placed mercury lamps leaped and flared from terrace to terrace. It was a brilliant spectacle, but a cruel trick on lovers. They had to search for their shadowed opportunity elsewhere. Tourists and the Tel Aviv smart set often found it in Omar Khayyam's, a night club built into a kind of catacomb at the base of the lowest terrace. The illumination within was predictably sepulchral. Cigarette smoke streamed and whorled about guitar players and jazz pianists. Waitresses in leopard-skin leotards circulated among the customers serving drinks and cold cuts.

For those with grosser appetites, there were other pleasures to be had outside. Lev, Rudick, and I walked slowly through the cobblestone alleyway, doing our best to remain inconspicuous among the tourists and other passers-by. The effort was unsuccessful. A dark-skinned Moroccan youth, wearing an Italian-style sport shirt and black, drain-pipe trousers, stared hard at Lev for a moment, then flashed a signal down the road. It was caught by the heavily painted slattern seated on a grapefruit crate against the wall. Instantly she jumped to her feet and disappeared into a doorway. Lev quickened his pace.

"Let's get round the corner before they do," he called to us. "I'll show you a real market."

He did not exaggerate. At intervals of approximately ten feet in the street opening before us, four or five young men had stationed themselves on the curbstone, and brazenly offered their "merchandise" to passing pedestrians. Most of the girls were still in their teens, and all of them were Orientals. The spectacle shocked me deeply.

"Are they Jewish, these youngsters?" I asked Rudick.

"Every one," he replied, smiling faintly at my astonishment. "Most of them are North Africans or Kurds. The pimps are Rumanians."

"But why aren't they cleared off the street? Why aren't they arrested?"

Here Lev explained matters. "The law isn't that simple," he pointed out. "We have to catch them in *flagrante delicto* or else we can't get them convicted. Watch." He inclined his head toward the procurers. The youths had suddenly and mysteriously dropped back against the walls. A few of them remained there, eyeing us furtively; the others strolled down the sidewalk with elaborate casualness. The girls stared morosely at the ground.

"You can see for yourself," Lev said. "We could arrest them on *prima facie* evidence. But we could never make it stick in court. Ask them, and they'll tell you they're out sniffing the night air. We'll try something else now."

Rudick and I followed the detective back to the original alleyway. There we entered Omar Khayyam's once again, passed through a rear door, and then climbed a long, all but interminable stone stairway. In a few minutes we reached the top floor. Lev pushed open the wooden trap door and we walked out onto the roof. It was an excellent vantage point. The view commanded the entire complex of streets and lanes at the base of HaShetach HaGadol. Apparently it had been under observation for some time; to my surprise, a man crouching at the edge of the roof suddenly straightened up and walked toward us out of the shadow. Lev introduced the newcomer, then turned briskly to the business at hand.

"What's the story?" he asked.

The man opened a notebook. "At seven forty Pinhas Lupescu's girl, Joulie, took a client to Sorek's," he read. "Finished twenty minutes later. At eight twelve Rbiqua, Mani Zilber's girl, took a client to the same place. Finished quarter of an hour later. She went back with a client a half-hour after that, and left just two minutes before you came."

Lev nodded. "Shade down to the bottom, I suppose?"

The plain-clothes man shrugged, and Lev grunted sourly. Rudick noted my bewilderment.

"Suppose we grabbed them," he said. "They'd tell the judge that they were sleeping with their boy friends. We'd get no help from their clients, either. They wouldn't admit visiting a prostitute."

"The one count we can occasionally catch them on is spreading disease," Lev added. "That's why I've got my man up here. It's the only time circumstantial evidence proves useful in court."

It was not the legality that bothered me, however. It was the sociology. I had seen occasional streetwalkers in Israel before, especially on Ben-Yehudah Street in Tel Aviv, and in the Arab quarter of Haifa. But I had never imagined that prostitution was so systematized.

"Too bad you couldn't have seen Edmond in action," remarked the plain-clothes man. "There was a man with a real system. He was a Tripolitanian immigrant, not older than thirty. Before we finally put him away he had ten whores working for him and was taking in a thousand pounds a week."

I must have sighed. Rudick put his arm around my shoulder amiably. "You haven't seen anything yet," he assured me.

Our next destination was the thoroughfare known as Rehov Shishim—Sixty Street. Even before we reached the main square, I had an inkling of what awaited us. We parked the car in a side alley. Lev radioed headquarters, and then we proceeded by foot. It was another world, a dark world of dark people. They clustered in small groups outside fetid saloons and smoke-filled card parlors. Most of them were North African. Some were Iraqi, Persian, and Yemenite. But the costume rarely varied: the striped sport shirt with flaring collar, the tightly fitting corduroy trousers, the pointed Italianesque shoes. Nor did the hair styles: long, heavily greased, often swept into duck tails in the back.

As the saloon radios blared Arab melodies up and down the street, the youths stood slack-limbed by the entrances, their eyes following the movements of passers-by with glittering, feral insolence. They recognized Lev, coldly returned his stare, but said nothing. Halfway down the street chairs suddenly overturned in a bar. A man shrieked in Arabic. Instantly his voice was drowned in shouting. By the time we reached the door the noise had stopped. We looked in. Four men had dropped back against the wall. A youth mopped blood from his cheek, glared at Lev for a moment, then turned away. The detective strode quickly to one of the card players, an older, fat man, and seized his wrist.

"Let me have it, Marzouk," he snapped, tightening his grip.

The man shrugged. "Ayn li," he mumbled. "Haven't got it."

Lev tilted the card table, and carefully examined the inner rim. Then he crouched on all fours and peered under the chairs. The sergeant ordered the bystanders to roll up their sleeves to the elbow. Lev inspected their forearms personally. Finding nothing, he whispered in the sergeant's ear. Then, loudly—"We're booking you for disturbing the peace."

He walked out of the saloon, leaving the sergeant to take down the

men's names. We continued on, walking in the middle of the narrow
street.

"Was it a knife you were looking for?" I asked.

"Opium, morphine."

We reached the terminal point of our journey, Rehov Shishim's central
square. I knew then without being told that I had reached the sinkhole of
Israel. Nothing in my experience matched it for sheer soul-numbing hope-
lessness—neither the poverty of the *ma'abarot,* the squalor of immigrant
settlement villages, nor even the desperation of the social-welfare waiting
rooms. There were beggars and drunkards here, of course. Prostitutes as
well. But there was also something else, something much worse. Thirty or
forty men, most of them Orientals, were seated back to back on orange
crates, or on the curbstone itself. They had once been alive. Now their
motor centers still functioned, but they were dead. Their bodies were
wasted and near-cadaverous. Their hollow eyes stared inward, and obviously saw nothing. Well, Rudick had warned me.

Another detective awaited us. Together he and Lev approached the
assemblage of human derelicts. Without saying a word, they lifted one
lifeless arm after another in search of the telltale needle marks. None of
the men protested. None spoke a word. Their sallow, emaciated faces
betrayed neither emotion nor awareness. Lev bent forward, thrust his mouth
next to an addict's ear, speaking quietly: "Where is it, Mimouni? Speak
to me and I'll take care of you."

The man coughed, the echo of spittle rattling up from his skeletal
breastbone. He stared vacantly into the detective's face and said nothing.
At the same time the second detective and the sergeant, who had rejoined
our party, methodically set about their hunt for stray packets or grains of
hashish. They found nothing. Perhaps they would have abandoned the
search if one of the men, a tall, pallid Ashkenazi, his head shaved close
to the skull, had not suddenly lurched to his feet, and started off at an
erratic trot for the beach. The plain-clothes man let him continue. Then,
when the man had put twenty yards behind him, Lev jerked his head.
The sergeant and the second detective started off in leisurely pursuit.

"They'll find it now," Rudick predicted confidently.

"But where do they get it?" I asked.

"It starts with the Arabs."

From camel caravans crossing the Negev, smuggling raw opium from
Jordan or Sinai. Other packets come from the Lebanon, or even through
the port of Haifa. From there Jews take over, usually veteran Sephardic
or Oriental families with well-developed Arab connections. Sometimes they
take possession of the dope at the border, sometimes at harbors. Yemenite
fishermen convey it down the coast to Jaffa, the cesspool of Israel crime.
And then individual dealers take over: Edmond, the Moroccan pimp; Aga
Cohen, "king" of the Jaffa underworld; Gastoune Boubaker, "wizard"
of aphrodisiacs.

Who were the buyers? They were sprawled out before us now. Rudick
and Lev were busy making up the account: "That's Naikil. We caught

him pandering on Ben-Yehudah Street, sent him up for three months to Ramle prison . . . Nissim Mahoula, there, with the bandage on his eye. Petty filching. We put him and his brother on probation just last June . . . Mordecai Youbert is in the middle. Look at him, he doesn't know where he is, poor kid. His mother is living with an Arab in Acre . . . Put down Imiliou Lopez for watching. He's been seen with Aga Cohen at the Laique Bar . . . Yes, there's Pinhas, he was with them. His wife's also living with an Arab now; two breaking and entering charges against him this year . . . we'll try a urine test on him, but I'm not optimistic . . . Jean-Jean and Elias, there they are, out like a light, both of them . . ." And more and more and more.

"When we have our first Jewish criminals," wrote Bialik, the eminent Zionist poet and essayist, "then we shall know we are a nation at last." Bialik would have turned over in his grave. The people I saw that day were all Jews, children of Israel, gentle people of the Book. There were hundreds of them, dope addicts and prostitutes, thieves and gamblers and drunkards and ruffians. In succeeding weeks I saw them in prisons, on work gangs, and in rehabilitation centers. One could become inured to hardened criminals after a while, to recidivists with square ears and prognathic jaws, to police-wary felons with cunning eyes and agile fingers. It was the children who demoralized you, however. The youngsters were flooding the probate courts and reform schools. They were the first evidence I had seen in Israel of incipient social cancer.

Ephraim Millo, chief of the national probation service, gave me the statistics. Between 1949 and 1962 the number of delinquents brought to probate court rose by 52 per cent. This represented 127 out of each 10,000 youngsters in the country. Fully half these youthful offenders were of European origin, and many of them were sabras, native-born. Yet when it came to the more serious disturbances, to such felonies as assault, robbery, arson, rape, and dope addiction, the statistics revealed a different picture: here most of the offenders—70 per cent—were children of Oriental immigrant families. A majority of these were North African.

The phenomenon terrifies Israel's European community. "The North Africans are wild people," they complain. "They look and act just like Arabs. A person risks his life whenever he walks through one of their neighborhoods. Just look at the crime rate. Look at the increase in venereal disease, in gambling and dope smuggling. Who brought all this to Israel if not they? We built a civilized community here, and these primitives are destroying it all." More than occasionally, too, European Jews will confess privately that they would like to see the influx of Jews from Moslem lands halted altogether. "The Orientals are swamping us," the argument goes. "Their birth rate is three times ours. In another decade they will have transformed this country into a Levantine State. Hitler certainly did his job better than he knew. Who ever dreamed Israel's population would be made up of these Arabized derelicts?"

II

No one did. Certainly not the ideologues and pioneers of Jewish settlement in Palestine. Before World War II few Zionist spokesmen gave more than fleeting attention to the squalid Jewish hinterland of North Africa or the Near East. Perhaps it was a natural oversight. As late as 1939, 90 per cent of world Jewry belonged to the Ashkenazic community. Europe was the power center of Jewish life. Between the Vistula and the Seine lived millions of educated, hard-working and resourceful men and women, ideal raw material for the Zionist renaissance. And upon this European Jewish population, as a result, the emissaries of the Jewish nationalist movement concentrated their efforts. Zionist societies, philanthropic federations, gymnastic clubs, hiking groups, musical and literary societies, training and emigration camps sprang up by the hundreds between communities as far apart as Moscow and London. Here was the *Yishuv's* most likely source of useful and productive immigrants.

The Nazis disposed of that source. In less than a half-decade the demographic structure of Jewish life was radically altered. The creative and dynamic Jewish communities of continental Europe were all but obliterated. Soviet Jewry survived, perhaps two-thirds intact, but hopelessly locked off behind the Iron Curtain. Thus it was that the State of Israel, born amid the debris of the "Final Solution," was suddenly compelled to search the backwaters of Jewish life for its potential citizens. For the first time the various Zionist agencies turned their attention to a world passed by, to some 800,000 Jews living in Moslem lands. Of these, nearly a half-million were to be found in the massive Berber littoral: 142,000 in Algeria, 109,000 in Tunisia, and 253,000 in Morocco. It was the single largest concentration of Jews in the Moslem world, and almost overnight it had become the single largest reservoir of immigrants to Israel.

The reservoir began emptying, more rapidly, more dramatically than had ever been anticipated. For the rising fury of Maghreb nationalism was sweeping across North Africa. From Algeria to Tripoli Jewish villagers and city dwellers alike discovered that the tenuous *modus vivendi* with their Berber neighbors was suddenly crumbling. As in the case of Syria, Yemen, and Iraq, moreover, economic and political insecurity was fused with a deeply rooted and urgent revival of Jewish messianism. Tens of thousands of devoutly religious families saw in the emergence of the Jewish State the true and certain omen of divine intercession. Pouring from the Maghreb at the rate of 20,000 and 30,000 a month, the Jews of North Africa burst upon the beleaguered Israel nation like a tidal wave. Within a decade after the State's founding, in fact, 211,000 Maghreb Jews had arrived in Israel. It was in large measure the impact of these North African fugitives which undermined Israel's Western foundations, and threatened to Orientalize and Levantinize the Jewish Republic—and thus jeopardize its very survival.

The newcomers were penniless, of course. Transported to Israel in vessels and planes chartered by the Jewish Agency, they brought with them a few duffelbags, the clothes on their backs, and nothing more. The rest of their pathetic belongings had been sold at desperation prices to provide a few weeks' subsistence money in Israel. Their educational level was among the lowest of any immigrant group. Indeed, many of the North Africans were totally illiterate. With all too few exceptions, their behavior was that of Arab primitives: cursing and fighting among themselves, shrieking and wailing in employment or social-welfare waiting rooms. They wrapped themselves in filthy jodhpurs and burnooses, swaddled (and nearly suffocated) their children in countless grease-stained blankets. Their food, even for those in the best of economic circumstances, was saturated in oil, and rarely included fresh vegetables or dairy products. Their notions of personal hygiene were often quite rudimentary.

Were they malleable? Could they be changed? Here the settlement authorities experienced their deepest misgivings. The Maghreb Jews seemed grateful enough to have arrived safely in Israel. But their gratitude apparently did not embrace a willingness to make crucial sacrifices for the nation's development. The Jewish Agency was prepared to guarantee them food, clothing, shelter, medical care, and, ultimately, a livelihood. It asked in return that the immigrants settle in areas crucial to Israel's security: in outlying co-operative or collective-farm communities; or in factories newly located in the southern part of the country.

The request anticipated too much. Congested for centuries in wretched ghettos, deprived of the opportunity to own or work the land, the North Africans had been compelled to earn their bread as small-trades men or artisans. The typical Maghreb Jew, as a consequence, was likely to be a leather worker, a cobbler, a silversmith—or, more commonly, a huckster, a small greengrocer, a fruit salesman, a sidewalk vendor of imitation jewelry and knickknacks, a porter, or a dealer in second-hand clothing. The vocations were marginal, but they were the only vocations the immigrants knew—and, in many instances, the only vocations they wanted to know. During the early years of their settlement in Israel, appeals made to their Jewish pride or their Zionist idealism apparently fell on deaf ears. If they were settled on new moshavim, given homes, agricultural tools, and training, the immigrants all too frequently pocketed their Jewish Agency loans and blandly drifted back to the cities. Ultimately no more than 10 per cent of the Moroccan and Tunisian immigrants remained in agricultural communities. The rest glutted the urban slum areas, and took their chances once again as petty traders or unskilled laborers.

It was surely difficult if not impossible to recognize in this semiliterate lazzarone the descendants of one of the most prosperous and fecund civilizations in Jewish history. Yet such was the heritage of Maghreb Jewry. Indeed, during the Islamic Renaissance between the ninth and thirteenth centuries, the comparative literacy of these ancient settlers (antedating even the Carthaginians and Romans), and their commercial connections with other Jewish communities in the Mediterranean basin, enabled them to achieve a reasonably high degree of economic security. At the end of the fifteenth century, moreover, their numbers were augmented by perhaps fifty thousand Sephardic Jews, refugees from the Inquisition and the Spanish expulsion decree. For these newcomers, North Africa proved a blessed oasis after the butcheries of Catholic Europe. Until well into the early modern era, therefore, Maghreb Jewry was one of the most favorably situated Jewish communities in the world.

Their cultural level was correspondingly high. During the Islamic Renaissance the Maghreb's galaxy of Jewish intellects very nearly rivaled that of Spain. In the celebrated capital of Kairwan (present-day Tunisia), Jewish scholars developed one of the most distinguished legal academies of the early medieval era. The city of Fez was the home of the eminent philologists Dunash ibn-Librat and Yehudah ibn-Hayouj, in the tenth century, and of Ishaq al-Fassi, the most celebrated rabbinical authority of the eleventh century. Fifty years later Fez served also as the temporary domicile of the world-renowned Jewish philosopher, Moses Maimonides; of the exquisite Fassi poet, Yehudah ibn-Abbas; and the mathematician Yusuf ibn-Aknin, who later was appointed astronomer to the Prince of Cairo.

Moreover, individual Sephardic families established vital commercial and diplomatic links with other lands. Early in the sixteenth century, Abraham Benzemirou, chief rabbi of the Portuguese Jewish community in Morocco, served as official intermediary between the Moroccan Moslem communities and the kingdom of Portugal. The merchant prince Samuel Pallash, ambassador of Morocco to the Netherlands in the sixteenth century, was one of the founders of the Jewish community of Amsterdam. Simultaneously, Ya'akov Sasportas, a native of Oran who became rabbi of Marrakech, was entrusted with another mission by the king of Morocco —this time to Spain, which was still burning its own Jews in autos-da-fé.

Thus, until the late eighteenth century, the Maghreb remained one of the most creative enclaves of Jewish life in the world. Its reputation as a center for scholarship and literature extended to all corners of Europe, and even to the Americas. And it was precisely the Arabized descendants of this celebrated community who now shuffled and whined their way through the back alleys of Israel's slum cities, who eked out their livelihoods as menial workers, or as peddlers of dope and women.

It was true that a pall had fallen on them two centuries before, during the period of the most savage religious reaction in North African history. *Dhimmi* (minority) taxes, always discriminatory, had been tripled then. Access to the sultan's courts had been cut off altogether. Jews had been locked in their *mellahs,* forbidden to travel. Indeed, they had been transformed into the serfs of the local Moslem *caïd,* their property subject to expropriation at the overlord's slightest whim. Within the space of one generation, the Jewish community of Morocco was reduced to semimendicancy. Within the space of one century, the largest majority of the country's Jews had forgotten how to read or write. In 1912, the French occupied Morocco. Under direct orders from Paris, the Jews were granted a few basic civil rights, and liberated from their most crippling indignities.

But by then the damage had already been done: Moroccan Jewry had succumbed to an almost total cultural atrophy. Moreover, within a few years of the Maghebric immigration to Israel, the citizenry of the Jewish State discovered another and perhaps even more fundamental ingredient of the North Africans' malaise. It was rage. They were slowly choking of pent-up rage.

III

The discovery could be dated quite precisely: July 9, 1959. It sprang from a sordid barroom brawl in Wadi Saleb, a slum quarter of Haifa. Police were called to the scene. In the ensuing melee a drunken Moroccan, one Ya'akov Akiba, was shot and wounded while resisting arrest. He was taken immediately to a hospital, where his condition was described as "serious but not dangerous." Nevertheless the rumor quickly circulated that Akiba had died, the victim of "police brutality." Early the next morning a large crowd of Moroccan immigrants surrounded the Wadi Saleb police station, waving black flags smeared with blood, and demanding "revenge." At first the police allowed the demonstration, evidently assuming that it would soon exhaust itself. But disorders flared up sporadically throughout the day. At last, shortly before 6:00 P.M., a police task force, wearing steel helmets and armed with truncheons, forcefully dispersed the crowds. By then thirteen policemen and two civilians were injured, most of them by stones thrown from roofs. Thirty-two persons were arrested, including four women. Extensive damage was caused to property in the lower slum areas of the city. A parked car was burned, a café wrecked, a restaurant damaged. A Mapai club and the Histadrut club were almost completely gutted. In the retail district four cars were overturned, and the windows in about twenty shops were smashed.

An account of the riots appeared on the front pages of all Israel's newspapers. It was quite apparent that some sort of mass protest was being registered by the Oriental community, with implications far deeper than a barroom fracas. Indeed, ensuing investigations of the riots made it plain that the shooting of the wastrel, Ya'akov Akiba, had served merely as a trigger for a long-repressed outburst of real or fancied grievances. Thus, on July 13, one Asher Hissin, president of the so-called "Association of North Africans in Israel," demanded a commission to investigate the housing, employment, education, and social status of his kinsmen in Israel. They were being discriminated against, Hissin insisted; it was their fully justified resentment which sparked the outburst of July 10.

Several days later the government appointed a nonparty committee to evaluate the more deeply rooted causes of the Wadi Saleb uprising. Witnesses were called. One of them, David Ben Haroush, offered a particularly grim account of personal and collective discrimination. He had arrived in Palestine from Morocco in 1947, he explained, and had served in the Israel army during the War of Liberation. After demobilization, he set about finding a home for himself. Then, according to Ben Haroush's testimony, he discovered that the authorities had allocated all the better accommodations to European immigrants. He himself had to settle for a squalid shanty in Wadi Saleb. Later he found employment in the police department; together with other Oriental policemen, however, his duties were confined to routine guard assignments, offering little opportunity for promotion. Eventually Ben Haroush left the police and opened a small café in Haifa. It was patronized exclusively by North Africans. Europeans never came near the place.

"You ask if there is prejudice in this country," Ben Haroush cried, his voice rising angrily before the packed committee room. "A North African is always down at the bottom of the list whenever he applies—whether to the development authority, the city administration, the welfare organization for the aged, or the Jewish Agency. It's always the European immigrants who get the most favored treatment." On being pressed, the witness admitted that the North Africans were often poorly equipped by education for the better-paying jobs. "Even so," Ben Haroush countered bitterly, "if I am unskilled, does that mean that I must raise a generation of porters? That people with academic training must automatically raise a generation of professionals? Where will it end?"

Ben Haroush's vehemence was by no means atypical. Other North African witnesses insisted that education seemed to be almost exclusively an Ashkenazic prerogative. By 1959 80 per cent of Israel's children reached the ninth grade—but only 25 per cent could afford to continue to the end of high school. The largest number of casualties were Orientals, for their families were the poorest, the ones most urgently in need of their children's earnings. What happened to these youngsters afterward? The answer was provided by the teachers and social workers who later testified. At first the drop-outs flooded the labor exchanges. In 1957, for example, of 2,000 young people looking for work at the Haifa youth labor office, 1,800 were from North Africa. Obviously there were not enough jobs for all of them. The rest were left to the street—and its consequences. With minor variations, the statistics were duplicated in nearly all of Israel's cities. Nor was there any evidence that the situation would become anything but worse. The pressure of a swelling population forced secondary-school authorities to become increasingly selective in admitting pupils. Those of lower cultural background or of lower I.Q. ratings were the first to be rejected—nearly always the Orientals.

These facts were no secret to the North Africans themselves. But lacking newspapers of their own, lacking so much as a single North African member of the Knesset, lacking almost any effective means of public expression, they had brooded in impotent silence. Their complaints generally reached no further than the ears of labor-exchange and social-welfare officials. Until Wadi Saleb.

It happened that the commission hearings coincided with the election campaign for the Fourth Knesset. Thus, the witnesses' grievances were followed with rapt attention by the country's politicians. In mid-August each party sought to outdo the other in expressing its concern for the

North African immigrants. Mapai, the powerful Labor Party which dominated the government coalition, proved especially solicitous—aware that the Wadi Saleb rioters had singled out the Mapai clubhouse for ransacking and burning. Social-welfare payments were increased to destitute Moroccan families. Popular Mapai figures including Moshe Dayan, the conqueror of Sinai, and even Ben-Gurion himself, were sent into Moroccan neighborhoods to offer assurances of social and economic help in the near future.

It is not unlikely, too, that the members of the commission which issued the final report in August, reflected this political awareness. The summary was remarkably circumspect. It announced that the riots were probably spontaneous, and developed out of a genuine sense of grievance. "The . . . picture that is presented by the North African immigrants is one of isolation or a feeling of isolation from the settled part of Israel's society . . . a deep feeling of failure in life—as regards income, housing, etc. . . ." The report concluded with a paean to the loyalty and patriotism of Israel's North Africans, and with an appeal to the government to provide the nation's Oriental population with supplementary educational and vocational guidance. "But more than anything else, the committee calls upon every citizen of Israel to make his contribution to the fusing of the immigrants from the various countries." The sentiment was heartily echoed the next day by editorials in all the country's leading newspapers.

The report was innocuous and misleading. If it failed to discuss at length the limitations the Moroccans themselves brought with them, it also ignored the unofficial, but nonetheless quite tangible and demonstrable instances of discrimination. To be sure, the Maghreb Jews were far from ideally equipped for well-paying jobs. On the other hand, labor-exchange officials rarely seemed willing to give the North Africans the benefit of the doubt. Perhaps they had been jaded by their experience with the newcomers. But it was not improbable, too, that the employment authorities had been affected, as had so many other Israelis, by the steady attrition of pre-State idealism. Since 1948 housing, food, and employment were increasingly secured through patronage and political connections. The Ashkenazim possessed those connections, and the Orientals did not. All too often the latter were assigned to jobs that minimized their potential competition with the older, Ashkenazic group.

The commission report also failed to come to grips with a rather more fundamental North African grievance. Their sense of injustice had not arisen simply as a result of economic and social inequality. After all, the imperfections in Israel's young democracy affected all Oriental immigrant groups—Yemenites, Iraqis, Persians, Kurds, Tripolitanians, as well as Moroccans and Tunisians. Yet with few exceptions it was the Moroccan protest which was the most vocal and violent. Why, then, should one group, backward and unfairly treated, but surely not more so than the others, have produced such a disproportionate share of delinquents and misfits, of sullen and explosive *voyous?* What could have been agitating them more unremittingly than the other Oriental minorities?

A great deal, actually. The truth was that the Moroccans expected more of Israel than almost any other of the State's newcomers. Frustration and bitterness had been eating away at their vitals throughout all the decades of French occupation—long before they departed from their Maghreb homeland. In the ghettos of Casablanca, Marrakech, Meknès, and Fez, the North Africans had nurtured a festering sore. In Israel they searched for a cure.

<h3 style="text-align:center">IV</h3>

A visit to the *mellah* of Casablanca offers only the faintest hint of the difficulty. Of course the place stinks. Some of the odor arises from food laid out in the innumerable tiny market stalls that line both sides of the narrow, winding streets: the fly-spotted vegetables, fruits, meats, fish, nuts, and treacly, dripping cakes and candies. Yet the stench is essentially of people: a swirling ocean of patched *abayas,* burnooses, turbans, skullcaps, and veils, obscenely sagging trouser seats and eyes black or blistered with trachoma, leaden patinas of dirt extending from ringleted hair to rag-bound feet. The place is cacophonous, too, with the harangue of sidewalk peddlers, the curses of donkey and camel drivers, the wail of beggars—their numbers are endless—casting their blind gaze upon hardly less wretched passers-by. They are all Jews.

One of them, a child, opened his eyes each morning in a room on Rue Djama Shluh. On his bed slept four other brothers. On the second bed lay three sisters. The adjoining room was his father and mother's. Grandfather and two other children shared the kitchen. It was the Hayot family, and if they were poor Bebert did not know it. He had his place on the bed. The kitchen tap poured cold water whenever he turned it. There was food: *shashlik, humus, techina, addas,* potatoes, pepper, and *arissa,* and all the oil one needed for frying. At times Bebert's head itched, and at times his eyes burned, but he was never hungry, and never seriously ill. A nickel-plated radio lay on the kitchen table, and the family heard music simply by turning a knob. When Bebert and the other children walked into the alleyway they wore shoes on their feet; the same could not be said for most of their playmates. Papa had a business of his own, a little printing press downstairs. Papa could even speak and write a little French. How many other Jews could say that for themselves? Arabic was the common jargon of the *mellah,* after all. (Poor old Grandpère, squatting in his turban and cassock, responded only to Judeo-Berber.) It was not an intolerable life.

Only the confinement chafed. All the more, the older one grew. The houses were old, yawing, crumbling down into the street. Like most of the neighboring thoroughfares, Rue Djama Shluh was only three and a half yards wide. Garbage cans lined the curbs, their fumes suffusing the wares of innumerable stalls and shops. The inhabitants grew more numerous each year. They grew more primitive, too, for they were Atlas Mountain Jews, terror-stricken refugees flooding in from the Berber hinterland. Perhaps there was no longer room for them in the *mellah;* yet there was no room for them anywhere else. In Casablanca, as in Fez, Meknès, Marrakech, Constantine, and the other cities of the Maghreb, Jews generally found it safer to remain in their ghetto. Berber knives were sharp.

The French, for their part, were unwilling to provoke their Moslem subjects unnecessarily. They appointed only Berbers as magistrates and policemen, for these were the positions that represented visible and tangible authority. A Jew involved in a dispute with a Moslem invariably lost his case in court. Indeed, a street argument rarely got as far as the courtroom; if the Jew was not manhandled by a Moslem policeman, a Berber mob settled the issue. To be sure, commercial relations between Jews and Moslems were generally unruffled. And there were occasional instances of genuine Moslem-Jewish friendship. One of Bebert's closest childhood friends was Mohammed Tijani, and the two were often guests at each other's homes. But in its larger contours the gulf between the two communities remained wide and unbridgeable. As late as the mid-twentieth century, the Jews were regarded as *dhimmi*s.

The best, the only hope remained the French. Bebert and his brothers and sisters had been taught to believe it. So had all their friends. The French had brought peace and order to Morocco. Perhaps they had not yet granted the Jews French citizenship, as in neighboring Algeria. But at least it was the presence of the French army in the larger cities which prevented anti-Jewish outbreaks. Moreover, the French had brought with them the promise of material and cultural progress for Jew and Moslem alike. Their superb roads, power stations, and office buildings, their spacious modern homes in the New City, all these were shining examples of the possibilities of Western enlightenment. So were their civil servants: efficient, honest, impartial, virtually impervious to the traditional Maghreb blandishments of baksheesh. Their schools were microcosms of everything rich and meaningful in the Gallic cultural tradition. There was no question about it: the French alone were capable of civilizing the benighted and slothful Maghreb.

Little wonder, therefore, that the Jews viewed their European protectors with admiration and gratitude. It was a gratitude amplified, too, by occasional gestures of official encouragement. Now and then a particularly well-educated Jew was engaged as a white-collar employee in the French administration. Jewish children of promising intellect were not infrequently accepted on scholarship in French government schools. Nor was it unheard-of for a French family to invite a Jew of "Western" education to their home—a significant and memorable social triumph for the guest. Accordingly, even children of the most impoverished *mellah* homes looked forward to attending school in the Jewish-sponsored Alliance system, for the teachers and language of instruction were French. Bebert and his generation were convinced: social equality and economic emancipation lay with the tricolor.

Here, then, was the heart of the problem. In his early youth Bebert, too, attended an Alliance primary school. With his classmates, he was introduced to the French language, to French literature and science, history and government. For the first time, too, he was permitted a vision of another world: a world of order, efficiency, and logic, of cleanliness and modernity. The experience was exalting. It was disconcerting, as well. As the years passed, Bebert discovered that the people who awaited his return from class each day were strangers. They were his parents.

There was Maman: bloated from a lifetime of childbearing and oil-soaked Oriental cooking, seated cross-legged on the *diwan* in her grease-stained purple kimono. Each time an older sister was married off Maman was transformed into a beaming ritual-impresario. There was the girl's hair to be dyed; then the ceremonial visit to the *hamman,* the public bathhouse, and the *mikveh,* the ritual pool. And finally the wedding banquet itself, ten days after daughter's period (ensuring fertility): shouting, drinking, tongue trilling, and amulet waving. Maman, with her *djebban* gown and silk *fouta* veil exorcising the djinn, painting herself with sticks of *ned,* dousing herself with incense, lumbering like an elephant to the frenzied music of cymbals, flutes, tom-toms and *darboukas.*

And Papa: at work in his blue beret and double-breasted sack suit. Or, on Jewish holidays, rocking back and forth in his filthy skullcap and Oriental robe, mouthing Berber incantations in the same breath with Hebrew prayers, whirling into ecstasies at the tombs of "wonder-working" rabbis. Papa, presiding like a king over his brood, paralyzing all conversation with a glance. Who in his right mind would have dared to discuss intimate matters with the ruler of the household? Or question Papa's dictates on ritual observances? Like his brothers, Bebert was handed a *tallith* (prayer shawl) and phylacteries on bar mitzvah day, and ordered to wear them three times daily thenceforth, praying as Papa dictated, shrill-voiced, invoking the protection of the Almighty against the Evil Eye.

Bebert performed these rites without complaint until well into his adolescence. Then his friends began to mock him: "Wave the chicken today, Bebert? . . . Tell us about it in class, will you? . . . Going to put on *t'fillin* [phylacteries] tonight, Bebert?" The jibes struck home. None of his schoolmates bothered any longer with the Judeo-Berber incantations and amulet wearing of their parents. That kind of hocus-pocus would hardly differentiate the Jews from their Moslem neighbors, after all—and how then could the French choose between them? Bebert's brother had long since rebelled against the *t'fillin* routine. The home had echoed to the bitter accusations and harsh threats of the father, the respectful but firm replies of the son. Eventually the boy had left home. Bebert remembered the day well; miraculously, the world had not come to an end.

When his own bar mitzvah was only two years behind him, therefore, he returned late one summer night from a "surprise party"—a necking and petting chivaree said to be the latest thing in Paris—and slept through his morning prayers. Father almost choked with rage. Bebert cowered in the corner like a whipped dog, but refused to put on his *tallith* or phylacteries. He went through the ordeal again a week later, and before the month was over his prayers were limited to the synagogue on the Sabbath. Papa barely spoke to him any longer, except for the phrase he repeated like a

litany, his jaw tight: "You were my last hope." Even when the recriminations stopped, the tension remained. It took its toll on the boy. The day after
his seventeenth birthday he dropped out of school and found a part-time
job in a grocery shop. At least he would not be dependent on Papa for
pocket money.

But the restlessness still gnawed at him. Beyond Rue Djama Shluh lay
the Moslem quarters. No hope there. A world away, across the city, lived
the French. No access there either. At least not directly. But perhaps it
was still possible to find an indirect approach to the New City. How would
a boy without resources, education, or connections act European, look
European, *be* European? Bebert and his friends thought they knew. They
made the effort—gropingly, within the framework of their pathetically
limited ghetto experience. Not for them the burnoose and cassock of their
grandparents, nor even the Levantine double-breasted sack suits and bead-
spangled chiffon dresses of their parents. Rather they adopted the "smart"
street attire they saw in the French-language films and picture magazines.
The boys adopted flaring sport shirts, drain-pipe trousers, and pointed
buckle shoes. The girls walked out by night in tight, form-fitting sweaters
and slacks. At weddings and religious events the traditional costumes
prevailed, even the rhinestone tiaras. But at swimming pools the bikini was
the new vogue.

And there were other changes, too. The more their parents remonstrated,
the more the smart set found refuge in the Nolly Bar on Rue de l'Horloge.
It was said the French were drinking *machiyah* these days, a powerful
concoction brewed of dry raisins and figs. Well, Bebert and his crowd
could hold their liquor as well as any European. Afterward, too, other
entertainments beckoned: "surprise parties" in private homes, gatherings
in dance palaces like Negresco's on Place Edmond Doutte or the Scehere-
zade on Rue de l'Horloge. The lights went out there, the young Jews and
Jewesses danced to the latest continental tunes in the approved apache
fashion, wedged tightly together, hands roaming freely. Afterward there
were the fashionable and secret pleasures of the bedroom. It was still a
closed world, of course. But there was at least one sure contact with the
French. The Forty-Eight was open, presided over by dependable Madame
Janeau. La Parisienne, too, offered attractive girls at quite reasonable prices.
Bebert himself preferred Le Cheval Blanc, near the harbor. Katy, "his" girl,
had been brought over straight from the Madeleine, and treated him as
if he too had been born and bred in Paris.

The young *voyous* of the *mellah* paid a price for their revolt. Bebert
twice came down with intestinal inflammations. The neighborhood apothe-
cary diagnosed the cause as hard liquor—too much and too early. Maurice,
Bebert's best friend, suffered an acute attack of gonorrhea, a gift of Le
Cheval Blanc. Others of the group were rounded up and beaten by the
Moslem police for "loitering," "pandering," or simply "antisocial behavior" (hardened Berber felons usually escaped the dragnet). The crisis
in family relations was considerably more painful. Jewish parents, shocked
and humiliated by the incomprehensible behavior of their children, reacted

in the only way they knew—with threats, curses, and beatings. Of course, the punishment merely exacerbated the problem. Noucha and Khmeissa, daughters of neighboring families on Rue Djama Shluh, fled their homes and became professional prostitutes in the New City. Maurice, Bebert's inseparable companion, was found beaten unconscious in a gutter, the victim, it was later discovered, of a Corsican pimp upon whose territory he had encroached.

And in the Hayot home, Papa's choked silence scorched and seared. Bebert found it unendurable. Eventually he left home, moving in with his Aunt Annette. His struggle for escape gained a final urgency there. He was burning inside. He could taste the flames licking at his gullet each time he bit into his oil-drenched meal of *pquela* (rice-stuffed sausage) and squash. The fire leaped up from his viscera each time he lit the olive oil Argand lamp for Aunt Annette's nightly prayers. The fumes were in the air around him as he strode, dark-browed, through the jibbering, gesticulating wretches who were his people—the "Chosen People." He had to get out.

"Get out, sure get out," said Maurice. "The first thing to do is loosen up."

They went to another "surprise party," got drunk, and slept with some girls. When Bebert awoke the next morning he found that sex did not help any longer.

"There's more than one way of letting off steam!" suggested Maurice. With four other companions, they skirted the Moslem quarters and went over to the *fondouks,* the Maltese tenements. There they picked a fight. It ended as it always had, with the mounted Berber police blowing their whistles and swinging their truncheons. Bebert and Maurice reached home with their clothing shredded and blood-soaked.

Finally one night Bebert took the risk, and ventured out of his own toward the New City. He entered a European bar and ordered a glass of pernod. The barman gazed at him for several moments, then asked: "How old are you, boy?"

Bebert shrugged. "You see how old." He motioned to a group of French youths drinking near-by. "I'm their age, no younger, am I?"

The barman's hand was already outstretched. "Let's see your identity card," he said.

Bebert gave it to him.

"Hayot," read the barman. "Yes, I know what you are. This is a European place. Clear out."

Bebert felt himself flushing. "Well, I'm not a Berber, am I?" he asked, his voice unnaturally high.

The barman pressed a buzzer. "Get out, *kiki,*" he said, "or you'll be in trouble."

A moment later a beefy doorman approached. Bebert saw him coming, but before he could move other hands were on his arms and neck. In a moment he was flat on his back in the street, the wind knocked out of him. He lay there silently, struggling to regain his breath. A middle-aged

European couple passed his way, fastidiously avoiding the prostrate figure.

"Ugh," said the woman.

"Sale Juif," said the man. "Serves him right for leaving his neighborhood."

Bebert's parents had learned the lesson during the war, when the administration sold out to Vichy, and passed anti-Jewish ordinances. But Bebert had been a mere child then, and hardly remembered. He had to learn his own lessons. He was persistent. But so were his teachers.

"*Kiki, kiki,*" shouted the French youngsters, when he and Maurice ventured into a cinema house in the New City.

"*Youtre,* move," warned the gendarmes in the Marine Dance Palace. Or simply silence, and no service, in the Parc Lyautey restaurant.

The hope slowly faded.

On the other side of the *mellah,* of course, in Ein Shook, Derb Sultan, Ben Dzeliah, Carrière, Bidonville, and the other Moslem quarters, there yawned only chaos. At first not every Jew was willing to believe it. A few community leaders—Leon Benzequen, Meyer Toledano, Joseph Ohana—were prepared to make common cause with the Istiqlal, the Moroccan independence movement.

"Moroccan freedom is a certainty," they argued. "We must join forces with the Berbers now, before it is too late."

But as far as the overwhelming majority of Moroccan Jewry was concerned, it was already too late. They knew that they had been *dhimmi*s too long in the eyes of their neighbors to be regarded as allies now.

Nor did it escape the Moslems that the Jews had traditionally been under the special protection of the French. To the followers of Istiqlal, Jews, even the most thoroughly Orientalized and Arabized among them, were to be distinguished from the hated Europeans only by their vulnerability. Ambushing a French convoy was a tricky matter. Pillaging a defenseless Jewish neighborhood was quite another. There were anti-Jewish boycotts. These were followed by riots. Then, in June of 1948, it was the eighteenth century all over: pogroms in the towns of Oudja and Djerada, forty-three Jews dead, and three times that many wounded. French patrols arrived—but too late, of course.

"Say your prayers, *yahudi,*" cackled the lowliest of Berber porters. "When *horea* [independence] comes, you'll get yours."

But the Oudja and Djerada massacres were desperation measures, too. The Berbers had learned of other alternatives open to the Jews. Elsewhere, the accounts had it, Jews had annihilated and enslaved Moslems by the hundreds of thousands. They had wrested land for themselves in the midst of the Moslem world. Even now the despised *dhimmi*s of the *mellah* were packing their bags, departing to claim the spoils of their kinsmen in Palestine.

In fact the opposite was the case. The first *émigrés* who left for Israel after 1948 were more concerned about their rewards in the next life than in this one. Even the young men and women of the second wave of emigration, arriving in Israel during the early 1950s, entertained few illusions about a radical improvement in their economic circumstances. It was another kind of freedom they were after.

One could breathe in Israel. A man could grow there. One's dignity was safe—from Arabs, from Europeans, even from one's parents. So Bebert had heard. The Zionist emissaries had come to the Alliance clubhouse and described the land. They had described the kibbutz, the vigor, the spaciousness, the purity, the pastoral freedom of the life. They had described heroes returning from battle—Jews in uniform, carrying their own weapons, parading smartly through city streets, applauded and cheered by thousands of adoring onlookers. As Bebert listened intently, his chest heaved with excitement. Little wonder that his friends were departing by the dozens, that each week boys—and girls—were enrolling in the *Youth Aliyah* registry, anxiously awaiting news of the next sailing.

"People like us can live the way they want to in Israel, Bebert," confided Maurice. "The old folks can't force anything down our throats. It's all part of the Zionist plan; the idea is to get away from the old traditions. That's for me."

Bebert did not bother to analyze his own reaction. He knew only that Israel was the answer to every problem, every frustration, every restriction he had ever endured. It was impossible now for him to live anywhere else. In September of 1952, he notified his mother. Maman grasped her breast as if she had suffered a seizure.

"Do not let me hear those words again," she gasped. "Jewish boys do not leave their families."

Bebert persisted, but a wail was Maman's only answer. Finally, with a quaking heart, he raised the issue with Papa. Papa did not lift his hand, did not so much as shout. Instead he opened a desk drawer and pulled out several letters.

"I will tell you what these are, boy," he said. "These are letters from Samwil, Azour's son from the tannery. You read."

Bebert did as he was told. In his crabbed Arabic script, Samwil the tanner described the life he had found awaiting him in Israel. It was a melancholy story: of *ma'abarot,* of squalor, unemployment, and discrimination. Not a ray of light crossed the dreary account, not an inkling of happiness or fulfillment, from the moment the unfortunate man had reached the Holy Land to this very day. Bebert handed the letters back.

"There are others," said the father, tapping a packet in the drawer.

"Doesn't matter," countered Bebert resentfully. "Serves them right for settling in the cities."

"My son, do not provoke me again," said Papa, ominously.

But the warning went unheeded. Bebert persisted. Every second or third day he returned home to plead with his father. There were scenes, shouting, curses, threats. Once, in desperation, Bebert forged Papa's signature on the *Youth Aliyah* waiver form. But the emissary was suspicious, and he checked with the father. For the first time since his childhood, Bebert received a thrashing—in public, right in front of the printer's shop. But this, too, availed nothing. In April of 1953, Maurice departed for Israel with a *Youth*

Aliyah group. As Bebert kissed his friend good-by, the impotent fury of the past years welled up within him, and he wept furiously. He ran home to his parents.

"Papa," he shouted, "Joulie has gone, and Chmyane, Noucha, and Boubaker have gone. Khmeissa has gone. Today Maurice has gone. I shall go, too. I shall go to Sfax or Oran and forge your signature there if I have to."

Papa's face was grave, but his tone was quiet, as if he had prepared his answer in advance. "I shall sign," he said. "I know that as soon as you reach Israel you will ask me for money to return. But you must find out for yourself."

The same afternoon Papa affixed his signature to the waiver form, and handed it over to the emissary at the *Youth Aliyah* office. Thereupon the Israeli instructed Bebert to return in two days for registration. And when the moment came, and the boy walked out of his flat, accompanied by his parents and younger brothers and sisters, he found all his neighbors lined up on the street, mingling their wails with those of his own family. It was the funeral ritual. Bissor, Papa's apprentice, dutifully photographed the rites. Then Bebert kissed his family good-by. He swung his duffelbag over his shoulder, and climbed aboard the waiting bus.

The embarkation camp was twenty-six miles northeast of Casablanca. During the war French soldiers had been quartered there. Now its rude barracks were crowded instead with three hundred Moroccan Jewish youngsters. Something of the original military atmosphere remained; the commanding officer was in fact a major in the Israel army, a bearded rabbi. It was he who assigned Bebert to his bunk, and then outlined for the boy a routine of housekeeping and clerical duties. There would be a delay before the next sailing. The food was bad, and the accommodations were worse. Yet the camp experience was not without its advantages. Together with nearly two thirds of the other youngsters, Bebert was treated by the camp doctor for trachoma. It was the first time he had ever really known modern, competent medical care. Terramycin ointment, applied to the surface of his eyeballs, all but eliminated the burning and itching which had afflicted him since early childhood.

On the thirteenth day after his arrival, Bebert was suddenly given a forty-eight-hour leave to visit his family. After that, the group would be sailing. The final two days with Maman and Papa were the worst of the boy's experience. Their grief was so intense, the terrors they envisaged in Israel so palpable, that for a brief moment Bebert's resolve was shaken. Then, stepping out for a breath of air, he was instantly surrounded by a group of neighborhood girls. Their admiration was written plainly on their faces.

"Are you really going to a kibbutz, Bebert?" they asked.

"Only for a short while," he assured them. "After that, I'm going into the Israel army."

The girls were awe-struck. "Will they give you a gun?"

Bebert laughed. "What a question! Who's to stop us from carrying guns there?"

When he walked into the house, he threw his clothing into his duffelbag
—then unpacked again. He was still a half-day too early.

But at last he sailed. The boat was the French steamer *Lyautey;* it was
little more than a floating Jewish dormitory. Not all the passengers were
pioneers. To his astonishment, Bebert learned that fully half the girls had
been shipped off in disgrace by their parents for living with Berbers. And
when, three days later, the ship arrived at Marseilles, Bebert's shock was
compounded by the Jews who awaited him. They were packed together in
the Agency transit station, the Camp d'Arenas, on the outskirts of the port,
and they had come from all corners of North Africa. There were sophisticated bank clerks from Alexandria among them, and illiterate hucksters
from Marrakech, multilingual currency dealers from Tangier and stuttering dope addicts from Misurata, pomaded dandies from Algerian coffee
shops and odoriferous, boil-infested camel tenders from the Atlas Mountains; the bad with the good, the shiftless with the energetic, the primitives
and the Levantines. Bebert had seen such people before in the Rue Djama
Shluh, and even all together. He had not expected to see them share a common voyage to Israel, the land of heroes.

The task of selection was left to others. Less than an hour after lying
down on his bunk, Bebert was approached by a fellow Moroccan. The man
had lived in Israel for two years, and now served as a Mapai Party emissary
to the transit camps.

"You look strong," he said to Bebert, in French. "Want to join a real
pioneering kibbutz?"

"Yes," cried Bebert, before the words had left the man's lips. "Just tell
me where."

It was in the Negev, the man explained, and it was called Dorot. The life
was hard there, but it was good, and the food was plentiful. It was a place
for young people. Boys and—pretty—girls were settling there by the dozens.
Best of all, a spirit of camaraderie suffused all the kibbutz's activities. Everyone loved his brother in Dorot. They were building something together.

From the moment he heard this dithyramb Bebert had thoughts for
nothing else. The next day he and the rest of the group sailed from Marseilles on the *Negba,* an Israel vessel. On shipboard he excitedly discussed
his future prospects with the other passengers. They shared his enthusiasm.
Most of them were young, carefully selected from the camp by Jewish
Agency experts. Like Bebert, they regarded themselves as the vanguard of a
new agricultural settlement in Israel. During the four days of their crossing,
national origins were forgotten. Even the brutish Sudanese began to smell
better, the closer Israel approached. They were comrades in the new venture.

Then, at last, six days later, Haifa port loomed across the bow. The wharf
was black with humanity. There were uniformed officials among them, and
—Bebert's heart leaped with joy—some of these were soldiers, wearing smart
berets and half-boots. It was a time to be alive. Nothing could take the
edge off the moment, not even the brusque official reception that followed,
the shouted instructions of harassed, overworked clerks, the moraine of files
and forms to be translated and filled out, the choking dust-billows of DDT

in the "disinfectant room," nor the probing, tapping, and thumping of Jewish Agency physicians.

"You still have a little residual trachoma," remarked one of the doctors to Bebert. "You'll have to go into quarantine for a couple of weeks until it's cleared up."

And off he went, to a camp outside the port, together with nearly half the other North African immigrants. It was squalid, even by the standards he had left behind. The barracks were as crowded as cages, the food was swill.

"You haven't seen anything yet," jeered the "veterans," the immigrants who had been sent back for recurrent eye inflammation. "Wait till you get to the *ma'abarot*. Then you'll learn what kind of reception they give Jews in this country. An Arab would have a better chance here."

Bebert listened, but the only words he heard were those of Aharon, the emissary. The man had returned in search of his original "protégés" from the Camp d'Arenas, and he identified Bebert immediately.

"Haven't changed your mind, have you?" asked Aharon with a smile.

"No, no, no."

The emissary repeated his description of the kibbutz. The words were music.

They were all true. Two weeks later Bebert was discharged from quarantine, and departed immediately by bus for the Negev. There he found Dorot exactly as he had expected it. The sun was hot, but the air was pure. The soil was harsh, but plants were already thrusting their way to the surface. The food was simple but plentiful. There were latrines and showers with hot water. And the barracks, too, were as Bebert had imagined them: Spartan, clean, smelling of fresh cedar and hot tar. He shared his room with three other youths. One of them was Egyptian, one a Casablancan like himself, and one a quite primitive Atlas Mountain boy. They got on well together. Each knew that there was no room for disharmony in the Promised Land. Yes, Maman and Papa, Bebert's heart sang in the fullness of his joy, every Jew is my brother here, and I am his.

v

Dorot, located midway between Rehovot and Beersheba, was ten years old. It had been founded during the Second World War. The kibbutz had been heavily shelled during Israel's War of Liberation, but since then had been rebuilt almost from the ground up. Dorot's land holdings had grown to four thousand dunams, its livestock to some two hundred cows, five hundred sheep, and fourteen thousand chickens. Its membership had grown, too, to nearly eight hundred. Nearly half of these were new immigrants.

Bebert worked with them in the fields, laying pipe. It was the hardest labor he had ever known or imagined. By the time he returned to his room at day's end, he was heaving and coughing with exhaustion. There was little enough time for relaxation or companionship during the week. Occasionally he mumbled a few words to his roommates. Now and then he dashed off a letter to his parents. Usually free time meant a chance to sleep. Even on the Sabbath the opportunities for friendship were limited. His Hebrew came slowly. Had it not been for the help of a gentle, fifteen-year-old Yemenite girl, he would not have made himself understood at all. If he developed few friendships among the Europeans, it was surely the language barrier that was to blame.

The months passed. Bebert's frame gradually filled out with muscle and sinew. So, too, did his reserve of energy. He began tentatively joining the evening sessions of the kibbutz youth group. The boys and girls folk-danced around the bonfire. He mastered the steps. They sang in Hebrew. He learned the words. Several times he entered into halting conversation with the youths who sat on either side of him. They smiled politely and answered him. Then he offered an apple to Sarah, the blonde, silken-haired Polish girl who lived in the barracks next to his. She smiled and refused. One weekend a group of Ashkenazic youngsters made plans for a picnic at the seashore. Bebert approached them and asked to come along.

"It's a kind of private party," explained one of the boys, with some embarrassment. "We're going to Naomi's uncle for dinner afterward in Tel Aviv. I don't think he'll have any more room."

It was surely the language difficulty. He worked harder with his little Yemenite friend. Once she suggested another possible reason. Bebert listened respectfully and then immediately began bathing each day. Of course relations with his fellow Moroccans were friendly at all times. Indeed, the North Africans apparently thrived on their own cohesiveness. So long as they received the same work, the same lodgings, the same food as the Europeans, most of them seemed quite satisfied. Once Bebert ventured to raise the matter with Aharon.

"Habibi," the emissary replied impatiently, "nobody's calling you dirty Jew here. You do your share, you'll get your share. Don't start looking for troubles you don't have."

Bebert did his best not to. Yet somehow the veteran kibbutz members failed to respond to his overtures of friendship. He did not admit it in his letters home, of course; his pride was involved. Besides, he had his own *hevra,* his own group of friends. If he wanted to take a weekend trip to the seashore or Tel Aviv he could always go with his fellow Moroccans. He was not lonely.

One Saturday night, waiting at Tel Aviv's central bus terminal for transportation back to Dorot, he noticed a youth strolling out of the neighboring Arabic-language cinema house. Bebert caught his breath, then hurriedly left his place in the bus queue and followed the young man into the bar. Their eyes met. Yes, he was not mistaken. It was Maurice. Instantly the two boyhood friends fell into each other's arms, exchanging wet embraces. For several moments they both spoke simultaneously. Finally, seated in a booth, they plied each other with questions. During the conversation, Bebert studied Maurice's face. It was puffed and ravaged, the eye pockets blue and sagging.

"The Agency tried to stick me on a moshav, but I wasn't much for farming," Maurice explained. "Our whole gang was in the Tel Aviv-Jaffa area, so I tried it here, too. The minute I left the farm the Agency cut me off without a piaster. Salauds! It's been hard since." He shuddered. Involuntarily, Bebert shuddered too.

In the beginning, Maurice had found a room with friends, and then registered at the labor exchange. They asked him what his skills were. He explained that he was a "merchant." They were not interested. Then the Histadrut offered to train him in stone masonry—if he would agree to work on a Solel Boneh housing project in Afula.

"Afula! Why not the Oued Guigo [the desolate central Atlas range of Morocco]?" He spat in recollection. "I didn't come to Israel for that."

"What did you do?"

Maurice spread his hands. "Here I am," he said. "I've gotten by, doing a little of this and a little of that. I delivered groceries at first. I chopped ice. It was black work," he muttered reflectively. "I'll never do it again."

"Then what did you do?" Bebert persisted.

"Well, I deal in foreign exchange," said Maurice.

"Banking?"

"A dealer in foreign exchange," repeated Maurice vaguely. "I exchange foreign currency at special rates. It's too complicated to explain." Then he thought for a moment. His eyes brightened. "Do you want to come in with me?" he asked Bebert suddenly. "There's a lot of territory I can't cover by myself. I'd give you the Tel Aviv port area. You could live in town."

Bebert was confused. Did Maurice make a living that way? Why did he not have his own office? And Maurice explained: his business obliged him to move around; the office was not as important as the contacts; business could be transacted anywhere, in a restaurant, a coffee shop, in a harbor, even in the streets.

"I don't think I want it," Bebert said thoughtfully. "I like it on the kibbutz. I can sleep nights. I never felt healthier in my life."

"But what can you do? Where can you go?"

"Never mind," Bebert insisted stubbornly. "We're building something."

Maurice laughed out loud. "Who are you building for, habibi? You'd better find out now how big your share will be. 'Building something!' That's a bad joke. Something for the Ashkenazim."

Bebert had heard enough. After a few minutes of labored conversation, the two friends parted. Several times during the bus ride back to the kibbutz Bebert shook his head disbelievingly. Was this the handsome lighthearted Maurice he had grown up with, with whom he had shared adventures and dreams? This flaccid bum, broken after only six months in the country? Bebert recalled their parting in Casablanca harbor and the tears that had been shed between them. The memory filled him with shame. His was a fresh, exciting new world now. So much the worse for those who turned their backs on it.

He awoke the next morning rested and at peace. The day was bright, the air clean. The fields were waiting, and his young, strong body was ready for them. In the distance he could hear the clatter of dishes from the dining hall. The girls were preparing breakfast. His comrades were stirring in the rooms next to his, some of them already awake and climbing into their work clothes. No, he had no qualms. He was among his people. Slowly, slowly, he was learning their language. He would speak to them, and they to him.

Indeed, the Europeans and Orientals chatted together amiably enough during the daytime. It was simply that, after the work hours, they broke off naturally and spontaneously into separate groups. I am not worried, Bebert reminded himself. They don't know me yet. They don't know that I am not Maurice. His smile did not fade, not even the day he wandered by accident past the swimming hole when the girls were changing clothes, and he heard the shriek: "Get down, a darkie's looking you over!" Nothing to worry about. It would not be long before all of them would respect him. His time was coming.

VI

Bebert's time came in December of the year. The military conscription office ordered him to report for his physical examination. To his delight, the army doctors passed him without hesitation, and his application to join the paratroops was accepted. He was formally inducted at the army reception center at Rehovot, and transferred the next day to the parachutist training camp of Tel Nof, near Chadera. Together with hundreds of other youths of all backgrounds and from all parts of Israel, Bebert was registered, classified by country of origin, weighed, measured, issued clothing, toilet articles, pocket money, fed in the cavernous dining hall, and finally sent on to his barracks. The experience was more confusing, more exhausting than on that unforgettable day, over a half-year before, when he had first arrived in Israel. Late in the afternoon he climbed into his uniform slowly and cautiously, then pulled on his cumbersome half-boots. Walking into the latrine, he examined himself thoughtfully in the full-length mirror. The outfit was not as dashing as he had hoped, but—there was no doubt about it—he was a soldier; no one would have mistaken him for anything else. He was on his way to becoming a paratrooper, a member of the elite of the Israel army. A slow, proud smile crossed his face.

There was little time for self-satisfaction in the weeks that followed. Bebert had been informed that basic training in the Israel army was the most grueling in the world. For a recent immigrant, that warning was an understatement. Fluency in Hebrew was still far off. Although he and other newcomers spent an extra two hours a night in the army language school, he was hard-pressed to understand even the most routine military orders. Had it not been for a barracks-mate, a Turkish boy who translated the commands for him into French, Bebert would have been altogether lost.

Moreover, the noncommissioned officers were pitiless. Under their stern gaze, no soldier ever walked—he ran. It seemed to Bebert, too, that they were especially hard on the Oriental boys. The emphasis on cleanliness drove the new immigrants frantic. There was bed inspection, of course, and pack inspection. But in addition the sergeants watched closely to ensure that the recruits showered each day, that teeth, ears, and noses passed daily scrutiny. It was humiliating. Yet the officers were relentless. They eased up only after the first two months, when the Moroccan and Persian boys began to adopt the ritual as a matter of habit.

And then there was the regular routine, the drill all recruits went through, Europeans and Orientals alike. Each day except the Sabbath they were awakened at 5:30 A.M., and lined up outside for inspection five minutes later. A two-mile run followed, then calisthenics. At 6:10 the men were discharged to make their beds, wash, and clean their rifles. Breakfast was served precisely at 7:00. At 7:30 the inspection of the day followed. Again, the sergeants bore down hard. If a conscript's rifle was dirty he was ordered to spend the following night taking his weapon apart and putting it together again—at half-hour intervals, changing his clothes each time.

At 8:00 A.M. Major Marcell took over. A tall, barrel-chested Austrian Jew, Marcell had spent ten years in the French Foreign Legion, and seven years after that in the British regular army. His torso was a clinical exhibit of old shrapnel wounds. Yet, although he was a grim and ferocious disciplinarian, the major treated all his boys alike, from the best-educated sabra to the most backward Kurdish youngster. And he asked nothing of the recruits that he would not perform himself. At 8:00 he was on the firing line with the trainees, leading them in rifle practice. At 9:00 he led them personally over the fences and parapets of the obstacle course. At 9:45 it was back to target practice, this time two hours with machine guns and mortars.

After an hour and a half for lunch and rest, the recruits were quick-marched back to the parade ground. This time it was judo practice, and bayonet close-in fighting. All the while Major Marcell led the instruction, shouting, warning, correcting, bullying, cajoling. The man was not human: his energy exceeded that of the youngest soldier. He left the men only after dinner. The conscripts remained in training even then, however. There were Hebrew lessons. There were occasional night marches (faces blackened, shoes packed with mud to prevent their squeaking), lessons in path-finding in darkness, and in reading the stars. It was a fifteen-hour day. Free time was all but nonexistent.

Bebert received his first furlough after three weeks in camp. He set out immediately for Dorot, and arrived near the dinner hour. Stepping out of the bus, he straightened his uniform, ran a comb through his hair, and tightened his belt. The muscles of his arms already were straining through his khaki sleeves. He felt like a soldier. Then he entered the compound of the kibbutz.

The children saw him first. With an excited shout, they clustered about him and escorted him to the dining hall. There the boys from his barracks rose to greet him. During the meal his friends listened intently as Bebert described (half in French, half in Hebrew) his experiences in basic training. Across the dining hall another soldier on furlough, a freckled Ashkenazic youth, was presiding over a homecoming ceremony of sorts with members of his family. Bebert winked at him companionably. After dinner a group of five admiring North African youngsters followed Bebert to the recreation room. They talked—on and on—until Bebert's heart was filled to overflowing, and until the boys began drifting off to their bunks.

Finally, after midnight, he stretched, arose, and walked back slowly toward his room. From the clover field he heard singing and laughter. A bonfire blazed; nearly twenty of the kibbutz's young people were dancing a hora. Avinoam, the other returning soldier, stood in the middle of the circle, clapping time gleefully. Sarah, the little blonde Polish girl, was among the group. So were the European youngsters who had greeted Bebert on his return. He watched silently for perhaps ten minutes. Then he entered his room, undressed, and lay back on the bed, his arms folded under the pillow. It is not enough that I understand them already when they speak, he thought; they still cannot understand me. He thought of his parents, and of their warnings. Maurice, too, was not absent from his thoughts. In the distance he could still hear the strains of the concertina, the blended voices of his generation.

Two days later he returned to camp. The training routine quickened appreciably now. The obstacle courses were tougher. Daily drills gave way to overland marches, some of them lasting ten days. Increasingly, too, night marches were scheduled. It was Major Marcell's practice to awaken his troops shortly after midnight, giving them fifteen minutes to prepare themselves. Each man was obliged to wash and shave with the cold water from his canteen. ("Take pride in yourselves; you are soldiers of Israel now.") Then there was a hot meal from the field kitchen. After that the men blackened their faces, jumped up and down as they listened carefully for telltale jingling in their pockets or the squeaking of shoes. Then guns were stripped down once more, cleaned, and reassembled—in darkness. Finally the soldiers moved out, on their bellies, probing carefully for barbed wire.

Bebert sensed what was happening to him. The most hazardous exercise no longer gave him pause, neither swinging across chasms by rope, nor dismantling mines, nor even carrying out assault missions under live ammunition. He could do anything the next man could do. He could even speak passable Hebrew. It had come slowly and painfully at first. But now, after eight months in the country, the language suddenly broke through. He followed orders without interpretation. He conversed freely. At night, during breaks in the overland marches he sat with his comrades around the campfire, chatting, singing, laughing. In the field, at least, there were no differences between them. They were elite troops, bound together in a common corps. Bebert's doubts faded during those wonderful moments. Major Marcell was his father. The soldiers beside him were his brothers.

After a month and a half of basic training, Major Marcell bade his men good-by. New officers took over. Parachute school began. Bebert and other recruits who had passed the rugged infantry course were introduced now to a completely new regimen. Their instructor was one Captain Zalman, twenty-five years old, a qualified pilot, and a veteran of over three hundred parachute jumps. He wasted no time with his charges. They, too, began jumping immediately—from towers, simulating the shock of opening parachutes. Zalman's patience was inexhaustible. He himself demonstrated the steel reflexes of a trained tumbler as he drilled the men again and again on the method of falling properly, of rolling rather than dragging with their open chutes. Most of the troops learned quickly. There was a large proportion of Moroccans among them. Like Bebert, their motivations in acceptance and prestige were intense.

Thirteen days after the course began, the trainees climbed into Dakota transport planes and made ready for their first "authentic" jump. Seated with Bebert on the metal benches were Captain Zalman, twenty-three nervous recruits, and a lieutenant. The lieutenant was a girl, an experienced parachutist. Whenever possible, the army included women in the training flights for morale purposes. It was a shrewd move. In the girl's presence, the men laughed, sang, and exchanged jokes.

The planes leveled off at 1,200 feet. The green lights went on in the cabins. The men linked their chutes to the cables and rose. Then the lights flashed red. In Bebert's plane it was the girl who jumped first. The men went next, in groups of three. When Bebert's turn came he followed his instructions carefully, leaning out into the wind, dropping with his head down. For three seconds he plummeted sickeningly toward earth. Then suddenly the harness under his arms jerked him upright. The chute had opened. He was floating under the great silken umbrella. Exhilarated, Bebert looked about him. On all sides men were swaying gently downward. He looked down. Officers stood by jeeps, their helmets glinting in the sun. See me, thought Bebert exultantly. Maman and Papa, see me!

"Flap your arms. Kick. Show me signs of life!"

It was an officer's voice, talking through the loudspeaker on the lead jeep. The dropping parachutists obeyed the order. Then the ground rushed upward, with unexpected speed. Bebert locked his feet together, as he had been trained. The impact was hard, but he rolled with it. Five minutes after landing he had dismantled his chute and folded it. Together with other members of his company, he reported to Captain Zalman. The officer returned their salutes.

"Not too bad," he observed, with a thin smile. "It's faintly possible you'll pass this course."

Bebert was certain that the compliment had been meant for him alone.

That afternoon the captain reviewed the jump, analyzing mistakes. Then the next day the men jumped again, in groups of four. And the next day they jumped again—this time with full kit and gun. In the succeeding weeks, night jumps followed. Inevitably there were accidents, an occasional broken ankle, one death. Bebert's leaps were nearly perfect. His co-ordination was effortless. His sense of direction in darkness was the wonder of his comrades. Nor did it escape his officers.

After five more night jumps, the parachute course was completed. There was a parade. A band played. Lined up at attention, the men were formally inducted into the parachute brigade, and presented with the coveted paratrooper badges and scarlet berets. As the colonel shook his hand, Bebert went light-headed with joy. Maman and Papa would soon know, and Maurice and the youth group from the kibbutz, and all the neighbors in the *mellah,* and those who had called him *yahud* and *youtre.* He was his own man. His chest swelled: this beret, this badge, Bebert Hayot has earned them.

His graduation present was a grueling new training program in infantry warfare. All maneuvers took place in the Negev now. There were assaults on hills under live fire, demolition raids with bazookas and bangalore torpedoes, fifteen-hour desert marches under full pack, classes in topography and cartography, lectures on the military history of Jewish and Arab settlements, training sessions with automatic weapons from all parts of the world —Russian and Czech guns, too, captured from the Arabs. And always there was the jumping, five and six times a month. It was an exhausting routine. But Bebert thrived on it. He was proving himself remarkably adept with a light machine gun, and already had become a favorite of his officers. In March, 1954, he was awarded his stripe as a private first class; only a third of the soldiers in his group shared this honor.

That same month, Bebert and his comrades spent the first night of the Feast of Passover in an open-air *seder* in the western desert. Seated with them as special guests were General Moshe Dayan, the chief of staff, and Dayan's wife and daughter. The famous one-eyed commander waived his rank that night.

"We are all one family, *chaverim,*" Dayan assured the soldiers. "There are no generals and no privates here, only brothers and sisters of Israel."

And Bebert believed him. Had he ever really been a *dhimmi?* Had he ever felt anything less than pride in his Jewish identity? The memory of those ghetto years was fading rapidly now. His companions at the table were men, strong men, among the bravest and best-trained soldiers in the world. They knew what they were defending. He would trust his life to them anytime, anywhere.

"The *mellah* is so far away," he wrote Maman and Papa the next day. "I can hardly bear to think of the way I had to live, never knowing where I belonged, what it meant to be free, really free. You *must* leave that place. Come here as quickly as possible. Even if life were ten times harder in Israel than it is, there would be no other place for a Jew. You owe it to my brothers and sisters to let them grow up here. This is our country. You cannot understand it until you come. Papa and Maman, I read of the troubles the Berbers are making in the back country. No Jew is safe in Morocco. Come quickly, I beg you."

But the answer was always the same. He read the letter, signed by Papa, but obviously transcribed in sister Lisette's schoolgirl French. "How can you speak of our troubles with the Berbers," he wrote, "when hardly a Jew in Israel can go to sleep in safety? Do not think we are ignorant of what is happening. We hear Radio Cairo every night. And Marsouk and Fatma Zadok came back only last month and told us of the *fedayin* raids. The Egyptians run through Israel as if it were theirs. Even Jews in the cities are not safe. It is not the 'only place' to raise our children, my son. It is the last place, with those trained killers about. Your Maman and I pray to God that He may keep you far from the path of such assassins."

VII

The danger was real. Crossing the Gaza Strip in growing numbers, and crossing nightly, the enemy shattered the peace of the land. First it was an isolated Jewish tractor driver shot dead. Then a farm wife in her kitchen. Then children in a classroom. Each week, each month, the number of casualties rose. By the summer of 1954 no Jew in his right mind ventured out alone at night in a border area; no one was safe from the lurking *fedayin*. Moreover, Jordan and Syria now followed Egypt's example, sending raiders of their own across Israel's borders. Occasionally the killers would be captured or slain. But apparently there was no effective way for the Jews to retaliate except by actual military raids into Arab territory, and that was one step they would surely not dare to take.

In this assumption, however, the Arab governments reckoned without the mounting fury of the "old man." Although he had retired as prime minister in 1953, David Ben-Gurion stayed on as chief of the Mapai Party. In this capacity, he remained the most powerful single influence in government affairs. Returning in June of 1954 from his desert retreat of Sdeh Boker in the Negev, Ben-Gurion conferred with Prime Minister Sharett and defense officials. The officials met with Moshe Dayan and members of the military general staff. The professional officers knew what had to be done. Evidently they also knew who were the troops to do it.

It happened that the week before, Egyptian *fedayin,* operating from the Gaza Strip, had begun systematically dynamiting the wells of Jewish settlements in the Negev desert. Now, therefore, the paratroops were alerted and briefed. There would be a retaliation raid. The generator of the Gaza waterworks was the objective. The honor would go to Bebert's squad.

On the first moonless night, the men were driven to the border. Climbing out of the trucks, they began treading their way silently across the rock-strewn frontier. After thirty minutes they reached their first objective, the British military cemetery located just on Gaza's outskirts. Directly to the left stood the small brick building which housed the generator. And sixty yards northwest of that, precisely as Intelligence had promised, were the Egyptian military barracks. Following his instructions, Bebert set up his light machine gun beside a carob tree. There he covered the troops as they moved cautiously toward the generator building. The moment the paratroopers reached the building's entrance, they encountered four Arab caretakers, who had been sitting in the darkness, smoking. Panic-stricken, two of the Arabs jumped up and rushed back into the generator room. Another dashed toward the military post, shrieking at the top of his voice: *"Yahud! Yahud!"*

Instantly the lights in the barracks went out. A moment later the Egyptian detachment loosed a hail of rifle and automatic fire in all directions. The fourth Arab civilian meanwhile stumbled erratically in Bebert's direction. Before the terrified man could give away the Jews' positions, however, Bebert leaned forward and smashed his pistol butt against the

Arab's skull. Thus far, the Israel soldiers had avoided firing a shot. Moving with precision, the paratroopers in the generator room laid their charge, lit the fuse, and then quickly regrouped by the carob tree. A that moment a squad of Egyptian soldiers rushed toward the generator building, firing their guns as they ran. They reached the entrance—just in time to be blown to bits. The raiders then beat a hurried retreat, changing directions in a zigzag pattern to avoid being cut off before reaching their home base. But there were no further clashes. Across the border their comrades were waiting to embrace and congratulate them.

Bebert had acquitted himself well in the action. Shortly afterward he was sent to noncommissioned officers' school. For the next four and a half months, his training exercises were all in the Negev; and they were nearly all at night. At times, he and his fellow trainees were on their bellies, crawling through mine fields in mock raids on air strips and radar installations. Frequently they were on their haunches, clinging to tanks that battered into fortified positions. But most of all they were falling through air, dropping on pin-pointed targets from troop transport planes. By the time the course ended, Bebert had jumped twenty-nine times at night. He was graduated with honors as a corporal.

His counterparts across the border were in continual training, as well. Infiltrating in darkness, the *fedayin* dynamited wells, maimed flocks of sheep and cattle, stole valuable irrigation equipment. Above all they killed: 1,300 Jewish civilian casualties by the winter of 1955—and more to come, if Radio Cairo could be believed. Israel's newspapers printed the colonel's speeches and his warnings verbatim. His vulpine smile was frozen in every daily on both sides of the border, and with each act of violence the grin grew wider and more confident. The Jews stared back at it in hypnotized fascination. The man's skill and relentlessness were uncanny.

For the Israel government it now became a matter of some urgency to convince Arab and Jew alike that Jewish territory was not to be violated with impunity. In February of 1955, therefore, following an especially severe Egyptian murder raid, a full company of paratroopers—Bebert among them—was sent back to the Gaza border. This time the objective was the Gaza military camp itself, the principal training base of the *fedayin*. Again, the action took place at night. The main force made its way toward the town. A second, smaller detachment was posted beside the road leading into Gaza, waiting in ambush for possible Egyptian reinforcements. Here Bebert crouched with his comrades, listening intently for the outbreak of fighting.

It came precisely on schedule, a roaring cacophony of machine-gun and mortar fire. The sky flickered and glowed with the explosion of Egyptian Very rockets. It would surely be only minutes before an Arab relief column came speeding down the road from the near-by military base of Khan Yunis. And indeed, hardly more than a quarter-hour after the main attack was joined, the Jewish ambush unit heard the sound of approaching trucks. Bebert saw them, a convoy of ten Dodge troop carriers, each loaded with perhaps twenty soldiers. As the lead truck drew near, Captain Mat, the

Israel operations officer, whispered the order. One of the Jewish soldiers pulled a cord. A napalm tank-can rolled onto the road and exploded in a liquefied wall of flame. Before the Egyptians had time to react, Bebert dashed forward with his squad and began machine-gunning the seated troops. The Arab driver and sixteen other men slumped over dead.

By now the Egyptians in the remaining trucks had managed to collect their wits. Jumping down, they fanned out in a half circle, attempting to surround their attackers. Hereupon Captain Mat ordered his troops to maintain their barrage of fire, but to withdraw slowly in a zigzag pattern. Enough time had to be consumed for the assault force in Gaza to complete its operation. Bebert kept his finger pressed hard on the trigger of his UZI submachine gun, sending bursts of hot lead into the advancing enemy; at the same time his men hurled smoke grenades at the Egyptians. The Arabs were well led, however. After a few minutes of intense counterbarrage, they suddenly broke off contact, regrouped, and moved on by foot toward the town of Gaza.

The Arab flanking action had begun too late. Several hours later, when Bebert and his companions returned safely to Israel territory, they learned that the principal mission against Egyptian headquarters in Gaza had been an almost unqualified success. The central military camp had been demolished, together with some thirty Egyptian officers and men. Two Egyptian ammunition trucks, fully loaded, had been captured and driven back across the border. The operation had not been an easy one. The Egyptians had fought well. Five Jews had been killed, and several times that many wounded. But the Israelis had acquitted themselves resourcefully; it was convincing proof of the thoroughness of their training. The day after their return, they were visited and personally congratulated by David Ben-Gurion.

"He shook my hand," Bebert wrote his parents, "and asked me how long I had been in the country. When I told him, he slapped me on the back and said: 'You are proving yourself a good citizen.'"

The retaliation actions registered effectively on Israel's neighbors. Each operation was followed by a brief pause in *fedayin* activity. Perhaps, in other times, the Jewish counterraids would have put a final stop to the Arab terror campaign. In the summer of 1955, however, the Egyptian dictator struck a bargain with the Soviet empire. Mortgaging his country's cotton crop to the U.S.S.R. for the next twelve years, Nasser acquired in return a supply of weapons and munitions which included two hundred and fifty jet fighter and bomber airplanes, three hundred heavy tanks, two submarines, two heavy cruisers, two destroyers. Simultaneously, a task force of Russian and Czech technicians and military advisers arrived in Egypt to train Nasser's forces in the use of the new war materiel.

Without delay the colonel set about exploiting this glittering armory to enhance his Pan-Arabist ambitions. His pressure—in funds, in clandestine arms shipments, in cajolery and open threats—soon proved remarkably effective. Intimidated by Egypt's fearsome new power, the Syrian government resigned in favor of a crypto-Communist regime openly friendly to

Nasser. Jordan's young King Hussein, in deference to Nasser's wishes, exiled his British military adviser, Brigadier John Bagot Glubb, on twenty-four hours' notice. Within three months, the Arab League was virtually transformed into an extension of the Egyptian Foreign Office. Only one sensational coup de main remained to consolidate Egypt's leadership in the Arab world: the obliteration of Israel. With complete outspokenness, the Cairo press and radio made it plain that a full-scale Egyptian assault on the Jewish State was in the final stages of preparation. Accordingly, *fedayin* raids increased in scope and intensity.

So, too, did the reprisal raids. The paratroopers played a role in nearly every action. One of the biggest of these, in January, 1956, was launched against the Egyptian police station in Khan Yunis. The Israelis crossed into the Gaza Strip in armored half-track troop carriers. While machine-gunners concentrated a raking barrage on the Egyptian watchtowers, Bebert and ten other men blasted open the doors of the police post with bangalore torpedoes. Lighting dynamite charges, they withdrew—and waited. The ensuing blast killed twenty-six Egyptian police. Four Jews died in the operation.

A week and a half later the paratroopers penetrated even deeper into Egyptian territory, this time against the great police fortress of Tzabcha, in the Sinai Peninsula. It was a night-long battle, with several hundred troops participating on both sides. The Egyptians counterattacked with tanks and light artillery. The ambush had been carefully laid, however. The Israelis shattered the Egyptian armor with napalm cans and bazookas. Five Jews were killed and eleven wounded. Some fifty Egyptians died, and twenty were taken prisoner. Large quantities of Egyptian ammunition and armored vehicles were also captured. It was a convincing demonstration of Jewish military power. Egyptian guerrilla activity briefly stopped.

Yet the other Arab states still were not convinced. *Fedayin* raids increased on the northeastern borders. Jewish fishermen who ventured out at dawn on Lake Kinneret were systematically picked off by Syrian snipers. The Israel High Command decided that another retaliation operation was called for. It was an ambitious one. The objective was to demolish the entire series of five fortified Syrian sniper nests that dominated the northeastern border of the lake. The combined action was to begin at 10:00 P.M.

It was a cold, rain-swept winter night. Bebert and his squad circled the western arc of the lake on foot. Then they dropped to their stomachs, awaiting the signal to move against their assigned objective, a network of three bunkers. When the lieutenant whispered the order, the troops crawled forward, quietly snipping the Syrian barbed wire. The aerial Intelligence photographs of the Arab position were accurate in every detail; each man found his target precisely in the right place. Suddenly the first enemy Very light went up, followed instantly by a wild barrage of machine-gun fire from the bunkers. The troops pressed on methodically toward the concrete emplacement.

Bebert's months of battle experience paid off now. A hardened "veteran" of nineteen, he drove his sinewy body close to the ground, routinely ignoring the sizzling lead that pitted the earth about him. When he reached the base of the Syrian gun emplacement, he and a comrade unfastened their bangalore torpedo, rammed the charge against the side of the wall, and set the firing mechanism. Bebert's retreat was by the book: legs driving like pistons, torso parallel to the ground. He watched with professional satisfaction as the bunker shattered into smoking fragments. A few shell-shocked Arabs rushed dazedly in the direction of their attackers. Bebert and his machine-gunner smoothly shot them dead. The rest of the twenty-seven Syrians flung up their hands in surrender. They, too, were gunned down. Not a Jew had been wounded. Moreover, at each of the other fortified positions, the operation was equally successful. For the time being, at least, the entire northeastern border of the lake was demilitarized. The Israelis returned to their bases.

There were other actions in the spring and summer that followed: bitter guerrilla skirmishes, cruel and violent ambushes and counterambushes, nightly murder raids and retaliation measures. It was war—long before October, 1956. But Bebert was out of it. In August his term expired. He was demobilized.

VIII

He returned to Dorot. The kibbutz looked good to him. The buildings had been repaired and a new water tower erected. Modern stainless-steel cooking vats had been purchased for the kitchen. Food was better. Each *chaver* was now provided with a new lamp for his room. In two and a half years of grueling military training, Bebert had forgotten the little pleasures and luxuries of civilian life. Now they were all his: a day's work and a night's rest; afternoon tea breaks with time for the daily newspaper (he read it without difficulty); quiet conversation and social gatherings in the dining hall. And, in sleep, silence during the hours of darkness. The long leisure of the Sabbath.

It was too long. There was too much leisure. Nothing happened. Bebert chatted with his roommates. In the kibbutz library he browsed aimlessly through the picture magazines. There were books on the shelves. Once he struggled through several chapters of an Aharon Meged novel—then, sighing, put the volume back; it was filled with philosophy, with ideas and allusions taught in the schools he had never attended. He walked out on the roads. The dust flared up beneath him. Twice he hiked to Migdal Ashkelon. The fumes of uncollected garbage and sizzling asphalt met his nostrils. Most of the town's inhabitants were illiterates. Seated in a local coffee shop with a few youths of his age, Bebert dispiritedly whiled away the afternoon playing *tric-trac* (backgammon). Some of the boys were demobilized soldiers like himself. They shared Bebert's unrest. It was still possible to eye a passing dark-eyed girl, of course, and even to find someone to talk to. But somehow the hunger remained.

Perhaps Nasser was to blame, Bebert speculated. If only a man could move freely with time and money for relaxation. But no matter where one traveled in this burned-out little country, the opportunities for release, for the most elementary recreational pleasures, vanished and shriveled before one's eyes. Yes, if it were not for Nasser, and the Egyptian boycott and army, Israel would long since have possessed the kind of sports palace Casablanca boasted, the dance halls, the emerald soccer fields. It was a Jewish land, after all. Jews weren't being kicked off the streets here. Why then did so few people own automobiles, or nice houses or private gardens? Why was everything gray and khaki and drab and workaday? Because Nasser made it so. He, only he, made the land hard. He ringed it with barbed wire, and intercepted the ships that brought comforts and luxuries from other nations. Wretched grinning reptile that he was, with his forked tongue and his unctuous lies. One could not trust him. One could not trust his murderous, scheming people. Moslems were Moslems, whether in Israel or Egypt or Morocco. With their confiscatory taxes, their insults, and now their *fedayin,* they had never meant anything but misery for the Jews.

The worst of it, Bebert reflected, was the way they scarred you from within. He would not forgive them for that. He and his people had lived among the Moslems too long. Now they resembled them, and sometimes—he admitted it now to himself—they acted like them. Bebert had been in Israel three years. Wide-eyed simpleton that he was, he had come full of sap and energy and romantic illusions about Jews being with Jews. Sometimes it worked—in the army, for example. But once on furlough or back in civilian life altogether, matters were very different. His friends were still the Orientals. In spite of all the overtures he had made to the Europeans, it still did not work. No use evading the fact any longer, it still did not work. Very well, he was a soldier. He would not whine. He would not lie silently in his bed bewailing his fate. Rather he performed his daily chores, stayed up late with the friends he could trust, and blotted everything else from his mind.

Only the vision of golden-haired Sarah intruded on his waking hours. During the morning breakfast recess, he paused before returning to the beet fields, and wandered past the nursery. The sight of her, walking the tots through the garden, filled his chest with the familiar sweet ache. Now and then he managed to find a seat at her table in the dining hall. When there was an evening of folk dancing, he arranged to be in her circle. Her eyes were sea-blue and her skin was a ripe peach. He worshiped her. Perhaps, then, a miracle would still happen. Finally, on a Sabbath afternoon in late August, Bebert plucked up courage and asked her to accompany him for a walk later in the evening. To his unspeakable joy, she nodded her agreement, her face solemn.

Before dinner he shaved carefully, then dressed himself in his Sabbath shirt and trousers. With his hand on the doorknob, he threw a last glance at the mirror. His crinkled black hair, freshly pomaded, glistened bright under the naked light bulb. Hard work and a good diet had strung hard muscles across his back and shoulders. The face—the face was dark, of course. The lips were full. Yet it was no more than a Jewish face, he decided. In the summer, he was hardly to be distinguished from the sunburned Europeans. For that matter, he was lighter than two boys from Odessa who lived in the kibbutz. His accent was Eastern; but so was the Sephardic mailman's whose family had lived in Palestine for five generations. Bebert tightened his belt. He was a sergeant in the paratroopers, that was the point. He left the room.

After dinner Bebert and the girl walked across the kibbutz compound, taking care not to venture beyond the barbed-wire limits.

"You've changed since you returned from the army, Bebert," she said. "You are quieter."

He nodded, momentarily tongue-tied.

"Are you thinking deep thoughts?" she asked teasingly.

Then he blurted it out: "I am thinking about you, Sarah," he said, looking straight ahead. "I think about you all the time."

Sarah said nothing.

"I see that you have no *chaver*," he continued, speaking as rapidly as he could draw breath. "I thought perhaps you and I could be *chaverim*. At motzait chen b'ainai—You find charm in my eyes."

"We are friends," she said quietly. Before he could speak again, she continued. "No, Bebert, listen to me. I knew why you wanted to see me tonight. I, too, wanted to talk to you." She was eighteen, but she sounded much older. "We can be friends, but we cannot be *chaverim*. It's not possible."

"Not possible," he repeated automatically, his heart sinking.

"We don't have enough in common." Although Sarah spoke briskly, her tone was kind. "We mustn't make more troubles for ourselves than we already have. These things never work out."

Bebert swallowed twice. "What haven't we in common?" he asked. "Are you a Christian or something? Am I?"

"Bebert—"

"You want to say I'm a new immigrant, don't you?" his voice rose. "So are you, aren't you? How long are you here from Poland—seven years?"

"It's not that," she protested, her voice rising too. "Please, why do I have to go into such detail with you? All the others don't ask these questions. They just accept things as they are."

Bebert laughed mirthlessly. "Well, how are things? You're Jewish. I'm not an Arab, you know. I am a real Jew, even—"

"Bebert, don't say it," she pleaded.

"—even if I'm not a real live Ashkenazi," he persisted. "I'm a better Jew than you are." He paused. "I know all the prayers, at least." It sounded lame. All his energy was suddenly gone; he felt quite stupid.

They walked on in silence. When they reached the nursery, she spoke again. "You're a good sort, you really are. You're the last person who should have any trouble finding a *chavera*. What about Shulamith [Bebert's little Yemenite friend]? She comes back on furlough in a few more weeks. You find charm in her eyes, you know?"

He would not listen to this any longer. Soon she would suggest Chaya, the Teheran girl, or even stinking Mamoulah, the Kurd. What did she take him for, a Berber, an Arab?

"I'll leave you here," he said. His stomach was burning.

"Don't be angry, please," she pleaded. "We'll see each other every day."

But he strode back quickly to his room. Slamming the door, he hurled himself onto the bed.

For several minutes he lay there silently, his chest heaving. Then he stared at his watch. Still early. He climbed to his feet and walked out again. This time he made for the road. Within moments he had flagged down a passing car.

IX

Motzei Shabbat—the termination of the Sabbath. Tel Aviv had burst into life once again. Under neon lights Dizengoff Avenue surged with movement, the vast "inspection" parade, the best value for one's money in all Israel. A half pound bought an *espresso* at a sidewalk coffee shop, and a seat at the edge of the arena. They marched past the glittering marquees by the hundreds and thousands. There were stolid, middle-aged couples in faded gray suits and shabby cotton dresses; teen-agers, nervous and tense in their slacks and inevitable Italian sport shirts; mop-haired, sunburned soldiers and soldierettes in brown khaki uniforms and rakish berets; gawking, wide-eyed kibbutz youths in blue Russian-style peasant blouses, corduroy trousers, and sandals. They stared at the seated coffee drinkers; the coffee drinkers stared at them. There was neither appraisal nor evaluation. It was frank, open, and unabashed. Here we are, the onlookers said to each other, count us and look us over. This is how far we have come.

Bebert elbowed his way through the crowd, seeing nothing. At Frischmann Street he veered left, walking rapidly toward Ben-Yehudah Street. He found what he wanted on the corner. Three women were standing there, two Orientals and one flaxen-haired European, all of them still in their teens. Without hesitation he approached the blonde.

"You're Minna?" he asked. "The Hungarian?"

She looked him over without expression, then nodded.

"My friend told me about you," he said. "I'm from Dorot. He said you'd take care of me."

The blonde cast a glance down the street. "B'Seder," she murmured, "all right, come on. We'll go to my place."

Bebert followed her to a downstairs room on the side street. It was no shabbier than dozens of other flats he had seen since his arrival. Only the odor was offensive, probably carbolic acid. Methodically the Hungarian girl removed her sweater, unrolled her stockings, and hung them on the chair by the cot.

"B'Seder," she said crisply, extending her hand. "That's ten pounds in advance."

"Don't be funny," he replied. "I know what the price is."

"Ten pounds," she repeated, her voice hardening.

Bebert sat down on the bed. "Come on, Minna," he persisted. "I know the facts of life. Joel Zucker was here just last week and you took five pounds from him."

"Ten pounds for Africans," she snapped. "That's final."

For a moment Bebert sat in paralyzed silence. The walls seemed to crack and buckle before his eyes. Then he leaped to his feet. "You . . . you . . ." he gasped, "you rotten—"

Minna's hand closed on a bread knife. "That's all," she warned, her voice shrill. "Clear out. I've handled your type before."

He could feel the cords knotting on his neck, his eyes bulging from his head. He wanted to speak, but no words came. Finally, half choking, he shouldered his way past the girl and dashed up the steps to the sidewalk. Then he ran, like a runaway horse, galloping off the curb and back again, oblivious to the shocked stares of bystanders.

He ran for nearly thirty minutes, until he reached the address his friend had sent him. Counting off the houses, he reached the apartment door, and pounded on it. There was no answer. Bebert sat on the steps and waited, his head in his hands. Another Moroccan, a youth of his own age, stopped and called to him.

"Looking for Maurice?"

When Bebert nodded, the boy beckoned him to follow.

And at last they found Maurice, at his favorite bar on Shishim Street. The two young men gazed at each other incredulously. Bebert, lean, bronze, and muscular, was no longer the skinny, pimple-faced youngster Maurice had left behind at the central bus terminal nearly three years before. And Maurice—neither was Maurice the hollow-eyed, slack-jawed bum Bebert remembered. He was well fed and clean-shaven. His shirt and jacket were of good quality. Tentatively, Bebert extended his hand. Maurice clasped it with a warm smile. Bebert grinned back weakly.

"That's the Bebert I remember," Maurice exclaimed delightedly. He put his arm around his friend's shoulder. "I almost gave up hope on you. Why didn't you answer my Chanukah card? I sent you my address. Where have you been?"

"In the army—in the paratroops."

Maurice whistled admiringly. Then, resorting again to French, Bebert told the whole story: of the training, the battle actions, his promotion to sergeant.

For a few moments Maurice remained silent. "A real hero," he murmured at last. "Well . . . I wasn't so lucky. The army didn't want me."

"What happened?"

Maurice leaned forward and whispered in his friend's ear. Bebert winced. Maurice sat back and laughed. "Don't worry, I keep it under control. I wouldn't want to get all my little girl friends in trouble."

"You look all right to me," said Bebert. "What's happened to you since I saw you last? You're a different man."

"Umm." Maurice nodded. "I got smart." Then described it. His career began with black marketeering in currency. Not much success there, too many official devaluations, one after the other. Then came the women. Better money there, but still not enough; the Europeans had their own women, the Orientals couldn't afford the price. At last a friend had tipped him off where the main chance lay. It was dangerous, but it was worth it. Sick people bought the stuff, and Arabs, too. Anyone with trouble. And the beautiful thing was that customers always had a way of finding the money.

"Do you want some?" Maurice asked.

Bebert shuddered. "What's the matter with you? Do I look sick?" he protested.

"Money, you idiot," shouted Maurice. "Money, to solve your problems." He looked at his friend carefully for a moment, then added: "You've got problems, I think."

Bebert nodded. For several moments he hesitated. And, then, suddenly, the grievances poured from him like a gusher: the frustrations and humiliations, the bruised ideals and shattered dreams. As Bebert spoke, Maurice filled his friend's glass, and filled it twice more. Finally, a half hour and a bottle of *arak* later, Bebert was spent. He stopped speaking. Maurice smoked quietly.

"What's got into you?" he asked, at last. "Was it any better back home?"

"Maurice!" Bebert was shocked. "I . . . we expected so much here. You know that."

"I'm not so sure." Anyway, Maurice continued, there was no point talking about the past. His eyes were on the future. There were deals to be made, and opportunities to be exploited for men with a little nerve. For Bebert, for example.

"Nothing doing." Bebert shook his head vigorously. "That stuff can kill a man."

"Army make you squeamish about killing?" asked Maurice, mockingly.

"Come on, Maurice. These are Jews we're talking about."

"Sure, Jews. The people who call you darkie, and wanted to send me to lay bricks in Afula." Maurice sighed. "Never mind, I see you haven't the guts for it. What do you want, money?"

"No, I said."

"What then?"

"Do you know some girls?" Bebert whispered, crestfallen.

Maurice threw up his hands. "Is that all?"

He arranged it, of course. Not once, but many times, each weekend that Bebert came to Tel Aviv. It was a powerful narcotic. A man could forget many things. The sting went out of Bebert's wounds. The edge, too, went off his vision of Israel. In Maurice's hands, he entered a world far darker than his private grievances. There were men there who killed for a gambling debt, who sold their sisters and peddled dope to their brothers: cowards, drunkards, thieves, whores, Jews every one, in the land of new hopes.

And early in the small hours of the Sunday mornings when he returned to Dorot, he saw the tiny frame buildings, the paint peeling from the shingles, the entire profile of the kibbutz frozen in the false dawn of the East. The guard was at his gun in the tower. Hardly a rooster yet crowed. Even the jackals and the owls were silent at last. How poor it all was, how small and terribly helpless. These patch-trousered youths and frizzle-haired girls rolling over on their iron cots, never tasting dessert with a meal, calling themselves fortunate if they saw a film once a month, groping dazedly now for their work boots and the rude promise of another sweat-stained day— they were on the committees and the assemblies who decided where he should work, what he should wear, when his guard duty would come, what his pocket money would be, and how he would spend his ten short days of precious vacation. His destiny was in the hands of these phlegmatic, tight-fisted Europeans, with their public ideals and private snobberies.

Perhaps not any longer. Maurice had offered him the chance for freedom. Ironically, his friend never raised the subject again—just smiled whenever he saw Bebert, fed him well, gave him good wine and black-eyed women, and said nothing. And Bebert, too, said nothing. But the unspoken offer conjured up visions of paradise. He saw himself returning to the kibbutz on a streamlined motor scooter, the blue-eyed daughter of Tel Aviv's mayor sitting on the pinion seat behind him. When the excited *chaverim* crowded around, he invited them all to his apartment on Rothschild Boulevard; there was always a bed and a meal for anyone there. In his closet hung suits of the latest style, and sweaters and trousers imported directly from Paris. And next door, in an apartment even larger than his own, Maman, Papa, and all his brothers and sisters made their home, gratefully seeking the advice and directives of Bebert, the breadwinner. The daydreams were tantalizing, intoxicating. Next weekend he would listen to what Maurice had to say.

X

Friday afternoon, the beginning of the weekend, was October 25. Bebert lay on his bed, his hands clasped behind his head. Suddenly his door was flung open and Raphael, one of the kibbutz members, walked in. His face was flushed and he was breathing heavily.

"Don't people knock anymore," growled Bebert.

"There's a general call-up," said Raphael urgently. "We just got the news through the switchboard. Your name is on the list." When Bebert stared at him uncomprehendingly, Raphael raised his voice in exasperation. "Mobilization, Bebert! You have to report to camp right now, immediately. Pack. Move. Quick."

Then the youth rushed out, the list in his hands, and continued on to the neighboring barracks.

Bebert was on his feet before the door swung closed. Within two minutes he had swept his toilet articles into a bag, pulled on a shirt, trousers, and sweater, and dashed out of his room. The kibbutz compound was already crowded with men hurrying toward the main gate with knapsacks on their arms. Some were accompanied by white-faced and tight-lipped women. Others were alone, evidently unable to find their wives before leaving. Bebert joined the group as it moved toward the bus stop on the east side of the dirt road. There was no need to wait for the bus, however. An endless chain of military vehicles passed by, stopping every few hundred yards to pick up the reserves. Bebert and the other kibbutz members found room in a caravan of four troop carriers. The procession moved northward.

Squeezed tightly with his comrades on the truck's wooden plank, Bebert gazed out in astonishment at the traffic. The Ashkelon road, never heavily traveled, was now suddenly churning with movement. Not all the vehicles were military. The motley procession included baggage vans, Eged buses, poultry wagons, taxicabs, private automobiles, fork-lift trucks, delivery carts, coal and ice lorries, vehicles ancient and modern, some of them purring smoothly, others coughing and stuttering their way along the gradient in second and first gears—but all of them packed to the gunnels with men and women. And, as it turned out, all of them, on every road in Israel, were moving toward military camps. In this fashion, within the space of twenty-four hours, sixty thousand Israel reservists were mobilized into their country's defense forces.

Switching to a bus at Ness Ziona, Bebert reached his destination ninety minutes after leaving Dorot. It was the paratroop staging center of Tel Nof, near Rehovot. Here the roadway to the gate was glutted exclusively by military transport. Within the base itself, the compound was lost to view in the congestion of new arrivals. Men were moving in all directions, some already in uniform, others carrying armfuls of khaki army issue equipment, but most of them still in civilian clothing, rushing to barracks and warehouses with procurement slips in their hands. Bebert was overwhelmed by the noise and excitement. Never in his life had he seen such a compression of humanity, neither at the soccer stadium in Casablanca, nor the Camp d'Arenas at Marseilles, nor the dock at Haifa, nor even at the induction center when he first entered the army.

"Bebert!" A man's voice suddenly shouted in his ear. He turned to find his former lieutenant, Oved, grinning at him. "Bebert," Oved repeated delightedly, "you didn't waste any time. Get over to the quartermaster's and outfit yourself. Then report to me here. You're assigned to my regiment."

"Oved, are these maneuvers?" Bebert shouted back over the din.

"Man, do these look like maneuvers?"

Indeed they did not. After two and a half years in the army, Bebert could recognize organization behind the frantic eddy of troops and machines. Officers and men moved with purpose; each apparently knew what his assignment was. Boxes of ammunition were being loaded into trucks. Cans of gasoline and oil were stacked at precisely measured intervals. Platoons and squads were falling into line. When Bebert reported to the warehouse, his name was already on the quartermaster's list, together with his measurements. Within moments his arms were piled high with clothing and equipment, including a new steel helmet, canteen, trench shovel, a fully loaded knapsack, and the latest model UZI submachine gun. When he reported back to the lieutenant he noted that most of his fellow conscripts were already outfitted with the same gear.

Then he was put to work loading and stacking ammunition. Yes, surely these were not maneuvers. The weapons were bazookas, recoilless antitank rifles with French markings. The rockets and shells were gleaming, new, loaded, and primed with detonator caps. Mortars and heavy machine guns, locally manufactured, were already mounted on their tripods and oiled for action. In the vehicle park behind the barracks hundreds upon hundreds of troop carriers, jeeps, and half-tracks were lined up in double column, awaiting their turn at the gasoline pumps. As Bebert fought his way through the agglomeration of troops and equipment, he stopped repeatedly to greet old friends, most of them comrades from his own paratrooper unit.

"What's up?" each questioned the other. "Where are we going, do you think? . . . Did you ever see a build-up like this before? . . . Look at all that new equipment. . . . Where did it come from, anyway?"

The questions flew back and forth. Yet only later did the men receive their first formal assurance that the mobilization was more than a practice exercise. Bebert and the other noncommissioned officers gathered together in the mess hall for an informal briefing session. Oved, the lieutenant, gave them the word: "No one is to leave the camp," he warned. "The gates are locked. No further contact will be permitted with the outside."

The men were disoriented. It was an action all right—but of such scope? With tens of thousands of reservists called up from all over the country? What could it mean? Where were they striking?

"I don't know any more than you do," Oved insisted. "Our job is simply to get the men classified and the equipment primed and loaded." Then, grinning for the first time, he added: "About the strike—I have a pretty good idea about that."

The sergeants and corporals began to smile, too. If, then, there were to be an action, no one could seriously doubt where it would take place. It would have to be on the eastern border. The Gaza frontier had been relatively quiet for the past six weeks, after all. The *fedayin,* although trained and equipped by the Egyptian army, had recently shifted their base of operations to the Hashemite Kingdom. And it was upon this frontier, in turn, that Israel's security forces had concentrated their most recent retaliation actions. Between July and October, Jewish shock troops had launched nocturnal attacks upon one Jordanian police fortress after another, shooting up Arab garrisons, dynamiting gun emplacements, until, sector by sector, the jagged eastern border had been demilitarized. Perhaps the Arabs would rebuild their fortifications, would once again launch terror assaults from them. But for the time being, at least, the Jordanians were too shaken to respond effectively to all-out war.

Moreover, only two weeks before, Cairo, Damascus, and Amman had issued a simultaneous, and ominous, announcement: henceforth all Arab military operations against Israel would take place under a unified, i.e., Egyptian command. This was co-ordinated action, the one threat which had never materialized during the original Palestine war, and the one peril the Jews feared most. Indeed, they feared it more than the nightmare of the *fedayin* raids, more even than the staggering quantities of Soviet planes and tanks that Nasser was massing in Gaza. Now therefore the Israel high command had apparently decided to abort the danger before it became mortal: to launch a pulverizing blow against Jordan, the weakest link in the tightening Arab chain.

In Tel Nof and other military camps throughout Israel, the thousands of mobilized reservists sensed what was afoot. In spite of the mounting intensity of preparations, a curious wave of relief seemed to surge through the troops. It was as if all the indecisions, the painful half measures of the past year and a half, all the terror raids, the sleepless, fear-racked nights were to be swept aside. The retaliation that counted most was now at hand; the issue would be joined at last in full-scale combat. For the next two days Bebert and his comrades at Tel Nof went about their assignments in high spirits. They studied, dismantled, and reassembled the new equipment with grim smiles on their faces and a ready stream of wisecracks on their lips. Even the greenest recruits were exhilarated by the prospect of a decisive thrust against the enemy, and snapped to their tasks with preternatural speed.

On the evening of October 28, eight hundred and fifty men of the Second Paratroop Brigade were ordered to report for briefing. They gathered at the southern end of the dining hall. An officer rose and the troops fell silent. Bebert's heart beat faster. It was his beloved Major Marcell. As always, too, Marcell captivated his troops from the first sentence.

"This is no maneuver, boys," he pointed out. "It's real war. We're going to play an important role in it, too. We're jumping tomorrow behind the enemy lines. Our purpose is to stop Arab reinforcements from getting through to the front. I can't tell you *where* we're going to jump. But it will test all our training as it has never been tested before. Every man will have to perform to the maximum. We'll be on our own. There will be no ground support, no logistical support. Everything we get, every can of gas, every mortar shell, every clip, comes to us by air."

Then, with diagrams on the blackboard, Marcell described the manner in which supplies would be dropped, how they were to be retrieved and unloaded. Gravely and carefully he explained, too, how the supplies would be hoarded; how, at all costs, water would have to be preserved; how camouflage would be laid during the daylight hours to guard against possible air attack. The instructions were hardly new. They were basic-manual field rules to every Israel soldier, and certainly the paratroopers had mastered these lessons, both in theory and practice, even in the earliest stages of their training. Coming from Major Marcell on the eve of battle, however, they commanded acute and urgent attention. Then the men were dismissed, with orders to be in their beds by 10:30 P.M.

The lights went out on schedule. But no one slept. Bebert and his comrades lay in their bunks, their eyes open, their throats dry with excitement. Some of the soldiers whispered to each other cautiously, speculating on the events of the next day. Others tossed and turned, smoking or fidgeting with their gear. Bebert lay rigid, his hands behind his head. His thoughts were of the new world he had entered, of his companions in Dorot, and the drudging, Spartan routine of the kibbutz—they began to look good to him now. He thought of Rue Djama Shluh, and the pepper and garlic reek of the *mellah*, of his bloated, oil-grimed aunts and uncles, his querulous, lachrymose mother and his grim, obdurate father; of his gentle, doe-eyed little brothers and sisters. He missed them. He loved them. He fell asleep thinking of them.

When the whistle blew it was 4:40 A.M. The barracks were still in darkness. The men jumped out of bed. Washing and dressing quickly, they strapped their guns and equipment on their backs, and trotted out to the compound for inspection. A hearty breakfast followed, then three hours of painstaking weapons-testing. At 9:00 A.M. the companies were ordered into final briefing sessions with their officers. Bebert and his comrades seated themselves in a large semicircle around Oved. The lieutenant's face was curiously flushed. Slowly he unrolled a large scroll of paper, which he framed carefully on a wooden easel. The men stared at the sheet for a long moment, and then began whispering to each other in astonishment. It was a map of Egypt. The sector was the Sinai Peninsula.

"Hold on to your safety belts, boys," said Oved. "The staff just gave me the information a couple of hours ago. It's Sinai you're looking at, all right. And here," his finger traced an arc deep inside Egyptian territory, some one hundred and fifty miles from the Gaza border, "is the 'Parker Memorial.' That's where we're going down—late this afternoon. We'll prepare our positions there tonight. Tomorrow morning we'll move on the Mitla Pass to stop all Egyptian traffic eastward."

He paused for a moment. The men remained silent. Some of them hardly breathed, so profound was their shock. Egypt! Egypt! It defied belief.

"We'll be carried over by Dakotas and Nords," the lieutenant continued. "Cover will be provided by jet aircraft all the way. The jump and regrouping marker on the ground will be a green flag. The moment we're down we run toward the sun. That's all." He sat down.

The troops began to stir. Suddenly a corporal leaped to his feet, beside himself with excitement.

"We're moving against Nasser himself, boys, you hear?" he cried. "Against Number One. Let's give the lieutenant three cheers, what do you say!"

Instantly all the men were standing, shouting at the top of their voices. Almost simultaneously, in other units throughout the camp, cheers were going up. The thrilled, enraged roar of thousands of men deafened the morning. Soldiers were leaping and dancing, hugging and kissing each other in exultation. They were moving against Number One, the arch-killer himself, the source of all their nation's grief and suffering. Bebert's happiness was uncontrollable. His arms closed around his bunkmate, Hershkowitz. Hershkowitz's handle-bar mustache closed wetly against Bebert's cheek. "Do you need anything, Hayot?" the man asked. "Can I get you anything?" "Nothing," came the reply, "but name anything I have and it's yours. I love you, Hershkowitz."

Yes, he loved them all. His comrades, his brothers in arms. The tears ran down Bebert's cheeks. He fought his way into an embracing throng of men, hugging and kissing the faces nearest him. "Do you need anything?" the questions rang back and forth between friends and strangers, Europeans and Orientals, among seventeen hundred men of the First and Second Paratroop Brigades, Jews and brothers. Oh, how Bebert loved them. His heart ached with the weight of it. He would not have changed places with any man alive. Glorious, inspired high command. Adored brigade, blessed land! May this moment endure forever!

A few routine chores remained. First-aid drills had to be run through once again. There were identification quizzes of enemy tank silhouettes. Lunch was served at 11:30. At 1:30 P.M. the men were lined up once again for final inspection. They stood there by the ranked hundreds, helmets fastened, weapons at the ready. The officers made few comments as they passed down the rows. At 2:00 P.M. the troops were ordered into the idling trucks. Equipment thudded and clattered as the men climbed aboard. Soon the caravan began to roll, scores upon scores of vehicles, moving slowly, bumper to bumper.

After two and a half miles the procession crawled to a halt before the Tel Nof maintenance center. The soldiers jumped down briefly again. Two hundred girls, wearing the blue epaulets of the air corps on their khaki uniforms, awaited them, standing at attention. Wordlessly the soldierettes handed over the packed chutes, and the men immediately strapped them to their backs. Then, as if obeying some inner, spontaneous signal, the girls broke ranks and surged forward, crying aloud, embracing the troops fiercely. The men's faces broke into smiles. The warmth of that farewell kindled their hearts. As the trucks rolled out, the girls ran after them, clinging to the paratroopers, shouting encouragement and words of endearment.

"Bebert!" A woman's voice penetrated the bedlam of good-bys. He stared at the slim dark girl in amazement. It was Shulamith, from Dorot. She stood there unexpectedly tall, corporal's stripes on her sleeve, black hair pulled taut under her beret, her large saucer eyes opened wide over the high cheek bones. Bebert swallowed several times. Then Shulamith clasped his wrist.

"Bebert, come back," she cried. "Take care of yourself."

"I promise," he replied. "I'll be all right."

"Bebert," she called again, running after the truck, "you find charm in my eyes. Be careful."

"Yes, you in mine," he shouted. "Don't worry."

There was no time for more. The procession continued for another mile and rolled to a stop beside the concrete apron at Tel Nof airport. The field was crowded with planes—transports—more than the paratroopers had ever seen before in Israel. There were the familiar squat Dakotas; and now, too, for the first time, nearly twenty French Nords, huge silver pelicans capable of seating forty men at a time. Officers stood on the ramps, lists in their hands. Without speaking, the troops lined up by squadrons before their assigned planes. Bebert, standing under the wing of a Dakota, watched the flight crew climb aboard. He recognized the copilot instantly: the celebrated Yael Finkelstein, a trim, red-haired lieutenant, the only woman aviator in the Israel air force. Bebert watched her take her seat, and begin the crisp, routine checkoff of instruments. Then Lieutenant Colonel Arik, the paratroop commander, pulled up in his jeep. Walking briskly down the lines of assembled men, he shook hands with each soldier.

At 3:00 P.M. the paratroopers boarded the planes and fastened their seat belts. Simultaneously, down the entire width of the airfield, propellers turned slowly, engines whined, coughed, then roared into life. As the transports moved down the tarmac the paratroopers began to sing. The singing continued as the Dakotas and Nords taxied to the end of the runway, turned, revved their engines a last time, then began the take-off run. The men fell silent. The planes folded their wheels and climbed slowly toward the sun.

XI

At the same time, elsewhere along the Sinai frontier, a massive spring began to uncoil. The drop of the paratroop battalion at the Parker Memorial was merely the first stage. One hour before the planes took off, the main body of the paratroop brigade, under the command of Colonel Ariel Sharon, began crossing the international frontier. Its task was to attack the enemy at Kuntilla, just across the border from the southern Negev. After seizing this town, Sharon's men would proceed further, overrunning the Egyptian fortified posts of Themed and Nakhl. If all went according to the high command's plan, Sharon's brigade would link up with the dropped battalion at Parker Memorial. From there the combined force would drive westward to invest the Mitla Pass, the snaggle-cliffed defile controlling lateral traffic in the peninsula. All Egyptian reinforcements to central and eastern Sinai could then be blocked at their one point of exit.

With the exception of Sharon's single brigade, however, to be loosed against Kuntilla simultaneously with the paratroop drop, the regular Israel field army would refrain from attack during the entire first day of operations. Thereby Egyptian forces in the Sinai Peninsula would be kept mystified about Jewish intentions, and—hopefully—be thrown off balance. It was on the fate of Sharon's paratroop brigade that General Moshe Dayan's final decision pivoted: whether or not to wage full-scale war against Egyptian Sinai, or to limit operations to a raid by this one brigade. If, as anticipated, the paratroop operations went well, then and only then would Dayan and his staff proceed with their principal objective. That objective was nothing less than the annihilation of all Egyptian strong points in Gaza and eastern Sinai. The main field army would thereupon strike out at the fearsome triangle of enemy fortifications in the northern peninsula: Rahfa and Al-Arish on the north coast; Abu Agheila on the Ismailia road, where the main Egyptian deployable strength lay, poised for the long-promised attack against Israel; and finally the *fedayin* nests of Gaza and Khan Yunis in the Gaza Strip.

The key, then, was the paratroop operation. And at the outset everything depended upon the ability of the air-borne battalion to reach its target, to block Egyptian movement from the Suez Canal area, and to sustain itself until Colonel Sharon's reinforcements arrived. The paratroopers' ultimate goal was the Mitla Pass, 156 overland miles from the Israel border. Unhappily the Pass ran for 870 yards between a saw-toothed hell of ranges and peaks, only 80 yards apart at their widest point. Accordingly, the Israelis had chosen for their drop zone the Parker Memorial, a British monument constructed sixteen miles to the east, a natural landmark surrounded by level, comparatively safe ground. Yet even without moving toward Egyptian positions in the Pass, the paratroopers would be hard put to defend themselves from attack until Sharon's main force arrived. The air-borne units were equipped with automatic light weapons, four antitank guns, two 120-mm. mortars and eight jeeps for reconnaissance. Nothing more. Even ammunition and foodstuffs would have to be dropped by air.

There was no assurance that the air itself would be clear. The drop was to be made by slow Dakota and Nord transports—fully a half-hour before sunset, within thirty-five miles of Egypt's Canal-based jet fighters. While the invading troop carriers were to fly low, in an attempt to avoid the Egyptian radar screen, the covering Israel jets would be obliged to make the longest part of their sortie several thousand feet higher, to conserve fuel. Thus the fighter planes would register on Egyptian radar at least one hundred miles off. The high command hoped to forestall the danger of interception by sending an advance fighter squadron on a north-south pattern ten miles inside the Canal Zone at varying heights. Presumably this would clutter up the enemy radar, and draw off those Egyptian pursuit planes that would otherwise speed toward the descending parachute squadron. But the success of the plan depended upon all variables operating in Israel's favor.

Without access to the total picture, Bebert and his companions nevertheless sensed their vulnerability in the lumbering, propeller-driven craft. As the flight leveled off, the men clutched their guns tightly and stared out the windows in silence. The unfolding Negev desert was only fifty feet below them, each furrow and dune brilliantly outlined by the rays of the setting sun. Occasional farm settlements passed beneath the Dakota's fuselage, lonely checkerboards of brown and green. Then Bebert sucked in his breath and pressed his brow against the glass. That was Dorot down below! He would have recognized it anywhere—the watchtower, the barley and clover fields, the cowshed, the poultry run and—yes, there it was—his own barracks, his own friends! They stood clustered in front of the secretariat building, waving frantically at the passing armada. Before he could lift his own hand, the kibbutz had vanished. His excitement was stillborn. A clinging gust of sadness passed over him. The plane droned on.

A half-hour later the Dakota reached the lower spine of the Negev. Suddenly, without warning, it banked sharply starboard, and moved eastward across open desert.

"Look at that, will you!" one of the soldiers cried out. "Those are our boys."

The other men turned in their seats, peering intently at the terrain beneath them. Several hundred trucks, jeeps, half-tracks, and AMX tanks were strung like a chain of beads, in double loops, around and through a collection of mud huts and earthworks. The vehicles were unmistakably Israel's; they all bore the freshly painted X identification on their roofs.

"That's Kuntilla," said Sergeant Major Schwartz, the jump master, as he examined his map. "Sharon's got it, right on schedule."

The paratroopers let out a whoop of delight, slapping each other's backs. Right on schedule! Good old Sharon, he wouldn't let them down! Bebert sat back, breathing deeply; by God, this was a military machine one could depend on. The other men shared his reaction. They settled in their seats again, smiles breaking on their taut faces. The plane's nose headed directly on toward the fireball of the sun. As the minutes passed the desert's coarse striations miniaturized into a black and lavender spider web. The Dakota was rising.

"Check your lines." It was the jump master talking.

The men went through the routine of examining parachute hooks, tightening buckles. Bebert looked at his watch: it was 4:43. Beneath the plane's right wing, Parker Memorial edged into view, a small stone obelisk protruding from a rectangular base. In the cabin the red light winked on. Sergeant Major Schwartz stood, lifting his thumb. "Everybody up. It's going to be all right, boys." The men bunched together in threes beside the open door at the rear of the fuselage. At precisely 4:45 the light flashed green. Within ten seconds all twenty-five men were out the door. Bebert was one of the last to go. During his instant on the aluminum jump bar, his eye encompassed a sky filled with planes: Dakotas and Nords flying in diamond four formation, pairs of Mystère jets revolving slowly, counter-clockwise, around each transport. Below, chutes were opening everywhere. Bebert leaned forward and fell free.

It was a routine drop. The harness snapped him erect within four seconds. The rest of the descent, from seven hundred feet, consumed another eighteen seconds. Yet he was out of practice. The landing was heavy, jarring his pelvis. For perhaps three minutes he sat without moving, in semi-shock. The noise of men about him gradually aroused him. Slowly he crawled to his feet. Stripping off his harness, he buried his chute and tightened his pack. Then, without further pause, he followed the others in the direction of the sun. His back ached. He refused to think about it. On his right, a soldier lay groaning. It was a friend, Yohanan, a farmboy from Kibbutz Yagur. His leg was broken. Bebert and three other men lifted the stricken paratrooper into a stretcher and carried him forward.

By now Bebert had reached his unit, Squad A. They followed their directions precisely—trotting directly westward toward the Memorial. Before them the sun had dropped below the horizon, only the afterglow remaining. Suddenly from up front a whistle blew, and then a familiar voice shouted an order: "Spread out and flatten, boys. There's a plane headed this way." It was Major Marcell.

The men dropped, motionless. The dun-brown of their uniforms blended with the rolling terrain. To the northwest an Egyptian air force Dakota climbed slowly into the dusk, then wallowed imperturbably toward the horizon. The whistle blew again, and the men got to their feet. By the time he reached the obelisk, Bebert was breathing heavily.

Darkness was falling fast. The officers immediately assigned the men to their positions. The battalion was divided into three companies, and each company was bivouacked on one of the three road prongs extending from the junction near the base of the monument. Explanations were hardly necessary now. Egyptian traffic would have to be stopped here and the junction itself defended until the arrival of Sharon's brigade reinforcements the next day. If all went successfully, the men would then move directly against the Mitla Pass. In the waning light Bebert could make out a bedouin encampment perhaps five hundred yards further east. Nothing much to worry about from them. The Arabs were probably accustomed to Egyptian paratroop maneuvers; they would not know one from the other. The Israelis set up their machine-gun emplacements on all six sides of the road junction. Ration cans were opened. Cigarettes were lit and carefully cupped. Soon the darkness was complete.

During the night none of the men slept. Israel cargo planes passed overhead in relays, dropping supplies by parachute. The supply operation was executed brilliantly, precisely according to plan. The equipment included cans of food and water, as well as heavier material: ammunition, mortars, fuel cans, five jeeps—the latter strung to clusters of chutes. All the chutes fell within the standard five-hundred-yard perimeter, and all of them carried tiny flashlights that gleamed brightly in the darkness. Nothing was lost. Not a single piece of equipment was damaged. The men unloaded the supplies quickly and efficiently. New ammunition clips, canteens, and rations were distributed. The jeeps were fueled. Mortar shells were stacked.

Shortly before midnight a scout on the northeast road gave a low whistle. In the distance a car's lights were approaching. Instantly the men crouched in battle position. As the vehicle drew parallel with the advance patrol, the paratroopers recognized the markings of the Egyptian signal corps. On command, an Israel corporal loosed a burst of automatic fire at the jeep. The car careened wildly for several moments, then stopped upright. The Israelis leaped onto the road, guns at the ready. But the two Egyptian passengers, both civilians, were quite dead. Within a quarter-hour the corpses were buried, the jeep stripped of its fuel and water cans, and the car itself driven under the camouflage net the Jews had prepared to cover their own vehicles.

Meanwhile Major Marcell, who had been scanning the bedouin encampment with infrared binoculars, clucked his tongue sadly: "The bedouin are moving west," he murmured. "They know who we are now. That means the Mitla garrison will be alerted." He lowered his binoculars. "We can expect an air strike by morning light," he added gravely.

There was an even more ominous possibility which the major left unspoken, but which the men sensed: the dispatch toward Parker of an

Egyptian armored column. Nothing could be done. With the advantage of surprise lost, the paratroopers were still pinned to their battle stations; the road junction had to be defended. The battalion was woefully undermanned and underequipped. But until reinforcements arrived, it was immobilized. Everything depended now upon the progress of Sharon's brigade.

In fact, the overland march of Sharon's relief column had started well enough. Kuntilla had surrendered after the feeblest of resistance. But at the same time nearly all Sharon's artillery had become mired in the sand, together with most of his tanks and ammunition trucks. The mishap threatened a loss of at least ten hours. The colonel recognized, however, that the dropped battalion at Parker was ill-supplied to defend itself for more than a single day. He decided not to wait until his heavy equipment was extricated by bulldozers. He would take the risk and press on. Thus, throughout the night, Sharon led his stripped-down column westward, toward the awaiting Egyptian fortification of Themed. He reached it at 3:45 A.M. on October 30. Themed was a powerfully defended cliff, ringed with mines, barbed wire, and guarded from its ridge by an Egyptian battalion equipped with heavy-caliber artillery. A frontal attack appeared to be suicidal. Yet again Sharon decided to gamble. The rising sun was in the enemy's eyes; the Israel column had raised vast dust clouds. Perhaps the defenders could be bluffed. The colonel ordered a heavy mortar barrage. Then, as his half-tracks and his seven tanks barreled at right angles toward the cliff, all guns blazing, Sharon dispatched a column of infantrymen against the Egyptian positions from the rear. The ruse worked. Confused and terrified by the fury of noise and movement, the Arabs collapsed altogether. Within the hour the fortified ridge was occupied by the Jews.

Sharon was sorely tempted now to await the arrival of his artillery and the main body of his tanks. Yet he rejected the possibility. There was no time left for a pause. The sun was rising fast, and every moment increased the vulnerability of the battalion at Parker. After the briefest of intervals for refueling and a little sleep, the commander ordered his troops to mount their vehicles once again.

The final obstacle on the road to Parker was the fortress of Nakhl, fifty miles to the west. The column reached its outlying defenses by 5:00 P.M. Fortunately for the Jews, the Egyptian positions here were not on high ground. Sharon's first instinct was to attempt a double-enfilading movement with his tanks and armored half-tracks. Even as he was about to give the order, however, one of his staff officers shouted delightedly and pointed to the east. Trucks and caissons were heading their way. It was an Israel artillery battery, one of those that had been mired outside Kuntilla. The arrival of this supporting cannonry decided the issue dramatically. Five minutes after reaching the column, the artillery pieces were detached from their caissons. The moment range had been taken, the twenty-five-pounders began laying down an intense barrage on Egyptian emplacements. Answering artillery fire was wild and altogether inaccurate. The enemy panicked and broke, leaving behind vast quantities of ammunition.

Sharon made no effort to intercept the fleeing Arabs. His column had been on the road twenty-four hours now, and Parker's Memorial and its defenders were at least another four hours away.

Meanwhile, throughout the previous night, the dropped battalion had waited in tense silence, certain that the terrified bedouin work gang had sounded the alarm at Egyptian headquarters in Suez. When dawn broke on the morning of the thirtieth, the paratroopers recognized that they were in quite acute danger. An hour passed, then two, and still no word from Sharon's column. At 8:10 A.M. a flight of eight Israel Mystère and Ouragon jets passed overhead, and radioed down to Major Raful's command car. A column of Egyptian armor was descending on Parker from Mitla, the squadron reported; the air force would now strafe it, but the troops below would do well to dig in. Then the planes vanished. Immediately Raful redeployed his battalion on the northwestern and southwestern prongs of the road junction. Within minutes the men heard the sound of prolonged automatic fire and aerial cannon to the west. Smoke curled slowly between the distant ridges. Somewhere an Egyptian convoy was taking a heavy strafing. Lay it on, Bebert whispered silently; cremate them.

The Egyptian column had indeed suffered a severe pounding. Scores of enemy vehicles had been destroyed. But not all of them. By 1:00 P.M. the paratroops caught their first glimpse of the enemy advance patrols. Jeeps and troop carriers were pulling to a halt about 1,500 yards to the west. Through binoculars, the Israelis could see soldiers dismounting, setting up mortars in the hills flanking both sides of the road. Among Raful's junior officers the temptation was strong to move against the enemy without delay, before the Egyptians had time to fortify their positions. The major was adamant, however; one hundred and fifty men without tanks would be sitting ducks on that highway. They would have to wait until Sharon's column arrived.

And so they waited, digging trenches, filling sandbags, munching listlessly on their rations, checking and rechecking their weapons. The hours passed. Darkness fell. A half-moon slowly reprinted the desert. Each company took turns sleeping. Once a flight of Egyptian Vampire jets whined overhead on the way to retaliate against the approaching Israel convoy. Bebert huddled under his blanket, his back turned away from the bitter night wind. At 9:30 P.M. he was awakened by shouting. All about him men were standing, pointing toward the east. He followed their outstretched arms. In the moonlight he saw what they saw: a column of dust rising from the dunes. Minute by minute the dust cloud grew until, a half-hour later, the first faint outlines of vehicles could be distinguished. And twenty minutes after that the machines rolled into Parker. It was Sharon's brigade—AMX tanks, half-tracks, jeeps, armored cars, caissons carrying mortars, recoilless rifles, tons of shells, small-arms ammunition, food, water, gasoline, and seven hundred beautiful, wonderful troops. Raful's men threw themselves upon the newcomers, embracing them gleefully, hugging and wrestling them to the ground.

Eventually supplies were distributed. Troops wounded by Egyptian strafing were given first-aid treatment. Two dead men were buried. New company assignments were announced, camouflage nets were erected to protect the parked vehicles, guards and patrols were redeployed. All was in readiness for the final jump-off against Mitla. All but Sharon's men themselves. They had been on the move, fighting and rescuing stalled equipment, almost continually for the past thirty-six hours. Their bloodshot eyes were starting from their heads. Some of the troops were literally asleep on their feet. The colonel, in over-all command now, gave the welcome order: the night would be used for rest. For the next five hours silence descended on the freezing desert.

XII

By ten the next morning, the reunited brigade was prepared to move. Fueled and loaded, the tanks and troop carriers started their motors. The engines growled quietly. In a moment the terrain was blanketed by a treble whine. It was not the sound of diesels. The men gazed skyward. Four Egyptian Vampires banked slowly overhead, wheeling leisurely, the sun glinting on their wings. Then the jets began the final approach toward the column. As the lead plane dropped into rocket range, it hung motionless for a moment. Suddenly its tail assembly floated free. Before the astonished eyes of the paratroopers, two Vampires yawed crazily, then dropped belly first onto the desert, exploding in bluish-yellow flame. The remaining jets struggled for altitude; but, too late, they disintegrated in mid-air. Seconds later two Israel Mystères soared out of the sun, dipping their port wings in salute, then roaring eastward. On the ground eight hundred and fifty paratroopers cheered wildly, waving their helmets until the jets had disappeared over the horizon.

Then the convoy began to roll. The first three miles went smoothly. Advance patrols reported that the Egyptian mortar teams had apparently withdrawn closer to the foothills. Sharon ordered the column onward, but more slowly. From the radio set in his command car he received a message from a Piper observation plane: the Pass itself looked clear. Five minutes later Mitla unfolded before the colonel: a tangled matrix of dun-colored cliffs, 1,500 to 2,500 feet high. And there, into the ravine, no more than eighty yards across at its widest point, snaked the desert pike. It was a natural death trap. All the more worth controlling, in that case. First it would have to be reconnoitered. For this mission Sharon picked Major Mordecai Gur, commander of the armored column.

"Take a task force into the gap," the colonel ordered. "At the first sign of an ambush, pull out. Don't try to shoot your way through under any circumstances. We'll take it from the cliffs if there's any trouble."

Gur immediately organized his unit. Balancing his strength carefully, he selected three rifle companies, to be carried by half-tracks, three AMX tanks, one battery of 120-mm mortars, and one motorized battery of twenty-five-pounder artillery. At 12:30 P.M. the major climbed into his jeep and personally led the procession westward. As the task force entered the defile, the clatter of half-tracks and tanks sent echoes flying uncannily back and forth from the rock facings. The convoy rounded a bend. Then a smoke ball lofted gently from the north parapet, leaving its tracer in the air. Lieutenant Aryeh Crespi's half-track suddenly erupted in flame, careened precariously, then settled on its side across the width of the road. Return movement out of the pass was blocked.

The canyon was thereupon transformed into a hell of flailing lead and steel: the task force was trapped in a classic cross fire from both cliff walls. Lieutenant Crespi lay prone under his vehicle, his head blown off. Several other men fell, pumping blood. The rest of the troops ducked for cover, squatting awkwardly under the bumpers of their carriers as bullets and shrapnel churned the earth about them. Gur appraised the situation instantly from his vantage point at the lead of the column. The faces of the cliffs were pocked with sangars—caves artificially hollowed out for gun emplacements. There must have been twenty of them at least on each side, and all of them were spitting flame. On the north side of the road, too, Gur detected a Russian-made half-track burrowed into the embankment, the twin machine guns of its turret firing point blank into the stalled column.

"Get a bazooka lined up on that half-track," Gur shouted to one of his lieutenants. "We'll provide covering fire from this end."

Distracted by the sudden, if inaccurate hail of bullets from Gur's embattled infantry squads, the Egyptians concentrated their barrage on the lead units of the task force. In the brief interval, a bazooka team focused its sights on the enemy half-track. The second rocket struck home; the vehicle belched smoke. Unexpectedly, too, a cache of Egyptian ammunition behind the half-track suddenly erupted in a roar. Gur had a moment's breathing space. He ordered the AMXs to elevate their guns and fire at the caves. The light tanks followed instructions and began lobbing shells into the cliffs. It was an impossible task, however; the trajectory was almost completely perpendicular. The unequal battle continued for an hour and a half. Speaking to Sharon by radio, the major issued a report of the situation.

"We're blocked and pinned down," he explained. "There's no way of moving until we get our disabled vehicles off the road. The caves will have to be silenced for that. I'm going to send some men up there, but we'll need plenty of reinforcements from your end."

Sharon agreed. His entire brigade was now strung out and immobilized, in and out of the Pass, for three miles. Gur's company blocked the operation. It would not suffice merely to rescue the trapped unit. Gur was right: one way or another the caves would have to be silenced. The colonel summoned to his side the commander of the Second Infantry Battalion, Lieutenant Colonel Aharon Davidi.

"Those sangars will have to be captured the hard way," Sharon pointed out. "Take your men up the cliffs, starting from here. You'll descend into the caves sideways or from above. Gur will try to infiltrate them from below. We'll send some jeeps as far into the canyon as we dare to evacuate the wounded."

Davidi immediately ordered his two hundred officers and men to dismount. On foot, they began the ascent of the northern ridge. Simultaneously, in the canyon itself, Gur sent his infantry squads racing toward the southern rock facing. Once there, they began lifting themselves up the ledges, hand over hand. It was a hopeless assignment. Accurate rifle and automatic fire from the sangars opposite picked the Israelis off, one by one. Gur ordered his men back to the cover of their vehicles. It was noon. All that could be done now was to await the cover of darkness, and to maintain a counterbarrage. In this fashion the Egyptians might be distracted from the relief battalion moving across from the east.

Everything depended upon the success of Davidi's operation now. Sweating under full pack, the troops followed the young infantry officer up the treacherous slopes of the northeastern promontory. Bebert was among them. He picked his way carefully among the rocks, grunting at the strain on his injured pelvis. None of the men said a word. An hour later, at 3:00 P.M., the battalion reached the crest of the ridge. The sound of battle grew loud in their ears. Davidi quickened his step now, and his troops swung their weapons to the ready. Then, a few hundred yards further, the entire battle arena suddenly opened before their eyes. Gur's vehicles were sprawled helplessly at all angles along the ravine. Beside them crouched the embattled troops, occasionally exposing themselves long enough to fire return volleys at the caves. The scene was somehow unreal. Streamers of smoke floated across the canyon like fog, dappling the carnage in shadows, even cloaking it momentarily. But it was no illusion. Men were trapped and dying down there.

"Let's go." Lieutenant Colonel Davidi gave the order matter-of-factly. Separating into companies, the soldiers began a unit by unit descent toward the sangars. Bebert followed his officer, Lieutenant Oved, toward the gorge. Only seconds after reaching the rock facing, however, the relief brigade was spotted. Instantly the Egyptians in the caverns opposite elevated their guns. A wall of flame flickered along the southern cliff. Rocks on the northern promontory suddenly were chewed loose or fragmented by the fearsome blast of lead and steel. Men dropped on every side. Bebert and his companions flattened on the ledge, dazedly setting their UZIs to semi-automatic fire, and then sniping back into the mouths of the caverns across the ravine. Some of the shots must have struck home. Two of the sangars directly opposite slackened their barrages.

At the same time one of the half-tracks on the road bed below, evidently struck by a mortar shell, rolled back unexpectedly into the embankment. Watching from the ledge, Davidi noted that a partial escape route had now opened for the convoy. Somehow Gur would have to be informed. Unfortunately, all radios had been shot out of operation in the ravine. Via his own portable walkie-talkie, therefore, Davidi communicated with the jeep company at the canyon mouth, asking for a volunteer to drive into the inferno and notify Gur to pull out. Ironically, it was Davidi's own driver, a twenty-one-year-old sabra, who accepted the mission. Jamming his car into high gear, the youth roared hell-bent into the valley. While he was still four hundred yards from the stranded convoy, however, his jeep was literally lifted from the ground by a savage fusillade. With bullets in his chest, stomach, and legs, the driver crawled the remaining distance, and reached Gur. Then he crawled back once again to the protection of his overturned jeep. The young courier was destined to linger for two months in a military hospital, where he was decorated, and died.

The effort was in vain. In the interval other wrecked vehicles were flung battered across the road. The task force remained in a vise. At Davidi's command, therefore, one of the relief companies retraced its steps to the east, then descended directly to the canyon floor beyond the range of the sangars. Bebert watched, dry-mouthed, as the men silently made their way along the base of the cliff, crouching, half-crawling toward the immobilized column. Following them closely, at Davidi's order, were several half-tracks and ammunition trucks from the canyon mouth—the latter intended to supply Gur's men and offer protection for the troops who now advanced on foot.

But they accomplished neither purpose. It was 4:10 P.M. Four planes, Meteor jets, suddenly approached from the direction of the sun. The Egyptian markings were clearly visible on their fuselages. Swooping low over the Pass, their engines deafening the valley, the planes loosed their rockets against the advancing company. The ammunition truck at once exploded with an ear-splitting blast, sending bullets and shell fragments ricocheting from one side of the road to the other. The planes banked above the eastern rim of the range in preparation for another swoop. Then, unexpectedly, they scattered, picking up speed toward Suez. A moment later four Israel Ouragons flew by in close pursuit.

No one on the ledge cheered. They could hear the stricken men below bellowing in agony. Without waiting for orders, Bebert and two companions clambered down the mountain wall, ignoring the bullets that stitched the rock facing about them. Dashing in a zigzag pattern toward the protection of the gutted half-track, they found the remnants of the company: men torn open from head to crotch, others breathing their last, digging their heads into the ground. One corporal was running in circles, a flaming torch. By now gathering dusk partially covered the descent, and others of the relief reached the base of the cliff. Lieutenant Colonel Davidi himself joined them. Then darkness fell altogether. The firing slackened. Along the length of the ravine, the paratroopers used the respite to administer first aid to their wounded.

Davidi was determined not to waste the opportunities of nightfall, however.

"Oved," he called to the lieutenant. "Take your squad and get to Gur's unit. Pull out as many wounded as you can. If his officers have other ideas for you, put yourselves under their command."

Within thirty seconds Oved and the twenty-two men of his squad were creeping forward, UZIs cradled tightly in their arms. Bebert was among them, guarding his lieutenant's right flank. The first hundred yards were covered without incident. Then the paratroopers saw figures before them.

It was a detachment of troops from the task force. One of the soldiers was Major Mota of the armored battalion. He seized Oved's hand in delight.

"Man, we can use you," he whispered. Then he pointed toward the north cliff. "There are their three worst bunkers, twenty meters high, about fifty meters apart. We've figured out that they have six or seven troops operating heavy machine guns in each one. Nothing's going to move in or out of this road till we take them."

A frown crossed Oved's handsome face. "I don't know," he protested. "Davidi said we should pull out the wounded."

Major Mota raised his voice. "Oved, our wounded are as important to me as they are to Davidi. But if we don't get those caves there will be a lot more dead men in this Pass. We'll move now, you hear."

Oved nodded. "We'll move," he agreed. He whispered instructions to his second lieutenant. The twenty-two men bunched together, listening to the order. Then, single file, they crept forward in groups of four to the base of the north cliff. Bebert remained at Oved's right. Together they began the ascent of the first ledge. Behind them the rest of the squad clambered upward, hand over foot. The surface of the mountain was well dimpled, but almost entirely perpendicular. The ascent was agonizing. Thus far all was silence, except for the labored breathing of the troops. Soon the ominous black cavern was visible, only ten more yards above them. Bebert felt as if his back were breaking into two pieces.

"Yosi," he grunted to Oved, "I've got to rest a minute."

"Move," whispered the lieutenant. Then louder: "You must."

Abandoning caution, Oved thereupon jammed his feet hard against the ledge, and charged his way straight upward to the cave entrance. His heavy-soled paratrooper's boots clattered against the rock. Alerted, the Egyptians in the sangar instantly began firing. The burst caught a young second lieutenant head-on, sending him toppling back into the ravine.

"I'm coming," shouted Oved furiously.

Pulling the detonator pin, he waited a moment, then hurled a grenade at the mouth of the sangar. The grenade missed, struck the wall, and bounced back toward the lieutenant himself. Its explosion tore Oved in half.

Bebert was senior officer now. He reacted instinctively to his training. Gathering six men about him, he flattened them against the cliff, then began inching sideways toward the cavern. From the corner of his eye he could see tracer bullets spitting from the sangar. Quickly he primed his grenade, paused the required three seconds, then leaned forward and lobbed the smoking apple into the cave. The effort was perfectly timed. The rock wall shuddered with the force of the explosion.

"Come on," Bebert shouted. Dashing into the smoke-filled sangar, the paratroops blasted away at the remnants of the Egyptian machine-gun crew. Following the letter of the infantry manual, Bebert unholstered his pistol and put a bullet into the head of each Egyptian body he could find. He missed one. The Arab stirred, then fired a burst from his Karl-Gustav point-blank into the chest of one of the corporals. Bebert dispatched the

Egyptian with two final shots of his revolver. The Jewish corporal was beyond help. Signaling his men to follow, Bebert moved on toward the neighboring bunker.

This one was easier; the ledge inclined upward, away from the cavern's line of fire. By loosing burst after burst at an angle into the sangar's entrance, the paratroopers managed to drive the Egyptian defenders back from their machine gun. Simultaneously a lieutenant from Gur's convoy grappled his way up from the road, and hurled a grenade flush into the mouth of the cave. It went off with conclusive effect, billowing smoke along the rock sidings. Bebert and his squad swung into the bunker immediately, gunning down the survivors.

"Take the last cave, will you, Eli," Bebert said to the lieutenant. "I'm going down to start pulling the wounded out." With that he began the descent into the ravine.

He jogged quickly along the road until he reached the main concentration of wrecked vehicles. The most seriously injured men lay there, partially sheltered by armored half-tracks. Bebert recognized one of the soldiers. It was a kibbutz youth named Nazaroff. His head and chest were bandaged tightly.

"How's your *matzav ruach* [morale], Nazaroff?" Bebert whispered, pressing his friend's hand. "Think we can carry you out of here."

The stretcher bearer, a Moroccan private, shook his head in a panic. "We've got to move him back," he shouted. "He's hurt bad. Look here," he switched on his flashlight, focusing it on Nazaroff's chest.

Bebert cursed, cracking the stretcher bearer across the face with the flat of his right hand, and snapping off the light with the left. But it was too late. A rifle bullet from the third sangar, still holding out, thudded into Nazaroff's breastbone. Simultaneously a machine-gun fusillade churned through the line of wounded men, tearing shards of metal from the half-tracks, sending needle-sharp stone fragments ricocheting from the southern cliff wall. Bebert staggered, then dropped to one knee. His groin was pouring blood. Fortunately his senses remained quite clear. Tearing open his pants' leg with his sheath knife, he pressed his thumbs down firmly on the artery center. The bleeding slowed. From his open knapsack, he removed a heavy gauze dressing, and fastened it by bandage to his inner thigh. The rock fragment would remain for the time being.

Bebert turned next to the men around him. Their faces were barely distinguishable in the dark, but their groans and death rattles identified their positions only too clearly. He groped for Nazaroff, and found him choking in a pool of blood.

"Nazaroff, hold on," Bebert gasped. "We're clearing the Pass. A little longer and we'll get you out."

Bebert was right. Capture of the first three sangars had knocked the hinge pin off the Egyptian defense network. Davidi's men were now entrenched in the lead bunkers of the northern cliff. Setting up their weapons behind the sandbags, they poured lethal salvos in a flat trajectory directly into the caves across the road. There was room for movement now. Sharon's armor rolled tentatively into the entrance of the ravine. By 7:00 P.M. bulldozers had cleared the wrecked vehicles off the outer fork of the escape route. Fresh squads and platoons of infantrymen now swarmed into the gap. Joining with the beleaguered troops in the canyon, they moved directly toward the ledges. The task was by no means concluded. The Egyptians fought bravely. Each cave had to be taken individually. During the next hour, Jewish casualties were nearly as heavy as they had been during the entire afternoon—34 men killed and 102 wounded. But the battle was on increasingly equal terms; 211 Egyptians were slain in their bunkers. By 9:30 Davidi's aggressive leadership had accounted for all but a handful of sangars on both sides of the canyon. It was a mopping-up operation now. The convoy began to move westward, investing the entire Pass.

Bebert's destination was eastward. He was loading the wounded on a weapons carrier, when his groin injury opened again without warning. As he pressed his thumbs on the artery, he noticed two small holes in his lower abdomen. Was this a new wound, he wondered? Then weakness suddenly overcame him and he stumbled. At this point Bebert's comrades forcibly lifted him into the caisson, ignoring his protests. Together with the other wounded, he was carried back to Parker Memorial. In his absence a field hospital had been set up there. Ten doctors were working continuously, ministering to emergency cases. Bebert was stretched out on a makeshift operating table and given a blood transfusion. A doctor and nurse sewed the artery closed.

During the night a landing strip was laid just east of the monument. Dakota troop carriers and tiny Pipers began arriving now at fifteen-minute intervals, ferrying new supplies, carrying out the wounded. Bebert was one of those evacuated. As the plane roared full throttle into the dawn, he lifted his head weakly for a moment. The fuselage floor was packed with men, most of them semiconscious under their blankets. Nazaroff was two stretchers away. Bebert attempted an encouraging smile. Nazaroff stared back, his glazed eyes unseeing. Bebert realized suddenly that his friend was dead. Panic overtook him. For a moment, as he turned his own head to the wall, he thought he saw the face of death: the hawk nose, the dazzling smile, opened like a trap, the eyes, rimmed with lashes black as *ned*, glittering hypnotically. "You djinn, you bastard, you will pay," said Bebert.

But in fact he had already paid. By the morning of November 1, Nasser's forces in the Sinai were all but shattered. Within four days Israel's mobile columns had overrun every major Egyptian stronghold in the peninsula. The morning after Sharon's force had crossed the frontier, an infantry brigade moved against the Egyptian fortress of Queisima, and captured it after a three-hour battle. From Queisima, in turn, an armored brigade set forth against the powerfully fortified hedgehog of Abu Agheila, closer yet to the northern coast. After a two-and-a-half-day artillery and tank duel, Abu Agheila's defenses collapsed. Almost simultaneously two powerful brigades of Israel infantry and armor were dispatched toward

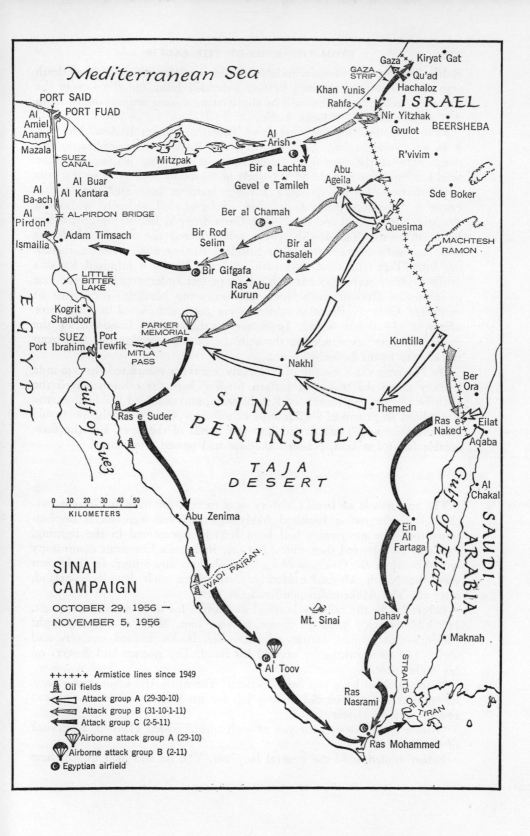

SINAI CAMPAIGN

OCTOBER 29, 1956 –
NOVEMBER 5, 1956

+++++ Armistice lines since 1949
Oil fields
Attack group A (29-30-10)
Attack group B (31-10-1-11)
Attack group C (2-5-11)
Airborne attack group A (29-10)
Airborne attack group B (2-11)
Egyptian airfield

Rahfa. This was the most formidable citadel in all Sinai, a reticulated death trap of no less than eighteen heavily defended hills, and the key to the Egyptian military complex within the narrow coastal strip running from Al-Arish to the city of Gaza itself.

Rahfa was the personal triumph of Brigadier Chaim Laskov. He took it in an overnight battle, confounding the Egyptians by infiltrating his troops between the mine fields under cover of darkness, then storming the final battlements under the very barrels of Egyptian artillery. The rest was anticlimactic. Al-Arish, Nasser's *fedayin* training base and the staging center for the long-planned invasion of Israel, fell virtually without a struggle. Khan Yunis and the city of Gaza dropped like ripe plums a few hours afterward. The Jewish troops who entered the abandoned depots took possession of more than four hundred Russian-made vehicles, including forty T-43 tanks and sixty armored cars. Nearly a hundred Russian artillery pieces were also left behind in perfect order, together with vast quantities of Russian shells, fuel supplies, army blankets—even cans of antifreeze. Only the Egyptian soldiers were gone, abandoned by their inept officer to the desert wastes. Israel air patrols spotted hundreds of the maddened wretches wandering through the dunes, dropping like flies from thirst, prey to the bedouin knives.

On November 4 a convoy of Tel Aviv reservists completed the 240-mile journey down the wastes of eastern Sinai. There the column seized the abandoned Egyptian fortress of Ras Nasrani, and pounded the final enemy stronghold of Sharm al-Sheikh into submission. Control of the peninsula and the Straits of Tiran passed into the hands of the Jews. For the foreseeable future, at least, Nasser's shadow had passed from Israel.

XIII

The magnitude of Israel's victory was more than military. It was psychological: the nation breathed freely again. There were social implications, too. The newcomers had been heavily represented in the fighting, and they had proved themselves. No one in Israel's European community would consider the Orientals cowards or slackers any longer. In their own way, the North Africans evidently cared about their Jewish homeland, after all. The Ashkenazim pondered the fact.

Bebert lay in the military hospital at Ramle, his torso encased in a cast. His kibbutz-mates came en masse to visit him. Many of them brought presents—tins of jam, cartons of cigarettes, books, knitted sweaters and socks. The men awkwardly pressed his hand. The women laid flowers on his night table.

"Can't wait to have you back, Bebert," Yonathan, the kibbutz secretary, murmured shyly. "You did quite a job for us. When you return you can rest up as long as you want."

"And a special dessert for you at each meal," added Hannah, supervisor of the kitchen.

Bebert smiled amid the general laughter. Yes, he was glad to see them too, he said. They needn't have traveled so far to visit him. He hoped the fields would be harvested on time, in spite of the departure of so many men. No need to worry about him; he would be on his feet sooner than they thought. To his parents' urgent cable, he sent the same response.

The doctor was not quite as optimistic. "We had to leave the rocks inside, Hayot," he explained. "Taking them out would have jeopardized the entire arterial and lymphatic complex. Never mind, they're clean. They shouldn't cause you any trouble. It's your back you'll have to watch. You see, the pelvis has been dislocated. You'll be in a cast at least another six weeks."

"Will I be able to jump again?" asked Bebert.

"Jump? Hardly likely. I should think you would have had enough of that."

But Bebert had not. Flat on his back during the past fortnight, he had found plenty of time for reflection. The visions and echoes flashed through his mind: the early months of basic training in 1954, the handsome boots and beret, the equalizing power of a UZI submachine gun, the retaliation raids, the warmth and camaraderie of nights around the desert bonfires, the Passover *seder* with General Dayan and his family. Above all he relived those breathless moments, less than three weeks before, when beloved Lieutenant Oved had announced their destination. It all came back again, the warm embraces, the brotherhood, the urgent need to offer each other help and companionship. There was the campaign itself: the lives risked, the wounds suffered, the sacrifices made—and no one asked for whom. They knew for whom: for each other. It was enough. In the Israel army it was enough. Yes, that was where he wanted to be. He was a man there.

When his officers visited him, he put the question directly to Major Marcell. "I want to stay in," he said. "I want to go to officers' training school. Will you second me?"

Marcell's scarred, weather-beaten face parted in a surprised grin. He put his hand fondly on Bebert's cast. "Will I! If you hadn't suggested it, I would have."

"It will be tough, Bebert," warned Colonel Arik. "Six months of the ruggedest training you've ever seen. Lots of written examinations, too. Courses in history and archaeology. But—I think your Hebrew is up to it. Anyhow, you qualify in every other way, no doubt about that. I'll back you, too."

In the last week of Bebert's convalescence he received an official letter from the ministry of defense. His application for officers' candidate school had been accepted. Maurice was with him in the hospital room when the letter arrived. The friend shrugged.

"I don't know," he said. "It's a hell of a life ahead of you. What do they pay?"

Bebert laughed. "About one eighty a month in training. More when I become a second lieutenant. Don't you ever think about anything except money?"

"Not very often," Maurice admitted. Then his face became quite serious. "It's an honor for our people that they've accepted you, I got to admit it. Any other Moroccan officers in the paratroops?"

"I'll be the first."

Maurice nodded. "It is an honor," he repeated. "I wish it was me."

The moment he was released from the hospital, Bebert departed for Jaffa. He reached Shulamith's room within the hour, and stayed there for the next three days. She had visited him daily since his return from Sinai, and had rented a room in anticipation of his return. Now their plans were firmly made. She would be discharged from the army in two months. After that she would go with him. Together they pored over the classified pages of the newspapers.

"Here's one," he said at length. "In Petach Tikvah. 'One and a half room flat, small kitchen. In perfect condition. Good neighborhood. I £2,000 key money. Phone 52084.'" He whistled. "Two thousand pounds! The army wouldn't put up more than half of that."

"My father and uncles will give us the rest," she said decisively. "Leave it to me. Call the owner and tell him you'll go over."

He made the phone call, and set up the appointment for the following morning. When the next day came, he saw Shulamith off to camp on the 6 A.M. army bus. Then he flagged a ride to Petach Tikvah. It was a medium-sized city of nearly fifty thousand people. Wolffsohn Street, his destination, was a spacious, well-paved thoroughfare, and centrally located. Bebert looked about him. It was a good neighborhood, all right. Nothing but houses and trees. Not even a school near-by to make noise. The passers-by were all European. He reached the address, a stone building of two floors, and rang the bell at the lower side entrance.

A stocky, bald man with a pink, well-fleshed face opened the door.

"Mr. Albrecht Friedenthal?" asked Bebert, pronouncing the name with difficulty.

The man nodded, staring at the paratrooper quizzically for a moment. "Oh yes," he began to smile uncertainly. "You are interested in the flat. Come in."

He showed Bebert through the premises. They were small, but adequate. The tiles in the kitchen and bathroom were all new. The walls in the bedroom had been freshly painted.

"It's nice," Bebert admitted. "I'm a little worried about the price. Can we talk about it?"

Mr. Friedenthal was looking at the campaign ribbon on Bebert's chest. "Sinai?" he asked. Bebert nodded modestly. The proprietor smiled again. "You boys did a grand job," he said. "My nephews were both there, in the same brigade. They took Al-Arish."

"That was a good action," Bebert murmured politely. "Congratulations."

"Where are you from?" asked Friedenthal.

"Kibbutz Dorot, in the Negev."

"No, no," Friedenthal persisted, "I mean before that. Iraq? Morocco?"

"Morocco," Bebert replied quietly, his guard suddenly up.

"You speak a good Hebrew," the landlord mused. "I've been in this country twenty-three years and I still break my teeth on it. Look here," his tone became brisk, "this place is all right, but it's not for a paratrooper who fought in Sinai. I own several flats that would be better for you. Please," he raised his hand as Bebert began to object, "you deserve it. I want to do everything I can for you boys." He scribbled an address on the back of an envelope and handed it to Bebert. "This one is in Tel Aviv proper. The same size, the same price—maybe even a little lower if you like it. Phone me after you see it and let me know if you're interested. We'll work something out." He extended his hand. Bebert shook it gratefully.

The address was Gimmel Street, Kfar Salame. Returning to Tel Aviv, Bebert asked directions at the Central Bus Terminal. He learned that his destination was in the southeastern part of the city, not more than a mile and a half away. The weather was cool and bright, and his back was giving him no trouble. He decided to walk. As he set out at a brisk pace, the buses passed him, two or three a minute, grinding through the narrow exits, flooding the alleyways with dense billows of diesel smoke. On both sides of the street, kiosk owners and *felafel* vendors blandly stuffed their *pitah* rolls with garlic and peppers, piling them high on the spotted counters. Pinch-faced little newsboys, ragged and scuff-shoed, darted through the crowds, bleating the day's headlines with grown men's voices.

The bedlam continued for three blocks. Then the traffic thinned. The neighborhood was industrial. Mechanics' hammers and electric drills pounded and rasped from tiny ironmongers' shops and motorcycle garages. Trucks and donkey carts passed in and out of asphalt driveways. Bebert walked on another four blocks. The road became dirt again, and was flanked by barracks-like stucco dwellings, most of them covered with galvanized tin roofs. On the front steps mothers sat nursing their children. The women were all dark. Many of them wore silk *foutas* and veils, their ears were pierced with tiny gold rings. Conversing in Maghreb Arabic or Judeo-Berber, they stopped short as Bebert walked by, smiling and nodding their heads in approval. Bebert paused, too, staring for a long moment at the street sign fastened to the corner barracks.

"Gimmel Street," he repeated the words dully.

At that moment a swarthy youngster passed by on a bicycle. He gazed curiously at the lean soldier in the maroon paratroop beret, then circled around and braked to a halt. "Can I help you, *chaver?*" he asked. "What number are you looking for?"

"Gimmel Street," said Bebert again, his voice thick.

"What number, *chaver?*" the boy repeated. Then his eyes opened wide. "What are you doing? What is it?" he asked, his mouth beginning to tremble. Bebert's fingers tightened on the handle bars, and his face drew close to the boy's.

"There is another Gimmel Street somewhere, isn't there?" he whispered.

"But there isn't, *chaver,*" pleaded the boy, his eyes filling with tears. "I wouldn't fool you. You're wrecking my bicycle."

The women on the front steps were standing now, muttering to each other in alarm. "Stop that, stop that, soldier!" shrieked one of them. "Leave the boy alone."

Then the bicycle dropped to the road, and the youngster was kneeling beside it, sobbing.

"Salaud! Cochon!" he shouted at Bebert's retreating back.

"Bondouk!" shrilled the women at the top of their voices, until the running soldier disappeared around the corner.

For two days Bebert remained beyond reach. Lieutenant Colonel Arik remonstrated with him: "I can't understand you. With your ability you could go right to the top. You ought to jump at a chance like this. How many people do you think we accept for officers' candidate school, anyway? It's an honor, Bebert. You'd be with the best boys in Israel. This is a real elite corps."

Bebert shook his head. No, he did not want it anymore. He was through with it all. Arik threw up his hands, then tried again. "I put my reputation on the line when I recommended you," he pleaded. "There aren't five boys a year I'd give the rating I gave you. You've got what it takes. Damn it, you'd make a great officer."

Bebert sat like a stone, neither agreeing nor disagreeing. Arik talked on, pacing the corners of his office, raising his voice, lowering it, at times pounding his fist on the desk. What would make a grown man act like a sullen child, he asked? A run-in with one miserable Yecke landlord? "You're too smart for that, Bebert," the officer insisted. "To hell with the little snob. Who needs him? We'll get you any flat you want, anywhere. Name the neighborhood, the price. We'll stand behind you. We're paratroopers, man." He put his arm on Bebert's shoulder.

"It's not that," said Bebert, at last, in a low voice. "I told you it's not just one landlord. I thought it would be different when I came here. It wasn't. I thought it would be different after the hospital. Now I know better. I'm through with giving and getting nothing back."

Arik argued for a few minutes more, then gave it up. Lieutenant Amnon Dagon tried next. "I want you to think for a minute," he explained gravely. "Only a fool would deny your people have troubles in this country. It's been a hard life for the newcomers. Some of it is our fault. Some of it is theirs." Bebert said nothing as Dagon continued. "Some North Africans think they'll never be anything but bootblacks or *felafel* salesmen. That's why they don't try to be anything else." The lieutenant's voice was urgent now. "Bebert, be our proof that a man with guts and brains can be anything he wants to be if he tries hard enough. Any man who can make it with us is a leader. Your people ought to know that they have leaders among them. You owe them that, Bebert. Every Moroccan kid who looks at you will know that there's another way besides Aga Cohen's and Shishim Street."

A door opened and Major Marcell walked into the room. After thirty months of service together, the powerful, bull-necked officer looked no less formidable now than on that cold December day in 1953 when Bebert had first walked into the induction camp at Rehovot, a green recruit. The major's shoulders still bulged under his khaki jacket. When he smiled, his face creased into a latticework of tiny pits and crevices. He was smiling now. "How are you, Hayot?"

Bebert nodded woodenly, but said nothing. He respected the major more than any man he had ever known. With fifty people like Marcell running the government, this would be a country worth living in. There would be no Gimmel Streets then, no discrimination in labor exchanges, no more handling the Arabs with kid gloves. Sinai would have taken place two years ago, after the first *fedayin* raid. But—Marcell wasn't in the government, just in the army. That's where they kept all the good men locked up.

Perhaps the major had read his thoughts: "You can go a long way in the army, Hayot," he said matter-of-factly. "You get back what you give there." And give back what you get? Did that follow, too? Is that what he meant?

Bebert rose and walked about the room in agitation, then stared out the window. The compound was filled with trim, erect soldiers, snapping through their drills with dispatch and precision. The officers stood like young lords, their bronze epaulets and paratroopers' insignia gleaming in the sun. Too bad the photographs he had sent Papa and Maman could not be in color; they missed the maroon of his handsome beret. Still, his parents had written that the pictures had created a sensation among all the neighbors of Rue Djama Shluh. He smiled wryly, and his hand instinctively groped at his thigh, where once his oiled leather holster had hung. Then he sat down.

"Never mind," he whispered to himself.

He sat without moving for another ten minutes. Arik watched him intently through veiled lids. Marcell smoked in silence, gazing at the ceiling. Outside recruits marched off the parade ground. The clatter of their weapons echoed from the barracks wall. Slowly then, with a shuddering, barely audible sigh, Bebert reached for the enlistment forms. Marcell smiled.

"Giving it another chance?" he asked, quietly.

Bebert nodded. Perhaps there was more than one way to cast a shadow in this land. "Another chance," he muttered. Just one more.

CHAPTER EIGHT

THE BANKER

P ASCAL LEVI, a smiling, round-faced Jew of Cairo, was accustomed to the good things of life. The son of a Syrian Jewish immigrant, he had been raised in a spacious apartment on Cairo's fashionable Abdul Aziz Street, and educated in the Collège Français, the city's finest *lycée*. As a young man directly out of school, he was accepted straightway as a junior executive in the currencies exchange division of Barclay's Bank. He married well. His wife, Amalia da Curial, was the daughter of one of the oldest Sephardic families of the capital, and she bore him two daughters. They made their home in an attractive four-room flat in Zamalek, Cairo's most exclusive residential neighborhood. Two servants ministered to the family's every need. Ibrahim, the senior retainer, drove Levi to the bank each morning in the family's Citroën sedan.

Evenings were rarely spent at home. During the social season, between November and March, there were performances of the Italian Opera to attend, or fashionable night clubs like the Auberge on Guizeh Street, or the Palace in Helmieh, or Badias in Opera Square. There were film benefits at the Metro, the Miami, or the Radio. And always, too, there were lavish private dinners at the better restaurants, and at the Gezira Country Club. The Club, the cynosure of the Jewish smart set, boasted a golf course, a racing course, three swimming pools, forty-two tennis courts, six squash courts, two polo courses, four bowling greens, three croquet grounds, and a cricket pitch. By far the largest part of Levi's social life centered around the Gezira. After a vigorous late afternoon of field hockey, he enjoyed nothing so much as dressing in his tuxedo, and escorting his handsome wife into the main banquet hall for eight-o'clock dinner. Resplendent in their evening gowns, mink coats, and jewelry, the women were the glittering ornaments of their husbands' success. Dinner companions at the club were usually Jews or members of the other European colonies, and conversation was invariably carried on in French or English (Arabic was reserved for servants).

For that matter, virtually all of Egypt's 75,000 Jews considered themselves "European," integral members of that elite economic and social circle which included 350,000 Greeks, 200,000 Italians, and 50,000 English, French, and Armenians. Nor was Jewish settlement in Egypt less recent than the European. In fact, except for a tiny minority who traced their lineage to the Alexandrian community of antiquity, the country's Jewish population had been almost negligible before World War I. Their numbers were slightly augmented after 1914 by several thousand refugees from the Ottoman provinces of Syria, the Lebanon, and Palestine. These were joined, too, by a sprinkling of *émigrés* from North Africa, Greece, and Corfu. Yet the largest migration wave of Jews did not arrive until the 1920s and 1930s. Most of the newcomers were born in the Near East, and were Near Eastern in background and traditions.

They had come to Egypt precisely and specifically to shed their Asian inheritance. The country offered refugee Jews the priceless opportunity of European status. After the outbreak of World War I, the French consuls in Egypt placed all refugees from Syria, the Lebanon, and North Africa under their special protection. Similarly, the British consuls assumed responsibility for immigrants from Aden, Yemen, and Corfu; while the Greek and Italian consuls also watched over their own. Later, to be sure, this privileged extraterritoriality was gradually withdrawn. For example, upon receiving their independence in 1935, Syria and the Lebanon promptly stripped all *émigrés* abroad of their former capitulatory status. At the same time, Mussolini summarily deprived all Italian Jews, within and outside Italy, of their Italian citizenship. Five years later, during the Second World War, Greek and Bulgarian Jews resident in Egypt were no longer accredited to the home countries, both of them within the Nazi orbit. Thus, by 1940, perhaps four fifths of the Jews resident in Egypt were stateless.

Yet, curiously enough, this loss of national identification created few problems for Egyptian Jewry. As "local subjects," they still enjoyed full legal protection in their personal life and business activities—without the corresponding responsibilities of citizenship. They were not required to serve in the army. In many instances they paid reduced taxes. Of course, the right to vote, or to participate in Egyptian political life, was denied them. But, in any case, what self-respecting Jew was concerned with the public affairs of that sodden and illiterate African morass? Even the darkest-skinned Sephardi had long since identified himself with the European world.

Entirely unencumbered, therefore, by their statelessness, the Jews proceeded rapidly to carve out economic security for themselves. They were almost exclusively a middle-class community. Beginning as petty merchants in East Cairo and Old Alexandria, they moved within a very few years to larger-scale proprietorship. Together with the Greeks and Italians, Jews soon managed, or owned, the finest shops on Suleiman Pasha and Ali Pasha Streets, and controlled the most important textile firms in the Musky commercial quarter. Hundreds of Jewish financiers served as executives in Egypt's banking system. Jewish brokers played prominent roles in the currency and cotton exchanges, and in the Bourse—so prominent, indeed, that the members of the Bourse traditionally elected a Jew as their president. Later, too, the economic boom of the Second World War consolidated their already formidable economic position. Together with the *nouveaux riches* of the other minority communities, Jewish families began purchasing homes in the attractive residential neighborhoods of Heliopolis, Daher, and Zamalek. Some Jews even managed to buy plots in Cairo's celebrated Garden City, wherein lay the palatial estates of the Moslem feudal landlords, the authentic rulers of the country.

Nor was their way to security and affluence ever barred by political obstacles. They rarely if ever encountered prejudice. Indeed, Egyptian officials, both in the government and in business, vied with each other in engaging Jewish executives; for Jews were known to be the cleverest and most soundly educated inhabitants of the country. Their children, after all, comprised fully 60 per cent of the Collège Français. Moreover, Jews were productive and law-abiding. They could be depended upon to develop the economy of the country. Their doctors, too, were known to be wonder-workers; the pashas unhesitantly entrusted their lives to Jewish physicians and surgeons. Jewish attorneys were by far the cleverest in the nation; no Egyptian could match their skill in guiding clients through the labyrinth of the laws. Above all, the Jews were esteemed as kind employers; they never laid a hand on a servant, never cursed or shouted. Perhaps nationalist hatreds simmered beneath the surface of Egyptian public life, but they were directed toward the British colonial officials, rarely toward the other peaceful and creative European minorities—and least of all toward the Jews, that most compliant of peoples. It was as a mark of public approbation and affection, therefore, that on the Jewish New Year the governor of Cairo traditionally paid a respectful visit to the synagogue of Chaim Nahum Effendi, chief rabbi of Egypt, and invoked the latter's blessing for the government and people of the land.

Levi and his friends reciprocated this tolerant affection. The Egyptian lower classes were gentle people, smiling, uncomplaining, loyal, unsurpassed as workers and servants; they deserved to be treated with compassion. Levi himself frequently extended small personal loans to his houseboys whenever they needed medical help for their children (a gesture few Moslem employers were likely to make). Occasionally he and Amalia invited one or another of the native clerks and their wives for dinner; and thereafter, he knew, the enraptured Egyptians never ceased to discuss the honor of their acceptance at a "European" home. Levi chuckled inwardly at the reaction. Why not, he thought? God has been good to us. He has given us this placid abode, the comforts we enjoy, the Gezira Country Club, our summer at the Lido in Mersa-Matruh. They are amiable people here. It's a good land.

It was the only land he ever considered for himself and his family. Of course he recognized, as did most of his acquaintances, that the Jews were *in* Egypt, but not *of* Egypt. He needed no reminder that his people were an island unto themselves. Indeed, none of the other minority peoples exceeded the Jews in cohesiveness or community discipline. Egyptian Jewry had established its own elaborate network of schools, clubs, hospitals, synagogues, and mutual-aid societies. As in nearly every other Near Eastern country, rabbinical courts decided matters of personal status. All Jews were in fact obliged by the government to pay "taxes" to support this autonomous community; and they did so willingly. Nor were Levi and his friends indifferent to the redemptive effort taking place in Palestine. They had long expressed a friendly interest in Zionism, had contributed generously to the Jewish National Fund, and had taken an active part in the Maccabee Club and other Zionist organizations.

During the early thirties, too, several hundred Egyptian Jews, intensely Zionist in their loyalties, made the decision to leave the country and settle in Palestine. In 1942, when Rommel's Afrika Korps camped outside the gates of Alexandria, three thousand others fled eastward for refuge. These numbers were matched shortly after the battle of El-Alamein—although this time Jews did not depart as terrified fugitives, but rather as voluntary settlers; they had been inspired to play an active role in the Zionist revival by the young Palestinian soldiers stationed in Egypt. As late as 1945, however, the majority of Egypt's Jews exhibited little willingness to make more than a moral and financial commitment to the Jewish National Home. Levi and his friends were well satisfied with the status quo.

And then, almost overnight, the birth of the State of Israel precipitated Egyptian Jewry's gravest emotional and political crisis. The battles in Palestine were taking place only two hundred miles away. King Farouk had dispatched his fellah armies there. None of the Jews of Egypt doubted that anything but naked territorial ambition motivated Farouk's adventure in Palestine. Nor were their own sympathies ever in doubt. They understood quite clearly that the men and women of Israel were defending more than their sovereignty; they were defending their homes and their lives. To Egyptian Jewry, the people dying in defense of the *Yishuv* were their own kinsmen, their own flesh and blood. So intense was this emotional identification that four hundred young Egyptian Jews suddenly departed from Cairo and Alexandria; ostensibly their destination was France, but in fact they remained in Europe only long enough to arrange transmigration to Israel, where they served in the Jewish defense forces.

Yet the largest part of Egypt's Jewish population was by no means prepared to make this drastic a personal commitment. On the contrary, their first and immediate concern was for their own safety. Regarding the outbreak of the Palestine war with frank horror, they instantly closed their Jewish National Fund offices, their Maccabee clubs, and imposed a strict moratorium on all Zionist or quasi-Zionist activities. Nothing would be said or done to furnish the government with evidence against them. Restraint, indeed complete and utter silence, would be the rule. Levi, for example, made it a point never to discuss Palestine with his non-Jewish colleagues, and this was a practice invariably followed by all Egyptian Jews.

There were incidents. From time to time ugly allusions to dual loyalty appeared in the press. Jewish shops in the poorer quarters of the larger cities were stoned. Occasionally Jews were arrested on suspicion of espionage. Several firms discharged their Jewish employees. And yet, discrimination was never officially inspired, nor did public disorders of any significance ever take place. For that matter, there were few "patriotic" demonstrations of any kind. It is doubtful if the fellah masses ever really knew what was happening in Palestine, or where, precisely, Palestine was. The Moslem aristocrats of the country knew, of course, but as a rule they were too busy with their polo matches, or winning favorable mention in the society columns of the English-language newspapers, to bother with the issue of Palestine or the Jews.

Nevertheless, the Egyptian Jewish community viewed even the occasional, scattered incidents of anti-Semitic unrest as warning of future danger. For all their insulation from the country's populace, few Jews had not witnessed at one time or another the mercurial rages of the street mob, the indolent sadism of the police. The threat was exacerbated, too, by the continued state of war between Egypt and Israel—long after actual hostilities had ceased. Would fighting be renewed? Egyptian Jewry wondered. Would a state of siege be imposed upon the country? Would the Jewish minority be quarantined as "unreliables?" The unanswered questions exerted intolerable psychological pressure on a minority people. Thus, between 1949 and 1951 some thirty thousand Egyptian Jews decided not to risk unknown and imagined perils. They sold their homes and businesses, transferred their holdings to European banks, and departed for France and Italy. From there ten thousand transmigrated to Israel. Most of the immigrants avoided the *ma'abara* squalor of other Near Eastern newcomers. With very few exceptions, they ended up as white-collar workers in Israel's banks, insurance companies, and other commercial enterprises.

But Levi remained in Cairo. He would not panic, as had so many of his friends, uprooting their families without tangible cause or need. By 1949, in fact, the signs of normalcy were visible everywhere around him. The Palestine war ceased to be a major topic of discussion in the press or radio. The routine of the pre-1948 period returned. The workers and fellahin still grubbed for a living. The Wafd cabinet still played its endless games of political musical chairs. The fat king bestirred himself from his torpor only long enough to consult procurers and erotica salesmen. In the cities there was money to be made in the currency exchange and in cotton futures. People lost interest in the Jews. The governor of Cairo again paid his routine visit to Rabbi Nahum on the Jewish New Year. The social life at Gezira and Mersa-Matruh revived.

Yet under the surface of Arab political life nothing was quite the same. Hatreds were stirring—against the West, and its agents. One of the symptoms of unrest was the growth of a sinister organization known as the Moslem Brotherhood. Self-proclaimed terrorists, the members of this band were openly dedicated to "cleansing" Western influence from the Near East, usually by assassinating the "puppets" of British imperialism. Ostensibly the Egyptian branch of the Brotherhood had been dissolved in 1948, after its agents murdered the pro-Western chief of the Cairo city police, Selim Zaki Pasha. That same month however, Prime Minister Nakrashy Pasha, who had ordered the organization's dissolution, was himself shot dead by a member of the Brotherhood. Assassination of other public officials followed during the next few years; no government functionary was safe from the fanatic cabal.

The Moslem Brotherhood represented merely the crest of a growing wave of public unrest. Moreover, anticipating the wave's force and direction, the Egyptian government itself began applying pressure on the British to remove their Suez garrison. The British, as it happened, were unwilling to negotiate. Insisting that the Canal was theirs by treaty right, they made clear their intention of keeping the garrisons at Suez indefinitely. On January 25, 1952, however, a skirmish between British troops and Egyptian police at Ismailia produced consequences that were destined to change the entire face of Egyptian public life. A current of xenophobia swept through the land. Riots erupted in Cairo, provoking the king to send the army into the streets, and to dismiss Premier Nahas Pasha. For another half-year two successive Wafd administrations tried vainly to cope with the aimless, surging fury of the nation's vast unwashed. The protest gained momentum: the government was rotten, so the charge went; it was a tool of the British and the property owners who worked in league with them; corruption in high places had disgraced national honor in Palestine, the Suez, and the Sudan.

On July 23, 1952, the unrest reached its climax. A military *coup d'état* suddenly overthrew the venal Wafd regime. Under the titular leadership of General Mohammed Naguib, a veteran of the Palestine war, the new junta of young officers immediately set about making a clean sweep of the symbols of the past. King Farouk was compelled to abdicate and flee the country. On June 18, 1953, Egypt was declared a republic. The titles of pasha and bey were abolished. The constitution was abrogated, and all political parties were suspended. Naguib, now prime minister, served notice that Egypt had embarked upon a new era of governmental reform, social improvements, and "national self-fulfillment."

The pronunciamento was not entirely empty rhetoric. Naguib was an able man, and his intentions were honest. Nor were his accomplishments unimpressive. The government summarily imprisoned wartime profiteers and perennial baksheesh takers. Feudal landlords were severely restricted in their opportunities for further land purchases. Indeed, many of the largest feudal estates were confiscated outright, and the funds realized from them applied to ambitious programs of public health and education. The tax rate of foreign-owned businesses was raised, too, although hardly enough to cause serious concern among the European minorities. Many of these measures were justified and long past due. By and large, the Italian, Greek, and Jewish communities shared the prevailing conviction that the new administration was a blessing for the country. In discussing the matter over cocktails at the Gezira Country Club, Levi defended this view: "A part payment now is better than bankruptcy later," he insisted. "You know what happens when the 'street' gets out of control. Naguib has stopped all that. And at least he's not beating the Palestine issue to death."

That much was true. Occasionally the government loosed a cliché-ridden broadside against the "Zionist bandits in Palestine." From time to time editorials in the nation's press renewed the promise to "right the wrong committed against our Arab brothers." But the diatribes were routine propaganda, and served primarily to maintain Egypt's membership in good standing in the Arab League. For the most part the subject of Palestine was ignored. Naguib was uninterested in provoking chauvinism. He made it clear, too, that Egypt's European communities could expect complete protection as long as they remained loyal and law-abiding inhabitants of the country. Egypt's Jewry had nothing to fear, Naguib added, provided they severed all ties with "international Zionism." Then, to prove his good will, the prime minister went so far as to pay a personal visit to old Rabbi Nahum on the eve of the Jewish New Year.

Unhappily, Naguib himself was out of date. The junta which had brought him to power possessed ambitions far transcending those of mere domestic reform. On April 18, 1954, the revolutionary committee suddenly evicted the genial premier from his office, on the charge that he had become a "tool of the Communists and the Moslem Brotherhood." Colonel Gamal Abd al-Nasser, who now succeeded Naguib as prime minister, was a personality of a very different type. Like his predecessor, Nasser was a veteran of the Palestine war; and like Naguib, he shared the revolutionary committee's determination to rid Egypt of corruption and economic oligarchism. The resemblance between the two men ended there, however. Nasser recognized that the entire Arab world from North Africa to Iraq was in flux, casting about for means to emancipate itself from the dead hand of political and economic colonialism. A clever leader, an imaginative and eloquent leader, might well succeed in exploiting this surging disaffection to carve out a Pan-Arabist empire for himself. Gamal Abd al-Nasser was convinced that he was such a man.

He began slowly, consolidating many of Naguib's innovations, tightening his own control over the government hierarchy, ruthlessly quashing the last remnants of the Moslem Brotherhood, on the one hand, and outlawing the Communist Party, on the other. By the summer of 1955 Nasser's grip on the country was secure. He now began making elaborate preparations to project his influence outward. Cautiously, but relentlessly, he set into motion a high-powered propaganda campaign, battering away by press and radio against Western "imperialism" in the Arab world. British control of the Suez Canal was one of his first targets. Israel was another. So, too, by indirection, was the European "monopoly" of Arab economic life. By government edict, Arabic was now recognized as the only official language in the schools, courts, and cotton and stock exchanges. As Nasser issued this fiat, a chill ran through Egypt's Greek, French, and Italian minority communities. They sensed what was coming. The finance ministry had already begun to block their access to the national markets.

Of all Egypt's minorities, none had reason to fear the new nationalism more than the Jews. Even as Nasser set about training and equipping his "Palestine liberation" forces, he made it clear that he regarded Egypt's Jewish community as a fifth column, potential agents of the Zionist cause. In the winter of 1954, only five months after Nasser's accession to power, a "cold pogrom" was launched against the country's forty thousand remaining Jews. Jewish storekeepers found their shops boycotted. On thinly disguised legal fictions, Jewish importers were deprived of their licenses. Underwriting houses severed their connections with Jewish brokers in the stock and cotton exchanges. Eventually Jewish businessmen found it expedient to hire Egyptians as front men. With growing frequency now, mobs paraded through lower-middle-class Jewish neighborhoods, shouting protests at Jewish "treason," occasionally hurling rocks through house windows. The police rarely intervened.

Indeed, the police themselves were being systematically indoctrinated by experts in Jew-hatred. They were German. Nasser had surrounded himself with an entourage of former Nazi officers, and these were the men who held the executive positions in his "State Security Cadre," the Egyptian military junta's equivalent of an SS. Thus, the commander in chief of Egypt's State Security Cadre was Lieutenant Colonel "Al-Nacher," formerly SS Grossaktionsleiter Leopol Gleim, who had once served as commander in chief of Hitler's SD-Geheimgarde. The Secret State Police was the largest and most important department of the State Security Cadre, and was directed by one Lieutenant Colonel "Habid Suleiman," formerly SA Gruppenleiter Heinrich Sellmann, who at one time had been chief of the Gestapo district headquarters at Ulm, Bavaria. The political section of this department was under the direction of Lieutenant Colonel "Ben Salem," formerly SS Bannführer Bernard Bender, who, owing to his knowledge of Yiddish, had functioned during the war as chief of the Gestapo special branch for detection of Jewish underground movements in Poland and Russia. The State Security Cadre's propaganda department was directed by SS Gruppenleiter Moser, a Sudeten German who had since changed his name to "Hassan Suleiman." Moser's right-hand man was SS Gruppenleiter Bubler, now Arabized into "Amman." The executive positions in the propaganda section were entirely manned by Germans holding Egyptian passports. It was this bureau which now concentrated its efforts against "Zionists," employing the Goebbels-Streicher method of garish posters and leaflet literature depicting hook-nosed, bearded Jews.

By the summer of 1954, therefore, it had become quite clear to Egyptian Jewry, even to perennial optimists like Levi, that the likelihood of maintaining a respectable, orderly existence under the Nasser regime had vanished. The only possible solution now seemed to be emigration. Unfortunately, it was not a simple matter to leave the country. There were businesses and homes to be disposed of. The market for them had collapsed. There were savings to be transferred abroad. The government blocked that possibility. The few hundred Jews who each month set sail for France and Italy carried with them the barest residue of what had once been quite impressive fortunes. Those who remained behind—they were still the majority—searched desperately, but with increasing futility, for a more effective technique of salvaging the remnants of their businesses and careers.

Early in July, Levi was visited at his home by Dr. Musa Marzouk, house physician at Cairo's Jewish hospital. Marzouk was a slim, well-proportioned man, quite handsome except for a nervously twitching cheek. He was only slightly younger than Levi, twenty-nine, and the two had been friends since boyhood. Over coffee, the young men anxiously discussed the plight of their families. Neither of them doubted that emigration was the only solution for Jews of their station. The question was how, with the exits closing on all sides. Then, cautiously, Marzouk broached a plan. He knew a man, he said, who had found a way of extricating Jews with their savings almost intact. It was a question of baksheesh, and for that a special fund had to be created. He, Marzouk, had already taken up a collection, but if the authorities discovered the existence of the money they would confiscate it out of hand.

Thereupon Marzouk opened his doctor's bag and dropped a sheaf of English bank notes on the coffee table.

"There are two thousand English pounds sterling here," he said. "I want you to hold it for us until I notify you otherwise."

"Why me?" asked Levi in confusion.

"Because you are a banker. If anything happens you will know how to mingle it in your bank's accounts. No one will be the wiser."

After further discussion, Levi agreed. For the time being, however, he kept the money locked in his family safe at home. Three days later Marzouk visited him again. This time the doctor brought a friend, a non-descript man in his mid-thirties who was introduced simply as Wien.

"This chap is one of us," Marzouk assured Levi. "He must have three hundred pounds of the money to make certain necessary purchases."

Levi handed the sum over and the men departed. They did not return to his home again. Perhaps they preferred to stay out of sight until police vigilance relaxed. It happened that during the past week several unexplained incidents had thrown the government and press into a turmoil. Five small bombs had been discovered in the mailboxes of the United States Information Service and the British consulate libraries both in Cairo and Alexandria. Presumably the culprits were Egyptians, venting their spleen against the continued presence of British troops in Suez. A few weeks later, rags soaked in inflammable material had been found in Cairo's Radio Cinema during the showing of a British-American double feature. The episodes were highly embarrassing to the Nasser regime; the Egyptian government, even then negotiating with London for the withdrawal of Britain's Suez garrisons, was made to appear incapable of protecting British interests in the country.

Indeed, fearful of the conclusions the West would draw, Nasser instantly ordered a massive crackdown on all known criminal and "antisocial" elements. Within a space of two weeks nearly twenty thousand men and women were rounded up and thrown into jails and makeshift concentration camps. Some of the prisoners were charged with smuggling and trafficking in narcotics; others with stealing telephone and telegraph wire. Nearly all of these, however, even the commonest felons, were carefully screened for possible connections with the recent bomb outrages. The police were not altogether inefficient. A watchmaker talked. Under "persuasion," a pharmacist talked. The information was meager, but it suggested dramatic political possibilities.

One afternoon late in July, Pascal Levi returned home from the bank. As he emerged from his garage, two waiting detectives seized him, hurled him roughly into a waiting automobile, and drove off toward the center of town. There Levi was clapped into Abbasiya military prison. For two days he remained in solitary confinement. Faint with terror, he implored the guard to notify his wife of his arrest—but he was ignored. On the third day an army officer and a detective entered Levi's cell and began to interrogate him.

"Do you know Philip Natanson?" asked the officer.

"Who?" said Levi.

The detective kicked him in the groin. When Levi recovered he was seated on his stool, and the interrogation continued. From their questions, he pieced together the circumstances of his arrest. Philip Natanson was a Jewish chemist. Evidently he had been discovered near the Radio Cinema with a "smoking bomb" in his possession. Upon arrest and questioning, Natanson had "confessed" his membership in a Zionist spy ring. Furthermore, he had implicated other members of his gang. There were fourteen in all. Levi was alleged to have been one of them.

"What have you to say to that, Jew Effendi?" snapped the officer.

The room whirled before Levi's eyes. "But this is absurd," he gasped.

"Where did you get seventeen hundred English pounds sterling?" asked the officer. When Levi stared at him, unbelievingly, the detective chimed in: "We opened your safe. We'll open you, too, unless we get the facts quickly."

Melting with fear, Levi immediately related the circumstances of his meeting with Marzouk, and later with the stranger, Wien. "It was just a providence fund to help innocent people leave the country," he whispered piteously. "We thought you would be glad to get rid of us."

The detective sighed, looked at his watch, then signaled to the guard. As the two men opened the door of the cell, the officer gazed contemptuously at Levi's quivering, gelatinous body. "We're going to hack all that fat off you, Levi Effendi, until we get every piece of information."

Levi raised his hand like a schoolboy. "Can I have a lawyer?" he pleaded.

The detective laughed. "Here are your lawyers," he said, waving to a quartet of military police who now entered. Then the two men left.

The military policemen pinioned Levi to the floor. With rubber truncheons they proceeded to flail the prisoner's chest and abdomen. "Going to speak?" they asked, between intervals of beating.

"Speak? What do I know?" Levi shrieked.

After a few minutes of this, the guards left, muttering in disgust. Levi crawled toward his straw mattress and collapsed.

The next morning a military doctor entered the cell, examined the prisoner to ensure that his body bore no telltale scars or bruises, then left without a word. Late in the afternoon the military police returned. Spreadeagling Levi on the floor once more, they repeated the beating. "I know nothing," Levi sobbed. "I am not a spy."

The ordeal was repeated each day. And each day the doctor examined Levi. The weeks passed. The prisoner lost weight steadily. By October he was a shambling ruin of a man.

On November 30, Levi was visited by a short, fat Egyptian in his mid-fifties.

"I am Ahmed Rushdi," the visitor said. "The court has appointed me as the defense counsel for the accused. Tell me everything you can. I will try to help you."

Levi began to weep. *"Now* you want to help me. I've been here four months. You could have come earlier."

"Sorry, my dear fellow," murmured the lawyer sympathetically. "I was only appointed yesterday. Don't worry, though. We've still got a fighting chance."

"What about my wife and children?" cried Levi. "Do they know what happened to me? Are they taken care of?"

"Everything's taken care of," Ahmed Rushdi assured him. "Your family was informed of your arrest the very next day. No one has bothered them. They are well. What about you?"

"They've tortured me."

"Have you confessed anything?"

Levi repeated what he knew, and what he had said. The lawyer clucked: "You can even repudiate that at the trial. We shall say that you were ill-treated. Do you know anything else?"

"Nothing, nothing, nothing."

Ahmed Rushdi arose, and handed the prisoner an envelope. "These are newspaper clippings. They will give you an idea of what the government has decided to make out of this case." He shook hands with Levi. "I shall try to help you," he promised again. Then he left, five minutes after he had entered.

Levi opened the envelope. The first clipping was dated October 17, and carried an official announcement by the minister of the interior, Colonel Zakharia Moheiddin. Thirteen Jews had been arrested as members of a large-scale Zionist spy ring. The prisoners had been interrogated for forty-three days. Several of the accused had attempted suicide, including one woman, Victorine Nino, who was seriously injured when she jumped out of a window. Colonel Moheiddin stated that the aims of the spy organization were: first, to assist Israel undercover agents in Egypt by supplying them with funds and jobs; second, to maintain contact with Israel by means of radio; third, to gather military, political, and economic information on Egypt; fourth, to organize disturbances contrived to sow confusion, promote a state of uncertainty in the country, and poison the political atmosphere against Egypt in the international arena.

In a later clipping, Moheiddin declared that the alleged spy ring had become active at the very period when an Anglo-Egyptian agreement was about to be concluded for the evacuation of Britain's Suez Canal base. Evidently Israel had organized the spy organization to launch subversive acts —thus demonstrating a state of instability in the country and worsening the relations between Egypt on the one hand and Britain and the United States on the other. The public prosecutor, General Hafez Sabek, alleged that the leader of the group, "Ibram" (i.e., Abram) Dar, alias John Darling, was an Israel army officer. The other members were residents of Egypt. They included:

Musa Lieto Marzouk, doctor of the Jewish Hospital

Samuel Bakhour Mazar, teacher

Victor Moses Levi, broker

Victorine Nino, alias Marcelle, a woman employed by a group of English-owned textile firms

Max Bennett, employed by the Anglo-Egyptian Motors Company

Paul Franck, employment unknown—and, like Dar, to be tried *in absentia*

Yusuf Zaafaran, insurance clerk

Philip Herman Natanson, aide of the firm of Elie Curiel

Robert Nissim Dassa, commercial clerk

Elie Jacob Naim, employed by the commercial firm of Schwartz in Cairo

Mayer Samuel Miogass, salesman of Alexandria

Cesar Yusuf Cohen, employed by Barclay's Bank

Pascal Nissim Levi, employed by Barclay's Bank central office

The entire "plot" had come to light, said the article, when Natanson was arrested with an incendiary bomb actually smoldering in his pocket. The government would demand the maximum penalties.

Levi read and reread the clippings. He felt strangely relieved. At least he knew now what the government had concocted against him; he was no longer in a vacuum. Of course the accusations must have been spurious. Bombs, incendiary material, secret radio transmitters—it was an insult to one's intelligence! The Cairo Jewish community was a close-knit one, and Levi knew most of the defendants quite well. They were all people of his station. Each of the accused was thoroughly and unshakably respectable. Even his friend Marzouk would have been the last to indulge in adventurous spy missions. Indeed, Levi recalled that it had required all the doctor's courage merely to solicit money for the emigration fund. If the prisoners had admitted their guilt, as the clippings stated, Levi could well imagine the circumstances. His ribs and abdomen throbbed with the memories of his own "confession." He anticipated further police persuasion.

Yet the day following the lawyer's visit, the beatings suddenly stopped. The food, too, improved markedly. Evidently the government wanted its Jews in presentable condition by the opening of the trial. Other prisoners were not as fortunate. From near-by cells, blood-curdling screams reverberated around the jail compound. The victims were members of the Moslem Brotherhood, and they were being systematically tortured to death by the guards. Once, on his way to the dispensary, Levi caught a glimpse of the man in the neighboring cell, a knot-boned wretch, curled on his pallet like a dying foetus. Only the face was still intact, and there was no mistaking it: the prisoner was Fuad Secaggedinne, formerly minister of the interior in the moribund Wafd government.

On December 15, Levi and the rest of the Jewish captives were transferred to the civilian prison near Cairo's Grand Union Station. Conditions here were far better. Levi had a bed to sleep on (he learned later that his family had paid for this privilege). The guards were correct. In fact, the time had come for the trial to begin. At noon of the same day a tailor entered, carrying the suit Levi had worn at the time of his arrest. Of course it was far too large now; but a few clever tucks, clips, and safety pins eliminated the slackness. Only the shirt suggested what the prisoner had endured. It was at least two sizes too large. Yet, in spite of his earlier beatings, Levi was in better condition than the other accused.

He saw them for the first time that same morning. Gaunt, pallid, and limping, they were loaded in a van and carried to the military court in Gouvernoral, a public building on Bab al-Khalk Circle. There they were hustled into the dock, and seated together on two benches. A platoon of dusky Egyptian police hulked large over them, carrying rifles slung over their shoulders, wearing great brass-buckled belts, high cloth collars, and fezzes, and exuding a sickly-sweet odor which soon permeated the entire courtroom. Among the prisoners, Marzouk was only a wraith of his former self, his face cadaverous behind a thick, unkempt mustache. Natanson sat like a statue, thin, erect, eyes bright with terror in his peaked, boyish European countenance. Max Bennett, an elegant, well-dressed Ashkenazic Jew, prematurely bald, nestled his chin against his chest and stared dispiritedly at the floor. The woman, Victorine Nino, still moderately attractive in a severe black dress, glared tensely at the photographers who flashed their light bulbs in her face. The others slumped in their seats like collapsed paper bags.

The three judges sat behind a massive, wooden curving tribunal. They were all in officers' uniforms. The chairman of the presidium, General Mohammed al-Digwi, was a balding, gravely handsome man; with his closely clipped mustache and immaculately groomed uniform, he seemed the personification of the British military tradition. Precisely at 9:30 A.M. al-Digwi announced that the trial had begun. After the co-judges and the counsel were sworn in, defense attorney Ahmed Rushdi arose to register a protest:

"Your Honors, may I respectfully point out that I was assigned responsibility for this case only two weeks ago. That is hardly enough time to prepare an adequate defense."

"You will be able to study the case during its hearings," General al-Digwi blandly assured the lawyer. "We will allow you to call a witness for the defense even if he is in Alexandria. The tribunal is at the disposal of Maître Rushdi."

"Thank you, Effendim," murmured Rushdi, and sat down.

Then the state prosecutor, Fakhri Abd al-Nabi, arose to present his argument. In a lengthy address, he informed the court that Israel, on behalf of international Zionism, was plotting to "destroy" Egypt; and to that end the Jewish State had sent into Egyptian territory one of its officers—i.e., Ibram Dar, alias John Darling—"to form a den of residents in the land to serve the cause of Israel." Repeating the detailed charges against the prisoners, the prosecutor thereupon insisted that, under Article 78 of the Penal Law, the accused were guilty of collaboration with Ibram Dar. Article 78, a sword of Damocles hanging over the head of every opponent of the Nasser regime, stipulated that anyone conspiring or communicating with a foreign state, or its agents, with intentions hostile to Egypt, or "with the object of facilitating an aggression" against Egypt, "will be punished by death whether the sought purpose was achieved or not achieved."

During the next few days al-Nabi elaborated upon his original charges. During the years 1951, 1952, 1953, and 1954, he declared, the accused engaged in criminal activity within the jurisdictions of Cairo and Alexandria. Ibram Dar was the brains behind the plot, directed by the Israel Intelligence. The ring he organized—the defendants—had as its goal the acquisition of secret information on Egyptian military plans and installations. Presumably the ultimate purpose of the plot was an attack upon Egypt. The spy group's secondary aim, however, was sabotage within Egypt, not excluding the disruption of Egypt's relations with England at a delicate phase of Anglo-Egyptian negotiations. Thus, Dar set up a laboratory for manufacturing explosives. Marzouk, Mazar, Victor Levi, Nino, Bennett, and Franck were declared to have participated in these activities. Dar's principal local agent was Marzouk. Mazar was his deputy in Alexandria, together with Victor Levi. Nino, Bennett, and Franck were members of the secretariat, charged with financing the operation, as were all the rest, from Natanson to Pascal Levi.

The prosecutor continued. When the incendiary materials were ready, the prisoners placed bombs in the Alexandria post office, in the United States Information Offices in Cairo and Alexandria, in the cinemas Rivoli and Radio, and in the buildings of the Grand Union Station in Cairo. The mere fact that the bombs failed to explode did not vitiate the crime, declared the prosecutor, which of itself surely justified the death penalty for all the defendants. But, he added, associated violations of the penal code were no less serious, and no less deserving of capital punishment. Natanson and Dassa had actually been sent to Israel for their training. The former, a photographic specialist, had been instructed in chemical techniques of bomb making. Upon his return to Egypt he transformed his apartment into a chemical laboratory. Victor Levi and Naim helped him.

Moreover, Victor Levi himself was said to have studied in Israel, specializing in radio and "geography." On his return to Alexandria, he assembled a radio transmitter in Mazar's apartment with materials supplied by Marzouk. For this purpose the group obtained two hundred pounds from Max Bennett. Mayer Miogass supplied another five hundred pounds for the installation of an explosives laboratory. Victorine Nino, alias Marcell, was the avowed liaison agent for the spy ring and Israel. In her jail "confession," she admitted having received from abroad one thousand pounds which she divided equally between the Cairo and Alexandria branches. She was also the direct liaison with Ibram Dar. As for Max Bennett, he had served in 1948 as a major in the Israel army, and was sent to Egypt by Dar himself. It was he who transmitted and received all the messages and mail between Egypt and Israel. Bennett, in fact, had also "confessed" working for Israel and Zionist agents in Italy and Iran. He, therefore, was the first to have met with Dar in Cologne. Finally, concluded the prosecutor (somewhat anticlimactically), the defendants had gathered a wide variety of information prejudicial to Egypt and had disseminated it throughout the world.

The detailed accusations created a sensation in the packed courtroom, and in the later press reports. So, too, did the "confessions" produced by the state attorney. In spite of this initial advantage, however, the prosecutor's cross-examination of the defendants did not move smoothly at first. Several of the prisoners repudiated their confessions. One of these was the dark-haired young Jewess, Victorine Nino. Unruffled on the witness stand, she flatly denied admitting that the organization's purpose was espionage for Israel. "Whatever I said before has no value," she stated quietly. "They maltreated me during the interrogation." This statement was ordered struck from the court record by General al-Digwi, president of the tribunal. Furious, the prosecutor bore down on her.

Prosecutor: "Do you know a person called John Darling (Ibram [Abram] Dar)?"

Nino: "I knew him in Egypt in 1951."

Prosecutor: "Hasn't he got a connection with Israel?"

Nino: "I don't know."

Prosecutor: "What is the reason for your acquaintance with John Darling?"

Nino: "I have nothing to say to this question."

President al-Digwi: "What do you mean you have 'nothing to say'?"

Nino: "It means that I don't want to reply to this question."

Al-Digwi: "Meaning, you know the answer, but you don't want to reply?"

Nino: (hesitating) "Yes."

Al-Digwi: "Why don't you want to reply to this question?"

Nino: "I just don't want to."

Prosecutor: "You admitted that he came to Egypt to work for the good of Israel."

Nino: "No."

Prosecutor: "What then is the reason for your acquaintance with him?"

Nino: "I have nothing to say to this question."

Al-Digwi: "Meaning, you know the answer, but do not want to reply?"

Nino: "I don't know the answer and I don't want to reply."

Prosecutor: "You have admitted, haven't you, that John Darling operated a group in order to serve Israel's interests in Egypt."

Nino: "I have nothing to say to this question."

Al-Digwi: "Meaning, you know the answer but you don't want to reply?"

Nino: "There is no answer and I know nothing."

And further interrogation produced nothing. The young woman remained firm. So, too, did Bennett. By the second week of the trial, however, the other defendants proved rather less intransigent on the witness stand. Confronted with the implacable hostility of the judges, who participated as actively in the cross-examination as the prosecution, several of the accused wilted visibly, throwing themselves on the mercy of the court. One of the first to crack was Musa Marzouk. Almost immediately after taking the oath, the young doctor willingly described his initial meeting with Ibram Dar, as far back as 1951. Dar's mission in Egypt, Marzouk insisted, was simply to form a club or union between Jews and Egyptians. Otherwise, he, Marzouk, would never have contemplated associating with an Israeli agent.

Here again, General al-Digwi initiated the cross-examination:

Al-Digwi: "Was there ill-feeling between the Jews and Egyptians?"

Marzouk: "I think yes."

Al-Digwi: "Very well, if it was your intention simply to form a club, why should your activities have been secret since it was for a good cause?"

Marzouk: "Dar told us that our mission must be kept secret, at least for a time."

Prosecutor: "Since you wanted to improve relations, why should your activities be secret? You have not answered the question."

Marzouk: "Indeed, I could not understand the reason for secrecy."

Prosecutor: "Why did each of the members of the group assume false names?"

Marzouk: "I did not understand this either but I thought this part of the secret plan."

Upon further cross-examination, the defendant admitted that he had met Dar in Paris, and that he had followed him later to Israel. There he had participated in an Israel army course in wireless operation, cartography, and cryptography. "But I never knew the reason behind it," Marzouk concluded, lamely.

Perhaps the most unimpressive performance was given by Pascal Levi himself. His turn came during the third week in December. As he took the stand, Levi saw his wife for the first time; she was sitting near the back of the room with her mother and brother. Amalia's eyes were swollen, but otherwise she looked well enough. Levi noted, too, with some relief, that she still wore her jewelry. Then, as he recited the oath (on the Torah), he decided instantly what he was going to say. With little coaching from the defense attorney, Levi used his opening statement to give the complete account of his meeting with Marzouk, and later with the man called Wien. The prosecutor wasted little time in attacking the story.

Prosecutor: "You say Marzouk gave you money for a providence fund. Why did he not keep it himself?"

Levi: "He said I could dispose of it better because I was in the banking field."

Prosecutor: "You knew this money was to be used to help smuggle Jews to Israel."

Levi: "No, Effendi. It never occurred to me that Israel would necessarily be their destination. I was told they were going to Europe."

Al-Digwi: "Why then did the money have to be hidden? We have never blocked emigration to European countries."

Levi: "Indeed, I could not understand the reason at the time. I never had any intention of breaking the law."

Al-Digwi: "You did not suspect that this so-called Wien might have been an Israel agent?"

Levi: "Indeed, Effendi, how would I know that?"

Al-Digwi (sharply): "You are not to question the court. Answer me."

Levi: "I knew nothing. I certainly had no idea that bombs or incendiary material would be purchased with the funds. I would never have made trouble for this country. I was born here. Egypt has been good to me. I still had my job. I would never knowingly have aided Israel. I never wanted to have anything to do with Israel. I did not want to make trouble. I love my country."

Prosecutor (contemptuously): "Sit down."

Levi: "Effendi, I would do nothing against Egypt."

Al-Digwi: "The accused will sit down immediately."

Levi's breakdown accurately reflected the nerve-shattered state of nearly all the defendants. On December 21, the morning before he was scheduled to testify, the urbane, apparently unshakable Max Bennett decided on another way out. Guards found him on the floor of his cell, his wrists slashed, and beside his lifeless body a letter to his wife, begging forgiveness. News of Bennett's suicide was the *coup de grâce* as far as the other prisoners were concerned. By the end of the month each was vying with the others in compliancy; they insisted to the court that their only purpose was to foster a Jewish-Egyptian friendship league; that they resented their exploitation by Israel agents; that it was the Israelis, not they, who (for all they knew) may have assembled radios, bombs, and other explosive devices.

Yet the state's attorney, with the active and vocal help of the judges themselves, maintained the pace of his attack. The trial was proving an incomparable opportunity to divine a monstrous Zionist plot against the nation, and, too, to solidify national support for the revolutionary government. The prosecution was not likely to forfeit its chance. Neither was the state press and radio, which each day described the courtroom proceedings in an ominous and inflammatory tone, conjuring up hair-raising visions of Jewish treachery and Israel cunning. Nor was the accusation of guilt limited to the hapless prisoners. The entire Jewish population of the country was now branded as a fifth column, undeserving of the "hospitality" of the Egyptian people.

Across the Sinai border, in Israel itself, these reports were followed with mounting trepidation and dread. It appeared quite obvious even to the most credulous observer that Cairo was using the hapless defendants to make political capital. Speaking in the Knesset in late December, 1954,

Prime Minister Moshe Sharett voiced his profound indignation, stigmatizing the Egyptian court proceedings as a "show trial," and the accusations of Israel espionage as "blatantly libelous." Editorials in Israel's leading newspapers speculated that Nasser, by proving his ability to deal with "Zionist intrigue," anticipated consolidating his influence not only in Egypt proper, but also in the Arab League. Meanwhile, in Israel's larger cities, crowds of outraged Egyptian-Jewish immigrants demonstrated in front of the American and British consulates, pleading for the Great Powers to intercede with the Cairo regime; for if thirteen Jews could be dragged before a military tribunal on such farfetched charges, what assurance was there that the remaining forty thousand of their kinsmen would not be imprisoned—and perhaps worse—at any moment? Film clips of these demonstrations were later shown on television and in newsreels in the Western nations. Editorials appeared in the press of France, England, and the United States, decrying Nasser's "Byzantinism," and urging him to treat the prisoners with justice. With varying degrees of success, the leading Jewish organizations in these countries appealed for action by their own governments. In Cairo proper, the American ambassador, Jefferson Caffery, secured Nasser's personal assurance that whatever the verdict the death penalty would not be imposed.

The decision of the court was not long in coming. The prisoners had been examined and cross-examined. The defendants had no longer demurred, but rather had pleaded their ignorance of the organization's true purpose. In the hands of the prosecution, the spy plot had been amplified into a vast international cabal, with headquarters in Israel. Now, at last, convinced that the case had been milked for its last ounce of publicity, the State Attorney ended his presentation, and the military judges retired to consider their verdict.

The officers returned ten days later. All the defendants were pronounced guilty. But since the prosecution had not leveled identical charges against each of the accused, the tribunal was left with discretion in the sentences. These, too, were issued, on January 29, 1955. Standing before the packed, silent courtroom, General al-Digwi announced the decision of the panel. It became clear, moreover, as the sentences were read in pairs, that they had probably been decided even before the trial had begun. "Ibram" Dar, alias John Darling, and Paul Franck were condemned to death—*in absentia*. Musa Marzouk and Samuel Mazar were sentenced to death by hanging (neither man flinched upon learning his fate). Victor Levi and Philip Natanson received life sentences; Victorine Nino and Robert Dassa, fifteen years at hard labor; Mayer Miogass and Yusuf Zaafaran, seven years at hard labor.

"Pascal Nissim Levi!"

The prisoner approached the tribunal. Al-Digwi gazed at him sternly, then spoke: "You have been found guilty of associating with agents of an enemy power, and of being an accomplice before the fact in their sabotage activities." Levi closed his eyes. The sentences had been descending in severity, and his was near the end; but he braced himself now for a minimum of five years. "This court has decided to spare you," al-Digwi continued, "on the assumption that you were probably an unwitting accomplice." And presumably on the assumption, too, that an occasional prisoner spared would attest to the quality of mercy in Egyptian justice.

Levi slowly opened his eyes. "Thank you, Effendim," he murmured, and walked out of the dock on rubber legs. Behind him he heard al-Digwi extend similar pardons to Elie Naim and Cesar Cohen.

As Levi entered the aisle, moving carefully toward his sobbing wife and brother-in-law, he heard a familiar voice behind him say, quietly: "Mabruk —Congratulations."

He turned, and stared for a moment at Musa Marzouk. Levi began to answer, but instead collapsed in a dead faint.

Two days later, despite the urgent intercession of the Western ambassadors, Marzouk and Mazar were hanged. A day of mourning was declared in Israel.

Pascal Levi spent the next week and a half recuperating at his home. He said nothing to his wife of what he had endured. She did not ask, but rather sat beside him night and day, alternately weeping and kissing his hands. At last he felt strong enough to venture out. There was no point in delaying the issue any longer; he had to find out if his job at the bank was still awaiting him.

As he maneuvered his Citroën through the downtown area, Levi fastened his eyes greedily on the familiar, comforting sights of his beloved Cairo: on the shops, the traffic islands with their superb overhanging palm fronds. He watched the pedestrians surge past: dusky fellahin and porters in their brown felt skullcaps and *gallabiyas,* striped skirts billowing over their buffalo-hide shoes; and the Westernized ones (the majority now) in their business suits and shiny patent-leather boots. Once Levi had dismissed them all, fellah and Levantine alike, as a malleable, shapeless mob, the "street" who needed the minorities to do their thinking for them. That era was gone—forever, he suspected. As the people of Cairo eddied by his cruising automobile, he watched them carefully, his face strained with fear and respect. That mud-colored rabble, they ran the country now. He stayed on by their sufferance.

He hesitated a long moment before entering the bank. Through the glass doors he could look straight across the marble foyer to the assistant director's office. Samuel Abarbanel used to sit there. Probably not any longer. Taking a deep breath, Levi walked through the entrance. In an instant every teller, cashier, and accountant fell silent, staring curiously at the reprieved prisoner who had once been their superior. Consciously ignoring their glances, Levi strode quickly to the paneled oak door at the end of the hall. He knocked, and then entered. Seated behind the desk was Subkhi ibn al-Arasa, once chief clerk of savings accounts, and an occasional guest in Levi's home.

"Come in, Monsieur Levi," he said cordially, standing and extending his hand. "I'm so glad you are back safely. Are you well? You've lost weight. Never mind, you'll be your old self again soon. You needn't rush back to work, you know. Your office is waiting, whenever you feel up to it."

Weakly, Levi pressed his forehead against al-Arasa's hand. Then, wiping his eyes with his handkerchief, he entered his office and returned to work.

He performed his duties with his old competence. He received his former salary. Wearing a fixed, glazed smile, he even carried on the same small talk with his fellow employees. In the evenings he and his wife visited with friends at Gezira, or at home. For a while, indeed, Levi persuaded himself that somehow life might be carried on as before, even if within narrower limits, and exercising restraint and caution.

His optimism was misplaced. Nasser made the point clear when he consummated his weapons transaction with the Soviet Bloc, in the summer of 1955. Egypt was now a nation of twenty-five million, the mightiest power in the Near East, declared the Egyptian dictator; the time had come for its voice to be listened to with respect. To the roaring accolades of his worshipful population, Nasser set about exerting his new-won strength: on the Suez Canal, which he sequestered outright; on Algeria, transshipping guns to the grateful insurgent armies there; on Syria and Jordan, subsidizing the politicians who promised to fulfill his vision of a Pan-Arabist empire under Egyptian domination; and, not least of all, on Israel, which he harassed continually with terrorist infiltrators, and which, by spoken and written word, he openly marked for destruction.

Even while completing his military preparations, the Egyptian ruler shrewdly allowed his people a safety valve for their awakened xenophobia. With official encouragement, businessmen now dropped their last Jewish employees. The press campaign against the "Zionist conspiracy"—i.e., local Jewish treason—reached new levels of virulence. Jews were openly cursed on the street. One day, in the early autumn of 1956, Ibrahim, Levi's house servant of the last twelve years, suddenly informed his employer that he was leaving.

"I do not work for dogs," he declared solemnly. "From now on the dogs work for us."

Levi remarked despairingly to his wife later: "It's a simple matter for them. If they leave, they move up. Ibrahim wouldn't walk out—'dogs or no dogs'—unless he had something better. Well, he does. Nissim Asoula was squeezed out of his garage concession yesterday for 'tax delinquency.' Ibrahim has the car washer's job. When it happens to me Abd al-Rahman Bastoni will step right up from the cashier's booth into my office. I don't blame the poor beggars."

They were surely not to be blamed. The forced "retirement" of Jews allowed Egyptians to move into supervisory positions for the first time, into the management of shops, and into lower level executive jobs in banks, insurance companies, and import-export firms. If tension with Israel was the excuse for driving the Jews out, then so much the better; let the state of war continue.

But the state of war worked both ways. On the night of October 29 the lights of Cairo were suddenly extinguished. In the streets all traffic was halted. By next morning the news had circulated through the city that severe fighting was taking place against Israel. Convulsed with excitement, the citizenry grasped wildly for clues or rumors of what was happening. The papers and radio reported "immense victories" over Jewish troops in Sinai—nothing more. Those who understood foreign languages received a rather fuller and more accurate version. During the next few days BBC and Radio Monte Carlo provided a complete and detailed account of Israel's pulverizing victory in the Sinai desert. And in the weeks that followed, demobilized soldiers and deserters began straggling back into the city; they told their own story of what had happened. The Jews had built tunnels under Egyptian army camps, the returning troops declared, then had sprung out of the ground. The Egyptian officers had deserted their men; those who had been captured were subjected to the final ignominy of imprisonment under the guard of Israel women soldiers.

The demoralization of Nasser's army was surpassed only by that of Egyptian Jewry. They sensed now that their time had come. On the twentieth day after the Sinai debacle Levi entered his office at the bank to find Subkhi ibn al-Arasa awaiting him. The assistant director was quite pale.

"Levi, my dear," he said, "your name has just appeared on the *Official Gazette*. They've confiscated all your securities here. I beg you to clear out quickly, for the sake of your wife and children."

Levi had been expecting this. "I shall go now," he promised. He was calm.

But he had no sooner begun clearing the drawers of his desk before three policemen entered. "You will come with us," said the sergeant. They walked out into the street, Levi between them. As they proceeded on foot toward the Cozzika police station, the sergeant quietly reviled the arrested man: "If you speak a word, Jew, I'll put a bullet into you. Dung heap, viper, mother raper, son of a bitch. You won't get off this time."

At the station Levi was ordered to stand with his face to the wall. He heard the sergeant phone the ministry of the interior and ask for Colonel Miniawy, chief of the anti-Zionist section. "I have Levi," said the policeman. "I await your orders."

When the answer came, Levi's final ordeal began. He was transferred by electric train to the Khazindra internment camp on the other side of town, then locked in a room with eighteen other Jews, all "political suspects." There he remained for two months. During the entire period he was not permitted to bathe. The food was worse than his original prison fare. Once he was allowed to receive a package of cheeses from his wife—who had evidently bribed one of the prison officials. Each day Levi gazed bleakly out the window. This surely must be the end, he told himself; there is little more that they can do to me.

He was right, as it turned out. On the sixty-second day of his internment, Levi and his fellow prisoners were transferred to the central railroad station. Surrounded by more than a hundred policemen, the nineteen Jews were marched into the train, handcuffed two-by-two. Three hours later they arrived in Alexandria, where another detachment of police vans was waiting. The prisoners were immediately carted off to Korneldick prison. There they were jammed together in one tiny, windowless cell. Four days after that the guards ordered the Jews to dress; they were about to leave Egypt. Levi was frantic. What of Amalia and the children, he wondered? How shall I leave without them?

But that matter, too, had been arranged. The family was waiting at the port.

"What's happened?" he shouted out to Amalia across the wire customs fence. "Are you coming along?" He noted with dismay that she was not wearing her jewelry.

"It's all taken care of," she cried back. "We have tickets. We're sailing together."

So, too, were nine hundred other Jews crowded together at dock-side. The government had ensured that they would pay for their own exile. Nearly all their possessions and savings had been sequestered. Levi and his family took with them three suitcases of clothes, 350 Egyptian pounds, and nothing else. Throughout the country, other Jews were undergoing the same ordeal. A mass migration had begun, voluntary in name only, as thousands of jobless, distraught Jewish families were allowed to "pay" for passage to Europe by the simple expedient of leaving behind everything they owned. Within the next two months nearly 25,000 Jews managed in this fashion to depart from the country. They were the fortunate ones. The 17,000 others who remained behind would not have another chance. Destitution, the forced closure of nearly all their community institutions, systematic terrorization soon followed. It was small consolation that not long afterward this fate was shared by Egypt's other minority communities.

On board the Egyptian steamer *Misr,* Levi was left with five days to make some hard decisions before reaching Naples. The Italian authorities would permit stateless passengers only one week in the country. After that what alternatives were there? He thought of Canada and the United States, then dismissed the idea. There were immigration quotas there—and in any case, he could not afford the passage. France? The country was in the throes of political upheaval; no place for a Jew under such circumstances. Very well, where then? He thought of Israel, of course. But curiously enough, years of Egyptian propaganda, the endless newspaper and radio accounts of starvation and discrimination in the Jewish State, had left their impact. Of course he knew that the story was deliberately biased. But—even so—might there not be a hard kernel of truth in it? Levi had always been a Zionist in principle. Yet the mere thought of living in an impoverished, arid, little Spartan nation, of working with his hands, possibly even of facing conscription as a common soldier—repelled and terrified him. He was thirty-six; it was not the age to begin pioneering.

The decision was made for him, however, and against his better judgment. Disembarking at Naples, the boatload of Jewish refugees found buses awaiting them, chartered by the Jewish Agency. From the harbor the newcomers were transported to the Hotel Bella Vista, a modest accommodation on Piazza Garibaldi—also chartered by the Jewish Agency. The food was good. So was the medical care provided by Agency doctors. Amalia was in tears.

"I want the children raised among people like these," she said. "They have stood by us."

"Yes," he smiled sourly, "they've helped us here. Here they have time for us. In Israel it would be a different story. Do you think we're the only people they have to worry about there?"

Amalia's face became set. "Pascal, I won't have our children raised among strangers," she warned. "We don't need a country club any more. We need safety. Whatever happens, these people are our people. At least *they* will never turn against us."

Levi sighed. "Anyway, it doesn't look as if we have much of a choice, does it," he said.

On the third day after their arrival in Naples, he was interviewed by a representative of the Association of Egyptian Immigrants in Israel. The man assured Levi that the Association would find him a job.

"You know, I was a banker," Levi interjected eagerly. "I have a great deal of experience in finance."

"Well, we can't promise you an executive position in a bank, you understand," the representative said. "But we've been rather successful so far in taking care of our people. Between us and the Agency we'll find you something."

"Something? What does that mean, monsieur? Forgive me, but I'm not a ditch digger, you know. After all, I'm not a Moroccan. I'm a European." Then he paused, noting the scowl on the man's face. Perhaps he had gone too far. The events of the last two years had badly eroded his self-confidence. "Please don't feel that I'm a special problem," Levi continued, this time deferentially. "I don't want to be any trouble, you understand?"

The representative smiled slowly and knowingly, and patted him on the shoulder. "Try not to be frightened any more, Monsieur Levi," he said. "In Israel Jews are not considered trouble."

The Egyptian refugees were received compassionately and resourcefully. No Israeli needed reminder of what these people had endured since Nasser assumed office. The carefully manipulated chauvinism, the boycotts, and expropriations had gained momentum from the first week of Nasser's incumbency; the Cairo spy trial and the Sinai campaign had served merely as the ultimate guarantee of future exodus. The Jewish Agency and Israel government had prepared for it—and now it had come, a new wave of exiles for the ingathering. However painful the motivating circumstances, the State was as grateful for the infusion of new citizens as the refugees themselves were to find sanctuary. The Israel economy was already strained to the limit, yet homes and jobs were somehow provided for the newcomers. The past was forgotten. A new world was in the making.

As the years went by, however, there remained one Israeli who persisted in casting backward glances, who would not allow himself to forget the details of a crucial episode in the Egyptian disaster; for the Cairo spy trial had profoundly affected his career. His name was Pinhas Lavon, and he was secretary-general of the Histadrut, the powerful Israel Federation of Labor.

A slim, handsome, white-haired man in his mid-fifties, Lavon had come to Palestine from his native Poland as a young man, and had worked his way up through labor politics to a position of eminence in the Mapai Party. As early as 1953 he was widely recognized as one of the three or four most influential members of the Party's central committee.

It was in that year that David Ben-Gurion stepped down from his joint responsibilities as chief of government and minister of defense, and retired to the desert kibbutz of Sdeh Boker for a long period of study and rest. Moshe Sharett now became prime minister. Lavon, who had been serving for some time as minister without portfolio, took over the defense ministry. It was not an appointment which was greeted with enthusiasm by the army. Unlike Ben-Gurion, who had been deeply involved in Haganah matters for years, Lavon was new to defense problems. He himself possessed almost no personal military experience; indeed, until 1948 he had been widely regarded as a "nonactivist," a disciple of the moderate Chaim Weizmann. Thus, when Lavon assumed his new duties, the general staff was compelled to start almost from the beginning in an attempt to initiate him in the complex problems of defending a small and poor country against almost insuperable odds.

Those were particularly difficult times. The British were even then completing arrangements to remove their garrisons from the Suez Canal Zone. *Fedayin* were killing Israel civilians in their sleep. The United Nations Truce Supervision officers were generally unsympathetic to Israel, for they had been angered by Jewish retaliation raids. To make matters worse, the Israel government was unable to find a single major power willing to sell it weapons. Yet in spite of these grave and mounting dangers, the new minister of defense seemed anxious to cut his own apprenticeship period short. He often took decisions without consulting the experienced soldiers who dealt with security problems on a daily and professional basis. Vain, short-tempered, unable to brook the slightest opposition from subordinates, Lavon soon began suspecting intrigue everywhere about him. Perhaps his suspicions were not altogether unjustified. The ministry's director-general Shimon Peres, made no secret of his resentment at losing his earlier freedom of action: Ben-Gurion had allowed him to operate the ministry virtually on his own. By the summer of 1954, in fact, Lavon and Peres were no longer on speaking terms, and all communication between the two was carried on in writing. Lavon's relations with the rest of the staff soon deteriorated badly. He further exacerbated this friction now by proposing the establishment of a security council, half of whose members would be civilians. The council presumably would function as high command in peacetime. At one point in these proposals, Moshe Dayan, the chief of staff, submitted his resignation. His colleagues persuaded him to withdraw it only after an impassioned appeal.

This was the situation when, in July of 1954, the "Zionist spy ring" in Egypt allegedly was discovered. The arrest of thirteen Jews on charges of plotting for Israel was of course ideal grist for Nasser's propaganda mills— and, by the same token, a catastrophe for Egyptian Jewry. Unknown to the citizens of Israel, however (and probably as well to the Nasser government), the Cairo spy trial was a crushing blow to the reputation of the Israel Intelligence apparatus. For within Israel's general staff, it was generally assumed that the captives in Abbasiya prison had indeed been in communication with Israel agents; their arrest by the Egyptian police, and their forced confessions of membership in a "Zionist spy ring," apparently added up to a grave indictment of mismanagement in the Israel defense ministry. It seemed clear that Pinhas Lavon could not avoid final responsibility for the disaster. Pressure began to mount for his resignation.

But Lavon himself had other ideas on the matter. He was convinced that the spy trial, far from being an indictment of him personally, served rather as convincing proof of the army's determination to sabotage his influence in the ministry. Thus, approaching Prime Minister Sharett directly, he demanded a secret commission of inquiry to investigate the facts behind the Cairo debacle. Sharett agreed, and on December 28, 1954, appointed a two-man committee, consisting of Yitzhak Olshan, justice of the supreme court, and Ya'akov Dori, president of the Haifa Technion (Institute of Technology), and formerly chief of staff of the Israel armed forces; both were men of unimpeachable integrity. Lavon was the first to appear before them. Although there is no authentic version of the defense minister's testimony, it is assumed that he provided historical background of the "incident."

Shortly after Nasser assumed the dictatorship of Egypt, in 1954, but during the period when the British still remained in their Suez garrisons, a committee in the intelligence division of the Israel defense ministry ostensibly worked out a plan to induce the British to stay on in Egypt. The alleged purpose of the scheme (also never authenticated) was to devise fake anti-British and anti-American incidents in Egypt, thus making it plain to the West that the Nasser regime could not be trusted to protect Western military and naval bases in his country. Presumably London would thereupon reject any further Egyptian demands for withdrawal of British forces in the Suez; and the British would stay on, a restraining influence on Egyptian military adventures in the Near East. Lavon, so the account went, approved the idea, and in February he reactivated an intelligence unit for work in Egypt proper. Breaking with precedent, however, Lavon insisted that the unit should not remain under the joint control of army and civilian intelligence; rather the defense ministry alone would determine its operations. At this suggestion the civilian Intelligence authorities protested vigorously. Intelligence and sabotage should never be mixed, they warned; saboteurs must be hirelings, for if they were caught they could not then jeopardize the larger Intelligence network. Lavon rejected the argument—fatally, as it turned out. To him, efficiency seemed to dictate unilateral control.

According to plan, in May 1954 Colonel Alexander Harari,* chief of army Intelligence, sent his deputy off to Europe to make final arrangements for the plan. The deputy, Major Motke Ben-Tsur, thereupon personally transmitted the orders to the person charged with reorganizing the Intelligence-

---

* At the request of the Israel ministry of defense, the author has agreed to withhold this man's true name.

sabotage team in Europe. The latter was Mordecai Wienman,* a part-time civilian employee of Israel army Intelligence, and a perennial adventurer with a rather unsavory record of dealing in confiscated Arab land. Whatever his personal background, Wienman possessed the connections and the burglar's nerve required for the mission. And yet the operation, as Ben-Tsur described it to Wienman (and as Lavon was said to have related it before the committee), far exceeded the mandate contemplated by the minister of defense.

Wienman was ordered to recruit his agents in Egypt. The most important of these was the Israel army officer Avram Dar, a light-skinned, English-speaking Yemenite Jew who operated under the alias of John Darling. Together, these men would arrange for the dispatch of bombs to United States Information Service and British consulate libraries in Alexandria and Cairo. Presumably the bombs—significantly bearing Egyptian markings—would not go off, and the finger of suspicion would point inevitably to Egyptian nationalists. In July it evidently all happened that way. As Lavon explained it, however, Wienman went further. Following Ben-Tsur's instructions, he arranged for a bomb to be thrown in a crowded cinema during the showing of British and American films. It was the misfire of this bomb which resulted in Natanson's arrest—and the eventual round-up of the entire Zionist undercover group. In his testimony before the Olshan-Dori committee, Lavon insisted that he was blameless for this fiasco: at no time had he given orders for any action so drastic and brutal as the detonation of a bomb in a cinema. He expressed outrage that such instructions could have been given behind his back.

The committee members were not notably impressed by this argument. Why, they asked, had Lavon not reacted at once upon learning that bombs had been placed in the mailboxes of the American and British libraries? Hereupon the minister of defense replied that he had considered these acts to be of a mild, indeed, a preliminary nature. Then precisely for this reason, the committee replied, and whether Lavon had ordered the cinema bombing or not, should he not have known that a much more serious deed might well follow the mail bombs? Why did the minister of defense overrule civilian Intelligence on control of the operation if he had not anticipated a major act of sabotage against the Nasser government? And why had he not requested this inquiry in July or August, immediately after the arrest in Egypt of the implicated Jews? Here Lavon stated that he had no way of anticipating Ben-Tsur's orders to Wienman; efficiency dictated unilateral control. Moreover, he had felt it best to postpone the inquiry until the Cairo spy trial had ended. Most of the Jewish defendants were entirely innocent of the charges against them, Lavon pointed out, and the rest certainly had not intended to commit violence of any sort. The defense minister's concern for the Jewish prisoners was his weakest argument. The trial was in fact still continuing.

Under oath of secrecy, other principals in the "mishap" testified before the Olshan-Dori committee. One of these was Colonel Harari, chief of Intelligence. In direct contradiction of Lavon, Harari insisted that he had taken no action without the direct knowledge and approval of the minister of defense himself. Indeed, Lavon had personally ordered him to initiate the proceedings in Egypt; the command had in fact been issued in Lavon's home, at a meeting attended by Shimon Peres, director-general of the ministry of defense, as well as by the deputy chief of staff, and other high army officers. At this point Harari submitted in evidence a copy of a letter he himself had later written to General Moshe Dayan, the chief of staff, who was absent from the country at the time of the Cairo debacle, and who, from abroad, had requested a full report. In this letter, Harari stated that the Egyptian undertaking had been carried out "according to the orders of the minister of defense." Wienman, also appearing now before Olshan and Dori, indicated that it was his understanding, too, that the entire idea had been Lavon's. When asked if he had been coached on his testimony by Harari, or Ben-Tsur, or other members of the intelligence section, Wienman assured the committee that he had not.

By now the committee members were convinced that neither the defense minister nor his subordinates had satisfactorily explained Lavon's role in the affair. Thus, in their official report, they declared themselves at a loss to decide where the responsibility lay. The report satisfied no one, least of all Lavon. Even so, the minister of defense might have allowed the matter to rest there had it not been for one witness who testified during the course of the hearings. This was Shimon Peres, director-general of the ministry. Peres had not been personally involved in the mishap himself, and, accordingly, it seemed clear that he was being asked to testify on the general state of affairs within the defense ministry and the armed forces—and in particular on the relations between the minister and his staff. At any rate, that is what Lavon assumed.

At this point, therefore, Lavon asked Prime Minister Sharett for permission to examine the minutes of Peres' evidence. Sharett flatly refused. Immediately the defense minister concluded that the director-general's testimony must have contained defamatory statements against him. Furious at what he considered his subordinate's disloyalty, Lavon insisted upon Peres' prompt dismissal, as well as the removal of Harari and Ben-Tsur. Sharett was unable to comply. And with good reason. The prime minister had in his hands a "nonpartisan" report issued by Yosef Sprinzak, Speaker of the Knesset, which stated that morale in the armed forces had declined ominously under Lavon's tenure in the defense ministry; his continuation in office might well have drastic consequences for the security of the country. Under these circumstances, Sharett decided that the furthest he dared go was to transfer Harari and Ben-Tsur to other branches of the army. Peres would remain. The moment the prime minister made known this decision, Lavon, outraged and humiliated, offered his resignation. To his complete surprise the offer was accepted. Hereupon Sharett issued an urgent appeal to Ben-Gurion to return to Jerusalem; and in February, 1955, the "old man" rejoined the government as minister of defense (eight months later he assumed the prime ministry, as well).

None of these hearings was made public. Indeed, the failure of the alleged espionage mission in Egypt remained a classified secret, known only to a small number of men in the top echelons of government. Moreover, the circumstances of the defense minister's resignation were by no means fatal to his career. The members of the Mapai Central Committee were fully cognizant of Lavon's unusual intellectual and administrative abilities. After several months of hesitation and deliberation, they eventually offered him the extremely influential position of secretary-general of the Histadrut, which he accepted.

In his new role as chief of the powerful labor federation, Lavon embarked upon a vigorous and imaginative program of reforms within the Histadrut. With typical aggressiveness, he proceeded to challenge some of the most powerful entrenched interests in the country, including the directorship of Solel Boneh, the wealthy contracting and building division of Histadrut. As usual, he made enemies, and was frequently bitterly criticized, both within and outside the labor federation and the Mapai Party. But even his most implacable foes respected him. Few of them ever imagined that he was vulnerable to attack for a failure in his earlier career, that his resignation from the ministry of defense had been other than voluntary.

But Lavon remembered, and brooded. As the years passed he watched helplessly as the most prized ministries in the government faded beyond his reach. It became increasingly evident that Ben-Gurion was grooming a number of younger protégés as his successors, and they were precisely the men whom Lavon had reason to remember with bitterness. One of them, Moshe Dayan, formerly chief of staff of the army and now—in his mid-forties—minister of agriculture, seemed a leading candidate for the prime ministry. The other, Shimon Peres, also in his early forties and now deputy minister of defense, appeared the logical choice ultimately to succeed Ben-Gurion as defense minister. Unlike Lavon, who represented the older "pioneer era" of the Third *Aliyah*—the East European immigration wave of the early 1920s—both Dayan and Peres were members of the "second generation" of political leadership. Both had been raised and educated in Israel. They seemed symbolic of the younger group which included nearly all the top officers in the army, the leading technical experts in most of the government ministries, in the Jewish Agency, and in the Mapai Party itself.

Yet the conflict was more than one of generations. It was no less a struggle to control the philosophy and character of the government following Ben-Gurion's eventual retirement. In large measure, the new group associated itself with the transformation of pre-State voluntary institutions into "official" government agencies. The army was an example of this kind of change. It was founded in 1948 on the base established by the Haganah and other clandestine, voluntary self-defense cadres. In 1948 these former underground units, including the leftist Palmach and the rightist Irgun Zvai Leumi, were dissolved. Since then the army had become professional and nonpolitical, its recruits supplied by national conscription. The revision of the school systems was another example. In the pre-State period schools were financed and staffed by the *Yishuv*'s major political parties—Labor (left), or "general" (right). or religious. Between 1952 and 1954, however, the schools were de-politicalized and placed directly under the supervision of the government. Finally, in 1959, the labor exchanges, formerly maintained by the unions themselves, were also taken over by the State. In every instance, the transformation proved logical and successful.

Yet one great bloc of pre-State institutions still remained untouched—and apparently untouchable. These were socialized medicine, many forms of social security, subsidized cultural activities, and bus transportation. The Histadrut controlled them all. Moreover, by maintaining its grip on nearly every labor union (in what has remained essentially a laboring country), Histadrut was able to exert a powerful, indeed, perhaps the most powerful influence on the economy of the entire nation. Here lay the seeds of a new conflict. The government, increasingly staffed by young, university-trained experts, favored a policy of strong austerity. The ministry of finance and the Bank of Israel urged that the standard of living be frozen to permit the shift of all available resources to export industries, absorption of immigrants, and development of the Negev. The veteran leadership of Histadrut opposed this; Lavon and his colleagues favored a rising standard of living for all working men. The government pressed for the separation of the wage level from the rising price index; the Histadrut successfully blocked this move. Important groups close to Ben-Gurion argued for wider salary and wage differentials to increase the incentives for professionals and skilled workers. The Histadrut, true to its old socialist ideology, vigorously opposed the idea.

Temporarily frustrated on issues of economic policy, the government nevertheless insisted that at the least the duplication of welfare functions ought to be ended. Kupat Holim, for example, the elaborate Histadrut network of clinics and hospitals which provided health coverage for two thirds of Israel's citizens—this surely belonged within the purview of the government. Ben-Gurion raised the issue with increasing frequency. So, too, did Dayan, Peres, and the younger members of the prime minister's circle. Possessing few if any personal attachments to the Histadrut, the members of the "second generation" were not overly concerned about the traditions, the vested interests, or the cherished loyalties and ideologies of the monolithic old labor federation. They were determined to pattern Israel's society on the needs of the 1960s, not of the 1920s or 1930s.

Actually, Lavon and his associates were by no means blind to the needs of the time. They had frequently demonstrated restraint and economic good sense in the wage raises they had sought for their constituents. Between 1955 and 1959 the secretary-general had himself introduced major changes into the structure of the Histadrut. These included the decentralization of Solel Boneh, the professionalization of staff, and new controls over the bus co-operatives. As a loyal member of the Mapai Executive, Lavon had thus far made a reasonable effort to preserve party unity. But he drew the line on the issue of health insurance. So far as Lavon could determine, Kupat Holim, with its incalculable medical advantages, was by far the Histadrut's most powerful inducement for membership. Once the health network was transferred to the government, the labor federation would remain only a hollow shell of its former self. So, too, would Lavon. It did not escape the secretary-general that the transfer to the government of this crucial public welfare instrument would decisively curtail his public leverage. The triumph of the "Dayan-Peres crowd" would then be complete.

In April of 1960 a crucial piece of information unexpectedly provided Lavon with a new lease on his political future. A young intelligence officer, Yosef Harel, happened to be examining the minutes of the 1954–1955 Olshan-Dori hearings, when he noticed two incongruities in Colonel Harari's testimony. He called them to Lavon's attention. Instantly the secretary-general recognized the significance of what Harel had found. The former chief of the Intelligence bureau had declared that Lavon himself had issued the order for the alleged cinema bombing at a meeting in his, Lavon's, home. Yet the meeting had in fact taken place a full week *after* the failure of the intelligence mission. There was something else: the copy of Harari's letter to General Dayan, containing the phrase "according to the orders of the minister of defense." The original of the letter, which Dayan had brought back with him, was now in the files—and did not contain this vital clause. Evidently the phrase which appeared in the copy, and which had been presented to the Olshan-Dori committee, was a forgery.

The following month, at a routine labor policy meeting with Ben-Gurion at the latter's home, Lavon drew the prime minister aside and revealed the new evidence to him. In the light of this information, Lavon pointed out, surely the time had come for him to be exonerated completely for the Egyptian debacle. Ben-Gurion was impressed, and promised to investigate the matter immediately. Lavon was temporarily mollified. He departed for Zurich a few days later to convalesce from a recurrent nervous disorder. Shortly afterward, true to his word, the prime minister appointed a committee of inquiry under the chairmanship of Chaim Cohen, a justice of the supreme court. Lavon, meanwhile, was kept well apprised of developments at home by his faithful aide and public-relations specialist, Levi-Yitzhak HaYerushalmi.

Because the matter under investigation represented a security issue of the highest importance, Cohen and his associates conducted the hearings in their alternate roles as army reserve officers. Shortly after the proceedings began, however, the Cohen committee found itself considering other evidence no less vital than the revelations supplied by Yosef Harel. In fact, the prime minister's awareness of the new material probably accounted for his willingness to grant Lavon an immediate investigation. A half-year earlier, in November of 1959, Mordecai Wienman—the Intelligence bureau's former European contact man—had been put on trial in the Jerusalem district court. The charge, which was heard *in camera*, was treason. Apparently Wienman had been a double-agent, escaping detention in Egypt by betraying his comrades there. During his testimony before the district court, Wienman had warned that he would not go down alone. By way of keeping his promise, he revealed that he had committed perjury before the Olshan-Dori committee. He had declared, in 1955, that he had not been coached by his superiors. But in fact he had. Upon his arrival from Europe, he had been met at Lydda airport by an emissary of Ben-Tsur, Harari's deputy. The emissary had provided Wienman with a detailed account of the hearings, and had advised him how to testify—against Lavon, of course. At that time Wienman had followed instructions. Now, in Jerusalem, facing a sentence of twelve years in prison (he was convicted), he was taking his revenge.

The evidence of this perjury was a bombshell. Upon first hearing of it, Ben-Gurion was said to have been shocked speechless. Although the Cohen committee conducted its investigation in the strictest privacy, confirmation of this earlier disclosure somehow managed to reach Levi-Yitzhak HaYerushalmi, and he promptly relayed it to Lavon. One may imagine the secretary-general's reaction. His day of revenge, too, was near at hand. In September, 1960, Lavon finally returned to Israel. At the airport he announced to the friends and reporters who greeted him that he would shortly have an important announcement to make. It was supposed that Lavon was referring to the simmering issue of government versus Histadrut control of Kupat Holim, and that he was once again about to resume his endemic feud with the prime minister.

Lavon had the prime minister on his mind, all right; but Kupat Holim was hardly the matter he wanted to resolve with him. Two days after returning home, Lavon's wife "leaked" the information of the Cohen committee investigation to *Ma'ariv*, the widely read afternoon newspaper. This, in turn, was followed by a press release, in which Lavon himself hinted darkly that he had been "framed" years earlier for political reasons. The following day, the secretary-general and Ben-Gurion finally met.

"I told you I wouldn't take this lying down," said Lavon. "You have all the evidence you need to give me a full exoneration immediately. I have every right to it. I've been living under a cloud long enough."

"Of course you have every right," agreed Ben-Gurion, not without embarrassment. "All I'm asking you to do is wait till the Cohen committee issues its report. Then it will be final and official."

Lavon was not placated by this reply. The hearings had been taking too long. Besides, he did not trust Cohen's objectivity. Returning home, he consulted with HaYerushalmi, and the two decided upon a new course of action. It was to demand a special meeting with the Knesset foreign affairs and security committee. Already mystified and titillated by the "leak" to *Ma'ariv*, the committee willingly agreed.

For several weeks afterward a dramatic series of hearings ensued. In specific detail now, Lavon elaborated to the committee precisely what had happened during the summer and autumn of 1955, and the manner in which he had been "slandered" and forced to resign from the government. He suggested, too, that he had been "framed" because his subordinates resented the loss of freedom they had enjoyed in the days when Ben-Gurion, serving jointly as prime minister and minister of defense, had left them to conduct the affairs of the ministry on their own. Although the hearings before this committee were ostensibly in executive session, extracts of each day's testimony somehow found their way into the daily press. Derogatory accounts of Lavon's period of office as minister of defense—inspired, he insisted, by officials of the ministry—also began to appear in the newspapers. Lavon himself issued almost daily press releases, striking back at every aspersion, real or imaginary.

The public was in a state of complete confusion. After all, the events of the espionage operation and its subsequent consequences, both in Egypt and Israel, were still top secret. Now, too, in 1960, the government censor carefully edited all newspaper reports. No reference was permitted (nor is it to this day in Israel) to the alleged underground mission in Egypt, to the disaster that followed. Names of the implicated parties, people like Harari, Wienman, Ben-Tsur, were never mentioned. All that could be revealed was the vague information that in 1955 an "unfortunate mishap" had occurred in the defense ministry, that Lavon had been blamed for it, that there had been hearings, that the minister had resigned under uncertain circumstances; that now, five years later, new evidence had suddenly come to light which Lavon was resolved to exploit; and that a major schism was opening between distinguished officials of the government and the Mapai Party. Yet even these scraps and smidgens of information were enough to create a growing feeling of public unrest. Had the reputation of an innocent man been besmirched for political reasons? Was Lavon another Dreyfus? How could these things have happened in a democracy, anyway?

Alarmed and embarrassed by the acrimonious controversy now developing publicly among its most respected leaders, the executive committee of the Mapai Party, too, recognized that urgent steps would have to be taken to settle the matter instantly and discreetly. In fact, for a moment the possibility of a settlement appeared encouraging. In October of 1960, Levi Eshkol, minister of finance, returned from a mission abroad. Eshkol was one of the government's and the Party's most respected figures. He had not been involved in the dispute on one side or another. He had hardly stepped off the plane, therefore, before he was asked to mediate the "Affair." To the relief of the Mapai central committee, he agreed.

Eshkol's task was made simpler by the Cohen committee, which at this point completed its hearings and issued its eagerly awaited report. Not surprisingly, the report concluded that a high-ranking officer still in active service, and another in the reserves, had suborned one of the crucial witnesses in the 1955 hearings to commit perjury. The report stated, however, that in view of the unofficial nature of the Olshan-Dori committee, and the long period of time that had since elapsed, no prosecution could now be initiated. Nor could the question be discussed of who had given the fatal order in 1954. Nevertheless, enough was known to make it clear that much of the crucial evidence submitted before Olshan and Dori could no longer be considered valid.

With this report in hand, Eshkol immediately paid a visit to Moshe Sharett, the former prime minister. Together the two men devised a compromise formula which appeared certain to resolve the imbroglio. In mid-October Sharett issued a public statement, declaring that if he had known in 1955 of the evidence now disclosed, he would have regarded it as a "weighty confirmation" of Lavon's version of the facts, although he would still have accepted the defense minister's resignation rather than agree to the dismissal of Peres. With this statement, both Lavon and his rivals, especially Dayan and Peres, would presumably be placated. And after some delay, Lavon did eventually issue a press release, declaring himself satisfied with Sharett's statement as far as the "slur on his personal integrity was concerned." With these concessions from both sides, the "Lavon Affair" apparently had come to an end.

But it was not to be that simple. Prime Minister Ben-Gurion had thus far remained in the background, unwilling to become involved personally in a dispute which was not of his making. Sharett's report infuriated him, however. The "old man" viewed it as nothing less than a slander against his beloved army. For one thing, it seemed intolerable to the prime minister that a martyr should be made of a man like Lavon, who was far from untainted by what had happened in 1954; who, in Ben-Gurion's view, had seriously undermined the efficiency and morale of the armed forces during his tenure as minister of defense. Most important, Lavon represented the Mapai "old guard." If he were now permitted to appear as the innocent victim of a sinister army intrigue, he might conceivably make enough capital of his "martyrdom" to undermine Ben-Gurion's younger protégés— as well as the economic and political views they advocated. Accordingly, in a statement issued to the Knesset in the last week of October, the prime minister publicly repudiated the "so-called finality" both of the Cohen report and of the Sharett statement. He called instead for the establishment of a new commission, a legal commission, to re-evaluate the case.

The cabinet was taken completely off guard by Ben-Gurion's unexpected outburst. What did the "old man" have in mind, they wondered? Did he wish to keep the nation in a turmoil merely to satisfy a point of political vanity? Nevertheless, after several emergency meetings the ministers decided to provide Ben-Gurion with a "cooling off" period, by appointing a seven-man nonpartisan commission from among its own members. Under the chairmanship of minister of justice Pinhas Rosen, this group was charged with reviewing once again all the facts attendant upon the "Lavon Affair." The nominal excuse for this tiresome prolongation of the case was the exclusively military nature of the Cohen committee, and the fact that Cohen and his associates had not investigated Lavon's responsibility for the original security "mishap."

Yet the ministerial committee's findings were hardly likely to mollify the prime minister. On December 7, Attorney General Gideon Hausner was sent to Paris to interview Dahlia Carmeli, Colonel Alexander Harari's former secretary in the Intelligence department. There, the young woman declared in a sworn affidavit that the words, "according to the orders of the minister of defense," had in fact never appeared in the original letter to General Dayan. Rather, Harari had added the phrase to the copy of the letter he had presented to the Olshan-Dori committee. It was a damning revelation. Together with the evidence already accumulated by the Cohen committee, it climaxed Lavon's case. On December 21, the ministerial committee pronounced its unanimous decision: Lavon had not given the direct order for the 1954 security "mishap." With equal unanimity, the members of the committee firmly, and hopefully, declared the matter to be closed.

But once again the ministers had not reckoned with Ben-Gurion's brittle and pugnacious temper. Quite beside himself with anger, the old prime minister flatly refused to accept the report as conclusive. What kind of an inquiry was it, he charged, which could examine and cross-examine members of the army—and at the same time spare Lavon himself from cross-examination? Only a legal investigation could probe the evidence with true thoroughness and impartiality. Did Lavon oppose such an investigation? Little wonder. His career as minister of defense had been a disgrace. He had ruined the morale of the armed forces. His responsibility for the "mishap" was far greater than any of the so-called committees had yet established. Let there be a legal inquiry, and whatever its conclusions might be, he, Ben-Gurion, would accept them. But nothing else would suffice.

At first the Mapai secretariat resisted the prime minister's demand. The members of the Party's central committee were weary and embarrassed by the unseemly public controversy. Each day that the "Lavon Affair" remained the subject of public discussion, the Party suffered an additional loss of prestige; and so, for that matter, did Ben-Gurion himself. Yet, strongly supported in his stand by Dayan and Peres, the prime minister remained obdurate. There were moments, indeed, when the very mention of Lavon's name sent him into paroxysms of rage. When the rest of the Mapai central committee still hesitated, therefore, the "old man" decided to bring them into line by unloosing his most powerful weapon: he threatened to resign. The shock value of this warning was all the prime minister could have hoped. Few of his associates had ever imagined that he felt this deeply on the Lavon issue. Confronted with his stern ultimatum, however, the executive members of the Party immediately began conducting marathon emergency sessions. Delegations were sent to the prime minister, pleading with him to reconsider. They followed him to his office, to his home, then to his desert retreat at Sdeh Boker. These maneuvers were unavailing. As far as Ben-Gurion was concerned, the Party would now have to choose between him and Lavon.

And so, reluctantly, it did. Over the opposition of such Mapai stalwarts as Golda Meir, minister of foreign affairs, and Pinhas Sapir, minister of commerce and industry, the majority of the Party's central committee fell into line. So, too, did most of Mapai's rank-and-file membership. It is worth noting, however, that their reaction was not dictated exclusively by loyalty to the prime minister. For the past three months even Lavon's warmest sympathizers had become increasingly irritated by the secretary-general's behavior. Perhaps he had been wronged in 1955. Perhaps his sense of injustice was legitimate. Nevertheless, Lavon seemed to luxuriate in his "martyrdom." Had his first loyalty been to the Party, he presumably would have made his case "within the family." Indeed, had he followed this course originally, exoneration might well have taken place quietly, without recrimination, and without the necessity of airing the "mishap" to the country and to the rest of the world.

But that was not Lavon's way. From the very moment of his return from Europe he had launched a systematic campaign of abuse and vilification against his "secret enemies." Moreover, he had insisted upon doing so publicly. Advised each step of the way by the shrewd Levi-Yitzhak HaYerushalmi, the secretary-general had issued endless press releases, ventilating his grievances to the population at large. Rebuked and warned by his Mapai colleagues, he had nevertheless insisted on speaking out against "army careerists," against the "opportunistic cabal" sprouting within the prime minister's office. Nor did Lavon restrict himself to the "injustice" committed against him five years earlier. Interwoven in his charges were strenuous warnings against the impending peril of "étatism," of "thought-control," of the "myth of the indispensable man" (referring here, of course, to Ben-Gurion). By January of 1961, it had become quite apparent that the secretary-general was embarked upon a belligerent and violent drive to undermine the prime minister's leadership, and perhaps at last to wrest from him control of the machinery of the Mapai Party.

The plan misfired. Appalled at Lavon's recklessness, the most respected Party leaders now severed their ties with him. Even within the Histadrut, his own bailiwick, Lavon's support ebbed rapidly. Both inside the labor federation and the Mapai Party pressure mounted for a vote of censure against the secretary-general. When Lavon's friends sought to warn him privately, he rejected their appeals, at times launching into shrill and only partially coherent diatribes against the enemies "plotting" against him wherever he turned. Ultimately Lavon's irascible press campaign proved his undoing. On January 25 three respected and influential members of the Histadrut Executive submitted their resignations; they had lost confidence in Lavon, they declared, and were unable any longer to work with him. Thereupon the Mapai central committee called a special session to discuss the Party crisis. During the meeting, both the secretary-general and Ben-Gurion himself appeared—once sitting on the same rostrum simultaneously (they refused to shake hands). Lavon came off badly in the interchange. His manner was typically splenetic; his sense of self-restraint seemed altogether to have vanished. It was obvious by now even to Lavon's most ardent supporters that the secretary-general's political career was heading rapidly for an abrupt and inglorious end.

Yet the evident failure of Lavon's offensive proved nevertheless to be a pyrrhic victory for Ben-Gurion and his supporters. As early as January a committee of distinguished professors from the Hebrew University issued a public denunciation of the prime minister's "dictatorial" methods. They viewed his rejection of the ministerial committee report, his threat to resign, as a serious danger to the democratic processes of the State. This protest was widely publicized in the press, as was a similar petition released by the Association of Students of the Hebrew University.

Rather more ominous was the mounting opposition of Israel's political parties. The non-Mapai members of the cabinet, in continuous consultation with their party colleagues, now gave serious thought to the possibility of withdrawing from the Mapai-controlled coalition. The issue came to a head on January 30, when representatives of three coalition partners, Mapam, Achdut HaAvodah, and the Progressives, notified the Knesset that they were "supporting the present government because it had stood up against the prime minister's attempts to reverse its approval of the ministerial committee's findings." This curiously involuted statement was in effect a vote of confidence in a government without Ben-Gurion. The results of this "vote of confidence"—which was of course essentially a vote of nonconfidence—were dramatic. The very next day, January 31, the prime minister formally announced his resignation.

Not surprisingly, the announcement sent the leadership of the Mapai Party into a state of near-shock. What ailed the "old man" they wondered. In all his political career he had never before been this neurotically thin-skinned. At first, therefore, Ben-Gurion's associates remonstrated with him, urging him to reconsider. On February 4, the central committee went further, officially notifying Lavon of his dismissal as secretary-general of the Histadrut (a purely formal gesture, for Lavon's authority in the labor federation had already been hopelessly undermined). But by mid-February the matter was already out of the Mapai's hands. The other coalition parties made it plain that they would not rejoin the present government so long as Ben-Gurion remained the Mapai candidate for prime minister. For their part, of course, the Mapai leadership had no intention of substituting anyone else, however respected, as their leader. Weeks of protracted interparty negotiations and maneuvers followed. Every effort was exerted to avoid the expensive and time-consuming ordeal of national elections. Mapai had emerged from the national elections in 1959 with the largest plurality in its history; its members were loath to jeopardize that leadership only a year and a half later. Yet all efforts at compromise were unavailing. Even the personal intercession of President Ben-Zvi proved useless. On March 7 the government formally announced that new elections would take place the following August.

Campaigning began listlessly, gaining momentum only in the early weeks of the summer. The opposition parties obviously were determined to make capital out of the "Lavon Affair," viewing it as perhaps the ugliest political scandal to reach the national scene since the Kastner Case of 1953. Mapai had become corrupt, they argued; Ben-Gurion's continuation in office would surely represent a growing threat to Israel's youthful democracy. Yet as the months passed, it became clear to the opposition that they dared not count on the "Lavon Affair" alone to overthrow the Labor government. Classical party arguments would also have to be exhumed. Thus, the Liberals (a recent joinder of the General Zionists and the Progressives) warned of the stultifying effects of a socialist economy. Herut, the right-wing revisionist party, heartily echoed this sentiment, adding to the list of charges Ben-Gurion's alleged failures in the area of foreign policy. The left-wing Labor parties, Mapam and Achdut HaAvodah, flailed away at the ostensible decline of pioneering idealism under the Ben-Gurion regime. And the religious parties remained true to form: the nation was becoming godless, they warned: corruption and delinquency could only be attributed to a cynical desertion of the ideals of the Torah.

Few of these arguments set Israel's citizens to dancing in the streets. They had heard all the charges and countercharges before—indeed, less than two years before. Nor were they unaware of the accomplishments that Mapai claimed for its administration: quiet along the Arab borders, a rising standard of living, accelerated development of the Negev desert. Still, the "Lavon Affair" irritated, if it did not unsettle, the voting population. The nation may not have had access to the actual facts of the Intelligence debacle of 1954, but that was unimportant. Even if the ominous warnings of Mapai corruption, of Ben-Gurion dictatorship were not quite the dangers the opposition represented them to be, it was nevertheless apparent that the great Labor Party was unable to maintain peace in its own household. More important, the factious public brawling of Mapai's leaders represented a kind of affront to the private citizen: as if the prime minister and his colleagues assumed that whatever they decided for Israel was a matter of their own private discretion, and not of the electorate which had given them their mandate. Perhaps the administration ought to be taught a lesson.

So it was. The chastisement was mild, but nevertheless significant. When election results were tallied in late August, it became clear that the Mapai had suffered a noticeable setback: a loss of five seats in the Knesset, from forty-seven to forty-two. Most of the other parties maintained their status quo, with the exception of the Liberals, whose representation in the Knesset rose from fourteen to seventeen, and Achdut HaAvodah, which picked up one additional seat. Fully two months were to pass before a patchwork coalition could be formed. Ultimately, and to no one's very great surprise, Ben-Gurion stayed on as prime minister. Yet this time the "old man" was compelled to base his government on a much narrower partnership than formerly; for the Liberals and Mapam remained outside the coalition. Thus, operating on a smaller base, the prime minister would now find his freedom of action more seriously curtailed.

What then would the election results mean in foreign and domestic policy? No one could yet be sure. Yet one fact was already certain, and it was made unmistakably clear when the new Knesset passed, as one of its first laws, a statute henceforth placing the ministry of defense under the special supervision of a new committee for security affairs. This committee would be composed exclusively of civilians. The population of Israel had served notice that it would not permit unlimited discretion to its professional military staff—even on the issues vitally affecting the nation's defense. Israel's taut, efficient army was one of the proudest accomplishments of the Jewish democracy. But it was the latter, not the former, which was sacred. The nation had not forgotten what it was defending.

Pascal Levi found a job in Israel. He earned two hundred and forty pounds a month as a night clerk in a C-class hotel on Tel Aviv's HaYarkon

Street. It was hardly the kind of work he was accustomed to, of course; but it was the best the Association of Egyptian Immigrants could find for him on short notice. As it was, he fared better than most of the twenty-five thousand Jews who shared his exodus from Egypt, who found the banks and insurance companies of the Jewish State overstaffed, and who now were digging ditches and laying pipes in development areas. The Agency had supplied his family with a modest flat in the outlying community of Holon, a half-hour's bus ride from Tel Aviv. His daughters were enrolled in school and were rapidly learning to read and speak Hebrew. The family had made a few friends among the French-speaking Rumanians and Moroccans who were their neighbors. Amalia, suffering from high blood pressure, was given excellent medical care by the local Kupat Holim doctors. They were secure.

On winter nights Levi sat behind the desk in the unheated lobby, a scarf wrapped tightly around his neck, staring morosely out the windows at the waves lashing the beach.

"I don't like to complain," he remarked to the guest who offered him cigarettes. "I know I'm better off than the friends I left behind. My family and I are alive. We have a roof over our heads. We eat—barely. Israel is poor. It can't afford to give us much, but it shares what it has."

He thought for a moment. "Yet I'm not asking for the moon, you know," he added. "If I have a job in Tel Aviv it doesn't seem like much for the Agency to get me a flat in town, instead of making me spend nearly two hours commuting each day. We can't go out on the Sabbath, of course. The Orthodox won't let the buses run then, and there's nowhere we can go on foot. I'm not complaining, you understand," he repeated, staring anxiously at his visitor. "I know I'm better off than in an Egyptian prison. Still— why can't Cécile, my oldest girl, go to an English school? She was making such wonderful progress in English before we left. What harm can it do to let her become fluent in a language the whole world is using today? I tried to enroll her in an Anglican mission school in Jaffa, and the roof nearly fell in on me. The Agency called me in and put pressure on me to remove her. The man at the labor exchange heard about it and glared at me as if I were some sort of traitor. Why are they so chauvinistic here? Where I was raised we were taught to be worldly, sophisticated, to absorb the best things of many lands. Sometimes I wonder if Israel is better in this respect than Egypt today . . ."

His words trailed off, and he stared moodily again at the sea, at the lights of a Greek freighter glowing in the distance.

"That boat," he said at last, "it belongs to one of the biggest import-export firms in southern Europe. I used to handle all their foreign exchange in Cairo. Their agents had tea with me quite often. A couple of months ago I wrote the company. I asked if they needed an experienced commercial representative here who knew languages. They answered me—said they had someone already, but they might have a future opening for a man who is also fluent in Hebrew." He laughed harshly, a half-cough. "'Fluent in Hebrew,' at my age!

"Now and then I've thought about applying for immigration permits to the United States and Canada. But I suppose there's really no point in that. Seems they have waiting lists years long. What they're really saying, though, is that Jews aren't wanted. Sometimes I go to Jaffa in the early evenings, before my shift here starts. I sit and stare at the churches, sometimes for hours, and I think: how different everything would be if I were one of *them*, if my children took *their* communion. We would hear from the American embassy within weeks then, you could be sure. Of course I would never do anything so foolish," he added hastily, staring anxiously once again at his visitor. "I just sit and look. I know I am a Jew. There are worse places for Jews than Israel. I know it well. Whatever happens, my family and I are safe here. No one is knocking at our door in the middle of the night. I don't tremble any more when I see a policeman. I know I'm . . . home." He swallowed. "Home, it *is* home, I suppose. It's only . . . that you have to live in it—up to the hilt, so to speak. They don't let you stand aside from the things that happen. They make such a point of . . . of . . . being involved. Like this election going on. The way these parties keep after me, one would think that the entire fate of Israel hangs on my vote. It gets awfully wearing after a while. You understand me, monsieur?"

Levi sat back. His drawn brows gave him away. Had he said too much? he wondered. Had he appeared disloyal? For a long moment he paused. Then he spoke again: "In my own way I love this country, monsieur," he assured his listener. "I do my duty here. I wouldn't want you to think otherwise. I hope you don't think I'm criticizing. Just night thoughts, so to speak. Nothing I could do would ever bother anyone. I'm too small a man to give anyone concern." He sighed. "I don't want to cause any trouble."

CHAPTER NINE

THE PHYSICIAN

WESTERNERS who visit the Near East are invariably struck by the courtesy and hospitality of their Arab hosts. They are impressed, as well, by the exoticism of Arab diet and dress, by the grace and charm of Arab architecture. Yet long after visitors from the Occident have forgotten the beauty, they remember the squalor. They recall the hordes of naked children, picking in dung pits for scraps of garbage; the beggars, skittering like flies through public thoroughfares, clamoring for a moment's attention and pity; the gaunt, sallow faces of peasant families, nourishing their brood on flour paste, oil, and dried lentils, then gorging themselves like famished animals during the happy intervals of wedding and feast days. More even than the poverty, however, it is the evidence of disease which leaves an ineradicable scar on the impressionable Westerner. In Alexandria, Cairo, Damascus, Aleppo, in Bagdad, Basra, even in Beirut, the last romantic illusions are dispelled the moment one leaves the fashionable thoroughfares and strolls through the back streets. For here the great majority of the city's inhabitants lives, and here alarming numbers of people are sick. Frequently they are dangerously sick. Their coughs are rasping and hollow. They expectorate blood. Children are covered with pustulant sores. They limp. They gasp. At times they crawl by with twisted limbs. Eyes are fogged with trachoma, scalps infested with boils and ringworm, stomachs racked by dysentery.

Surveys conducted by the World Health Organization have concluded that disease is more than widespread in the Arab world. It gallops, it rages. In Egypt alone, in 1962, notwithstanding the Nasser government's considerable efforts in the field of public health, an estimated 6 to 11 per cent of the population were afflicted by such enteric diseases as typhoid, paratyphoid, and murine typhus. Fifty-two per cent suffered from viruses of the Coxsackie and ECHO varieties, from intestinal amebiasis, and from amebic hepatitis. An even larger number, often estimated as virtually the entire rural population, have at one time or another fallen victim to zoonoses and such pest-borne diseases as West Nile and relapsing fever. In Syria and Iraq, children suffer "Aleppo" and "Jericho" boils, ringworm, and

367

bilharziasis as casually as Western youngsters endure measles or chicken pox. Venereal disease is still the rule rather than the exception among the slum population of the port cities. Pestilence has been an accepted fact of life—and death—in the Near East for centuries, and so indeed it is today.

With the singular exception of Israel. Of course the population of the Jewish nation is heterogeneous. The medical histories of its people vary. The gulf is wide between the bronzed, muscular sabra, born and raised in the Mediterranean sun, in the physical security of the Zionist homeland, and the European refugee, still unrecovered from the trauma of Nazi concentration camps; between sparrow-limbed Yemenites, thousands of whom were felled by tuberculosis within months after arriving in Israel, and obese Moroccan housewives, their arteries slowly thickening with the cholesterol of oil-soaked Berber diets. Even wider is the gap between all the Jews—Europeans and Orientals—on the one hand and Israel's Arab minority on the other; among Arab village dwellers it is only now that the most elementary notions of hygiene are gaining general acceptance. Yet for all of these, the native-born, the crippled D.P., the former denizen of the fetid *mellah*, the Negev bedouin, Israel offers medical care not inferior to that provided by the most advanced Western nations.

For one thing, the more serious communicable diseases are usually stopped before they can begin. In the Jewish State preventive medicine is applied with a near-religious zeal. In every corner of the land laboratory technicians are testing water, studying insects, inspecting foods and plant fibers. Engineers are laying out sewage disposal systems in new settlement areas. Every possible breeding point for mosquitoes or rodents is assiduously drained and then sprayed with toxic compounds. Inspectors from the ministry of health investigate every bakery, every abattoir, every dairy. All bottled milk is pasteurized. X-ray stations are located in every population center, and each employee is required to have his chest photographed at least once every four years. Nothing is left to chance.

Nor are the curative services in any sense inferior to the preventive. This little State of 2,250,000 people boasts no less than 1,000 clinics, 100 hospitals, and 500 mother-and-child health centers. There are, in addition, some 5,000 doctors in Israel, thus providing the country with one doctor for each 420 inhabitants, by far the highest ratio of its kind in the world. Accordingly, Israel is free from the ravaging epidemics of its Arab neighbors. Malaria, typhus, typhoid, tuberculosis have been effectively stamped out. An elaborate network of medical facilities has kept the adult Jewish population in remarkably good health. The children, carefully supervised by school doctors and nurses, radiate vigor and energy. The nation's youth, most of them toughened by army service, are in demonstrably better physical condition than the great majority of American teen-agers. This is Israel, a Near Eastern country, the neighbor of peoples to whom no death is premature. Surrounded by disease and semi-invalidism, the Jewish Republic is quite obviously an outpost of more than democracy on the rim of Asia.

It was not always thus. During the first period of Zionist settlement, between 1881 and 1914, the Jewish inhabitants of Palestine suffered the identical physical torments of the Arabs. They, too, knew the fever-racked agony of malaria and typhoid, the torture of bilharziasis and trachoma. They sickened and died by the hundreds, went blind by the thousands. In the beginning, the medical facilities available to them were limited in Jerusalem to three badly understaffed Orthodox hospitals: the Rothschild and Bikur Holim hospitals in the Old City, and the Wallach (later She'are Tzedek) hospital in the New City. Elsewhere medical services were restricted to a handful of tiny Christian mission hospitals in Tiberias, Nazareth, Safed, and Jaffa—small comfort to Zionist families living far off in the Sharon or lower Galilee. In any case, Orthodox Jews feared death rather less Church doctors.

There were, at the same time, a small number of Jewish physicians who arrived in Palestine even before the turn of the century. Their efforts on behalf of the pioneer Zionist settlement fulfilled the most heroic traditions of frontier medicine. Prominent among them were Dr. Hillel Yoffe and Dr. Ya'akov David, distinguished malariologists whose field of battle was the Galilee and the Plain of Sharon; Dr. Helena Kagan, the first Jewish pediatrician of Jerusalem; Dr. Saul Tchernichowsky, who is remembered today as one of the most celebrated Hebrew poets of the Zionist renaissance, but whose patients recall him as a skilled and dedicated healer. There were others: Doctors Asherman, Avigdori, and Ticho, youngsters newly arrived from Europe who endured unimaginable hardships and dangers during their itinerant rounds of Baron Rothschild's PICA (Palestine Colonization Association) settlements. The physicians' severest ordeal, however, was neither wretched transportation, Arab bandits, nor even the plagues that laid them, as well as their patients, on their backs for weeks at a time. It was the absence of adequate facilities. Their "clinics" were wretched slate huts, their equipment pathetically inadequate even by Near Eastern standards. Water for instruments was carried from wells in jugs, and then boiled over an open hearth. Patients slept on straw mattresses on the floor.

It awaited the vision of an American Jewess, Henrietta Szold, for a serious effort to be launched to provide adquate medical care in Jewish Palestine. The daughter of a Baltimore rabbi, a resourceful educator, Henrietta Szold was the founder and animating spirit of Hadassah, the Women's Zionist Organization of America. It was she who persuaded Hadassah's members to make treatment of the ill their special concern. Under her guidance, Hadassah opened a district medical service in the Old City of Jerusalem in 1913. Three years later, during the blockade of World War I, Hadassah dispatched a special medical team to minister to Palestine's starved and disease-ridden Jewish population. Immediately following the armistice in November, 1918, moreover, Henrietta Szold's followers assumed the responsibility for the Rothschild Hospital in the New City of Jerusalem —and later embarked upon the construction of hospitals and mother-and-child health stations in most of the other larger cities in the country.

By then the American Zionist constituency had grown both in numbers and resources. During the comparative security of the Mandatory period, therefore, Hadassah managed to extend its activities by opening a fully equipped medical center on Mount Scopus outside Jerusalem, and by establishing scores of district clinics throughout Palestine. The government of Israel and various local authorities have since taken over these facilities. But even today, the major portion of medical care in Jerusalem and its surrounding villages is provided by Hadassah. The responsibility is a formidable one, for it embraces more than a quarter of a million people, and the population of the region is fast-growing. The care, too, is all-inclusive, offering preventive services for expectant mothers, for infants and school-children, as well as diagnostic and curative services for patients of all ages. Most important of all, this remarkable women's organization has constructed and maintains the superbly equipped Hebrew University-Hadassah Hospital, ministering to the inhabitants of the entire Jerusalem area.

Yet invaluable as the Hadassah contribution has been, it was the indigenous Jewish community of Palestine itself which ultimately made possible a standard of medical care unsurpassed elsewhere in the world. Health insurance was the key, and it developed quite naturally out of the egalitarian Labor-Zionist philosophy which has shaped nearly every phase of Jewish Palestine's political and economic life. Today 83 per cent of Israel's population are guaranteed full medical and surgical coverage as members of nation-wide voluntary health-insurance programs. Not surprisingly, by far the largest and most important of these programs is sponsored by Histadrut, Israel's all-powerful Federation of Labor. It is known as Kupat Holim (the Sick Fund), and its growth faithfully reflects the *Yishuv's* transformation from a disease-racked community, on the brink of semi-invalidism, into an astonishingly healthy and vital nation of farmers, workers, and soldiers.

The reasons for the universality of participation in Kupat Holim are not difficult to find. For one thing, membership is automatic the moment one joins the Histadrut. And in Socialist Israel 70 per cent of the population belong to the mighty labor federation. Moreover, in nearly all instances employers share equally the cost of their employees' coverage. Finally, membership fees to the Histadrut, and by indirection to Kupat Holim, are graded according to the worker's salary; if he earns less he pays less. Yet whatever the employee's contribution, his benefits match those of the wealthiest capitalist in the land. For the term "medical care" is interpreted in its widest meaning. It includes treatment by a physician either in clinics or at home; full hospitalization in institutions belonging to Kupat Holim, or, when necessary, in government, municipal, or Hadassah hospitals; free medicines in the pharmacies and dispensaries of Kupat Holim, as well as artificial limbs, hearing aids, and other mechanical devices; convalescent care, payment for sick leave, mother-and-child preventive health service, medical treatment in case of accidents at work; and, finally, care of the chronically ill.

While Kupat Holim deals with every aspect of medicine, its work revolves primarily around the outpatients' service, provided through more than a thousand clinics in all parts of Israel. The country is divided into a number of regions, each served by a main regional clinic equipped with specialized services (laboratories, X-ray stations, pharmacies, physio-therapy institutes, mother-and-child welfare stations) and linked to the regional hospital of the same district. The general practitioner in each clinic thus can rely on an integrated system of specialized modern facilities and services to which he can refer patients whenever necessary. Moreover, Kupat Holim doctors, clinics, and hospitals have been carefully located even in the remotest rural and development areas—in striking contrast not only to the early days of pioneer settlement in Palestine, but also to medical services in other lands where rural communities have been notoriously un-cared for.

Most significantly, in Israel the lower middle class has not been the victim of crippling medical and hospital expenses. Whenever local services are not adequate—for example, in the event of rare diseases or experimental surgery—Kupat Holim will spare no expense either to import foreign specialists for consultation and treatment, or even to send the patient abroad. All for the price of the six or seven pounds the Israeli pays monthly for his health insurance. These rates are low for everyone. No patient need ever view an impending operation as a mortgage on his economic future.

Of course, extensive and modestly priced as the health program is, medical care in Israel is ultimately only as good as the doctors who administer it. Most of them are very good indeed. The time has long since passed when a good doctor—any doctor—was worth his weight in gold, when dedicated pioneer physicians like Hillel Yoffe, Ya'akov David, or Helena Kagan were greeted as near-Messiahs by their patients. During the 1920s several hundred physicians arrived with the third and fourth immigration waves from Eastern Europe. And during the Hitler epoch in the 1930s over two thousand superbly trained doctors arrived as refugees from Germany, Austria, and Czechoslovakia. By the eve of the Second World War, in fact, the Jewish community of Palestine actually found itself over-supplied with medical practitioners. Several hundred immigrant doctors were now compelled to abandon their profession and earn their livelihoods as laborers, kibbutz members, or bus drivers. (A not entirely apocryphal anecdote was told in that period of the passenger who fainted during a bus ride. Im-mediately a score of fellow passengers rushed to his side, each proclaiming, "I am a doctor." "But I, too, am a doctor," insisted the driver, stopping the bus and hurrying to the stricken man. Whereupon the unfortunate patient opened his eyes and announced somewhat impatiently: "Stop crowding me. I'm a doctor and I'll take care of myself.")

It was the sheer surplus of foreign-trained physicians which accounted, in 1939, for the decision of Hadassah and the Hebrew University to limit the curriculum of their new teaching hospital to postgraduate studies. There was no need, after all, to add to the surplus of practitioners. Not until ten years later, when the State of Israel was established and inundated by hundreds of thousands of new immigrants, did the medical school finally decide that the renewed demand for doctors justified a full program of undergraduate as well as graduate study. Unfortunately, the hospital, on Jerusalem's Mount Scopus, was no longer available; the Jordanian army blocked access there. And so a new hospital was built, financed almost exclusively by the contributions of Hadassah members and their families in the United States. An immense, fifty-million-dollar structure, it is located today in the suburb of Ein Kerem outside Jerusalem, and it is perhaps the outstanding enclave of medical science in all of Asia—and surely one of the finest in the world. Here study young sabras and veteran European-trained scientists. Their facilities in this monumental cluster of stone-and-glass buildings are very nearly ideal, and include such sophisticated equipment as a cobalt bomb and a radioactive isotope laboratory for the most advanced cancer treatment. Faculty members are sent to the United States periodically on fellowships. Instructors and guest lecturers from other lands share teaching responsibilities with the Israel personnel. Under the sponsorship of the ministry of health, postgraduate courses and refresher courses are offered here for Israel's general practitioners and specialists.

Yet study opportunities for the nation's doctors are not limited to the Ein Kerem medical complex. The hospitals and medical associations of each of Israel's three major cities maintain their own programs. Thus, in Jerusalem, Haifa, and Tel Aviv, weekly lectures are offered in all phases of medical practice, together with clinical and pathological conferences. Most of the various medical branches of each community conduct bimonthly seminars and symposia. Perhaps most important of all, Kupat Holim sponsors a postgraduate program for its own physicians at the modern, well-equipped Beilinson Teaching Hospital in Petach Tikvah, near Tel Aviv. Once every three years, Kupat Holim physicians are sent to Beilinson for intensive six-week refresher courses in their own specialties. Members of the Beilinson faculty are themselves periodically sent abroad for advanced research.

In almost every area, therefore, Israel provides its doctors with adequate, and usually better than adequate opportunities for service and study. The resources of powerful health-insurance organizations permit effective and thorough treatment of all the nation's citizens, whatever their income. Moreover, the government and population are, by and large, receptive to even the most radical and expensive of medical innovations. For there is no public obscurantism where health is concerned; physical well-being has long been an axiom of Zionist policy. Perhaps the climate of medical practice is best summarized by Professor Artur Ber, chief of the department of endocrinology at Beilinson Hospital, and one of the world's most distinguished authorities in his field.

"In some respects Israel is a medical paradise," he observes. "I can't think of any other country where needs of health take such priority. It's not just a Zionist tradition, either; I suspect that it is more of a Jewish tradition—the sacredness of life, and all that." He smiles at the observation, his almond, slightly Oriental eyes creasing at the corners. "Anyway, one sees the emphasis on saving life everywhere one turns. Obviously people could subsist a lot more comfortably here if we didn't have to spend so much curing the immigrants." He reflects for a moment, then nods slowly. "It's really very touching. From the physician's point of view, I must say

I'm quite moved by it. All these clinics, all these mother-and-infant dispensaries. They bring me patients from the poorest Oriental families—imagine, not to some young interne in a slum clinic, but to me!" His gaze travels for a moment to one of his bookshelves: it is packed with volumes and articles on endocrinology—of his own authorship. "They bring them to me."

It is a nation intent upon ministering to the ill. Of all the members of its society, therefore, none should have found more intellectual and spiritual satisfaction than its doctors. The opposite is the case.

The town in which Artur Ber was raised was one of the most attractive in Poland. Located high on a hill overlooking the Vistula, Plotzk was famous for its cobblestoned medieval lanes, its handsome church spires. Boats passing from Cracow to Danzig frequently stopped there, allowing tourists to open their picnic baskets on the green, undulating meadows beside the riverbanks. Plotzk was a market center, and its thirty thousand inhabitants were mildly prosperous by East European standards. Even the town's nine thousand Jews lived well, sharing the trade and artisanry of their Christian neighbors. Of course, Jews and Poles did not live in the same streets, nor did they intermingle socially. Yet there was little friction between the two peoples.

Ber's childhood reflected the casual interaction of both cultures. His father, a small merchant, sent him to a Jewish school—where the language of instruction was Polish. Secular as well as Jewish subjects were taught, and both Christians and Jews served on the faculty. One of these non-Jewish teachers, a handsome, eloquent history instructor, imbued the youngster with a fervent hatred of the country's Russian overlords, and a deep and abiding Polish patriotism. This loyalty was intensified during the First World War, when Pilsudski's mixed German-Polish army drove the occupying Russian garrison from the town of Plotzk. Euphoric with happiness, young Ber rushed into the street to greet the liberators of his "motherland." General Pilsudski himself, tall and resplendent on a white charger, bent over in his saddle and patted the boy's head. It was the touch of the Messiah. In the years immediately following the war, not even rumors of Pilsudski's anti-Jewish pogroms in eastern Poland and the Ukraine shook the youth's confidence in the essential decency of the Polish people.

Then, in 1924, having passed his matriculation exams—with the highest marks in the history of his Gymnasium—Ber made preparations to depart for the University of Warsaw. There he would fulfill his lifelong ambition of studying medicine. There, too, alas, the facts of life awaited him. Polish universities maintained a strict numerus clausus for Jewish students: in the case of the medical school, the quota of fifteen was filled. Ber was rejected. Instead, he spent the next two years listlessly studying philosophy and literature, supporting himself by tutoring medical students in chemistry. Finally, in 1926, with the help of a Jewish doctor possessing the proper "connections," Ber was accepted into the school of medicine—veterinary medicine.

He put the ensuing years to good use. Swiftly establishing himself as the ablest student in the school, he translated from German several source works on veterinary medicine, thus providing the University of Warsaw with its first Polish-language textbooks in the subject. At the same time he undertook original research in the field of veterinary pathology. Eventually he secured an assistantship to Professor Szygmond Shimonowski, a kindly Socialist who took a keen personal interest in his brilliant pupil. In 1931 Ber received his doctorate. By then the medical school found it impossible any longer to deny him admission. He enrolled as a first-year student, at the age of twenty-four.

Routine study occupied the smaller part of his time. Ber had found his métier as a researcher. In the ensuing six years he turned out twenty-nine original papers, ranging the field from bacteriology to oncology and hematology. He was the recipient of several grants from the League of Nations Committee on Hygiene, and on its behalf conducted a number of significant experiments dealing with the effects of undulant fever. Even before he received his medical degree, Ber had prepared the outline for his first volume, *Compendium of Endocrinology in the Light of Contemporary Investigations,* a four-hundred-page work which, when eventually published in 1938, won instant recognition as a definitive source book on the subject.

There were other satisfactions. In 1932 he married Irena Makowska, an attractive dramatics student whom he had met in his sister's home. The new bride had come from an intensely Zionist home and had received a rudimentary training in Hebrew; indeed, she had once belonged to HaShomer HaTzair, the left-wing Zionist movement. Neither she nor Ber found time to renew their Jewish cultural interests after marriage, however, and the memory of that early Hebrew education was now filed away with Sabbath observance, synagogue rites, and other discarded relics of the past.

On the other hand, the young couple were never allowed to forget that they were Jews. During his university career, Ber was pointedly excluded from both the veterinary society and the medical society, although his publications had already won wide recognition from the Polish Medical Association. Several times he was discharged from jobs when it was discovered that he was Jewish. Once, when Ber held a municipal position as an abattoir control employee, his fellow workers warned him to clear out lest he suffer an "accident." He himself narrowly escaped the fate of several Jewish classmates, who were forcibly thrown out of their laboratories by Polish students. Many of the faculty endorsed the prevailing anti-Semitism of the University of Warsaw. "Give them their coats," mocked Professor Loth, as Jews were hustled out of his anatomy lecture. "It's cold outside." Not infrequently Jewish students were beaten with brass knuckles in the classrooms, as the instructors blandly looked on. When the university rector protested the excesses, he was stoned in the streets. In 1937 Jewish undergraduates were submitted to the final indignity of ghetto benches in the university lecture halls. Had it not been for the special protection of fearless old Professor Shimonowski, Ber probably would have been unable to conduct his research, perhaps even to complete his studies.

The experience scarred him deeply. Upon receiving his M.D. in 1937, he decided not to apply to the medical school for a research post in endocrinology, although this had long been his cherished ambition. Rather, he secured private employment in several Jewish-owned drug firms, and in 1939 was promised a job with the soon-to-be-established Jewish Institute of Pathology. Unfortunately this institute was not opened in time, and Ber was obliged to carry out his research on a voluntary, nonpaying basis in the medical school's histology department. It was there, nevertheless, working with Dr. Josef Flaks, that Ber embarked upon the celebrated experiments that laid the basis of his international reputation. Thus, Ber was the first to confirm the inhibiting influence of male hormones on breast cancer. He was the first to discover the technique for producing antigonadotropin, a drug capable of inhibiting the hormone which stimulates the sex glands. Other, equally promising discoveries appeared certain to follow from this series of experiments. But in 1939 Hitler suddenly loosed his armies on Poland.

Within two hours of the Nazi invasion, Ber reported to the nearest enlistment center to register as a medical officer. His decision was instinctive; the humiliations of the past years notwithstanding, it was still his country. Still an ungrateful one. He was refused a commission, and inducted instead as a common soldier—although with the responsibilities of a doctor. Ber had hardly taken leave of his wife before he was ordered on the road with the Polish army. The movement was eastward: it was a general withdrawal. For twelve days the troops continued to retreat along the refugee-packed highways. Frequently they were strafed by Nazi Stuka dive bombers.

By the time they reached eastern Poland, the soldiers discovered that they had entered Soviet-occupied territory. The country had been effectively partitioned between the Germans and the Russians. The Polish troops now found themselves captives of the Communists. The enlisted men were sent home. The officers were kept in custody. When his profession was discovered, Ber was given an "honorary" commission and promptly sent off to the Ukrainian prison camp of Kozielsk. There, for a month and a half, he and forty other medical officers were kept in the confinement of a single room. They occupied themselves by delivering lectures on their specialties.

Eventually the Nazis and the Soviets reached agreement on the captured soldiers. In late November the prisoners were loaded on a slow train, and delivered back to German-occupied territory. This time the exchange lasted long enough only for the Poles to be switched from one train to another, and then dispatched to the concentration camp of Sagan, in Silesia. Here, for the first time, Jews were singled out for special quarters: tents instead of the huts reserved for Polish soldiers. Throughout the agonizing cold of the winter, the Jewish prisoners huddled together, massaging each other's bodies to survive. Then, in late February, Ber was suddenly granted a reprieve. The German camp doctor had read his papers, and had been impressed by them. He allowed Ber to return home, even supplying him transportation as far as Poznan. The rest of the journey was made by foot.

By the time he arrived in Warsaw, he was as ragged as a tramp. Footsore and hollow-bellied, he shuffled slowly through the streets until he found the apartment of his wife's parents. It was Irena who answered his knock. She went faint. Until that moment she had not known her husband was still alive. Nearly a half-hour elapsed before intelligible conversation between them was possible. Later Irena described the plight of the city's Jewish population after the Nazi conquest. There had been special ration cards, confiscations, curfews. She herself had managed to buy food only by selling part of her husband's library.

"Anyway, there are certain privileges money can't buy," she added wryly.

Ber followed her gaze to the blue six-pointed star sewn on her sleeve. The sight of that ghetto badge shocked him more profoundly even than his imprisonment of recent months, or the poisonous academic Jew-hatred of his university career. There was more to come, of course. At first Ber earned a passable livelihood as a resident in the local Jewish hospital. Then his salary was cut. In the spring of 1940 so were food rations—for all Jews. The number of patients increased, then the number of corpses. And in the summer the Germans conscripted labor gangs to work on a wall. It was the beginning of the Warsaw ghetto. When the wall was finished the entire Jewish population of the capital was moved inside; later the inhabitants of every Jewish village in the district were transported there. Ber's parents were among the newcomers.

It was the outbreak of typhus in the town of Plonsk which probably saved Ber's life. In July of 1941 he was summoned to Plonsk by the Judenrat (the puppet Jewish council) to fight the epidemic. Apparently the German occupation authorities found it inconvenient for plague to be sweeping through their district; they even sent one of their military command cars for Ber. In Plonsk he was greeted by Ramek, president of the Judenrat. Ramek was a beefy, jovial man; he had lived well under the Nazis.

"Do join me for lunch, doctor," he said cordially, waving his hand at a table piled high with delicacies.

Ber stared at the repast in silent horror. "Thank you," he said at last, picking up his hat, and leaving the house.

Turning immediately to his task, Ber set about reorganizing the medical life of the community. With drugs purchased from Germany, the local pharmacy was restocked with the proper medicines. Homes were disinfected and public buildings transformed into clinics and dispensaries. Nearly a hundred townswomen were trained to administer injections or serve as practical nurses. Men were conscripted to dig sewer systems—and graves. It was endless, driving work for Ber. Indeed, he himself came down with typhus, but miraculously recovered within two weeks. A month after that he felt confident enough to send for Irena. The epidemic was broken.

For a full year Ber and his wife were permitted to remain in Plonsk. They even persuaded themselves that the worst of the Nazi danger was over. In that town, at least, Jews seemed to be going about their affairs unmolested, however abject their poverty. Occasional rumors were heard of starvation and killings elsewhere. The name Oswiecim (Auschwitz) had been mentioned. But there was no evidence of systematic executions. Then in June of 1942 a tubercular wreck of a man knocked at the door of the Ber apartment. It was Irena's brother, all but unrecognizable. That night, after resting and eating, he gave them an eyewitness account of mass starvation in the Warsaw ghetto, of tens of thousands of families shipped by rail to "death camps." The brother himself had been packed into a boxcar with his parents. Ber's parents were there, too. Their destination had been Treblinka.

"I saw it all," he said, tonelessly. "The old ones went first. Your parents, Artur. Then Irena's and mine. I saw our white-haired mother naked, driven in line to the gas chamber. Your sister and her children were next. I probably was scheduled after that. But they sent a group of us young men to the forest to cut wood. I took a chance and ran. Here I am—for the while. They are emptying the towns now."

Ber nodded. I suppose I should have known, he thought. So many of his patients, countless friends and neighbors, had mysteriously disappeared during the last few weeks, some "for treatment in the district hospital," others presumably selected for migration elsewhere. It was only too obvious now what had happened to them. In bed that night he lay silently and remembered his parents and sister. Finally, too, he remembered his obligation to live. Without informing Irena, he arose and wrote to his old professor and patron, Shimonowski, now living in Warsaw. ". . . Gentile Warsaw is the last place they would look for Jews," he wrote. "Can you take in Irena and me? Of course I'll work in your laboratory."

The reply came four days later. It was affirmative. The Bers made their plans immediately. On the next moonless night they packed and hurried to the rail depot. No one stopped them. It seemed almost too easy. Indeed, it was. Under flickering arc lights some 1,600 Jews—the last remaining Jews of Plonsk, as it turned out—were also waiting on the station platform. None spoke in more than a whisper. They were standing in lines that extended for many hundreds of yards on both sides of the track. SS guards in black death's-head caps patrolled the ranks of captives, occasionally snapping their quirts, rarely speaking. Ber seized Irena's wrist. His first instinct was to turn back. It was too late, however. One of the guards had recognized him.

"Get in line, Herr Doktor," said the Nazi. "If you and your wife have any ideas about leaving us, Asta here will tear your guts out." He patted a huge glowering police dog as he spoke. Without another word the couple joined the rest of the Jews.

The Nazis moved with impressive speed and efficiency. Within an hour the entire throng was loaded into two connected trains. Most of the prisoners were crowded into the corridors of the rail carriages, and into the baggage cars. Ber and his wife were more fortunate. The conductor, a kindly Pole, had once been a patient of Ber's. Immediately he assigned the couple to a compartment with six other people. Irena gasped: one of the passengers was Ramek. When the president of the Judenrat recognized his traveling companions he lowered his eyes and turned his face away. A half-hour later the locomotives began to move. The Jews were taking their final trip.

Not the doctor and his wife. The chance recognition by the Polish conductor had been their salvation. Ber's brain was working. By the time the train reached the suburbs of Warsaw he had decided on another gamble. Outside a slight drizzle fell. The capital itself was quite dark; presumably the authorities were conserving electricity. And beyond Warsaw there would be a forest. Ber walked out into the corridor. When the conductor passed his way, the two whispered briefly. Upon a signal, Irena joined them outside the compartment door. The train continued moving deliberately, a great clacking funeral hearse. Then a thick, matted foliage of bushes and trees loomed past the windows. Under the revolving locomotive light, the waters of the Vistula gleamed fitfully. It was Grodno, Warsaw's afforested suburb. The train slowed almost to a standstill.

"Come on," Ber whispered, then pushed Irena from the platform of the carriage. In a moment he joined her. The two tumbled and rolled down the rail embankment, into the protective shelter of the woods. For a moment they lay side by side, gasping for breath. Yet neither was injured, not even scratched. There was a sharp report, as of a rifle shot. Almost at the same moment, however, the train picked up speed. In three minutes the last rail carriage had vanished into the tunnel of the forest. Ber and Irena ran on into the woods, until they reached a cemetery. There, suddenly and totally exhausted, they stretched out and slept.

Dawn came. Irena stirred. "My mother appeared to me," she whispered with a shudder. "We must leave quickly."

Reluctantly Ber arose. With his bare hands he hollowed out the earth, then buried his papers. He lifted his wife to her feet, and together they walked in the direction of Warsaw. By 7:00 A.M. they had reached the first tram station. The conductor, a woman, stared at them suspiciously. Ber paid the fare with several used razor blades, which the woman accepted without comment. A half-hour more of travel, by streetcar and foot, and the destination was reached. Ber rang the bell of Shimonowski's apartment.

A woman in her mid-thirties opened the door. It was the professor's daughter. Her eyes opened wide as she recognized Ber, the man she had once loved. Then she saw Irena, and embraced her.

"Come in, quickly," whispered the daughter, her voice choked.

Shimonowski entered from a back room. He and Ber stared unbelievingly at each other. The pupil was a gaunt scarecrow. The teacher's thick mop of unruly hair and walrus mustache had turned completely white. Their greetings were calm, but their hands trembled with emotion.

"You'll work for me, Ber," said Shimonowski later, in a tone that brooked no argument. "I'm getting by doing urinalyses and blood tests. The laboratory is in the kitchen. From now on you're my assistant. The money won't be enough to keep the two of you alive—it's not enough for us—but we'll get you other jobs."

The other "jobs" were door-to-door peddling of saccharine for Ber, labor in a cosmetics factory for Irena. Somehow they earned enough for their food and lodgings. The difficulty arose in finding lodgings that were safe.

There were rooms to be had. Within Warsaw proper the likelihood of discovery by the Germans was not high. The danger lay with the Poles. At first the couple stayed with the Shimonowskis—until a Polish neighbor who despised the professor's socialism became suspicious, and alerted the Gestapo. The Nazis arrived only minutes after Ber and Irena had departed for their "outside" work. After that there was no question of returning. Shimonowski purchased a false passport for the Jewish couple, but it was not enough. A sympathetic Polish landlord in Marshal Kosciusko Street lost his nerve when he discovered that his tenants were Jews, and ordered them out. On another occasion a landlord's wife recognized Irena and notified an acquaintance in the SS. Instead of turning the couple in, however, the Nazi resorted to blackmail. Ber was forced to part with his instrument bag. Irena gave up her last "spare" shoes and sweater.

During the next two years the Bers moved through a nightmare world of intrigue and suspicion, changing their address no less than twenty times, often simply on the instinct that they were being watched. Not infrequently, too, they encountered Jewish acquaintances in the street, and steeled themselves to avoid offering even a hint of recognition. The experience was more than nerve-wracking. For Ber it was degrading. He and his wife were obliged continually to lie, to falsify their life histories, to spend an hour each night studying fake biographies, to learn the catechism better than the Poles themselves. It left a wound on both of them deeper than physical misery.

It affected their very will to survive on the Passover of 1943.

Irena cried out in sudden alarm. "I hear shooting. It might be a firing squad."

"Don't leave the room," her husband warned. "I'll take a look."

He investigated and returned, deeply shaken. For a while he could hardly speak.

The Jews behind the ghetto wall had embarked upon a frantic, all-but-hopeless revolt. They were exchanging gunfire with the Nazi troops.

"They are mad," Ber whispered. "They won't gain a day's respite that way."

Yet the uprising was destined to continue for another thirty-three days. In the beginning everything that happened was insulated from Gentile Warsaw. Soon the Poles became inured to the sounds of firing, the dull hollow explosions of Nazi demolition squads, even the occasional plaintive shriek of dying Jews. For several weeks there was nothing to be seen, however. But one Sunday morning in late April, smoke suddenly billowed from the other side of the ghetto wall. Standing near a group of picnicking Poles, Ber and Irena watched in paralyzed silence as the upper floors of Jewish tenement buildings sprouted flame. Then, within full view of on-lookers on both sides of the wall, a woman climbed out of her third-story window. She clutched a child in her arms. Deliberately she kissed the infant, then dropped it to the street. In a moment she, too, leaped from the sill. Immediately afterward, other Jews, eyes streaming and mouths gasping in suffocation, dropped silently to their deaths. The smoke obscured the view. Soon the battle went underground into the sewers, where a small band of men and women managed to survive a few more days.

The Bers all but lost the power of speech for weeks afterward: the memory of those falling bodies had apparently numbed their senses and reflexes. Several times Irena was nearly detected as a Jewess; she stumbled on her carefully rehearsed "biography." Her husband recognized the death wish for what it was. He himself might have succumbed, had it not been for persistent rumors of liberation. By the autumn of 1943 German hospital trains returning from the Russian front passed through Warsaw. The demoralized faces of the wounded soldiers revealed the extent of the Nazi defeat. It was only a matter of time now.

The months passed. The trickle of returning German and Hungarian soldiers became a flood tide. With the spring crocus came the first news of the Russian advance into eastern Poland. Instantly the Underground in Warsaw began making preparations for an insurrection; it was vital that the Poles be in control of their own capital before the Soviets arrived. Weapons were smuggled in from the government-in-exile in London. By midsummer a partisan army had been organized. During the last week of July the detonations of Russian artillery could already be heard in the distance. Roaring through Warsaw's streets, truckload after truckload of crack Nazi troops sped toward the eastern front. And on August 1, the signal for the uprising was given. Instantly bands of Polish irregulars, wearing red-and-white arm bands, moved into position, seizing public buildings and the main traffic arteries.

The old patriotism seized Ber. After all the years of disillusionment and betrayal, it refused to be stilled. Poland was his country. It was reviving. He would join the revolt. He presented himself to the insurrectionist head-quarters.

"I am a doctor," he announced. "Put me to work anywhere. I'm at your service."

The medical officer, a tall, close-shaven dentist, nodded impassively. "Let me see your credentials."

After some hesitation, Ber handed over his false documents. The Pole pursed his lips. "But there's nothing here about your being a doctor," he murmured.

"Pani, I am a Jew," Ber replied. "These are the only papers I dared keep in my possession. Ask Professor Shimonowski, or any one of your colleagues who attended the University of Warsaw Medical School. They will tell you about me."

The medical officer remained impassive. "Well, you have already told me," he remarked, tersely. "This is a Polish uprising. When we need foreign help we'll ask for it."

But within three days that "foreign" help was needed. Under orders from Moscow, the Russian army stopped short at the very outskirts of Warsaw. Exactly as Moscow wished, the Germans immediately proceeded to do the Soviets' dirty work for them: i.e., to annihilate the Polish nationalist move-ment—and with it all possible opposition to a future Communist regime.

The destruction was fearsome. During the next ten days two thirds of Warsaw was blasted into rubble by Nazi cannon. Nearly 100,000 Poles were slaughtered. Another 400,000 fled the capital.

When the fighting reached its peak intensity, a courier from the Underground arrived at the Bers' room. "Can you come, doctor?" he asked. "We're badly short of people in the emergency wards."

Irena clutched her husband's arm. "Artur, don't you dare," she whispered. "We owe them nothing."

Ber shrugged her off and arose. Furious, but silent, she joined him.

They were assigned to the northern part of the city, to what had once been a Catholic hospital. It was a charnel house now. The wounded were stacked three in a bed. Food supplies were all but exhausted. So were the stocks of drugs. During the succeeding week, as the building rocked and shuddered from German shell blasts, Ber performed scores of operations —without benefit of anesthesia, and often at night, with candles as his only illumination. His wife, serving as a nurse, fashioned bandages from the patients' shirts, dresses, and petticoats. The corridors stank of pus and blood. Twice Irena collapsed, once from exhaustion, once from a shrapnel wound in her thigh. Ber himself was nicked by flying shrapnel in the midst of surgery, but somehow managed to finish stitching his patient's gaping abdomen.

It was largely wasted effort. At the end of the week the hospital was captured by Lett and Ukrainian irregulars, allies of the Nazis. Many of the patients and staff were identified as partisans and shot. Others curried favor with the soldiers by informing on their fellow prisoners. Several of the doctors saved themselves by revealing that two Jews were in the hospital.

But Ber and Irena had anticipated this. They escaped minutes before the hospital was captured. For the next two days they joined the swarm of refugees fleeing the city. When hunger and exhaustion made further movement impossible, they stopped at the neighboring town of Korskie. And there Ber managed to find employment as a laboratory worker.

The job lasted only six weeks. Someone recognized Irena, and immediately both the director of the laboratory and the owner of their room ordered them out: no Jews wanted. In mid-October Ber and his wife moved on to Cracow. But there was no work for a doctor. Indeed, there was little work for anyone. The city was on the verge of starvation. Irena scavenged in the streets. Her husband occasionally found an odd job as a veterinarian on neighboring farms. It was not enough to feed them both. By the end of December, Ber and Irena were too weak to leave their room. It was a curious irony. They had survived the German nightmare for five years. Now, as they lay silently on their beds, listening to the rumble of Soviet artillery in the east and Nazi troop carriers fleeing westward on the highway outside, starvation had found the key to their room at last and approached their bedside. "So unfair," Irena murmured once. Ber waited uncomplainingly for the end to come.

The end of the war came first. In January, 1945, Russian troops—most of them middle-aged men and girls—entered the city. The Red Cross and other relief organizations followed, opening soup kitchens and dispensaries. The Bers waited only long enough to regain their strength. Two weeks later they boarded a refugee train with several hundred other Jewish survivors and departed for Lublin; a Joint Distribution Committee camp had been established there. The moment he reached the JDC office, Ber filled out an application form for transport to Palestine.

When Ber's turn came to be interviewed he handed over the application without comment.

"Dr. Artur Ber?" The clerk gazed curiously at the ragged figure before him. "If you are Dr. Artur Ber of Warsaw we have a message for you."

Ber opened the note. When he finished reading it, tears misted his eyes. "It's from Shimonowski," he told Irena. "I didn't even know he was still alive. Here he is in Lublin, and he wants to see us."

The meeting took place an hour later. It was joyous beyond expression. The old man's family had survived intact. He himself was in good health and brimming with energy and optimism.

"It's a new world, dear Ber," he exulted. "The Russians are giving us money to open a university here. I'm developing a medical school for them, and *you* are going to be in it: I've arranged for you to be chairman of the department of pathology of the faculty of veterinary medicine, nothing less. We'll have everything we want, freedom for research, good laboratories, everything we've ever dreamed of. What do you say to that? I won't let you turn me down."

"But I must, Dr. Shimonowski," Ber replied. "Irena and I have decided to leave this country. We've endured more from the Poles than from the Germans. For the last ten years of our lives all that we can remember is suffering. We're only flesh and blood, after all. We can't live in the midst of enemies all our lives."

The old professor nodded sympathetically. "You are right, my dear," he agreed. "No man should be forced to live among enemies. I personally think that the new people's regime will be friendly—indeed, I see it already—friendlier than any Polish government of my lifetime. I think they will make this a hospitable land for Jews. I'm sure of it. But I can't force you to believe it. What I do say, my boy, is to give it a chance. Stay a little longer and see what develops. If Poland remains the Poland we've always remembered, then you can leave. I won't hold you back. But stay a little longer, Ber. Help me, too, now. I need you."

Ber found it impossible to refuse that appeal. He agreed to stay on temporarily. Indeed he remained in Lublin less than a year. The Communist regime apparently was determined to spare neither effort nor money in elevating Polish science and medicine to the level of the Western nations. New universities and research institutes were founded. One of the most important was in Lodz. Shimonowski was given the responsibility of building a medical school there. He took Ber with him, this time as professor of endocrinology. Two months later, in fact, Ber was offered the chairmanship of a superb new endocrinological institute, the first of its kind in Europe. His salary was higher than he had ever imagined, much higher even then Shimonowski had promised. His laboratory facilities were unexcelled. Less than six months after Ber and Irena had nearly starved to death in Cracow, they found themselves settled in a spacious, well-appointed apartment, served by a maid, and driving their own automobile. Shimonowski had not exaggerated. Working and living conditions were "everything we've ever dreamed of."

Ber was by no means oblivious to the other, uglier, face of the "People's Government," to the regimentation, the obsequious deference to the leader principle, the arrogance of Party officials, the spoliation of Polish natural resources for Russian needs. Yet neither could he ignore the forthrightness with which the Communist regime rectified or eliminated many grave abuses and anachronisms. The official suppression of anti-Semitism was surely one of the new government's major accomplishments. Moreover, the vast land holdings of the Church were now sequestered and distributed among the peasantry. So were the fiefdoms of the "Leviathan," the reactionary association of aristocrats and industrialists who had subsidized prewar Polish fascism. Free compulsory education was now available to all children. Medical care was extended to everyone without cost. New hospitals were erected now by the scores—and soon by the hundreds. Laboratories and library facilities took priority over apartments in the nation's building program.

Ber luxuriated in the new society, in the personal and professional opportunities that now were his. During the next few years he hurled himself once again into research, conducting experiments of a sophistication he had not dreamed possible in the prewar era, and publishing nearly a hundred articles and monographs. Irena gave birth to a daughter and son, and raised them with every material comfort. All the ordeals and agonies of the war years faded now into the haze of an ancient nightmare. So vanished, too, the fleeting postwar notion of departure for Palestine.

Other Jews made the same commitment to their Polish homeland. These were not the majority of the survivors, to be sure. Approximately 160,000 men, women, and children (most of them repatriated from Russia) fled westward in horror from the graveyard of their families, from the poisonous Judeophobia of the Polish people. But a minority, perhaps 50,000, remained. A very small number of these were hard-core Communists, convinced that a Leninist society offered the only hope for a progressive social order. Some of these Jewish Marxists now assumed important positions in the Polish Communist Party. Yet a much larger number of those who stayed in Poland were intelligentsia, men and women possessing administrative or technical skills vitally needed in the reconstruction of the Polish State. Communism as a dogma was altogether repulsive to them. Nevertheless, physically and emotionally exhausted by the degradation of the war years, they found it impossible to resist the opportunity of earning decent, well-paid livelihoods as officials in the civil service, as chemists, engineers, doctors, plant managers, or newspaper editors. Perhaps 70 per cent of these people were settled in the former German territory of Upper Silesia, a desolated region which the government hoped to restore in large measure through Jewish talents. The rest of the Jewish repatriates, like the Bers, stayed on in the larger cities of integral Poland.

Ber himself experienced mixed feelings about many of these survivors. Those who held key posts in the Communist Party he despised; not merely for their communism, but for the arrogance with which they lorded it over Poles and Jews alike. Yet there were others, non-Communists, who simply dropped their Jewish associations and interests, who raised their children as Poles, without attachment to any religious tradition whatever. These were Ber's friends. Many were colleagues of his on the medical faculty. He did not presume to judge them, for he shared their ambivalence. He and Irena may have registered with the Jewish committee of Lodz, but they realized perfectly well how meaningless the gesture was. Their children, too, were raised as Poles, without the slightest contact with Jewish traditions or customs. In the old days, of course, anti-Semitism would have forced Jewish families into some kind of ethnic or religious identification. But that problem hardly existed any longer; official anti-Semitism had been stamped out by the new regime. Insults and threats were not unheard of; but in the early postwar era, at least, these were rare. All in all, Ber was grateful for the new state of affairs. He preferred not to have his children reminded of their ancestry, either affirmatively or negatively.

In his favored university position, moreover, Ber was almost entirely insulated from the change in Jewish status when it finally came. It began in 1948, with the sudden prohibition of all further Jewish emigration to Palestine. It gained momentum during the next few years in the guise of an officially sponsored policy of "anti-Zionism." Had Ber been alert, he probably would have detected this "anti-Zionism" for the façade it was. Jewish communal organizations of a purely religious or philanthropic character were ordered closed. A number of prominent Jewish Communists were suddenly purged from their Party posts. Indeed, in 1951 and 1952, nearly every important Jew in the Communist bloc, including Rudolf Slanski, secretary-general of the Party in Czechoslovakia, and Anna Pauker, foreign minister of Rumania, were expelled from the Party organizations.

By 1952 even the most sanguine Jewish Marxist realized what was happening. Following Moscow's lead, the governments of the satellite regimes began launching thinly disguised assaults against "cosmopolitanism," against "Zionist parasitic elements." Almost invariably the "cosmopolitans" bore Jewish names: and when the names were not Jewish, the accusations specifically identified the culprits as being of "Jewish origin." The danger became far more palpable on January 13, 1953. On that day Tass, the Soviet news agency, announced that nine doctors, six of them Jewish, had "confessed" to the murder, four and a half years earlier, of Andrei Zhdanov, a prominent Bolshevist and member of the Politburo. The "murder" was said to have been committed on behalf of Zionism, and at the orders of the American intelligence service. Almost immediately the revelations of the so-called Doctors' Plot became the signal for the most furious anti-Semitic campaign in Soviet history. Throughout the entire Communist orbit, Jews by the hundreds, then by the thousands, were deprived of their jobs. These were not merely Jewish Party-members. They were Jewish civil servants, teachers, factory managers, even occasionally technicians. With complete impunity now, Russians, Poles, and Rumanians openly reviled their Jewish neighbors, desecrating their cemeteries, insulting their children.

In some measure, perhaps, Stalin's morbid but genuine fear of "deviationism" may have accounted for the anti-Semitic campaign. The Soviet dictator was convinced that all Jews were secretly Zionists, that Zionism was little more than a cat's-paw for Western "imperialism." Stalin's thinking was also probably influenced by a second factor, as well—a classic one: anti-Semitism as a diversionary technique for domestic difficulties. Since the end of World War II those difficulties were all too evident. The Marxist system was incapable of feeding its populations adequately, of housing or clothing them. There had been agricultural failures, breakdowns in the production of vitally needed consumer goods. A scapegoat was needed—and the Jews were historically ordained for the role. Finally, too, the Soviets had discovered yet another Nazi weapon: the projection of an international enemy as a *raison d'être* for international expansion. "Zionist imperialism" was construed as such a world-wide menace; obviously only world-wide communism was capable of rooting it out.

Fortunately for the Jews, Stalin died only two months after the notorious Doctors' Plot trial. Almost immediately the gravest danger to their physical security receded. The arrests and dismissals tapered off. The anti-Semitic press campaign lost some of its virulence. Yet the warning signs had been all too evident. Few Jews anticipated any longer that the militant crusading egalitarianism of the early Communist movement would ever be revived. And without it, they knew they would be left prey once again to the traditionally brutal prejudices of the surrounding populations.

Ber himself survived the "time of troubles" without undue grief. He was a distinguished scientist; and in Communist Poland (unlike the Soviet Union) scientists were largely immune to discrimination. Moreover, Ber could never have been accused of overt hostility to the Communist regime. He had gained too much from it. Indeed, with Shimonowski, he had willingly affixed his signature to Communist-sponsored peace petitions, and had written his colleagues abroad, urging them to combat Western "imperialism." His difficulties, rather, were of another nature, and arose primarily from his scientific integrity.

In the winter of 1950 he attended a congress of biology in the city of Zakopane. The gathering was an impressive one, consisting of the most respected biologists in Poland, as well as delegates from the Soviet bloc of nations. Here, for the first time, the Lysenko theory of genetics was presented to a Polish audience. Ber listened in silence as one speaker after another arose to echo the official Communist line—Lysenko's—that heredity could be influenced by external stimuli. The doctrine was tailor-made for Communist purposes, of course. It appeared to validate the Marxist contention that social and economic change was capable of altering even genetic development. At the end of the fourteen-day colloquium Ber mounted the platform to deliver his scheduled address. The speech was short but pungent: Lysenkoism was nonsense, Ber declared; there was not a shred of evidence to support it; politicians would do well not to meddle in scientific matters. Then he sat down. His Polish colleagues gave him an uproarious standing ovation. Later the proceedings of the congress were published by the ministry of health; of course the most critical of Ber's remarks had been censored.

A half-year later the Polish endocrinological society gathered for its first convention in Lodz. Again, Russia and the other satellite nations sent delegates. And once again Ber delivered a sharp anti-Lysenko speech. This time, however, the address was published, for Ber was president of the society and editor of its journal. Indeed, reprints of his address were circulated throughout the entire Communist world. After that Ber was watched much more closely, his articles carefully censored. The following year he was not invited to address the biological congress. Neither were any of his fellow endocrinologists; for by now it was clear that the Communists were interested in relegating the field of endocrinology to a minor science. Apparently in the study of gland functions too much emphasis was placed on pure chemistry—which seemed to have unalterable laws of its own. Conversely, the science of neurology was given renewed official attention, for here it was possible to give dramatic proof of the nervous system's reaction to external stimuli.

"External stimuli may be important," protested Ber angrily, "but the brain alone can't affect gland secretions. Glands don't react like nerve endings. The Lysenkoists will never prove otherwise."

If Ber had lived in Russia he probably would have been sent to Siberia for his theories. In Poland, repression was rarely carried that far. Indeed, Ber was permitted to conduct his research without interruption, and even to continue as chairman of the endocrinological society. In 1953, shortly after Stalin's death, he re-articulated his anti-Lysenko views at the Lodz meeting of the Pavlovian society: nerves and external stimuli would never control all human behavior, he insisted. Suddenly, in the midst of his address, he was interrupted by a Russian colonel—now an officer in the Polish army—who was sitting in on the meeting as an "observer."

"Professor Ber is expressing discredited ideas," remarked the colonel, in his heavy Russian accent. "I might even say dangerous ideas. Perhaps he would like to reconsider."

For a moment Ber remained silent. Then, in cold fury, he measured off his words: "Perhaps the colonel would like to give me the courtesy of letting me finish my speech—either that or learn Polish, so that he will at least know what I'm talking about."

The audience rose spontaneously, cheering at the top of their voices. Within a matter of days news of the incident circulated throughout Poland's scientific community. Ber found himself something of a national hero. He elaborated on his views a few months later in a two-part article entitled "Pavlovism under the Microscope." These were, of course, devastatingly critical analyses of the Pavlovian (and Lysenkoist) theories. The pamphlet was priced at one zloty. Forty-eight hours after its appearance, its price had soared to ten zlotys—and then all copies were gone. By now, however, Ber had pressed his reputation and luck too far. Under instructions from the government, the university senate publicly condemned him, and ordered its condemnation published at all scientific meetings. Detectives began attending Ber's class lectures, diligently taking notes. His friends, too, gradually lost their nerve and dropped away; their wives and children avoided Irena and her youngsters in the street. Ber sensed for the first time that he was in grave danger of being dismissed from his post, and perhaps worse.

It may have been Stalin's death that saved him. The passing of the Soviet dictator brought with it a notable political and intellectual "thaw." In Russia itself the most serious of the police-state restrictions were eased. People congregated, spoke, and in some instances wrote more freely. The new mood was instantly sensed in the satellite nations. Hesitantly at first, then more deliberately, the Polish government eased many of its former repressive measures. Thus, early in 1955, Ber was officially "rehabilitated" by the central committee of the Polish Communist Party. The university senate condemnation of 1953 was similarly repudiated.

"It was bound to happen," Ber declared exultantly to his wife. "You can't keep the blinders on these people forever. What a moment to be a Pole! We'll see some real progress now. I'll have my students throw those detectives out of the classroom if they ever come back."

But they did not return. Once released, totalitarian controls could not be restored. Indeed the pressure continued to mount for a complete and final end to dictatorship in Poland. The climax was reached in the summer and early autumn of 1956. On June 28 of that year the industrial workers of Poznan staged a general strike. Marching on the local Communist headquarters, a procession of some fifty thousand employees and their families clamorously demanded free elections and the withdrawal of Russian troops from Polish soil. Violence was inevitable. The police fired on the marchers. In the ensuing riot fifty-three people were killed. Now, indeed, the nation was keyed for revolution. The Communist Central Committee sensed the danger, and was determined to abort it at all costs. Apparently the only hope of preventing a full-scale uprising was to install a new party secretary—a liberal. It was no secret to the members of the Party that Wladyslaw Gomulka was that man.

On October 21 Gomulka was unanimously elected chairman of his Party. Leaving no doubt now where he stood, the new Polish leader immediately demanded, and received, Moscow's approval for the resignation of Russian Marshal Rokossovsky as Poland's minister of defense; soon thereafter all Russian officers in the Polish armed forces were replaced by Poles. After that, too, Cardinal Wyszynski was released from internment, and returned to Warsaw as primate of the Polish Catholic hierarchy. Religious instruction was introduced again in the schools. Poland was not yet free. But its people were freer to express themselves than at any time since 1939. Ber was surely right: it was a moment to be a Pole.

But not a Jew. People gave vent at last to the hostilities and grievances they had repressed since the end of the war. As it happened, no hatred was more deeply rooted than anti-Semitism. Ber, who had lived in the secluded, privileged retreat of his laboratory all these years, was astounded at the transformation in the Polish citizenry. Of course he had known that the Poles were traditionally hostile to their Jewish minority. Yet he had hardly imagined that a liberalized government would prove incapable of keeping Jew hatred within legal bounds. Now, however, to the shocked dismay of Ber and the rest of Polish Jewry, two well-known anti-Semites were added to the Gomulka cabinet. Jewish civil servants in several key ministries were dismissed. For the first time since 1945, poison-pen letters, urging the Jews to clear out, appeared in several newspapers. While Ber and Irena themselves did not suffer directly from the renewed Judeophobia, they recognized the danger to their children. The Gomulka government had permitted Catholic religious instruction to be reinstated in the schools. Virtually the only youngsters who did not attend these classes were Jews. For the first time, the Ber son and daughter would have to be set apart from their classmates. It was an uncomfortable prospect, one the parents were not prepared to face.

Indeed, for Artur and Irena Ber the revolution of 1956 was the final and ineradicable moment of truth. Poland was Poland. Poles were Poles. Whatever the regime, whatever the social programs, whatever the laws, here was a people which would never change, which was incapable of ever dealing fairly with its minorities. For a Jew there was simply no future in this land.

"What am I supposed to do, then?" Ber asked his wife. "Give up everything I've built here: my position, my laboratory, my private practice? This apartment, your maid, our vacations?"

"Where has it gotten us?" Irena sighed.

Of course she was right. It seemed little to sacrifice in return for the children's security. The problem was only how to get out. Since 1948 tens of thousands of applications for exit permits to Israel had been gathering dust at the ministry of the interior.

But for Jews, the sudden and favorable attention now given their applications was the other, brighter face of the 1956 revolution. Gomulka was no anti-Semite (indeed, his wife was Jewish). The Party secretary deplored the prejudices of his countrymen no less than the Jews themselves. But what was he to do? If restraints were loosened, people would express themselves; and that was the way the Poles were. The more he thought about it, however, the more Gomulka was convinced that—in all conscience—he could not deny exit to Jews who were determined to leave the country. If they still wished to depart for Israel, he would not be the one to place further obstacles in their way. In fact, this might be the best method after all of ending the unremitting friction between the two peoples. The moment he reached this decision, Gomulka ordered the ministry of the interior to begin processing the applications.

Within a matter of days the news had circulated throughout Poland's Jewish population. Thousands of Jews rushed to the nearest passport offices to complete the necessary formalities. The applicants included, as well, a large number of repatriates from the Soviet Union, families that had been permitted to return to their homes during the thaw following Stalin's death. The emigration began slowly, for adequate transport was lacking; the government's *volte face* had taken Jewish Agency officials entirely by surprise. Trains had to be provided, as well as shelter and food en route to the south-European ports. The machinery of exodus was costly and complex. Several months passed before the Israel authorities were able to cope with the unexpected wave of emigrants. In spite of the inevitable confusion, and the more than occasional inadequacy of Jewish Agency immigration officials, however, the departure of Polish Jews rapidly assumed major proportions. In all, between 1956 and 1958, no fewer than forty-three thousand Jews streamed out of Poland en route to Israel. It was an *aliyah* of the first magnitude.

Although Ber was one of the first to learn of the government's change of policy, he hesitated at first to apply for an exit permit. There were certain difficulties. The ministry of the interior allowed no funds to be taken out of the country, only furniture and personal effects. Presumably the Jewish Agency would cover the cost of transport to Israel. But there was the problem of survival in Israel after arriving. How could he earn a living, he wondered, or find opportunities for research? Ber decided to visit the Israel legation in Warsaw, and ask the advice of the officials there.

Katriel Katz, chief of the legation, was a stocky, sandy-haired man in his mid-forties. During his incumbency, he had steered a delicate course between the suspicions of the Communist government on the one hand, and the hungry curiosity of the Polish Jewish community on the other. If he remained too circumspect in his dealings with his fellow Jews, he ran the risk of extinguishing their faith in Israel and their dreams of emigrating there. If he encouraged them overtly, indeed if he maintained more than the most casual and discreet contact with them, he risked official denunciation—perhaps even expulsion—as a "Zionist-imperialist agent." Far more serious, too, was the danger of retaliation against Polish Jewry itself; and it was this fact which inhibited the local Jewish inhabitants in their dealings with him. The situation was cruelly unnatural. When Katz appeared at the Warsaw synagogue during the High Holy Days, for example, he and his fellow worshipers were compelled to greet each other as polite strangers. When he attended Polish state functions, he scrupulously avoided chatting for more than a few moments with a local dignitary of Jewish extraction.

The situation had changed somewhat for the better in recent months. The Warsaw regime evinced a willingness to relax its strenuous anti-Zionist position. Public denunciations of Israel no longer appeared with monotonous regularity in the press. Israel's recent invasion of the Sinai Peninsula had been roundly condemned, of course. But—had Katz merely imagined it?—there seemed to be a tone of grudging admiration in the newspaper accounts of Israel's victory. From what he had heard, the Polish population had been curiously impressed by the military and agricultural accomplish-ments of the Jewish Republic. "These are not the kind of Jews we remem-ber," was the usual comment. Who could explain it? Perhaps their consciences were guilty. Gomulka himself had paid a number of friendly visits to Israel exhibits in the recent trade fair and film festival. And now, at last, the emigration ban was actually being lifted.

Katz was still cautious. "I don't want to give you too much encourage-ment, Dr. Ber," he explained to his visitor. "The decision to leave Poland has to be yours. I'm not persuading you one way or the other."

"I understand that," Ber replied. "All I want to know is what the possi-bilities are of my resuming my practice and my research in Israel. Will I have such a chance?"

Katz shrugged. "Look here, Israel is a poor country," he replied patiently. "We're heavily staffed already with professional people of all sorts, and especially doctors. Unquestionably you won't live there as well as you do here. You won't have the same salary, the same subsidies. You probably won't even have the same prestige. These are facts you must face."

Ber nodded soberly. It was surely no time for illusions. During the past few months several of his doctor friends had departed for Israel with grandiose notions of what they would find there. He had heard from many of them already. Their shock was a profound one. Ber would not make the same mistake. He would carefully prepare in advance.

Fortunately that very week the first secretary of the Israel legation, Bar-Mor, was about to depart for a brief home leave. Well aware of Ber's distin-guished reputation, he promised the doctor to investigate the possibility of a special arrangement for him. And indeed, when Bar-Mor returned in December, it was with good news. There seemed every likelihood that a man of Ber's stature could be assured of research possibilities, with an in-come of at least six hundred pounds a month—plus an option on a good apartment. Of course, the sum was little enough in comparison with a medical professor's earnings in Poland. But in Israel, at least, the salary was an impressive one. Ber discussed the matter with Irena, and she agreed; they would take a chance.

He informed the ministry of health of his decision to leave. The authori-ties were shocked. Did the honored professor know what he was saying? Did he realize what he was giving up? Surely Dr. Ber had not been offended by the stray remarks of a few prejudiced and ignorant people? He must be aware that he was the most honored figure in Polish science. The nation's medical reputation could survive the departure of other doc-tors and chemists—but not Dr. Ber, by no means Dr. Ber. Nor were the authorities the only ones to protest his decision. The moment the news was revealed, he was deluged by letters from scientists throughout Poland. They needed him; endocrinology would profit from his research wherever he might live, but Poland needed the moral courage of a man who could single-handedly defy the entire ideological apparatus of Communist pseudo-science.

But he had made up his mind. The entreaties of his colleagues no longer concerned him. Neither did the economic hardships that awaited the family in Israel. His thoughts were now of his older child, his daughter. She was ten years old, and she did not know that she was Jewish. Neither Ber nor Irena had ever had the courage to tell her. They were not proud of the fact. It was one thing to leave the children at home when they, the parents, accepted an occasional Passover invitation, to eat pork in their own apartment, scrupulously to avoid mention of Jewish subjects when the children were present. Perhaps this faintheartedness could be forgiven under the circumstances. Jewishness had meant nothing but grief and agony to the Bers all their adult lives; quite unconsciously they had come to associate it with the canards and accusations of their enemies. But Ber wondered if he really could be forgiven for having gone so far: he had actually allowed the girl to believe she was Catholic. During the school hours she had been permitted to attend Catholic instruction—even more, to attend church with the maid on Sundays. Well, what was he to do? The youngster was blonde and snub-nosed. She wrote and spoke such beautiful Polish. Could he allow her to know that her classmates were not her people, that she would never belong to them?

Then in May, 1957, the exit permits were delivered. The automobile, the furniture, and the books were packed and shipped. There could be no further procrastination.

"Kristina, we are going to Israel," he explained.

"It's in Arabia, isn't it, Daddy? Shall we be there long?"

"We shall live there."

She shook her head. "Why Israel? Is it a place for Polish people?"

"No, no," the mother explained. "It is a Jewish country. We are Jews, Kristina."

"What are Jews?"

They offered an explanation. It was a lame one, filled with vapid historical references to the Bible, and to a deity that was one rather than three. No mention was made of grief or persecution. Of course the definition was beyond the child's understanding, and eventually they gave it up. She would simply have to learn by living among Jews, in a Jewish land. Fortunately, there would be no problem with the boy. He was of kindergarten age, and would probably readjust quickly.

On September 14, 1957, the Bers departed. A large crowd of friends and students had gathered at the Lodz railway station to see them off. The farewell was a Slavic one, lacking neither embraces nor tears. Then the city was behind them. From Warsaw the family changed trains for Vienna. And at Vienna representatives of the Jewish Agency were waiting with tickets and currency. After that there remained only Venice and the *Messapia,* a comfortably appointed steamer packed to the rails with Jews, Polish Jews. Many of them recognized the famous Professor Ber, and doffed their hats.

"We are going home, Pan Doctor," they cried gaily. "Quite a feeling, eh?"

He smiled. "That's right," he called back, "going home." He listened to the sound of the words, but they conjured up his apartment in Lodz. He repeated them again, silently, and this time he saw his father's house in Plotzk, and the river traffic moving leisurely along the Vistula below. Suddenly hot tears filled his eyes, and he stared intently at the sea.

The boat arrived in Haifa on September 26. The day was hot, and the afterglow of the Near Eastern summer intensified the anxieties of disembarkation and registration. The usual Jewish Agency officials were there, lists, forms, and files stacked on the tables before them. The newcomers were interrogated, their names checked, and credentials examined. Ration cards were distributed, then small sums of money. Some of the immigrants found relatives waiting to take them in hand. But most of them were alone, except for the families who accompanied them. They were allotted now to waiting buses, and sped from the port to settlement centers. Here the Agency's social workers would show them their homes, assign them their jobs, register them for loans.

For a small minority of highly trained professional people, other arrangements were occasionally made. Ber was one of these privileged few. He was handed one hundred and fifty pounds by an Agency official, then sent off with his family to Beit Brodetsky, a hostel near Tel Aviv reserved for people in his "category." The two and a half rooms were not uncomfortable—so long as they were temporary. He was certain that Bar-Mor's assurances were reliable. At any moment now he would surely be visited by a representative of the ministry of health. Indeed, four days later he was.

"Of course we know all about you, Professor Ber," the man explained respectfully. "Mr. Bar-Mor spoke to us some months ago. For the time being, we've come up with a spot for you in Haifa. It's a very nice—small—hospital."

Ber was confused. "Is it a university hospital? A research hospital?"

"A plain and simple hospital for sick people, doctor," the representative replied. "Research facilities in this country are still quite limited."

Politely but firmly Ber rejected the offer. He had not given up the directorship of a world-famous institute to become a house physician. On his own, he paid a visit to the Hebrew University Medical School. He was invited to lunch. The faculty members expressed a courteous interest in his research.

Ber pressed the issue. "Do possibilities for research exist here?" he asked. "I should think this is the logical place to continue my work."

The tenor of the conversation changed immediately. The professors were obviously embarrassed. One of them stated the issue bluntly, however. "We don't get the kind of state subsidies you've been accustomed to, doctor. This is a pioneering country. It's all we can do to keep up with all the latest developments. Research projects of any size are just beyond our capacities now." Then he added pointedly: "All our spare funds go into the immigration—immigrant clinics, you understand."

When Ber left he was trembling with anger and frustration. Perhaps he had not awaited a gala reception in his honor. Yet he was hardly a country doctor. He would have expected more deference from medical professors, his colleagues. His illusions were rapidly dispelled, however; during the next few weeks he became an expert in swallowing his pride. On his own, he made appointments with directors of the most important hospitals in the country. The answer was always the same: they were overstaffed; they had been for years, ever since the late 1930s.

One afternoon Ber sat despairingly in the office of Dr. Joshua Cohen, assistant director-general of the Israel ministry of health, and chairman of the medical placement committee. Cohen, a sympathetic young Scottish Jew, did his best to explain the situation. Nearly five hundred doctors had arrived from Eastern Europe during the last year and a half, he pointed out. Of course they all asked to be placed in the larger cities. But that was out of the question. Many even of the smaller rural communities were oversupplied. If newcomers wanted employment they would simply have to allow the committee to place them: viz., at posts in village clinics or outlying development areas.

"Of course, one *could* develop a private practice in the city," Ber speculated, half to himself.

"Dear Doctor Ber," Cohen replied earnestly, "private medical practice hardly exists in this country. Nearly everyone here belongs to an insurance program of one sort or another. Why should people spend money on a private doctor when Kupat Holim can give them one just for the cost of membership? Of course some immigrants have tried to start private practices of their own. You can talk to them. I assure you they are not making a living."

Ber knew this was true. Anyway, he was already in his middle age. It was no time for ventures on his own. Cohen, in turn, suspected that Ber's aversion to a rural practice stemmed from more than a need for adequate research facilities. Like the other refugees from Eastern Europe, he probably assumed that the Israel farm settlement was a kind of *kolkhoz*—just the sort of Communist village most of them were fleeing from. Ultimately the newcomers discovered the difference between a kibbutz or a moshav, on the one hand, and a *kolkhoz,* on the other. It was precisely the difference between voluntarism and nonvoluntarism; they learned it from family and friends who lived there. But it took time.

Language inadequacy was another, more serious problem. No one was more aware of this than Cohen. In the early days of the Polish immigration, he had sent doctors out to clinics before they could speak more than a few words of Hebrew. As a direct consequence of that shortsightedness (he admitted it now), the physicians failed from the very outset to establish the crucial rapport with their patients. Unsuccessful in fulfilling the necessary father image, many of the newcomers cracked, suffering nervous breakdowns. Cohen and his colleagues were obliged to devise new techniques. One of the most promising was the medical ulpan (Hebrew language school). Here the refugee doctors were enrolled in special three-month "acclimatization" classes at various hospitals throughout the country. During the mornings they visited the wards with the physicians who shared their specialties, studying local hospital methods, the ailments peculiar to

Israel's polyglot population and climate. In the afternoons, however, the immigrant doctors concentrated exclusively on the study of Hebrew. The program was financed jointly by the government and the Jewish Agency; books and instruments were provided by a special doctors' loan fund. The project showed every likelihood of success.

Ber had heard of the medical ulpan. He was perfectly willing in principle to participate. The question was: At which hospital? If it was simply another Haifa prospect, there would be no point in it. Somehow he would have to find an institution possessing adequate laboratory facilities. He was in the full maturity of his intellectual powers. He had much to give. It was unthinkable that his research career should come to an end now. He would wait, and keep searching.

The decision was not easily taken. At the end of the month his funds were gone. For the first time since the war he and his wife were forced to dispose of personal possessions. Some of their most valuable books and *objets d'art* were sold for food. When Ber approached the Jewish Agency for an apartment loan, he was ordered to find two co-signers; and even with these guarantors he would receive less than half the seventeen thousand pounds he had requested. Through friends, he began negotiations with the Society for Refugee Scientists; but the organization's funds were seriously depleted. If Ber was willing to be patient, there was the possibility of a four-hundred-pound loan, sometime within six weeks. . . .

But his patience was exhausted.

"I was wrong," he admitted despondently to Irena. "I took a chance and it didn't work out. It's no time to stand on false pride. We'll have to go back."

"If they will still take us back."

Ber fondled the boxes of letters from his friends and colleagues. "I am not worried about that," he said.

He was not worried about reappointment as director of the endocrinological institute, nor about regaining the use of his former laboratories. He could endure the humiliation of returning as a failure, even the propaganda the government was certain to make of his disgrace. His concern was much more basic: raising his children in Poland. No matter which way he rationalized it, the welfare of his children was the crucial issue. What would happen to them if he returned? They would have enough to eat, of course. But they would have enough in Israel, for that matter—if their father was willing to settle for second best. He considered the idea for a while. And finally, in bed late at night, he decided that he had almost forgotten why he came.

"Yes, hold out a little longer," murmured his unsleeping wife.

On an impulse, Ber wrote to the Israel legation in Warsaw. Soon thereafter a letter from the legation arrived at the desk of Golda Meir, Israel's foreign minister. Mrs. Meir agreed to receive Ber at her home in Jerusalem. During the course of the interview, the doctor explained his predicament, and warned of the disastrous propaganda consequences that might follow his return to Lodz: If the most eminent scientist in Poland could not make a living in Israel, what encouragement would other Polish Jews find to migrate there? The foreign minister was not insensible to the argument. She sent a note to the Jewish Agency. The Agency, in turn, agreed to give Ber special consideration. Thus, a handsome, modern apartment was finally provided for his family in Tel Aviv, at the nominal rental of ninety pounds a month. The Agency assured him, too, that somehow a remunerative post would be found for him—with research facilities.

That promise was kept. Several weeks later Ber received an invitation to meet with the directors of Beilinson Hospital near Petach Tikvah, the central training hospital of the Kupat Holim health insurance organization.

"We have a little research money from the Rogoff Foundation," one of the doctors explained. "We hadn't thought in terms of endocrinology. However, we agree with the Agency that it would be a mistake not to take advantage of your availability. We'll put a small laboratory at your disposal, and perhaps one full-time assistant. It's not what you are used to, of course," he added apologetically. "But Kupat Holim generally doesn't go in for research of that sort, and for us it's a lot."

Neither was Ber used to the salary. His monthly payment came to six hundred pounds, and this included remuneration for his daily endocrinological responsibilities at Beilinson. After taxes, he was left with three hundred fifty pounds. Never mind, he would accept the arrangement for the time being. He was not ungrateful. It could hardly have been a simple matter for the Agency and the Kupat Holim to break all precedents on his behalf. He understood their financial problems.

But he understood his own, too, and they plagued him continually. Professor Artur Ber, world-renowned scientist, a wealthy man in his native land, a voluntary immigrant to Israel—now subsisting with his wife and two growing children on three hundred fifty pounds a month! He discussed the problem with friends: "How can I pay for my daughter's music lessons?" he asked. "Or her English and swimming lessons? How can we go to a concert or theater, or even buy a book—or pay for a life-insurance premium? I'm already in debt thirty-five hundred pounds. You see how small the apartment is. We have one room for both children. Our bed is in my study. I'm selling off some of my most priceless books, my entire Sienkiewicz and Zeromski collections, first editions of Tuvim and Raymont. What's left for us? We're educated, cultured people, and we're giving up the only things that make life worth-while for us.

"There is a good side to Israel, too, of course," he added. "We *are* free, and we never forget it. And you can almost taste the idealism here—in spite of all the chaos and inefficiency. Imagine that Yemenite convict risking his neck to stop the *fedayin* escape at Shatta prison. You read about it the other day? He was already under life sentence, but his country came first. One must admire that. And the bravery of the Israel army, something I never expected. The workers get good protection here, too, better than in Poland; almost cradle-to-grave security. That is *true* socialism. Old Shimonowski would have liked that."

But there was so much that was bad in the Jewish State, so much that could not be forgotten or forgiven. He thought especially of the uncon-scionable inefficiency and impersonality of Israel officialdom. Whatever public benefits the government and Agency conferred, these were dissipated by the bureaucrats' grudging rudeness, their susceptibility to "influence." Perhaps the Party structure was responsible. It was inconceivable that a nation could support so many political parties and still survive. Everything one touched here had a political wire attached to it—it was almost Balkan.

The nation was Balkan in some of its tyrannies, too. As a nonreligionist, Ber was horrified by the pressure tactics of the Orthodox politicians, their ability to paralyze the country on the Sabbath, their absolute control of personal and marital affairs in Israel. Many of the Bers' friends had brought Polish—Catholic—wives with them. These women were frequently snubbed by their Jewish neighbors. Under moral circumstances, their children might have been raised and educated as Jews. But the Orthodox remained ob-durate; the children were Gentiles, and with their mothers were beyond the pale of Jewish marital or burial privileges.

"I may attend Chanukah or Passover functions," Ber pointed out, "but only as national holidays, not as religious ones. That's the way the children are learning Hebrew and Jewish history in school: strictly as a national language and a national history. I want no Orthodox mumbo jumbo mixed up with it. They won't attend Yom Kippur services. Johnny, my youngest, will not have a bar mitzvah."

"Except under strong social pressure," Irena cautioned.

"I'm not so sure," Ber replied, momentarily forgetting his children's re-ligious classes in Warsaw. "If we had wanted the easy way we certainly wouldn't be here."

In the winter of 1962, four years after their last meeting, the author paid a return visit to Artur Ber and his family. To outward appearances little had changed. It was the same apartment, cluttered, overcrowded with old furniture and books. Irena was still an attractive woman, tall, brown-haired, fresh-complexioned. Ber was perhaps a little stockier, and had shaved off his mustache; but his eyes still sparkled when he warmed to his subject. His manner, too, remained patient and courtly. The children had grown well: the daughter was a slim, ethereal youngster of nearly fifteen, the boy a vigorous, happy extrovert, a typical sabra.

But there were differences, of course. For one thing, all conversation was carried on in Hebrew. The children spoke it perfectly, Irena with some difficulty, and Ber himself with surprising ease and fluency. Upon being complimented, the doctor shrugged modestly: "I studied Hebrew as a boy, don't forget," he remarked. "I had a basis for the language. Now I even lecture in Hebrew to young doctors."

But he had progressed in other ways, too. As he described his career during the past few years, it became clear how and why he had regained his peace of mind.

"I am a professor again," he declared, with justifiable pride. "All students doing research in endocrinology at Beilinson have to pass my examinations.

I'm now chief of the department of endocrinology at the hospital, you see. It's a wonderful feeling. My salary hasn't gone up, but I've been able to resume a private practice of sorts. This has enabled me to begin paying off my debts to the Agency. That's important psychologically."

Ber's satisfactions were more than professional. He had thrown himself actively into the public life of his new country. Within the space of four years he had been elected to the secretariat of the doctors' division of the Histadrut, chairman of the Histadrut's health department for the kibbutzim and moshavim, and a member of the steering committee of the Union of Polish Immigrants.

"I'm a citizen, after all." He laughed. "I have to assume the responsibilities of a citizen."

"Yes, but he's working like a crazy man," Irena interrupted. "He suffered a heart attack two years ago—he didn't tell you that. He won't slow down. A doctor ought to know better."

"Never mind that." He dismissed her complaint. "It would have happened to me wherever I live. I enjoy my work, and I enjoy working hard. I can't change."

The Bers took especial pride in the children. They had adjusted to the country better than they had ever imagined. Kristina was the outstanding student in her Bible class. Her Hebrew poems had been published in the school paper. She had many friends. Johnny belonged to a youth group and excelled in sports. He would soon be old enough to join the Boy Scouts, his burning ambition of the moment.

"Johnny, stand on your head for the gentleman," his mother commanded. With alacrity, the youngster performed the stunt, then sat back proudly amid laughter and applause.

"No more complaints then?" the doctor was asked. "Evidently you've lost most of your misgivings about Israel."

Ber looked surprised. "I have the same misgivings now that I had four years ago," he said. "You know, there are more things wrong with this country than right with it. I haven't changed my mind about anything— except that we're staying here and fighting it out. My friends and I have talked it over, you see, and we decided that fighting it out is the only way. Either we make our weight felt in this country or no one will take us any more seriously than—" he grimaced—"the Moroccans or the Iraqis." He shook his head vigorously. "No, my friend, I'm an educated Westerner. I'm not ready to become just another immigration statistic—not Professor Artur Ber." He sighed. "I'm at peace with myself, you might say—but not with Israel. For example, my situation is better than it was when I first came. But it's still far from good. It always will be difficult for me, you see, because I'm a doctor. I can live here. I can do my research. I can cure people." His face began to darken. "And my colleagues and I can be exploited more unmercifully than any other group of citizens in the State. It's a scandal and an outrage. They squeeze us till the pips squeak."

The salaries Ber described were no secret. They had been the subject of acrimonious public discussion for years. Upon first arriving in the country, he had refused to believe his senses when the wage scale was described to him. There was no mistake, however. The rates were official, fixed jointly by the Histadrut doctors' division, the government, and the Israel medical association. Internes received a take-home pay of I£195 monthly. Very well, they might be twenty-five years old, married, and fathers—but internes were internes. Afterward, too, however, general practitioners beginning their careers in their late twenties received a net take-home pay of no more than I£250 per month. Ultimately this would rise to a maximum of I£305, and perhaps I£30 more each ten years after that. Financially, at least, the general practitioner henceforth was a forgotten man. Even physicians who had spent five years of hospital work qualifying for a specialty rarely earned more than I£450 net a month in Kupat Holim. These were men in their mid-thirties, who were beginning their careers without having accumulated so much as a single retirement or insurance benefit—although the average worker had already received such increments for the past eighteen years.

If the physician was asked to continue at the hospital as a senior staff-member, he would draw a maximum salary of I£500 monthly, but still without overtime or pension benefits, although he might be approaching forty. In fact, it was only when he had reached his early forties, and possibly had been appointed director of a clinic or deputy director of a hospital department, that his income began to mount, perhaps to I£570, with associated retirement and insurance rights. Someday, if he were particularly skilled or fortunate, the full responsibility of directing a hospital department might be his, and with it a take-home pay of I£630 monthly. At that, the salary was I£280 higher than the national average for practicing physicians. It was flat and final, with no supplements or tax deductions. And it was exactly 80 per cent higher than the income of a skilled laborer! Or, put another way, the ratio of an Israel physician's earnings compared to those of a skilled laborer was less than two to one. In Western Europe and the United States it was eight to one.

"In Poland and the Communist countries it's fifteen to one," Ber pointed out. "And these are Communist countries, mind you."

Ber was a latecomer on the scene. The indignation of the nation's physicians had been rising long before he and hundreds of other doctors arrived with the Polish immigration. Each year there had been medical committee meetings both within and outside the Histadrut. Petitions had been drawn up. Threats had been openly made. Several times the Association of Academic Workers—the doctors' union within the Histadrut—had warned the parent organization that the situation was becoming altogether intolerable. If drastic changes were not made in the ratio, the only alternative might be a physicians' strike. No one was happy about that possibility. It ran counter to the deepest traditions of the medical profession.

"What can we do?" protested Ber. "It's not a question of social prestige with us. We must have a higher standard of living simply to be good doctors, to purchase the books we need, to maintain our educational level, to travel to meet other doctors. Many of us would like our children to continue in the medical profession. How then can we afford the high school, university, and medical school education that they must have?"

To these complaints the government and Histadrut had responded, in turn, by pointing out that the basis of Israel medical practice had always been health insurance; and that, as a consequence, doctors had no alternative but to accept salaried positions in the insurance funds. Moreover, they received the highest salaries the State's economy could bear. They were better off, surely, than physicians in private practice. They earned more than engineers, and usually more than lawyers. Too much discrepancy simply could not be allowed between the professional classes and the working classes—if the nation intended to maintain a sound, healthy society.

As far as the arbiters of Israel's political and economic life were concerned, this last point was the crucial one. From the earliest days of the Second and Third *Aliyot,* the powerful Labor Zionist bloc had successfully prevented the revival in Palestine of the kind of Jewish society that had existed for centuries in the Diaspora: a society of merchants and scholars, of soft-handed intellectuals and *luftmenschen.* The Zionist homeland required workers and farmers and fighters. *Their* needs would take priority. And for the past forty years they had. The Histadrut and the Labor parties made their position clear: the dignity of physical work must be rewarded; the Jewish intellectual was still a marginal man.

Of course, ideologies more often reflect than shape realities, and this was especially true of Israel. Had there been a shortage of skilled physicians, as in pre-World War I days, for example, the laws of supply and demand would surely have been translated into higher doctors' salaries. But as it was, the medical profession had never recovered from the hardships of overabundance. It was evident, too, that Ber and his Polish colleagues were hardly in a position to solve the problem. Indeed, they compounded it. Whatever the justice of their own case, they were confronted with an inescapable dilemma: wages would have to remain low if the large-scale professional unemployment of the 1930s was not to be repeated. "We are willing to provide you with jobs," the directorate of Kupat Holim continually reminded the newcomers. "But if you want work you must take it where and how we give it. We are determined that not so much as a single immigrant physician will have to abandon his profession. We want no doctors driving buses, as they did in the days of the German immigration. Employment will entail sacrifices, however, and you must be prepared to make them."

As far as the doctors were concerned, they had already made too many. In 1959, and again in 1962, they announced their intention to strike. In both instances, as it happened, last minute concessions avoided a national medical walkout. But the concessions were minor ones. In 1962, for example, salaries were raised by a maximum of 7 per cent.

"Just in time for the devaluation of the pound," Ber remarked angrily. "They gave us the increase with one hand and took it away with the other. Someday soon this country is going to learn what the Communists learned years ago; physicians are not proletarians. If doctors don't receive the security they deserve for all their years of training and responsibility, no one will go into this profession anymore. Then you'll see the results a generation from now. There will be a shortage of physicians, I promise you. The health standard of this country is one of our proudest accomplishments. It will decline."

Much of his leisure time was now taken up with committee work. There were facts and statistics to be assembled, arguments to be prepared. Somehow the conscience of the nation had to be reached. This was his mission, and it drove him relentlessly. "A doctor is not a mechanic or a greengrocer, you know. People must understand that."

He started to amplify the point, but at that moment an assistant knocked at the door of his office, interrupting his train of thought. "Professor Ber, they've brought the baby for you to look at."

He replaced his note pad and walked down the corridor to the examination room. The pediatrician was waiting at the entrance. They shook hands cordially.

"I wanted you to see the child," the pediatrician explained. "I've tentatively diagnosed a classic adrenal hyperplasia—she's only eight months old. Ovarian activity seems unlikely to me."

"It certainly sounds like an adrogenital syndrome," Ber agreed.

They walked in. Ber smiled sympathetically at the mother. She was a young woman. This was her first child. The baby lay whimpering on the examination table. Yes, it was either the adrenals or the ovaries, not much doubt about that. There were the symptoms: premature puberty, enlarged clitoris, facial acne, weight already eighteen pounds.

"We'll make lab tests immediately," Ber decided. "Twenty-four-hour urine specimens, and fifteen cc. of blood," he instructed his assistant. "I want the corticoids tested."

The chemical tests were duly carried out. The report was in Ber's hands the next afternoon. It was the adrenal hormones, all right. He reached the pediatrician by telephone.

"So far, so good," he reported. "The lab reports a tremendous overproduction of 17-ketosteroids, something like fifty in the urine alone. At this age, bilateral hyperplasia seems quite likely. May I suggest that the child receive five milligrams of dexamethasone each day for the next six or seven days. Restricted sodium diet, of course. I should like to see her again in a week."

The week passed, and the baby was returned for examination. The mother said nothing, but her face was gray with anxiety. This time the pediatrician had brought three medical students with him.

"I don't like it at all," he whispered to Ber, when the mother was out of earshot. "You can see for yourself. All the clinical symptoms are still there."

Ber nodded. There had been no change whatever. He picked up the laboratory report.

"Is this from today?" he asked in astonishment. The adrenals were still pumping four times the normal level of hormones.

"Sixty-two 17-ketosteroids as of this morning," replied the pediatrician.

Ber considered a moment. "Well, doctor, this is no hyperplasia," he said finally. "Dexamethasone surely would have suppressed it."

The pediatrician cleared his throat uncertainly, then asked: "You are surely not suggesting that it's a tumor, Professor Ber? Not in a child this age?"

"I suspect a tumor," Ber answered firmly. "Of course, we'll want a picture. But I definitely suspect an adrenal tumor, doctor."

The baby was prepared for the X-ray room. Delicately the roentgenologist thrust his needle into the space behind the abdominal cavity. The injection of air would outline the retroperitoneal area clearly.

Yet when the plates were developed, they showed nothing out of the ordinary. Not a sign of an adrenal tumor on the films. The pediatrician seemed relieved.

"I didn't relish the thought of abdominal surgery on an eight-month-old child," he confessed.

"Doctor, I still recommend it," said Ber. "Those tests convince me that we have a tumor here."

The pediatrician hesitated. "Of course I wouldn't argue with you, Professor Ber," he said at last. "But the absence of X-ray evidence seems surprising, to say the least."

It was a fair objection. Surgery was rarely carried out on the basis of chemical tests alone. As recently as three or four years earlier it would have been unthinkable. Still, Ber was a distinguished scientist; his research had contributed in large measure to the reliability of hormone evidence. The pediatrician really had little choice in the matter. After additional consultations with Professor Nathan, chief of surgery at Beilinson, the decision was taken.

On the morning of the operation Ber found eight other doctors in the scrub room, two of them students of his. News of the case had evidently circulated through the hospital. As he lathered his hands slowly and deliberately, it occurred to him that he must have sounded quite dogmatic to his colleagues. Still, it was not the first time he had risked his professional reputation; he would not retreat from his original diagnosis. In the operating room itself, the sight of the helpless little body saddened him further. Sodium pentathol had already been administered, the anesthesia tube was in the child's mouth, her abdomen swabbed yellow. Professor Nathan bent over the operating field. With one sure transverse stroke of his scalpel he opened the muscle wall. The assistant followed the incision with his sponge. A few more strokes along the same line and the entire abdomen lay open.

With great delicacy now, the surgeon severed the attachments around the spleen. Thus far there were few bleeders. Only two hemostats were necessary and the field was quite clear. With his hand, Professor Nathan gently lifted the spleen and pancreas, then the splenic artery and vein; the second assistant held the organs firmly. There it was, the left adrenal clearly in view. The gland was no larger than a pea. It was obviously normal. Ber began to perspire. He heard someone cough. For a moment his eye caught the pediatrician's. Then he concentrated again on the child.

By now a half-hour had gone by. Professor Nathan paused for a report from the anesthesiologist. It was good, only a slight drop in blood pressure. Immediately the surgeon and the first assistant changed sides at the table. They would proceed toward the right adrenal. With two fingers of his left hand the surgeon forced the kidney downward. The assistant gently nudged the liver in the same direction. The scrub nurse handed Professor Nathan his scalpel again. This time he made the incision in the glistening white membrane covering the back wall of the abdomen. It was a rectangular "trap-door" opening, and it required time and exquisite precision. Instinctively some of the doctors edged forward. Ber was on his toes, his neck craned forward. There was a murmur of excitement. Ber took a deep breath, a half sigh. Behind the vena cava the right adrenal was emerging. It was gray-white and the size of a peach: pure tumor, obviously malignant.

Professor Nathan and the assistant moved swiftly now. They required less than ten minutes to free the adrenal. With a simple sponge forceps the surgeon lifted the neoplastic—tumorized—gland. The remaining attachments to the kidney would have to be cut, as well as all the adhesions to the abdominal wall. The task consumed an additional forty minutes; there were many bleeders here. But finally it was done. The malignancy was dropped into a damp towel and passed to Ber for inspection.

"Mazel Tov," whispered the pediatrician, peering over Ber's shoulder. "Congratulations."

They both grinned weakly behind their masks, then sent the growth on to the pathology laboratory.

The rest was anticlimactic. Professor Nathan left the sewing-up to his assistant. Ber stayed to the end.

"Blood pressure eighty over fifty," announced the anesthesiologist, before the child was wheeled away. Ber followed the rolling table into the recovery room. He himself administered the first cortisone injection. For nearly three minutes afterward he continued to gaze fondly at the unconscious baby. Saline solution would maintain her body chemistry. The pulse was good. Within twenty hours she would be out of the recovery room. As he walked into the corridor, Ber greeted the child's parents, who thanked him warmly. Both were in tears.

"The pathologist told us it looked semimalignant, Professor Ber," said the mother. "Are you sure Dr. Nathan got it all?"

"Almost positive," Ber replied with conviction. "The adrenogenital syndrome should fade out within forty-eight hours. The rest is simple now. With the right cortisone ratio we'll have a fine, healthy baby on our hands in no time."

He let them enter the recovery room, and then continued the walk back to the elevator. The husband was shabbily dressed, he thought. What could that young couple be earning between them? Perhaps four hundred pounds, five hundred? Not more. It hardly mattered. The operation, the hospital and steroids were frightfully expensive, but at least the burden would not fall on the parents. The people would bear it—the nation which had allowed nothing to block effective and thorough action on Artur Ber's diagnosis. That was worth something. He experienced a few such triumphant moments each week, and the exhilaration of them lightened his step. There were worse places, he admitted.

⇥⇥⇥ I I ⇤⇤⇤

Ha-Tikvah

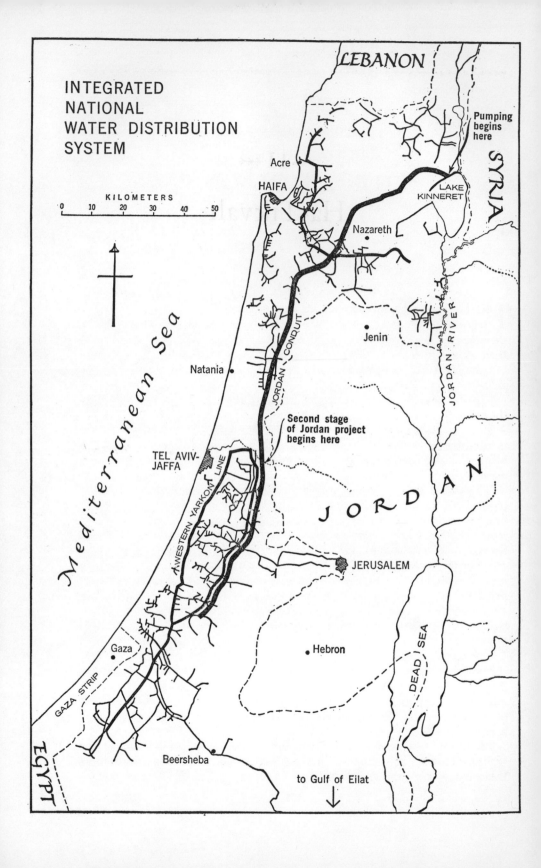

INTEGRATED
NATIONAL
WATER DISTRIBUTION
SYSTEM

KILOMETERS
0   10   20   30   40   50

LEBANON

SYRIA

Pumping
begins
here

Acre

HAIFA

LAKE
KINNERET

Nazareth

Mediterranean Sea

Jenin

JORDAN RIVER

Natania

JORDAN CONDUIT

Second stage
of Jordan project
begins here

TEL AVIV-
JAFFA

WESTERN YARKON LINE

J O R D A N

JERUSALEM

Gaza

GAZA STRIP

Hebron

DEAD SEA

EGYPT

Beersheba

to Gulf of Eilat

CHAPTER TEN

THE ENGINEER

IN JULY of 1932 my parents checked into Jerusalem's Eden Hotel. Exhausted by the long bus ride from Haifa, and thoroughly enervated by the summer heat, they hurried through the formalities of registration, and then walked quickly to the protective coolness of their suite.

"Ah," said my father gratefully, as he opened the door to a spacious, well-ventilated double room.

"Thank heavens," murmured my mother, surveying the tile bath and shower.

Then, as my mother still enjoys telling the story, she turned the faucet in the bath—and waited. No water. She tried the shower faucet. Nothing. Muttering and perspiring, my father wrenched and twisted the taps in the wash basin. Still not a drop.

"I'll call the desk," he said at length. "They probably forgot to open the pipe to our room." He lifted the telephone: "Hello desk! We're not getting water here. We've tried all the faucets." He listened silently for several moments, then replaced the receiver. "They say it's not the bathing hour!" he explained to my mother. "It's the same in every hotel."

" 'Not the bathing hour?' " said my mother indignantly. "They can't tell me when to take a bath. Let me have that. Hello, desk. What's going on here? I don't care about other hotels. Now look, we're tired, and we're hot. We must have a bath. No, now. Good." She hung up triumphantly. "Wait a couple of minutes and then try the faucet again," she said. "They promised us water."

The management kept its promise. Ten minutes after the first telephone conversation, there was a knock at the door. My mother opened it. No one there. She walked to the end of the hall. Still not a sign of life. Only upon returning to the room did she see the vessel, parked neatly at the threshold of the door. It was a stone urn, slightly less than two feet high, filled to the brim with water.

"Welcome to Palestine," cried my father—and then leaned against the wall, convulsed with laughter. In the nine years since he had last been in the country, some things had still not changed.

405

Nor, in certain respects, have they yet. Today one can turn the faucet in a hotel bathroom with reasonable certainty that water will issue forth. But the guest is encouraged not to abuse the privilege. "Please do not waste water," appeals the sign above the basin. "Help us irrigate the Negev." It is a genteel way of making the request. Few hotel proprietors would be so gauche as to suggest that each additional drop of running water adds to their overhead. It is true, though. No utility in an Israel hotel or home is as expensive as water. Thus, in cities far from sources of water—in Jerusalem, for example—it is the practice of bathers to wet themselves only long enough to work up a quick lather. Afterward they swiftly rinse, stoically refusing the Western indulgence of a luxurious water-massage.

And yet, as hotel proprietors suggest, this restraint is undoubtedly a matter of national as well as personal self-interest. In movie theaters, during the brief recess when advertisements flash on the screen, the final slide invariably displays a dripping faucet, with the warning underneath: "Chaval al Kol Tipah—a shame to waste a single drop." The advertisement is sponsored by the National Water Board, and it reflects the government's ceaseless determination to conserve this most precious of the nation's resources. Indeed, when the winter rains fail to arrive on schedule, concern is palpable in every corner of the nation. Newspapers report the crisis on page one. Farmers gaze at the sky in mute anguish. City dwellers discuss the water level as if their very livelihoods depended upon the replenishment of wells and storage reservoirs—which, of course, is not far from the case. In the reclaimed desert-land of Israel, water is life, and hence is sacred.

Consider its limitations. There is no precipitation whatever throughout the long summer months. The Jewish Agency states that the annual (winter) rainfall decreases from north to south, attaining its maximum intensity of forty inches a year in the Galilee, and dropping steadily to eight inches at Beersheba—then to nothing at all at the tip of the Negev desert. Even of the rainfall that does reach the ground, moreover, only the smallest fraction remains on the surface, or is absorbed into it. No less than 60 per cent is returned to the atmosphere by soil and plants. Of the rest, 35 per cent is soaked up by the ground; while the remaining 5 per cent flows down the roaring winter streams that discharge either into the Mediterranean or into the Jordan River. But thus far even the Jordan's waters are a dead loss. They empty into the sulphurous inland lake called the Dead Sea—where they evaporate. Actually, most of the water available for drinking or irrigation is subterranean, and must be pumped up to reach the land. Unfortunately, the one area of the country which best lends itself to irrigation is the south; and here, underground water resources hardly exist at all.

Can anything be done, then, to slake the thirsty land? Until the most recent decades few of Palestine's inhabitants thought so. Under the Ottoman regime, irrigation was limited exclusively to the coastal plain; small oil engines pumped water from shallow wells to the local orange groves. For domestic uses, settlers carried water on donkey back or in horse-drawn carts. Towns like Jerusalem continued to subsist, as in ancient times, on rain water collected in underground cisterns from the roofs and gutters.

Not surprisingly, it was the Zionists who first attempted something better. By 1914 the Jewish colonies of Petach Tikvah and Tel Aviv began piping water supplies into their groves from a small plant erected on the Yarkon River. The generator was a seventy-five horsepower diesel; it was the largest water venture of its day. During the first years of the British Mandate, the Jewish National Fund concentrated primarily on deepening the wells in the coastal area. The results of that effort were not unimpressive. Within a single decade after the establishment of the Mandate, the Jews managed to quadruple Palestine's supply of water. Indeed, together with tree planting, well drilling virtually became the symbol of the Zionist renaissance. The one major departure from the well-digging technique was the construction, in 1928, of a hydroelectric power station at Naharayim on the Jordan River. Unhappily, this plant was destroyed by the Arab Legion during the 1948 invasion of Israel.

Renewed progress in water development awaited the 1930s, when a large influx of Jewish immigration brought fresh manpower and funds into Palestine. Advanced methods of well drilling, pipe laying, and reservoir construction were put into use. Thus, exploiting the supply of electric power from the Jordan River hydroelectric power station, and from thermal stations in Tel Aviv, Jewish engineers were able to carry out large-scale pumping economically and dependably. For the first time, too, water was piped from springs in the Valley of Jezreel, from the Jordan and Yarmuk rivers, and even from wells sunk in the rock formations of the hills. Where needs could not be met by the resources of a single village, regional systems were established, as in the Jordan and Yavneel valleys, the Harel Bloc, and the coastal plain.

In 1936, after detailed surveys and negotiations, the Jewish Agency and the Histadrut pooled their resources to establish a national Jewish water company, known as Mekorot. Within a month after its incorporation, the new company embarked upon its first project: constructing a waterworks for the city of Haifa, and a pumping station for the Valley of Yizreel. Meanwhile, the Mandatory authorities, whose headquarters were located in Jerusalem, high in the Judean mountains, decided that it was strategically dangerous for the government to depend any longer upon local cisterns for its water supply. Accordingly, British engineers set about installing a long pipe line, to run from the Rosh HaAyen spring near Petach Tikvah, directly into the Romema reservoir, on the outskirts of the isolated capital. (Twelve years later Britain's pro-Arab government would have reason to regret that decision.)

It was not, however, until 1943 that the exploitation of Palestine's total water resources was made the subject of serious and detailed research. The project was directed by Mekorot from its small office in Tel Aviv, and one of its first staff members was Aharon Wiener, the man who was destined ultimately to become the driving force and chief engineer of water development in Israel. A gentle, dark-eyed, bushy-haired introvert, Wiener had arrived in the country only seven years earlier, from his native Czechoslovakia. He had been reared in Brno, the son of a prosperous textile manufacturer, and had received a first-rate scientific education at the city's

Czechoslovak Engineering College, from which institution he received his degree in 1935. An ardent Zionist, Wiener waited only a year after his graduation before departing for Palestine.

He arrived at a bad time. Civil war had broken out between Arabs and Jews, and the paralysis of economic life apparently foreclosed any employment opportunities in his own profession. During his first sixteen months in the country, Wiener supported himself only by accepting occasional odd jobs as a draftsman and surveyor. Not until 1939, fully three years after reaching Palestine, did he receive his first engineering commission, planning settlements for the Jewish Agency in the Hulah Valley. He carried out the assignment with meticulous care and efficiency. Other projects soon came his way: constructing bridges over the tributaries of the Jordan; planning office buildings for the Haifa refineries; designing army camps and roads (after the outbreak of World War II), and later mock-ups of Italian beaches and coastal installations—in preparation for the British invasion of Italy. Appointed resident engineer of the Gaza district, Wiener proved an expert administrator, especially in dealing with the bedouin who were his principal supply of manpower. By 1943 his professional reputation was established.

It was in that year, therefore, that he was approached by his friend and colleague, Nachman Kaplansky, with an offer to join Mekorot. The proposed salary was hardly an inducement. But apparently there were other challenges.

"The war won't last forever, Aharon," Kaplansky explained. "When it ends we'll have to find new ways of absorbing immigrants and stimulating our economy. Water will be the key. There has to be some hard, long-range thinking on a master water plan, and we want you to help us. From your point of view, this is an opportunity to use your best talents."

Wiener was less impressed by Kaplansky's rhetoric than by the men who comprised the directorate. The company's general manager was the able Levi Eshkol (later to become minister of finance and then prime minister in the government of Israel). The general secretary was the equally competent Pinhas Sapir (later to become minister of commerce and industry); chairman of the board was Dr. Abraham Granat, the renowned land expert and chairman of the Jewish National Fund. The staff of engineers and designers represented the best talent of its kind in the country. Indeed, Simcha Blass, the chief consulting engineer, was widely recognized as something of a genius, one of those rare personalities in whom professional skill was blended with administrative resourcefulness and political expertise. Blass had foreseen the possibility of exploiting Palestine's water resources long before most of his colleagues. It was he, in fact, who had originally convinced the Jewish Agency and the Histadrut to establish a national water company.

Yet for all Blass' prophetic intuitiveness, the vision of bringing water to the parched and arid homeland was as old as the Zionist movement itself. In fact, it was Theodor Herzl, the founder of political Zionism, who first gave expression to that dream. In his novel *Altneuland,* written in 1902,

Herzl projected the grandiose—but not altogether farfetched—notion of irrigating Palestine by tapping the Nile; the river's waters would be piped under the Suez Canal, then pumped on in a conduit across the Sinai Peninsula. A disciple of Herzl's, the Russian-Jewish engineer, Pinhas Rutenberg, conceived the rather more likely idea of exploiting the 1,400-meter fall of the Jordan River to the Dead Sea, thus irrigating Palestine and providing the country's electric power at the same time. In later years the chief geologist of the Mandatory government, George Blake, issued a report which declared Palestine's water resources to be far more extensive than had formerly been recognized. Blake was killed by bedouin in 1937—before he succeeded altogether in puncturing the argument, used by the Colonial Office for political purposes, that Palestine was too arid to support a larger Jewish population.

Now, therefore, in the 1940s, the opportunity had fallen to Blass and a new generation of engineers to deal with the perennial challenge of irrigation. Wiener willingly joined them in their effort. Yet from the very outset the Mekorot engineering team was faced with several nearly insurmountable obstacles. One was the lack of even the most rudimentary information about Palestine's water resources. The British had accumulated some data on the Jordan's rate of flow; but there appeared to be little likelihood of harnessing that flow for irrigation purposes so long as the river ran through Arab territory. The engineers knew, however, that untapped ground water probably existed on the coastal plain. Perhaps, then, this reserve offered the best immediate possibility of watering Jewish villages and fields. It is worth noting that as late as 1943 only 240,000 dunams, less than 25 per cent of Jewish-owned land, were irrigated. The majority of the Zionist settlements still resorted to dry farming.

Accordingly, studying the reports of European and American hydrologists, and then working closely with their own geologists, the Mekorot engineers managed to gather some crucial information about the nature of ground water. Its origin was rain—but rain which apparently penetrated only absorbent soil and granular rock. Thus, sandstone, gravel, or "percolation-type" rock offered the surest clues to the presence of ground water. If untapped, this water flowed slowly underground back to the sea. Some of these subterranean deposits may have been millions of years old; yet, far from stagnating beneath the earth's surface, they were continually circulating back to the sea, replenished in a steady cycle by winter rains. By painstaking experimentation, the engineers discovered, too, that the rate at which ground water could be tapped had to be precisely and mathematically adjusted to the amount of rainfall. If the natural cycle of flow was too drastically interrupted, if more water was tapped than could be "recharged" by rain, then the well would be drained dry. Moreover, if the underground water level dropped too suddenly, sea water would flow back in, polluting the soil.

The engineers collected their data, dispatched geologists to search for "percolation" soil and rock, and then conducted flow and replenishment tests. The methods were by no means foolproof in the 1940s, and the first charts were far from reliable. Nevertheless, enough likely sites were located to make feasible a number of regional drilling programs, especially in the Valley of Jezreel and the northwestern Negev. Yet here a new and more serious obstacle was encountered, and it was not technological. It happened that the Jewish farm holdings were located between large Arab-occupied areas. Suspecting (quite rightly) that Jewish agricultural ambitions were political no less than economic, the British authorities urged Arab landowners to refuse the Jews permission to extend pipes across their territories.

In September of 1946 a major attempt was made to bypass this obstruction. During the Second World War twelve Jewish farm settlements had been established in the northern Negev. For three years they subsisted exclusively on dry farming. In 1946, however, wells were discovered in the Beersheba area, and the time had come to extend water pipes to these outposts. As anticipated, the British persuaded many of the Arab sheiks to deny the Jews the required easement. Fortunately, the problem was partially solved with an ancient and time-proven equalizer: handsome bribes, paid to the sheiks by the Jewish Agency. And when the Arabs themselves were given access to Jewish water at quite reasonable rates, they dropped their opposition altogether.

Nevertheless, it was still necessary for the pipes to cross wasteland. And because this was Crown territory, the Mandatory government blocked further passage by simple administrative fiat. Yet once again the Jews managed to counter, this time by an ingenious exploitation of Ottoman land law (which had been inherited by the Mandatory regime). It was a technique which had already been perfected during the establishment of "illegal" kibbutzim. Working in moonless darkness, Mekorot engineers and laborers fitted the steel tubing together at breakneck speed, cloaking the sparks of their acetylene torches with damp blankets. Simultaneously, Haganah scouts decoyed the police by creating noisy disturbances in neighboring areas. Occasionally, too, Jewish girls managed to lure British security officers into nightlong drunken parties. In the morning, when the police discovered what had been done, they were too late to order the installations removed. No legal action could be taken against "improved" wasteland. Determined not to be outmaneuvered, however, the Mandatory regime organized mixed British-Arab police units, and sent them out on special night patrols. Again the effort was unavailing; Haganah units almost invariably succeeded in decoying the police elsewhere. By the summer of 1947, a series of pumping stations had been constructed and 130 miles of pipes laid, with outlets in each of the twelve kibbutzim.

During the Palestine war of 1948–1949, water from these pipes literally kept the beleaguered outposts alive, and with them the Jewish claim to the Negev desert. At times the transfusion was a precarious one. Shortly after crossing the Israel frontier, the Egyptian invaders demolished the central Negev pumping station at Niram. The Jewish settlements were instantly deprived of irrigation water, while reserves of drinking water dropped rapidly and alarmingly. Yet, rather than attempt to rebuild the station elsewhere (which probably would have been impossible under the circumstances), Wiener immediately designed and constructed a portable water pump. Every two or three weeks, under cover of darkness, engineers smuggled the ingenious machine to the wells behind Arab lines. There it pumped water to the settlements for several hours, and the kibbutzim thereby succeeded in replenishing their tanks for another fortnight. Today the legend of the "Wiener gadget" is enshrined in Israel folklore, together with the epic of the "Davidka," the homemade mortar which repelled the Arab Legion in Jerusalem.

The role of water during the battle for Jerusalem was, if possible, even more crucial and dramatic. The story is best related in *The Faithful City,* a masterful account of the siege written by Dr. Dov Joseph, military governor of the capital during the Israel War of Liberation. Joseph pointed out that Jerusalem's main water supply came from the Rosh HaAyen springs near Lydda, some forty miles down the mountains. Unhappily, the four pumping stations were all located in Arab-held areas; and if the Palestine Civil War of 1936–1939 had taught one lesson, it was that the Arabs would not hesitate to damage or even destroy these stations to undermine Jewish resistance. To compound the danger, the British had announced their intention to leave shortly. There was now every likelihood that Jerusalem would soon be cut off from the Rosh HaAyen springs altogether, and thrown back almost entirely upon its own water resources.

These resources were quite meager. They consisted of a single reservoir, in the suburb of Romema, with a capacity of a mere twenty thousand cubic meters. It was quite evident that this pitifully minimal quantity would not have lasted the Jewish population of Jerusalem more than forty-eight hours. But Dr. Joseph was determined to find other supplies. On December 19, 1947, he dispatched a secret request to the Jewish householders of the city, ordering them to scour the cisterns at the base of their houses "in preparation for the impending winter rains." Under normal circumstances the order would have raised eyebrows. To be sure, stone and concrete cisterns had once served to capture the overflow of rain from roofs and gutters; but they dated from the time when rainfall was the only source of water, except for goatskins delivered by Arabs from near-by wells. Moreover, these ancient catch basins were quite unreliable, and certainly not the last word in hygiene, for they had been out of use for years. Nearly all the Jewish inhabitants of Jerusalem recognized that Joseph's stated reason was purely a ruse, however. Instead of relying upon the weather, the governor was determined to fill these cisterns clandestinely with water from the Rosh HaAyen pipe line.

Dr. Joseph's scheme was by no means farfetched. His engineers had been making some careful calculations; they estimated that the supply of available water could be increased to 115,000 cubic meters—providing that all the cisterns in Jewish Jerusalem were repaired, and enough tin were imported to fashion additional tanks for each home. Of course, by itself even this enlarged storage capacity would not meet Jerusalem's needs in the event of a prolonged siege. Checking their slide rules carefully, however, Joseph's engineers were convinced that if the replenished tanks and cisterns were immediately sealed, and if water were subsequently doled out at the rate of ten quarts per person per day, the city would be able to subsist on its own resources for perhaps one hundred and fifteen days. It was worth trying. Admittedly the project would be terribly expensive; Joseph knew, too, that the Jerusalem municipal budget could hardly be stretched that far. Without delay, therefore, the governor paid an urgent visit to Ben-Gurion in Tel Aviv. He explained his plans to the prime minister designate, and pleaded for five thousand Palestine pounds. To Joseph's very great surprise, Ben-Gurion, who ordinarily never dealt personally with financial matters, opened a desk drawer and calmly wrote out the check. Less than twenty-four hours later Jerusalem's municipal engineers began an intensive drive to purchase the necessary materials, to inspect and repair cisterns, and to supervise the construction of tin water tanks.

There was not much time. Joseph recognized that the task would have to be completed within five weeks, before the British began their staged withdrawal and turned the pipe line over to the Arabs. Moreover, the entire project would have to be carried out in the strictest secrecy. The Mandatory authorities could not be allowed to know that extra water would shortly be pumped into their main pipe line specifically for the purpose of replenishing Jewish supplies—they would unquestionably have prevented this operation had they learned of it. Here the municipal water engineer, Avi Leibowitz, took steps to outwit the British. He began holding back some of the city's water, thus enabling his men to fill the cisterns at night. It was a tricky operation. Once, in late February of 1948, the commander of the British military garrison in Jerusalem complained sharply to the municipality that his men were not getting their regular water supply. Little did he imagine where it was going.

Then, on March 1, the development Dr. Joseph feared most took place. Three hundred Arab guerrillas seized the abandoned British army camp adjoining the Rosh HaAyen waterworks. They remained there, poised to cut Jerusalem's water supply at their own discretion. Seven weeks later, a detachment of armed Iraqi infiltrators ordered the station's Arab employees to stop pumping water. Immediately the Jewish authorities protested to the Mandatory government. The British in turn promised to take over the operation of the station themselves. But they never did. And finally, on May 15, two hours after the British Mandate officially terminated, the Arabs severed the pipe line. For the beleaguered Jewish inhabitants of Jerusalem, isolated and under heavy attack in the blazing months of the Palestine summer, the moment of their gravest peril had arrived.

Joseph's carefully laid plans worked well enough in the beginning. By May the cisterns and tanks had been filled with the anticipated reserve of 115,000 cubic meters. In early June, when water from the depleted Romema reservoir ceased flowing through the city's pipes, engineers broke the seals on the private cisterns and transferred their contents to larger tanker-trucks. From then on these trucks were charged with distributing the daily water rations to Jerusalem's householders. The drivers were men of authentic heroism. Despite continual shell fire and sniping, they followed their daily rounds into every district of the city. People learned to depend on them, lining up with their containers each day at specified distribution centers, grimly ignoring the bullets that occasionally whined by them. The water tankers rarely failed to arrive on schedule.

Nevertheless, the siege proved to be murderous even beyond Dr. Joseph's worst expectations. Hospitals rapidly filled to capacity; additional water supplies were soon desperately needed for medical purposes. Moreover, Israel soldiers, defending the city's ramparts in a smoke-filled inferno of artillery and mortar bombardment, were beginning to stumble and faint from thirst. As a result, Dr. Joseph ordered the daily ration cut from ten quarts to eight quarts, and later to six quarts. The authorities issued instructions on saving water, offering advice on cooking, drinking, and washing. But after a while people devised their own means of using and re-using their supply. A favorite technique was to remove the stopper from the kitchen sink and place a bucket underneath the vent; the water trapped in this fashion was used to wash floors and then to flush the toilet. By midsummer the Jerusalemites had long since forgotten the luxury of a bath. Now and then an occasional bucket of the precious liquid could be purchased from nuns and priests in the near-by churches. But this supply, too, was soon exhausted. It was not uncommon during those days to see ragged, barefoot Oriental children wandering from house to house, begging for a glass of water. Rare was the family that could spare these pitiable urchins even half a glass.

The first United Nations Truce in Palestine had come into effect as early as June 11, 1948. The fighting in Jerusalem stopped. But not the ordeal of thirst. By the terms of the armistice agreement, the Arabs undertook to resume the pumping of water to Jerusalem. They did not honor this commitment, in spite of the furious protests both of Dr. Joseph and Count Folke-Bernadotte, the United Nations truce supervisor. On July 6, Joseph wrote Bernadotte: "Twenty-five days of the twenty-eight-day truce period have already elapsed without our having received a single drop of water, although for a considerable time now there has been no technical obstacle in the way of resumption of the flow of water." No technical obstacle, perhaps, but an obvious strategic one. The Arabs expected to resume the attack the moment the truce expired. Thus far their military assaults had failed. Clearly their best chance of breaking the Jewish defense, therefore, was to maintain the blockade intact.

Fortunately for the citizens of Jerusalem, alternate plans had already been laid for the replenishment of their water supplies. The pumping station of Latrun was in Arab hands. But the other stations, the plants at Saris, Shar Haggai, even Rosh HaAyen itself, were now firmly under Jewish control— the result of savage fighting during the first weeks of the Palestine war. The problem, consequently, was to find a new source of water, and to construct a new pipeline between the available pumping depots. After hurried investigation, Aharon Wiener found his source in Kibbutz Hulda, which possessed its own well. In addition, it was now possible to gain access to Jerusalem through the recently completed "Burma Road," extending from

Deir Muheisin to Bab al-Wad. What remained to be done, therefore, was to link the Hulda well with the three pumping stations, and thus to transfer water along the length of the newly opened Jerusalem highway into the city's Romema reservoir. Unfortunately, this project required thirteen miles of new pipe line.

The construction of the makeshift pipe line was one of the epics of the war. Wiener sent his skeletal force of workers on a frantic hunt to collect every spare piece of pipe they could find in their stocks, or forage from other installations. Of course, standardization was out of the question under the circumstances. Some of the pipes were ten inches in diameter, some twelve inches. Some were perilously thin at the surface. Nevertheless, they were all joined, somehow. Pumps were manufactured in a small factory near Tel Aviv, using overhauled diesel engines from abandoned British army stocks. When manpower ran low, Ben-Gurion issued a special order allocating a hundred soldiers to the project.

It was, in fact, the actual installation of the equipment which proved the most rugged ordeal of the entire undertaking. The "Burma Road" had still not been graded, and supply trucks were continually breaking down in its craters and potholes. Pipes, too, cracked repeatedly, for there was no time to dig the proper ditches for them, or install the proper anchoring. The heat was unrelenting; strong men reeled and collapsed. Nevertheless, Wiener drove his workers mercilessly. At last, on August 11, the final stretch of pipe reached Jerusalem's Romema reservoir. As Wiener sent the order back to Hulda for pumping to begin, a large crowd of several thousand citizens drew near the reservoir, their faces pale with heat and thirst. Minutes passed, a half-hour, then three quarters of an hour. Nothing happened. Wiener was momentarily overcome by nausea. Some of the townspeople began praying compulsively. Others began sobbing as their discipline, intact during the harrowing months of the siege, gave way at last under this final ordeal. Then, with a sudden gurgle, the pipe spouted forth. Water began to pour. The cheer that went up from the crowd could be heard halfway across the city. In the ecstasy of the moment people hugged and kissed each other, as if the hour of final salvation had arrived. For Jerusalem, in fact, it had.

The lesson of the Negev kibbutzim and the Jerusalem pipe line was not lost on the Israel government When the fighting eventually drew to a close, in the late winter of 1949, a list of priorities was drawn up for the impending armistice negotiations. And when the Israel plenipotentiaries met with their Arab counterparts on the Island of Rhodes, they held fast to the first and basic point on that list: the inclusion of Palestine's key water resources within Israel territory. Indeed, even as the iron and coal deposits of Alsace-Lorraine were the key to the Franco-Prussian peace treaty of 1871, so water proved to be the central issue in the discussions terminating the Palestine war. Thus, by the provisions of the United Nations Armistice, the protruding finger of northeast Palestine was awarded to Israel, including the key tributaries of the Jordan River. Whatever developed in the future, whatever peace treaties were ultimately worked out between Arab and Jew, the victorious

Israelis of 1949 recognized that water was the one resource without which their newly independent nation could never be viable.

The urgency of irrigation could hardly be overstated. From the moment of the declaration of the State, immigrants began pouring into the country by the tens of thousands, then by the hundreds of thousands. Between 1948 and 1952 Israel doubled its population. Three hundred new villages were established in the northern and central regions of the country. Nearly every square dunam of farm land was placed under cultivation; for without sufficient hard currency for purchases abroad, Israel's food staples would have to come almost exclusively from her own soil. If that soil were to produce, however, water would be needed—water in quantities heretofore undreamed of.

This was the problem foreseen by the Royal Commission of 1937. Upon investigating the causes of Arab-Jewish tension in Palestine, the Commission had warned that the country's chronic water shortage precluded the possibility of unlimited immigration. The report had infuriated the Zionist authorities. Determined to disprove the Commission's basic contention, therefore, the Jewish Agency had promptly set about gathering expert testimony to support its own—much larger—claims for the absorptive capacity of the land. One of the first witnesses for the Zionist cause was the distinguished American soil conservationist, Dr. Walter Lowdermilk. Visiting Palestine several times during the late 1930s, Lowdermilk eventually published his conclusions in a detailed and solidly documented book. It was this celebrated "Lowdermilk report" which laid the basis for all subsequent water planning in Palestine—and later in Israel. After suggesting a number of preliminary measures for the exploitation of ground water, Lowdermilk concentrated upon evaluating the potentialities of the Jordan River. The river's rate of flow was sufficient, he insisted, to allow a major diversion of its winter rain surplus to the arid regions of the south. In this fashion enough land could be cultivated to support a population of five million.

Lowdermilk's proposals were later endorsed, and considerably refined, by another American, James Hayes, former chief engineer of the Tennessee Valley Authority. In 1945, Hayes spent four months gathering data in Palestine at the invitation of the Jewish Agency. The following year he outlined his ideas in a small volume entitled *TVA on the Jordan*. Subscribing essentially to Lowdermilk's approach, Hayes offered a gradualistic plan. It began first with the utilization of ground water, moved on to the exploitation of the Yarkon River, and concluded with the ambitious scheme of irrigating both the Jordan Valley and the northern Negev desert with the winter surplus of the Jordan River.

The Mekorot engineers had been deeply impressed by the Lowdermilk-Hayes scheme. Yet in those days the notion of carrying it out in its entirety seemed farfetched; the British and Arabs would surely have blocked any attempt to tamper with the country's basic water sources. That was before 1949, however. A war had been fought and won. The British, and most of the Arabs, were gone. Now, at last, decisions on the allocation of Israel's water resources would be made by Jews alone. Moreover, to ensure that all decisions would be made efficiently, the Israel government divided Mekorot in two: the water company itself was assigned the implementation of the master plan; but a special board of experts, called Tahal (the initialed abbreviation of "Water Planning for Israel"), was empowered to decide what the master plan would be. Wiener was appointed general manager of Tahal. The final professional decisions on where and how water would flow were now his.

Wiener himself had long been an adherent of the Lowdermilk-Hayes scheme. Yet he was too astute an engineer to recommend any venture except after the most detailed consultation with specialists. Thus, in the summer of 1949 he flew to the United States to meet with the senior staff members of the American Bureau of Reclamation. After a series of prolonged and valuable discussions, Wiener was invited to meet with a hulking, taciturn Californian named John Cotton. Cotton, who held separate degrees in civil, structural, mechanical, and electrical engineering, was widely regarded as one of the outstanding water engineers in the world. An immediate rapport developed between the two men. Indeed, they possessed many of the identical characteristics: modesty, tenacity, scrupulous devotion to technical detail. When Wiener invited Cotton to visit Israel for three or four months as consulting engineer to Tahal, the American enthusiastically agreed. Ultimately those seasonal visits were extended for six additional years.

As early as the winter of 1950, however, Cotton and Wiener had blocked out the working blueprint for Israel's water development; and in December of that year they flew back to the United States for a week-long meeting with a consulting board of American water engineers, led by Professor Abel Wohlman of Johns Hopkins University. The plan was subjected to detailed scrutiny and evaluation. Eventually it was approved. In essence, it was the original Hayes scheme, modified to conform with Israel's new borders and a decade of new information. The project consisted of a list of priorities. These included:

1) The intensive utilization of ground water, as well as river water for areas adjoining rivers. Because ground water was usually located near the sea, emphasis was to be placed first on the coastal area. Afterward, this coastal ground water would be piped inland, and distributed gradually over a wider agricultural area. In later years the same pipe network could be utilized for the Jordan and Yarkon waters, when the time came to exploit them.

2) Reclamation of intermittent flood flows, and reclamation of sewage through chemical depolution.

3) A group of intermediate irrigation projects, including the construction of pipe lines from the Yarkon River to the Negev, and a plan for irrigating the Kishon and Beit She'an valleys. Both these undertakings would consume more time and funds than the ground water project, but far less than the much larger Jordan Valley Project.

4) And finally the mighty Jordan Valley Project itself, the last and most important phase of the entire master plan.

As Wiener returned to Israel with the committee's approval in his pocket, he recognized that the success of the enormous venture depended in large measure upon adequate manpower. Hundreds of trained engineers and technicians would be needed, as well as several thousand foremen and skilled laborers. Fortunately, in the same winter of 1950–51 nearly four hundred refugee engineers arrived in Israel from Poland. During the next two years, with the active help of American Point Four experts, many of these immigrants were given intensive retraining in the field of hydrology. Technicians, too, were enrolled in Point Four seminars. As a direct result of this training program, no less than 450 engineers, 800 technicians, and 4,000 workers were ultimately employed on the water scheme.

American aid did not extend as far as free equipment, however. Neither, on the other hand, did Israel possess sufficient foreign currency for purchases abroad. It was eventually decided, therefore, that all available capital funds would be invested in the local production of irrigation supplies. In this fashion, too, thousands of additional jobs would simultaneously be provided for Israel workers. For example, the town of Migdal Ashkelon was actually brought into existence when Mekorot constructed a concrete pressure-pipe factory on the Ashkelon dunes. Similar plants were erected in Ramle, Acre, and Naharia, all devoted to the production of steel and asbestos pipes and electric pumping motors.

The water plan is incomparably the most expensive public project Israel has ever undertaken. No other national undertaking has even approached it in annual or long-range cost, not even the acquisition of modern jet aircraft or rockets. When Wiener submitted his estimated budget to the government in 1951, he forecast an ultimate expenditure of $175,000,000—a truly fantastic sum for a struggling little nation. Some of the funds, to be sure, were destined to come from outside sources: from German Reparations, United States government counterpart funds, World Bank loans, and Israel bond investments. But even in the case of these, the money would have to be taken from a common national pool—and the loans repaid later with interest. Whatever help might be received from abroad, the largest part of the cost would surely be borne by the Israel people themselves. Yet none of these considerations gave the government pause. Indeed, it is significant that the cabinet and the Knesset passed the water plan unanimously. Each year since 1951, too, Wiener's annual submitted budget has been approved after only the briefest *pro forma* discussion. The Knesset would no sooner have challenged water development than national defense, or Israel's very right to exist.

In 1951, Wiener and his colleagues turned immediately to the project's first phase, the utilization of ground water. They were well aware that their research of ten years earlier was by now hopelessly out of date. Although the location of ground water had been fairly well charted, its actual quantity was still unknown. Far more extensive and sophisticated investigation was needed. Fortunately, the Israelis were not entirely dependent upon their own research. During the past decade hydrologists in the Netherlands and Algeria had devised a number of new, and strikingly effective, techniques for ground water measurement. The Tahal engineers were not slow in profiting from this research—nor from the services of Israel's own geologists and physicists. Under the direction of Professor Leo Picard of the Hebrew University, for example, a team of talented young geologists undertook a detailed study of Israel's rock structures. Relying heavily on the science of micropaleontology—the study of microfossils—Picard's team successfully determined the geologic age of underground formations, and thereby acquired vital evidence on the extent of subterranean pools and streams. Geophysicists of the Weizmann Institute later supplemented this information with the imaginative use of electrical resistance soundings, seismic reactions, and gravimetric measurements.

Invaluable as modern electronic equipment proved to be, however, the most important data were usually acquired through painstaking laboratory tests. Even under ideal circumstances, the measurement of underground flows remained the most complex and demanding challenge to the hydrologist's skill. The water rarely moved freely. Rather it circulated through wand, the porous and mercurial sandstone uniquely characteristic of the Palestine soil profile. Wiener's men collected samples of this sandstone, and then methodically studied the size of the different grains, submitting them to water examination in order to measure the rate of flow between them. Glass tubing, lowered into wells, measured the gradients and changes of water elevation. Isotopes and dyes were infused into inland water sources; when the dyes reappeared again on the coast, the speed of the underground cycle was then tabulated with reasonable accuracy.

The work was slow, and at times uncertain. Techniques useful in one area could not be duplicated in another. Occasionally entire experiments had to be discarded when earlier soundings proved unreliable. Not infrequently the collapse of a substratum buried thousands of dollars of crucial equipment. Nevertheless, Tahal's engineers doggedly continued refining their techniques until their rate of error was reduced to less than 10 per cent, the most impressive record of its kind in the world. By the winter of 1953–1954, virtually all underground sources in the Israel coastal area had been charted, together with the "rock" flows of the interior. During the past decade that water has been almost completely exploited, tapped, piped, and at times "stored" in reserve for future use. In 1948 Israel utilized 240,000,000 cubic meters of ground water annually. At the date of writing the annual rate approaches 850,000,000 cubic meters. This represents nearly two thirds of the nation's entire known water supply.

Even as ground water resources were being developed, Wiener and his men embarked upon preliminary experiments to reclaim the waste waters of Israel's major towns. The prospects were encouraging: in the country's three large cities alone the amount capable of being reclaimed annually was estimated at more than 90,000,000 cubic meters—perhaps 5 per cent of Israel's total water resources. Thus, a pilot plant was erected in Haifa. The squat, ungainly looking cylinder treated the city's sewage biologically, then promptly transferred the purified residue into the surrounding farm communities for irrigation. The experiment's results were remarkably good. Mekorot engineers immediately began work on a larger plant, and completed it in 1963. Other such plants are scheduled for construction between 1963 and 1968 in Tel Aviv, Jerusalem, and a number of smaller urban centers.

The purification of sewage, while not insignificant in the total water scheme, nevertheless was overshadowed by the far more extensive Yarkon-Negev and Kishon Valley projects, carried out during the middle 1950s. The Yarkon would hardly have been dignified by the title of river anywhere but in the arid Near East. A runty little stream, hardly more than seven miles in length, it snaked westward from the Petach Tikvah springs, forming a northern boundary of sorts for Tel Aviv as it discharged into the Mediterranean. Yet in spite of its unimpressive size, the Yarkon's annual flow of 170,000,000 cubic meters represented a pure bonanza for Israel's water planners, and they exploited its surplus to the maximum. Between 1952 and 1955, Mekorot engineers constructed a dam and pumping station at the Petach Tikvah springs, then laid a fat, sixty-six-inch pipe line for some seventy miles along the coast. In this fashion fully 100,000,000 cubic meters of the Yarkon's flow were rechanneled southward to the Negev. An additional seventy miles of branch piping distributed the water evenly among the Negev's sixty-five agricultural colonies. Thereupon the strategic ring of desert outposts was transformed almost immediately into a necklace of viable, productive farm settlements; their 200,000 dunams of dry soil turned green within weeks after the water arrived.

The Kishon Valley Project, completed soon afterward, produced even more dramatic results. Conceived as a forerunner of the larger Jordan Valley Project, the Kishon scheme was based on the surplus of rainfall which each winter deposited forty inches of water in the rivulets and streams of the Galilee hills. Most of the flow ended up in the Jordan, or in flash floods that emptied into the Mediterranean. Some of it, however, found its way to the so-called Kishon River, a tremulous little creek arising west of Afula during the winter rains, and meandering slowly northwestward to the sea. Wiener and his colleagues were determined to harness this winter surplus for the use of the Valley of Jezreel (the Emek) and the Haifa industrial region. Immediately, therefore, Mekorot engineers set about laying pipes directly to Haifa from the wells and springs of the mountain area. Later, they constructed a packed-earth catch basin at the headwaters of the Kishon, a reservoir capable of storing some 8,000,000 cubic meters of the Galilee run-off. From this tiny artificial lake, in turn, a network of pipes was laid into the Emek. When the pumping began in 1957, conveying 160,000,000 cubic meters of water into the Valley of Jezreel, the Emek was rapidly transformed into the most completely irrigated stretch of land in Israel, and surely the lushest and greenest. An ancillary undertaking, completed in 1958, utilized the springs at the foot of the Gilboa mountains to irrigate the humid, semitropical Beit She'an area, in the southern Jordan Valley. With the usual combination of pipes and pumping stations, an additional 40,000,000 cubic meters of water were now made available to 50,000 dunams of formerly marginal agricultural soil.

It must not be assumed that the blessings of irrigation descended like manna from heaven upon Israel's farm settlements. Mekorot was a public utility, after all; at least part of its enormous capital expenses would have to be defrayed by consumer income. Indeed, the water bill of a partially irrigated settlement often ran as high as three or four agorot (one or one and a half cents) for each cubic meter of water. A fully irrigated moshav usually consumed between 15,000 and 16,000 cubic meters per settler annually. Each farmer, in turn, was obliged to pay a yearly water bill of between 500 and 700 pounds (170 and 240 dollars)—a heavy expense by Israel standards. The cost of irrigation proved especially formidable in hill areas; thus, hill settlements were discouraged from raising marginal-value crops. On the other hand, precisely because the government and Jewish Agency held controlling shares in Mekorot, they were in a position to adjust water rates when issues of public policy were involved. This was the case in the Judean mountain and Negev areas, where the cost of water ran prohibitively high for individual farmers. Yet because settlement in these regions was crucial for security reasons, the government extended loans to Mekorot, enabling the water company to lower its rates.

Perhaps in ten or fifteen years the necessity for special subsidies to arid-zone farm communities may diminish radically. This will depend almost entirely, however, upon the success of the Jordan Valley Project, the final and culminating phase of the master plan. The vast undertaking is based upon the Israel government's decision to settle and cultivate the Negev desert. It was a hard decision to make. Actually only half the country's total virgin acreage lends itself to irrigation, and it might be assumed, therefore, that the Jewish State would have concentrated its reclamation efforts upon the more accessible, and certainly more temperate, northern and central areas. And yet this alternative was rejected out of hand from the moment the water plan was first mooted.

For one thing, Wiener and his colleagues recognized that the soil of the northern Negev was potentially quite fertile. Moreover, it formed a continuous and extensive area, embracing no less than 1,500,000 dunams of flat tableland. Such a plateau was eminently suitable for mechanized cultivation, as well as for pipe laying and road building. Then, too, while other regions could rely, at least partially, on rainfall for their crops, this was hardly possible in the bleak and sun-scorched Negev desert. Thus the incremental benefit of irrigation was markedly higher in the Negev than elsewhere in Israel. This factor, together with the very range and continuity of the terrain, would permit valuable savings in marketing, public services, and soil research. From the point of view of agriculture alone, therefore, the Negev became the logical site of the nation's major irrigation program.

But there were other factors, social and military, that dictated the government's choice. It was anticipated that the population of Israel would grow at the rate of a million each decade for the next thirty or forty years. Space for this burgeoning humanity surely could no longer be found in the congested north-central areas of the country. The Negev was the only solution. Indeed, the wilderness demanded settlers: without an extensively inhabited belt of rural and urban communities, the southern half of Israel would remain likely prey for Arab infiltrators. It is highly probable, of course, that industry rather than agriculture offers the key to the Negev's future settlement. Nevertheless, water is in every respect as crucial for the development of factories and cities as for the irrigation of plantations and farms.

If there remained little question that the Negev deserved first priority in the master plan, neither was the source of that water in doubt. Lowdermilk knew the answer in the 1940s, and his proposal had been unanimously seconded by Hayes, Cotton, Wiener, and the consultative committee in the United States. The water would have to come from the north, from the Galilee area wherein winter rains provided the celebrated forty-inch annual "surplus." Because the largest proportion of that surplus flowed into the Jordan, it was quite obvious that the storied river would have to be tapped, its reserve extended by pipe and conduit through the Emek to the coastal plain, and from there pumped along the coastal plain to the northern desert.

The task was an immense one. The entire Jordan River system was distinctive, for it refused to follow the pattern of Israel's other rivers. It did not flow westward toward the Mediterranean where its currents could be more easily exploited. Instead, the Jordan moved in a southerly direction, ultimately draining into the Dead Sea. And from the Dead Sea there was no outlet; the water stopped. Moreover—again unlike Israel's other streams —the Jordan was in reality a confluence of three tributaries and two rivers. Not all of these originated within Israel proper. Rather, the Jordan's headwaters arose from a kind of delta, consisting of the so-called Hasbani River, which began in the mountains of the Lebanon; the Litani (Dan in Hebrew), originating in Israel territory a short distance from the Syrian border, at the foot of Mount Hermon; and the Banyas River, arising in Syria. All these tributaries converged in the Jordan a few miles to the north of the Hulah Canal (formerly a lake). From then on a single river, constituting the border between Israel and the Hashemite Kingdom of Jordan, proceeded for another ten miles in a steep and narrow gorge descending some eight hundred feet, until its waters emptied abruptly into Lake Kinneret.

As the Jordan continued its flow from the southern exit of Lake Kinneret, it junctured with the Yarmuk River, a little less than a mile below Tiberias. The Yarmuk in turn formed the northern border between Syria and the Hashemite Kingdom, and crossed Israel diagonally for perhaps two and a half miles before losing its identity permanently in the larger Jordan. Actually, the Valley of the Jordan, through which the waters continued their gradual descent southward, was considerably wider than the Jordan River itself. More important, it was higher, bounded on the west by the Judean hills and on the east by the hills of Moab (or the mountains of Edom, as they were occasionally called). As a consequence of this perverse and seemingly unnatural juxtaposition of river and valley, the farmers of antiquity had found it impossible to utilize the Jordan's currents: water has never yet flowed upward. Instead, the ancient cities depended for irrigation upon the Persian technique of Kanat, the skillful use of canals dug into hills to strike ground water.

For the modern Israelis, in any case, the post-Yarmuk course of the Jordan was a matter of little interest. For the river left Israel only sixteen miles after the juncture, and from then on continued its leisurely descent into the Dead Sea through Hashemite territory. As far as Wiener and his colleagues were concerned, all attention focused on the upper stretch of the river, the portion which emptied into the Kinneret. Here the engineers laid their elaborate irrigation plants. Here, too, unfortunately, any diversion of the river's upper waters would affect the flow which subsequently reached Hashemite soil—and the Arabs, for their part, warned that they were determined to prevent such a diversion "at any cost." Thus it was that the Jordan Valley Project, formidable enough as a challenge to engineering skills, raised equally complex issues of sovereignty between the two riparian states.

Under normal circumstances, a simple agreement between the adjacent nations would have allocated a fair share of the water to each. In this fashion, for example, the United States and Mexico had reached an understanding on the division of the waters of the Rio Grande and Colorado rivers. Similar agreements had been reached by the United States and Canada to allocate power and navigation rights on the St. Lawrence River system. Alas, matters could not be resolved as expeditiously in the Near East. Israel and the Kingdom of Jordan were still in a state of war with each other. And although both countries were in urgent, even desperate, need of the Jordan River's irrigation potential for their own development plans, the absence of a peace treaty between them apparently blocked all possibility of negotiation.

It did not escape the Great Powers, on the other hand, that if Jews and Arabs could be persuaded to co-operate on a purely economic venture of mutual interest, the political hostility between them would inevitably be lessened. To that end, in 1953, the American government sent to the Near East Mr. Eric Johnston, an experienced public official and negotiator, and more recently personal emissary of President Eisenhower. In his briefcase, Johnston carried a plan formulated by an American engineering firm for the development of the entire Jordan River basin. In some respects the scheme was based on the old Hayes blueprint, except that it was strongly— and intentionally—biased in favor of the Arab states. Thus, while Israel insisted that the water would have to be allocated according to political, economic, and engineering principles, Johnston (speaking for the United States State Department) added a fourth principle—that of "morality." The largest share of the Jordan's flow should be assigned to the Hashemite Kingdom, Johnston explained, for it would be "morally" wrong to divert water from one river basin—in this case, the Jordan—to another, that is, the western basin draining into the Mediterranean. As Johnston envisaged it, the water would be used exclusively in the Jordan Valley; and in that sector, at least, Israel's needs would obviously be much smaller than the needs of the Arab neighbor.

The Government of Israel indignantly rejected this argument. Its legal experts quoted numerous instances in which water had been diverted from one basin to another. Wiener drew especial attention to agreements worked out by the United States itself. One of these was the Colorado River Project, wherein the American and Mexican governments equitably divided the waters of the Colorado, leaving to the discretion of each nation the use of its respective share; as it proceeded toward Mexico, therefore, the river's flow was diverted from its original basin to the Los Angeles watershed area. Similarly, the waters of the Sacramento River had been diverted into the San Joaquin Valley. Dozens of other precedents were cited, from the United States and elsewhere. The "morality" factor was demonstrably hollow, Wiener insisted, a fiction devised to appease the Arabs.

Johnston was taken aback by the vehemence of Israel's reaction. Evidently he had anticipated that the Hashemite Kingdom would be the major stumbling block; once the Arabs acquiesced, he believed, the Jews would gratefully affix their signatures to any "reasonable" compromise. Undaunted, however, by this initial failure, the American emissary returned to the United States in the hope of devising a more palatable scheme. He flew back to the Near East three times during the next three years, skillfully and patiently negotiating with representatives of the Israel and Jordanian governments. To placate the Jews, Johnston eventually dropped the "moral" factor from his proposed water plan. Now there remained only Arab intransigence to grapple with. In fact, the Hashemite representatives raised no points of disagreement on the economic provisions of the scheme. Rather, their opposition was based exclusively on a political principle: refusal to accept the Zionist State as a *fait accompli*. Accordingly, it required all of Johnston's considerable diplomatic resourcefulness to convince the Arabs that a joint water venture would not necessarily imply recognition of the State of Israel, nor even the *status quo* of the existing Arab-Jewish boundaries. Eventually Johnston succeeded in persuading the Jordanian delegates. Once this hurdle was overcome, technical questions alone remained. And indeed, by December of 1955, the date of Johnston's last visit to the Near East, these problems had been largely resolved. Both sides were close to agreement on the final utilization of the Jordan's waters.

It was just at this point, when the two governments were on the verge of signing a formal agreement, that a political bombshell burst over the Near East. It was the announcement by Cairo of the massive Soviet arms deal with Egypt. Suddenly, virtually overnight, the entire balance of power in the Moslem world shifted radically. The Hashemite Kingdom, frozen in its tracks by the looming, terrifying shadow of Gamal Abd al-Nasser, "postponed" further negotiations with Israel; at that delicate juncture, Jordan was not willing to provoke the anger of the Egyptian dictator. It is one of the tragedies of contemporary diplomacy that the "postponed" negotiations were never again resumed. Thus vanished a historic opportunity not merely for a project of supreme economic benefit for the peoples of the Near East, but very probably for a *de facto* Jordan-Israel peace treaty, and an end to the threat of war between Arabs and Jews.

Predictably, Israel's reaction to this last-minute *volte face* was one of chagrin and outrage. For three frustrating years the Jewish representatives had negotiated in good faith, postponing construction, accepting compromise after compromise in the growing likelihood of reaching agreement with their Jordanian neighbors. Now the fruits of this painstaking diplomacy apparently were to be swept away by naked *Realpolitik*. As far as the Israelis were concerned, the time for forbearance was past. By the terms of the abortive Johnston Plan, the Israel water project formed an independent unit, based on the master blueprint worked out by Wiener, Cotton, and the American committee. From the engineering point of view, it was possible to implement the project with or without Arab co-operation. Now, therefore, construction would begin—without that co-operation. Whatever the objections from other quarters, the Government of Israel insisted that it was unwilling to procrastinate any longer; a nation had a legitimate right to self-development.

As we have noted, the principal objective of the Jordan Valley Project is to transfer the surplus of the river's northern waters through the Valley of Jezreel, on to the coastal plain, and from there to the northern Negev. To that end an enormous conduit is in the process of construction, traversing two thirds the length of the country, absorbing local surpluses and supplementing local deficiencies en route. Lake Kinneret will serve as the mouth of the conduit. A dam, constructed at the southern exit of this tiny inland sea, will permit the accumulation and regulation of the rain-swollen influx of the upper Jordan. Thus, functioning as a seminatural reservoir, the Kinneret can be tapped during the warm season, its waters sluiced into a tunnel extending westward to the lower Galilee hills north of Nazareth. Here the water will be pumped through a short stretch of pipe to an elevation of five hundred feet above sea level.

Once reaching the Nazareth hills, the current will end its upward journey. Indeed, from then on its course should be comparatively level. At the western drainage point of the Battauf Valley north of Nazareth, a small operational reservoir will store the water at strategic intervals. Later, when the summer irrigation begins, an enormous concrete pressure pipe (the author has driven a jeep through sections of it) will funnel the water on through the Emek, piercing the hills south of the Carmel range in a four-mile tunnel. Henceforth the conduit will run parallel to the coast until it reaches the northern edge of the Negev, near the Lachish area. From this point, large distribution lines will circulate water through the northern Negev as far south as Beersheba.

Along the full course of this extraordinary water system, moreover, there will be strategic outlets for irrigation. The largest number of them are planned for the coastal plain and the northern Negev, where existing facilities are not yet sufficient. Ultimately, the entire flow of water through Israel will be controlled by a central station in Tel Aviv. With the use of electronic computers, Wiener and his colleagues will be able to determine precisely the amount of moisture each part of the country will require, and when and where it should be distributed. Water will be pumped, piped, or stored in the network of underground reservoirs (most of them natural), at the exclusive discretion of Wiener's engineers.

By the time the Jordan Valley Project is completed, in 1968, it will be possible to supply the nation with an additional 320,000,000 cubic meters of water annually. This will represent a 25 per cent increase in supply. For the Negev, in fact, the increase will come to 75 per cent, and will surely vastly augment, if not revolutionize, the possibilities for industrial and agricultural development in the northern desert. Communities like Ashdod, Ashkelon, Kiryat Gat, Beersheba, and Dimona, will be able to meet the mounting water requirements of new factories and municipal services. For Israel as a whole, the completed water scheme should ultimately irrigate enough land to feed a population of three million—entirely from the country's own food production. By 1970, in fact, Israel should be producing a larger agricultural output per ton of water than any other nation in the world. Nor does this anticipated increase of production take into account alternate methods of irrigation.

Yet it should be noted here that those alternative methods are being carefully explored. Near Eilat, the ministry of development has established a pilot plant to test the so-called Zarchin process—i.e., the desalinization of sea water by vacuum freezing. Near Beersheba the Weizmann Institute and the Arid Zone Research Station are conducting experiments in electrodialysis, separating salt from water as the fluid passes through electrically charged membranes. Elsewhere in the Negev other techniques, ranging from cloud seeding to the development of drought-resistant plant species, are under investigation (see Chapter 12). Until now, none of these methods has proved to be economically feasible on a large scale. But the experiments go on. Meanwhile the Government of Israel has continued to devote its principal resources to the vast irrigation program, for thus far the pipe seems to be the only validated and reliable technique of watering the Negev economically.

There has been no procrastination in launching the Jordan Valley Project, the final and most important stage of the master irrigation plan. Less than a week after the collapse of negotiations with the Arabs, the Prime Minister's office ordered Mekorot to begin immediate installation of the first pipe. The task had long since been divided into two stages. The first included all the necessary pumps, pipes, and tunnels for transferring the surplus of the Jordan to the Tel Aviv area. From Tel Aviv the two Yarkon conduits were already available to convey water to the Negev. The target date for the completion of this phase is the winter of 1963–1964. The second stage, requiring an additional three years, will permit the installation of a much larger pipe line extending from the Tel Aviv area to the desert.

One need only glance at a topographical map of Israel to understand the discrepancy in the timetable of the two stages. Part Two will be carried out over comparatively level terrain. But Part One has required huge electric pumps to boost water from Lake Kinneret up to the hills of Galilee, and then from Nazareth to the Carmel range. Tunnels are bored in solid rock and lined with concrete. Pipes ascend mountains and cross treacherous ravines. Moreover, it was necessary to design and test these pipes, to construct the factories that produced them, before so much as a single mile of actual installation could begin. This proved to be a task no less formidable than the actual digging and tunneling. A full three meters in diameter, the pipes were constructed of pre-stressed concrete, and had to be capable of withstanding pressure of up to 170 pounds per square inch.

And yet these difficulties have been surmounted. At the date of writing the first phase of the Project has all but been completed. It has cost ninety million dollars, and tens of millions of man hours of labor. One who traces the course of this monumental undertaking from its source, in the reservoir of the Kinneret, to its present (and temporary) terminus near Tel Aviv, who drives parallel to the gaping concrete tunnels that traverse gorges and penetrate mountains, the deep-hulled conduits that stretch, arrow-straight, for mile after mile through soil, rock, and water, can only express wonderment and admiration for engineers who conceived this awesome design and brought it to fruition; and for an impoverished little nation willing to devote the largest part of its meager resources to a task that offers neither the possibility of short-term gain nor the promise of ultimate prosperity. A 25 per cent increment in water, after all, hardly represents a guarantee of prosperity, or even of solvency.

Indeed, the Israel government readily admits that, whatever the economic advantages implicit in the Jordan Valley scheme, they may well be counterbalanced by the threat of military hostilities. The Arabs have been outspoken on this issue: Israel can divert water from the Jordan only at its own peril, they warn; in the absence of a signed agreement between the riparian states, the Jews dare not tap a common river without provoking a *casus belli*. Despite the urgency of its tone, however, the Arab ultimatum singularly fails to impress the Israelis. By the terms of the abortive Johnston Plan, they point out, the Kingdom of Jordan was granted its maximal demand: a continuous annual flow into Hashemite territory of 100,000,000 cubic meters of Jordan River water. Agreement or no agreement, that rate of flow would still be scrupulously respected. Under no circumstances would Israel pump more from the Lake Kinneret reservoir than its proposed share of 40,000,000 cubic meters. The Jews insist, too, that if any nation is violating the spirit of international law it is Jordan. For Jordan is tapping the Yarmuk River for its own irrigation program, thereby diminishing the rate of flow of that portion of the river which enters Israel territory.

In any case, the Jews add, the Arabs failed to sign the original Johnston Plan not because they disagreed with its projected allocation of water, but purely and simply for reasons of political hostility. When water negotiations between India and Pakistan reached a similar political impasse, in 1952, the Nehru government nevertheless proceeded with its own irrigation scheme—as if the agreement between the two nations had actually been signed. The Government of Israel, asserting that every nation has an "inalienable" right to self-development, has left no doubt that it will follow this precedent. Accordingly, when the first phase of the Jordan Valley Project is completed, in the winter of 1963–1964, Wiener and his engineers are grimly determined to begin their pumping operations.

What steps are Israel's Arab neighbors likely to take then? Their threats have been typically ominous. The moment so much as a single cubic meter of Jordan water flows into an Israel pipe, they warn, the Arab nations will "reserve unto themselves the right of collective action." In the case of the Hashemite Kingdom, this action is not likely to take the form of more than a strenuous diplomatic protest, possibly an appeal to the United Nations Security Council. King Hussein, whose throne is quite precarious, is understandably wary of tangling with the Israel army. Nor does he view with equanimity the possibility of Jewish counteraction—i.e., blocking Jordan's Yarmuk River scheme.

The Government of Israel takes somewhat more seriously the Syrian threat to dam the Hasbani, one of the three tributaries that flow into the Jordan River. If the Syrians should erect such a dam, the Israel army or air force presumably would attempt to destroy it—and full-scale war could thereupon erupt between the two nations. Few of Israel's foreign office experts are persuaded, however, that the mercurial and unstable Syrian government will accept this risk—certainly not for the mere will-o'-the-wisp of Arab "solidarity." But in view of the recent intensification of Syrian attacks on Israel border settlements, the chance is not altogether remote.

It was in anticipation of this danger, in fact, that the Jews abandoned their original scheme for developing cheap electric power in the Galilee. The first master plan envisaged the construction of a canal along the River Jordan north of Lake Kinneret. The Jordan's waters, dropping through the canal a sharp 1,200 feet into the lake, would have spun the generators of a giant hydroelectric plant, thereby providing cheap current for all of northern Israel. Unfortunately, such a canal would also have run to within one hundred yards of the Syrian border. The Syrians could easily have demolished it with artillery and mortar fire, while claiming that Israel was guilty of aggression—for stretches of the canal would surely have traversed the no man's land and neutralized zone along the frontier. After protracted and agonizing debate, the Israel government eventually decided not to run this risk. The plans for a canal and hydroelectric plant were abandoned.

Instead, as we have seen, the Israel engineers moved south, to the northwestern shore of Lake Kinneret itself. There, capacious underground tunnels, already hewn out of the granite mountains at prodigious expense and effort, will siphon water from the lake rather than directly from the river. The shift represents more than a political concession by the Jews, more than a willingness to stay clear of the demilitarized zone and well within Israel sovereign territory. It is also a strategic decision of profound significance. For the entire apparatus of irrigation—pumping machinery, power generators, water conduits, and suction pipes—are now safely housed in the extensive network of underground tunnels. And the tunnels, concrete-sheathed and lying deep in the bowels of three parallel mountain ranges, are virtually indestructible. They cannot be damaged by artillery fire, probably not even by an atom bomb.

Yet, by itself, the construction of well-protected tunnels offers no guarantee against a generalized war between Israel and its neighbors. The Arabs stand firm on their position. They insist that canal or no canal, tunnels or no tunnels, even the siphoning of water from the lake will affect the Jordan's flow, and thus will infringe Arab sovereignty. Actually it is Egypt, the largest nonriparian Arab State in the Near East, which has issued the most explicit and unequivocal warnings, and they are taken most seriously of all by Israel. Nasser made plain his intentions in a special cabinet meeting of November, 1959:

> I know [he said] that Israel has been working on the project for the diversion of the Jordan waters since we first rejected the Johnston Plan in 1953, and I know that some Arab States are implementing plans connected with the Israel project on the basis of the Johnston Plan. But I do not think we can have war and sure victory now. . . . Not yet having built up our military strength to the level of overwhelming superiority, we cannot launch an offensive war and proceed to destroy Israel's installations. . . . I think that the decisive year will be 1963 or 1964. . . . If we then take action against Israel, we will be defending our rights and can thus guarantee that world public opinion and the United States will be on our side; moreover, our military preparations will be complete and our forces ready. By that time we shall ourselves have manufactured the jet bombers we need, and also the rockets. The Arab political situation, especially in Algeria, will be different . . . when I start a war I want to take it to the only end I accept—decisive victory.

In the face of this openly stated determination to launch a "third round" against the Jews, and of dangers that are probably not entirely illusory, will the Israel government hesitate before permitting its engineers to throw the lever in the Lake Kinneret pumping station? Hardly likely.

"If there must be a war," says Wiener, in all sobriety, "then let it be for this. We have staked everything on that water. It is our blood, our life."

One recalls those words each time the admonition flashes on the screen of an Israel movie theater: "Chaval al Kol Tipah—a shame to waste a single drop."

CHAPTER ELEVEN

THE SAILOR

IN THE afternoons, when school had ended for the day, a young boy removed his shoes and walked along the beaches of Tel Aviv and Jaffa. He watched the ebb and flow of the waters, the gulls wheeling and skimming over the tide, the drunken jig of buoys marking shoals and sand bars. Most of all, he watched the ships floating offshore. There were freighters and tankers among them, packet boats and small passenger liners. They bore the markings of strange and exotic lands: of Italy, Greece, Turkey, England, France, even of Russia and Japan. The boy stared, open-mouthed, as the tiny Arab dinghies unloaded cargo and passengers, loaded the familiar yellow crates of citrus fruit and winter vegetables. He thrilled to the penetrating hoot of steam whistles, the slowly rising billows of smoke from the towering stacks, the rattle and thump of anchor chains. In his dreams, he stood on the bridge of each vessel, sailed the Mediterranean with them, passed through the Suez Canal en route to the Indian Ocean, and through the Straits of Gibraltar to the New World.

The period was the 1930s. The boy's name was Yehiel Yitzhak Aronowicz, but his friends called him simply Ike. His parents, Polish immigrants, understood and encouraged their youngster's love of the outdoors, his hikes with the HaBonim youth group, his weekly outings with the sailing club. It did not cross their minds, nor Ike's, that his love of the sea would ever develop into anything more than a hobby. In the entire country there were only a handful of Jewish tuna fishermen, and a few Jewish-owned passenger ferries. The British would permit nothing more.

Until the Second World War. Ships were needed, and sailors to man them. In 1942, at the age of nineteen, Ike managed to secure a berth as deck hand on a 1,200-ton freighter, the *Sophia*. Purchased by Jews and operating under British charter, the tiny vessel plied the eastern Mediterranean, carrying military supplies to British army camps in eastern Eritrea and along the Red Sea coast. The weather was deathly hot, the crew's quarters cramped and fetid, and Ike was wildly, gloriously happy. The churning wake behind him was burying the limitations and frustrations of his youth. The world was his highway. He shared it equally with admirals and merchant princes of the Gentile lands. So long as he lived, he knew then, his destiny was charted.

In November of 1942, Ike collected his pay check in Port Saïd and returned to Haifa by train. There, to his delight, he learned that the Palmach —the shock troops of the Jewish Underground—had recently founded an auxiliary "naval" unit, the Pal-Yam. The first training course had begun a month earlier, in a small encampment near Caesaria. Ike joined it forthwith. The instructor, Shmuel Tarkus (later to become commander of the Israel navy), was self-taught, as were most of the officers of the Underground. And like most of these men, too, Tarkus' practical experience was extensive. For the next four months he drilled his thirty-eight students in the fundamentals of navigation, seamanship, and ocean rescue. The equipment consisted of three battered sailboats and one ancient motor launch. During the winter, outings in these makeshift vessels proved quite dangerous, and there were frequent capsizings. But Tarkus was relentless; experience was everything, he insisted. Someday his boys would encounter graver dangers than the waves off Caesaria. There would be treacherous nocturnal beachings and possibly armed encounters with British destroyers. In fact, the postwar rescue of European Jewry was the fixed and uncompromising purpose of the entire training course.

When the first class was "graduated," in March of 1943, none of the youths were permitted to apply for maritime employment—lest their Pal-Yam training be divulged to the British. The one exception was Ike. Because his proficiency as a sailor was based on an open record of commercial sailing, Tarkus allowed him to return to sea. And at sea Ike remained, for the next three and a half years. In spite of the continual danger of torpedo attack, these were perhaps the happiest years of his life. They were spent aboard Norwegian and British tankers, shuttling oil between Haifa and Tripoli, and later Abadan, Bombay, Calcutta, and Capetown. The work, as a deck hand, was not particularly difficult, and often the captains allowed Ike to try his hand at odd jobs around the ship, and even to take an occasional turn at the wheel. The other sailors had a liking for the little Palestinian. He was only five feet, six inches tall, but he was exceptionally wiry and energetic; and behind that curiously youthful, diffident face, a quick brain was incessantly at work, storing every fact, every detail of the sailor's trade. Ike wore his Jewishness without a trace of self-consciousness. He talked freely and enthusiastically about his people and his dreams for their freedom. The other crew members respected that pride.

His most exciting moments were the stopovers at foreign ports. It hardly mattered at which harbor the ship docked, there seemed always to be a sizable community of Jews, even in India. Almost invariably, too, they were passionate Zionists. Ike was their honored guest. He was lavishly entertained—and supplicated for every last morsel of information about life in Palestine. His own curiosity was hardly less intense; he filled several diaries with notes on these trips. Ike returned home for extended shore leave only twice during the war; but on his first visit, in the winter of 1944, his former comrades in the Pal-Yam called a special "congress" in his honor at the Caesaria training school. Nearly two hundred men gathered for the affair, including the Palmach commanders, Yitzhak Sadeh and Yigal Allon. No Jew of their acquaintance had ever enjoyed so wide or varied a maritime career. For three hours they questioned Ike about his travels. India was the subject of special fascination for them. How powerful was the Indian nationalist movement? they asked. Did it seem likely that the British would be driven out? Did the Indians feel the same kinship for the Zionists that the Zionists felt for them?

Ike made a few discoveries of his own. The Pal-Yam experiment, begun tentatively the year before, had now developed into a valuable adjunct of the Underground effort. Every four months new and larger classes were being trained. Many of the graduates found employment in various functions at Haifa harbor. Already fifteen were working on a Jewish-owned coastal freighter. Half that many obtained berths on a Turkish tramp steamer, and managed to smuggle back weapons into Palestine on their return trips from Alexandretta. The others temporarily accepted nonmaritime jobs, and impatiently awaited the moment to begin the long-delayed rescue operation from Europe. In normal times few of these youths would have qualified as first or even second mates. Indeed, it was not Shmuel Tarkus' intention that they serve as officers even later. Rather, the Pal-Yam graduates were trained to act as Haganah agents on refugee vessels; they would take the place of hired seamen only in the event of emergencies. In the last years of the war, no serious thought was yet given to a future Jewish merchant marine, or to the possible mercantile advantages to be gained from a local cadre of seamen. The *Braichah*, the rescue of European Jewry, remained the single, consuming purpose of the Jewish Agency and Underground leadership.

The opportunity for action came with the surrender of Nazi Germany. In the ensuing months Haganah agents fanned out through Europe in search of Jewish survivors. Their quest was thorough; they found nearly 300,000 Jews still alive, and managed to direct the great majority of them to the Displaced Persons' camps of Western Germany. At the same time, the Pal-Yam trainees set about purchasing ships, hiring crews, and then transporting nearly 30,000 refugees to embarkation ports in southern France and Italy. There the D.P.s were dispatched "illegally" to Palestine. In the beginning, during the summer and autumn of 1945, several of the refugee boats actually succeeded in eluding the British blockade, and successfully unloaded their human cargoes at night on remote beaches.

By the winter of 1946, however, hardly one of these derelict vessels was able any longer to escape interception by the Royal Navy, and most of their passengers were carried off forthwith to internment camps in Cyprus. Nevertheless, although the voyages were invariably exhausting and frustrating, the Jewish Agency was determined to maintain, even intensify the *Braichah*. Each time the British boarded one of these pathetic little refugee ships, international attention was focused on the plight of the D.P.s. World opinion was a weapon, too. Accordingly, new boats were needed, new crews —and additional Jewish seamen.

In the autumn of 1946 Ike Aronowicz was completing a three-month course at London's Prince Edward VII Maritime College. In September, shortly before receiving his papers as a second mate, he was summoned to a meeting with Shaul Avigor, chief of the Jewish migration operation in Europe.

"How long before you get your mate's papers?" Avigor asked him.

"Two more weeks. But I'm ready to leave now if you like."

"No, finish up," said Avigor. "Then try to find a way to get to the United States. Have you a ship?"

"With second mate's papers, I can get on any British ship sailing in that direction," Ike replied confidently.

Avigor nodded. "Phone the Jewish Agency office there when you arrive. Ze'ev Szynd will be in touch with you and will tell you what to do then."

The interview terminated. Within three days after receiving his mate's certificate Ike secured a berth on a freighter. Twelve days after that he reached Norfolk, Virginia. Szynd, a stocky, red-haired little Palestinian, was waiting for him on the dock.

Together the two men traveled on to Baltimore, where Szynd introduced Ike to Captain William Ash, his "contact" man. Ash was a beefy, cigar-smoking Brooklyn Jew, who had once served as director of the United States Merchant Marine Academy at King's Point; more recently he had been elected secretary of the masters, mates, and pilots union. He made no secret of his Zionist sympathies.

"Ze'ev said you needed a passenger boat, and I got you one," said Ash. "With a few adjustments here and there you should be able to squeeze three to four thousand people in her."

Ike was uncertain that he had heard Ash correctly. Three to four thousand people! Until then the Haganah had crowded its refugees into reconverted Liberty ships or even tramp freighters. After those leaking tubs, any kind of passenger vessel would have been a dramatic improvement. But a ship capable of accommodating three to four thousand passengers defied belief; an entire D.P. camp could be loaded into that kind of space.

"What have you bought, anyway—the *Queen Mary?*" Ike asked.

Szynd smiled sourly. "Not quite," he replied. "You'll see."

The three men walked over to the Pratt Street Pier. Ash pointed to the dark silhouette outlined against the dusk. "There she is," he said proudly. "The S.S. *President Warfield.*"

"It's a ferry," added Szynd hastily. "She used to navigate the Chesapeake Bay. We got her a week before she was to be sold for junk."

Cautiously, Ike approached the ship. For several minutes he hardly knew whether to laugh or weep. It was surely the ugliest, most ungainly vessel he had ever seen. The entire dead-weight tonnage could not have exceeded four thousand tons. Yet the hulking, antiquated superstructure, culminating in a single, incongruously elongated smokestack, belonged on a passenger liner five times heavier. Indeed, in Ike's eyes the *President Warfield* seemed nearly as tall as it was long. The entire bow, too, was covered with rust and barnacles—the crust was clearly visible above the water line. Somehow the monster floated; but it hardly seemed capable of sailing even the length of the harbor.

"Don't be discouraged, Ike," Szynd whispered. "She's in better shape than she looks. We have a good-sized crew working on her already. In another two months she'll be seaworthy." He hesitated, then added apologetically: "I know she rides a little high in the water. But even that can be an advantage, don't forget."

Ike nodded. His practiced eye had taken it all in, and he was making calculations quickly. If all the leaks could be plugged, at least the ship would be hard to sink. Moreover, that whalelike bow offered a lot of protection against ramming. Ash was right too; preposterously high as it was—rising no less than four decks—the superstructure did provide sleeping space for several thousand passengers. The hold could be saved for supplies.

"Anyway, it's the only thing you've got to work with," Szynd added. "I want you to supervise repairs and train the crew. We'll have a captain for her before she's ready to leave."

From then on the responsibility was Ike's. Szynd's calculations had been too optimistic. Nearly every one of the vessel's moving parts had to be replaced. Additional time was consumed scraping the hull, and then girdling it with a steel fender. Huge stores of food and blankets had to be purchased from army surplus depots—enough for four thousand passengers. Then, too, the crew had to be trained and briefed. Of the thirty-five young men under Ike's command, all but five were unpaid volunteers. One of them was non-Jewish; he was John Grauel, a Unitarian minister from Worcester, Massachusetts, and a passionate Zionist. The rest were American-Jewish naval and merchant marine veterans, as well as several members of Zionist youth groups who worked as general handymen around the ship. All the crew members went about their work with unflagging enthusiasm—a remarkable feat inasmuch as the repairs, far from being completed in two months, consumed nearly a half-year.

Finally, in March of 1947, the ship was completely reconditioned. A Honduran flag of registry was procured, as well as a captain—a taciturn German-American in his late sixties. On the seventh of the month the S.S. *President Warfield,* loaded with ballast, moved slowly out of its Pratt Street dock and lumbered its way across Chesapeake Bay. In the ship's log the port of destination was listed as Shanghai. There, ostensibly, ownership would be transferred to a Chinese river-ferry company. But the fiction was hardly necessary. Neither city nor federal authorities bothered to investigate the wallowing tub. It was obviously not going far.

In fact, the ship sailed exactly 350 knots. On its first day out, heavy weather struck. Almost immediately water began flooding the hawsepipes and pouring through loose rivet holes. Without hesitation the captain issued the order to return. Twenty hours later the *President Warfield* limped into Norfolk harbor. Whereupon the captain signified his opinion of the ferry by resigning.

An additional two weeks were needed before the *President Warfield* was repaired and ready to sail again. A new captain was hired, a friendly, younger man who was unfazed by the vessel's earlier mishap. He checked the boat over quickly, then gave the order to sail. And this time Ike's hopes were justified. All went well. The steamer plowed its way uneventfully across the Atlantic. On April 10, 1947, thirteen days after departing from Norfolk, the *President Warfield* reached Marseilles. There, by prearrangement, the captain left the ship.

Ike's first visitor on shipboard was Shmaryahu Zameret, the brilliant young Haganah chief of operations in France.

"Welcome to the new captain," were his first words to Ike. "You're now permanent commanding officer of this ship."

"Are you out of your mind?" Ike gasped. "I've never commanded a ship before."

"There's a first time for everything." Zameret grinned. "I'm afraid there's just too much riding on this ferry to leave matters to outsiders. Anyway, no professional would assume responsibility for what you're going to do. I've been told forty-five hundred people can be squeezed in here. That's how many you're going to carry."

As Zameret explained it, the voyage of the *President Warfield* would be the single most important crossing since the illegal migration effort began. Its significance lay not simply in the unprecedented number of passengers aboard. There would probably be fighting. Ike must under no circumstances passively allow the boat to be intercepted. World attention would be seized by the throat on this one.

"Tell your Americans to keep their mouths shut from now on," Zameret warned. "British agents are watching everything we do. They've plugged all loopholes here. You won't be able to outfit the ship in Marseilles. Proceed to Porto Venire, instead. It's an inlet seven miles from La Spezia—I'll give you a map."

"Where will I get fuel for the trip?"

"You'll find it."

They foraged the port area for the next three days, purchasing six hundred drums of oil, and loading the ship by hand. Ike thereupon ordered the boilers fired and the anchor hoisted. Carefully, he maneuvered the ferry back into the Mediterranean. As the *President Warfield* reached open sea, the twenty-three-year-old captain suddenly felt a wave of exhilaration surge through him. By God, he would pull it off; he was as sure of success as he was of life.

The crew members, too, had reached their maximum efficiency and now were eager for action. The first leg of the trip went well. The ship reached Porto Venire in forty hours, and anchored successfully in the tiny cove. There, to Ike's astonishment and delight, he was greeted by Avraham Zakkai, an old classmate from Pal-Yam days. The two had not seen each other since the 1944 gathering at Caesaria. Zakkai was now supply officer of the rescue operation. He had made arrangements with a small local shipyard, and promised to refit the ship within two months.

There was much to do. Thirty carpenters were hired to install bunks for 4,500 people. A pipe, perforated with tiny holes, was welded along the entire circumference of the ship, and then attached to the central steam bent; if the British attempted to board they would find a hot surprise awaiting them. Special high-pressure fuel pipes were also installed to add scalding oil to the welcome. A steel plate three millimeters thick was bonded to the stern, as further protection against collision. Finally, an extra anchor was hauled on board to serve as a makeshift battering ram if the occasion demanded. Of course, all this equipment was to be used only as a final emergency measure. Ike's primary intention was to land his passengers, and to that end he was prepared to accept a limited British boarding party if necessary. Later, within reach of the Palestine coast, his crew would disarm the British, turn up the speed, and make a dash for the beach.

Evidently the British were determined to abort the sailing at the outset, however. Within two weeks after the ship's arrival, CID agents began swarming through Porto Venire. There was no time to waste now. After hasty consultation with Avraham Zakkai, Ike decided that the best course was to return to France the moment the protective devices were installed. Four days later, the last bolt was riveted into place, and Ike gave orders to cast off. Yet, no sooner had the *President Warfield* steamed out of Porto Venire than two British destroyers began trailing it. A day and a half after that the ferry docked at Port de Bouc, near Marseilles. Immediately the destroyers dropped anchor near-by. When the Jewish crew members visited cafés during the evenings, the British sailors were on hand to taunt them with anti-Semitic remarks. Once there was a fist-fight, and several men on both sides were injured seriously.

"We'll see you again, Jew boys," the British shouted, after the French police had broken up the brawl. "The next time we get hold of you there won't be any gendarmes to protect you."

The ship remained in Port de Bouc for nearly a month. When all necessary supplies were finally loaded, on July 6, several Haganah agents came on board to discuss the berthing arrangements for the passengers, and to make final plans for possible future emergencies. Gad Hilb, captain of an earlier Haganah ship which had beached successfully in Palestine, advised Ike on the currents prevailing near the Tel Aviv coast. Yosi Hamburger, the Haganah security officer assigned to sail with Ike, went ashore to supervise the transfer of the refugees to the port. Three days later Hamburger sent word to Ike, requesting him to proceed to the near-by inlet of Sète; there the passengers would be waiting. Immediately the *President Warfield* crawled out of Port de Bouc, docking in Sète two hours later. Hamburger rushed aboard, flushed with excitement.

"They're all here," he announced triumphantly. "We got them down from the German border in less than three days. We'll load them tonight."

It was Ike's turn to marvel at Hamburger's authentic genius for organization. At 2:00 A.M. a rubber bridge of dinghies extended from the shoreline to the ferry. Across that bridge passed 4,500 Jews. There were small children and infants among them, old men and women, pregnant mothers and invalids, many of them badly crippled. Silently, in perfect order and discipline, the refugees allowed themselves to be hauled aboard, and then took their appointed places in the makeshift dormitories. By 8:00 A.M. the entire operation was completed. Rations were passed out among the passengers, instructions given in several languages, a clinic and kitchen schedule announced. Ike entered the steering cabin to make final preparations for departure.

"Wait a moment."

Hamburger's voice was tense, and he pointed to a French police barge pulling alongside. Ike clutched his head in his hands. "That's all we need," he muttered—and then dropped a ladder for the visitors. A score of gendarmes immediately climbed on deck. Without a word, the officer in charge led his men into the engine room. There, blandly ignoring Ike's outraged protests, the police systematically confiscated the ship's burners— and then departed as swiftly as they had come. The ship was immobilized. For several moments so was its crew.

Suddenly collecting his wits, Ike ordered a dinghy lowered. Hurrying to a telephone onshore, he put through an urgent long-distance call to Haganah headquarters in Paris. It was Shaul Avigor who supplied the answer.

"Bevin [the British Foreign Secretary] is in Paris, Ike," Avigor explained. "He's got all the facts and figures on the boat. He's pressured the French government into stopping it."

"But that's fantastic!" Ike exploded. "With all the world problems Bevin has to solve, he has to make *us* an international issue? Can't you do anything?"

"We've tried every trick we know, every contact we have," insisted Avigor. "It's no use, he's got us blocked this time. You'll have to find a way out on your end."

"Thanks very much."

Yet by the time Ike returned to the ship an idea had occurred to him. Opening his locker, he removed a handsome captain's uniform. He had saved it for such an emergency. One of the woman passengers was hastily recruited to sew an extra two stripes on his sleeves. Then, looking for all the world like a young boy masquerading as an admiral, Ike hurried back to shore, where he commandeered one of the Haganah jeeps, and roared off at full speed toward the town of Montpellier, the capital of the district of Provence. Fifty minutes later he entered the office of the district governor. In his makeshift French, Ike explained that he and his countrymen, "Hondurans," were prevented from returning home because the police had arbitrarily removed the burners from the ship's engines. This was obviously an unforgivable, indeed a "disastrous" breach of international law.

The governor, a stocky jovial man in his mid-fifties, listened patiently. "To 'Honduras,' eh?" he murmured, a smile slowly creasing his face. "Thousands of people waiting to get to 'Honduras,' what do you know." Thereupon he signed a slip of paper, ordering the return of the burners. Handing the note to Ike, he commented again: "We mustn't let these British tell us French what to do. People have a right to sail to 'Honduras' if they want to."

By 2:00 P.M. the burners were restored. The only problem remaining now was to clear the port. Unfortunately, as Ike soon learned, all the licensed harbor pilots were under strict instructions to avoid the refugee ship: the *President Warfield* was political dynamite. Later in the afternoon, however, with the help of a Greek intermediary, Ike and Yosi Hamburger were introduced to a retired pilot. For a flat million francs, the Frenchman promised to guide the ship out under cover of darkness. Arrangements were made to meet at 1:00 A.M. near an abandoned lighthouse.

The two Palestinians turned up on schedule. But the pilot did not. Ike and Hamburger waited for forty-five minutes. Finally, in desperation, the men began whistling, waving a flashlight, even calling out loud; there was always the remote possibility that they had misjudged the meeting place. It was wasted effort.

"You'll have to take her out yourself, Ike," said Hamburger.

Ike nodded glumly. The task would have been dangerous even in daylight. Only the most experienced pilots were acquainted with the treacherous reefs and sand bars. In pitch darkness the risks were all but insurmountable. Nevertheless, there was apparently no other alternative; returning to the ship, Ike called the crew together and explained what had to be done.

"What about the three French soldiers on the dock?" asked John Grauel, the Unitarian minister. "The moment we get steam up they'll start shooting."

"You're a sympathetic type," Ike grinned. "Maybe you can dissuade them."

Grauel resorted to most un-ministerial methods. Joining the soldiers on the dock, he engaged them in lively conversation, and then produced a flagon of cognac. The moment the liquor was consumed another bottle mysteriously appeared. By 3:00 A.M. the soldiers were *hors de combat*. When Grauel returned to the bridge all was in readiness. The boilers had been fired, and cruising steam pressure had been reached. No one was available on the dock to help cast off, however, and so Ike ordered his men simply to cut the ropes. That turned out to be a mistake. The propeller began churning slowly—and then ground to an abrupt halt. Peering over the stern, Bernie Marx, the first mate, called back: "It's fouled, Ike. The rope is all twisted up in the propeller."

The crew groaned: apparently the ship was trapped at the very outset. For the next two hours Ike desperately revved the engines back and forth, attempting to grind the rope to pieces by sheer power. Remarkably enough, the technique worked. By 5:30 A.M. the ferry eased out of its dock. With wooden poles, the crew literally "felt" the ship through the Sète beds. That hazard, too, was cleared. But not the next one. Before the *President Warfield* reached the harbor's narrow exit, the prevailing current washed the vessel onto a shoal. And there it remained, in spite of all efforts to power it into deep water.

"What now?" asked Hamburger.

Ike shrugged. There was no choice but to wait for the tide to come in— at daybreak. The opportunity for a secret escape had now vanished. Three and a half hours later, in bright sunlight, the water level rose. Artfully using the vessel's shallow draft and powerful engines, Ike finally nudged the hull off the sand bar. A few minutes later the boat reached the harbor exit, and the wide, hospitable Mediterranean. Several of the crew members began to cheer. Ike silenced them with a glance.

"A little late for that," murmured Bill Bernstein, the third mate, as he pointed out to sea.

Six British destroyers were drawing near. Within minutes they surrounded the ship, one fore, one aft, two on each side. The starboard destroyer was the *Ajax;* eight years before, it had helped sink the Nazi pocket-battleship *Graf Spee.* Now, as the warship pulled closer to the wallowing Jewish ferry, the captain of the destroyer called out by loudspeaker: "Can we help?"

Ike politely declined the offer.

During the next week, as the destroyers clung like limpets to the *President Warfield,* the exchange of greetings became somewhat less cryptic. Five times a day the *Ajax* called out to the passengers in English, German, even in a labored quasi-Yiddish: "We must warn you that we shall board your ship the moment Palestine territorial waters are reached," the announcement repeated. "Under no circumstances are you to obey the orders of the Jewish Underground. All attempts to resist our boarding party will be sternly suppressed."

To each warning the Jewish loud-speaker promptly replied with a recorded version of "God Save the King." Occasionally, as passing ships swung close to inspect the extraordinary phenomenon of a British naval task force shepherding a tiny river steamer, Ike flashed out a message in semaphore: "What do you think of our escort? Even His Majesty the British King does not rate a bigger escort than this."

Nevertheless, during the first week of crossing, there was no violence or threat of violence. The British stayed close, but affected only solicitude for the Jewish passengers. Two days before reaching the Palestine coast, one of the women on the *President Warfield* gave birth to a daughter. In spite of the best efforts of the several refugee doctors on board, the woman died shortly afterward. There was a funeral. As the mother's body, wrapped in the Zionist flag, was dropped at sea, the British destroyers immediately lowered their own flags to half-mast. Ike deliberately created the impression that he was taken in by these gestures of sympathy. Placidly, he steered his ship on a direct course for Haifa; no hint was offered that the transfer of passengers would be other than peaceful. And yet, sailing perilously close to the shore lines of Sardinia, then Pantelleria, and finally Egypt, Ike shrewdly tested the destroyers' ability to match the *President Warfield's* shallow draft. They could not. It was an encouraging sign. The British would be unable to press the chase to the very coast line of Palestine.

At 1:00 A.M. of the seventh day, the ship's Haganah navigator made his scheduled calculations and reported that Gaza beach lay forty-two miles due east. Ike nodded but said nothing; at least an hour and a half remained before reaching the three-mile limit. Suddenly, completely without warning, the destroyers turned their searchlights on the refugee vessel. The boat's crew were blinded in the concentrated glare. Simultaneously the clipped accents of the task force commander were heard once again on the loud-speaker: "You are now entering the territorial waters of Palestine. Our personnel will immediately board your ship. Do not resist. I repeat: do not resist."

Ike was stunned. The violation of international law was flagrant and brazen. Then, seizing his own microphone, he shouted back: "Liars! You are liars! We're at least forty miles west of Palestine! Bloody pirates, if you want a fight we'll give you one!"

Thereupon he ordered the Zionist flag run up, together with the pennant bearing the vessel's new name: *Exodus—1947.*

Pulling the steam whistle, Ike signaled an immediate hard turn to port. The great klaxon became stuck, however, and for the next few minutes its wild blast lent the final nightmare ingredient to the confusion and violence. Even before the boat could begin its turn, the windows of the bridge shattered, spraying glass throughout the bridge. A pattern of machine-gun bullets stitched along the bulkhead. Miraculously, no one was hit. At the same moment the boat shuddered violently; the destroyers had begun their ramming. In the glare of searchlight beams, a party of eight British marines swung by ropes onto the top deck near the steering room. They carried leather shields and clubs tipped with lead.

"You know what to do now," Ike shouted. "Smother them, disarm them, quickly."

The crew and a phalanx of male passengers rushed the marines, who flailed back savagely with their clubs. In the ensuing melee Ike's leg caught a bruising clout. Almost simultaneously Bill Bernstein staggered and dropped unconscious, his head pouring blood. Crawling on all fours, Ike dragged the prostrate mate into his own cabin. By the time he returned to the deck, the marines had already been disarmed. Instantly he ordered them locked in the wheelhouse. But the battle had only begun. During the next few hours the destroyers continued their attack, methodically ramming the Jewish vessel until it appeared certain to capsize. The steel plating offered sufficient protection, however. It was, rather, the armory of other defense weapons that proved less effective. The steam pipe failed to operate properly. Nor was the hot oil spray powerful enough to repel boarding parties. Only the spare anchor was an unqualified success; dropped on the top deck of one of the destroyers, it killed seven British sailors.

Thus far the battle was a stalemate. Each time a group of marines swung aboard the *Exodus* they were met blow for blow by the infuriated passengers. Tear-gas bombs, lobbed from the warships, were promptly hurled back at the British. In addition the refugees dropped heavy wooden lifeboats on the decks of the destroyers. When larger numbers of marines at last began to reach the steering room, Ike rushed aft and disconnected the wires attached to the wheel. From then on he maneuvered the ship by direct manipulation of the rudder.

As the hours passed the vessel began to tilt. The continual ramming was finally achieving its effect. Although the ship was still seaworthy, it could no longer be steered. A quick conference with the doctors brought Ike more serious news. The number of wounded passengers had mounted drastically. Several of them were critically injured. Bill Bernstein had already died of brain concussion. A man and a boy had died of bullet wounds. The doctors warned that they would no longer be able to cope with the situation if the fighting continued. Ike looked at his watch. It was nearly 8:00 A.M. For seven hours the unarmed little ferry had successfully resisted six British destroyers. Consulting with Yosi Hamburger, Ike agreed that there was no longer any alternative to an armistice.

Hamburger carried out the negotiations. He offered to accept a boarding party in return for immediate medical care of the Jewish wounded. The British agreed. Within minutes twenty marines swung down on the deck of the *Exodus*. Simultaneously the more gravely wounded of the refugees were transferred to the destroyers. As the exchange was taking place, Ike dispatched a long radio message to the Haganah receiving station in Haifa. In full detail, he described the battle that had taken place. "Let there be no concern," he concluded. "The ship is not sinking. We have made the barbarians show their true faces. The world now knows them for what they are. Take courage. Soon we shall be among you." Kol Haganah, the Jewish Underground radio station in Palestine, broadcast Ike's words at the moment they were uttered. Throughout the country—in homes, in factories, in coffee shops and restaurants—Jews listened breathlessly to the incredible drama taking place less than forty miles offshore. Ike's parents were among the listeners. Until that moment they had been certain that their son was still in the United States.

The trip to Haifa consumed another five hours, but it was uneventful. The ferry reached Haifa (under its own power) on the afternoon of July 18. British army units succeeded in hustling all the refugees ashore, and into the large detention pens that had been set up for them near the ducks. Most of the American crew mingled anonymously with the passengers, and went undetected. Only Bernie Marx was recognized; but as an American, he later secured his release. Then the CID began its search for Ike, Yosi, and the other Haganah agents. Provisions had been made for such an emergency, however; a small hiding-room had been tunneled out of the gravel ballast in the lower hold. British investigators passed that way several times, but saw nothing. During the next two days several Haganah agents came on board, dressed as members of the cleaning and disinfecting crew. They smuggled food to Ike and the others. At the end of the week British vigilance finally relaxed. Ike and his companions swung down a rope ladder under cover of darkness, and swam to safety.

It was only upon reporting to Haganah headquarters, several hours later, that Ike learned the fate of the refugees. Foreign Minister Bevin had decided to make an "example" of the *Exodus* passengers. They had all been transferred to another boat, and were even then being transported back to Germany. When Ike heard the news he thought at first that he would faint.

"Try to see the thing in perspective," the Haganah officer urged him. "I'll show you the papers that have come in by air. For the last three days the *Exodus* story has been front-page news in nearly every country in Europe. We're convinced that Bevin has hanged himself on this one."

That conviction was borne out.

Reporting to Palmach headquarters at Juara, Ike and Yosi Hamburger gave a detailed account of their recent mission to a picked group of Underground leaders. They urged, too, that extensive use be made of American Jews as crewmen for the refugee ships; the Americans had proved to be far more intensely committed on the Zionist issue than the Palestinians had ever imagined. Ike and Hamburger recommended, as well, that the scale of naval training be enlarged immediately—not only for the "illegal" voyages that lay ahead, but also for the massive transshipment of displaced persons that would surely follow the solution of the Palestine question. The Underground leaders ultimately approved both suggestions. During the next two months, additional numbers of Palmach youths were assigned to the Pal-Yam training courses at Caesaria and Yagur, while Haganah emissaries in the United States actively recruited Jewish naval and merchant marine veterans for the rescue operation. In all, some ten vessels were staffed primarily by American-Jewish crewmen.

In September Ike was informed of his new assignment. He was ordered to leave immediately for Constanta, Rumania. There he would assume command of the *Pan Crescent,* a former United Fruit Company freighter. With its sister ship, the *Pan York,* the vessel had recently been purchased by the Jewish Agency for the refugee traffic. Actually several D.P. boats had already departed from Constanta, but the migration from that port still represented the smallest trickle in the escape operation. Even then, approximately 15,000 Jews were sitting on their suitcases in Joint Distribution Committee camps near the harbor, anxiously awaiting the blessed moment of departure for Palestine. Not the least of the Haganah's difficulties was Rumania's inaccessibility. In recent months its border had been sealed off from its nearest neighbor, Hungary. As a result, eleven weeks went by before Ike managed to smuggle and bribe his way from Paris to Prague to Budapest to Belgrade, and finally to Bucharest and Constanta.

Unfortunately, by the time he arrived at the Black Sea port, the British blockade had reached the peak of its efficiency. A direct sailing to Palestine itself was now out of the question. Nor was it really necessary any longer. The United Nations Partition Resolution had been passed only the month before; within less than a half-year an emergent Jewish State would assume full freedom of action on immigration. Accordingly, Moshe Shertok, political director of the Jewish Agency, issued orders for the ships to make directly for Cyprus, without provoking the usual ordeal of interception off the Palestine coast. The major Haganah goal now was to concentrate as many Jews near Palestine as possible. The moment the British Mandate terminated, these refugees would be available for the Jewish defense effort.

Even following the Partition Resolution, however, Haganah emissaries found their way barred by innumerable political obstacles. Ike, arriving in

Constanta on December 22, was informed by the Communist authorities that the D.P.s would not be permitted to depart from Rumanian ports, whatever their destination. It was a shattering disappointment. As rage and frustration welled up within him, Ike momentarily contemplated ordering the refugees out on a mass hunger strike. Then he immediately abandoned the idea; the Communists could not have cared less whether the Jews lived or died. He searched for other alternatives—and found one the same day. Just before the ship's planned departure, he managed to arrange for the 15,000 Jews to be transferred by rail to the Bulgarian harbor of Burgas. There, within twenty-four hours, the refugees were loaded into the *Pan Crescent* and the *Pan York*—for the ships had sailed down the Black Sea coast to meet them in accordance with the new plan. The *Pan York* was under the command of Gad Hilft, Ike's friend and companion from Pal-Yam days. Both vessels were dependable old single-stackers of 6,000 tons each. Although built in 1901, they were still quite seaworthy; indeed they were among the most valuable recent additions to the Haganah "merchant marine."

The new arrangements notwithstanding, the fate of both the ships and the refugees themselves still remained in doubt. Only twelve hours out of Burgas, the *Pan Crescent* and *Pan York* reached the Turkish coastal check-station of Buyukdere, guarding the entrance to the Bosphorus. And here the Turkish police boarding party informed the Jewish captains that entrance into the Straits would not be permitted. Moreover, if the boats should even drop anchor within Turkish territorial waters they would be seized, and their passengers interned. Immediately Ike communicated with Gad Hilft by radio.

"Something smells," Ike said. "It's a violation of international law. The Straits have to stay open for all merchant and passenger shipping. I've got the maritime code right in front of me. Even Soviet ships go through."

"I suppose the British have gotten to them," replied Hilft. "They didn't try anything like this last year."

Ike thought for a moment, then decided on a gamble. "Gad, let's threaten to drop anchor," he said. "They may be frightened of the British, but I have a hunch that the prospect of feeding and housing fifteen thousand refugees will frighten them a lot more."

Hilft agreed. Ike promptly notified the Turkish police that the ships were about to heave to, that even internment in Turkey was a fate preferable to the "horrors" of life in Rumania. It was the one answer the Turkish lieutenant had not expected. Visibly losing his composure, the officer hurried back to shore and referred the matter to authorities in Ankara. When the reply arrived—nearly a half-day later—it was apparent that the bluff had worked. The ships were allowed to proceed through the Straits.

Apparently the British themselves had foreseen this contingency. The moment the refugee vessels passed through the Golden Horn, reaching the Mediterranean, they were joined by two British destroyers. One of the warships pulled to within a hundred yards of the *Pan Crescent*.

"We understand that you are under orders to bring these two ships to

Cyprus," the commanding officer called out by loud-speaker. "Please confirm."

This time it was Ike's turn to refer to headquarters. He promptly radioed Haifa, asking for instructions. The answer came back immediately: he was at liberty to confirm. Thereupon Ike notified the British that Cyprus was in fact their destination.

"We will cause you no trouble," the officer replied, "providing that you allow our boarding parties in your steering room the day before arrival at Famagusta harbor."

By now Ike was well aware that the British feared "trouble" far more than he. He called back: "We have means of resistance but will not use them if no attempt is made to identify members of our crew."

The British agreed. Both sides kept their bargain. On the day before arrival at Cyprus, the boarding parties mounted the refugee ships without incident. And once the vessels finally docked at Famagusta, on January 4, 1948, the passengers were unloaded peacefully, and carried off by British army lorries to internment camps. Ike and Hilft remained on deck with their crews. No efforts were made to arrest them. Indeed, the British hardly considered that necessary, they had made other plans for the *Pan York* and *Pan Crescent*. The steamers were "temporarily" confiscated by the Admiralty.

The moment these orders were conveyed to him, Ike ran down the gangplank, hired a taxi, and sped off to the governor's office. When the Englishman received him, Ike brushed aside the man's amenities. "The ships are our property," he shouted. "They carry the Panamanian flag. They are owned by the Jewish Agency. We agreed not to carry refugees to Palestine. What more do you want? Is this an example of British fair play?"

The governor was unperturbed. "This is simply a necessary precaution to avoid the overextension of our facilities here and in Palestine," he explained. "The arrangements are purely temporary."

Presumably the ships would be returned on May 15, when the Palestine Mandate terminated. Yet when Ike pressed him on this point, the official remained noncommittal. Determined, therefore, to protect the boats from possible British sabotage, Ike and Hilft decided to remain on board—the entire five months.

From that moment a cat-and-mouse game began between the Jewish captains and the British authorities. Ike was obliged to find means of keeping the *Pan York* and *Pan Crescent* in a state of continual readiness, for departure could not be delayed beyond the target date of May 15. At first, the task of maintaining a continual vigil seemed all but hopeless. The crews, most of them hired Italians and Spaniards, decided to leave. Obviously replacements could not be imported from Palestine. British soldiers were stationed on deck to ensure that no attempt was made to smuggle the boats out of the harbor, or to load them with supplies or fuel. Occasionally destroyers exploded depth charges around the hulls to deter refugees from swimming out to the boats.

In spite of these formidable obstacles, however, years of Underground training enabled Ike and Hilft to keep a step ahead of their wardens. Each day they cadged small quantities of fuel from the British for "safety" purposes, in case of storm. Those supplies were carefully hoarded. Whenever British inspectors took soundings of the fuel tanks, their testing sticks struck false bottoms. Similarly, the Jewish captains recruited D.P.s with naval or engineering experience from the camps. The refugees, in turn, managed to board ship by posing as carpenters or electricians who were needed for "repairs" to keep the boats from leaking. By spring both vessels were adequately fueled, stocked, and manned for immediate departure to Palestine. All that remained now was to await May 15.

When the fateful day came, the Israel flags were immediately raised on the *Pan Crescent* and *Pan York*. It was an emotional moment. Watching the ceremony from shore, the Jewish internees shouted, sang, applauded with near-hysterical fervor. Then Ike and Hilft paid a formal visit to the British governor in Nicosea, and demanded immediate permission to sail. Again the official was noncommittal: "The United Nations have insisted that Palestine be partitioned peacefully," he explained blandly. "We cannot be sure that the ships will be used for peaceful purposes."

"You don't have to be sure," Ike replied, barely controlling his voice. "You British are not our legal guardians any more, nor the guardians of our morals for that matter. We are sovereign now."

Yet it required an additional two weeks of haggling, and the threat of legal action, before the governor grudgingly released the ships from internment. But not the refugees. The British were flatly determined that no Jews of military age would leave the island—lest the Arab war effort be jeopardized. Thus Ike and Hilft returned to Palestine with near-empty boats, at a time when soldiers were desperately needed for the *Yishuv*'s defense. Not until the second United Nations Truce, on July 18, did the English finally lift their ban on the free departure of refugees. And then, at long last, without encountering further harassment, the *Pan York* and *Pan Crescent* returned to Cyprus. During the ensuing weeks Ike and Hilft made four round trips between Famagusta and Haifa, emptying the internment camps of their 25,000 occupants, and conveying the refugees to their new homeland.

"Nothing came easily in those days," Ike recalled. "We had lived and worked under conspiratorial conditions so long that we were never certain whether our sovereignty would be taken seriously or not. For the first few months after May 15, we sailed in a kind of twilight world. Sometimes Israel was recognized as a State by port authorities; sometimes not. But we were not returning to Honduran or Panamanian flags under any conditions. Those ships were ours now, and so were the people we were bringing."

Other nations slowly adjusted themselves to the idea. For most of them, the sight of those ancient, reconverted freighters, flying the Israel flag, represented the first tangible proof of the existence of the Jewish State. In the majority of instances, too, that maritime introduction preceded diplomatic relations. Some of the vessels loaded weapons for the Jewish defense effort. But most of them loaded passengers. For during the year and a half following May 15, 1948, the immigrant traffic was the single most important fact in Israel's life. Ike, of course, was still deeply involved in that migration: loading 3,000 refugees in Yugoslavia, another 4,000 in Italy, again 4,000 in Italy—until, by the end of April, 1949, his vessel, the *Pan Crescent,* had transported some 28,000 passengers to Palestine. Yet even these trips played but a small part in the immense process of ingathering. Buying and chartering freighters, oilers, ferries, rickety tramp steamers, wherever they could be found, the Jewish Agency supplied passage for no less than a half-million refugees between May, 1948, and December, 1951. Indeed, it was this unprecedented influx of human cargoes, beginning "illegally" in the postwar years, and continuing openly after the birth of the Jewish State, which was almost exclusively responsible for laying the basis of the Israel merchant marine.

No one in the top echelons of the Israel government ever doubted that a strong commercial navy deserved highest priority in the nation's economic planning. The country was small and poor, with severely limited agricultural and industrial potentialities. The only frontier, therefore, where Israel was not restricted either by space or natural resources was the sea itself. Greece and Norway, nations similarly unendowed with natural wealth, had long since learned the importance of developing large fleets for the carrying trade; the sea had traditionally been an open market for any country capable of exploiting it. In the case of Israel, moreover, important political and military factors dictated the need for a merchant marine. The Jewish State possessed no overland trade routes, for the Arabs had sealed its borders. With its back to the water, sorely beset by hostile neighbors to the north, east, and south, Israel found it a matter of the most desperate urgency to maintain its relations with friendly countries in other parts of the world— as well as with Jewish communities in other lands. A shipping line was the best and probably the only dependable means of avoiding almost total physical isolation.

Yet reliance could hardly be placed any longer upon the ancient tubs that had served as carriers for the refugee traffic. Only a year after the establishment of the State, the one remaining vessel considered seaworthy for passenger shipping was the tiny, 3,500-ton *Kedma*. Shortly afterward two other obsolete boats were purchased and reconverted, the *Negba* and the old *Jerusalem*. These hardly sufficed, even for immigration purposes; while cargo shipping had to be left almost entirely to the fleets of other nations. In spite of these urgent maritime needs, however, Israel's financial circumstances, woeful to the point of near-bankruptcy in the early 1950s, limited purchases to a handful of tiny, English-made cargo vessels.

Then, in 1952, the German Reparations Agreement made available to the Jews $820,000,000 worth of capital goods. Not surprisingly, the Government of Israel immediately gave top priority to the purchase of cargo and passenger vessels from West German ship-building firms. In later years, moreover, the nation's steadily improving financial situation allowed shipping orders to be placed in other countries, particularly in Japan, France, and the

Netherlands. As a consequence of this sudden acceleration of purchases, the Israel merchant fleet, consisting in 1949 of four rusting freighters totaling 6,000 gross tons, grew by 1963 to seventy-seven carriers, with a deadweight tonnage of 710,000, and valued at $170,000,000. The average age of the ships in 1963 was four years, thus providing Israel not only with the fastest-growing fleet in the world, but also the most modern. The list of vessels includes five trim, speedy passenger liners, the *Theodor Herzl,* the *Jerusalem,* the *Artza,* the *Moledet,* and the *Shalom;* and two mixed passenger-and-cargo ships, the *Zion* and the *Israel.* The boats share combined transport accommodations of 5,000 passengers, and they are invariably booked to capacity—usually by enthusiastic American-Jewish tourists for whom the excitement of a voyage on an Israel carrier is more important than the elegant and experienced service of older shipping lines. In addition, two Japanese-built oil tankers, constructed for the Eilat-Persian Gulf run, reach the formidable tonnage of 45,000 each. According to present development plans, the Israel merchant fleet will total at least a million and a half dead-weight tons by 1970. Even by 1963, however, Israel boasted the fourth largest merchant fleet among the Mediterranean nations.

This burgeoning maritime strength was perhaps the single most dramatic phenomenon in the not undramatic growth of the Israel economy since 1948. Yet its results are not to be measured simply by accumulated tonnage. Less than 1 per cent of Israel's seaborne foreign trade was carried by Jewish vessels in 1948. In 1963 the figure reached 36 per cent—and fully 78 per cent of all sea passengers. In the Mediterranean, Jewish ships accounted for 73 per cent of all trade between Israel and the Mediterranean countries, and 91 per cent of the passenger traffic. Israel's tankers now import 32 per cent of the country's oil. The Zim Company, the nation's principal shipping line (jointly owned by the Jewish Agency, the Histadrut, and the government) has extended its activities throughout the entire world. Today its vessels anchor regularly in hundreds of ports—in Piraeus, Naples, and Marseilles; in Rotterdam, Cherbourg, Le Havre, Bremen, Hamburg, Danzig, Malmo, Liverpool, and Helsinki; in Philadelphia, New Orleans, Houston, Tampa, Los Angeles, San Francisco, and Seattle; in Rangoon, Kobe, and Manila.

For several years, too, Zim has been opening out a promising import-export trade in the virgin hinterland of Africa. Vessels of the company's West African Line ply the torrid and exotic coastal route to Nigeria, the French Cameroons, the Ivory Coast, Gabon, and Ghana. Dropping anchor in the makeshift, ramshackle harbors of Monrovia and Freetown, Abidjan, Accra, and Takoradi, the Israel vessels unload their cargoes of light industrial equipment, and take on vast quantities of timber logs, hides, beef, and cottonseed—all to be processed later in Jewish factories. A virtually identical traffic is carried out by Zim's Eilat-Africa Line, beginning at the southern tip of the Negev and calling at virtually all the major East African ports, including Massaua, Djibouti, Mogadiscio, Mombasa, Tanga, Zanzibar, Dar es Salaam, Mozambique, Lourenço Marques, Durban, and Capetown. Eight ships are used on the East African run alone, with approximately four sailings a month from Eilat.

This "explosion" of shipping capacity has measurably stimulated employment in subsidiary industries, including electronic equipment firms, dry
docks, repair companies, ship chandlers—in addition to the six thousand
employees who work as stevedores, repairmen, and construction laborers in
the ports of Haifa, Eilat, and Tel Aviv. Even these harbors, their capacities
expanded many times over since 1948, no longer offer sufficient docking
space for the scores of ships that anchor off the Israel coast each month.
Accordingly, for several years a "crash" program has been under way to
construct a vast new harbor at Ashdod, eleven miles north of Ashkelon.
Once the project is completed, hopefully in 1965, Ashdod will rank only
behind Alexandria as the largest and most fully equipped deep-water port
in the eastern Mediterranean.

Impressive as these achievements have been, they do not yet satisfy
Israel's maritime planners. Thus far the nation's merchant fleet transports
only 28 per cent of the country's total foreign commerce. Determined,
therefore, to increase Israel's share of the carrying trade, Zim has in recent
years devised the entirely unprecedented technique of negotiating partnership arrangements with the companies of other maritime nations. At first
these agreements were worked out with the newly emergent countries,
especially those of Africa. It was a mutually satisfactory arrangement on
both sides. The recently liberated African nations far preferred to borrow
from Israel's quite limited mercantile experience, than to depend on the
help proffered by England, France, or Italy. The reason was not difficult to
fathom, of course. The Western Powers were suspect as former colonial
overlords. Little Israel presented no threat to the Africans' hard-won
independence.

Accordingly, the first such contract was negotiated with Ghana, in September, 1957, and resulted in a company entitled, not inappropriately, the
"Black Star Line." By terms of the agreement, the Government of Ghana
held 60 per cent of the line's stock, and Zim 40 per cent. Management,
however, remained exclusively in the hands of Zim, whose staff trained
Ghanian sailors, directed a newly founded maritime school in Accra, and
provided the officers for the Black Star Line's four vessels (as well as for
President Nkruma's private yacht). Some of the Israel instructors were
themselves but recent graduates of naval courses. The trust and co-operation
of their African students compensated in some measure for their own lack
of self-confidence. Indeed, the entire joint venture proved a quite remarkable success. It is significant that the new company plied the route not only
between Ghana and Israel, but also between West Africa and Britain. In
this fashion, the Jews succeeded in capturing back a share of the trade
Britain had formerly pre-empted on the sea routes to Israel itself. Similar
agreements are pending between Israel and Nigeria and Liberia, and have
in fact already been consummated between Israel and Burma.

Moreover, in its drive for a larger share of the world carrying trade,
Israel has not overlooked the possibility of joint undertakings with well-
established maritime powers. Thus, in 1958, the Gold Star Line came into
existence, co-managed by Israel and Japan. Operating out of Hong Kong,

the company sends its vessels to Osaka, Yokohama, Kobe, Singapore, Rangoon, Lourenço Marques, Durban, Capetown, Takoradi, Abidjan, and Conakry. A subsidiary company, the Seven Star Line, ships cargoes between Israel, Africa, and Japan; while yet another venture, the Great Lakes Line, enables Zim to act as partner in a joint Israel-American company navigating the St. Lawrence Seaway. By 1963, there was hardly a port in the world in which a vessel fluttering the Star of David had not dropped anchor.

Ike Aronowicz's career reflected this proliferating maritime traffic. After a brief period of further study in London, he returned home to receive his master's license from the newly established Israel Board of Naval Examiners. Immediately afterward he shipped out to sea once more. Between 1950 and 1958 he commanded nearly every type of freight ship and passenger ship in the Israel merchant marine, carried every variety of cargo, dropped anchor in most of the major harbors of three continents—and acquired, at the same time, a revealing insight into the attitudes of other peoples toward his country. In many instances, especially in the larger American cities, the response was perfunctory, or at best mildly curious. In the Netherlands and Scandinavia, on the other hand, in Italy and France, sailors and townspeople alike expressed an unusually friendly interest in the Israelis, insisting upon buying them drinks, and often extending home hospitality.

Elsewhere, reactions were mixed. In the early fifties, stopovers at German harbors proved to be quite uncomfortable. Ike lectured his men in advance, warning them to remain together in groups when ashore, to exercise the utmost restraint in the presence of Germans. They followed those instructions. Yet wherever the Israel crew members walked, they could see and feel the astonished glances of bystanders, the fingers pointed at the Hebrew lettering and the Jewish stars on their caps, the muffled whispers behind their backs. And when they entered cafés or bars, sitting only a few feet from groups of German sailors, tension mounted at times to the breaking point. Usually the Germans began with remarks among themselves: "What are they? Jews? . . . No, they call themselves Israelis now . . . Big shots . . ." And then, after a few drinks, the taunts began. "Hey, Jakey, who do you get to run your ships? . . . Yids, who let you in?"

The Israel crew endured the baiting in silence only twice. The third time, in Hamburg, Ike personally gave the signal to strike back. A wild fist fight ensued, until the police rushed in to separate the infuriated men. The Jewish sailors were not booked—neither at Hamburg, nor at other ports where fights erupted. Indeed, there was one incident at Bremerhaven when Ike's third mate, a powerful veteran of the Yugoslav partisans, walked over to an aggressive German stevedore and smashed the man flat with one punch. The German died shortly afterward of a brain hemorrhage. Again, the police scrupulously refrained from pressing charges. After a number of such encounters, the Germans learned a grudging respect for the Jewish mariners. Drinks were never exchanged between the two groups; but, after a while, neither were blows.

Ironically, Ike himself was obliged to enter into a more extended and "diplomatic" relationship with the Germans. In 1955 he arrived at the

Eisfleth shipyard, on the Weser River, to supervise the final stages of the construction of his "kibbutz ship," the *Palmach*. The owner of the yard, Heinz Behrendt, was an ex-Nazi. In his initial dealings with Ike, the German maintained an attitude of strained correctness, which Ike reciprocated in kind. As the two men worked closely together during the ensuing weeks, Behrendt discovered, to his surprise, that the Israeli's knowledge of marine engineering more than equaled his own. Indeed, Ike's suggestions for improvements and alterations were more imaginative than any Behrendt had previously encountered. When the German ventured at last to ask a few circumspect questions about Ike's nautical experience, he was given the full story. The shipyard owner was awe-struck by the account of the *Exodus-1947*.

"But, Herr Kapitan, you are another Felix Graf von Luckner," exclaimed Behrendt, in astonishment. "I have never heard anything like that in my life."

"There were many such episodes," Ike replied drily, "and not only at sea."

Whereupon he described the Warsaw Ghetto uprising. When he finished, the German remained silent for several minutes.

"I won't insult your intelligence by saying I had to be a Party member," Behrendt said finally. "They promised us things I wanted. I even believed the stories we heard of the Jews. I was wrong, of course. Because I have met you, I am one of the few who know how wrong we all were. I would like to know the right things now. Will you tell me something about Israel?"

Ike told him. They sat in Behrendt's home at night, eating and drinking together. Others of the German's family and friends joined them, listening intently to Ike's descriptions of life in Israel, the sacrifices of the Jewish pioneers, the ideals of Labor Zionism, the philosophy and sociology of the kibbutz, Ike's dream of co-operative shipping. They questioned him incessantly. The boys and younger men seemed particularly entranced by Ike's account of kibbutz life.

"Will your government let us visit Israel?" they asked. "We would like to work on a kibbutz."

Ike shook his head. "You will have to inquire for yourselves," he replied. "Perhaps someday the time will come."

In later years Ike learned that several of these youths did, in fact, visit Israel, spending their summers on collective settlements.

By the end of Ike's seventh week at Eisfleth, the freighter had passed its final inspection, and was ready to be turned over to the Israel crew. Following the protocol customary on such occasions, the shipyard prepared a festive launching ceremony. Ike took his place on the platform and delivered the expected speech of thanks on behalf of the Zim Company. His tone was sober.

"None of us in Israel can ever forget the sufferings the Nazis inflicted on our people," he told the assembled workers. "In my opinion nothing can ever atone for that tragedy, certainly not reparations alone. Nevertheless, we have received splendid co-operation from this shipyard, and our relations with Herr Behrendt and the workers have been excellent. I can only hope that our association here is an indication of a new generation growing up in Germany. If that is the case, then someday our two nations will be friends."

In the silence following these remarks, Behrendt ordered the shipyard band to play "HaTikvah," the Israel national anthem. The German workmen stood at rigid attention. At this point, however, the Israel crew members began shaking their heads. Several of them gazed imploringly at Ike. The massed drums and trumpets had not yet sounded; but the Jews listened and heard the distant strains of the "Horst Wessel" song. As the conductor raised his baton, Ike laid a restraining hand on the man's arm. "Please don't," he said quietly. "The time has not yet come for that."

Before boarding the ship, Ike took his final leave of Behrendt. "We'll meet again someday, Herr Kapitan," the German assured him emotionally. "I shall never forget our friendship."

Ike grasped the man's hand warmly, then ascended the gangplank. Later, as the vessel moved down the Weser, he watched silently from the bridge. Behrendt and the German workmen were cheering. Tugboats on the river blew their horns in salute. From ships docked along the riverbank German sailors waved their hats in greeting. The experience was bittersweet for Ike and his crewmen. A new epoch was by no means opening. But perhaps an old one was closing.

In a sense, the experience was reversed in the Soviet Union. Ike paid his first visit to Russia in January, 1953, when he sailed the Zim freighter *Tzfonit* and its cargo of oranges into Odessa. He had looked forward to this trip for years. Fully 70 per cent of the population of Odessa port (as distinguished from the city proper) were Jewish; the opportunity of establishing contact with Russian Jewry was better here than in almost any other Soviet city. At first, however, the presentiments were not favorable. Even as the *Tzfonit* cruised between the buoys flanking the entrance to the sparkling, placid harbor, it was met by a Zim sister ship, the *Hadar,* churning out into the Black Sea. The captain of the departing vessel was Steve Hernandorena, a non-Jewish veteran of the Spanish Loyalist army, and now an Israel citizen. He called out his greeting to Ike on the loud-speaker: "If you have any secret documents on board, hide them," Hernandorena warned. "The Soviet police will turn your ship inside out."

Then he sailed by. Duly alerted, Ike instructed his crew to dispose of any literature that the Communists might consider "provocative." The routine was familiar; he had learned it well years before in his dealings with the British harbor police. It occurred to him at that moment, too, that he had not been so tense since the early days of the refugee sailings. Indeed, no sooner was the *Tzfonit* tied down at his assigned dock than, true to Hernandorena's warning, a Soviet colonel and four soldiers came on board and entered the steering cabin. A perfunctory search was made. During the first few minutes of the search the officer spoke to Ike in Russian, while a crew mate translated:

"Your documents say your name is Aronowicz," said the colonel.

"That is correct. Yehiel Yitzhak Aronowicz."

"A Jewish name. But the other captain was not a Jew."

"No," Ike explained. "He is Spanish in origin. But we consider him an Israeli, just like all the rest of us."

Then, to Ike's astonishment, the colonel suddenly grinned and began speaking in flawless Hebrew. "Welcome, *chaver,*" he said, pumping Ike's hand vigorously. "You can't be too careful these days. I'm a Jew, too, as you see. We are proud and honored to have a ship here from Israel. I can promise you a warm welcome."

It was an understatement. A few minutes later the assistant port director boarded the *Tzfonit.* He, too, was a Jew.

"My name is Victor," he said in Yiddish, flashing a gold-toothed smile. "Our city is at your disposal. Unload your cargo and then come down to the Seamen's Club. We shall do everything possible to make you comfortable here."

That evening Ike and his crew followed Victor into the clubhouse. The welcome was a royal one. Most of the hostesses were intelligent, attractive Jewish girls. They vied with each other in lavishing attention, food, and wine on the Israel seamen. The non-Jewish sailors and port officials were hardly less friendly. They admired the poise and self-assurance of the Israel visitors, and were flattered by the Jews' remarkably detailed knowledge of classical Russian literature. But, inevitably, it was the local Jewish population which provided by far the most effusive hospitality. Each night during the next week and a half, Ike and his shipmates were dinner guests in various Jewish homes. The experience was a memorable one. After one or two drinks hosts and visitors alike usually dissolved in tears, and began embracing each other fervently.

"You can't imagine what we went through here," the local householders explained in Yiddish. "The Germans slaughtered a hundred thousand Jews in the Odessa region alone. Although we're still a large community down here in the port area, elsewhere we're only a shadow of what we once were."

"And since 1945?" asked the Israel sailors.

Here the replies usually became evasive. "Since 1945? . . . Things have been difficult for everyone . . . There are shortages, of course . . . For Jews? Perhaps not so easy. There are certain rights we would like, national rights, like the Ukrainians, the Georgians, and the others . . . Never mind . . . in time we shall get them."

But as the night wore on and intimacy deepened, fears and hopes were voiced with increasing frankness. At first they took the form of probing interrogation about life in Israel. Was not the regime there imperialist? . . . Had it not betrayed the Marxist ideals of the early Labor Zionist settlers? . . . Was there not discrimination against Oriental Jewry? However they were phrased, the questions reflected the impact of skilled and effective Soviet propaganda. Few of Odessa's Jews had actually believed what they had heard; but the doubts had nagged and haunted them. Now, gratefully, they listened as Ike and the other Israel sailors provided detailed—and transparently sincere—answers. Life in Israel was by no means a paradise, the visitors pointed out. But surely no ideals had been betrayed: Israel was a free country; a man could live there without fear, expressing to the full his individuality as a human being and a Jew; the Socialist experiments of the kibbutz and moshav were still intact; it was a Labor Zionist government even now; the Orientals were slowly but surely being acculturated.

And by the small hours of the morning all inhibitions were dropped. In fact, stated the hosts, they and all their Russian-Jewish friends urgently desired to leave the Soviet Union. Their passion to emigrate was consuming, nearly unbearable in its intensity; but who would even dare to predict when the time for free departure would come? The hosts revealed that when the State of Israel was born, the Jews of Russia had been transported into a near-euphoria of happiness, singing and dancing in the streets, weeping and embracing for joy. Since that memorable, unforgettable moment, however, hardly any meaningful news of Israel had ever reached the Soviet Union again, except for the horror tales released by the official Communist news bureaus; accurate, detailed information about the Jewish Republic had been almost totally lacking until these Israel merchant vessels began to arrive. Now, at last, the facts could be heard at firsthand, for here were Jewish sailors, living proof of the freedom and dynamism of the Zionist nation across the seas. Little wonder, therefore, that the arrival of Ike and his comrades was nothing less than a public holiday for the Jews of Odessa.

During the next few days, as the *Tzfonit* loaded its cargo of wheat and timber, Jews from communities in all parts of southern Russia arrived at the port city. They crowded so insistently around the Israel vessel that the harbor police were eventually summoned to clear work space for the stevedores. Every few hours, too, a crew member would return from town carrying a box filled with letters for relatives in Israel. Ike promised to have all this correspondence delivered, and he kept that promise. Unfortunately, less could be done for onlookers who begged the crew for information about missing relatives: a daughter last seen in Bialystok in 1942, a father lost in the retreat from Simferopol, a sister said to have been repatriated through Poland—would the honored brethren from Israel have information about these missing dear ones? But the appeals were in vain. With a single memorable exception. An aged woman and her daughter stepped from the crowd and approached one of the sailors, who had just descended from the *Tzfonit*.

"Please, young man, I have come all the way from Baku to meet this ship," the old woman said. "I am seeking information about my son. I haven't seen him in twenty years, but I'm sure he is in Israel, because I used to hear from him before the war."

"A lot of Jews in Israel, little lady," the sailor replied patiently. "What's his family name?"

"Mellman."

The sailor drew closer. "I know a Mellman," he answered cautiously, "but not from Baku."

"No, no," the woman explained, "of course not from Baku. His father took him on ahead of us to Shanghai shortly after he was born."

"David Mellman?"

"My God, yes," mother and daughter cried out together. "Where is he?"

The sailor, a powerful bosun in his late twenties, remained silent for several moments. Twice he attempted to speak, but no words came. Finally he regained his voice, and answered, in strangled tones: "He is standing before you, Mother."

The onlookers surged closer. There was shouting, then a gale of sobbing, then songs of thanksgiving. Total strangers embraced each other. Dancing, cheering, applauding, the crowd triumphantly escorted the reunited family into town. Later in the day a gala celebration was arranged at the Seamen's Club. Ike and the entire crew participated. It was 2:00 A.M. before they returned to the ship and tipsily mounted the gangplank.

Ike was awakened five hours later by an urgent pounding on his cabin door. Before he could answer, Victor, the assistant port director, entered. His face was quite pale. A newspaper was clutched in his hand.

"Too bad you can't read Russian, my friend," he said. "I'll have to translate this for you."

As Victor read, Ike slowly sat up straight in bed. Was this Nazi Germany? Apparently nine doctors had just "confessed" the 1949 "murder" of Andrei Zhdanov and Alexander Shcharbakov, both prominent officials in the Soviet hierarchy. Six of the physicians were Jews. Indeed, there was no doubt on this point—for they were identified as Jews. Then, as Ike listened, incredulous, Victor read on: the murder was committed, the doctors "confessed," in collusion with Zionists and by order of American Intelligence; this was but another in a long list of crimes committed by the heinous international network of Zionist imperialism, which exploited Russia's "rootless cosmopolitans" for its sinister purposes.

"What does it mean?" Ike asked at length.

"It means," said Victor, after a long pause, "that Stalin has decided to make anti-Semitism official. We've been used to discrimination for a long time. But obviously something much worse is brewing now. Much worse." He thought for a moment, then added: "Please don't think we feel differently about you and your crew, Ike. We love you and bless your country. But these visits, the celebrations . . . we have to be careful, you see . . . perhaps, for a while . . ."

"Yes, I understand," said Ike sadly.

He understood better when he walked out on deck. Bad news traveled fast. Down below, the wharf was all but deserted. Of the crowds that had packed the dock during the past week, only a handful of aged men and women and a few small children remained. Nor was this sudden absence of visitors a false alarm. At the Seamen's Club later in the day the Israel sailors sat alone. The Russians ignored them completely. The Jewish port officials briefly exchanged pleasantries, but followed these with embarrassed excuses, and returned to their tables. Invitations to Jewish homes stopped altogether. During the five remaining days in port, the crew members of the *Tzfonit* were boycotted as if the vessel had been touched by the plague. Only one vestige of the former routine remained. At night, as the Israelis wandered listlessly through the streets of the harbor, they were approached furtively by local Jews, who slipped them the names and addresses of relatives in Israel, and then rushed off into the darkness.

On the morning of the *Tzfonit*'s scheduled departure, Victor ascended the gangplank for a final "official" inspection of the ship. He completed his duties in silence. For a moment he hesitated in the steering cabin, then walked over to Ike, shook his hand—and finally embraced him, weeping freely. Ike felt the lump rising in his own throat.

"It won't always be like this, Victor," he assured his friend. "We know what you really feel, and you know what is in our hearts. We are one people."

"One people," Victor sobbed, "and we have to treat each other like strangers."

"Never mind, it won't last forever."

As Victor returned to the dock, he cast a last glance up to the bridge. Suddenly, ignoring the suspicious glances of the harbor police, he shouted to Ike in Yiddish: "Keep those ships coming, captain."

Ike waved back wordlessly. As the tugs nudged the *Tzfonit* out into the harbor, he could see the public buildings and—further back—the houses of Odessa extending toward the northern hinterland. The morning sky was bright, the weather clear, the bay all but empty of traffic. Nevertheless Ike ordered the steam whistle blown twice. He watched intently as stevedores on the docks paused and looked up. He was certain, too, that the hostesses in the Seamen's Club must have halted their conversation for that brief moment and raised their heads. So, surely, did men and women in countless Jewish homes along the waterfront. They heard it, as he wanted them to. Someday we shall be back, someday you who wish to sail with us will board our ships. This was his thought. But until the *Tzfonit* cleared the harbor he could not bring himself to speak.

A man needed an occasional change of scene. Even in the new Europe the earth moaned with the cadavers of one's kinsmen; and in bondaged Europe, with the silent terror of an *émigré* people. In every port, hopes were commingled with memories. Which were the harbors that knew not a Jew from an Israeli, welcoming both, virgin alike to European technology and the Hebrew conscience? Ike cruised the southwestern shoulder of that promised land in the spring of 1952, and returned a year later. The *Tzfonit* took its first soundings off the inlet of Takoradi, Ghana, then dropped anchor to pick up a shipment of logs for the plywood factory of Kibbutz Afikim. The coast was steaming hot and barbarously poor; but its resources were plentiful, and not the least of them were its people.

Ike steered the boat inland the next year, following the course of the Benin River northward into Central Nigeria. Anchoring off the desolate little trading village of Sapele, the *Tzfonit* loaded hides and logs for two days. On the morning of the third day Ike was about to cast off when a delegation of Negroes suddenly called to him from the riverbank. In pidgin English they explained that the king of the local Benin tribe had invited the captain and his officers to visit his palace; native bearers were waiting to carry the guests there. Ike hesitated for several moments, then decided to accept the invitation—but smilingly declined the offer of bearers.

The town was the usual collection of mud huts with thatched roofs. The palace was a somewhat larger building, also of mud, and located on a hill surrounded by a high wall. Yet the king himself was anything but the typical African chieftain. A handsome, ebony giant in his mid-thirties, the tribal ruler proved to be English-educated, and remarkably cultivated.

"I have read a great deal about Israel, you know," said the king. "I'm a great admirer of your country."

"Thank you, Your Majesty," Ike responded in kind. "It is good to know that we are not entirely overlooked among the great nations of the earth."

"On the contrary," insisted the king. "In my opinion Israel has far more to offer us than the colonial States do."

Whereupon the ruler began plying his visitors with questions about their homeland. How had the Jews succeeded in liberating themselves from the English? How had Israel organized its government so quickly? How had the Israelis managed to launch their economy in the early years of State-hood? How large a role did the Labor Federation (the chieftain used the Hebrew word Histadrut) play in Israel's life?

Ike and his companions answered as fully as possible. As the animated discussion continued, it became clear that the chieftain had chosen Israel as the model for his own people.

"You have done so much in so short a time," he explained. "And your problems in absorbing a backward immigrant population are not unlike the problems we shall face when we have won our freedom. It is well known that you are pioneers in social justice at home. You see, that is how we know that you are one people who have not come to exploit us. We would welcome more contact with Jews."

Ike did not forget that conversation. In later months, the *Tzfonit* opened up other associations on the Dark Continent. Indeed, in the case of Israel, trade usually followed shipping; for as the little Jewish freighter explored Africa's western coastline, Ike discovered unprecedented markets for Israel cements, irrigation equipment, chemical fertilizers, and textiles. There were, in addition, plentiful sources of raw materials—logs, hides, cocoa, beef— available more cheaply in Ghana, Liberia, the Ivory Coast, Nigeria, and Sierra Leone than anywhere else in the world. The information, relayed to Israel businessmen and government officials, ultimately proved valuable beyond Ike's fondest hopes. Yet he did not permit himself to be dazzled by trade opportunities alone. The king's remark had left an ineradicable impression on him: "You are one people who have not come to exploit us."

Israel sailors were under strict instructions to justify that confidence. For example, it was the custom of the British, French, and Italian shipping lines to pick up local work gangs of Negro stevedores in Sierra Leone, and then to keep them on board as cheap labor while the boats worked their way down the West African coast. The European crews treated these blacks hardly better than pack animals, compelling them to sleep on straw in the cargo holds, feeding them rice, bread, and water, and paying them a miserable pittance. Of course, the resources of the Zim Line hardly matched those of its European competitors. Even so, for Ike and the other Israel captains it was a matter of principle to provide their Negro stevedores with minimal living conditions—with mattresses in the vestibules of the crew's quarters, the same food eaten by the Israel sailors, and a few English pounds a month as payment. Many of the natives were quite primitive; they stole and became drunk on the slightest pretext. Nevertheless, speaking to these workers in pidgin English, the Jewish crew members respected their dignity, joked with them, and scrupulously refrained from the time-honored practice of beating or humiliating them.

The reputation of the Zim vessels spread rapidly through the bush. Wherever the *Tzfonit* docked, hundreds of Negroes crowded the shore, shouting, applauding, pleading to be hired. "Jew ship, Jew ship, wanna work on Jew ship," they chanted. Ike and his comrades grinned each time they heard that plaintive refrain. The expression was hardly new to them: hostile and suspicious harbor officials had uttered it during the period of the illegal migration; and, until recently, so had German sailors in Hamburg and Bremen. In the mouths of these illiterate half-starving wretches, however, "Jew ship" was a term of hope and gratitude. Ike welcomed the visits hardly less than the native workers themselves. Each time he hoisted anchor he carried back with him something more precious than cargo. It was the ignorant, hopeful expectancy of a dark and imprisoned world, eagerly waiting for the people of Israel to fulfill its destiny there.

During those years of marine diplomacy, one of Ike's principal assets was his crew. Israel sailors were incomparably better educated than those of other shipping lines, and were still relatively immune to the brutalizing influences of the port cities. The time had long since passed when 35 per cent of Israel's seamen were hired mercenaries from other lands. By 1963 the Israel merchant fleet employed 4,000 men, and only 5 per cent of them had to be hired abroad. For the first time, too, the largest number of captains and officers were locally trained. In 1948 the Israel Maritime College had been founded near Caesaria, under the direction of Captain Enrico Levi, a former commander in Italy's Istria Line. Students who enrolled in the college were intensively trained for five years in the latest techniques of marine engineering, navigation, meteorology, and radioelectronics. Annually since 1953, the school's graduates had been taking their places on the bridges of the nation's merchant fleet. Their ranks were supplemented, as well, by veterans of the Israel navy.

Yet it was not enough. The fleet's rate of growth rapidly outstripped the available supply of trained manpower. By 1963 the Zim Line alone experienced a shortage of nearly 100 officers and 195 ratings each year. Although Israel's ratio of one maritime officer per 6,400 inhabitants was high (the ratio in the United States was one officer per 13,200 inhabitants), it hardly matched the soaring annual increase in merchant tonnage. By the late 1950s there were already indications that the sea, once a magnet for the nation's adventurous youth, had begun to lose some of its attraction. The moral and educational level of Jewish sailors was still impressively high; but it was beginning to slip nevertheless. Fly-by-nights were infiltrating the ranks of professional seamen. Occasionally these were simply young men eager to accumulate a quick nest egg before settling down to routine jobs on land. But not infrequently, too, semicriminal types were drawn by the opportunity of smuggling foreign goods into Israel's black market. Other merchant navies had traditionally recruited a large proportion of their manpower from the dregs of society. Until recently, however, none of Israel's economic planners had foreseen this possibility in their own country. The surprise was an unpleasant one. Years earlier it might have been possible to staff a fleet with drifters; but hardly any longer, when modern ships required skilled electricians, refrigeration, electronic, and hydraulic engineers.

Ike Aronowicz was certain that he had devised a solution to the manpower problem; for nearly a decade, in fact, he had nurtured a pet scheme for attracting Israel's most talented youngsters to the merchant marine. He recognized, of course, that in recent centuries seafaring had hardly exercised a traditional appeal to Jews. But neither had agriculture, for that matter, and yet, in Palestine, Jews had been transformed into first-rate farmers through the imaginative use of collective and co-operative methods. Why then could the same techniques not be used in the merchant marine? If crewmen were offered part ownership of their vessels, surely they would develop an *esprit de corps* unique among merchant mariners. Admittedly, the experiment had never been tried before. Yet the newness of Israel's fleet was its very advantage. Unlike other countries, Israel was not hobbled by outmoded traditions and vested interests.

When Ike first broached the plan to friends and colleagues, they raised immediate objections. Egalitarianism might work satisfactorily on a kibbutz, they pointed out, but at sea the safety of passengers and cargo was at stake. Discipline was essential; there was no room on a ship for work committees and elections. Ike agreed. Rank would be preserved, from the captain on down. Even more, remuneration would be adjusted according to a man's training and seniority. Nevertheless, each crew member would be a part owner of the vessel, sharing equally in its profits after salaries had been paid out. In this fashion the ship's efficiency would become a matter of common concern. Initiative would be encouraged. Featherbedding, the meaninglessly rigid division of labor which prevented a sailor in one department from sharing responsibilities in another—all would be eliminated. Most important, crew members would be accompanied by their wives, who would work in the ship's catering department as stewardesses, cooks, laundresses— exactly as they did on collective settlements in Israel proper. With this last and most crucial of inducements, responsible married men would no longer find it necessary to shun the merchant marine as a livelihood. The family unit, a matter of considerable importance in Jewish life, could be maintained at sea.

Ike's scheme failed to impress the management of the Zim Company. The directors pointed out that they had already developed a large and successful organization along conventional business lines; whatever its weaknesses, whatever the shortage of manpower, the company was functioning with reasonable efficiency. Leave socialism to the kibbutz, they advised. Which was precisely what Ike did. He brought his proposal to friends in Kibbutz Ma'agan Michael, near Caesaria. They were more than interested; the idea soon had them wild with excitement. Soon afterward, pooling their communal funds with the savings of another collective settlement, Ein Harod, the kibbutz members secured enough collateral to open negotiations with the government for a loan. Their prospects were improved in 1955 by the availability of German Reparations money. Ike's prestige and articulateness clinched the matter. The ministry of transport eventually advanced the group enough credit to finance the construction of four small freighters. By 1959 those boats were all sailing.

Ike commanded the "flagship." It was the *Palmach,* constructed in Behrendt's shipyard, at Eisfleth. Sailing the Adriatic Mediterranean run, the little cargo vessel proved a financial and "sociological" success from the very outset. With the exception of the veteran bridge officers, the crew consisted almost entirely of families from Ma'agan Michael. They administered the ship's services efficiently, lived together in peace and harmony, went sightseeing together at ports of call, and gratefully sent the *Palmach's* modest profits back to their kibbutz. By the time the ship made its third voyage, between Haifa and Trieste, its reputation had preceded it. At every harbor en route, journalists and photographers were waiting, eager to secure a firsthand account of the "floating kibbutz." Indeed, among other seamen and marine officials, the *Palmach* was something of a sensation. Carefully— and at first skeptically—they inspected the boat, interrogated its crew, examined its log. But the record was flawless. The experiment evidently worked.

Not to Ike's satisfaction. It had never been his intention to recruit his staff exclusively from kibbutz members, and certainly not to send all the vessel's profits back to Ma'agan Michael itself.

"I'm a sailor, not a Socialist doctrinaire," he explained to the executive committee of HaKibbutz HaMe'uchad, the parent federation of collective settlements. "I certainly never intended to lure members away from existing kibbutzim, or simply to transplant farmers to the sea. I wanted to enlarge our merchant marine, and improve it. I want crewmen from the cities, imaginative youngsters from the youth movements. Give those people a chance to share in our profits, and we'll have the finest and probably the most efficient collection of seamen on the Mediterranean. We can't let this experiment remain exclusively in the hands of a few kibbutzim."

Yet the members of the executive committee were adamant. The *Palmach* and its sister ships were their prerogative, they insisted, as much their communal enterprise as a banana field or a jam factory operating on the premises of the kibbutz itself. The enlargement and improvement of the Israel merchant marine was not their primary concern; an additional source of revenue for their kibbutz was. Ike remonstrated, cajoled, threatened. But it was wasted breath. Finally, chagrined and disillusioned, he decided to give up his command.

The year was 1958. Ike was thirty-five years old, married, and the father of two little girls. It was not a time to start experimenting with his career. Although his relations with the Zim Line had been strained by his departure for the "floating kibbutz" venture, Ike was still their ablest captain. The company would have welcomed him back gratefully had he chosen to return. Yet the step seemed retrogressive. After seventeen years of maritime service as crewman and captain, he hardly cherished the thought of going back to routine sea duty on a conventionally operated ship. He had attempted to influence policy both at Zim and at HaKibbutz HaMe'uchad, but had failed. Management was not willing to give ear to a man whose entire experience was maritime, rather than administrative. Perhaps, then, the time had come to seek a formal education in transportation and business administration.

After several months of correspondence, Ike made his decision. In the autumn of the year he departed with his wife and children for the United States. There he enrolled in Georgetown University's department of international transportation, and registered for courses in maritime economics, harbor management, and labor relations. During his year and a half in Washington, D.C., he supported himself and his family by working as chauffeur and night watchman for the Israel Embassy. Study time was limited. Ike made it suffice. At the end of his school term in the winter of 1960, he was graduated from Georgetown with the highest scholastic average in the history of the department.

Immediately afterward Ike was admitted as a scholarship student to the Columbia University Graduate School of Business, and received his Master's Degree in February, 1961. Curiously, during his three-year stay in the United States, few of his classmates or friends were aware of his earlier accomplishments. It awaited the publication of the best-selling novel *Exodus* (a book Ike despised) and later the release of the film of the same name, to draw attention to his true identity. He found his sudden celebrity a painful experience.

In fact, he was still the same wiry, intense, extraordinarily youthful sailor who had boarded his first freighter twenty years earlier. For all his combination of practical experience and academic training, his love of the sea was still the little boy's who had once watched the freighters from the sands of Tel Aviv and Jaffa. Yet returning home now on the *Israel* (a vessel he had once commanded), Ike knew that his sailing days were probably over. Zim had offered him an important executive position in the company's head office. The ministry of transport was considering appointing him deputy director-general; or alternatively, manager of the port of Ashdod, destined to become Israel's largest and most important harbor. Ike himself no longer doubted that he would accept one of these assignments. Perhaps the weight of administrative responsibility would mellow him.

Even as he was considering these possibilities, however, he was approached by Israel Libertovsky, a friend of many years' standing. Libertovsky, an experienced engineer, a veteran of the illegal immigration and the Palmach, had won a distinguished reputation for himself by supervising the installation of the first pipe line from Eilat to Beersheba, and later by completing Mekorot's entire irrigation scheme in the north—both in record time. Now he was charged with a new, and perhaps his most challenging, responsibility: the establishment of a national shipyard. He wanted Ike as one of his managers.

"This is one of the biggest things Israel has ever undertaken," Libertovsky pointed out to Ike. "In fact, it's slated to become the fourth major industrial enterprise in the country. The government is pouring a hundred million pounds into it. We'll employ three thousand people by next year [1962]. Our plans, very simply, are to build ships—our own ships—up to thirty thousand tons each by 1963, and a lot bigger than that by the end of the decade."

The project was unprecedented for a country of Israel's size. Even as Libertovsky was explaining it, however, Ike had already grasped the entire picture. Israel's merchant marine was the fourth largest in the Mediterranean. Of course it was unthinkable that a nation possessing 700,000 tons of shipping, with a million additional tons on order, should depend continually on other nations for its equipment. Whatever the future of the maritime traffic, a national shipyard could easily be kept busy constructing fifty thousand tons of shipping a year—simply to replace depreciating vessels. Anyway, there was surely every likelihood of far larger orders. Zim was expanding. So were smaller private companies like El-Yam and Somarfin. Undoubtedly they would prefer to buy their vessels at home, if costs and quality were competitive.

Did Israel possess the human resources necessary for a major shipbuilding program? Ike was acquainted with at least twenty-five Israel naval architects and twice that many marine engineers. He knew that Israel possessed a higher ratio of these specialists per population than even the United States. In any case, from his own experience, he was well aware that shipbuilding was less a matter of technical proficiency than of organizational and managerial skill—avoiding the peaks and valleys of employment, keeping the labor force steadily at work in a well-spaced program of construction. No, his people did not lack for such skill. The possibilities were intriguing. Ike decided to accept the offer.

The promise of government support certainly had not been exaggerated. Ike was astonished at the quantity of land set aside for the project: over five hundred dunams at the mouth of the Kishon River, at the northern arc of Haifa Bay. That was space enough for a truly huge shipyard by the standards of any country. The budget was there for equipment of the latest design, everything that would go into the shipyard and the ships. And Ike purchased the material, from all over the world: a 15-ton plate-straightening machine; an enormous crane capable of lifting 40 tons, and two smaller ones of 15-ton capacity; a 100-ton lathe; a 40-ton boring and drilling machine; a 600-ton press; a drydock of 1,200-ton lifting capacity; three ultramodern slipways for the construction of 30,000-ton vessels; two enormous prefabrication sheds. And additional equipment was still on order or under construction at the shipyard itself.

Even as the buildings and machines were being installed, moreover, Libertovsky, Ike, and the managerial team began driving ahead on ship construction. The orders were small, at first, for the yard's capacity was still limited. As a rule, the commissions included tugs and barges for the Dead Sea Works, or tenders and landing craft for the navy, as well as occasional repair jobs in the drydock. But the immediate and primary goal was to provide the staff of engineers and workers with experience, to "break them in," together with the machinery; in this manner, skills would be developed for more economical, large-scale production. Yet even now the staff had acquired sufficient confidence in its abilities to make competitive bids for several rather larger projects. Thus, by 1962, the shipyard had already begun work on a 3,000-ton freighter for Zim, and was negotiating a contract with El-Yam for the construction of three additional vessels of the same size. Perhaps most promising of all, arrangements had virtually been completed to build two 7,000-ton freighters for Ghana.

Occasionally Ike indulged himself in the vision of Israel as another Netherlands or Italy, launching a succession of powerful and graceful ocean liners, achieving a reputation as a maritime giant among the nations of the earth. It was whimsy, he knew. His tiny country would do well merely to retain its fourth ranking in the Mediterranean. Nevertheless, there were moments when no dream seemed impossible. In late December of 1962, for example, the shipyard completed its first assignment. It was a small tank-carrier for the Israel navy. Ike himself took over the wheel during the seven-hour shakedown cruise. It was a good feeling. He had not stood on a bridge for nearly four years. The vessel handled exceptionally well, too, almost better than he had hoped. There were minor "bugs," an occasional loose valve in the engine, a few rattles and sighs from the starboard bow plates. That was normal, easily repaired.

Gently, he eased the ship into half-speed. The turquoise surface of the harbor bubbled gray-white behind the stern. Bat Galim, the southernmost arc of Haifa Bay, was clearly visible on the port side. For a moment Ike caught a glimpse of another landing craft, somewhat larger than his own, perched high on wooden supports—on dry land. It was the *Af Al Pi Chain,* a rusting souvenir of the illegal immigration. As a gesture of defiance to the British, the ship had transported its cargo of refugees to Palestine immediately after the *Exodus-1947,* and had suffered the same fate. Poised now like a statue at the highway entrance to Haifa, the fragile little vessel was a permanent monument to the *Braichah*—the Escape—and the passengers and crews who had broken the grip of an empire. Ike remembered well the endless, tortuous negotiations that had preceded the departure of the *Af Al Pi Chain,* and the *Exodus-1947,* and every other creaking relic his people had dared sail in those years before the State. Perhaps the tank-carrier beneath his feet would not have attracted second glances even in the smallest African river harbor. Yet it had been constructed and launched by pride of sovereignty, and its flag was welcome now at every port in the free world.

He rang the telegraph for three-quarter speed. The turbine spun, the

propeller bit cleanly into the wake, and the boat surged forward under renewed power. It moved backward, as well—far beyond the refugee convoys
of the twentieth and nineteenth centuries, beyond the wretched derelicts
clustered in the holds of aging leviathans, and the ritualized ordeal of innumerable earlier migrations. To the Renaissance era when the world's most
respected and distinguished navigators were Sephardic Jews. When Abraham Zacuto, Astronomer Royal to the Court of Portugal, plotted the course
that guided Vasco da Gama on the sea route to India. When earlier, in
1492, as professor of astronomy at the University of Salamanca, Zacuto
served as consultant and final authority for Christopher Columbus on the
eve of the latter's voyage to the New World. Financial backing, too, for
Columbus' epic journey was advanced by Don Isaac Abravanel, by Luis de
Santagel, and a small group of wealthy Jewish marranos. Refugees from the
Spanish Inquisition, a handful of Jewish crew members shared the perils
of that ocean crossing, and one of them, Luis de Torres, was the first European to set foot on the soil of America.

In his memoirs, Amerigo Vespucci, after whom the New World was
named, dwelled at length on his debt to Gaspard de las Indias, Admiral to
the Viceroy of Goa in India, and perhaps the most respected navigator in
the Portuguese fleet. Gaspard was a Jew, forcibly baptized by Vasco da
Gama; his reckonings were scrupulously followed by Amerigo Vespucci on
the voyage to South America. Indeed, Gaspard's book on navigation was
scripture for virtually every mariner who, during the next three centuries,
followed the uncertain ocean route westward. Many of the commanders
were Jews, Spaniards and Portuguese exiles. Settling in the West Indies
and on the American mainland, they transferred their ships to Christians,
and took up nonmaritime careers. Documents in the American Library of
Congress and in the City of Philadelphia record the bills of sale of these
early Jewish captains.

The vessel moved back, as well, beyond the early modern era, to 1419,
when Prince Henry the Navigator invited Judah Crescas—known as
Maestro Jacomo de Majorco—to become the founder-director of the Nautical
Obervatory at Sagrès, Portugal, the first nautical observatory in Christen-
dom. For generations Crescas' family had produced maps and nautical
instruments on the island of Majorca. Indeed, cartography, navigation, and
instrument making were hardly less than the monopoly of Majorca's large
Jewish population. During the fourteenth century, the Jews of this island
were widely recognized as the foremost cartographers of the Western world.
(At their hands, a century later, the young Christopher Columbus received
his first apprenticeship in mathematics.)

And back beyond that, to the early 1200s, when Roger Bacon offered the
Jerusalem Talmud and the Zohar as evidence that the earth was in fact a
globe, rotating on its own axis. Throughout the early Middle Ages, moreover, Jewish scholars continued to effect improvements upon the astrolabe,
the remarkable instrument which simultaneously measured the attitude of
the sun, the stars, and the planets. The device had been introduced to the
Moslem world via a translation, in Greek, of the writings of Mashaala, the

celebrated Jewish scholar of the eighth century. The quadrant, too, which determined bearings by calculating the attitude of the sun, was so improved by Rabbi Jacob ben Makhir in the thirteenth century that his new instrument became known as Quadrans Judaicus; later, further improved by Rabbi Levi ben Gershom, the quadrant acquired the sobriquet "Jacob's Staff." It was indispensable to all subsequent explorers; indeed, the British admiralty kept the "Jacob's Staff" in use well into the eighteenth century. For that matter, nearly all the accepted astronomical tables of the Middle Ages were either translated or compiled by Jews; the most important of them were entirely of Jewish authorship.

Jewish mariners tested the configuration of the sea by practice no less than theory. Throughout the early centuries of the Diaspora, their very existence as settled communities in the outlying corners of the earth encouraged and at times required them to pursue shipping on an international scale. Actually, sea-borne commerce was an undertaking long experience had prepared them to meet; for they were still the veteran fishermen of Galilee, the sinewy Mediterranean sailors of Israel and Judea. The Bible and Talmud were filled with their rich and colorful seamen's lore, the two hundred and more technical terms that described their vessels, their crews and harbors, their rollicking chanties and legends, even their maritime superstitions. They were King Solomon's crewmen, plying the trade routes between Ashdod and Tyre, Joppa and Tarshish, Eilat and Ethiopia. The sea was their kinsman.

So it was for their descendant off the coast of Bat Galim. Since childhood he had memorized the exploits of his forebears. Standing on the bridge of the little vessel, Ike gazed fondly at the whitecaps breaking and foaming toward the western horizon. He loved that heaving, churning, wind-blasted thoroughfare. He loved its amplitude, its unrevealed secrets, its tenuous, fickle horizon; he loved the impartiality of its cruelty. It was his sea—he would never be convinced otherwise. Every dip and swell in its treacherous surface bore the imprint of an ancestor's keel. Jonah and Hezekiah and Benjamin of Tudela and Moses Montefiore had made that route their own —and his. It was still his, and his people's. It was still the Jews' Highway.

CHAPTER TWELVE

THE PROPHET

COLONEL *Ben-David met me at the top of the stairs. "You are in luck this time," he said. "I was able to postpone his next appointment. That should give you a little more leeway."*

"Very good of you," I said to the aide. "I hope he knows what it's all about."

"You can tell him. Go in now, please."

The office was large and comfortably furnished. Oriental carpeting covered the floor. The chairs were wood and leather. Behind the desk a large map of Asia and Africa covered most of the wall. The State of Israel had been etched in black, purposeful reminder that the tiny nation's isolation was the presiding factor in all decisions taken here.

The stocky little man rose and shook my hand cordially. Then he waved me to a seat at his left hand. We exchanged amenities until the maid finished serving Turkish coffee.

"So, what is it this time?" he smiled tolerantly. "Foreign Policy? Defense? Relations with the Diaspora?"

"Something a little closer to your heart, I think."

He continued smiling.

"It is the Negev," I said.

"Ah," his white eyebrows rose. "An important subject. Closest to my heart? I don't know about that. But—a very big subject, very important. What makes you think it's my favorite?"

"I read your speeches."

He laughed heartily, and the pinkness of his complexion seemed for a moment to deepen. "Well, I'm glad to know that someone takes my speeches seriously." He paused, then nodded vigorously. "You are right, too. I mean every word I say about that desert. It will make us or break us. Either we conquer it or it conquers us. There is no compromising with the Negev. You wanted my views. There they are, black on white. Do you agree with them?" He sat back, waiting for me to speak.

"I am not really sure I know enough about the subject," I replied. Then, taking a chance—"I wonder if anyone really knows enough about the

464

*Negev. Even people who have lived there for years consider it an unknown
quantity. And the British, too—"*

"What about them?" he interrupted, with sudden asperity.

*"Sir, they were here for thirty years. If they had felt that the Negev
offered possibilities, surely they would have prospected there, offered concessions—at least to their own people, don't you think?"*

*The old man's expression was quizzical again. "You think they did not?
Maybe they knew more than they were telling. The moment they opened
that desert, wouldn't our people have moved in?"*

The British had known something. S. H. Shaw, consulting geologist to the
Mandatory government, had investigated the terrain, had charted it
roughly, and had drawn tentative conclusions about its mineral properties.
Then he locked the report in the files of his Jerusalem office, and awaited
instructions from his superiors. The orders arrived in May, 1948, during
the last chaotic days of British rule in Palestine. "You are to burn all
geological data in your possession forthwith," the message stated. "Under
no circumstances must the contents of your files fall into the hands of
the Jews."

Shaw was no Zionist. But the order outraged his scientific conscience.
Besides, he had learned to respect the Jewish geologists; they could squeeze
water from a stone. After several days of painful indecision, Shaw made up
his mind. He scribbled a note, then dropped it in the mailbox of a friend.
As he anticipated, the note was delivered into the hands of the Haganah,
the Jewish Underground. Thirty-six hours before the Mandate was due to
expire, Shaw set fire to a large sheaf of papers in his office.

"My files," he explained casually to his subordinates, as he left the
building.

The burning papers were in fact the worthless contents of Shaw's waste-
can. A few minutes later several Haganah soldiers, guns drawn, forced
their way into the building, and into the geologist's office. There they shot
open the locked files, and carried off the contents in canvas bags. It was a
vital *coup* for the Jews. The moment affairs were settled in Palestine they
would act decisively on the captured information. The incident affected
Shaw's life no less significantly. He was promptly dismissed from British
government service. For years thereafter he was unable to secure a position
in his own country.

As it happened, the Jews were unwilling to wait until fighting ceased
before evaluating Shaw's data. From the military point of view, no time
could be lost in exploring the desert. Crucial battles had been fought and
were being fought in the Negev's northern sector. Now, too, in the autumn
of 1948, the United Nations Truce supervisor, for the sake of a peace treaty,
was actively considering the possibility of trading off part of the Negev
to the Arabs. The Israel authorities were not likely to make this concession.
But for diplomatic as well as economic reasons, it was indispensable to them
to know what the territory encompassing no less than 6,500 square miles,
60 per cent of the land surface of Israel, was actually worth.

Thus, in Jerusalem, geologists of the Hebrew University pored over the Shaw material. It was not without value. The basic contours of the desert had been charted. Likely sources of water had been listed, together with prospective lodes of iron and manganese. But the data was rough and haphazard. Accurate topographical measurements had not been carried out. Detailed mineral samplings had not been analyzed. Not one agricultural or meteorological experiment station had been located south of the soil area. For that matter, not so much as a single highway had been laid. During the Second World War, when Rommel's Afrika Korps had penetrated British defenses as far as the gates of Alexandria, General Sir Claude Auchinleck had authorized the construction of a retreat highway from the Sinai Peninsula to Beersheba. But Auchinleck's successor, General Montgomery, had promptly countermanded this plan. The Negev remained trackless.

Thus, in October, 1948, the Israel government decided that no further time could be lost in preparing a detailed survey of the desert. The responsibility was turned over to Dr. Ya'akov Ben-Tor, a member of the Hebrew University's department of geology. Ben-Tor, an energetic German Jew in his mid-thirties, was serving at the time as mobilization officer of the city of Jerusalem. It was a comparatively sedentary post, and he chafed at its restrictions. The opportunity to chart the wilderness came to him as a godsend; indeed, the fact that units of the Egyptian army still remained in the southwestern sector of the Negev, that fighting still continued there, simply added to the challenge.

For his initial staff, Ben-Tor recruited Dr. Yitzhak Vroman, an associate from the Hebrew University, Dr. Chaim Dostrovsky, of the Weizmann Institute, several students of geology and biology, a few drivers, guides, first-aid men, and a radio operator. The Israel defense forces provided the group with five jeeps. In preliminary explorations, however, ground transportation proved of but limited value; one axle after another cracked on the murderous terrain. Ultimately major reliance was placed on a Piper Cub airplane, supplied by the air force. Two ruggedly built command cars occasionally followed—but more often remained stationary at fixed camp sites.

The expedition set out in the third week of December. The Piper Cub took off from the Rehovot landing strip with Ben-Tor seated beside the pilot. As the tiny plane gained altitude, the Negev's dun-colored rock dunes slowly revealed themselves in the southern distance. How close it was, and yet how little he, Ben-Tor—or any other Jew—knew of the desert except for the bare official statistics provided in the Mandatory handbook. The Negev [it declared]: divided into (1) the coastal strip forming a rectangle between the Gerar River on the north, the Wadi Shenek on the east, the Egyptian border on the south, and the sea on the west; (2) the Negev Plateau, a broad plain encircling the town of Beersheba, its surface broken here and there by hills and mounds covered with stones and rubble; (3) the hills of the Negev, rising from the tableland along the triangle and then descending to the Arava; (4) the Arava Valley, the long cleft descending from the Dead Sea to the Gulf of Akaba; and (5) the integral desert, a continuation of the wilderness of Judea.

As far as Ben-Tor or anyone else knew, only the first two of these zones were considered fit for cultivation of any sort. And even these were viewed as most unlikely prospects, for they, too, descended below the rainfall line, the point beyond which precipitation dropped to less than 250 millimeters a year (giving the area its name: Negev—Dryness). Their soil was saline, the sand and wind ravaged plant and animal alike. As for the remaining zones, there was nothing to be said or done: they were windy and barren, as gashed and pock-marked as the surface of the moon, their rock crust scorched by day and frozen by night. It was wilderness out there, the Great Unknown. Ben-Tor and his pilot gazed down in awed silence as the mighty emptiness yawned before them.

The survey began in the most hospitable region, the territory around Beersheba. From there it progressed laterally and southward toward the three "terror" zones. Each trip consumed approximately two weeks. The men were often compelled to prepare airstrips with their own muscle power, shoveling rocks and chipping away at escarpments. Every morning they were up at dawn, making a quick air survey of each new sector, then settling down for the tedious and exhaustive work of measuring the terrain with dipmeters and range finders. All relevant weather factors were recorded—temperature variations, the rate and moisture of prevailing winds, the density of dew concentration at night. Referring continually to the Shaw data, Ben-Tor's men checked with special care for likely underground water sources or mineral veins. Then each night the team gathered in the camp car to sort and examine rock and soil specimens, to transcribe their notes, and to prepare their draft maps. Ben-Tor made it his practice never to go to bed until he had summarized the day's efforts in his log.

The survey continued for thirteen months. During this period, with rare exceptions, the group lived on army rations and slept in tents. It was a grim ordeal. Some of the men collapsed under the desert heat. Others succumbed to respiratory diseases, a result of the bitter nighttime cold. Occasionally, members of the expedition were bitten by vipers and scorpions, and had to be flown back to Rehovot for immediate hospitalization. There were other dangers, too. Twice, the Piper Cub collided in mid-air with eagles and nearly crashed. And one afternoon, as the men were surveying the area between Beersheba and the Dead Sea, Dr. Pinhas Selah, a member of the geological team, strayed out of sight of his colleagues and did not return. His body was found later, throat slashed ear to ear by a bedouin knife.

But finally the task was completed, in January, 1950. It was a momentous achievement. The configuration, density, and surface properties of every one of the Negev's 6,500 square miles were now recorded in exact scale. The face of the wilderness had been mapped.

"We were not happy with what we found," Ben-Tor recalled. "Even along the coastal strip the so-called 'soil' was eighty per cent sand. The rest was nothing more than clay, salt, and loess [rock dust]. In the northern plateau, the loess content alone reached twenty per cent. It's the wind blowing loess and sand that accounts for those ferocious Negev sandstorms —and the resultant erosion. Without water, the prospects for farming looked pretty bleak."

"Ben-Tor said it was not encouraging," I reminded the old man.

"How does Ben-Tor know? Is Ben-Tor a farmer?" he asked, with some annoyance. "Are you?"

"Of course not." I laughed nervously.

He leaned forward. "Well, I am," he said. "I was a farmer from the moment I came to this country. How much water do you think we had in the Sharon or the Galilee in those days? We dry-farmed." He pounded a stubby index finger on the desk for emphasis: "And that's exactly what they are doing in the Negev this very minute. With a little imagination you can raise quite a respectable crop without water. Today in Europe the highest prices are being paid for winter vegetables—small potatoes, greens, tomatoes. Those vegetables come out of the Negev, my friend. Not from the rich soil of Europe. Not even from the irrigated areas of Israel. From the Negev. Think about that." Before I could speak, he pressed on: " 'Not encouraging.' What is there to encourage us here? Who waits for encouragement? I can tell you that those young families who went down to the 'G'vulot' in 1943 were not waiting for a guarantee of rain. They just went down on faith and farmed."

That was not quite accurate. In fact, the youths had been sent out by the Jewish National Fund to establish and operate three agricultural experiment stations in the northern Negev. For several years they conducted soil tests there under the supervision of the Jewish Agency's department of soil chemistry. Only later, after the possibilities of dry farming had been validated, did other young men and women venture down from the settled regions. By 1948 sixteen kibbutzim had been carved out of the coastal strip and northern Negev plateau. Several of them produced respectable wheat and vegetable crops. Even these, however, were conceived less as farms than as strategic outposts of Jewish settlement, a staked Zionist claim on the barren hinterland.

It was the merest beginning. Following the establishment of the State, a chain of new villages sprang up in the northwestern quadrant of the Negev, facing the Gaza Strip. By 1963 no less than fifty-one collective and co-operative settlements, supporting a population of 50,000 people, had effectively sealed the western corner of the "Great Dryness" against Arab penetration. Yet this time strategy alone was no longer the determining factor. The plain truth was that the nation desperately needed more food for its burgeoning population. Somehow, at all costs, the shallow, loessal soil had to be made to produce. By 1963, as a result, over 110,000 acres of Negev wasteland had been turned over to cultivation, most of it to dry farming. The results, if unspectacular, were not entirely unimpressive. During the winter season enough wheat and vegetables were raised to augment the needs of the neighboring industrial communities. Even the least successful colony managed to feed itself.

Of course it was not enough to satisfy the visionaries. The most tenacious and single-minded among them could be found at the Arid Zone Research Station in Givat, several miles outside Beersheba. Here the vigorous young directress, Dr. Hadassah Avigdori, planned the experiments that seeded the station's 3,000 dunams with cereal grains, fruit, and vegetables. Various "families" of sheep and cows, imported from twelve different countries, were set out to forage in clover and grass pasture. In the fields complex and expensive instruments measured subsoil temperatures, wind pressures, angle of rainfall, rate of crop growth, water retention and consumption. A modern, handsomely equipped laboratory permitted detailed analysis of the Negev's wide variety of soils. Quite obviously the ministry of agriculture had spared no expense in providing Dr. Avigdori with material, equipment, and manpower. Indeed, some two hundred Moroccan and Yemenite farm hands toiled here under her direction. The investment was a costly one. The government protected it by requiring all farmers living below the 250-mm. precipitation line to incorporate the station's recommendations into their planting schedules—as a matter of law.

It was costly for Dr. Avigdori, too. She was approximately thirty years old when I met her. These were the best years of her life. If her ambition had been comfort and social opportunity, she could undoubtedly have spent them to better advantage elsewhere. Her hair drawn back in a tight, dry bun, her skin flaking under the desert sun, she moved briskly between the steaming vegetable patches, their bulbs and roots corkscrewing toward the surface, and the animals bleating plaintively in their rancid cattle sheds. That moistureless purgatory was her entire life now. She had made the choice voluntarily.

"When Mekorot gets the water down this way things should be a little easier for you," I suggested.

"We shall use this information where the pipes stop," was her crisp reply.

One could admire her confidence without sharing it. The government had spoken of a million settlers in the Negev. In that case, one quarter of them would have to be farmers—or the remaining 750,000 would not eat. It did not seem likely without water.

"Oh, I do not say that the possibilities for agricultural growth are unlimited," the old man admitted. *"But dry farming is only one of the alternatives. The pipes will be coming down in a few years. That will give us twenty-five per cent more water right there. Then there are other irrigation techniques,"* he added. *"I presume you've read Nelson Glueck's book,* Rivers in the Desert?"

"Yes, interesting."

"There, you see!" he said triumphantly. *"If the ancient Nabateans could irrigate that whole area with their primitive terraces, just think what modern farmers can do. And that is exclusive of the Zarchin process."* He looked at me intently for a moment. *"I suppose you know what this is?"*

"I know the idea is to desalinize sea water," I replied. *"Don't ask me to explain it scientifically."*

*That struck him as funny. He laughed, twice, like a dog barking. "And
if you could, would I understand it?" He guffawed. "Even Weizmann [Dr.
Chaim Weizmann, the scientist who was Israel's first president] couldn't
make these matters clear to me. No, no. If the scientists say it has a chance,
that's enough for me. And they say this has a chance. Um, ummm, just contemplate what that would mean." He shook his great head at the wonder
of it. "Our arable land would be tripled, quadrupled—far below the rainfall
line. Cattle could graze. We would have meat as well as vegetables. That's
it, our food problem would be solved. I'm very optimistic," he added, super-
fluously. "We have good people working on these problems."*

Two of them were Dr. Hugo Boyko, director of the department of
ecology at the Beit Dagan agricultural research station, and his wife, Dr.
Elizabeth Boyko. Through research dating back to 1947, the Boykos proved
that certain varieties of vegetables and fruit, as well as many types of
industrial crops, can be grown successfully in sandy soil irrigated by plain
sea water. The technique, revolutionary in its simplicity, has excited the
interest of botanists throughout the world.

"Until now," explains Hugo Boyko, "the idea has been to get rid of sea
water in the development of coastal land. I am proposing a completely new
idea, namely, the *use* of sea water. The traditional danger of sea water is
that the salt accumulates in the soil as the water evaporates; the concentration finally gets so high that nothing will grow. My method is to use
so *much* sea water that the salt is washed out of the soil."

If the method can be applied successfully to a wider range of plants, an
additional half-million acres of desert land may yet be salvaged for agricultural use. No one is dancing in the streets on the strength of the Boyko
data. Israel's citizens, reflecting the mood of the government, are cautiously
optimistic. The Beit Dagan investigations are carried out under semi-labora-
tory conditions. In the Negev, unfortunately, the results of experiments
cannot always be duplicated on a large scale. People await firmer evidence.

Perhaps the best testimony is historical. It may be hidden in the ancient
Nabatean towns of Ovdat and Subeita, in the central Negev hill region.
During an aerial survey of this area in 1959, the distinguished plant phys-
iologist, Professor Michael Evenari of the Hebrew University, discovered
the key to the agricultural techniques of the ancient Nabateans. Apparently
this talented pre-Arabian people had devised an ingenious irrigation
network to trap the short, sharp, flood flows of winter. The soil was loessial
—grim bacterialess rock-flour. Rainfall totaled less than four inches a year.
Yet by a cunning use of terraces, conduits, and catch basins, the Nabateans
had managed to channel and concentrate the meager flow from the surrounding slopes. Thus, a light sprinkling of four inches of rain, falling on
thirty acres, could be directed into a single acre of loessial valley land—
thereby equaling a total of 124 inches of water. This was apparently the
method by which Nabatean farmers produced an eightfold barley and
sevenfold wheat yield from every seed they planted.

Or so Evenari believed. Determined to test this theory, he recruited a handful of students, and laboriously reconstructed a Nabatean farm at Ovdat, down to the identical terraces, canals, and cisterns. Then he began planting. The following winter, Evenari and his wife sowed the crops and labored with the same primitive wooden plows the ancients had used. Modern mechanical devices or artificial fertilizers were taboo. By December all was finally in readiness for the first rain of the season. In the Negev hills it fell on January 5, 1961—one fifth of an inch. A week later the scientist and his wife issued an announcement which was instantly published on the front pages of the country's newspapers.

> On January 11, 1961, Professor Michael Evenari reported excellent wheat and barley crops and promising fruit orchards at his restored Nabatean farm at Ovdat, following last Thursday's one-fifth-inch rainfall. This was in contrast to the loss of the entire Negev winter crop due to insufficient rainfall. Evenari directed rain water descending from the hills surrounding his three-dunam farm into Nabatean channels, and had enough water after Thursday's rain virtually to flood his land.

Upon reading of the experiment's success, water experts elsewhere wondered how they themselves had failed to devise so simple and obvious a solution: one constructed an irrigation network. In Israel itself, however, people who knew the Negev did not consider the solution a simple one. A middle-aged man and his wife had been obliged to live for ten months in the parched and searing wilderness to prove it. And if, in years to come, 50,000 others joined them, what would their labor be worth? That many people till the soil now in the more tolerable coastal and northern plateau regions of the Negev. The income from their crops is estimated at less than two million dollars annually. Presumably there arrives a time in a person's, and a nation's, life when labor must be valued as more than the ability merely to survive.

"No, we were never persuaded that agriculture was our best hope down there," Ben-Tor admitted. "The prime minister has his passion for clearing rocks. I wanted to use those rocks. By the time the survey was finished, it was pretty clear what we had. When we informed the ministry of development they immediately 'institutionalized' us." He chuckled. "All mineral, hydrological, and petrological investigations became our province. We informed the companies where we thought the prospecting would be good, and they acted on our suggestions. When the companies submitted their reports, we evaluated them and either recommended or vetoed government loans. And sometimes when private investors failed to move into a promising area fast enough, we asked the ministry of development itself to set up a corporation. We knew even then that our best hope lay in mineral deposits."

"Did one have to be a genius to figure that out?" the old man scoffed. "Of course we expected to dig for what we wanted. I never believed oil or honey would flow from the desert. Who did? Did you?"

He was back to that again. This time I kept my composure, merely shaking my head.

"Of course we expected to dig," he repeated. "Now look what we have found: potash, bromine, magnesium," he ticked them off on his fingers, "flint, clay, gypsum, copper, limestone. These resources are not gold or silver, but people need them and are willing to pay for them. Jews earn their bread in this country digging those minerals out and processing them. Other Jews supply these workers and their families. There you have a community growing up and establishing a settlement. It is happening all the time now in the Negev—just the way it happened in other parts of the country. Why must we talk in terms of idealism or self-sacrifice? Create jobs and people will work. It's an economic law."

I wanted to shift the conversation back to the original subject. "Sir, I have spoken to a number of experts about this," I observed, "Ben-Tor and Joseph Weitz of the Jewish National Fund, among others. They agree that minerals offer the best hope. But they don't believe that we ought to exaggerate their importance."

"Exaggerate?" He looked at me reprovingly for a moment. "But who is exaggerating? Either we have these substances or we do not. If I may say so, you are spending too much time talking to people who live in Jerusalem. You would do better to talk to the people who live in the Negev. Ask them what they think." He smiled. "In the end, they are the only ones who know what it's all about."

Gershon Segelman was a chunky, blue-eyed American in his early forties. A trained agronomist, he had come to the Negev in 1946 as a kibbutz member, and later joined the Dead Sea Works as director of market research. Seated now in his modest Beersheba apartment, he discussed the future of his company with me.

"It's remarkably good," insisted Segelman, with typical enthusiasm. "The Dead Sea is unquestionably the single most important source of mineral wealth in this country. Its quantities of potash, bromine, magnesium, and salt are all but unlimited. Take potash. Our plant at Sodom produced 150,000 tons of the stuff a year, and we've hardly begun. Potash is the key ingredient in chemical fertilizer, you know, and today the demand for fertilizer is growing at a prodigious rate. The population explosion is responsible. People have to be fed. Land and water by themselves are no longer enough. But add fertilizer to an acre of soil, and the yield jumps by another twenty-five per cent. The developing countries are beginning to learn this—especially the African nations. They depend upon agriculture for their survival. The United Nations sends experts to teach them to use fertilizer. So do we. We've sent soil engineers to nearly every state in Africa. Also to Greece, Iran, and Burma, more recently. The results have really been quite exciting. I would estimate that we can triple our production in the next five years.

"Then there is another factor," he continued. "The ideal fertilizer contains potash, nitrogen, and phosphates. Yet until recently we've exported raw potash alone. The foreign countries purchase their nitrogen phosphates elsewhere, and blend them with potash on the spot. It's a complicated process for them, and a loss of potential income for us. Of course, there are very few countries that can produce the single ideal chemical fertilizer economically. They can produce nitrogen from the air, and add potash—if they have it. But in any case they usually don't have phosphorus, and if they have them both, the potash deposits are so far from the phosphorus that the transportation cost of carting one to the other for synthesis is prohibitive. In Israel, however, we are in a unique position. We have discovered large quantities of phosphates in Oron. Oron is exactly twenty-eight miles from Sodom, where our potash plant is. Midway between the two we are building a new factory." Segelman grinned delightedly. "Do I have to tell you what that factory will be?"

Of course he did not. The new plant would combine nitrogen, potash, and phosphorus into the single ideal fertilizer. The production and transportation costs would assuredly be among the most economical in the world, and the resultant low price of the finished product undoubtedly would place Israel's fertilizers in a formidable, perhaps commanding, position on the international market. There would be other consequences, too. The fertilizer factory would become the hub of an important new settlement in the desert, the town of Arad.

I visited Arad twice in 1961, and once in 1962. It is located on a plateau of the Judean hills, just before the range drops precipitously toward the Dead Sea. During my first visit, in March, the inhabitants of Arad consisted of six surveyors and engineers, living in a single camp trailer and two tents. By the time of my second visit, in December, three architects and a sewage technologist had joined the original group. For the truth was that Arad did not yet exist, except on the drawing boards of the ministry of development. The town was wholly and entirely the conception of government planners. Aware that the rising factory would employ a work force of nearly eight hundred, the development engineers and architects were laying the groundwork for a town of ten times that many people. Blueprints had been prepared, specifying the location of streets, cisterns, commercial and residential areas, a hotel, a service and medical center. Construction finally began in September, 1962, the date of my third visit, with the cornerstone-laying of the hotel and a block of twenty homes. Building would not stop —so the government dignitaries who spoke at the occasion assured us— until the entire city had been planted, full-grown, on the rim of the wilderness. At the date of writing, Arad's population has climbed to five hundred.

"It's not a question of optimism," insisted Segelman. "The Dead Sea region is only at the beginning of its growth. In five years Oron will be producing 150,000 tons of phosphates annually. Add to that 600,000 tons of potash, 75,000 tons of magnesite for refractory bricks, 15,000 tons of bromine for use in pesticides, medicinals, and films, and 20,000 tons of salt—and you have a respectable industrial nucleus."

Segelman was not exaggerating. The entire southwestern shore of the great salt sea was a jungle of steel pipes, cracking towers, storage tanks, warehouses, machine shops, garages, and barracks. It was a boom area. The single, winding road leading from Sodom was clotted by an army of diesel trucks, straining up the mountainside under their burdens of chalk-colored mineral dust. Here were the basic raw ingredients of sea and earth, none of them more sophisticated than a routine compound—and solid, dependable hard-currency earners, every one.

But Segelman was not content merely to speculate on current development projects. His eyes bright with enthusiasm, he was already envisaging elaborate processing factories for the minerals.

"With gas, chlorine, and bromine, we can produce synthetic rubber ourselves," he assured me. "With gas from the Zohar fields we can use electrolysis to manufacture caustic soda right out of the salt. With the proper equipment we can also turn out magnesium and potassium industrial salts. There's no reason for us to leave the production of chlorinated hydrocarbons to others. We can make the same insecticides with our own gas and chloride. We've already got men drawing up plans for a huge polyethylene plant in Arad; the raw materials for it are right here. Just imagine, today the Dead Sea brings in about sixty-two million dollars for Israel. That's more than our entire annual citrus crop is worth."

"What percentage of Israel's total export income—net income—does that represent?" I asked, somewhat irreverently.

"Between two and three per cent. But by 1970 we expect to raise that to eight per cent."

By 1970, too, it was the government's plan to have a million people settled in the Negev, hopefully two fifths of Israel's population. I made a mental note of the figures. Forty per cent of the population earning 8 per cent of the nation's income. Somehow, I was not impressed.

"Fifteen per cent," Ben-Tor corrected me later, when I quoted the figures to him. "Fifteen per cent will come out of the Negev," he explained. "Segelman was speaking only of the Dead Sea area. We have other resources. Agriculture aside, there's the Ramon Crater, right in the desert's dead-center. That means clays, glass sands, and—further south—copper. In fact, by the time we finished that survey we knew pretty well how much of it there was and what it was worth."

"That is what I have already told you," the little man reminded me patiently. "All those other materials are there, too. Naturally, it would be nice if they were all concentrated in the Dead Sea basin, like potash, bromine, and phosphates. But the main thing is that we have them. What we need now are men willing to go deep into the desert to dig them out. That's the point."

His eyes twinkled impishly, but I held up my hand this time before he could say it. "Not I," I admitted.

Michael Skidelsky, a tall, white-haired engineer in his mid-fifties, was probably the sort of man he had in mind. Skidelsky handled the jeep the morning we drove off together from Beersheba for HaMachtesh HaGadol, the so-called Great Crater in the central-eastern Negev plateau. As we ground and roared our way through the dust, Skiddy bellowed his greetings

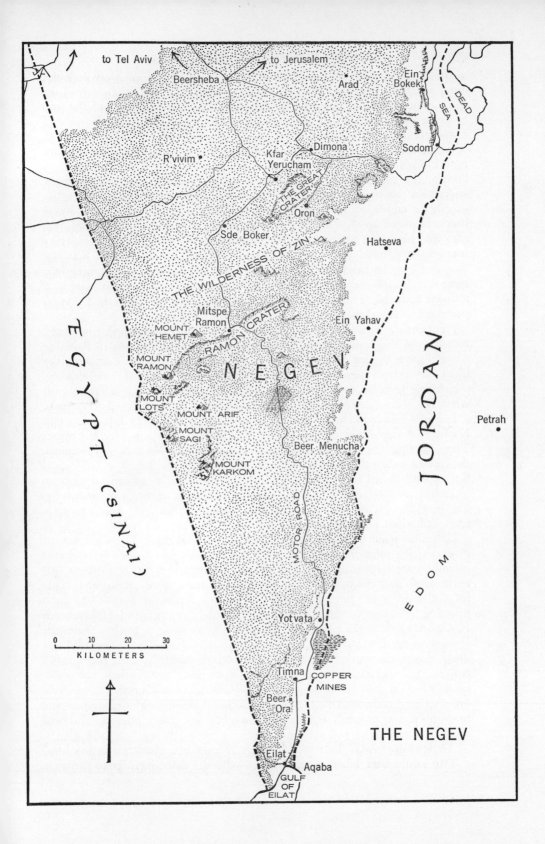

to Tel Aviv   to Jerusalem

Beersheba

Arad   Ein Bokek

DEAD SEA

R'vivim   Kfar Yerucham   Dimona   Sodom

THE GREAT CRATER

Oron

Sde Boker   Hatseva

THE WILDERNESS OF ZIN

Mitspe Ramon   Ein Yahav

MOUNT HEMET   RAMON CRATER

MOUNT RAMON   N E G E V

MOUNT LOTS

MOUNT ARIF   Petrah

MOUNT SAGI

MOUNT KARKOM   Beer Menucha

E D O M

MOTOR ROAD

EGYPT (SINAI)

JORDAN

0   10   20   30
KILOMETERS

Yotvata

Timna   COPPER MINES

Beer Ora

THE NEGEV

Eilat   Aqaba

GULF OF EILAT

to the fleeting images we passed en route; he seemed to know every bedouin, every grizzled desert rat by name. We paused at an ancient flour mill, its huge stone wheel paralyzed by the drought. Skiddy climbed out of the jeep to shake hands with a half-dozen Arab cronies who squatted at the edge of a moribund well. Then we moved on.

We talked about ourselves during the trip. I had the better of the bargain, for Skiddy's autobiography was a fascinating one. He had been born in Siberia, the son and grandson of enormously wealthy coal mine owners. Indeed, in the years just preceding World War I, the Skidelsky properties in Siberia employed no fewer than 25,000 laborers. The Bolshevik Revolution changed all that, of course. Fortunately for the Skidelsky children, they had been sent off to England early in 1917. There Michael Skidelsky was educated, receiving a degree in engineering at Cambridge. Between 1929 and 1939 he lived in Harbin, Manchuria, working as an engineer in a mine which ultimately produced a million tons of coal a year, and operated its own railroad. The mine was the family's: the Skidelskys had always possessed a remarkable faculty for landing on their feet.

He spent the Second World War as an officer in the British Army. Once, returning to England on furlough in 1943, he stopped off briefly in Palestine to visit some distant relatives. The experience changed his life. Skidelsky liked the people he met there. They were the kind of hard-driving, pioneering Jews his own family had been. He decided to pay a return visit when the war ended. He paid many more. In 1949 he decided to remain.

His first employment was as engineer for the Phoenicia Glassworks in Haifa. It was pleasant enough work, but far too restricting for his tastes. Then, in 1950, the Solel Boneh Contracting Agency, owners of Phoenicia, decided to prospect for glass sands in the Negev; the Ben-Tor Geological Survey had found important samplings in the desert's east-central plateau. Skidelsky was offered the job of project chief. He accepted it gratefully. For him, the Negev was virgin Siberia and Manchuria all over again. A man had room to breathe there.

He found what he wanted near HaMachtesh HaGadol. The silica was of exceptionally pure quality. The problem was to get it out in sufficient quantities for large-scale testing in Haifa. Unfortunately the equipment was antiquated, and there would be none better until the decision was made for full-scale production. Skidelsky lived with Arabs in Beersheba. Each morning he arose at dawn to make the three-hour trip to HaMachtesh HaGadol. Once at the Crater, he directed a work gang of twelve Moroccan Jews, loading the sand on a fleet of aging trucks. If the machinery did not break down, the trucks did. If the equipment remained intact, men would collapse from exhaustion or sunstroke. Somehow, nevertheless, the daily quota of eight tons of loading was maintained. After four months of this ordeal, the run-through in Haifa was declared positive. Modern automatic machinery was ordered. By then Skiddy had lost forty pounds, and was black as a bedouin.

"Delightful period," he recalled wryly. "Never had more fun in my life."

Two hours later I had an inkling of what he must have gone through.

We reached the Great Crater. The new equipment was already installed. Six workers operated the levers and pulleys of a gleaming automatic German glass sand cleaning plant. The machines turned out three hundred tons of silica a day. The kitchen and sleeping facilities, in a large camp trailer, seemed reasonably comfortable. In any case, the men did not spend their nights here, for a new road enabled them to commute from their homes in Dimona, only an hour's drive away. But for all the improvement in the crew's circumstances, it was the same Crater. One choked on its dust, reeled under the polarized rays of its white, disklike sun. The desolation of its streaked and mottled hills was absolute and fearful. Not a camel, not a buzzard could be seen. Not an echo returned to punctuate that fiendish silence. Woe to the man who was not at peace with himself here.

Yet HaMachtesh HaGadol was only the beginning. We moved south now toward the Ramon Crater, the huge declivity which marks the Negev's midpoint. Partially dehydrated, and thoroughy enervated by the heat, which seemed to dance in shock waves around me, I fell into a half-stupor. By now I was insensible to the pounding of the jeep against spine and kidneys. The journey passed by like a dream: a marble quarry looming up before us, hydraulic pile drivers crushing the rock into pulverulence; chalk dust transforming the muscular Oriental crew into a mobile frieze; innumerable ledges and ridges flaked white, ricocheting the glare into my burning eyes.

"Limestone, the one thing we have in abundance here," Skiddy's voice murmured, as if from a distance. "It's the basis of the world's chemical industry, you know."

He had slipped out of the jeep, and now chipped away briefly at the sediment with a tiny, sharp-edged hammer.

"Ceramic soft-stone, best and purest there is," the voice continued. "We're going to quarry it on an open-pit basis."

The jeep rolled on, and so did the dream. It was an ancient earthquake before us. Mountains climbed on each other's backs, twisted and tortured, folded, humped, and warped with the scars of an ancient catastrophe. The lesion opened in the earth, a monstrous fissure crawling its way toward the horizon.

"There it is, HaMachtesh HaRamon," he said. "There's my beauty."

It looked better later in statistics. The Ramon supplied Israel with nearly all its flint clay, rich in aluminum oxide, unexcelled for strengthening structural steels; and 8 per cent of its pure ceramic clay, smooth enough for tiles and plumbing surfaces, tough enough for the coating of high-temperature refractories, for steel and glass furnaces, jet-engine and ship's-boiler parts. There was gypsum here, too, the world's largest supply, the principal ingredient in plaster of Paris, wall plaster, casts, a vital additive for the cement industry. No time had been wasted in setting up quarries. Workmen were blasting away with dynamite charges and automatic dredges, with pneumatic drills, mechanized winches, scrapers, and compressors.

"Just the beginning," Skiddy assured me. "We have to wait until the overseas markets jell. I estimate that we can ultimately mine two hundred tons of this stuff a day. It's hard to say what it will be worth to us. With luck, five or ten million dollars a year, perhaps. It depends on the export market. Of course, right now our profit is rather slim." He became vague.

By the most optimistic standards, five or ten million dollars a year. The output of one middle-sized American corporation. Perhaps then, nothing more could have been expected of clays and rock dusts. The old man had said it, after all; these were not deposits of gold or silver, not even of coal or iron. Not a precious metal in the lot.

There was a single glimmer of real hope, but it was much, much further south. From Beersheba the trip by automobile required eight hours, from Sodom only an hour and a half less than that. One reached it by following the great cleft of the Wadi Arava from its sub-sea-level floor near the Dead Sea, climbing steadily into the mountains of the Wilderness of Zin, and then descending slowly along the scorched riverbed of Wadi Jeib straight on toward the Gulf of Akaba. Occasional acacia trees, tamarisks, Christ's thorn, and broom-plant grew along the way. For the rest, the Wadi Arava smelled of death. To the biblical chronicler, this was indeed the prototype of the "Valley of the Shadow."

Nelson Glueck, the eminent American archaeologist, discovered the site by an imaginative use of biblical clues. King Solomon's copper mines were reputed to have been located near the ancient Red Sea port of Etzion Geber, a few miles from present-day Eilat. For several years Glueck painstakingly scoured the area until, in 1935, he finally unearthed the ruins of a huge copper smelter. Pottery shards near-by confirmed the period. The relics surely belonged to the Solomonic monarchy. It was an epic discovery. Yet for many years its significance appeared to be entirely antiquarian. Shortly after the birth of the State of Israel, however, metallurgists returned to Timna, where Glueck had made his historic find. If the smelter was there, the deposits themselves surely were close by. Drilling and laboratory examination supported this hope, and eventually confirmed it. The earth was saturated with copper ore.

By October, 1958, an open pit had been dug at Timna and three small plants erected near-by. Mining operations, begun tentatively three years earlier, now moved into full-scale production. Ore was extracted from the pit, and later from the tunnels. The rock was crushed to powder, then leached in sulphuric acid. Finally, converted into copper sulphate, the powder was conveyed by belt to a scrap-iron "launder" pan where it emerged as granular copper cement—80 per cent pure. The process was an expensive one. Aside from the $20,000,000 required for the initial plant and equipment, a labor force of five hundred men, working in three shifts, had to be paid, housed, and transported to and from the city of Eilat, where they lived. An additional two hundred workers required training each year. As late as 1962 the total annual production had not exceeded seven thousand tons of copper cement annually. It was not enough even to meet domestic needs. Nevertheless, Timna officials bubbled with optimism. For an additional investment of a "mere" $7,500,000 they insisted, output could be doubled, and the cement converted into 100-per-cent metallic copper—

thus adding substantially to the product's earning value. What would that be? The experts estimated the sum at $80,000,000 annually by 1965. Gross, not net income.

The Timna enterprise was unquestionably an impressive one. Surrounded by the gaunt, lonely rock pillars of the southern wilderness, the sprawling complex of mills and heavy machinery, of hundreds of engineers and workers methodically squeezing blood out of stone—what was this if not the apotheosis of the Zionist ideal, a distillation of everything that had been taught, preached, and polemicized of the Jewish renaissance? It was all of that, surely, and more. But not less. Not yet a simple business proposition, a hard-headed cash investment for cash dividends. The promises were invariably issued in good faith. But somehow even the most "realistic" of project engineers spoke of huge future profit as if it were already deposited in the Bank of Israel. By what right? On the basis of these painfully wrested earth scrapings? Was this ruined and petrified cinder of desolation to be seriously considered as a guarantor of the nation's viability? My misgivings had been growing in recent weeks. I expressed them to Skidelsky. He shrugged noncommittally, but withheld comment. Our jeep pulled slowly out of the boulder-strewn diadem, and back to the main road.

The next morning at dawn we drove northward. Neither of us spoke much. The way back was a long one, and energy was best conserved. Besides, Skiddy himself had doubts about the final stop on our itinerary. Perhaps because he held no proprietary interest there. It was a curious *volte face* nonetheless: HaMachtesh HaKatan, eight miles southwest of the Dead Sea, was the one Negev crater that seemed to me to offer the most dramatic possibilities. We reached it early in the afternoon. Had it not been for the high-pitched whine of its generators, we might have passed it; from a distance of more than fifty yards the tiny outpost was swallowed in the lavender haze of the surrounding mountains.

Twenty-five helmeted men grunted and sweated over a "joy-rig," a swiftly rotating carborundum tip attached to a zinc-plated steel drill. It was not clay or rock dust they were looking for here. Inside one of the trailers two bearded young geologists were conducting tests. Their equipment seemed more than ample. From wall to wall the mobile laboratory was packed with sinks, tubes, and glass piping, with elaborate charts and petrological tables, ultraviolet petroloscopes, oscilloscopes, and electric microscopes. Skiddy smiled tolerantly at the apparatus.

"The march of progress," he murmured.

"Exactly that," responded one of the scientists, with equal good humor. "The samplings are first-rate. We're quite optimistic."

"Um." Skiddy had been hearing those reports for years now.

In fact, the gravimetric and seismic surveys had always been encouraging. Nor could one argue with results. For on September 23, 1955, the Lapidot Company had struck oil in the Heletz field, seventeen miles south of Ashdod. By August, 1960, a total of forty wells were already active in the Heletz region, pumping 156,000 tons of high-grade petroleum annually. A month after that the Lapidot team scored again, this time near Kibbutz

Negba, thirty miles south of Tel Aviv. Petrologists estimated that the second strike added a potential of another 150,000 tons a year to Israel's oil reserves. Was that not progress?

It was, of course. If hard-boiled mining engineers like Skidelsky had reservations, their conservatism was by no means shared by the rest of Israel's population. Already 15 per cent of the nation's oil needs were being supplied by local wells. Better yet, other sources of domestic fuel had recently been discovered. Three years after the first Heletz oil strike, the Naphtha Petroleum Company began sinking shafts into the Zohar field, eleven miles west of the Dead Sea. At first the effort was judged a failure; not a trace of oil could be found. Not a trace of oil but—as the drilling proceeded— rich, astonishingly plentiful quantities of another ingredient: high-grade methane gas.

The discovery was in some ways far more promising than the original oil strikes. For gas could perform many of the functions of petroleum. Gas could power machinery, could heat, refrigerate, could even be piped as easily as oil to the furthest reaches of the country. Indeed, by 1963, direct lines from the Zohar fields were fueling the Dead Sea works at Sodom, the textile plants of Dimona, the phosphate works in Oron, and the emergent city of Arad. The Naphtha Company was pumping gas at the caloric equivalent of 140,000 tons of oil a year, and the estimates of its total reserve continued to mount. The latest calculation listed it as the equivalent of 2,500,000 tons of high-grade crude petroleum.

It was all in the future, of course. When I first visited the Zohar field in the summer of 1960, there was little yet to distinguish the drilling camp from its counterparts at Heletz or HaMachtesh HaKatan. It was small, consisting of no more than thirty men, most of them Orientals or immigrants recently arrived from Eastern Europe. Only four drills were working; thus far no funds were available for additional equipment. Living conditions were rude. Abandoned buses served as barracks and dining hall. The climate was an inferno. But, as always, the project engineers were euphoric.

"Our gas can do anything oil can do," insisted the director, Moshe Karabildnik, shouting to make himself heard above the churning engines. "It can do it better and cleaner."

"Like lubricating a car," I shouted back.

"Come on," he laughed. "Like providing power." Then he added: "Gas is more than power, too. It's the basis for a vast new chemical industry. Methane molecules are the key to plastics, the basis for industrial acetylene, acetone, orlon fibers, synthetic rubber, and methyl alcohol. We've already started negotiating contracts for plants. That big petrochemical complex going up at Arad is built entirely around our gas."

"But fuel is the big money-earner, right?"

"Fuel, yes," he agreed.

It sounded promising. What, then, was bothering men like Skidelsky?

"I'll tell you," Ben-Tor explained to me later. "There are people in this country who still expect miracles. When they hear that gas and oil have been discovered, they go into ecstasies. 'That solves all our economic problems,' they think. 'Israel is another Iraq or Kuwait, sitting on a common Near Eastern sea of black gold. All we must do now is export it—or withhold it for bargaining purposes—as the Arabs do. Our troubles are over.' But of course the facts are exactly the opposite. You've seen the pipe lines we've laid from Eilat to the Haifa refineries. They run just one way. We still import most of our oil. By the most optimistic calculations, there is only enough oil and gas combined in this country to cover a quarter of our pathetically small domestic needs. It saves us fifty or sixty million dollars a year in fuel purchases. But it earns us nothing."

During the weeks of my desert journeys, I had exerted myself to match the apparently limitless optimism of my traveling companions. Now, however, when Ben-Tor uttered those words, I somehow felt a door slamming on the Negev. He sensed my reaction, and smiled.

"You mustn't write the desert off," he reassured me. "I surely haven't. It's true, of course, that by the time we finished that survey, in 1950, my colleagues and I no longer shared Ben-Gurion's naïve belief that the Negev was a vast storehouse of hidden wealth, another Congo or Yukon. But we knew that something was there. And you've seen that there is. It gives us one per cent of our income today. In another twenty years it may account for ten or fifteen per cent. That's quite a respectable figure, I should say. But . . . of course . . . we shall have to work devilishly hard to reach it."

"And what is wrong with that?" the old man said, when I repeated this to him. "Hard work never hurt anybody, as far as I know."

"Sir, if people are going to work hard, wouldn't they prefer to do it in a pleasanter climate?"

He wagged his finger impatiently. "You have just made the first and basic mistake everyone makes when he discusses the Negev—and that applies to Weitz, Ben-Tor, and all the other so-called 'experts.' The Negev climate is not unpleasant." He paused, allowing me a moment to absorb this surprising intelligence. "In fact, the weather in the Negev is the best in all Israel. I'm told it's very much like your California." When I let that pass, he continued, with growing animation. "Look here, do you know that the weather is very dry there? That doctors send patients with respiratory complaints down there? And it isn't all that hot, either. We get a very pleasant western breeze for several hours in the afternoon—as far south as Sdeh Boker. My wife hangs out the washing then because she knows it will dry quickly." We both smiled. "And the nights are dry and cold, wonderful for sleeping. It's true, of course," he added, "that we have a dust storm now and then; but certainly they aren't more frequent than those awful humid spells up north. Do you think Tel Aviv is pleasant in the summer? Ghastly, isn't it— I can't stand the place at any time, if you must know. But in the summer you can die there."

I decided to interject. "Adon Rosh HaMemshalah, we are both agreed that the Negev is not a source of endless riches. Rich or poor, hot or cold, it has to be settled, I think that is the point."

"That is precisely the point," he agreed emphatically. "On the one hand, the desert cannot be left open to Arab infiltration. On the other hand, tens of thousands of Jews are pouring into this country every year, and there is simply no possibility of accommodating them any longer in the north-central region. No more room. Yes, that is the point."

He had left me the opening. "If hundreds of thousands of people are to be settled there," I said, "employment must be created for them. Presumably that employment will be mainly industrial. There doesn't seem much likelihood that the resources of the Negev itself are sufficient to support large-scale industry. Where then would the factories come from? Are you suggesting that they be established there artificially?"

"Artificially?"

"That is, established in the Negev to process materials that do not actually come from the Negev itself?"

"I understand you," he nodded. "And my answer to that is: Why not?" It was a Jewish answer. "What natural resources does Tel Aviv have?" he continued. "Do we not have industry in Tel Aviv? You know, I can remember perfectly well when there was no Tel Aviv. When I came to this country there was nothing but sand dunes where a city of four hundred thousand now stands. I hope the point is clear. Of course we can establish industry—I won't say artificially—but on a decentralized basis. With very few exceptions all the industry we have in Israel today is decentralized. Well, then, why should we not do the same thing in the Negev?" He leaned forward and wagged a finger. "We will not force the immigrants to go south. We don't force anyone to do anything in this country, except serve in the army and pay taxes." He smiled. "They will move to the desert of their own accord, exactly because there will be jobs for them there. Isn't that what we have done in Beersheba? You know Beersheba? Yes, all right, of course. You were impressed with it, I hope?"

"Deeply. More than I can say."

"Yes, a bustling, energetic city of fifty thousand, and due to double in population within ten years. But I remember it when it was a bedouin town of four thousand. What a mud hole it was in those days. Phew, a sleepy cesspool! I am not exaggerating."

He had described it exactly, then and now. Indeed, by October 21, 1948, when Beersheba was captured from its occupying Egyptian garrison, the bedouin population of the town had dwindled to less than two thousand. And few, even of these, were willing to remain under Jewish authority. The celebrated "gateway to the Negev" consisted of several hundred abandoned, fly-specked Arab huts, coffee shops, and mosques. One did not need to set foot outside the town in those days for a reminder that the frontier had been reached. The Great Emptiness intruded wherever one turned. Its sand somehow penetrated one's canteen. Its wind storms lashed the screens off barracks windows. The danger of *fedayin* attack was manifest in the gun holsters of soldiers and civilians alike. HAVE YOU REMEMBERED YOUR GUN AND AMMUNITION? read the signs leading to and from the town.

Even now, the older coffee shops still bear the notches of rifles that way-farers once stacked against the walls.

Today this rough-and-ready frontier quality is not always as apparent. For one who enters Beersheba in the afternoon or early evening, the first impression is of a wide expanse of handsome, modern factories, hotels, apartment buildings, hospitals, clinics, recreation and swimming centers. The Arab homes and mosques that survive in their dilapidation accentuate rather than belie the clean, gleaming functionalism of the new city. Yet one need not wait long for proof that Beersheba, for all its mushrooming size and streamlined modernity, is still an outpost on the edge of the wilderness, still an overgrown frontier town.

One sees it in the early morning, in the agglomeration of its people. They mill through the central thoroughfare of the "downtown" area, and they include fiercely mustachioed bedouin, black smocks draped over white woolen tunics, torsos crisscrossed with silver-handled daggers, rifles, and bandoleers of cartridges, strolling about the street in groups of two and three, stopping occasionally to shake hands with Jewish acquaintances; East European merchants, standing hopefully in the entrances of jerry-built shops that are exact replicas of the general stores of the American Wild West, the pots, pans, pails, toys, sunglasses hanging in profusion outside windows where they can be seen; Oriental *felafel* makers and shoeshine boys; swaggering young Moroccan toughs in pointed shoes and skin-tight velveteen trousers; blue-jacketed air force men on leave from their bases deep in the Negev; khaki-clad soldiers back from patrol, bronzed, hair sun-flecked and dust-grimed, goggles attached loosely to Arab-style *kaffiyahs,* fingers playing lightly over the machine guns that swivel from their jeeps and half-tracks. And along this packed and teeming artery, heavy with the odors of sizzling Near Eastern food and acrid loess dust, alive with the bawling of Persian sidewalk vendors and brightly clad Tunisian and Tripolitanian mothers, the endless whine and roar of jet fighter planes above and diesel engines below—along this life line one's eye follows and enters directly into the seared and fulvous desert awaiting beyond. Beersheba is still its gateway.

It is more than that, however. Sparked by a dynamic and imaginative mayor, David Tuviyahu, the frontier outpost rapidly exploited its strategic location between north and south to become a commercial and industrial boom town. Ceramic factories, using Negev materials, employ thousands of men and women, as do brick, plastic, textile, pesticide, and insecticide plants. Trucking companies are among Beersheba's most important profit makers, hauling the supplies that link the two Israels, settled and frontier. Government research stations, Jewish Agency settlement offices, the administrative offices of the Dead Sea Works, add other hundreds of wage earners to Beersheba's population. So, too, does the army, which has established the headquarters of its southern area command in this city. By far the most important source of income, however, is the building industry. Construction never stops in Beersheba. At the date of writing, six new hotels are going up, four new factories, two office buildings, and—most important—scores of new apartment houses. For the last five years, the city's population has grown at the rate of eight hundred a month. Officials of the Solel Boneh and Rassco building companies (the nation's two largest) estimate that three years of steady construction are needed merely to provide adequate shelter for Beersheba's present inhabitants. The prospects for the future are apparently limitless.

With few exceptions, the citizens of Beersheba are immigrants. Yet several hundred of the city's inhabitants are sabras, or veteran settlers in Palestine. They have been attracted in part by choice job openings. In part, but not altogether. For most of them have also been influenced by the challenge of a new environment, the excitement of developing virgin territory, escaping the congestion of the northern cities and breathing freely at last under limitless skies. They are a special breed: pioneers, adventurers, spiritual anchorites, individualists by conviction or temperament, fugitives from family responsibilities and past failures. Beersheba is the catch basin for them all. . . .

For Leon, proprietor of the Last Chance saloon, a former American marine, whose postwar career included gun running in the Philippines, buying and selling surplus American bulldozers in Paris (where he met his common-law wife, Betty), operating a fleet of combines for farmers in the Negev—which sent him into bankruptcy—and ultimately opening his bar on a Beersheba side street. It is rather a striking establishment: the decorations are composed entirely of petrified Negev wood, twisted and interlaced into intriguing patterns by the desert wind; a hangman's noose is suspended delicately from the ceiling's central rafter; while a three-piece Moroccan dance band supplies tango and paso doble rhythms for the hard-drinking patrons. Occasionally a customer will become drunk and disorderly. Leon smiles then, runs a thumb across his scarred and broken nose, and smashes a massive fist against the offender's chin. If, as has occasionally happened, the matter is not settled forthwith, the fight will range the length of the bar, and even the width of the street outside.

"My clients wouldn't respect me unless I took care of these matters myself," he grins, revealing two missing front teeth. "I like to do things my own way. That's why I came out here."

The city is home for Nehemia, chief designer for Beersheba's huge ceramic works, a bearded, powerfully built sculptor in his early forties. For all his years of study in Europe, Nehemia Aza returns continually to the spare, angular Negev style, which he incorporates into his factory's pots, urns, ash trays, and vases. The themes are biblical. The colors are the subdued brown and lavender pastels of the desert, twisting and winding over the surface of his work rather in the manner of the Negev's rock formations.

"I never doubted where I would live," he recalls. "As early as 1938 I began sculpting in and around Beersheba, using local themes. Occasionally I would ride one of my father's horses deep into the desert to find the clays I needed. I fell in love with the Negev then."

During the War of Liberation, Nehemia commanded an infantry unit there. Between battles he enjoyed walking alone in the hills, naked except for sandals, a pistol belt, and his long beard. Bedouin who caught a glimpse of this apparition fled in terror, convinced that he was the devil himself.

"I'll tell you what the Negev is to me." His expression softens, his eyes become warm, and he waxes sentimental. "It is a living, breathing animal, tortured and anguished, which cries out in the wind storms of the night and changes its colors with the shifting sun. It is a place for people with imagination. Ask me what the Galilee is and I'll tell you, too. It is a place for people without imagination: heavy, stolid people, or artists like Castel who live in the memory of the past. When a man travels in the Galilee he goes from one place to another. He knows where he is going. But how does one travel in the limitless expanse of the Negev? Like the bedouin, crossing the dunes on his lone starved camel, unequipped except for a rifle, a bag of wet grain, and a few tea leaves. 'Where are you going?' I ask him. 'South,' is his only reply. And that is enough for me, too. No borders, no limits. Where am I going? Where does my art lead? South. I wouldn't want to be bound."

Beersheba is home, as well, for the American-born sculptress, Hava Mechutan, who draws her materials exclusively from local Negev dust wood and basalt; for "Buddha," a sabra conservationist (born Yohav Oren), who drudges away each day at a patch of government land outside the city, growing drought-resistant plants for the local farmers; for the agronomist Saul Feldman, an American Ph.D. from Purdue University, who has lived in Beersheba since 1950, commuting daily to his agricultural research station near the Gaza Strip, testing weed killers and ignoring *fedayin* infiltrators. The city is home for Gershon Segelman, Mike Skidelsky, Hadassah Avigdori, and for scores of other nonconformists who have found on the frontier, and beyond, the answer to private and mysterious needs. Most of them know each other, and prefer each other's company. They are a clique.

With the exception of this elite group, however, the citizens of Beersheba by and large have been recent immigrants from North Africa and Eastern Europe. Idealism has not influenced their choice of settlement. Arriving in Israel quite penniless, they allowed themselves to be transplanted to Beersheba purely and simply for guaranteed employment opportunities there. It was part of a government plan. With the revival of large-scale immigration in 1956, no less than 70 per cent of the newcomers were funneled directly from their ports of arrival into southern "development" areas. Security reasons dictated the choice. So did economic factors. No further procrastination could be permitted in settling the Negev; guarantee the new arrivals work, said the planners, and willingly or unwillingly they would come. It was astute reasoning. Thus far most of the immigrants have come—unwillingly.

The largest majority were settled in and around Beersheba. But nearly 20,000 others were relocated elsewhere: in co-operative and collective farms in the northern Negev plateau and in the western coastal zone; in remote and isolated industrial towns far below the 250-mm. precipitation line. Dimona is one of these. Located midway between Beersheba and Sodom, this newly established community boasts a large, modern textile plant, and several blocks of well-equipped apartments for the families of men employed in the Dead Sea Works and the Oron phosphates factory. Most of these people are Rumanians, and they are hard-working, well-behaved citizens. As the Dead Sea enterprises grow, so will the population of Dimona—probably to 30,000 by 1970. The town's development has been so encouraging, in fact, that the Jewish Agency's public relations staff is fond of citing Dimona's growth as "typical."

Rather more typical, actually, is the mining community of Kfar Yerucham, eight miles west of Dimona, and directly astride the central Negev highway. It was founded in 1951 as an encampment for the glass sand and kaolin workers of HaMachtesh HaGadol, and its first inhabitants all were newcomers from Rumania. They were joined in succeeding years by immigrants from Morocco, Iran, and Poland. Few of those early inhabitants will ever forget the ordeal of settlement. Their original living conditions were quite horrifying; probably the worst in the entire country. For two years the town possessed neither water nor electricity. Drinking water had to be hauled in twice weekly by tanker truck. On several occasions the wretched immigrant families were on the verge of mutiny. Several women committed suicide. Fortunately, circumstances improved somewhat after 1953. A generator was installed, then a water-distilling plant. Later a textile mill was erected, followed by a small glass-cutting and diamond-finishing factory. Today the experts predict that, as production gains momentum at the Great Crater, Kfar Yerucham's current population of 3,000 will increase tenfold within the next decade. The growth cannot come too soon. Even now, the scorched loneliness of that forlorn little collection of box houses, the drudging monotony of its days and nights are heartbreaking merely to contemplate.

Yet for me, at least, Kfar Yerucham was but a tepid prelude to what lay ahead. Mitzpeh Ramon, as its name suggests, is perched on the lip of the Ramon Crater. Like Kfar Yerucham, Mitzpeh Ramon is a mining town. Clay and gypsum quarries provide employment for the 600 people who live there. Some of the workers volunteered for the "mission" when the encampment was founded, in 1953. Predictably, these were sabras, former residents of Kibbutz Sdeh Boker. In later years, however, all the inhabitants were jobless immigrants. The largest number of them were Moroccan and Tunisian Jews, and when they first arrived in Mitzpeh Ramon they were frightened and quite desperate men and women. Indeed, during their first year of isolation in that dead-center of the Negev, a few of them actually were driven berserk by the loneliness, and required confinement in mental homes. Most of the settlers were persuaded to remain, however, by the simple inducement of the highest wages in all Israel. Even those who fled northward found it difficult to resist the lure of fat pay envelopes; they returned to Mitzpeh Ramon now and then as "supplemental" laborers. Today half the encampment's population consists of these drifters. Many are illiterate. Presumably they form the basis for the "population of 12,000" which government and Jewish Agency planners glibly project for the Mitzpeh Ramon of the future. It will surely not be the near future. Not enough police or social workers can be spared from the rest of the country.

Only a few years earlier, in fact, the planning authorities discovered that wilderness outposts produced more than their share of inflamed social problems. Beer Tsofer was a case in point. Beer Tsofer was no Beersheba, or even Dimona. Founded as an experimental water-drilling station midway between Sodom and Eilat, the tiny settlement could hardly have been more isolated had it been located in the bowels of the Sahara. Michael Rothem, director of the encampment, was a wiry little major who had formerly served as military commander of the Eilat district. His army background proved invaluable at Beer Tsofer. Living and working conditions were indescribably bad. Food consisted of army rations. Water was trucked in from Eilat. Housing was limited to canvas tents. Not infrequently men collapsed at their jobs from "salt stroke" or "sand-fly fever." Yet they remained. They had no choice. Originally Rothem had assumed that his twenty-five workers—all of them North African and Iraqi immigrants—had volunteered for the task to escape the squalor and indigence of their *ma'abarot*. He learned later that they had signed up to escape the police. Nearly all of them had criminal records. At Beer Tsofer they reverted to type: drinking, thieving, and fighting among themselves.

"Sometimes they even came at me with knives," Rothem recalled. "I was forced to pistol-whip them. I was never without my gun, day or night. You know the old expression: it hurt me more than it did them." He sighed. "It was certainly no permanent solution. Later on I embarked upon a 'rehabilitation campaign.' In the evenings I seated them around a campfire and told them about the hardships, the hunger, and malaria, suffered by the first Jewish settlers in Palestine. Then I read them some of the memoirs from the First and Second *Aliyot,* and the famous Zionist poems of Alterman, Bialik, and Greenberg. The men were deeply moved. Believe me when I tell you that some of them wept. During all the months they had vegetated in their misery, apparently no one had told them how much our early pioneers had gone through. My toughest cases came to me later and apologized."

Yet the campfire sessions by themselves were hardly enough to make life endurable at Beer Tsofer. Taking a chance, Rothem decided to permit occasional women visitors. Some of the women were wives. Some were not.

"We weren't running a monastery." Rothem shrugged. "These men were in exile. They had to survive."

Yet in the beginning the visitors created as many problems as they solved. Not among the workers, but rather among the men they left. It happened that most of the girls were former prostitutes, and they, too, were escaping—in this case from their procurers. From time to time a jeep would approach on the desert road. Rothem knew what to expect; a pimp was coming to get his woman back. The routine rarely varied. The car pulled to a stop and the man climbed out, usually a tough, sullen Rumanian or Bulgarian.

"I'm looking for a friend," warned the thug, fingering a switch-blade suggestively.

"That's nice," replied Rothem with a friendly smile. "But first meet a friend of mine." He flipped open his holster, removing an army revolver.

Within minutes the jeep was on its way back north.

"There you have it," I told him. "These are the kind of derelicts you will have to depend on to settle that void. They aren't the type of pioneers you remember, surely, the ones who opened the Galilee and the Sharon?"

"Well, of course they are not," he replied with some astonishment. "Did you really believe I was so naive? First of all, they are not as young as we were. It's not a simple matter to be a pioneer when one is middle-aged. Then, don't forget they were never given our Zionist indoctrination. Don't blame them for that. Blame the world in which they were raised, their parents, their teachers, the governments that forbade these teachings. No, no, these are not pioneering types. For them it is a matter of bread and butter, nothing more. They will stay only as long as they have to."

I had lost his train of thought. "Are you writing them off, sir?" I asked. "Then where are the ones you plan to depend on?"

"Where are they? All around us. They are the young people. Our children. Sabras, even children of the immigrants. The ones who have gone through the youth movements, the Gadnah [a paramilitary sports organization], the army. These are the ones who are coming down."

"Coming down into the Negev? But are they?"

He arose from his seat, and walked over to the window. As he stared out, the morning sunlight illuminated the billowing tufts of white hair that framed his great head. His hands clenched and unclenched in agitation behind his back. I wondered if perhaps I had not gone too far. But when he finally spoke, his voice was subdued, still matter-of-fact.

"It's true," he admitted. "They are not yet coming in the numbers we had expected or hoped for. This generation is a problem for us. The so-called 'golden youth.' " He nodded sadly as he pronounced the words, "sitting around the coffee shops of Tel Aviv, playing cards—and worse. They are not what we hoped for, definitely not." He returned to his chair, changed his mind, then walked back to the window. "I have not given up on them, though," he murmured. "There is still a force in this land, a rest-less pioneering spirit which is far from dead. You once had it in the United States, in the old days. Today, unfortunately, most Americans are interested only in their Cadillacs and television sets. I'm sorry, it's true." He smiled at me, watching my diffident grin.

"Well, take Israel," he continued. "We are a poor land, poorer than the United States, poorer than almost any country in Europe. But what can we do? Moses picked this piece of territory for us and we have loved it and suffered for it ever since. Now then, our youngsters of today may have experienced a loss of idealism because the dramatic challenges of the old

days—the challenges that were ours in the Sharon and Galilee only three or four decades ago—seem to have diminished. But I ask you to watch carefully during the next few years. We have opened a new challenge for them. It is the Negev, of course. Already it is beginning to appeal to the imagination of the younger generation. Not to all of them, perhaps, not as many as we would like—but many, more and more. As soon as we formulate our plans and projects for the area they will jump at the chance to go down there and pioneer. Believe me, they have only been waiting for the chance."

It seemed like a particularly sublime example of wishful thinking. I wanted to say something, but at this moment Colonel Ben-David entered the room, and stood silently beside the desk. My time had expired. As I rose to leave, however, the old man impatiently waved me back to my seat. His enthusiasm waxed high now.

"All that our youth needs is a real challenge," he insisted. "They were faced with a challenge in the Sinai war and they met it. Now, in peacetime, they will respond to the challenge of the Negev. You think not? Look here, I want to tell you a story." He paced quickly to an end table, and riffled through the contents of a file. When he had found what he wanted, he handed it to me. It was a photograph of himself and his wife, climbing into an air force helicopter.

"I recognize the picture, Adon Rosh HaMemshalah," I said. "It was in all the newspapers last week."

"That's the one. They wrote that we were flying down to a wedding at our kibbutz, Sdeh Boker. But they did not know the story behind that wedding. I want you to hear this. It was a most interesting couple because the boy, a youngster of about twenty-one, was an only son. Unfortunately, his parents had been divorced for many years. Now, the young man hoped that at least his parents would return for his wedding. The mother was willing. But the father refused to come because he was not on speaking terms with his son. And why not? Because several years ago the boy, who had lived in Tel Aviv with his father, suddenly took it into his head that he wanted to live in Sdeh Boker. The father was furious. He was a wealthy man and had planned a university education for his son. 'If you go through with this crazy scheme,' he warned the boy, 'I'll cut you off. You'll never see me again.' But the boy was a stubborn type; he came down to our kibbutz anyway. And the father kept his promise. Relations between them were cut off.

"Now, this upset me. The boy's courage deserved the warmest approval of his father, and instead it was the cause of separation between them. And so, on an impulse, I called the father long distance. 'Look here,' I said, 'can you come and see me at my office tomorrow? I'll send a car for you.' 'Thank you,' the father said, 'I can come in my own car.' " The old man chuckled. "He must have known what was in store for him. At least he kept the appointment, though. I sat him down and said to him: 'What's the matter with you? This boy is your only son. Why won't you come for his wedding? You know how much it will mean to him.' So the

father hemmed and hawed, then finally went through the whole megillah again: that his son was a stubborn type, that he threw away the priceless opportunity of a university education, and why did he have to go to a wilderness like Sdeh Boker anyway, and so on."

Quite excited now, the old man re-enacted the little episode, banging his fist on the desk, as he had with the father. "Believe me, I told him, all right. I told him his son was a pioneer in the truest sense, and that boys like him were the best hope for Israel's future. And finally I said to him: 'I'm going to lock you in this office and not let you out until you agree to go to that wedding.' I was only half joking, too. We argued a little longer, but to make a long story short, he finally agreed to come. It was a happy wedding after all. The father made peace with his son, too. Hmmm"—he beamed with the recollection of it—"it was a little thing, but very few accomplishments have given me greater satisfaction. You see now, not everyone who comes down is a derelict. With people like this boy and his young bride, we'll make the Negev a homeland for a million Jews and more."

"I hope they will all be like him," I observed somewhat wryly.

"All? They won't all have to be like him." He blinked at me for several moments. "How many people are there like him anywhere? I would settle for a few thousand adventuresome young men and women. That's all we need to get matters started. And we have them. Depend on it, we have such people."

I had seen some of them. They were the men and women of the Negev's agricultural settlements, the drab, wind-swept little outposts of Kisufim, Nirim, Ein HaShloshah, and sixty others. Many were Americans, Canadians, and South Africans, restless young idealists searching for their own character in the desert's inferno. The challenge was compounded by loneliness: not the loneliness merely of bleak terrain or harsh living conditions, but of danger, as well, the heat-impregnated silence cloaking the *fedayin* attack, the nocturnal grenade and machine-gun blast. One did not escape it by movement. In the Negev it lay in wait, no matter where one traveled.

We sensed that loneliness during the trip southward to Sdeh Boker and Yotvata. As we drove, my companion, Mica Hermoni, a young water engineer, kept his eye sharp by shooting down quail with his army pistol. By the time we reached the 250-mm. precipitation line the desert heat had waned. The jeep seemed to cling to the asphalt ribbon of its own accord. In our eyes, occasional packs of camels and their bedouin masters, starved and emaciated by the drought, were barely distinguishable now from the desert's lifeless catalogue of rock and petrified scrub vegetation. Vagrant flights of locusts passed us by. We left the road and jounced over the sharp angular ribs of the central Negev plateau. In the distance a white and forlorn Arab house slowly turned black in the vortex of a cloud: the locusts were claiming another victim.

The dull kettle-drum roll of cannon gradually roused us from our torpor. After several minutes we saw the antlike French AMXs and Super-Shermans on the eastern horizon, wheeling and churning through a tornado of dust, their gun nozzles blossoming languid yellow flame. Tank maneuvers, and somehow no one had warned us. Perhaps two hundred yards to the north, the crest of a rock dune shattered into smithereens. The detonations grew louder for several minutes (long to be remembered), then faded behind us. The jeep careened on at full speed for nearly a half-hour after that. Mica and I continued laughing hysterically, our clothes bonded to our flesh with perspiration.

The rest was anticlimactic. What were Sdeh Boker and Yotvata, after all, but the typical garden variety of struggling, rather drab kibbutzim? Neither possessed more than the usual Spartan collection of concrete and wooden huts, austerely furnished slate-gray dining halls and nurseries. The fields were marginal. The yield of fruit and vegetables did not match the output of other kibbutzim, either in quantity or quality. As for the settlers, they, too, were replicas of countless other kibbutz members in every part of the country: lean, taciturn, grim in work and diffident in relaxation, plain-spoken, brutally frank in appraisal and self-appraisal. Once, when I made the mistake of equating their efforts with self-sacrifice, they cut me short with the answer I deserved. I had heard it before from Skiddy, Gershon, from Nehemia, from the farmers of the coastal area near the no man's land of the Gaza Strip, from the youngsters who raised cattle in the marsh jungle of Na'ot HaKikar south of Sodom, and from the engineers and workmen who labored in the oven of the Dead Sea Works. "Don't give us that nonsense," they insisted. "There are no pioneers here. This is a livelihood. We're in it for ourselves."

By all means. Why could I not accept their assurance that their effort—the entire redemptive effort in the desert—was a business, self-interest pure and simple? They made a good case for it in the port city of Eilat, at the Negev's southern tip. From a distance, it was a nacreous haze against the enameled blue of the gulf. Only two miles to the east, the bleached, forlorn little Jordanian port of Akaba nestled within view. Five miles south along the inlet, the barren wastes of Egyptian Sinai shimmered silently in the sun's blaze. And within the compressed little wedge of Jewish Eilat the desert abdicated altogether to the sea. The lapping of gentle waters sustained this overgrown fishing village. Each vessel dropping anchor here was a promise from the outside world, a tantalizing assurance of friendship from strangers beyond the Arab hinterland, another transfusion of life's blood from the artery of international commerce. Eilat was building on that hope.

Indeed, the community was apparently thriving. Oil tankers of 12,000 and 15,000 tons' displacement were nose-threaded docilely to the anchorage, pumping their cargo into the huge aluminum vats that supplied the Eilat-Ashdod pipe line. Two and a half miles further south along the bay, a picket line of concrete piles was being sunk to berth the 40,000-ton monsters that had recently joined Israel's merchant fleet. Within four years, so the experts said, Eilat would rival Haifa in the scope of its maritime traffic and port facilities. Thus, anticipating the raw materials that would soon be flowing through this neck in the Negev's bottle, the ministry of development was constructing a number of small plants along the water's edge: a tannery to process African hides; evaporation pans to produce salt from the bay's residue; a refinery for the edible oils extracted from Israel's sunflower seeds; quarries for Timna granite; a factory to grind bone and fish meal from the marine life that abounded in the gulf itself; as well as a small shipyard and dry dock to service the vessels that tracked the Red Sea's succulent tuna as far as the shores of Ethiopia. Two luxury hotels and three neat, comfortable youth hostels had sprung up to accommodate Eilat's swelling tourist traffic. More were planned, for the gulf's sparkling waters and dazzling coral formations were a magnet for Israelis and foreign visitors alike.

For the permanent settlers of Eilat there were other incentives. Good housing was one. The port community was perhaps the only city in Israel in which nearly every family enjoyed a spacious, modern, air-conditioned apartment, underwritten by the government at the most nominal of rents. Wages, the highest in the country, were partially tax-exempt. Nearly a third of Eilat's employees were permitted a free round-trip flight to Tel Aviv every two months. And yet, far from representing a policy of largesse, these social advantages were the irreducible guarantees without which the population of Eilat could not have reached its present size of 9,000. The climate was still murderously hot. With the exception of a single recreation hall and two movie theaters, cultural opportunities were all but nonexistent. In spite of recent improvements in living conditions, Eilat still lacked the vital inducement of direct communication with the rest of the country. Life there was lived in isolation.

It was hardly surprising, as a result, that as late as 1963 Eilat remained an unknown quantity to most of Israel's citizens. Indeed, the town did not so much as exist in the pre-State era. Its history began on March 10, 1949, when two companies of Israel troops completed a 150-mile trek across the Negev wasteland, and planted their country's flag on the roof of an abandoned British police fortress. This was the final military "operation" of Israel's War of Independence. During the next eighteen months Eilat remained a military outpost. Still unconnected by road to the north, the tiny army garrison continued living under field conditions, in tents, on army rations, dependent for drinking water upon a portable distillation plant, and upon supplies flown in to the makeshift airstrip. Guns were never out of reach, for the attitude of the British unit in Jordanian Akaba, only two miles distant, was an uncertain factor.

Predictably, the first civilians who appeared in this encampment area were rugged individualists, the usual species of desert rat for whom Eilat's loneliness and isolation were its most compelling attractions. David Sachs, the tall, ferociously mustachioed sabra who in 1950 assumed the "governorship" of the port area, was typical of this breed. Grandiloquently styling his clapboard hut "Government House," Sachs dearly enjoyed closing his "office" before noon, climbing into a jeep, and racing out into the Negev to hunt wolves, wild boar, and eagles. Danny Harhabait, supervising the construction of an army road to Beersheba, laid cunning ambushes for unsuspecting travelers who approached his way station; armed with a submachine gun, he suddenly leaped into the path of the approaching jeep, waved its passengers out, and "ordered" them to drink coffee with him before proceeding on their journey. A Gentile Texan, known simply as Jimmy, opened a horse ranch outside Eilat shortly after completing his tour of duty as a volunteer in the Israel army. Jimmy's entire operation was run Texas-style, down to branding irons and the pearl-handled revolvers he strapped to his waist. Arieh Tadmor, the "monkey man," was an ex-soldier turned botanist; continually in search of specimens, he drove Eilat's authorities haggard by disappearing in the desert for days at a time, living on roots, reptiles, and insects—"just like a monkey," he insisted, somewhat inaccurately.

So long as Eilat remained an outpost, it proved irresistible to the routine Negev variety of adventurer, eccentric, and plain and simple drifter. The Sinai Campaign of November, 1956, changed all that. Routing Egypt's armies on the battlefield, dismantling the Egyptian artillery that overlooked the Straits of Tiran, the Jews smashed the blockade of Eilat and secured international guarantees for the free passage of their shipping in the Red Sea. The trade routes to the Orient and Africa were opened. Freighters and tankers began to arrive and depart. Oil pipe lines were laid, connecting with the pumping stations of Ashdod and the refineries of Haifa. Immediately and dramatically a tiny frontier settlement was transformed into a dynamic port city. Eilat's population grew by several hundreds each month. Soon the colorful and restless wanderers of the earlier pioneer period were swallowed in the waves of sober engineers, technicians, factory managers, cannery workers, shopkeepers, and immigrant families who now poured into the gulf area, anxious to lay the basis of their financial security in favored and promising territory. Of course, in their own way they, too, were pioneers. Yet their most pressing family needs were now being met by air-conditioned houses, schools, playgrounds, and clinics. The challenge of isolation may have remained—but no longer the challenge of authentic physical hardship.

The adventurous ones have not yet vanished from the scene. They return on the tuna boats, grizzled and sun-blackened from weeks of cruising off the East African coast. Others arrive in jeeps, dust-grimed and raw-skinned from patrolling the oil pipe lines through wind storm and bedouin encampment. Tight-lipped ranchers and farmers come in horsecarts, stubbornly dumping their watermelons in the town square, taking their chances on open-air haggling. Cursing, guffawing sailors sit under flickering electric bulbs in coffee shops, gambling at cards with the Ghanian shipmates who have become their brothers in the holds, unloading Ethiopian mahogany and loading Dead Sea potash. Newlyweds come, too, deep-sea diving for sponges and coral gems within swimming distance of Egyptian Sinai; kibbutz members and soldiers and members of youth groups, amateur archaeologists and numismatists for whom school vacation is the opportunity to search the relics of King Solomon's garrisons. On the beach at night they light bonfires just beyond rifle range of the Jordanian sentries, and serenade the desert:

> *Right and left,*
> *Only sand and more sand,*
> *The desert is yellow without end.*
> *A caravan passes,*
> *The silence is moving,*
> *A primeval, wonderful dream.*
> *The sound mounts,*
> *Descends abruptly,*
> *Camels moving in unison*
> *Against a melancholy horizon:*
> *Tinkle, tinkle, tinkle, tinkle—*
> *This is the wayfarer's song,*
> *Clip, clop, clip, clop—*
> *Be silent and bear your burden.*

The strains of the concertina rise and fall. Love is made and passions are spent. The youths stretch out on their sleeping bags, fold their *kaffiyahs* under their heads and gaze languorously at the canopy of stars arching into enemy territory. The land is so small. Its borders squeeze the breath from one's lungs. The desert is open, of course, but even now its mystery is half resolved. In another ten years what will be left? Energy and curiosity are still waiting to be expended. Where, then, if not beyond the frontier, as the stars point? Someone hums it, another utters the words, and soon the concertina takes up the melody:

> *Oh HaSelah HaAdom, HaAdom,*
> *Oh HaSelah HaAdom, HaAdom,*
> *Oh the Great Red Rock, the Red One*
> *Oh the Great Red Rock, the Red One*
> *Over the hills and the desert*
> *There is a place, so the tales say,*
> *From whence no one has ever returned alive,*
> *A place called the Great Red Rock.*
> *Oh HaSelah HaAdom, HaAdom,*
> *Oh HaSelah HaAdom, HaAdom.*

The verses are sung quietly, almost in a whisper. For by order of the minister of defense, the song is forbidden. Young people are impatient and irresponsible. They chafe at boundaries and restrictions. The minister of defense knows. Curb your wanderlust, he warns them sternly. Channel your energies into the tasks that are yours, the efforts that lie ahead. If it is challenge and adventure you seek, you will find enough of that in the portion of desert which is ours. The less you dream of the Red Rock, the longer you will live.

Will they listen? They have not always. It is one of the authentic wonders of the world, the Red Rock, a castlelike monument, 130 feet high, carved in the stone base of an enormous cliff. And it is renowned not merely for its size, nor for the delicacy of its cameolike façade, but also for a remarkable and unique ability to capture the luminosity of the dying sun. The Arabs call this marvel Khaznet Firaun, the Treasury of Pharaoh. But in fact the Great Red Rock is not an Arab creation at all. Rather, it is a product of the ancient Nabateans, whose empire, in the centuries before Roman and Islamic domination, stretched from Madain Salih, the present-day Saudi Arabia, to the gates of Damascus.

Skilled agriculturists, as we have already noted, the Nabateans were hardly less accomplished in the arts of commerce, brokerage—and piracy. As their territory increased, they cached their loot and caravan tolls in the numerous caves and warehouses of Petrah, their capital city. The hiding place was a safe one. Petrah was beyond question the most inaccessible citadel ever inhabited by any people, ancient or modern. Travelers seeking entrance were obliged to make their way through the Siq, a notorious, mile-long slash in the Edomite mountains (the mountains of biblical Edom). The passageway was hundreds of feet deep, and often it narrowed to a width of a few yards. At some places, overhanging masses of flaming sandstone shut out the sky altogether.

Thus it was that this cliff-girt bastion remained hidden and totally abandoned for centuries following the collapse of the Nabatean empire. It is virtually certain that no European ever laid eyes on Petrah—until the city's epochal discovery, in 1812, by the Swiss traveler, John Lewis Burckhardt. What Burckhardt found, and described, in this isolated mountain fastness instantly captured the imagination of romantics throughout the Western world. There were mighty temples and palaces, he wrote, banquet halls and amphitheaters, pillars, obelisks, and giant urns all carved in the incredible red sandstone that marled the area and gave it its sobriquet. Perhaps other voyagers would have followed Burckhardt's trail. But if the "rose-red city, half as old as time" was unapproachable in ancient days, it was hardly less so in the nineteenth and twentieth centuries. Hostile bedouin tribes and an all but lethal climate hopelessly compounded the difficulties of travel.

For the Jews of modern Israel, especially, access to the Great Red Rock would appear altogether unthinkable: Petrah lies within the territory of the Hashemite Kingdom of Jordan, still in a state of war with the Israelis. And yet—Petrah is also a mere twenty-seven miles from the Negev's south-eastern border encampment of Beer Menucha. The very nearness of the fabled bastion has exerted a curious fascination for the youth of the Jewish State. They know that, except for itinerant Arab patrols and the bedouin who make their home in the Edomite mountains, the terrain leading to Petrah is no less deserted than the bleakest stretches of their own desert. Accordingly, their imaginations have been kindled: by the challenge of escaping from the suffocating confinement of a tiny land, of transcending the political and military blockade imposed by their Arab neighbors, perhaps even of proving to themselves no less than to their enemies that their destinies as Israelis, a reborn, sovereign people, lie in their hands alone. To ensure that this temptation does not prove altogether irresistible, the Government of Israel has threatened would-be border crossers with stiff fines and jail sentences. The lives of the nation's youth are too precious to be dissipated in hare-brained adventures. Still, not surprisingly, the dangers on both sides of the border have proved to be less of a deterrent than a stimulus. Occasionally a youngster or two will try it. They know it can be done. A girl proved it.

She was Rachel Z'vorai, a robust, sandy-haired daughter of Kibbutz Ein Harod, outspoken, tomboyish, and altogether uninhibited. During the War of Independence Rachel served as a member of the Palmach, the shock troops, and participated in the battles for Jerusalem and the Negev. After demobilization she returned to her farm at Ein Harod, and to the routine of feeding and milking the cows. It was on weekends and vacations that she indulged her first love, hiking through the countryside with her girl friends Gila and Aviva, exploring for exotic reptiles and archaeological relics. The love had been cultivated long before the war, at a time when hikers continually ran the risk of Arab ambush. Now the danger was gone. So, in some measure, was the excitement. The Negev was open, to be sure. Rachel explored it extensively with her friends. Nevertheless, by the early 1950s the bedouin were pacified; for all the desert's wild beauty, the only challenge remaining was one of endurance.

Several times the subject of Petrah arose. Even from Israel one could see the mighty Jebel Haroun, the Mount of Aaron. Petrah was said to be hidden behind it. Among Rachel's acquaintances were two older couples who had been there shortly before the Palestine war. Their descriptions of the legendary citadel enthralled her. Only twenty-seven miles from Beer Menucha! Of course, the territory was enemy. Presumably Arab patrols were on watch every mile or so along the frontier. Even so, a secret visit was surely not impossible.

Then, in March, 1953, shortly after Rachel's twenty-seventh birthday, a fellow kibbutz member casually mentioned to her that he had once crossed the central-western protuberance of Jordan, on a hike from Jerusalem to Ein Gedi.

"Weren't there guards, Meir?" she asked.

"Of course, but we moved at night. It wasn't too difficult to keep out of sight."

"What was the terrain like?"

"Nothing much. The Negev is a lot more interesting."

Never mind that, she thought to herself; there was Meir, a youth of nineteen, and he had crossed over undetected. If it could be done in the heavily populated agricultural plain of Jordan, it surely could be done in the barren wilderness east of the Negev. She questioned her friend further, checking his answers with her own considerable knowledge of the area's geography. By evening she had made up her mind. Yet she hardly dared to broach the subject directly.

"Meir," she said at length, "would you be interested in trying another trip sometime? Let's say to—"

"Petrah?" he exclaimed delightedly. "I wondered how long it would take you to get around to it. I'm game."

She devoured every book she could find about the citadel. The Israel Army Handbook was helpful. It described the likely military routes of ingress and egress. Especially fascinating was a little volume by Joseph Braslovsky, *Do You Know Israel?,* which dwelled at some length on the history and topography of Petrah. Meir was in the army at the time. Whenever he returned on furlough, the two pored over military maps, carefully folding and hiding their charts whenever others approached. By April they had laid out their basic route. Equipment and food supplies had been carefully calculated. They would wear khaki shirts and trousers, carry knapsacks, canteens, six cans of army rations, and a single Sten-gun with ammunition. Their departure only awaited Meir's next leave.

It came on April 30, and they left at dawn of the next day. Proceeding by bus as far as Tel Aviv, Rachel and her friend then hitchhiked to Beersheba. From there they flagged another lift, to Scorpion's Pass, just three miles east of the Great Crater. It was 6:00 P.M. Within the light of a single day the young adventurers had traversed half the length of their country. Yet their schedule called for them to reach Ein Chusub before midnight, and the armed agricultural settlement was another twelve miles distant. Rachel and Meir were experienced hikers, however. Following the sunken military road by touch as much as vision, they reached their destination with twenty minutes to spare. And at 4:30 the following morning, after a few hours' sleep and a hot breakfast, they persuaded a passing kibbutz truck to carry them further south.

The ride lasted three hours. By midmorning the shallow loess cleft of the Arava Valley vanished in the spume of the truck's exhaust. The bleak, tortured hills of the southern Negev crouched in readiness.

"Lech'i, Lech'i," cried several of the kibbutz youngsters mockingly. "It's the Sternists." Their fingers pointed through the slat boards to the tiny encampment lying directly athwart the road. It was Beer Menucha. Ostensibly a work camp, the tiny settlement was in fact a kind of Cave of Adullam for disgruntled right-wing activists who needed the breadth of a desert between them and the despised Labor government in Jerusalem.

"We'll get off here," Meir remarked suddenly to the driver.

"Here? Are you crazy?" he protested. "These are Sternists. What do you want with them?"

"Nothing, nothing," Rachel chimed in. "It's just a brief stopover."

"We thought we'd climb Har Hemda on the way down," improvised Meir, referring to a small mountain to the west of Beer Menucha. "We'll catch another lift later. Nothing to worry about."

Still suspicious, the driver nevertheless pulled the truck to a halt in front of the wooden shack that served as the camp's headquarters. Exchanging a cool greeting with the workmen on the ground, he waited only long enough for Rachel and Meir to dismount. Then he drove off.

"So, what can we do for you?" asked the camp director, a stout, sunblackened ox of a man with an enormous handle-bar mustache.

"Just a rest until evening," explained Meir. "Then we thought we'd head west and see what Har Hemda looks like."

"Suit yourselves." The director shrugged. "You can sleep in one of the tents there. When you get hungry the cook shack is open. Take whatever you need." He walked back to his workmen, who resumed their grading of the road.

Inside the tent the young hikers unfolded their map. Only now did they realize how ill prepared they were. With the frontier a mere two miles away, the directions that had seemed detailed enough back in Ein Harod now suddenly appeared hopelessly inadequate. The wadis and passes were sketched only in the most rudimentary fashion. Nowhere was the path leading to the Jebel Haroun clearly indicated. The great Siq of Wadi Musa was entirely missing. How was a trek through Arab territory even remotely possible with this meager intelligence? How were they ever brazen enough to imagine that they could try it? The thought remained unspoken. Each was ashamed to admit doubt or faintheartedness to the other. Instead, for perhaps the twentieth time, they reviewed their plan of movement. The main idea, Meir insisted, was to rely on his "marvelous" compass. Rachel was too exhausted to argue. They both fell asleep.

A good rest and a hot meal worked wonders. By 8:15 P.M. Rachel and Meir moved out again, settling quickly into their tested four-mile-an-hour pace. It was maintained with some difficulty here, for the terrain had become quite rough. On every side enormous granite boulders intruded into their path. Still, by all calculations, this was the shortest route eastward to the hill which was to be their first check-point. A half-hour later Meir paused for a moment, and tapped Rachel's shoulder.

"We are in Jordan," he remarked quietly.

For the next three hours the two continued by dead reckoning, wholly dependent upon Meir's "marvelous" compass. The awaited hill failed to appear. As if by compensation, however, Rachel caught sight of a narrow trail, probably a bedouin goat track, snaking through the rocks in the same southeasterly direction. They decided to trust their luck to it. By 11:00 P.M. the moon had climbed high. The shadows of the escalating mountain range cast a warped and eerie pattern across the ravine, hopelessly camouflaging all the anticipated check points. During the next few hours Meir stopped twice to calculate the azimuth. Finally, as the false dawn defined the ledges of the approaching peaks, he called back to Rachel: "We've gone wrong somewhere. Let's retrace our steps for a while till I spot that hill. There should be enough light to see it from the distance. Then we can get a bearing."

They returned northwestward. During the next two hours light flooded through the twisted ravines, etching the pitted granite boulders and the occasional clumps of juniper trees with diamond-like brilliance. The landscape was wild in its beauty—and dangerous in its luminosity.

"We'll have to take cover, I'm afraid," Meir remarked suddenly. "This light makes us vulnerable."

"What a shame we didn't bring our camera," Rachel commented dryly. She was very tired.

They sat down in the cleft of a large hill, partially sheltered by the limbs of an overhanging juniper. Then they slept, from 6:00 A.M. until nearly 11:00 A.M. Yet they dared not move till late afternoon, when shadows had grown long enough to provide cover. Then they circled west around the mountain. After forty-five minutes they reached a track. Camel tracks were still fresh in the loess dust. Eastward, as they followed the trail, small clusters of cactus sprouted along the base of the mountains. For the first time, too, an occasional lone bird flew by—another good sign. Suddenly Rachel pointed toward the crest of a northern mountain: an airplane was droning overhead, probably a Jordanian transport on its way to the military airstrip at Akaba. The couple froze against the ledge until the plane had passed. As they waited, Meir made a discovery of his own: his eye crossed a glittering little mountain pool only fifty yards to his left.

"This is the best clue we've had so far," he commented, as they filled their canteens. "Any caravan route would be sure to pass this way."

Unfortunately the trail soon disappeared in the cul-de-sac of three adjoining mountains. The map offered no hint of a convenient approach to the Wadi ed Deir, the dry riverbed leading to the cliffs of Petrah. The only likely alternative now was to ascend the mountains as they came, pressing due eastward. The ridges each grew higher than the next, some rising to 1,200 and 1,400 feet. One of the tallest, a double-humped terror, must have reached 1,800 feet, all sheer granite.

"Let's have a look at that again," muttered Meir, opening the map.

"Two humps," said Rachel. "It might be Jebel-i-Ded."

He nodded. "It is. Let's hurry."

They reached the top before darkness. There in the eastern distance loomed the peak they had been waiting for, the highest mountain of the entire range. It was the Jebel Haroun, the Mount of Aaron, gateway to Petrah.

Too excited now to eat or rest, Meir and Rachel clambered rapidly down the far slope of Jebel-i-Ded. Awaiting them at the bottom was a wide, superbly level wadi, its central gradient worn smooth by innumerable thousands of passing camels. At the far turn of the flattened riverbed a faced-stone stable appeared, still reasonably intact. Rachel recognized it immediately as Byzantine.

"The main road." Meir sucked in his breath. "The Wadi ed Deir, right on the button." He marked it on the map.

Rachel gazed at the stable for a long moment. "I'm sorry," she said at length. "All I see now is a nice place to lie down."

There they slept, peacefully, uninterruptedly, for nearly five hours. It was hunger alone that aroused them at 1:30 in the morning. Against their better judgment the youths finished off half their rations before leaving the stable. Finally, strapping on their knapsacks once again, they moved out into the moon-drenched wadi. The track was clear, but it was tortuous, for the wadi was frequently blocked. At times it spiraled around the mountains; more often it ascended them. Rachel carefully marked the location of each rise on the map before proceeding to the next; the speed of their return, perhaps their very survival depended on it. Meir, in turn, concentrated upon more immediate dangers. At each turning, stone terraces bore witness to the presence of human beings. Twice he heard the barkings of dogs in the distance. It required only an hour and a half after that to reach the mountain's topmost ledge. Unfolding beneath them was a riotous jungle of orchidaceous rock. In every direction, as far as the eye could see, the gradations of red vied for supremacy along walls, ridges, facings, caverns, declivities, crests.

"Boker Tov—Good morning." Meir snapped Rachel from her spell. "It's eight o'clock by my watch. We can rest now and wait till dark or chance it and go ahead. What do you say?"

"I'm hungry. Our one can of rations says we move on."

"Then stick close to the wall."

They descended the northeast slope of the Jebel Haroun. Several yards before reaching the path at its base, Meir suddenly grasped Rachel's arm and pressed her against the side of the wall. He had caught a glimpse of a bedouin shepherd tending a flock of goats in a distant field. They remained there motionless, for perhaps thirty seconds, until the shepherd's *kaffiyah* flashed white in the sun, and it became apparent that the man's back was to the mountain. The instant the base was reached, however, danger became far more palpable. The footprints on the path were human this time. Following Meir's example, Rachel stepped forward at a three-quarters angle, keeping the terrain on her flank continually in view. There was much to be seen. To the southwest a crater, more than four hundred feet in diameter, slowly unfolded before them like a great petrified boil. At its easternmost lip, an enormous fortress rose perhaps two hundred feet into the sky, pillars and battlements blazing red in the sun.

"The Umm el-Biyara?" Rachel asked.

"Yes. We'll reach the Wadi Musa any minute. If anyone sees us now, act casual, like a tourist. We'll speak only English to each other."

There were other signs of life, but all from antiquity. On the right of the pathway a stone archway and two stone villas bore the classic markings of Nabatean design. So, further on, did several long, narrow stables, as arrow-straight as if they had been constructed by modern engineers. The mountains narrowed over the fissure of the Wadi Musa, and cave entrances dappled the wall facings. These, too, were marled amber-violet. Rachel sucked in her breath. Through the cleavage of the mountains, shearing away almost directly beneath her feet, was a superbly preserved stone amphitheater, its lavender terraces warped gently into a giant crescent. This, then, was Petrah, the citadel itself. Meir pointed beyond the amphitheater's southern parabola, and eastward.

"Elohim!"

"Shh. Is it the 'Great High Place'?"

Rachel nodded dazedly. Here was the site of the sacred Nabatean blood rites: a vast courtyard, containing four basalt altars, encrusted with black stone emblems of the sun god, Dusares, and flanked by the two immense tapering pillars, shaped like obelisks, that had been quarried away from the mountain around them. The rays of the climbing sun ricocheted from

mountain to fortress to amphitheater, to the obelisks of the Great High
Place, each igniting the other until the entire outer necklace of the ancient
city reflected the glow of the sky. Rachel and Meir, too, were etched like
cameos against that disc. It was no place for them to be. They hurried
forward into the shallow parapet of the Wadi Musa.

Even now they could see the Siq's narrowing tunnel awaiting them less
than three hundred feet away. As they reached the sandstone entrance,
Meir unbuckled his knapsack, removing a flashlight. For several moments
he aimed its beam into the descending corridor. Then, switching it off, he
motioned Rachel to follow. Even in the semidarkness, the passageway
gleamed a dull, burnished mauve, the striations twisting along the wall
facings like a latticework of veins.

"Just a few hundred yards more," said Meir confidently.

It was closer to a mile, actually, most of it through a passageway no wider
than three yards across at its broadest point. Every fifteen or twenty feet
the rock facing was indented by cave entrances, their inner linings streaked
in brilliant red and violet, resembling the hollow of a conch shell or a snail.
The climax was yet to come. They reached it within a half-hour, and when
they saw it the ordeal of the past three days faded from memory. It was
the Khaznet Firaun, the Treasury of Pharaoh—it was HaSelah HaAdom,
the Great Red Rock.

From their stance at its base, the mammoth colonnade seemed to Rachel
and Meir endless in its vault toward the darkening sky. The twin terraces,
one on top of another, bulged like the epic minaret balconies of Old
Jerusalem's Mosque of Omar. And at the summit, a swelling eagle's egg
perched on an eyrie, was the capacious urn in which the treasure of the
Nabatean rulers had once been stored. It was 5:14 P.M.—Meir noted the
exact minute—and the sun was setting behind the Khaznet Firaun. Rapidly
now, the sandstone façade became translucent. The mineral *venae* coiled
into burnt-amber nodes and whorls. Suddenly it was afire, the entire luminous shell, from its bedrock foundation to the inverted cupola at its peak.
The tendrils of marl glowed purple, then lavender, then violet, and finally
a rich luminous garnet, transforming the colors from apex to base until
the mighty rock formation bloomed like a dew-struck flower.

"Meir, am I dreaming?"

"It's red all right. Fantastic!"

Etched in the wall near the base was a spiderwork of names—signatures
—carved by knife, some in Latin letters, others in Arabic. Impulsively,
Rachel and Meir added Hebrew characters to the Red Rock's collection.

Then they walked out. In the dusk the bowl-shaped valley of El-Khubtha
was still clearly visible, as well as the arches and pillars of a crumbling
palace and urn temple sheltered within its corona. There were other ruins
to explore. But time had run out, and so, very nearly, had the food rations.
The young hikers had seen the Red Rock, and had left evidence of their
visit. There was not a moment to be lost now in returning. Squatting behind a boulder, they waited only until the darkness was complete. Then
at 8:00 P.M. they began retracing their steps toward the Siq.

Not more than five of those steps were taken, however, when a powerful Lux light suddenly switched on a mere dozen yards away. Diving behind a near-by rock, Meir and Rachel waited, trembling, as the beam flooded El-Khubtha's basin, sent rays hovering momentarily over the distant Corinthian Temple, then angled away toward the Wadi Musa. The voices of men could be heard quite distinctly, conversing phlegmatically in monosyllabic Arabic. Then the light and the voices grew dim and moved steadily back toward the Siq. Rachel began shaking uncontrollably. Meir's hand, tugging at her wrist, was slick with perspiration. Obeying him, she rose, and together they treaded their way cautiously northward, in the opposite direction of the mountain pass.

"We can't go back in there," Meir whispered. "The only thing to do now is circle the town from the north."

"But all our markers and guide posts—" she protested.

"Heading west will get us to the border," he insisted. "That's all we need. We don't have to find another Petrah. Come on, don't argue."

"Can we swing down to the Es-Siyagh?" Rachel whispered. "According to the map, it's only about a hundred yards from here."

Meir agreed. Half-walking, half-crawling, the two managed to find the secondary trail, precisely where it was supposed to be. Then, straightening up, they edged their way through a ganglion of boulders, clutching each other tightly each time the narrow path unexpectedly led them to the brink of a mountain. By two o'clock in the morning the danger of interception seemed less urgent. They rested.

"I'm a little faint," Rachel muttered apologetically.

"We might as well finish off the rations now," Meir said. "If we don't reach the border in twenty-four hours food won't help us anyway."

They ate, emptying the contents of their final can. Then they fell asleep. They did not awaken until the sunrise. Rachel stared at her watch, jumped up with a start and nudged Meir. Quickly they strapped on their knapsacks, and proceeded westward. They had lost precious time, but neither blamed the other. The rest was worth it. Besides, the terrain had become less difficult now. The worst of the mountains were behind them. With the sun at their backs, they could see the distant shadows of the western gullies crisscrossing into the flat land. The border would not be more than ten miles away.

Those were the longest ten miles of Rachel's and Meir's lives. The shadows deepened unaccountably. The sun grew mottled, then passed from view. Each step dragged like lead. Meir was breathing heavily. Rachel's chest began heaving with exhaustion.

"What is this, a *khamsin?*" she gasped.

"I—don't think so." Meir studied the sky for several moments. "It could be a sandstorm coming on," he declared at last.

"Meir!" Rachel pointed toward the plateau. "That's the shepherd we passed on our way here."

The Arab was hardly more than a hundred yards ahead of them. This time he carried a rifle. His mouth was open, and he was calling someone.

"Shem! Shem!" Over the rush of the wind, his voice could be heard, shouting in evident terror to an unseen companion. "Shem! Shem!"

There was no answer, and the bedouin lurched erratically to his right, crossing the hikers' path at an oblique angle.

"Has he seen us, do you think," whispered Rachel.

Meir shrugged. "Maybe. He must have a couple of days ago, or he wouldn't be carrying that gun. Stay low. He doesn't want to meet us any more than we want to meet him."

The shepherd was apparently as confused as he was frightened, for he continued turning now in wide, aimless circles. He was quite young, hardly older than Rachel.

"Shem! Shem!" he cried repeatedly. "Shem—" Then he stopped short, opening black eyes wide in horror and disbelief. The two Jews stared back at him expectantly. Meir's Sten-gun was cocked, aimed directly at the Arab's chest. Frozen with tension, they waited on opposite sides of the narrow wadi, each certain that the other would make the first move.

It was the desert that spoke first. The roar was dull, pierced by a rasping whistle. The sand whirled, then cracked like a whip between sky and earth. There was nothing more to be seen. Squinting and blinking, the young Israelis held fast to each other's wrists, then stumbled on in the general direction of the western horizon. Several times during the next three hours, Meir attempted to study his "marvelous" compass; but the crystal had been knocked off, and the needle was berserk, spinning and leaping as the wind struck it. Parched and half-strangled by the sand, Rachel opened her canteen. It was blown from her grasp. The weight of her knapsack was becoming unbearable. Finally, when she was certain she could go no further, she felt Meir's hands on her back, unstrapping the load.

"It won't do us any more good," he shouted over the storm. "I'm leaving mine, too."

They struggled on, battered continually by the furious wind.

Neither could remember when the storm subsided. Rachel rolled over and saw Meir prone beside her. The shirt had been stripped from his back. Weakly, she shook his shoulder. He stirred.

"Storm's over," she whispered.

He looked up. The sun was indeed shining again. The wilderness was silent. They both lay back and breathed deeply. After a few more minutes Meir looked at his watch. It was 3:10 P.M.

"We must have walked at least seven hours," he said. "The border can't be far now."

"I hope not too far," said Rachel apologetically, "because we've been going the wrong way." She pointed to the sun. It was behind them.

With a groan, Meir climbed to his feet. He was very weak. Now it was her turn to offer encouragement. "You could still be right, you know," she explained, rising with him. "Maybe it only happened a little while ago."

But it had happened longer ago than that. They trudged westward for the next two hours without catching a glimpse of the Beersheba-Eilat highway. By now each of them was impervious to the danger of Jordanian border guards. The only thing that mattered was water. If their thirst were not soon quenched they would die. It was the unspoken thought between them, and neither would utter it. The desert might as well have been the Sahara. Vistas of sun-scorched limestone extended endlessly westward. Nothing remained as consolation, not even a mirage. Gazing wanly at Meir's taut, pale face, Rachel decided that he had aged ten years during these last four days. Good, decent fellow that he was, he would not have been in this but for her. It was likely, too, that Meir was the last person she would see in her life.

But by two o'clock the next morning they had reached the highway. Inspecting the terrain carefully, both Rachel and Meir agreed that Beer Menucha probably lay to the south. If they were wrong, or failed to reach the camp by dawn, they would lie down on the road. A passing vehicle might find them before they dehydrated.

Three hours later the sentry at Beer Menucha heard a feeble cry. Snapping off the safety catch of his rifle, he peered intently into the half-light. Then he saw them: two figures, half-naked, weaving and reeling on the edge of the highway. They collapsed before he could reach them. Other workmen rushed over to carry the youths into a tent.

Two days passed before Rachel and Meir were fit for travel again. The Sternists bedded them down, forced water into their throats, and fed them bland, dry food. Avinoam, the stocky foreman, refrained from questioning the young hikers until they were on their feet again.

"Now then," he asked, at last. "Tell me about 'Har Hemda.' Had a nice climb, did you?"

Disdaining Meir's warning, Rachel decided to tell everything. The other workmen gathered close. They listened to the account without uttering a word.

When Rachel finished, Avinoam sighed. "You are a couple of idiots, wild idiots," he remarked slowly. "Absolutely insane. In fact," he added with a smile, "I wish we had more crazy youngsters like you in our outfit."

It was the universal reaction. News of the exploit traveled fast. By the time Rachel and Meir were returned to their kibbutz, an army intelligence officer was waiting for them.

"You can relax," the man said. "We've decided not to make trouble for you. But we want a report of everything you saw."

They gave it to him, down to the last detail.

"Very interesting," the officer said, packing his notes into his briefcase. "I wouldn't advise you to do it again, though. Leave those explorations to us."

"We will now," remarked Rachel, with a mocking smile.

Then it was the turn of others. On successive weekends nearly a hundred youths poured into Ein Harod from all parts of the country. They had come for a firsthand account of the incredible exploit. Patiently, Meir and Rachel told all. Gila Ben-Akiva, Rachel's old hiking partner, was one of the listeners. Later, in the privacy of her room, Gila asked for the map.

"I'm going to try it, Rachel," she stated, matter-of-factly.

"Uh, uh," Rachel warned, "we've left our calling cards. The Arabs will be on the lookout now."

But Gila persisted and Rachel, who knew her friend too well, finally handed over a copy of the map.

On August 15, less than six weeks later, Gila set out for the south with four other farm youths. Among them were three boys—Arik, Eytan, and Alex—and a girl, Miriam. The group stopped briefly at Kibbutz Giv'at Brenner to attend the Palmach congress. It was the last time any of their friends saw them alive. Four days after their departure from Giv'at Brenner, Radio Ramallah, the State Broadcasting Service of the Hashemite Kingdom of Jordan, announced that five Jewish "soldiers" had been killed at Deir Malkoor, eleven miles within Jordanian territory. The following Saturday the bodies of the young Jews were sent to Eilat via the United Nations Truce Commission. As far as could be determined, none of the corpses had been mutilated. Returned with Miriam's body was a bullet-punctured copy of the Bible; with Arik's a small volume of poems by Frishmann, folded at the song "In the Desert."

It was Miriam's trip, not Rachel's, which became the subject of Israel folklore—the citizens of the Jewish State do not bother to venerate live heroes. A song was written memorializing her crossing. Unaccountably, the lyrics described the audacious little band of explorers as three youths, rather than five.

> *Three started out at sundown—*
> *Facing them the mountains of Edom burned—*
> *Taking with them an old dream, a map, and a canteen,*
> *Precious baggage on the way to the Great Red Rock.*

But no one doubted who its true subjects were, nor where they had gone. Although the word Petrah was not mentioned, the tragic fate of the young travelers was graphically rendered: the dream-struck image of the rock face, the blaze of the sun, the sudden, short bursts of fire, the twisted mouths stuffed with sand, the final tortured vision of the Khaznet Firaun. And the great petrified Lorelei of the desert, waiting, beckoning—

> *Over the hills and the desert*
> *There is a place, so the tales say*
> *From whence no one has ever returned alive,*
> *A place called the Great Red Rock.*
> *Oh HaSelah HaAdom, HaAdom*
> *Oh HaSelah HaAdom, HaAdom.*

Have others tried it since? No one speaks of the Petrah crossing openly any longer, for the prison sentence can be very stiff. The Jordanian State Radio, too, has kept silent on the subject, as if fearing to admit that the Hashemite frontier can be penetrated even briefly. But if I had any doubt that the mighty fortress still exerts its old fascination, it was dissipated in the early summer of 1961. I had stayed late one evening at my office on the second floor of Beit Hillel, the student center of the Hebrew University. As I left, about 8:30 P.M., I found myself unable to reach the main stairway. Students had packed every available square foot of the building's large auditorium, and now were fighting for space in the foyer outside. In all my years in Jerusalem I could not remember ever having seen a student crowd of this size—certainly not during pre-exam week.

"What's happening?" I asked a young man.

"Ze'ev Vilnay is giving a travel lecture, with slides," he replied.

Dr. Ze'ev Vilnay was the most distinguished guide and travel authority in Israel. There was no doubt that the man was a brilliant lecturer. But even so, a crowd of such size—

"Well, what's he lecturing about?" I persisted. "The Folies-Bergère?"

"It's about Petrah," the youth laughed.

Petrah! Of course, Petrah! By returning to the entrance of my office and craning my neck, I could barely make out the screen at the far end of the auditorium. The slides were faded, obviously of prewar vintage. Moreover, they struck me as quite pedestrian: the usual flat picture-postcard views of the celebrated temples, urns, and monuments—and in black and white, at that. The students hardly seemed to mind. Indeed, for me at least these young men and women, rather than the slides and lecture, were the authentic spectacle of the evening. Normally rather stolid and phlegmatic, their faces that night were rapt beyond anything I had ever seen outside a championship soccer match. Mouths were open, necks and eyes strained, fingers clutched tight on backs of chairs or skewered between clenched teeth. When the Khaznet Firaun—the Red Rock—flashed at last on the screen, a sudden murmur arose from the audience, as if an electric current had passed through the room. So far as I could see, no one was taking notes on Vilnay's lecture. Nevertheless, judging from the captivated, near-mesmerized expressions on those youthful faces, every syllable of his remarks, every furrow in that Red Rock, were chiseled cleanly and sharply in their minds. Their words and intentions were unspoken, but surely they must have echoed Rachel's the moment she staggered, delirious, into the hands of the work crew at Beer Menucha: "That desert, red, the redness, big . . . big . . . our names on the Red Rock . . ."

It was getting late. Colonel Ben-David had returned once more to the desk, and stood there in silent insistence. As I rose again, the P.M. courteously accompanied me to the door. Then, almost in afterthought, he paused briefly by a large map of Israel hanging on the side wall. Tapping his finger significantly against the desert area, he did not consider it superfluous to remind me that we had been discussing half of Israel that morning.

"Perhaps not the richest half," I ventured, "but at least the future half. I'm sure we are agreed on that."

"The future half and the richest half," he countered, rapping off the words with the same index finger. Then he smiled, shaking his head ruefully: "Why are you so hard to convince? You know, if your ancestor, Joel Moshe Solomon, had been the pessimist that you are, there wouldn't be a

Jew living in Jerusalem today. I say it again: the future and the richest half. We're getting wonderful material from down there. And it is as nothing compared to what we can produce in the next ten years."

On the verge now of leaving, it hardly seemed the best time for me to review the statistics again, or the testimony of geologists and economists. But I was vexed and frustrated. How could he stand there and make such remarks, especially after having read the innumerable reports and statements that crossed his desk, knowing full well that the Negev's supplies of oil, gas, gypsum, salt, flint clay, even of potash and phosphates, did not, and by the most sober and expert evaluation would not, provide his country with more than 15 per cent of its crucial hard currency? Was he totally indifferent to all this painfully accumulated evidence? How glibly the words rolled off his tongue: "The future half and the richest half. . . . We are getting wonderful material from down there. . . ." I had done my best to elicit a realistic appraisal from him, to learn his plans for colonizing and exploiting the desert in spite of its meager resources. Yet here he was, palming off on me that well-worn routine about the Negev's inexhaustible riches—as if I were an eager feature writer for the Israel Tourist Corporation. Well, never mind, he was aging. The miracles he had accomplished in his day were political and military. If, figuratively speaking, he had once squeezed blood from stones, why should he doubt his ability to do it again, this time in the Negev? He had earned the right to his grandiose dreams.

I thanked him for his time. We shook hands, exchanged regards and the usual amenities, and I left.

"So, did you get what you wanted?" Colonel Ben-David asked, as we returned through the corridor.

"It was very interesting," I replied. "Whether one agrees or disagrees with him, one always has the same feeling of sitting in the presence of greatness. It was wrong of me to press him on so many technical details. I should have left that to the technicians."

The colonel smiled. "That is all technicians are for," he said.

For the next three months my work kept me in Tel Aviv. I was not overly fond of the city. Its climate, its noise, its brassy exuberance, its lack of charm and tradition, all depressed me. Still, for an unmarried man Tel Aviv offered important compensations after a hard day of research and writing. There were places to go. The Habima and Cameri theaters were enjoying a reasonably good season. As always, the Israel Philharmonic was superb; its programs included some of the world's most distinguished guest soloists. The performances of the Ramat Gan Chamber Music Society were a pure delight. The Helena Rubenstein Art Gallery had recently been opened in the city's handsome cultural center, and its latest exhibition of French impressionist painting rivaled the best I had seen in New York or Boston. Eminent diplomats and literary figures frequently lectured at Zionist House.

And, too, there were people to see: lawyers, physicians, engineers, artists, writers, professors, musicians, businessmen, army officers. Certainly Tel

Aviv boasted a larger cultural community, numerically if not proportionately, than any other city in the country, not excluding Jerusalem. One met them everywhere: in comfortable, modern apartments, in good restaurants, at private weekend parties, at the beach, the swimming pool, at dinner clubs and night clubs, at hotel bars. They were there to be met and known. They streamed by the coffee shops of Dizengoff Street on late Friday afternoons and Saturday evenings by the thousands, the tens of thousands.

Now and then I would join them at the fashionable Bar California, near the juncture of Frishmann and Dizengoff Streets. Shlomo was there, and D'vorah and Uri and Menahem, Naomi and Ze'ev and Dov and Esther, Tal, Daniel, and Yehezkal, Reuven, Benjamin, Itamar, and Gad. The descendants of kings, priests, prophets, judges, patriarchs and matriarchs and warriors, the children of the Zionist pioneers—they were all there, Tel Aviv's smart young set now. One consulted them for the latest news of when, where, and to whom things were happening. They knew what picture was playing at the Chen, what singer was performing at HaMoadon HaTeatron, what guitarist was plucking at Omar Khayyam's, what stripper was peeling at the Hinga Bar, who had won the latest prize at the lottery, who owed whom money at cards, who was carrying on an affair with whom. One asked them. They had the answers. And to my shame, I listened.

"I'm meeting him tonight at the Artists' Club," confided a chic, elaborately coiffed young blonde. "I wouldn't trust him to pick me up at my place."

"We're going to the Accadia Pool Saturday morning," remarked a slim, mustachioed youth, elegantly togged out in shantung trousers and Japanese sandals. "Admission went up to three and a half pounds last week, but you wouldn't catch me dead on the beach."

"There goes Shaul in his new Opel. What do you think he paid for it? What? Restitutions? Oh, one of those."

"Shulamith is going to Europe this summer."

"Ruchama just got back."

"Have you heard the new band at the Avia? Not bad at all."

"Damn, I just broke a nail."

"Eli had a party at his new flat. I wasn't impressed. The usual crowd."

"That American furniture manufacturer is staying on an extra week at the Sheraton. I'd give my right arm to meet him."

"Going to the Dolphin House for your vacation? Better learn to play golf, then."

Should any of this have surprised me? By now only a fool or a stranger would have expected the youth of Tel Aviv to stalk through their daily activities in a posture of perpetual heroism, as if they were somehow larger than life, epic wish fulfillments of Diaspora insecurity. A nation could live on crisis and idealism only so long, after all. Israel's citizens had surely earned the right to the same pleasures and indulgences, the same foibles and petty weaknesses of other peoples. Anyway, in a national emergency even these young pub crawlers and coffeehouse sitters were as capable of grandeur as their forebears had been, the men and women of the early *aliyot*, Joel Moshe Solomon, Chaim Chissin, Rachel Yannait, Yehudah Almog, farm-bred sabras like Yigal Allon and Moshe Dayan, and the other giants of Zionist redemption. It was simply that, for all the youth could see, a national emergency did not exist at the moment, and they were determined not to manufacture one. Life was difficult enough as it was, what with army reserve service, high taxes, steep rents, climbing prices, bureaucratic ineptitude, the routine drudgery of life in an unprosperous little republic, still fighting for breath in a state of economic siege.

No, if anyone were to blame them it surely could not be I, who had never endured what they had endured, who had never known the mortal terror of an invaded homeland or the torment of prolonged hunger or thirst. It could not be I, whose tentative return to the bedrock of Zion had awaited the thirtieth year of my life, who had erred and stumbled along the path to Jerusalem and the grave site of my great-grandparents, and who even now kept one foot rooted safely in the other world. The privilege of reproach was not mine.

To the southeast, an Arkia Airlines DC-3 climbed slowly from the Ramat Aviv airstrip. Flashing silver as it banked over our heads, the dependable little transport settled on its routine course southward, the thrice-daily "milk run" to Eilat. It was spring. Most of the passengers in that plane would be tourists. From their cabin windows they would see what Ben-Tor had seen from his Piper Cub many years ago. There would be sand and dunes, hills and mountains, wadis and craters. There would be silence and desolation. The trip would consume no more than an hour, and it would be all the Negev most of these visitors would ever see. Perhaps it would be enough for their purposes. The ministry of development and the Israel Bond office would supply the necessary statistics about mining and quarrying, manufacturing and pumping. An eight-hour drive through the desert could be quite enervating in that weather.

But it occurred to me, too, that the shadow of the plane's wings would pass over much that was not described in the charts. Unseen below, the agronomists still dug their knees into earth: Hadassah Avigdori in Givat, Saul Feldman at the Gaza Strip, Michael Evenari in Ovdat, patiently matching the ingenuity of the ancients, and their own, against the miserly loess of the desert. The farmers were there, in sixty kibbutzim and moshavim scattered from the perimeter of Egypt to the Wadi Arava, raising crops that were marginal and children that were bronzed masterpieces. In the factories of Dimona, in the mineral pans of Sodom, in the quarries of Kfar Yerucham and Mitzpeh Ramon immigrants from Rumania, Poland, Egypt, Morocco, and Tunisia were melted and re-minted in a common inferno.

Yehudah Almog's craggy profile was carved forever in the renovated fortress of Masada. The ashes of Mike Skidelsky's cigarettes traced the course of the flint-clay hammer through the Negev's innermost viscera. In the oil and gas fields Moshe Karabilnik and Danny Kimche pressed on in their quest for a liquid El Dorado. Square pegs drifted through the clamorous jungle of shovels, derricks, and bulldozers: Leon, finding his niche in a frontier saloon; Nehemia and Hava, seeking pattern and form in the wild loneliness of the Negev plateau; David Sachs, Jimmy, "the monkey man," elbowing room for themselves in the pinched wedge of Eilat; pimps, whores, felons, and misfits rebuilding their dignity and self-respect in the purgatorium of the wilderness; archaeologists like Yadin, soldiers like Rothem, hikers and adventurers like Rachel, Meir, and Gila, recovering the ancient testimony of Hebrew audacity and imagination, and proving it by deed once again. There was a race!

"Boker Tov," said Avigdor, tapping his lemonade glass with a spoon. "Good morning. What are you smiling about?"

"Was I? Sorry, my mind was on something else."

On Ben-Gurion's final remark to me:

"I say it again: the future and the richest half. We're getting wonderful material from down there."

That crafty old man. He knew.

Ashkelon
June 16, 1963

ABOUT THE AUTHOR

Howard Morley Sachar was born in St. Louis, Missouri, in 1928. He was graduated from Swarthmore College and received his M.A. and Ph.D. from Harvard University in the field of modern European and Near Eastern history.

Dr. Sachar served as a member of the History Department at the University of Massachusetts, and as director of the B'nai B'rith Hillel Foundations at U.C.L.A. and Stanford University. He has studied and traveled extensively in Europe and Israel, and has been a contributor to a number of journals and magazines, among them the *New Republic,* the *American Historical Review,* and the *Journal of Modern History.*

The Course of Modern Jewish History, his first book, published in 1958, is now recognized as a standard work in the field. *Aliyah: The Peoples of Israel,* which was published in 1961, is a study of fifteen of the settlers in Palestine before 1948, through whose lives the rebirth of the Jewish State is examined.

Dr. Sachar is currently serving as director of Brandeis University's Jacob Hiatt Institute in Israel.

THIS BOOK WAS SET IN

GRANJON AND GARAMONT TYPES,

PRINTED, AND BOUND AT THE PRESS OF

THE WORLD PUBLISHING COMPANY.

DESIGN IS BY LARRY KAMP